Infant & Toddler Health Sourcebook

Infectious Diseases Sourcebook

Injury & Trauma Sourcebook

Learning Disabilities Sourcebook, 2nd Edition

Leukemia Sourcebook

Liver Disorders Sourcebook

Lung Disorders Sourcebook

Medical Tests Sourcebook, 2nd Edition

Men's Health Concerns Sourcebook, 2nd Edition

Mental Health Disorders Sourcebook, 3rd Edition

Mental Retardation Sourcebook

Movement Disorders Sourcebook

Muscular Dystrophy Sourcebook

Obesity Sourcebook

Osteoporosis Sourcebook

Pain Sourcebook, 2nd Edition

Pediatric Cancer Sourcebook

Physical & Mental Issues in Aging Sourcebook

Podiatry Sourcebook, 2nd Edition

Pregnancy & Birth Sourcebook, 2nd Edition

Prostate Cancer Sourcebook

Prostate & Urological Disorders Sourcebook

Public Health Sourcebook

Reconstructive & Cosmetic Surgery Sourcebook

Rehabilitation Sourcebook

Respiratory Diseases & Disorders Sourcebook

Sexually Transmitted Diseases Sourcebook, 3rd Edition

Sleep Disorders Sourcebook, 2nd Edition

Smoking Concerns Sourcebook

Sports Injuries Sourcebook, 2nd Edition

Stress-Related Disorders Sourcebook

Stroke Sourcebook

Substance Abuse Sourcebook

Surgery Sourcebook

Thyroid Disorders Sourcebook

Urinary Tract & Kidney Diseases & Disorders Sourcebook, 2nd Edition

Vegetarian Sourcebook

Women's Health Concerns Sourcebook, 2nd Edition

Workplace Health & Safety Sourcebook

Worldwide Health Sourcebook

Teen Health Series

Alcohol Information for Teens

Allergy Information for Teens

Asthma Information for Teens

Cancer Information for Teens

Complementary & Alternative Medicine Information for Teens

Diabetes Information for Teens

Diet Information for Teens, 2nd Edition

Drug Information for Teens, 2nd Edition

Eating Disorders Information for Teens

Fitness Information for Teens

Learning Disabilities Information for Teens

Mental Health Information for Teens, 2nd Edition

Sexual Health Information for Teens

Skin Health Information for Teens

Sports Injuries Information for Teens

Suicide Information for Teens

Tobacco Information for Teens

Alcoholism
SOURCEBOOK

Second Edition

Health Reference Series

Second Edition

Alcoholism
SOURCEBOOK

*Basic Consumer Health Information about
Alcohol Use, Abuse, and Dependence, Featuring
Facts about the Physical, Mental, and Social Health
Effects of Alcohol Addiction, Including Alcoholic
Liver Disease, Pancreatic Disease, Cardiovascular
Disease, Neurological Disorders, and the Effects
of Drinking during Pregnancy*

*Along with Information about Alcohol Treatment,
Medications, and Recovery Programs, in Addition
to Tips for Reducing the Prevalence of Underage
Drinking, Statistics about Alcohol Use, a Glossary
of Related Terms, and Directories of Resources
for More Help and Information*

Edited by
Amy L. Sutton

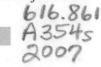

Omnigraphics

615 Griswold Street • Detroit, MI 48226

Bibliographic Note

Because this page cannot legibly accommodate all the copyright notices, the Bibliographic Note portion of the Preface constitutes an extension of the copyright notice.

Edited by Amy L. Sutton

Health Reference Series

Karen Bellenir, *Managing Editor*
David A. Cooke, M.D., *Medical Consultant*
Elizabeth Barbour, *Permissions and Research Coordinator*
Laura Pleva Nielsen, *Index Editor*
Cherry Stockdale, *Permissions Assistant*
EdIndex, Services for Publishers, *Indexers*

* * *

Omnigraphics, Inc.

Matthew P. Barbour, *Senior Vice President*
Kay Gill, *Vice President—Directories*
Kevin Hayes, *Operations Manager*
David P. Bianco, *Marketing Director*

* * *

Peter E. Ruffner, *Publisher*

Frederick G. Ruffner, Jr., *Chairman*

Copyright © 2007 Omnigraphics, Inc.

ISBN 0-7808-0942-4

Library of Congress Cataloging-in-Publication Data

Alcoholism sourcebook : basic consumer health information about alcohol use, abuse, and dependence, featuring facts about the physical, mental, and social health effects of alcohol addiction, including alcoholic liver disease, pancreatic disease, cardiovascular disease, neurological disorders, and the effects of drinking during pregnancy; along with information about alcohol treatment, medications, and recovery programs, in addition to tips for reducing the prevalence of underage drinking, statistics about alcohol use, a glossary of related terms, and directories of resources for more help and information / edited by Amy L. Sutton. -- 2nd ed.
    p. cm. -- (Health reference series)
  Includes bibliographical references and index.
  ISBN 0-7808-0942-4 (hardcover : alk. paper) 1. Alcoholism--Popular works. 2. Consumer education. I. Sutton, Amy L.
    RC565.A4493 2006
    362.292'86--dc22
                                                                    2006020700

∞

Table of Contents

Visit www.healthreferenceseries.com to view *A Contents Guide to the Health Reference Series*, a listing of more than 12,000 topics and the volumes in which they are covered.

Preface xiii

Part I: Facts about Alcohol Use and Abuse

Chapter 1—Questions and Answers on
Alcohol Consumption 3

Chapter 2—Facts and Figures on Alcohol
Consumption and Alcohol-Related
Health Effects 9

Chapter 3—Overview of Alcohol Abuse and Alcoholism 17

Chapter 4—A Family History of Alcoholism:
Are You at Risk? 25

Chapter 5—The Genetics of Alcoholism 29

Chapter 6—Underage Drinking 33

    Section 6.1—The Public Health
Challenge of Underage
Drinking 34

    Section 6.2—Tips for Teens: The
Truth about Alcohol 44

    Section 6.3—Youth Drinking Trends
Stabilize But Consumption
Remains High 47

    Section 6.4—Adults Are Most Common
Source of Alcohol for Teens 49

Chapter 7—Alcohol Advertising and Youth 53

Chapter 8—Drinking on College Campuses 65

        Section 8.1—What Parents Need to
                  Know about College
                  Drinking 66

        Section 8.2—The Hidden Consequences
                  of College Drinking 71

        Section 8.3—College Alcohol Problems
                  Exceed Previous Estimates 72

Chapter 9—Alcohol Abuse in Men 75

Chapter 10—Alcohol: An Important Women's Health Issue 79

Chapter 11—Alcohol and Minorities 85

Chapter 12—Alcohol and Aging 91

Chapter 13—Other Factors Associated with Alcohol
           Consumption 95

        Section 13.1—Delayed Alcohol Use
                  Linked to Fewer Problems
                  with Abuse or Dependence
                  as Adults 96

        Section 13.2—Alcohol Use Patterns
                  Associated with Body Mass
                  Index 98

        Section 13.3—Alcohol's Sight and Smell
                  Cues Increase Consumption ... 100

Part II: Preventing Alcohol Abuse, Dependence, and Alcohol-Related Injuries

Chapter 14—How to Cut Down on Your Drinking 105

Chapter 15—Talking to Your Child about Alcohol 109

Chapter 16—For Teens: Organizing a Substance-Free
           Party 123

Chapter 17—Changing the Culture of Campus Drinking 127

Chapter 18—Preventing Impaired or Drunk Driving 131

        Section 18.1—Understanding Blood
                  Alcohol Concentration and
                  Alcohol Impairment 132

Section 18.2—Alcohol and Transportation
Safety 135

Section 18.3—Lowered National Blood
Alcohol Concentration Limit
for Impaired Driving 140

Section 18.4—Tips for Preventing
Drunk Driving 144

Section 18.5—Get the Keys: How You
Can Intervene 146

Section 18.6—Strict Licensing Laws
Associated with Less Teen
Drinking and Driving 147

Chapter 19—Approaching Alcohol Problems through
Community-Based Prevention Programs 149

Part III: The Physical Effects of Alcohol

Chapter 20—How Alcohol Affects the Body 161

Chapter 21—Hangovers 167

Chapter 22—Alcohol Overdose 173

Chapter 23—Alcohol and Nutrition 177

Section 23.1—The Role of Alcohol in
the Diet 178

Section 23.2—Diet Quality Linked
to Alcohol Drinking
Patterns 180

Chapter 24—What Are the Myths and Facts about
Alcohol and the Liver? 183

Chapter 25—Alcoholic Liver Disease 187

Chapter 26—What You Need to Know about Cirrhosis
of the Liver 197

Chapter 27—Testing the Liver for Signs of Damage
or Disease 203

Chapter 28—Alcoholism: A Common Cause
of Pancreatitis 207

Chapter 29—What You Need to Know about Cancer
of the Pancreas 213

Chapter 30—Alcohol's Role in Gastrointestinal
　　Tract Disorders 219

Chapter 31—Alcohol's Damaging Effects on the Brain 227

Chapter 32—Alcohol and Heart Disease 237

Chapter 33—Alcoholic Cardiomyopathy 241

Chapter 34—Alcohol and the Immune System 245

　　Section 34.1—How Does the Immune
　　　　System Work? 246

　　Section 34.2—The Influence of Alcohol
　　　　and Gender on the
　　　　Immune Response 254

Chapter 35—Alcohol Consumption, Kidney Disease,
　　and High Blood Pressure 261

Chapter 36—Alcohol Consumption and Nerve Damage 265

Chapter 37—Alcohol and Sleep 271

Chapter 38—Alcohol and Cancer 275

　　Section 38.1—Overview of Alcohol
　　　　Consumption and the
　　　　Risk of Cancer 276

　　Section 38.2—Confusion Regarding the
　　　　Alcohol-Cancer Link 278

　　Section 38.3—Ingredient in Alcohol Related
　　　　to the Formation of Cancer 282

Chapter 39—Alcohol's Long-Term Effects on Bone 285

Chapter 40—Alcohol and HIV/AIDS 289

Chapter 41—The Interactions between Alcohol
　　and Medicines 295

　　Section 41.1—Harmful Interactions:
　　　　Mixing Alcohol with
　　　　Medicines 296

　　Section 41.2—Aging, Medicines, and
　　　　Alcohol 300

Part IV: Alcohol Use during Pregnancy and Its Effect on Fetal Development

Chapter 42—Drinking Alcohol during Pregnancy 305

Chapter 43—Understanding Fetal Alcohol Spectrum
        Disorders 311

Chapter 44—Frequently Asked Questions about
        Prenatal Alcohol-Related Conditions 319

Chapter 45—Caring for a Child Diagnosed with Fetal
        Alcohol Syndrome (FAS) 325
        Section 45.1—If Your Child Has FAS 326
        Section 45.2—Diagnosing FAS 332
        Section 45.3—Health Concerns of
                     Children with FAS 333
        Section 45.4—FAS through the Years 336

Chapter 46—Behavioral Issues and Other Conditions
        Associated with FAS 353
        Section 46.1—Understanding FAS and
                     Behavior 354
        Section 46.2—Secondary Conditions
                     Associated with FAS 358

Part V: Mental Health Problems Associated with Alcohol Use

Chapter 47—Alcohol and Mental Health 363
        Section 47.1—Mental Illness and
                     Problem Drinking 364
        Section 47.2—The Prevalence and
                     Co-Occurrence of Alcohol,
                     Drug, Mood, and Anxiety
                     Disorders 370

Chapter 48—Alcohol Use and Depression 373
        Section 48.1—Depression Linked to
                     Alcohol Dependence 374
        Section 48.2—Suicide, Depression, and
                     Youth Drinking 377

Chapter 49—Anxiety and Alcohol Use 381
        Section 49.1—Researchers Shed Light
                     on Anxiety and Alcohol
                     Intake 382
        Section 49.2—Social Anxiety Disorder
                     and Alcohol Use 384

Chapter 50—Post-Traumatic Stress Disorder
and Problems with Alcohol Use 389

Chapter 51—Childhood Attention Deficit Hyperactivity
Disorder and Alcoholism during the Teen
Years 393

Chapter 52—Alcohol Use and Its Association with Other
Dangerous Substances 397

    Section 52.1—Almost Half of People
in Addiction Treatment
Had Both Drug and
Alcohol Abuse 398

    Section 52.2—Alcohol and Nicotine Abuse
May Be Influenced by Same
Genes 400

    Section 52.3—Alcohol and Tobacco Use 402

Part VI: The Effects of Alcohol on Family, Work, and Society

Chapter 53—How Alcohol Affects the Family:
The Impact of Substance Abuse
on Families 409

Chapter 54—Coping with an Alcoholic Parent 419

Chapter 55—Alcohol and Substance Use in the Workplace 423

Chapter 56—Alcohol and Violence 437

    Section 56.1—Alcohol Use and
Violence in Youth 438

    Section 56.2—Domestic Violence and
Alcohol Use 442

Chapter 57—Substance Use and Risky Sexual Activity 445

Chapter 58—Alcohol and Sexual Assault 455

Chapter 59—Driving under the Influence 463

Part VII: Treatment and Recovery from Alcohol Dependence

Chapter 60—Recognizing and Helping Someone Who
Might Have a Drug or Alcohol Problem 469

Chapter 61—Screening for Alcohol Use and
　　　　　　Alcohol-Related Problems 475

Chapter 62—Barriers to Alcoholism Treatment 487

Chapter 63—Brief Interventions for Alcohol Use 491

Chapter 64—Inpatient and Outpatient Treatment for
　　　　　　Alcoholism or Substance Abuse 501

Chapter 65—Substance Abuse Treatment for Children
　　　　　　and Adolescents 519

Chapter 66—Physical Symptoms of Alcoholism Recovery 523
　　　　　　Section 66.1—Alcohol Withdrawal 524
　　　　　　Section 66.2—Delirium Tremens 528

Chapter 67—Medications for Treating Alcohol Dependence 533
　　　　　　Section 67.1—What Medications Treat
　　　　　　　　　　　　Alcoholism? 534
　　　　　　Section 67.2—Drugs to Treat Alcohol
　　　　　　　　　　　　Dependence 535

Chapter 68—The Secret of the Twelve Steps:
　　　　　　Spirituality's Role in Substance Abuse
　　　　　　Prevention and Treatment 545

Chapter 69—Alternative and Complementary Medicine
　　　　　　Treatments for Alcoholics 549

Chapter 70—Improving Access to Treatment for People
　　　　　　with Alcohol Use Disorders 555

Part VIII: Additional Help and Information

Chapter 71—Glossary of Terms Related to Alcoholism 565

Chapter 72—Directory of Government and Private
　　　　　　Resources That Provide Information
　　　　　　about Alcoholism 577

Chapter 73—State Substance Abuse Agencies 589

Index **601**

Preface

About This Book

Moderate drinking—defined as a drink or two a day—has been associated with positive health benefits, such as a reduced risk of heart attack or stroke. Drinking more than moderately, however, places a person at risk for a variety of health problems. In the short term, excessive alcohol consumption leads to a loss of coordination, slowed reflexes, distorted vision, memory lapses, and even blackouts, coma, or death from acute alcohol poisoning. Chronic abuse of alcohol can also lead to life-threatening health concerns, including liver disease, gastrointestinal cancer, heart disease, and stroke.

In addition, alcohol abuse is linked to mental illnesses, such as depression, anxiety, and addiction disorders. Furthermore, prolonged alcohol dependency may make it difficult for a person to maintain employment or personal relationships with parents, spouses or partners, or children.

Despite the sobering facts about how alcohol abuse impairs physical and psychological health, there is good news. Many people who abuse alcohol can halt the cycle of self-harm with medical assistance and the use of inpatient, outpatient, and self-help recovery programs.

Alcoholism Sourcebook, Second Edition presents comprehensive information about the use and misuse of alcohol among men, women, youth, and seniors, and it describes the effects of alcohol exposure on fetal development. The physical and emotional problems associated with alcohol dependency and alcohol's impact on family relationships, work, and society are discussed. A section on treatment describes medications and recovery programs. The book concludes with a glossary of terms and directories of resources able to offer assistance and additional information.

How to Use This Book

This book is divided into parts and chapters. Parts focus on broad areas of interest. Chapters are devoted to single topics within a part.

Part I: Facts about Alcohol Use and Abuse answers common questions about alcohol use and defines terms such as binge drinking, moderate drinking, and heavy drinking. It offers statistics about the prevalence of alcohol abuse among youth, men, women, and seniors. This part also describes factors that may place a person at risk for alcoholism.

Part II: Preventing Alcohol Abuse, Dependence, and Alcohol-Related Injuries offers tips on reducing alcohol intake and guidance for discussing the risks of alcohol use with children. This part also identifies strategies that parents, youth, and community members can take to prevent impaired or drunk driving and alcohol-related injuries.

Part III: The Physical Effects of Alcohol describes hangovers, alcohol overdose, and other consequences of acute alcohol intoxication. It also explains how chronic alcohol abuse affects the liver, pancreas, kidneys, brain, heart, immune system, nerves, bones, and other body systems. Alcohol's impact on nutrition and sleep and its interactions with medications are also discussed.

Part IV: Alcohol Use during Pregnancy and Its Effect on Fetal Development examines the risks of drinking alcohol during pregnancy and the role that alcohol plays in the development of fetal alcohol syndrome and fetal alcohol spectrum disorders. Information for caregivers of stricken children is also provided.

Part V: Mental Health Problems Associated with Alcohol Use describes the relationship between depression and problem drinking. It also details other mental illnesses commonly associated with alcohol abuse, including anxiety disorders, post-traumatic stress disorder, attention deficit hyperactivity disorder, and addiction disorders.

Part VI: The Effects of Alcohol on Family, Work, and Society includes information about alcoholism's effect on an individual's ability to function within the family or in the workplace. It offers insight into alcohol's role in crime, domestic violence, and risky sexual activity. Tips for children and teens on coping with an alcoholic parent are also included.

Part VII: Treatment and Recovery from Alcohol Dependence provides information on recognizing alcoholism and encouraging someone who abuses alcohol to seek treatment. Inpatient and outpatient programs, medications, barriers to intervention, and the physical symptoms of recovery are described. The role of spiritual programs and alternative and complementary medicine practices for alcoholism treatment are also discussed.

Part VIII: Additional Help and Information includes a glossary of important terms, a directory of government and private organizations that provide help and information, and a list of state substance abuse agencies that offer referrals for local alcohol abuse treatment programs.

Bibliographic Note

This volume contains documents and excerpts from publications issued by the following U.S. government agencies: Centers for Disease Control and Prevention (CDC); National Cancer Institute (NCI); National Highway Traffic Safety Administration (NHTSA); National Institute of Allergy and Infectious Disease (NIAID); National Institute of Arthritis and Musculoskeletal and Skin Diseases (NIAMS); National Institute on Aging (NIA); National Institute on Alcohol Abuse and Alcoholism (NIAAA); National Institute on Diabetes and Digestive and Kidney Diseases (NIDDK); National Institute on Drug Abuse (NIDA); National Institutes of Health (NIH); National Women's Health Information Center (NWHIC); Substance Abuse and Mental Health Services Administration (SAMHSA); U.S. Department of Veterans Affairs (VA); and the U.S. Food and Drug Administration (FDA).

In addition, this volume contains copyrighted documents from the following organizations and individuals: A.D.A.M., Inc.; The Advertising Council; American Academy of Family Physicians; American Association for Clinical Chemistry; American Association of Kidney Patients; American Heart Association; American Institute for Cancer

Research; American Liver Foundation; American Medical Association; American Psychological Association; American Society of Clinical Oncology/People Living With Cancer; John Brick, Ph.D.; Center on Alcohol Marketing and Youth at Georgetown University; Rebecca Clay; Eastside Domestic Violence Program; Deb Evensen; Gale Group; Hazelden Foundation; Institute of Alcohol Studies; Henry J. Kaiser Family Foundation; March of Dimes Birth Defects Foundation; Minnesota Department of Health; National Business Group on Health; Nemours Center for Children's Health Media/TeensHealth.org; Partnership for a Drug-Free America; Rutgers University Center of Alcohol Studies; University of Michigan Health System; and the World Health Organization.

Full citation information is provided on the first page of each chapter. Every effort has been made to secure all necessary rights to reprint the copyrighted material. If any omissions have been made, please contact Omnigraphics to make corrections for future editions.

Acknowledgements

Thanks go to the many organizations, agencies, and individuals who have contributed materials for this *Sourcebook* and to medical consultant Dr. David Cooke and document engineer Bruce Bellenir. Special thanks go to managing editor Karen Bellenir and permissions and research coordinator Liz Barbour for their help and support.

About the Health Reference Series

The *Health Reference Series* is designed to provide basic medical information for patients, families, caregivers, and the general public. Each volume takes a particular topic and provides comprehensive coverage. This is especially important for people who may be dealing with a newly diagnosed disease or a chronic disorder in themselves or in a family member. People looking for preventive guidance, information about disease warning signs, medical statistics, and risk factors for health problems will also find answers to their questions in the *Health Reference Series*. The *Series*, however, is not intended to serve as a tool for diagnosing illness, in prescribing treatments, or as a substitute for the physician/patient relationship. All people concerned about medical symptoms or the possibility of disease are encouraged to seek professional care from an appropriate health care provider.

Locating Information within the Health Reference Series

The *Health Reference Series* contains a wealth of information about a wide variety of medical topics. Ensuring easy access to all the fact sheets, research reports, in-depth discussions, and other material contained within the individual books of the *Series* remains one of our highest priorities. As the *Series* continues to grow in size and scope, however, locating the precise information needed by a reader may become more challenging.

A Contents Guide to the Health Reference Series was developed to direct readers to the specific volumes that address their concerns. It presents an extensive list of diseases, treatments, and other topics of general interest compiled from the Tables of Contents and major index headings. To access *A Contents Guide to the Health Reference Series*, visit www.healthreferenceseries.com.

Medical Consultant

Medical consultation services are provided to the *Health Reference Series* editors by David A. Cooke, M.D. Dr. Cooke is a graduate of Brandeis University, and he received his M.D. degree from the University of Michigan. He completed residency training at the University of Wisconsin Hospital and Clinics. He is board-certified in Internal Medicine. Dr. Cooke currently works as part of the University of Michigan Health System and practices in Ann Arbor, MI. In his free time, he enjoys writing, science fiction, and spending time with his family.

Our Advisory Board

We would like to thank the following board members for providing guidance to the development of this *Series*:

- Dr. Lynda Baker, Associate Professor of Library and Information Science, Wayne State University, Detroit, MI

- Nancy Bulgarelli, William Beaumont Hospital Library, Royal Oak, MI

- Karen Imarisio, Bloomfield Township Public Library, Bloomfield Township, MI

- Karen Morgan, Mardigian Library, University of Michigan-Dearborn, Dearborn, MI

- Rosemary Orlando, St. Clair Shores Public Library, St. Clair Shores, MI

Health Reference Series *Update Policy*

The inaugural book in the *Health Reference Series* was the first edition of *Cancer Sourcebook* published in 1989. Since then, the *Series* has been enthusiastically received by librarians and in the medical community. In order to maintain the standard of providing high-quality health information for the layperson the editorial staff at Omnigraphics felt it was necessary to implement a policy of updating volumes when warranted.

Medical researchers have been making tremendous strides, and it is the purpose of the *Health Reference Series* to stay current with the most recent advances. Each decision to update a volume is made on an individual basis. Some of the considerations include how much new information is available and the feedback we receive from people who use the books. If there is a topic you would like to see added to the update list, or an area of medical concern you feel has not been adequately addressed, please write to:

Editor
Health Reference Series
Omnigraphics, Inc.
615 Griswold Street
Detroit, MI 48226
E-mail: editorial@omnigraphics.com

Part One

Facts about Alcohol Use and Abuse

Chapter 1

Questions and Answers on Alcohol Consumption

What is alcohol?

Ethyl alcohol, or ethanol, is a psychoactive drug found in beer, wine, and hard liquor. It is produced by the fermentation of yeast, sugars, and starches.

What does alcohol do to the body?

Alcohol is a central nervous system depressant. It is rapidly absorbed from the stomach and small intestine, passes into the bloodstream, and is then widely distributed throughout the body. The effects of alcohol on the body are directly related to the amount consumed. In small amounts, alcohol can have a relaxing effect. Adverse effects of alcohol can include impaired judgment, reduced reaction time, slurred speech, and unsteady gait (i.e., difficulty walking); When consumed rapidly and in large amounts, alcohol can also result in coma and death. In addition, alcohol can interact with a number of prescription and non-prescription medications in ways that can intensify the effect of alcohol, of the medications themselves, or both. Furthermore, alcohol use by pregnant women, can cause serious damage to the developing fetus.

"Questions and Answers on Alcohol Consumption," Centers for Disease Control and Prevention, National Center for Chronic Disease Prevention and Health Promotion, January 31, 2005.

What is a standard drink?

A standard drink is one 12-ounce beer, one 5-ounce glass of wine, or one 1.5-ounce shot of distilled spirits. Each of these drinks contains about half an ounce of alcohol.

Is beer or wine safer to drink than hard liquor?

No. One 12-ounce beer has about the same amount of alcohol as one 5-ounce glass of wine, or one 1.5-ounce shot of liquor.

What is moderate drinking?

Based on current dietary guidelines, moderate drinking for women is defined as an average of 1 drink or less per day. Moderate drinking for men is defined as an average of 2 drinks or less per day (U.S. Department of Agriculture, 2000).

What is heavy drinking?

Heavy drinking is consuming alcohol in excess of 1 drink per day on average for women and greater than 2 drinks per day on average for men (National Institute on Alcohol Abuse and Alcoholism [NIAAA], 2004).

What is binge drinking?

Binge drinking is generally defined as having 5 or more drinks on one occasion, meaning in a row or within a short period of time (Naimi, 2003). However, among women, binge drinking is often defined as having 4 or more drinks on one occasion (NIAAA, 2004; Wechsler, 1998). This lower cut-point is used for women because women are generally of smaller stature than men and absorb and metabolize alcohol differently than men do.

What is alcoholism?

Alcoholism is a primary, chronic disease with genetic, psychosocial, and environmental factors influencing its development and manifestations. The disease is often progressive and fatal. It is characterized by continuous or periodic: impaired control over drinking, preoccupation with the drug alcohol, use of alcohol use despite adverse consequences, and distortions in thinking, most notably denial (American Society of Addiction Medicine, 2001).

What is alcohol abuse?

Alcohol abuse is characterized by recurrent alcohol-related problems, including problems with relationships, job performance, or both; the use of alcohol in hazardous situations (e.g., while driving a car); or some combination of these (*DSM-IV*, 1994).

Why are some people more sensitive to alcohol than others?

Individual reactions to alcohol can vary greatly and may be influenced by many factors, including age, gender, race, ethnicity, physical condition, the amount of food eaten before drinking, the use of drugs or medicines, family history of alcohol problems, and many other factors as well. Therefore, while drinking guidelines and definitions of drinking patterns can be very helpful in identifying risky patterns of alcohol use, personal decisions about whether to drink, and if so, when and how much, should take into account these individual factors as well.

What does it mean to drink too much?

A person may be said to be "drinking too much" or engaging in "excessive drinking" if they exceed either the guidelines for daily alcohol consumption, or the guidelines for average daily alcohol consumption. Among men, excessive drinking may be defined as more than 4 drinks per day, or an average of more than 2 drinks per day over a 7 or 30 day period. Among women, excessive drinking may be defined as more than 3 drinks per day, or an average of more than 1 drink per day over a 7- or 30- day period (NIAAA, 2004). However, current guidelines specify that certain individuals (e.g., youth under age 21 years, pregnant women, and persons recovering from alcoholism) should not drink at all. Among these individuals, any alcohol consumption may be too much. In addition, anyone who chooses to drink should be aware that individual reactions to alcohol can vary greatly. Therefore, when in doubt about whether it's appropriate to drink, and if so, how much, it is always best to consult one's own personal physician.

What does it mean to get drunk?

Drunkenness or alcohol intoxication is caused by an overdose of alcohol. However, the number of drinks that an individual needs to consume to get drunk varies based on a number of factors, including age, gender, physical condition, and the amount of food eaten before drinking, the use of drugs or medicines, and many other factors. However, binge drinking (i.e., for a man, consuming 5 or more drinks per occasion, and for a woman, consuming 4 or more drinks per occasion) typically results in intoxication.

What does it mean to be above the legal limit for drinking?

The "legal limit for drinking" is the alcohol level above which an individual is subject to legal penalties (e.g., loss of a driver's license). Typically, this alcohol level is measured in blood or breath, using either a blood alcohol test or a breathalyzer, respectively. Legal limits are defined by a government entity (e.g., state legislature or regulatory agency), and are specific to the situation that a person is in (e.g., driving a car) as well as the characteristics of the person themselves (e.g., their age). For example, in most states, the current legal limit for operating a motor vehicle is 0.08%, or 80 mg/dL among drivers who are age 21 years or older. However, there is zero tolerance for drivers who are under age 21 years, meaning that they are not allowed to operate a motor vehicle with any alcohol in their system. In contrast, the legal limit is 0.04% or 40 mg/dL for commercial truck drivers. Different legal limits also apply to airline pilots, bus drivers, and to persons operating recreational watercraft. However, it is important to recognize that the legal limit does not define a level below which it is safe to operate a vehicle or engage in some other activity rather, the legal limit is intended to define a level at or above which an individual is subject to legal action under a specific set of circumstances. Therefore, decisions about the appropriate level of alcohol consumption in a particular situation should begin with a careful assessment of whether it's appropriate to be drinking at all.

What are common health effects of drinking too much?

Excessive drinking, including binge and heavy drinking, has numerous chronic (long-term) and acute (short-term) health effects. Chronic health consequences of excessive drinking can include liver cirrhosis (damage to liver cells); pancreatitis (inflammation of the pancreas); various cancers, including cancer of the liver, mouth, throat, larynx (the voice box), and esophagus; high blood pressure; and psychological disorders. Acute health consequences of excessive drinking can include motor vehicle injuries, falls, domestic violence, rape, and child abuse (Naimi, 2003).

How do I know if it's OK to drink?

The current Dietary Guidelines for Americans recommends that if you choose to drink alcoholic beverages, you do so in moderation (see definition of moderate drinking). However, these guidelines also specify that there are some people who should not drink alcoholic beverages at all. These people include:

- children and adolescents;
- individuals of any age who cannot restrict their drinking to moderate levels;
- women who may become pregnant or who are pregnant;
- individuals who plan to drive, operate machinery, or take part in other activities that requires attention, skill, or coordination; and
- individuals taking prescription or over-the-counter medications that can interact with alcohol.

Therefore, when in doubt about whether it's appropriate to drink, and if so, how much, it is always best to consult one's own personal physician.

How do I know if I have a drinking problem?

Drinking is a problem if it causes trouble in your relationships, in school, in social activities, or in how you think and feel. If you are concerned that either you or someone in your family might have a drinking problem, it is important that you consult your personal physician.

References

1. American Society of Addiction Medicine. http://www.asam.org/ppol/Definition%20of%20Alcoholism.htm, accessed April 21, 2004.

2. *Diagnostic and Statistical Manual of Mental Disorders—Fourth Edition* (DSM-IV), published by the American Psychiatric Association, Washington D.C., 1994.

3. Naimi T, Brewer B, Mokdad A, Serdula M, Denny C, Marks J. Binge Drinking Among U.S. Adults. *JAMA* 2003;289:70–5.

4. NIAAA. Helping patients with alcohol problems: A health practitioners guide http://www.niaaa.nih.gov/publications/Practitioner/HelpingPatients.htm#step1A, accessed April 6, 2004.

5. U.S. Department of Health and Human Services, National Institutes of Health, National Institute on Alcohol Abuse and Alcoholism. Newsletter, No. 3. Winter, 2003.

6. U.S. Department of Health and Human Services, U.S. Department of Agriculture. *Nutrition and your health: dietary guidelines for Americans.* 5th ed. Home and Gardening Bulletin No. 232. Washington D.C.: U.S. Government Printing Office; 2000.

7. Wechsler H, Austin SB. Binge drinking: The five/four measure. *J Stud Alcohol* 1998;59:122–124.

8. Wechsler H, Nelson TF. Binge drinking and the American college student: what's five drinks? *Psychol Addict Behav* 2001; 15:287–291.

Chapter 2

Facts and Figures on Alcohol Consumption and Alcohol-Related Health Effects

Measures of Alcohol Consumption and Alcohol-Related Health Effects from Excessive Consumption

Current Drinking

- Current drinkers are those who consume alcohol-containing beverages.

- In 2002, 54.9% of U.S. adults (18 years and older) reported drinking at least one drink in the past month. The prevalence of past-month alcohol consumption was higher for men (62.4%) than for women (47.9%).

Binge Drinking

- Binge drinking is generally defined as having 5 or more drinks on one occasion, meaning in a row or within a short period of time. However, among women, binge drinking is often defined as having 4 or more drinks on one occasion. This lower cut-point is used for women because women are generally of smaller stature than men, and absorb and metabolize alcohol differently than men.

Excerpted from the fact sheet "General Alcohol Information," by the Centers for Disease Control and Prevention (CDC), National Center for Chronic Disease Prevention and Health Promotion, January 31, 2005. For a complete list of references, see www.cdc.gov.

- About 1 in 3 adult drinkers in the United States report past-month binge drinking, and this ratio has changed very little since the mid-1980s.

- In 2001, there were approximately 1.5 billion episodes of binge drinking in the United States. Binge drinking rates were highest among those aged 18 to 25 years; however, 70% of binge drinking episodes occurred among those aged 26 years and older.

- Binge drinkers were 14 times more likely to report alcohol-impaired driving than non-binge drinkers.

- Binge drinking is associated with a number of adverse health effects, including unintentional injuries (e.g., motor vehicle crashes, falls, burns, drownings, and hypothermia); violence (homicide, suicide, child abuse, domestic violence); sudden infant death syndrome; alcohol poisoning; hypertension; myocardial infarction; gastritis; pancreatitis; sexually transmitted diseases; meningitis; and poor control of diabetes.

Heavy Drinking

- Heavy drinking is consuming alcohol in excess of 1 drink per day on average for women and greater than 2 drinks per day on average for men.

- In 2002, 5.9% of U.S. adults reported heavy drinking in the past 30 days; the prevalence of heavy drinking was greater for men (7.1%) than for women (4.5%).

- Heavy drinking is associated with a number of chronic health conditions, including chronic liver disease and cirrhosis, gastrointestinal cancers, heart disease, stroke, pancreatitis, depression, and a variety of social problems.

Alcohol Dependence

A person is defined as being dependent on alcohol if he or she reports three or more of the following symptoms in the past year.

- tolerance (e.g., needing more alcohol to become intoxicated)

- withdrawal

- alcohol use for longer periods than intended

- desire and/or unsuccessful efforts to cut down or control alcohol use

- considerable time spent obtaining or using alcohol or recovering from its effects

- important social, work, or recreational activities given up because of use

- continued use of alcohol despite knowledge of problems caused by or aggravated by use

In 2002, 3.7% of past-year drinkers were alcohol-dependent.

Underage Drinking

- As of 1988, all states prohibit the purchase of alcohol by youth under the age of 21 years. Consequently, underage drinking is defined as consuming alcohol prior to the minimum legal drinking age of 21 years.

- In 2003, 44.9% of 9th through 12th graders reported drinking alcohol on one or more of the past 30 days; prevalence of current drinking was higher for females (45.8%) than among males (43.8%).

- In 2003, 28.3% of 9th through 12th graders reported binge drinking (having five or more drinks of alcohol in a row or within a couple of hours) at least once during the past 30 days. The prevalence of binge drinking was higher for males (29%) than among females (27.5%).

- Alcohol use is a leading risk factor in the three leading causes of death among youth: unintentional injuries (including motor vehicle crashes and drownings); suicides; and homicides. Other adverse consequences of underage drinking include risky sexual behavior and poor school performance.

- Zero tolerance laws, which make it illegal for youth under age 21 years to drive with any measurable amount of alcohol in their system (i.e., with a blood alcohol concentration (BAC) $\geq$0.02 g/dL), have reduced traffic fatalities among 18 to 20 year olds by 13% and saved an estimated 21,887 lives from 1975 through 2002.

Alcohol Use and Women's Health

- For women of childbearing age, the consequences of excessive alcohol consumption, particularly binge drinking, includes

11

unintentional injuries, domestic violence, risky sexual behavior
and sexually transmitted diseases, unintended pregnancy, and
alcohol-exposed pregnancies.

- In 2001, 11.8% of women aged 18 to 44 years reported consuming alcohol within the past month, and 11% reported binge drinking (5 or more drinks on any one occasion).

- Women with unintended pregnancies were 60% more likely
  to binge drink during the three months before conception than
  women with intended pregnancies.

Alcohol-Impaired Driving

- In 2002, 2.2% of U.S. adults reported alcohol-impaired driving in the past 30 days.

- In 1993, there were approximately 123 million episodes of alcohol-impaired driving in the United States.

- In 2001, there were approximately 1.4 million arrests for driving under the influence of alcohol or narcotics. This is an arrest rate of 1 of every 137 licensed drivers in the United States.

Alcohol-Related Health Effects from Excessive Alcohol Consumption

Total Deaths due to Alcohol

- In 2000, there were approximately 85,000 deaths attributable to either excessive or risky drinking in the United States, making alcohol the third leading actual cause of death.

- Alcohol-related deaths in the United States vary considerably by state, and are directly related to the amount of alcohol consumed and the pattern of alcohol use.

Alcohol Motor Vehicle Crash Deaths

- In 2002, 17,419 people in the United States died in alcohol-related motor vehicle crashes, accounting for 41% of all traffic-related deaths.

- In 1995, 36% of all crash fatalities among youth aged 15 to 20 years were alcohol-related.

- From 1997 through 2002, 2,355 children died in alcohol-related motor vehicle crashes; 1,588 (68%) of these children were riding with a drinking driver.

Alcohol and Unintentional Injuries

- Alcohol-related unintentional injuries and deaths include motor vehicle crashes, drownings, falls, hypothermia, burns, suicides, and homicides.

- Approximately 31.1% of those who die from unintentional, non-traffic injuries in the United States have a blood alcohol concentration of 0.10 g/dL or greater.

- Patients treated in an emergency department (ED) for an unintentional injury are 13.5 times more likely to have consumed 5 or more alcohol-containing beverages within 6 hours of their injury compared to age and sex matched community controls.

Alcohol and Violence

- In 1997, about 40% of all crimes (violent and non-violent) were committed under the influence of alcohol.

- In 1997, 40% of convicted rape and sexual assault offenders said that they were drinking at the time of their crime.

- Approximately 72% of rapes reported on college campuses occur when victims are so intoxicated they are unable to consent or refuse.

- Two thirds of victims of intimate partner violence reported that alcohol was involved in the incident.

- Nearly one half of the cases of child abuse and neglect are associated with parental alcohol or drug abuse.

- Approximately 23% of suicide deaths are attributable to alcohol.

Alcohol and Pregnancy

- Adverse health effects that are associated with alcohol-exposed pregnancies include miscarriage, premature delivery, low birth weight, sudden infant death syndrome, and prenatal alcohol-related conditions (e.g., fetal alcohol syndrome and alcohol-related neurodevelopmental disorders).

- In 1999, 12.8% of women aged 18 to 44 years reported any alcohol use (at least one drink) during pregnancy, and 2.7% reported binge drinking (5 or more drinks on any one occasion).

- Alcohol-related neurodevelopmental disorder and alcohol-related birth defects are believed to occur approximately three times as often as fetal alcohol syndrome (FAS).

- Fetal alcohol syndrome is one of the leading causes of mental retardation, and is directly attributable to drinking during pregnancy. FAS is characterized by growth retardation, facial abnormalities, and central nervous system dysfunction (i.e., learning disabilities and lower IQ), as well as behavioral problems.

- The incidence of FAS in the United States ranges from 0.2 to 1.5 per 1,000 live births.

- Any maternal alcohol use in the periconceptional period (i.e., during the three months before pregnancy or during the first trimester) is associated with a six-fold increased risk of SIDS.

- Binge drinking (five or more drinks at a time) during a mother's first trimester of pregnancy is associated with an eight-fold increase in the odds that the infant will die of SIDS.

Alcohol and Sexually Transmitted Disease

- Alcohol use by young adults is associated with earlier initiation of sexual activity, unprotected sexual intercourse, multiple partners, and an increased risk for sexually transmitted diseases.

- Among teens aged 14 to 18, 20% of those who reported drinking before age 14 also reported being sexually active compared to 7% of those who did not report drinking before this age.

- In 1998, an estimated 400,000 college students between the ages of 18 and 24 had unprotected sex after drinking, and an estimated 100,000 had sex when they were so intoxicated they were unable to consent.

- Among adults aged 18 to 30, binge drinkers were twice as likely as those who did not binge drink to have had two or more sex partners.

- People who abuse alcohol are more likely to engage in risky behaviors, such as having unprotected sex, having more sex partners, and using intravenous drugs. In a single act of unprotected sex with an infected partner, a teenage woman has a 1% risk of acquiring HIV, a 30% risk of getting genital herpes, and a 50% chance of contracting gonorrhea.

Hepatitis C and Chronic Liver Disease

- Alcohol consumption can exacerbate the HCV infection and accelerate disease progression to cirrhosis. Alcohol may also exacerbate the side effects of antiviral treatment for HCV infection, impairing the body's response to the virus.

- In 2003, there were 12,207 deaths from alcohol-related chronic liver disease (CLD). Approximately 75% of those deaths occurred among men.

- Approximately 40% of the deaths from unspecified liver disease in the United States are attributable to heavy alcohol consumption.

Alcohol and Cancer

- Alcohol-related cancers include oral-pharyngeal, esophagus (squamous cell type), prostate, liver, and breast. In general, the risk of cancer increases with increasing amounts of alcohol.

- Excessive drinkers are 3 times more likely to develop liver cancer than non-drinkers.

- Excessive drinkers are 4 times more likely to develop esophageal cancer than non-drinkers.

- Oral cancers are six times more common in heavy alcohol users than in non-alcohol users.

- Compared to non-drinkers, women who consume an average of 1 alcoholic drink per day increase their risk of breast cancer by approximately 7%. Women who consume an average of 2 to 5 drinks per day increase their risk of developing breast cancer by approximately 50% compared to that of non-drinkers.

Effective Prevention Strategies for Alcohol-Related Health Problems

Alcohol Taxes

- A 10% increase on the tax for alcohol containing beverages could reduce the number of binge drinking episodes per month by 8%.

- For every 1% increase in the price of beer, the traffic fatality rate declines by 0.9%.

- A 25% increase in the 1992 federal beer tax would have reduced work-loss days from non-fatal workplace accidents by 4.6 million and lost productivity by $491 million.

- Raising state beer tax from 10¢ per case to $1 per case would increase the probability of graduating from college by 6.3%.

Minimum Legal Drinking Age Laws

- All states and the District of Columbia have enforced 21-year-old minimum drinking age laws. In 2002, an estimated 917 lives were saved in traffic crashes as a result of the age 21 minimum drinking age laws.

- Increasing the minimum drinking age from 18 to 21 has reduced both drinking and traffic crashes among youth by 10% to 15%.

Comprehensive Community Programs

- Comprehensive community-based programs have reduced past month alcohol consumption among underage youth by 7%.

Intervention Training Programs for Servers

- Server training programs have reduced alcohol sales by 11.5% and sales to pseudo-intoxicated buyers by 46%.

- Server training programs have reduced single vehicle nighttime injury crashes by 23%.

Screening and Brief Intervention

- Brief physician advice to reduce alcohol consumption has reduced the number of binge drinking episodes in the past 30 days more than 40%.

- The U.S. Preventive Services Task Force (USPSTF) recommends regular screening in primary care practices for alcohol misuse among adults and pregnant women.

Chapter 3

Overview of Alcohol Abuse and Alcoholism

What is alcoholism?

Alcoholism, also known as alcohol dependence, is a disease that includes the following four symptoms:

- craving—a strong need, or urge, to drink;

- loss of control—not being able to stop drinking once drinking has begun;

- physical dependence—withdrawal symptoms, such as nausea, sweating, shakiness, and anxiety after stopping drinking; and

- tolerance—the need to drink greater amounts of alcohol to get high.

For clinical and research purposes, formal diagnostic criteria for alcoholism also have been developed. Such criteria are included in the *Diagnostic and Statistical Manual of Mental Disorders, Fourth Edition*, published by the American Psychiatric Association, as well as in the International Statistical Classification of Diseases, published by the World Health Organization.

"FAQs on Alcohol Abuse and Alcoholism," by the National Institute on Alcohol Abuse and Alcoholism (www.niaaa.nih.gov), September 23, 2005.

Is alcoholism a disease?

Yes, alcoholism is a disease. The craving that an alcoholic feels for alcohol can be as strong as the need for food or water. An alcoholic will continue to drink despite serious family, health, or legal problems.

Like many other diseases, alcoholism is chronic, meaning that it lasts a person's lifetime; it usually follows a predictable course; and it has symptoms. The risk for developing alcoholism is influenced both by a person's genes and by his or her lifestyle.

Is alcoholism inherited?

Research shows that the risk for developing alcoholism does indeed run in families. The genes a person inherits partially explain this pattern, but lifestyle is also a factor. Currently, researchers are working to discover the actual genes that put people at risk for alcoholism. Your friends, the amount of stress in your life, and how readily available alcohol is also are factors that may increase your risk for alcoholism.

But remember: Risk is not destiny. Just because alcoholism tends to run in families doesn't mean that a child of an alcoholic parent will automatically become an alcoholic too. Some people develop alcoholism even though no one in their family has a drinking problem. By the same token, not all children of alcoholic families get into trouble with alcohol. Knowing you are at risk is important, though, because then you can take steps to protect yourself from developing problems with alcohol.

Can alcoholism be cured?

No, alcoholism cannot be cured at this time. Even if an alcoholic hasn't been drinking for a long time, he or she can still suffer a relapse. To guard against a relapse, an alcoholic must continue to avoid all alcoholic beverages.

Can alcoholism be treated?

Yes, alcoholism can be treated. Alcoholism treatment programs use both counseling and medications to help a person stop drinking. Most alcoholics need help to recover from their disease. With support and treatment, many people are able to stop drinking and rebuild their lives.

Which medications treat alcoholism?

A range of medications is used to treat alcoholism. Benzodiazepines (Valium® , Librium®) are sometimes used during the first days after a person stops drinking to help him or her safely withdraw from alcohol. These medications are not used beyond the first few days, however, because they may be highly addictive. Other medications help people remain sober. One medication used for this purpose is naltrexone (ReVia®). When combined with counseling naltrexone can reduce the craving for alcohol and help prevent a person from returning, or relapsing, to heavy drinking. Another medication, disulfiram (Antabuse®), discourages drinking by making the person feel sick if he or she drinks alcohol.

Though several medications help treat alcoholism, there is no "magic bullet." In other words, no single medication is available that works in every case and/or in every person. Developing new and more effective medications to treat alcoholism remains a high priority for researchers.

Does alcoholism treatment work?

Alcoholism treatment works for many people. But just like any chronic disease, there are varying levels of success when it comes to treatment. Some people stop drinking and remain sober. Others have long periods of sobriety with bouts of relapse. And still others cannot stop drinking for any length of time. With treatment, one thing is clear, however: the longer a person abstains from alcohol, the more likely he or she will be able to stay sober.

Do you have to be an alcoholic to experience problems?

No. Alcoholism is only one type of an alcohol problem. Alcohol abuse can be just as harmful. A person can abuse alcohol without actually being an alcoholic—that is, he or she may drink too much and too often but still not be dependent on alcohol. Some of the problems linked to alcohol abuse include not being able to meet work, school, or family responsibilities; drunk-driving arrests and car crashes; and drinking-related medical conditions. Under some circumstances, even social or moderate drinking is dangerous—for example, when driving, during pregnancy, or when taking certain medications.

Are specific groups of people more likely to have problems?

Alcohol abuse and alcoholism cut across gender, race, and nationality. Nearly 14 million people in the United States—1 in every 13 adults—abuse alcohol or are alcoholic. In general, though, more men than women are alcohol dependent or have alcohol problems. And alcohol problems are highest among young adults ages 18 to 29 and lowest among adults ages 65 and older. We also know that people who start drinking at an early age—for example, at age 14 or younger—greatly increase the chance that they will develop alcohol problems at some point in their lives.

How can you tell if someone has a problem?

Answering the following four questions can help you find out if you or a loved one has a drinking problem:

- Have you ever felt you should cut down on your drinking?
- Have people annoyed you by criticizing your drinking?
- Have you ever felt bad or guilty about your drinking?
- Have you ever had a drink first thing in the morning to steady your nerves or to get rid of a hangover?

One "yes" answer suggests a possible alcohol problem. More than one "yes" answer means it is highly likely that a problem exists. If you think that you or someone you know might have an alcohol problem, it is important to see a doctor or other health care provider right away. They can help you determine if a drinking problem exists and plan the best course of action.

Can a problem drinker simply cut down?

It depends. If that person has been diagnosed as an alcoholic, the answer is "no." Alcoholics who try to cut down on drinking rarely succeed. Cutting out alcohol—that is, abstaining—is usually the best course for recovery. People who are not alcohol dependent but who have experienced alcohol-related problems may be able to limit the amount they drink. If they can't stay within those limits, they need to stop drinking altogether.

If an alcoholic is unwilling to get help, what can you do about it?

This can be a challenge. An alcoholic can't be forced to get help except under certain circumstances, such as a violent incident that results in court-ordered treatment or medical emergency. But you don't have to wait for someone to hit rock bottom to act. Many alcoholism treatment specialists suggest the following steps to help an alcoholic get treatment:

Stop all cover ups. Family members often make excuses to others or try to protect the alcoholic from the results of his or her drinking. It is important to stop covering for the alcoholic so that he or she experiences the full consequences of drinking.

Time your intervention. The best time to talk to the drinker is shortly after an alcohol-related problem has occurred—like a serious family argument or an accident. Choose a time when he or she is sober, both of you are fairly calm, and you have a chance to talk in private.

Be specific. Tell the family member that you are worried about his or her drinking. Use examples of the ways in which the drinking has caused problems, including the most recent incident.

State the results. Explain to the drinker what you will do if he or she doesn't go for help—not to punish the drinker, but to protect yourself from his or her problems. What you say may range from refusing to go with the person to any social activity where alcohol will be served to moving out of the house. Do not make any threats you are not prepared to carry out.

Get help. Gather information in advance about treatment options in your community. If the person is willing to get help, call immediately for an appointment with a treatment counselor. Offer to go with the family member on the first visit to a treatment program and/or an Alcoholics Anonymous meeting.

Call on a friend. If the family member still refuses to get help, ask a friend to talk with him or her using the steps just described. A friend who is a recovering alcoholic may be particularly persuasive, but any person who is caring and nonjudgmental may help. The intervention of more than one person, more than one time, is often necessary to coax an alcoholic to seek help.

Find strength in numbers. With the help of a health care professional, some families join with other relatives and friends to confront an alcoholic as a group. This approach should only be tried under the guidance of a health care professional who is experienced in this kind of group intervention.

Get support. It is important to remember that you are not alone. Support groups offered in most communities include Al-Anon, which holds regular meetings for spouses and other significant adults in an alcoholic's life, and Alateen, which is geared to children of alcoholics. These groups help family members understand that they are not responsible for an alcoholic's drinking and that they need to take steps to take care of themselves, regardless of whether the alcoholic family member chooses to get help.

You can call the National Drug and Alcohol Treatment Referral Routing Service (Center for Substance Abuse Treatment) at 800-662-HELP for information about treatment programs in your local community and to speak to someone about an alcohol problem.

What is a safe level of drinking?

For most adults, moderate alcohol use—up to two drinks per day for men and one drink per day for women and older people—causes few if any problems. (One drink equals one 12-ounce bottle of beer or wine cooler, one 5-ounce glass of wine, or 1.5 ounces of 80-proof distilled spirits.)

Certain people should not drink at all, however:

- women who are pregnant or trying to become pregnant
- people who plan to drive or engage in other activities that require alertness and skill (such as using high-speed machinery)
- people taking certain over-the-counter or prescription medications
- people with medical conditions that can be made worse by drinking
- recovering alcoholics
- people younger than age 21

Is it safe to drink during pregnancy?

No, drinking during pregnancy is dangerous. Alcohol can have a number of harmful effects on the baby. The baby can be born mentally retarded or with learning and behavioral problems that last a lifetime. We don't know exactly how much alcohol is required to cause these problems. We do know, however, that these alcohol-related birth defects are 100-percent preventable, simply by not drinking alcohol during pregnancy. The safest course for women who are pregnant or trying to become pregnant is not to drink alcohol at all.

Does alcohol affect older people differently?

Alcohol's effects do vary with age. Slower reaction times, problems with hearing and seeing, and a lower tolerance to alcohol's effects put older people at higher risk for falls, car crashes, and other types of injuries that may result from drinking.

Older people also tend to take more medicines than younger people. Mixing alcohol with over-the-counter or prescription medications can be very dangerous, even fatal. More than 150 medications interact harmfully with alcohol. In addition, alcohol can make many of the medical conditions common in older people, including high blood pressure and ulcers, more serious. Physical changes associated with aging can make older people feel high even after drinking only small amounts of alcohol. So even if there is no medical reason to avoid alcohol, older men and women should limit themselves to one drink per day.

Does alcohol affect women differently?

Yes, alcohol affects women differently than men. Women become more impaired than men do after drinking the same amount of alcohol, even when differences in body weight are taken into account. This is because women's bodies have less water than men's bodies. Because alcohol mixes with body water, a given amount of alcohol becomes more highly concentrated in a woman's body than in a man's. In other words, it would be like dropping the same amount of alcohol into a much smaller pail of water. That is why the recommended drinking limit for women is lower than for men.

In addition, chronic alcohol abuse takes a heavier physical toll on women than on men. Alcohol dependence and related medical problems, such as brain, heart, and liver damage, progress more rapidly in women than in men.

Is alcohol good for your heart?

Studies have shown that moderate drinkers—men who have two or less drinks per day and women who have one or less drinks per day—are less likely to die from one form of heart disease than are people who do not drink any alcohol or who drink more. It's believed that these smaller amounts of alcohol help protect against heart disease by changing the blood's chemistry, thus reducing the risk of blood clots in the heart's arteries.

If you are a nondrinker, however, you should not start drinking solely to benefit your heart. You can guard against heart disease by exercising and eating foods that are low in fat. And if you are pregnant, planning to become pregnant, have been diagnosed as alcoholic, or have another medical condition that could make alcohol use harmful, you should not drink.

If you can safely drink alcohol and you choose to drink, do so in moderation. Heavy drinking can actually increase the risk of heart failure, stroke, and high blood pressure, as well as cause many other medical problems, such as liver cirrhosis.

When taking medications, must you stop drinking?

Possibly. More than 150 medications interact harmfully with alcohol. These interactions may result in increased risk of illness, injury, and even death. Alcohol's effects are heightened by medicines that depress the central nervous system, such as sleeping pills, antihistamines, antidepressants, anti-anxiety drugs, and some painkillers. In addition, medicines for certain disorders, including diabetes, high blood pressure, and heart disease, can have harmful interactions with alcohol. If you are taking any over-the-counter or prescription medications, ask your doctor or pharmacist if you can safely drink alcohol.

How can a person get help for an alcohol problem?

There are many national and local resources that can help. The National Drug and Alcohol Treatment Referral Routing Service provides a toll-free telephone number, 1-800-662-HELP, offering various resource information. Through this service you can speak directly to a representative concerning substance abuse treatment, request printed material on alcohol or other drugs, or obtain local substance abuse treatment referral information in your state.

Many people also find support groups a helpful aid to recovery. The following list includes a variety of resources:

- Al-Anon/Alateen
- Alcoholics Anonymous (AA)
- National Association for Children of Alcoholics (NACOA)
- National Clearinghouse for Alcohol and Drug Information (NCADI)

Chapter 4

A Family History of Alcoholism: Are You at Risk?

If you are among the millions of people in this country who have a parent, grandparent, or other close relative with alcoholism, you may have wondered what your family's history of alcoholism means for you. Are problems with alcohol a part of your future? Is your risk for becoming an alcoholic greater than for people who do not have a family history of alcoholism? If so, what can you do to lower your risk?

What Is Alcoholism?

Alcoholism, or alcohol dependence, is a disease that includes four symptoms:

- Craving—A strong need, or urge, to drink.

- Loss of control—Not being able to stop drinking once drinking has begun.

- Physical dependence—Withdrawal symptoms, such as upset stomach, sweating, shakiness, and anxiety after stopping drinking.

- Tolerance—The need to drink greater amounts of alcohol to get "high."

From the brochure by the National Institute on Alcohol Abuse and Alcoholism (NIAAA), August 2005.

Many scientific studies, including research conducted among twins and children of alcoholics, have shown that genetic factors influence alcoholism. These findings show that children of alcoholics are about four times more likely than the general population to develop alcohol problems. Children of alcoholics also have a higher risk for many other behavioral and emotional problems. But alcoholism is not determined only by the genes you inherit from your parents. In fact, more than one half of all children of alcoholics do not become alcoholic. Research shows that many factors influence your risk of developing alcoholism. Some factors raise the risk while others lower it.

Genes are not the only things children inherit from their parents. How parents act and how they treat each other and their children has an influence on children growing up in the family. These aspects of family life also affect the risk for alcoholism. Researchers believe a person's risk increases if he or she is in a family with the following difficulties:

- an alcoholic parent is depressed or has other psychological problems;
- both parents abuse alcohol and other drugs;
- the parents' alcohol abuse is severe; and
- conflicts lead to aggression and violence in the family.

The good news is that many children of alcoholics from even the most troubled families do not develop drinking problems. Just as a family history of alcoholism does not guarantee that you will become an alcoholic, neither does growing up in a very troubled household with alcoholic parents. Just because alcoholism tends to run in families does not mean that a child of an alcoholic parent will automatically become an alcoholic, too. The risk is higher but it does not have to happen.

If you are worried that your family's history of alcohol problems or your troubled family life puts you at risk for becoming alcoholic, here is some commonsense advice to help you.

Avoid underage drinking—First, underage drinking is illegal. Second, research shows that the risk for alcoholism is higher among people who begin to drink at an early age, perhaps as a result of both environmental and genetic factors.

Drink moderately as an adult—Even if they do not have a family history of alcoholism, adults who choose to drink alcohol should do so in moderation—no more than one drink a day for most women, and no more than two drinks a day for most men, according to guidelines from the U.S. Department of Agriculture and the U.S. Department of Health and Human Services. Some people should not drink at all, including women who are pregnant or who are trying to become pregnant, recovering alcoholics, people who plan to drive or engage in other activities that require attention or skill, people taking certain medications, and people with certain medical conditions.

People with a family history of alcoholism, who have a higher risk for becoming dependent on alcohol, should approach moderate drinking carefully. Maintaining moderate drinking habits may be harder for them than for people without a family history of drinking problems. Once a person moves from moderate to heavier drinking, the risks of social problems (for example, drinking and driving, violence, and trauma) and medical problems (for example, liver disease, brain damage, and cancer) increase greatly.

Talk to a health care professional—Discuss your concerns with a doctor, nurse, nurse practitioner, or other health care provider. They can recommend groups or organizations that could help you avoid alcohol problems. If you are an adult who already has begun to drink, a health care professional can assess your drinking habits to see if you need to cut back on your drinking and advise you about how to do that.

Chapter 5

The Genetics of Alcoholism

Research has shown conclusively that familial transmission of alcoholism risk is at least in part genetic and not just the result of family environment. The task of current science is to identify what a person inherits that increases vulnerability to alcoholism and how inherited factors interact with the environment to cause disease. This information will provide the basis for identifying people at risk and for developing behavioral and pharmacologic approaches to prevent and treat alcohol problems.

A Complex Genetic Disease

Studies in recent years have confirmed that identical twins, who share the same genes, are about twice as likely as fraternal twins, who share on average 50 percent of their genes, to resemble each other in terms of the presence of alcoholism. Recent research also reports that 50 to 60 percent of the risk for alcoholism is genetically determined, for both men and women. Genes alone do not preordain that someone will be alcoholic; features in the environment along with gene-environment interactions account for the remainder of the risk.

Excerpted from *Alcohol Alert* No. 60, a publication of the National Institute on Alcohol Abuse and Alcoholism (NIAAA), July 2003. For a complete list of references, see www.niaaa.nih.gov.

Research suggests that many genes play a role in shaping alcoholism risk. Like diabetes and heart disease, alcoholism is considered genetically complex, distinguishing it from genetic diseases, such as cystic fibrosis, that result primarily from the action of one or two copies of a single gene and in which the environment plays a much smaller role, if any. The methods used to search for genes in complex diseases have to account for the fact that the effects of any one gene may be subtle and a different array of genes underlies risk in different people.

Scientists have bred lines of mice and rats that manifest specific and separate alcohol-related traits or phenotypes, such as sensitivity to alcohol's intoxicating and sedative effects, the development of tolerance, the susceptibility to withdrawal symptoms, and alcohol-related organ damage. Risk for alcoholism in humans reflects the mix and magnitude of these and other phenotypes, shaped by underlying genes, in interaction with an environment in which alcohol is available. Genetic research on alcoholism seeks to tease apart the genetic underpinnings of these phenotypes and how they contribute to risk.

One well-characterized relationship between genes and alcoholism is the result of variation in the liver enzymes that metabolize (break down) alcohol. By speeding up the metabolism of alcohol to a toxic intermediate, acetaldehyde, or slowing down the conversion of acetaldehyde to acetate, genetic variants in the enzymes alcohol dehydrogenase (ADH) or aldehyde dehydrogenase (ALDH) raise the level of acetaldehyde after drinking, causing symptoms that include flushing, nausea, and rapid heartbeat. The genes for these enzymes and the alleles, or gene variants, that alter alcohol metabolism have been identified. Genes associated with flushing are more common among Asian populations than other ethnic groups, and the rates of drinking and alcoholism are correspondingly lower among Asian populations.

Genes, Behavior, and the Brain

Addiction is based in the brain. It involves memory, motivation, and emotional state. The processes involved in these aspects of brain function have thus been logical targets for the search for genes that underlie risk for alcoholism. Much of the information on potential alcohol-related genes has come from research on animals. Research has demonstrated a similarity in the mechanisms of many brain functions across species as well as an overlap between the genomes of animals—even invertebrates—and humans.

Genetic Studies in Humans

Knowledge gained from animal studies has assisted scientists in identifying the genes underlying brain chemistry in humans. Much research suggests that genes affecting the activity of the neurotransmitters serotonin and GABA (gamma-aminobutyric acid) are likely candidates for involvement in alcoholism risk. A recent preliminary study looked at five genes related to these two neurotransmitters in a group of men who had been followed over a 15-year period. The men who had particular variants of genes for a serotonin transporter and for one type of GABA receptor showed lower response to alcohol at age 20 and were more likely to have met the criteria for alcoholism.

Another study found that college students with a particular variant of the serotonin transporter gene consumed more alcohol per occasion, more often drank expressly to become inebriated, and engaged more frequently in binge drinking than students with another variant of the gene. The relationships between neurotransmitter genes and alcoholism are complex, however; not all studies have shown a connection between alcoholism risk and these genes.

Individual variation in response to stressors such as pain is genetically influenced and helps shape susceptibility to psychiatric diseases, including alcoholism. Scientists recently found that a common genetic variation in an enzyme (catechol-0-methyltransferase) that metabolizes the neurotransmitters dopamine and norepinephrine results in a less efficient form of the enzyme and increased pain susceptibility. Scientists in another study found that the same genetic variant influences anxiety in women. In this study, women who had the enzyme variant scored higher on measures of anxiety and exhibited an electroencephalogram (EEG) pattern associated with anxiety disorders and alcoholism.

The drug naltrexone has been shown to help some, but not all, alcohol-dependent patients reduce their drinking. Preliminary results from a recent study showed that alcoholic patients with different variations in the gene for a receptor on which naltrexone is known to act (the mu-opioid receptor) responded differently to treatment with the drug. This work demonstrates how genetic typing may in the future be helpful in tailoring treatment for alcoholism to each individual.

Scientists are searching for alcohol-related genes through studies of families with multiple generations of alcoholism. Using existing markers—known variations in the DNA sequence that serve as signposts along the length of a chromosome—and observing to what extent specific markers are inherited along with alcoholism risk, they have found "hotspots" for alcoholism risk on five chromosomes and a protective area on one chromosome near the location of genes for alcohol dehydrogenase. They have also examined patterns of brain waves measured by electroencephalogram. EEGs measure differences in electrical potential across the brain caused by synchronized firing of many neurons. Brain wave patterns are characteristic to individuals and are shaped genetically—they are quantitative genetic traits, varying along a spectrum among individuals. Researchers have found that reduced amplitude of one wave that characteristically occurs after a stimulus correlates with alcohol dependence, and they have identified chromosomal regions that appear to affect this P300 wave amplitude. Recently, researchers found that the shape of a characteristic brain wave measured in the frequency stretch between 13 and 25 cycles per second (the "beta" wave) reflected gene variations at a specific chromosomal site containing genes for one type of GABA receptor. They suggest that this site is in or near a previously identified quantitative trait locus (QTL) for alcoholism risk. Thus, brain wave patterns reflect underlying genetic variation in a receptor for a neurotransmitter known to be involved in the brain's response to alcohol. Findings of this type promise to help researchers identify markers of alcoholism risk and ultimately, suggest ways to reduce the risk or to treat the disease pharmacologically.

Genetics Research

Even from the first drink, individuals differ substantially in their response to alcohol. Genetics research is helping us understand how genes shape the metabolic and behavioral response to alcohol and what makes one person more vulnerable to addiction than another. An understanding of the genetic underpinnings of alcoholism can help us identify those at risk and, in the long term, provide the foundation for tailoring prevention and treatment according to the particular physiology of each individual.

Chapter 6

Underage Drinking

Chapter Contents

Section 6.1—The Public Health Challenge
of Underage Drinking 34

Section 6.2—Tips for Teens: The
Truth about Alcohol 44

Section 6.3—Youth Drinking Trends
Stabilize But Consumption
Remains High 47

Section 6.4—Adults Are Most Common
Source of Alcohol for Teens 49

Section 6.1

The Public Health Challenge of Underage Drinking

From "Underage Drinking: Why Do Adolescents Drink, What Are the Risks, and How Can Underage Drinking Be Prevented?," *Alcohol Alert* No. 67, a publication of the National Institute on Alcoholism and Alcohol Abuse (NIAAA), January 2006. For a complete list of references, see www.niaaa.nih.gov.

Alcohol is the drug of choice among youth. Many young people are experiencing the consequences of drinking too much, at too early an age. As a result, underage drinking is a leading public health problem in this country.

Each year, approximately 5,000 young people under the age of 21 die as a result of underage drinking; this includes about 1,900 deaths from motor vehicle crashes, 1,600 as a result of homicides, 300 from suicide, as well as hundreds from other injuries such as falls, burns, and drownings.

Yet drinking continues to be widespread among adolescents, as shown by nationwide surveys as well as studies in smaller populations. According to data from the 2005 Monitoring the Future (MTF) study, an annual survey of U.S. youth, three-fourths of 12th graders, more than two-thirds of 10th graders, and about two in every five 8th graders have consumed alcohol. And when youth drink they tend to drink intensively, often consuming four to five drinks at one time. MTF data show that 11 percent of 8th graders, 22 percent of 10th graders, and 29 percent of 12th graders had engaged in heavy episodic (or "binge") drinking within the past two weeks. (The National Institute on Alcohol Abuse and Alcoholism [NIAAA] defines binge drinking as a pattern of drinking alcohol that brings blood alcohol concentration [BAC] to 0.08 grams percent or above. For the typical adult, this pattern corresponds to consuming five or more drinks [men], or four or more drinks [women], in about 2 hours.)

Research also shows that many adolescents start to drink at very young ages. In 2003, the average age of first use of alcohol was about

14, compared to about 17½ in 1965. People who reported starting to drink before the age of 15 were four times more likely to also report meeting the criteria for alcohol dependence at some point in their lives. In fact, new research shows that the serious drinking problems (including what is called alcoholism) typically associated with middle age actually begin to appear much earlier, during young adulthood and even adolescence.

Other research shows that the younger children and adolescents are when they start to drink, the more likely they will be to engage in behaviors that harm themselves and others. For example, frequent binge drinkers (nearly 1 million high school students nationwide) are more likely to engage in risky behaviors, including using other drugs such as marijuana and cocaine, having sex with six or more partners, and earning grades that are mostly Ds and Fs in school.

Why Do Some Adolescents Drink?

As children move from adolescence to young adulthood, they encounter dramatic physical, emotional, and lifestyle changes. Developmental transitions, such as puberty and increasing independence, have been associated with alcohol use. So in a sense, just being an adolescent may be a key risk factor not only for starting to drink but also for drinking dangerously.

Risk-Taking. Research shows the brain keeps developing well into the twenties, during which time it continues to establish important communication connections and further refines its function. Scientists believe that this lengthy developmental period may help explain some of the behavior that is characteristic of adolescence—such as their propensity to seek out new and potentially dangerous situations. For some teens, thrill seeking might include experimenting with alcohol. Developmental changes also offer a possible physiological explanation for why teens act so impulsively, often not recognizing that their actions—such as drinking—have consequences.

Expectancies. How people view alcohol and its effects also influences their drinking behavior, including whether they begin to drink and how much. An adolescent who expects drinking to be a pleasurable experience is more likely to drink than one who does not. An important area of alcohol research is focusing on how expectancy influences drinking patterns from childhood through adolescence and into young adulthood. Beliefs about alcohol are established very early in life, even before the child begins elementary school. Before age 9, children generally view alcohol negatively and see drinking as bad, with adverse effects. By about age 13, however, their expectancies shift, becoming more positive. As would be expected, adolescents who drink the most also place the greatest emphasis on the positive and arousing effects of alcohol.

Sensitivity and Tolerance to Alcohol. Differences between the adult brain and the brain of the maturing adolescent also may help to explain why many young drinkers are able to consume much larger amounts of alcohol than adults before experiencing the negative consequences of drinking, such as drowsiness, lack of coordination, and withdrawal/hangover effects. This unusual tolerance may help to explain the high rates of binge drinking among young adults. At the same time, adolescents appear to be particularly sensitive to the positive effects of drinking, such as feeling more at ease in social situations, and young people may drink more than adults because of these positive social experiences.

Personality Characteristics and Psychiatric Comorbidity. Children who begin to drink at a very early age (before age 12) often share similar personality characteristics that may make them more likely to start drinking. Young people who are disruptive, hyperactive, and aggressive—often referred to as having conduct problems or being antisocial—as well as those who are depressed, withdrawn, or anxious, may be at greatest risk for alcohol problems. Other behavior problems associated with alcohol use include rebelliousness, difficulty avoiding harm or harmful situations, and a host of other traits seen in young people who act out without regard for rules or the feelings of others (i.e., disinhibition).

Hereditary Factors. Some of the behavioral and physiological factors that converge to increase or decrease a person's risk for alcohol problems, including tolerance to alcohol's effects, may be directly linked to genetics. For example, being a child of an alcoholic or having several alcoholic family members places a person at greater risk for alcohol problems. Children of alcoholics (COAs) are between 4 and 10 times more likely to become alcoholics themselves than are children who have no close relatives with alcoholism. COAs also are more likely to begin drinking at a young age and to progress to drinking problems more quickly.

Research shows that COAs may have subtle brain differences which could be markers for developing later alcohol problems. For example, using high-tech brain-imaging techniques, scientists have found that COAs have a distinctive feature in one brainwave pattern (called a P300 response) that could be a marker for later alcoholism risk. Researchers also are investigating other brainwave differences in COAs that may be present long before they begin to drink, including brainwave activity recorded during sleep as well as changes in brain structure and function.

Some studies suggest that these brain differences may be particularly evident in people who also have certain behavioral traits, such as signs of conduct disorder, antisocial personality disorder, sensation-seeking, or poor impulse control. Studying how the brain's structure and function translates to behavior will help researchers to better understand how predrinking risk factors shape later alcohol use. For example, does a person who is depressed drink to alleviate his or her depression, or does drinking lead to changes in his brain that result in feelings of depression?

Other hereditary factors likely will become evident as scientists work to identify the actual genes involved in addiction. By analyzing the genetic makeup of people and families with alcohol dependence, researchers have found specific regions on chromosomes that correlate with a risk for alcoholism. Candidate genes for alcoholism risk also have been associated with those regions. The goal now is to further refine regions for which a specific gene has not yet been identified and then determine how those genes interact with other genes and gene products as well as with the environment to result in alcohol dependence. Further research also should shed light on the extent to which the same or different genes contribute to alcohol problems, both in adults and in adolescents.

Environmental Aspects. Pinpointing a genetic contribution will not tell the whole story, however, as drinking behavior reflects a complex interplay between inherited and environmental factors, the implications of which are only beginning to be explored in adolescents. And what influences drinking at one age may not have the same impact at another. As Rose and colleagues show, genetic factors appear to have more influence on adolescent drinking behavior in late adolescence than in mid-adolescence.

Environmental factors, such as the influence of parents and peers, also play a role in alcohol use. For example, parents who drink more and who view drinking favorably may have children who drink more, and an adolescent girl with an older or adult boyfriend is more likely to use alcohol and other drugs and to engage in delinquent behaviors.

Researchers are examining other environmental influences as well, such as the impact of the media. Today alcohol is widely available and aggressively promoted through television, radio, billboards, and the Internet. Researchers are studying how young people react to these advertisements. In a study of 3rd, 6th, and 9th graders, those who found alcohol ads desirable were more likely to view drinking positively and to want to purchase products with alcohol logos. Research is mixed, however, on whether these positive views of alcohol actually lead to underage drinking.

What Are the Health Risks?

Whatever it is that leads adolescents to begin drinking, once they start they face a number of potential health risks. Although the severe health problems associated with harmful alcohol use are not as common in adolescents as they are in adults, studies show that young people who drink heavily may put themselves at risk for a range of potential health problems.

Brain Effects. Scientists currently are examining just how alcohol affects the developing brain, but it's a difficult task. Subtle changes in the brain may be difficult to detect but still have a significant impact on long-term thinking and memory skills. Add to this the fact that adolescent brains are still maturing, and the study of alcohol's effects becomes even more complex. Research has shown that animals fed alcohol during this critical developmental stage continue to show long-lasting impairment from alcohol as they age. It's simply not known how alcohol will affect the long-term memory and learning skills of people who began drinking heavily as adolescents.

Liver Effects. Elevated liver enzymes, indicating some degree of liver damage, have been found in some adolescents who drink alcohol. Young drinkers who are overweight or obese showed elevated liver enzymes even with only moderate levels of drinking.

Growth and Endocrine Effects. In both males and females, puberty is a period associated with marked hormonal changes, including increases in the sex hormones, estrogen and testosterone. These hormones, in turn, increase production of other hormones and growth factors, which are vital for normal organ development. Drinking alcohol during this period of rapid growth and development (i.e., prior to or during puberty) may upset the critical hormonal balance necessary for normal development of organs, muscles, and bones. Studies in animals also show that consuming alcohol during puberty adversely affects the maturation of the reproductive system.

Preventing Underage Drinking within a Developmental Framework

Complex behaviors, such as the decision to begin drinking or to continue using alcohol, are the result of a dynamic interplay between genes and environment. For example, biological and physiological changes that occur during adolescence may promote risk-taking behavior, leading to early experimentation with alcohol. This behavior then shapes the child's environment, as he or she chooses friends and situations that support further drinking. Continued drinking may lead to physiological reactions, such as depression or anxiety disorders, triggering even greater alcohol use or dependence. In this way, youthful patterns of alcohol use can mark the start of a developmental pathway that may lead to abuse and dependence. Then again, not all young people who travel this pathway experience the same outcomes.

Perhaps the best way to understand and prevent underage alcohol use is to view drinking as it relates to development. This "whole system" approach to underage drinking takes into account a particular adolescent's unique risk and protective factors—from genetics and personality characteristics to social and environmental factors. Viewed in this way, development includes not only the adolescent's inherent risk and resilience but also the current conditions that help to shape his or her behavior.

Children mature at different rates. Developmental research takes this into account, recognizing that during adolescence there are periods of rapid growth and reorganization, alternating with periods of slower growth and integration of body systems. Periods of rapid transitions, when social or cultural factors most strongly influence the biology and behavior of the adolescent, may be the best time to target delivery of interventions. Interventions that focus on these critical development periods could alter the life course of the child, perhaps placing him or her on a path to avoid problems with alcohol.

To date, researchers have been unable to identify a single track that predicts the course of alcohol use for all or even most young people. Instead, findings provide strong evidence for wide developmental variation in drinking patterns within this special population.

Interventions for Preventing Underage Drinking

Intervention approaches typically fall into two distinct categories: (1) environmental-level interventions, which seek to reduce opportunities for underage drinking, increase penalties for violating minimum legal drinking age (MLDA) and other alcohol use laws, and reduce community tolerance for alcohol use by youth; and (2) individual-level interventions, which seek to change knowledge, expectancies, attitudes, intentions, motivation, and skills so that youth are better able to resist the prodrinking influences and opportunities that surround them.

Environmental approaches include:

- **Raising the Price of Alcohol.** A substantial body of research has shown that higher prices or taxes on alcoholic beverages are associated with lower levels of alcohol consumption and alcohol-related problems, especially in young people.

- **Increasing the Minimum Legal Drinking Age.** Today all states have set the minimum legal drinking at age 21. Increasing the age at which people can legally purchase and drink alcohol has been the most successful intervention to date in reducing drinking and alcohol-related crashes among people under age 21. NHTSA [National Highway and Traffic Safety Administration] estimates that a legal drinking age of 21 saves 700 to 1,000 lives annually. Since 1976, these laws have prevented more than 21,000 traffic deaths. Just how much the legal drinking age relates to drinking-related crashes is shown by a recent study in New Zealand. Six years ago that country lowered its minimum legal drinking age to 18. Since then, alcohol-related crashes have risen 12 percent among 18- to 19-year-olds and 14 percent among 15- to 17-year-olds. Clearly a higher minimum drinking age can help to reduce crashes and save lives, especially in very young drivers.

- **Enacting Zero-Tolerance Laws.** All states have zero-tolerance laws that make it illegal for people under age 21 to drive after any drinking. When the first eight states to adopt zero-tolerance laws were compared with nearby states without such laws, the zero-tolerance states showed a 21-percent greater decline in the proportion of single-vehicle nighttime fatal crashes involving drivers under 21, the type of crash most likely to involve alcohol.

- **Stepping up Enforcement of Laws.** Despite their demonstrated benefits, legal drinking age and zero-tolerance laws generally have not been vigorously enforced. Alcohol purchase laws aimed at sellers and buyers also can be effective, but resources must be made available for enforcing these laws.

Individual-focused interventions include:

- **School-Based Prevention Programs.** The first school-based prevention programs were primarily informational and often used scare tactics; it was assumed that if youth understood the dangers of alcohol use, they would choose not to drink. These programs were ineffective. Today, better programs are available and often have a number of elements in common: They follow social influence models and include setting norms, addressing social pressures to drink, and teaching resistance skills. These programs also offer interactive and developmentally appropriate information, include peer-led components, and provide teacher training.

- **Family-Based Prevention Programs.** Parents' ability to influence whether their children drink is well documented and is consistent across racial/ethnic groups. Setting clear rules against drinking, consistently enforcing those rules, and monitoring the child's behavior all help to reduce the likelihood of underage drinking. The Iowa Strengthening Families Program (ISFP), delivered when students were in grade 6, is a program that has shown long-lasting preventive effects on alcohol use.

Selected Programs Showing Promise

Environmental interventions are among the recommendations included in the recent National Research Council (NRC) and Institute of Medicine (IOM) report on underage drinking. These interventions are intended to reduce commercial and social availability of alcohol and/or reduce driving while intoxicated. They use a variety of strategies, including server training and compliance checks in places that sell alcohol; deterring adults from purchasing alcohol for minors or providing alcohol to minors; restricting drinking in public places and preventing underage drinking parties; enforcing penalties for the use of false IDs, driving while intoxicated, and violating zero-tolerance laws; and raising public awareness of policies and sanctions.

41

The following community trials show how environmental strategies can be useful in reducing underage drinking and related problems.

The Massachusetts Saving Lives Program. This intervention was designed to reduce alcohol-impaired driving and related traffic deaths. Strategies included the use of drunk-driving checkpoints, speeding and drunk-driving awareness days, speed-watch telephone hotlines, high school peer-led education, and college prevention programs. The 5-year program decreased fatal crashes, particularly alcohol-related fatal crashes involving drivers ages 15 to 25, and reduced the proportion of 16- to 19-year-olds who reported driving after drinking, in comparison with the rest of Massachusetts. It also made teens more aware of penalties for drunk driving and for speeding.

The Community Prevention Trial Program. This program was designed to reduce alcohol-involved injuries and death. One component sought to reduce alcohol sales to minors by enforcing underage sales laws; training sales clerks, owners, and managers to prevent sales of alcohol to minors; and using the media to raise community awareness of underage drinking. Sales to apparent minors (people of legal drinking age who appear younger than age 21) were significantly reduced in the intervention communities compared with control sites.

Communities Mobilizing for Change on Alcohol. This intervention, designed to reduce the accessibility of alcoholic beverages to people under age 21, centered on policy changes among local institutions to make underage drinking less acceptable within the community. Alcohol sales to minors were reduced: 18- to 20-year-olds were less likely to try to purchase alcohol or provide it to younger teens, and the number of DUI [driving under the influence] arrests declined among 18- to 20-year-olds.

Multicomponent Comprehensive Interventions. Perhaps the strongest approach for preventing underage drinking involves the coordinated effort of all the elements that influence a child's life—including family, schools, and community. Ideally, intervention programs also should integrate treatment for youth who are alcohol dependent. Project Northland is an example of a comprehensive program that has been extensively evaluated.

Project Northland was tested in 22 school districts in northeastern Minnesota. The intervention included (1) school curricula, (2) peer leadership, (3) parental involvement programs, and (4) community-wide task force activities to address larger community norms and alcohol availability. It targeted adolescents in grades 6 through 12.

Intervention and comparison communities differed significantly in "tendency to use alcohol," a composite measure that combined items about intentions to use alcohol and actual use, as well as in the likelihood of drinking "five or more in a row." Underage drinking was less prevalent in the intervention communities during phase 1; higher during the interim period (suggesting a "catch-up" effect while intervention activities were minimal); and again lower during phase 2, when intervention activities resumed.

Project Northland has been designated a model program by the Substance Abuse and Mental Health Services Administration (SAMHSA), and its materials have been adapted for a general audience. It now is being replicated in ethnically diverse urban neighborhoods.

Conclusion

Today, alcohol is widely available and aggressively promoted throughout society. And alcohol use continues to be regarded, by many people, as a normal part of growing up. Yet underage drinking is dangerous, not only for the drinker but also for society, as evident by the number of alcohol-involved motor vehicle crashes, homicides, suicides, and other injuries.

People who begin drinking early in life run the risk of developing serious alcohol problems, including alcoholism, later in life. They also are at greater risk for a variety of adverse consequences, including risky sexual activity and poor performance in school.

Identifying adolescents at greatest risk can help stop problems before they develop. And innovative, comprehensive approaches to prevention, such as Project Northland, are showing success in reducing experimentation with alcohol as well as the problems that accompany alcohol use by young people.

Section 6.2

Tips for Teens: The Truth about Alcohol

From the Substance Abuse and Mental Health Services Administration
(SAMHSA), August 2004.

Facts about Alcohol

Slang terms for alcohol include booze, sauce, brews, brewskis, hooch, hard stuff, and juice. Here are some other facts about alcohol:

- **Alcohol affects your brain.** Drinking alcohol leads to a loss of coordination, poor judgment, slowed reflexes, distorted vision, memory lapses, and even blackouts.

- **Alcohol affects your body.** Alcohol can damage every organ in your body. It is absorbed directly into your bloodstream and can increase your risk for a variety of life-threatening diseases, including cancer.

- **Alcohol affects your self-control.** Alcohol depresses your central nervous system, lowers your inhibitions, and impairs your judgment. Drinking can lead to risky behaviors, such as driving when you shouldn't, or having unprotected sex.

- **Alcohol can kill you.** Drinking large amounts of alcohol at one time or very rapidly can cause alcohol poisoning, which can lead to coma or even death. Driving and drinking also can be deadly. In 2003, 31 percent of drivers age 15 to 20 who died in traffic accidents had been drinking alcohol.[1]

- **Alcohol can hurt you—even if you're not the one drinking.** If you're around people who are drinking, you have an increased risk of being seriously injured, involved in car crashes, or affected by violence. At the very least, you may have to deal with people who are sick, out of control, or unable to take care of themselves.

Before You Risk It

- **Know the law.** It is illegal to buy or possess alcohol if you are under age 21.

- **Get the facts.** One drink can make you fail a breath test. In some states, people under age 21 can lose their driver's license, be subject to a heavy fine, or have their car permanently taken away.

- **Stay informed.** Binge drinking means having five or more drinks on one occasion. Studies show that more than 35 percent of adults with an alcohol problem developed symptoms—such as binge drinking—by age 19.[2]

- **Know the risks.** Alcohol is a drug. Mixing it with any other drug can be extremely dangerous. Alcohol and acetaminophen— a common ingredient in OTC pain and fever reducers—can damage your liver. Alcohol mixed with other drugs can cause nausea, vomiting, fainting, heart problems, and difficulty breathing.[3] Mixing alcohol and drugs also can lead to coma and death.

- **Keep your edge.** Alcohol is a depressant, or downer, because it reduces brain activity. If you are depressed before you start drinking, alcohol can make you feel worse.

- **Look around you.** Most teens aren't drinking alcohol. Research shows that 71 percent of people 12 to 20 haven't had a drink in the past month.[4]

Know the Signs of a Problem

How can you tell if a friend has a drinking problem? Sometimes it's tough to tell. But there are signs you can look for. If your friend has one or more of the following warning signs, he or she may have a problem with alcohol:

- getting drunk on a regular basis
- lying about how much alcohol he or she is using
- believing that alcohol is necessary to have fun
- having frequent hangovers
- feeling rundown, depressed, or even suicidal
- having "blackouts"—forgetting what he or she did while drinking

What can you do to help someone who has a drinking problem? Be a real friend. You might even save a life. Encourage your friend to stop or seek professional help. For information and referrals, call the National Clearinghouse for Alcohol and Drug Information at 800-729-6686.

Questions and Answers about Alcohol

Aren't beer and wine safer than liquor?

No. One 12-ounce bottle of beer or a 5-ounce glass of wine (about a half cup) has as much alcohol as a 1.5-ounce shot of liquor. Alcohol can make you drunk and cause you problems no matter how you consume it.

Why can't teens drink if their parents can?

Teens' brains and bodies are still developing; alcohol use can cause learning problems or lead to adult alcoholism.[5] People who begin drinking by age 15 are five times more likely to abuse or become dependent on alcohol than those who begin drinking after age 20.[6]

How can I say no to alcohol? I'm afraid I won't fit in.

It's easier to refuse than you think. Try: "No thanks," "I don't drink," or "I'm not interested." Remember that the majority of teens don't drink alcohol. You're in good company when you're one of them.

The bottom line: If you know someone who has a problem with alcohol, urge him or her to stop or get help. If you drink—stop! The longer you ignore the real facts, the more chances you take with your life.

It's never too late. Talk to your parents, a doctor, a counselor, a teacher, or another adult you trust. Do it today!

1. Traffic Safety Facts 2003 Data: Young Drivers, National Highway Traffic Safety Administration. U.S. Department of Transportation, 2004.

2. Prevention Alert: The Binge Drinking Epidemic. Substance Abuse and Mental Health Services Administration, 2002.

3. Harmful Interactions: Mixing Alcohol with Medicines. National Institute on Alcohol Abuse and Alcoholism, 2003.

4. 2004 National Survey on Drug Use and Health. Substance Abuse and Mental Health Services Administration, 2005.

5. Underage Drinking: A Major Public Health Challenge. National Institute on Alcohol Abuse and Alcoholism, 2003.

6. The NSDUH Report: Alcohol Dependence or Abuse and Age at First Use. Substance Abuse and Mental Health Services Administration, 2004.

Section 6.3

Youth Drinking Trends Stabilize But Consumption Remains High

"Youth Drinking Trends Stabilize, Consumption Remains High," from a press release by the National Institute on Alcohol Abuse and Alcoholism (NIAAA), September 14, 2004.

Although the prevalence of underage drinking has decreased since its peak in the late 1970s, drinking by youth has stabilized over the past decade at disturbingly high levels. The findings, part of a new analysis of youth drinking trends by researchers at the National Institutes of Health (NIH), appear in the September 2004 issue of *Alcoholism: Clinical and Experimental Research.*

"While these data confirm the reduction in underage drinking rates since the 1970s, they also underscore the need to redouble our efforts against this important problem," says Ting-Kai Li, M.D., Director of the National Institute on Alcohol Abuse and Alcoholism at the NIH. "The authors have demonstrated an important means for monitoring long-term changes in alcohol use patterns that will serve us well in these efforts."

Since 1975, information about drinking by persons age 18 and younger has been collected by a number of ongoing national surveys, including the Monitoring the Future (MTF) study, the Youth Risk Behavior Survey (YRBS), and the National Household Survey on Drug Abuse (NHSDA). These surveys have shown that almost 80 percent of adolescents have consumed alcohol by the time they are 12th graders, and that about 12 percent of 8th graders have consumed five or more drinks on a single occasion within the past two weeks.

Although year-to-year differences in drinking patterns in these surveys are often statistically significant, such short-term comparisons provide little useful information about long-term trends or changes in drinking habits over multi-year periods.

In the current study, researchers Vivian B. Faden, Ph.D., of the NIAAA, and Michael P. Fay, Ph.D., of the National Cancer Institute applied "joinpoint" statistical methodology to analyze trends in youth drinking data collected in three surveys: the MTF, the YRBS, and the NHSDA. Joinpoint analysis uses sophisticated statistical methodology to look at all available years of data from a survey simultaneously to identify significant changes in direction in trends.

"We applied this technique to three different surveys to see if joinpoint statistics tell the same story in terms of trends across surveys," explains Dr. Faden, Associate Director of NIAAA's Division of Epidemiology and Prevention Research. "This approach reveals information about trends in underage drinking heretofore unavailable, and strengthens the conclusions we draw regarding underage drinking trends."

The analyses showed an increase in youth drinking in the late 1970s, followed by a long period of decreases until the early 1990s. The authors note that the decline in underage drinking rates during this period probably reflects the increase in the minimum legal drinking age from 18 to 21. Since the early 1990s, all three surveys included in this analysis indicate relatively stable prevalence rates for underage drinking.

"Stable is better than up," notes Dr. Faden. "However, the current stability in youth drinking prevalence is quite worrisome." Rates for any alcohol use in the past 30 days range from 19.6 percent of 8th graders to 48.6 percent of 12th graders. The data also show that more than 12 percent of 8th graders and nearly 30 percent of 12th graders report drinking five or more drinks in a row in the past two weeks.

"Much remains to be done to get those numbers moving down again," says Dr. Faden. "We need to re-examine the approaches we have taken to prevent underage drinking, so that in another ten years we can report a downturn in this high-prevalence behavior instead of a stable situation."

As policy makers implement strategies to target underage drinking, the kind of trend analyses demonstrated by Drs. Faden and Fay will help provide the most comprehensive and reliable information on trends in alcohol use by underage drinkers.

The National Institute on Alcohol Abuse and Alcoholism, a component of the National Institutes of Health, U.S. Department of Health and Human Services, conducts and supports approximately 90 percent of the

U.S. research on the causes, consequences, prevention, and treatment of alcohol abuse, alcoholism, and alcohol problems and disseminates research findings to general, professional, and academic audiences. Additional alcohol research information and publications are available at www.niaaa.nih.gov.

Section 6.4

Adults Are Most Common Source of Alcohol for Teens

The American Medical Association (AMA) released the results of two nationwide polls that reveal how underage youth obtain alcohol, as well as how easily and often. The polls also show parental opinions and behaviors about providing alcohol to teenagers and perceptions on how youth acquire alcohol. The polls were funded as part of the AMA's partnership with The Robert Wood Johnson Foundation.

"From a public health standpoint, these findings are frankly disturbing," said J. Edward Hill, M.D., president of the AMA. "While it is of great concern to see how easily teens, especially young girls, get alcohol, it is alarming to know that legal-age adults, even parents, are supplying the alcohol."

The poll of teens, aged 13 to 18, found that nearly half reported having obtained alcohol at some point. In all age groups, girls nearly always ranked higher than boys in obtaining alcohol. In the adult poll, about one out of four U.S. parents with children, aged 12 to 20 (26%), agree that teens should be able to drink at home with their parents present.

"Policies and law enforcement efforts to stop minors from obtaining alcohol are important, but this data reveals how easily avoided those policies and laws can be when legal-aged buyers are the leading source of alcohol for children," said Hill. "And even parents who do not buy for their children could be unwitting sources if their alcohol at home is left unsecured."

Two out of three teens, aged 13 to 18, said it is easy to get alcohol from their homes without parents knowing about it. One third responded that it is easy to obtain alcohol from their own parents knowingly, which increases to 40 percent when it is from a friend's parent. And one in four teens have attended a party where minors were drinking in front of parents.

"Parents allowing underage children to drink under their supervision are under a dangerous misperception," said Hill. "Injuries and car accidents after such parent-hosted parties remind us that no parent can completely control the actions of intoxicated youth, during or after a party. And the main message children hear is that drinking illegally is okay."

Other key findings of the two polls include:

- Nearly one in four teens, aged 13 to 18, and one in three girls, aged 16 to 18, say their own parents have supplied them with alcohol, and teens who have obtained alcohol reported that, in the past six months, parents were the suppliers three times on average.

- While 71 percent of parents with children, aged 12 to 20, disagreed with the statement that teen drinking was okay if a parent were present, 76 percent think it is likely that teenagers get alcohol from someone's parent—and they knew about it.

- One out of four parents of children, aged 12 to 20 (25%), say they have allowed their teens to drink with their supervision in the past six months. Approximately one in 12 (8%) indicated they have allowed their teen's friends to also drink under their supervision in the past six months.

- While only eight percent of parents of children aged 12 to 20 indicated that they allowed their teen and his/her friends to drink with supervision in the past six months, 21 percent of teens attended a party where the alcohol was provided by someone else's parents. And 27 percent of teens attended a party where youth were drinking with parents present. This discrepancy suggests parents are unaware that other parents are allowing their own children to drink.

"The AMA applauds parents who discourage and disallow underage drinking," said Hill. "We hope that such parents willing to stand up for their children's health will be more vocal in their communities, letting children and other parents know that no adult should substitute their judgment for a teen's own parents. Drinking is not a rite of passage. Fatal car accidents, injuries and assaults, and irreversible damage to the brain are not rites of passage for any child."

According to the National Institute on Alcohol Abuse and Alcoholism, underage drinking is a leading cause of death among youth, including car accidents and fatal injuries. The U.S. Department of Health and Human Services also found that alcohol is linked to two thirds of all sexual assaults and date rapes of teens and increases the likelihood of contracting HIV or sexually transmitted diseases. An AMA report reveals the long-term damage that drinking does to teen brains, which continue developing until age 20.

The AMA said the poll results underscore the need for physicians to counsel parents on the health risks of alcohol use, as well as to advocate for policies to restrict access to minors.

"Parents and physicians do not bear the burden alone for reducing high-risk drinking," said Hill. "A teen's desire to drink is also important to address, and the alcohol industry should be ashamed of itself for its extensive and aggressive promotion of products to those too young to buy them. The alcohol industry makes a parent's job much harder when it flaunts products at sporting events, festivals, and concerts with little regard for the social and health consequences."

A study released in 2004 by the Center on Alcohol Marketing and Youth revealed that the number of alcohol commercials seen by young people, aged 12 to 20, continues to grow. And underage youth saw 48% more magazine advertising for beer and ale than legal-aged adults in 2003.

"Alcohol is everywhere," said Steven Harris, a 14-year-old from San Bruno, California. "Young people see ads everywhere. We see drinking on TV and in the movies, and we see it at parties and at home. And it is probably harder for teens to get into an R-rated movie than to get alcohol. It's a joke."

Chapter 7

Alcohol Advertising and Youth

Alcohol: Our Kids' Drug of Choice

Alcohol is the most commonly used drug among America's youth. More young people drink alcohol than smoke tobacco or use marijuana

—*National Research Council / Institute of Medicine, 2004.*

- Each day, more than 5,400 kids in the United States under age 16 take their first drink.

- One in six eighth-graders is a current drinker.

- One in five youth, ages 12 to 20, binge drinks (five or more drinks on one occasion).

- Most kids drink to get drunk: More than 90% of the alcohol consumed by 12- to 20-year-olds is drunk when they are bingeing.

Underage Drinking Harms and Kills Our Children

Alcohol use by children, adolescents, and young adults under the legal drinking age of 21 produces human tragedies with alarming regularity.

—*National Research Council / Institute of Medicine, 2004.*

- Each day, three teens in the United States die from drinking and driving, and at least six more die from other alcohol-related causes.

- Teenage girls who binge drink are up to 63% more likely to become teen mothers.

- Underage drinking costs the United States $53 billion a year in medical care, lost productivity, and the pain and suffering of young drinkers.

Alcohol Advertising: Reaching Kids Where They Live

While many factors may influence an underage person's drinking decisions, including among other things parents, peers, and the media, there is reason to believe that advertising also plays a role.

—Federal Trade Commission, 1999.

- A *USA Today* survey found that teens say alcohol ads have greater influence on the desire to drink in general than the desire to buy a particular brand.

- A study published in the *Journal of the American Medical Association* found that the number of beer and distilled spirits ads tended to increase with a magazine's youth readership. For every 1 million underage readers ages 12 to 19 in a magazine, researchers generally found 1.6 times more beer advertisements and 1.3 times more distilled spirits advertisements.

- A study of children ages nine to 11 found that children were more familiar with Budweiser's television frogs than Kellogg's Tony the Tiger, the Mighty Morphin' Power Rangers, or Smokey the Bear.

Institute of Medicine Calls for Industry Reforms and a Public Health Watchdog

In the committee's opinion, alcohol companies should refrain from displaying commercial messages encouraging alcohol use to audiences known to include a significant number of children or teens when these messages are known to be highly attractive to young people. It is not enough for the company to say: "Because these messages also appeal to adults, who will predominate in the expected audience, we are within our legal rights."

—National Research Council / Institute of Medicine (IOM), 2004.

- IOM called on the industry to move to a standard of not placing ads where underage youth are more than 15% of the audience— the proportion of youth in the population.

- IOM called on the U.S. Department of Health and Human Services to monitor alcohol advertising and report its findings to Congress and the public.

Why the Alcohol Industry's 30% Threshold Fails to Protect Youth

Because youth, ages 12 to 20, are only 13.3% of the national TV viewing audience, the alcohol industry's current threshold of not placing ads where underage youth are more than 30% of the audience allows alcohol ads to be placed on programs where there are more than twice as many youth as in the viewing population.

Youth Exposure to Alcohol Ads

Using standard advertising industry databases and methods, the Center on Alcohol Marketing and Youth (CAMY) at Georgetown University has documented widespread exposure of underage youth to alcohol ads and marketing on television, radio, and the Web and in magazines.

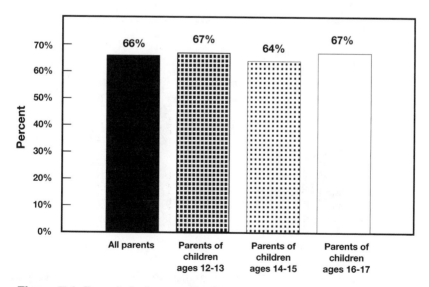

Figure 7.1. Parents believe seeing/hearing alcohol ads makes teens more likely to drink alcohol. Source: Peter D. Hart Research Associates/American Viewpoint, 2003.

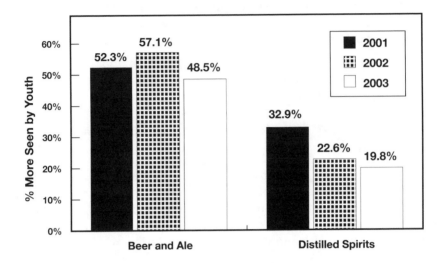

Figure 7.2. *Underage youth saw more alcohol ads than adults in magazines, 2001 to 2003. See camy.org for details; per capita comparison based on gross ratings points. Sources: TNS Media Intelligence, Mediamark Research Inc.*

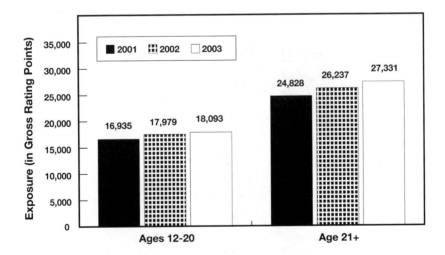

Figure 7.3. *Underage youth saw more than three beer ads for every five seen by adults on TV, 2001 to 2003. See camy.org for details; per capita comparison based on gross ratings points. Sources: TNS Media Intelligence, Nielsen Media Research.*

Television: A Vast Adland for Alcohol

- More than 750,000 alcohol ads aired on television from 2001 to 2003.

- Underage youth saw three alcohol ads on TV for every five ads seen by adults.

- More than 180,000 of the 750,000 alcohol ads were more likely to be seen by underage youth than adults on a per capita basis on programs such as Comedy Central's *Crank Yankers*, Fox's *MADtv*, and Comedy Central's *South Park*.

Table 7.1. Teens and Television Ads for Alcohol

	2001	**2002**	**2003**
Number of televised alcohol ads	192,423	282,273	286,651
Ads more likely to be seen by youth	48,624	66,924	66,384
Total spending	$773,735,471	$927,915,571	$813,181,159

Sources: TNS Media Intelligence, Nielsen Media Research

Top 15 Teen Programs Have Alcohol Advertising

In 1999, the Federal Trade Commission (FTC) reported that alcohol ads had appeared on "at least three of the 15 television shows reported to have the largest teen audiences." According to the FTC, "These shows may be among the best ways to reach teens, although they often have a majority legal-age audience."

The alcohol industry placed ads on all 15 of the 15 television shows most popular with teens in 2003, according to a CAMY analysis: 2,583 ads at a cost of more than $28.4 million. The programs included *Smallville*, *Fear Factor*, and *My Wife and Kids*.

Alcohol ads are among teens' favorites. Teens have ranked ads for Budweiser among their top 10 favorite TV advertisements in studies done in 2000, 2002, and 2004. [Source: Teenage Research Unlimited.]

Out of Balance: Alcohol Ads Outnumber Responsibility Ads 32 to 1

- Underage youth were 96 times more likely per capita to see a TV commercial promoting alcohol from 2001 to 2003 than an industry-funded responsibility ad regarding underage drinking.

- Responsibility advertising on television continues to be drowned out by the sheer volume of product advertising.

Table 7.2. Comparison of Spending on Alcohol Ads and Responsibility Ads

	2001	2002	2003
Number of responsibility ads	9,306	6,217	8,641
Number of alcohol product ads	192,423	282,273	286,651
Spending on responsibility ads	$36,532,918	$24,686,013	$30,534,007
Spending on alcohol product ads	$773,735,471	$927,915,571	$813,181,159

Note: "Responsibility" ads have as their primary focus a clear, unambiguous message warning against driving after drinking, encouraging use of a designated driver, advising viewers to drink responsibly, or informing them about the legal drinking age of 21. Sources: TNS Media Intelligence, Nielsen Media Research.

Alcohol Websites: Cyber Playgrounds for Kids

Alcohol websites attract large numbers of underage youth. Alcohol company websites received nearly 700,000 in-depth visits—visits that went beyond the age-verification page on the site—from young people under the legal drinking age in the last six months of 2003 alone. In fact, 13.1% of all in-depth visits to 55 alcohol websites were initiated by underage youth.

Games, cartoons, music, and high-tech downloads fill alcohol websites. Video games such as a water-balloon toss, pinball, car races, shooting aliens, and air hockey, as well as customized music downloads and IM (instant messaging) accessories were found throughout alcohol company websites, especially beer and distilled spirits websites.

No effective "carding" on the Internet. Alcohol industry marketing codes hold out the promise of limiting access to only legal-age adults by working with the computer industry. However, underage youth have easy access to alcohol websites since the majority of parental control software programs are largely ineffective at preventing youth from visiting these sites. A CAMY report for 2003 showed that as many as 76% of the alcohol brands eluded parental controls half the time or more.

Alcohol Radio Ads: Tuning in to Kids

In 14 of the 15 largest media markets CAMY studied in the summer of 2003, young people ages 12 to 20 heard more radio alcohol advertising per capita than adults over age 21. In five of these top 15 markets, underage youth also heard more radio alcohol advertising than young adults ages 21 to 34 on a per capita basis.

In its study, CAMY analyzed more than 50,000 radio ads airing in 104 markets across the nation. CAMY's analysis shows that 28% of these airings occurred when underage youth were more than 30% of the listening audience. According to revised industry marketing codes announced in September 2003, underage youth should not constitute more than 30%—a change from 50%—of the audience for alcohol ads.

Magazines: Alcohol Marketing Reaches Youth

- America's youth saw far more alcoholic beverage advertising in magazines than did people of legal drinking age from 2001 to 2003 on a per capita basis.

- Alcohol companies placed their ads in magazines with high youth readership, including *Rolling Stone, Vibe, Maxim, InStyle,* and *Sports Illustrated.*

- Between 2001 and 2003, alcohol companies spent $990.3 million to place ads in magazines. Distilled spirits advertising is especially prevalent in magazines because of the broadcast television networks' voluntary ban on distilled spirits ads. During that time, distilled spirits advertisers accounted for 75% of the dollars spent on alcohol advertising in magazines.

Table 7.3. Magazines with High Youth Readership and Alcohol Advertising, 2001 to 2003

	Average % youth readership	Total alcohol ad spending
Rolling Stone*	31.8%	$45,919,010
Vibe*	39.2%	$15,100,412
Maxim	24.5%	$67,667,310
InStyle	21.7%	$24,028,300
Sports Illustrated*	24.0%	$123,949,321

*Note: Composition and spending based on national editions. Sources: TNS Media Intelligence, Mediamark Research Inc.

Girls and Alcohol Advertising: Exposure to Alcohol Ads Is a Girl Thing, Too

Given the latest public health data on the closing of the gender gap in underage drinking, parents have even more reason to worry. Their daughters are being overwhelmed with alcohol ads portraying drinking as glamorous and fashionable.

> —*David H. Jernigan, Ph.D., Research Director,*
> *Center on Alcohol Marketing and Youth.*

A study conducted by CAMY and published in the *Archives of Pediatrics and Adolescent Medicine* found that in 2002, underage girls were even more overexposed to alcohol advertising in magazines than boys, and that girls saw more alcohol advertising in magazines than women age 21 and over.

CAMY's study found that underage girls saw 68% more beer advertising than women, age 21 and over, on a per capita basis. The difference in overexposure was most striking for ads for alcopops: Girls saw 95% more advertising than legal-age women on a per capita basis.

African-American and Hispanic Youth: No One Left Behind When It Comes to Kids and Alcohol Advertising

African-American kids and alcohol advertising. African-American youth have historically had lower rates of alcohol use and abuse than other youth, and African-American communities have been proud of that. That is what makes the Center's report striking and upsetting. African-American parents, teachers, health professionals and clergy do not need to have their hard work and success in protecting their children undermined by the alcohol industry's advertising and marketing.

> *—Dr. David Satcher, M.D., Director of the National Center for Primary Care, Morehouse School of Medicine, and former U.S. Surgeon General.*

Alcohol advertising was placed on television programs most popular with African-American youth. Alcohol advertisers spent $9.9 million in 2002 to place ads on all 15 of the programs most popular with African-American youth, including *Bernie Mac, The Simpsons, King of the Hill*, and *My Wife and Kids*.

Alcohol advertising in magazines and on the radio overexposed African-American youth. Compared to non-African-American youth, African-American youth saw 66% more beer and ale advertising and 81% more distilled spirits advertising in magazines in 2002. On radio, they heard 12% more beer advertising and 56% more ads for distilled spirits than non-African-American youth on a per capita basis.

Hispanic youth and alcohol advertising. The Center found that Latino children were even more likely than other youth to see alcohol ads in English-language magazines, and more likely to hear distilled spirits and alcopop ads on the radio. . . . The alcohol companies need to do a better job of self-regulating and stop inappropriate advertising. The Institute of Medicine recommends that the industry move its ads to better ensure that adults are more likely to see, hear, and read them than young people—an obvious solution that is long overdue.

> *—U.S. Congresswoman Lucille Roybal-Allard and David H. Jernigan, La Opinión.*

Alcohol advertising was placed on a majority of the TV programs most popular with Hispanic youth. Alcohol advertisers spent $18.3 million to place ads on 12 of the 15 programs in English and Spanish that were most popular with Hispanic youth in 2002, including *Las Vias del Amor, Ver para Creer, That '70s Show*, and *MADtv*.

Hispanic youth saw and heard even more alcohol advertising in magazines and on the radio than non-Hispanic youth. Hispanic youth saw 24% more beer and ale and 24% more distilled spirits advertising than non-Hispanic youth in English language magazines in 2002. Hispanic youth heard 11% more distilled spirits advertising and 14% more advertising for alcopops on English language radio than non-Hispanic youth on a per capita basis.

Taking Action to Protect Our Kids

Growing concern about the continued high rates of underage drinking in the United States and the role played by alcohol industry advertising practices has pushed policymakers and communities to take action. Efforts to reduce the exposure of underage youth to alcohol advertising range from the introduction of legislation in Congress to the passage of local ordinances to the adoption of new state rules to the creation of task forces by state attorneys general. Here are examples of how policymakers and communities are trying to protect our youth:

- The "Sober Truth on Preventing Underage Drinking Act," or "STOP Underage Drinking Act," first introduced in July 2004, was re-introduced on February 16, 2005 by a bipartisan group of U.S. senators and representatives. The STOP Underage Drinking Act employs many of the well-tested policies and programs recommended in the Institute of Medicine's September 2003 report to Congress. It funds measures that will reduce alcohol's availability to teens, better enforce drinking laws, and provide more resources for local community efforts. It also funds a small pilot media campaign that could serve as a model for a national adult-oriented campaign to educate parents about this issue. It provides for public health monitoring of the amount of alcohol advertising reaching our youth.

- Philadelphia's City Council unanimously passed in December 2003 an ordinance banning future alcohol advertising on city-owned property. By adopting this ordinance, the City Council banned alcohol advertising from the public transit bus shelters used by many schoolchildren when traveling between school and home each day. The City of Philadelphia owns all public transit bus shelters and administers the seventh-largest public school system in the United States.

- The State of Ohio adopted in May 2004 an administrative rule prohibiting alcohol billboards within 500 feet of schools, parks, and churches. Previously, billboards could have been within 500 feet of a school, park, or church as long as they were not visible from them. Ohio Parents for Drug Free Youth championed this reform and was supported by many other groups. While alcohol industry trade associations call for the 500-foot limit in their marketing codes, the Ohio rule is more specific, and makes the industry's voluntary ban enforceable.

- The National Association of Attorneys General created in the summer of 2004 the Youth Access to Alcohol Task Force to reduce underage drinking. The mission statement for the task force states: "The Task Force studies youth exposure to alcohol advertising and access to alcohol, educates state Attorneys General on ways to reduce access and change social norms about underage drinking, and partners with national and state entities to augment and enhance on-going efforts to stop underage drinking. The Task Force examines the alcohol industry's marketing practices, including television, radio, Internet and print advertising, and the effectiveness of the industry's self-monitoring programs, and works with the industry to reduce access. The Task Force compiles data on best practices related to liquor enforcement, legislative initiatives, parental education, and campus enforcement and education programs, and exchanges information among states regarding these programs and initiatives. The Task Force tracks Congressional and federal agency efforts to respond to the problem of underage drinking."

To learn more about these initiatives and other actions being taken to reduce underage youth exposure to alcohol advertising, visit http://www.camy.org/action.

Chapter 8

Drinking on College Campuses

Chapter Contents

Section 8.1—What Parents Need to
Know about College Drinking 66

Section 8.2—The Hidden Consequences
of College Drinking 71

Section 8.3—College Alcohol Problems
Exceed Previous Estimates 72

Section 8.1

What Parents Need to Know about College Drinking

Excerpted from the brochure "What Parents Need to Know About
College Drinking," by the National Institute on Alcohol Abuse and
Alcoholism (NIAAA), September 23, 2005.

A Snapshot of Annual High-Risk College Drinking Consequences

What do we know about the extent and impact of alcohol abuse on
college campuses? The data compiled below illustrate that each year
the consequences of college drinking are more significant, more destructive, and more costly than many Americans realize. It is also
important to remember that these consequences may affect your son
or daughter whether or not they drink.

- **Death:** 1,400 college students between the ages of 18 and 24 die
  each year from alcohol-related unintentional injuries, including
  motor vehicle crashes.

- **Injury:** 500,000 students between the ages of 18 and 24 are unintentionally injured under the influence of alcohol.

- **Assault:** More than 600,000 students between the ages of 18 and
  24 are assaulted by another student who has been drinking.

- **Sexual Abuse:** More than 70,000 students between the ages of 18
  and 24 are victims of alcohol-related sexual assault or date rape.

- **Unsafe Sex:** 400,000 students between the ages of 18 and 24
  have unprotected sex and more than 100,000 students between
  the ages of 18 and 24 report having been too intoxicated to
  know if they consented to having sex.

- **Academic Problems:** About 25 percent of college students report academic consequences of their drinking including missing

class, falling behind, doing poorly on exams or papers, and receiving lower grades overall.

- **Health Problems/Suicide Attempts:** More than 150,000 students develop an alcohol-related health problem and between 1.2 and 1.5 percent of students indicate that they tried to commit suicide within the past year due to drinking or drug use.

- **Drunk Driving:** 2.1 million students between the ages of 18 and 24 report driving under the influence of alcohol last year.

- **Vandalism:** About 11 percent of college students report that they have damaged property while under the influence of alcohol.

- **Property Damage:** More than 25 percent of administrators from schools with relatively low drinking levels and over 50 percent from schools with high drinking levels say their campuses have a "moderate" or "major" problem with alcohol-related property damage.

- **Police Involvement:** About 5 percent of 4-year college students are involved with the police or campus security as a result of their drinking. An estimated 110,000 students between the ages of 18 and 24 are arrested for an alcohol-related violation such as public drunkenness or driving under the influence.

- **Alcohol Abuse and Dependence:** 31 percent of college students met criteria for a diagnosis of alcohol abuse and 6 percent for a diagnosis of alcohol dependence in the past 12 months, according to questionnaire-based self-reports about their drinking.

Parents: A Primary Influence

As a parent you continue to be a primary influence in your son's or daughter's life. You are key in helping them choose the right college so that they get the best education possible. At the same time, you also need to ensure that when they go off to college they live in a safe environment. There are three distinct stages in which you, as a parent, contribute in critical ways to the decision making involving your college-bound son or daughter.

For Parents of a High School Student: Choosing the Right College

- As you examine potential colleges, include in your assessment inquiries about campus alcohol policies.

- During campus visits, ask college administrators to outline in clear terms how they go about enforcing underage drinking prevention, whether the school sponsors alcohol-free social events, what other socializing alternatives are available to students, what procedures are in place to notify parents about alcohol and substance abuse problems, what counseling services are available to students, and how energetic and consistent the follow-up is on students who exhibit alcohol abuse and other problem behaviors.

- Inquire about housing arrangements and whether alcohol-free dorms are available.

- Ask whether the college/university employs student resident advisors (RAs) or adults to manage/monitor dormitories.

- If there are fraternities and/or sororities on campus, inquire about their influence on the overall social atmosphere at the college.

- Ask if the school offers Friday classes. Administrators are increasingly concerned that no classes on Friday may lead to an early start in partying on the weekends and increased alcohol abuse problems.

- Find out the average number of years it takes to graduate from that college.

- Determine the emphasis placed on athletics on campus and whether tailgating at games involves alcohol.

- Find out the number of liquor law violations and alcohol-related injuries and deaths the campus has had in previous years.

- Finally, consider the location of the college and how it may affect the social atmosphere.

Influence of Living Arrangements on Drinking Behavior

The proportion of college students who drink varies depending on where they live. Drinking rates are highest in fraternities and sororities, followed by on-campus housing. Students who live independently off-site (e.g., in apartments) drink less, while commuting students who live with their families drink the least.

Environmental Influences

A number of environmental influences working in concert with other factors may affect students' alcohol consumption. Excessive alcohol use is more likely to occur in colleges:

- where Greek systems dominate (i.e., fraternities, sororities);
- where athletic teams are prominent; and
- located in the Northeast.

For Parents of a College Freshman: Staying Involved

- Pay special attention to your son's or daughter's experiences and activities during the crucial first 6 weeks on campus. With a great deal of free time, many students initiate heavy drinking during these early days of college, and the potential exists for excessive alcohol consumption to interfere with successful adaptation to campus life. You should know that about one third of first-year students fail to enroll for their second year.

- Find out if there is a program during orientation that educates students about campus policies related to alcohol use. If there is one, attend with your son or daughter, or at least be familiar with the name of the person who is responsible for campus counseling programs.

- Inquire about and make certain you understand the college's "parental notification" policy.

- Call your son or daughter frequently during the first 6 weeks of college.

- Inquire about their roommates, the roommates' behavior, and how disagreements are settled or disruptive behavior dealt with.

- Make sure that your son or daughter understands the penalties for underage drinking, public drunkenness, using a fake ID, driving under the influence, assault, and other alcohol-related offenses. Indicate to them that you have asked the college/university to keep you informed of infractions to school alcohol policies.

- Make certain that they understand how alcohol use can lead to date rape, violence, and academic failure.

For Parents of a College Student Facing an Alcohol-Related Crisis: Getting Assistance

- Be aware of the signs of possible alcohol abuse by your son or daughter (e.g., lower grades, never available or reluctant to talk with you, unwilling to talk about activities with friends, trouble with campus authorities, serious mood changes).

- If you believe your son or daughter is having a problem with alcohol, do not blame them, but find appropriate treatment.

- Call and/or visit campus health services and ask to speak with a counselor.

- Indicate to the Dean of Students, either in person or by e-mail, your interest in the welfare of your son or daughter and that you want to be actively involved in his or her recovery despite the geographic separation.

- If your son or daughter is concerned about his or her alcohol consumption, or that of a friend, have them check out www.alcoholscreening.org for information about ongoing screening for problems with alcohol.

- Pay your son or daughter an unexpected visit. Ask to meet their friends. Attend Parents' Weekend and other campus events open to parents.

- Continue to stay actively involved in the life of your son or daughter. Even though they may be away at college, they continue to be an extension of your family and its values.

In 1999, a majority of college and university presidents identified alcohol abuse as one of the greatest problems facing campus life and students.

Section 8.2

The Hidden Consequences of College Drinking

From the brochure by the National Institute on Alcohol Abuse and Alcoholism (NIAAA), September 23, 2005.

As college students arrive on campus in the fall, it's a time of new experiences, new friendships, and making memories that will last a lifetime. Unfortunately for many, it is also a time of excessive drinking and dealing with its aftermath—vandalism, violence, sexual aggression, and even death.

According to research summarized in a College Task Force report to the National Institute on Alcohol Abuse and Alcoholism (NIAAA), the consequences of excessive drinking by college students are more significant, more destructive, and more costly than many parents realize. And these consequences affect students whether or not they drink.

Statistics from this report indicate that drinking by college students aged 18 to 24 contributes to an estimated 1,700 student deaths, 599,000 injuries, and 97,000 cases of sexual assault or date rape each year.

Early Weeks Are Critical

As the fall semester begins, parents can use this important time to help prepare their college-age sons and daughters by talking with them about the consequences of excessive drinking.

This rapid increase in heavy drinking over a relatively short period of time can contribute to serious difficulties with the transition to college.

Anecdotal evidence suggests that the first 6 weeks of the first semester are critical to a first-year student's academic success. Because many students initiate heavy drinking during these early days of college, the potential exists for excessive alcohol consumption to interfere with successful adaptation to campus life. The transition to college is often difficult and about one third of first-year students fail to enroll for their second year.

71

Parents Can Help

During these crucial early weeks, parents can do a variety of things to stay involved. They can inquire about campus alcohol policies, call their sons and daughters frequently, and ask about roommates and living arrangements.

They should also discuss the penalties for underage drinking as well as how alcohol use can lead to date rape, violence, and academic failure.

Section 8.3

College Alcohol Problems Exceed Previous Estimates

Excerpted from a press release by the National Institute on Alcohol Abuse and Alcoholism (NIAAA), a part of the National Institutes of Health (NIH), March 17, 2005.

The harm caused by alcohol consumption among college students may exceed previous estimates of the problem. Researchers report that unintentional fatal injuries related to alcohol increased from about 1,500 in 1998 to more than 1,700 in 2001 among U.S. college students aged 18 to 24. Over the same period, national surveys indicate the number of students who drove under the influence of alcohol increased by 500,000, from 2.3 million to 2.8 million.

"This paper [published in the *Annual Review of Public Health*] underscores what we had learned from another recent study—that excessive alcohol use by college-aged individuals in the United States is a significant source of harm," said Ting-Kai Li, M.D., director of the National Institute on Alcohol Abuse and Alcoholism (NIAAA), part of the National Institutes of Health (NIH).

"The magnitude of problems posed by excessive drinking among college students should stimulate both improved measurement of these problems and efforts to reduce them," added the report's lead author Ralph W. Hingson, Sc.D, professor at the Boston University School of Public Health and Center to Prevent Alcohol Problems Among Young People.

Dr. Hingson and other researchers reported in 2002 that alcohol contributed to an estimated 1,400 injury deaths among college students age 18 to 24 in 1998. A subsequent change in college census methodology that increased the estimated number of 18- to 24-year-olds who were college students in 1998 led to an upward revision of that estimate to about 1,500 deaths. The same methods were used to calculate the 2001 estimates in the review article.

Dr. Hingson and colleagues gathered information about drinking and its consequences among college students for the year 2001. Their analyses included data from the National Highway Traffic Safety Administration, the Centers for Disease Control and Prevention, the National Household Survey on Drug Abuse, and the Harvard College Alcohol Survey, as well as national coroner studies and census and college enrollment data for 18- to 24-year-olds. They compared the 2001 data with similar analyses of 1998 data that they published in 2002.

"In both 1998 and 2001, more than 500,000 students were unintentionally injured because of drinking and more than 600,000 were assaulted by another student who had been drinking," said Dr. Hingson. "We must remember, however, that since the 18- to 24-year-old non-college population vastly outnumbers the college population, they actually account for more alcohol-related problems than do college students. For example, while 2.8 million college students drove under the influence of alcohol in 2001, so too did 4.5 million college-aged persons who were not in college."

Dr. Hingson and his colleagues propose data collection practices that they believe would improve future analyses of the consequences of college drinking. For example, they call for alcohol testing in every injury death in the United States.

"The data already collected on the numbers of alcohol-related fatal crashes annually in each state has proven invaluable to researchers seeking to study the effects of state-level legislative interventions to reduce alcohol-related traffic deaths," they note. "Unfortunately, without comprehensive testing for alcohol and determination of college student status of all persons who die from falls, drownings, poisoning, homicide, suicide, and any other kind of injury, we lack the most dependable yardstick by which to measure the magnitude of alcohol-related fatal injuries among college students, and whether this figure is changing over time."

The researchers conclude that greater enforcement of the legal drinking age of 21 and zero tolerance laws, increases in alcohol taxes, wider implementation of screening and counseling programs, and comprehensive community interventions are among the strategies that can reduce college drinking and associated harm to students and others.

Chapter 9

Alcohol Abuse in Men

Alcohol abuse in men oftentimes begins early in their lives. School years, especially high school and college years, are especially difficult for many boys, as they are facing concerns about body image, sexuality, and athletic performance. And at this critical time in their lives, they are more likely than women to have more opportunities to use alcohol and drugs.

Consider how men and women react differently to alcohol and drugs:

- Although both men and women are equally likely to become addicted to cocaine, heroin, hallucinogens, tobacco, and inhalants, men are more likely to abuse alcohol and marijuana.

- Men become dependent on drugs more slowly than women. The effects of cocaine on the brain and on the risk for stroke have been found to be more severe in men than in women.

- Men in drug treatment programs are more likely to have graduated from high school and to be employed and have fewer other health problems than women.

- More men than women are alcohol dependent or have alcohol problems. And alcohol problems are highest among young adults ages 18 to 29 and lowest among adults ages 65 and older.

Excerpted from "Alcohol and Drug Abuse in Men," by the National Women's Health Information Center (NWHIC, www.womenshealth.gov), June 2005.

We also know that people who start drinking at an early age—for example, at age 14 or younger—greatly increase the chance that they will develop alcohol problems at some point in their lives. Young men (and women) who abuse alcohol often take risks that endanger their health and the health of others, especially with having unsafe sex. Having unsafe sex can lead to teen pregnancy or to unwanted pregnancy, or to getting sexually transmitted diseases (STDs), such as HIV/AIDS. If you have a problem with alcohol, know that you are at risk for these diseases, which can cause serious, even life-threatening health problems.

What is alcoholism?

Alcoholism, also known as alcohol dependence, is a disease that includes the following four symptoms:

- **craving**—a strong need, or urge, to drink
- **loss of control**—not being able to stop drinking once drinking has begun
- **physical dependence**—withdrawal symptoms, such as nausea, sweating, shakiness, and anxiety after stopping drinking
- **tolerance**—the need to drink greater amounts of alcohol to get high

Research shows that the risk for developing alcoholism runs in families, but lifestyle factors, such as having friends that use or abuse alcohol, having a high amount of stress in your life, and having alcohol easily available to you also are factors. Knowing you are at risk is important, though, because then you can take steps to protect yourself from developing problems with alcohol. And with support and treatment, many people are able to stop drinking and rebuild their lives.

What is alcohol abuse?

A person can abuse alcohol without actually being an alcoholic—that is, he or she may drink too much and too often but still not be dependent on alcohol. Some of the problems linked to alcohol abuse include not being able to complete tasks for your job, school, or family; drunk-driving arrests and car crashes; and drinking-related health problems. Sometimes, even social or moderate drinking can be a problem—such as drinking and driving.

Is there a safe amount of alcohol for men?

For most adults, moderate alcohol use—up to two drinks per day for men seems safe. (One drink equals one 12-ounce bottle of beer or wine cooler, one 5-ounce glass of wine, or 1.5 ounces of 80-proof distilled spirits.)

You shouldn't drink at all though if you:

• plan to drive or engage in other activities that require alertness and skill (such as driving and using high-speed machinery)

• take certain over-the-counter or prescription medications (ask your doctor or pharmacist if it is safe to drink alcohol while taking them)

• have a health problem that can be made worse by drinking

• are a recovering alcoholic

• are younger than age 21

Is alcohol good for a man's heart?

Studies have shown that moderate drinkers—men who have two or less drinks per day—are less likely to die from sudden cardiac death. Sudden cardiac death usually happens when the heart begins beating too fast or chaotically to pump blood in the right way. Small amounts of alcohol might help protect the heart by cutting the risk of blood clots in the heart's arteries and by reducing problems with the heart's rhythm. Heavy drinking, though, can actually increase the risk of heart failure, stroke, and high blood pressure, and cause many other health problems. If you don't drink alcohol, you should not start drinking solely to benefit your heart.

The only way out of addiction is to recognize that there is a problem and that you can get help from others. Talk to your parents, doctor, nurse, teacher, counselor, or any adult you trust. Although it won't be easy, you or your friend can stop using alcohol. Don't be ashamed. Everyone needs help at some point in life. Asking for help could be the best decision you ever made.

Chapter 10

Alcohol: An Important Women's Health Issue

While it's true that men are more likely to drink alcohol and more likely to drink greater amounts, women have a higher risk of developing problems from alcohol consumption. When a woman drinks, the alcohol in her bloodstream typically reaches a higher level than a man's even if both are drinking the same amount. This is because women's bodies generally have less water than men's bodies. Because alcohol mixes with body water, a given amount of alcohol is less diluted in a woman's body than in a man's. Women become more impaired by alcohol's effects and are more susceptible to alcohol-related organ damage. That is, women develop damage at lower levels of consumption over a shorter period of time.

Considering that about one-third of American women report regular alcohol consumption and 2.3 percent, or 2.5 million women, meet the criteria for alcohol dependence, it is clear that research to better understand the effects of alcohol in women is critical.

Adolescence—Setting the Stage

Results from national surveys show that alcohol use is prevalent among both adolescents and young adults. And while heavy drinking remains more common among young men, the number of young women who drink heavily is alarmingly high.

From "Alcohol: An Important Women's Health Issue," *Alcohol Alert* No. 62, a publication by the National Institute on Alcoholism and Alcohol Abuse (NIAAA, July 2004). For a complete list of references, see www.niaaa.nih.gov.

Adolescence is a critical stage of development. Rapidly changing body systems may be especially vulnerable to alcohol's effects. Drinking during this time of accelerated brain and hormonal maturation may have long-term consequences.

During adolescence, striking physical changes occur in the brain. The prefrontal cortex, the brain region thought to be involved in various goal-directed behaviors, undergoes substantial changes. The amygdala, the brain structure believed to be involved in a person's emotional reactions and coordinating the body's response to stress, also undergoes developmental changes. Changes in these systems have a powerful effect on adolescent psychological functioning and behavior. As a result, some adolescents may be more likely to engage in risk-taking behaviors, such as experimenting with alcohol and other drugs.

In adolescents with significant alcohol use problems, the volume of the hippocampus, a brain region important for learning and memory, has been found to be significantly smaller than in control subjects. Limited research suggests that women may be more susceptible than men to shrinkage of brain regions. Whether this is true in adolescent girls is not yet known.

Adolescence is a time of dramatic changes in hormone levels and patterns. Gender differences in the body's hormonal response to stress also begin to emerge. Some girls may be at particular risk for emotional difficulties, depression, and problems with self-image as well as an increase in risk-taking behaviors. In addition, during early adolescence, girls may be especially vulnerable to stress. Levels of perceived stress have been found to be the most powerful predictor of alcohol and other drug use, after peer substance use.

Finally, evidence from animal studies suggests that alcohol may affect adolescents differently than adults. Adolescents do not become as uncoordinated or sleepy when drinking alcohol as adults do. Adolescents do, however, appear to be more sensitive to alcohol-induced disruptions in certain types of memory. Clearly, more research is needed to explain how gender differences may influence the way alcohol affects the developing adolescent brain and other body systems. What is known, however, is that the younger a person begins drinking, the more likely he or she is to develop a problem with alcohol later in life.

The Reproductive Years

Alcohol use may have effects on female reproductive function at several stages of life. Some research suggests that the growth spurt and normal timing or progression of puberty may be at risk in human adolescents who consume even moderate amounts of alcohol on a regular basis. Heavy drinking has been shown to disrupt normal menstrual cycling and reproductive function. The reproductive consequences associated with alcohol abuse and alcoholism range from infertility and increased risk for spontaneous abortion, to impaired fetal growth and development.

The Dietary Guidelines for Americans recommend no more than one drink per day for women, and no more than two drinks per day for men. Drinking at these levels usually is not associated with health risks and may prevent certain forms of heart disease.

Fetal Alcohol Syndrome

Maternal alcohol use during pregnancy contributes to a wide range of effects on exposed offspring, including hyperactivity and attention problems, learning and memory deficits, and problems with social and emotional development. The most serious consequence of maternal drinking during pregnancy is fetal alcohol syndrome (FAS). Children with FAS have a distinctive set of facial anomalies, growth retardation, and significant learning and/or behavioral problems. Even children prenatally exposed to lower levels of alcohol may exhibit learning and behavioral problems. Thus far, a threshold below which no fetal damage will occur has not been established. In the absence of such information, following the Surgeon General's recommendation that women abstain from drinking alcohol during pregnancy remains the safest course.

Breast Cancer

One of every eight American women will develop breast cancer in her lifetime. Some evidence suggests that alcohol consumption may increase the risk of breast cancer. Although the risk is relatively small, the benefits of moderate alcohol use should be weighed against the risk of developing cancer, especially in women with a family history of breast cancer, who appear to be at particular risk, even at low levels of drinking. Likewise, postmenopausal women who drink moderate amounts of alcohol have a higher risk of breast cancer if they use hormone replacement therapy (HRT), a known risk factor for breast cancer.

Alcohol and Older Women

The cessation of ovarian function at menopause and the accompanying decline in the production of the sex steroid hormones secreted by the ovaries are marked not only by characteristic signs and symptoms but also by a loss of estrogen's protective effects against osteoporosis and coronary heart disease. Alcohol use affects the health of postmenopausal women in two ways—directly, through its impact on organ systems such as the liver, brain, and gastrointestinal tract, and indirectly, by altering the blood levels of sex steroids that affect the risk for disease. Both the pattern and amount of alcohol that a woman drinks influence whether alcohol has a beneficial or harmful effect on her body.

Heart Disease

Coronary heart disease (CHD) is the number one killer of American women. One in every three American women dies of CHD. Several studies suggest that in pre- and postmenopausal women, light-to-moderate alcohol consumption may increase blood concentrations of estrogen and its metabolic byproducts—which may serve to protect against CHD. In fact, the incidence of CHD remains low until after menopause, apparently because abundant estrogen protects women against CHD. After menopause, however, women's risk of CHD increases, approaching that of men. A large body of epidemiological evidence strongly suggests that light-to-moderate alcohol consumption significantly reduces the risk of CHD in both genders. Although the exact mechanisms remain unclear, alcohol has been found to improve the risk factors and conditions associated with CHD, such as reducing the LDL, or "bad" cholesterol, and increasing the HDL, or "good" cholesterol; and reducing blood clotting and the "stickiness" of platelets, small cells that play an important role in clot formation. It is clear, on the other hand, that heavy drinking can damage the heart.

Bone Disease

Osteoporosis is a skeletal disease characterized by low bone mass, increased bone fragility, and susceptibility to fracture. Nearly half of all women over age 50 will have an osteoporosis-related fracture in their lifetime. At about age 35, people reach their "peak bone mass"—the point at which their bones are as strong as they will become. After age 35, women lose 0.5 to 1 percent of their bone mass each year. At menopause, when the ovaries stop producing estrogen, the rate of bone loss increases to about 3 to 7 percent per year.

Some epidemiological studies suggest that light-to-moderate alcohol consumption may be associated with increased bone mineral density and decreased fracture risk in postmenopausal women. This effect has not been found in animal studies in which the amount of alcohol consumed as well as other lifestyle factors could be controlled. On the other hand, heavy alcohol use clearly has been shown to compromise bone health and to increase the risk of osteoporosis by decreasing bone density and weakening the bone's mechanical properties. These effects are especially striking in young women, whose bones are still developing, but chronic alcohol use in adulthood also can harm bone health. In addition, animal studies suggest that bones do not overcome the damaging effects of early chronic alcohol exposure even when alcohol use is discontinued.

Other lifestyle factors, such as tobacco use, also may increase the risk of osteoporosis and fractures. People who drink are 75 percent more likely to smoke, and smokers are 86 percent more likely to drink. This combination of habits significantly compounds osteoporosis risk.

The greatest risk factor for the development of osteoporosis in women is menopause. Previous research found that postmenopausal HRT protected against the loss of bone density and greatly reduced the risk of osteoporosis-related fractures. However, findings from the Women's Health Initiative—a large study on the risks and benefits of strategies that may reduce the incidence of heart disease, breast and colon cancer, and fractures in postmenopausal women—found that when weighed against the risk of other types of disease, such as cancer, there was no net benefit for using HRT, even in women who have a high risk of fracture. Other factors, such as weight-bearing exercise and increased body mass, do have beneficial effects on bone health.

Memory and Brain Function

Alzheimer's disease (AD) is the most common form of dementia among older people. It is characterized by progressive changes in cognitive ability, memory, and mood. Women appear to be at greater risk than men for AD, although women's longer life spans may contribute to this higher risk. Heavy alcohol consumption is known to result in memory deficits. Heavy alcohol consumption also may increase the risk for AD in both genders and in women in particular, as they appear to be more vulnerable than men to alcohol-induced brain damage. At present there is no evidence to suggest that brain function is negatively affected by moderate alcohol consumption. In fact, some researchers believe that moderate drinking may even protect the blood vessels in the brain, in a way that is similar to how it protects the vessels in the heart against CHD.

Chapter 11

Alcohol and Minorities

Patterns of alcohol use and its consequences vary widely among minority groups. Although more research is needed, evidence suggests that prevention and treatment efforts may be more effective when based on an understanding of the ethnic context of drinking behaviors and their development. This text summarizes research on differences in alcohol use and problems, selected determinants of drinking, and the development of targeted prevention and treatment programs with respect to the four main minority groups in the United States: African Americans; Hispanics; Asian Americans and Pacific Islanders (AAPIs); and American Indians/Alaska Natives (AI/ANs). It is important to note that these categories include hundreds of distinct ethnic or racial populations which differ markedly in cultural characteristics and drinking behavior. Consequently, research does not support broad generalizations about specific subpopulations, many of which have not been studied individually.

Ethnic Differences in Drinking Patterns

Data from nationwide surveys of adults show that both current drinking (defined as consumption of 12 or more drinks in the past year) and heavy drinking (heavy drinking is defined as five drinks on a single day at least once a month for adults and five drinks in a row at least once during the previous two weeks for adolescents) are most prevalent among

From "Alcohol and Minorities: An Update," *Alcohol Alert* No. 55, a publication of the National Institute on Alcohol Abuse and Alcoholism (NIAAA), January 2002. For a complete list of references, see www.niaaa.nih.gov.

AI/ANs and Native Hawaiians and lowest among AAPIs. Alcohol use is increasing significantly among Asian Americans, who constitute one of the fastest growing U.S. minority populations. Among adolescent minorities studied nationwide, African Americans show the lowest prevalence of lifetime, annual, monthly, daily, and heavy drinking, as well as the lowest frequency of being drunk. Hispanic adolescents have the highest annual prevalence of heavy drinking, followed by Whites. Among all age and ethnic groups, men are more likely to drink than are women, and to consume large quantities in a single sitting.

Ethnicity and Alcohol Problems

Medical Consequences. Research on alcohol's health effects on minority groups has concentrated largely on cirrhosis, a progressive and often fatal liver disease usually attributable to long-term heavy drinking. Analysis shows a strong correlation between death rates from liver cirrhosis, regardless of cause, and drinking levels nationwide. Consistent with this association, deaths from chronic liver disease and cirrhosis are about 4 times more prevalent among AI/ANs than among the general U.S. population. However Hispanics are approximately twice as likely as Whites to die from cirrhosis, despite a lower prevalence of drinking and heavy drinking. The reason for this discrepancy is unclear. Evidence exists that Hispanics tend to consume alcohol in higher quantities per drinking occasion than do Whites, resulting in a higher cumulative dose of alcohol. In addition, Hispanics have a higher prevalence than do Whites of hepatitis C, a serious infectious liver disease that greatly increases the risk for liver damage in heavy drinkers.

Social Consequences. According to data from a nationwide survey, the prevalences of drinking and driving in the past year were 19 percent among AI/ANs, 11 percent for both Whites and Hispanics, 7 percent for African Americans, and less than 6 percent for AAPIs. Alcohol-related fatal crashes are three times more prevalent among AI/ANs than among the general population, constituting one of the 10 leading causes of death among AI/ANs, along with alcohol-related suicide, homicide, and cirrhosis.

Contributors to Ethnic Differences

Social Factors. The availability of alcohol, as measured in terms of the geographic density of alcohol sales outlets, has been linked to patterns of alcohol-related traffic crashes in communities. Studies have shown that greater densities of liquor stores are found in segregated minority neighborhoods. However, the apparent association between minority status and alcohol problems in some areas may reflect the disproportionate concentration of alcohol outlets in low-income communities rather than ethnicity per se.

Another factor contributing to minority drinking patterns is acculturation, the partial or complete adoption of the beliefs and values of the prevailing social system. Through acculturation, the original drinking pattern of an ethnic group tends to change to resemble more closely that of the overall population. However, acculturation also is influenced by gender, religious beliefs, family traditions, personal expectations, and country of origin. Some researchers have advanced the concept of "acculturation stress," whereby drinking increases in response to the conflict between traditional values and beliefs and those of the mainstream culture. Conversely, others have pointed out that many people, especially youth, learn to draw on support and resources from both cultures for protection against alcohol problems.

Biological Factors. People vary in their vulnerability to the effects of alcohol. Some of these differences result from genetically determined variations in the body's ability to break down (i.e., metabolize) and eliminate alcohol. For example, after drinking, many Asian subpopulations experience flushing of the skin, nausea, headache, and other uncomfortable symptoms. Those symptoms result primarily from inactivity of aldehyde dehydrogenase-2 (ALDH2), an enzyme involved in a key step of alcohol metabolism. A study of Asian males born in Canada and the United States found that those who had inherited the gene for the less active form of this enzyme drank two thirds less alcohol, had one third the rate of binge drinking (i.e., consumption of more than 5 drinks per day), and were three times more likely to be abstainers than a group of Asian males who possessed the more active enzyme. However, some people develop alcohol problems despite possessing the inactive form of ALDH2, demonstrating the importance of additional factors in the development of drinking patterns and consequences.

Among some African Americans, genetically determined variability in another alcohol-metabolizing enzyme, alcohol dehydrogenase-2, appears to affect the degree of vulnerability to alcoholic cirrhosis and alcohol-related fetal damage.

Prevention

Some alcohol prevention programs that have demonstrated success in the general population have been modified to be more culturally relevant for specific ethnic groups. The following two programs have been scientifically evaluated to compare the effectiveness of the culturally sensitive version with that of the generalized version for the populations in question.

School-Based Prevention. The school-based Life Skills Training (LST) program was designed to help adolescents cope with social influences that encourage use of alcohol and other drugs (AODs). Researchers compared the standard LST program with a modified version based on both the traditional and current cultural heritages of African American and Hispanic inner-city youth. Data collected two years after program initiation indicated that participation in either program produced significant decreases in measures of alcohol consumption. However, the culturally focused approach produced significantly greater improvement than did the generalized LST approach.

Family-Based Prevention. Since its inception as a generic program for White and multiethnic children of alcohol- or other drug-abusing parents, the Strengthening Families Program (SFP) has been modified for use with specific ethnic populations. The modified program generally has been found effective in reducing family problems and alcohol use among rural and urban African Americans and to a lesser extent with urban Hispanics. Among Native Hawaiians, however, comparison of the generic SFP with a culturally modified format produced inconclusive results.

Alcohol Availability. The high density of alcohol outlets in minority neighborhoods is noted above. However, the effect of limiting alcohol availability to reduce drinking problems among specific minority groups is not known. An exception to this situation is found among Alaska Natives, where geographic isolation and diversity of local alcohol control policies have combined to enable controlled research on naturally occurring experiments.

Studies of local alcohol control laws in remote Alaska Native communities have shown that prohibiting the sale, importation, and possession of alcohol by adults as well as by adolescents (i.e., dry communities) is associated with total and alcohol-involved injury-related death rates and alcohol-related outpatient visits. In contrast, a study of American Indian reservations in the northwestern United States suggests that alcohol-related deaths may be reduced more effectively by restricting the sale and use of alcoholic beverages rather than by prohibiting them. This conclusion is supported by results of a study that mapped the locations of alcohol-related deaths in a "dry" Navajo reservation in New Mexico. Most such deaths occurred among intoxicated pedestrians along roads leading to border towns, suggesting that those residents were returning from places outside the reservation where they had gone to obtain alcohol.

Treatment

The Community Reinforcement Approach is a highly flexible treatment intervention that can be adapted to ethnic or cultural minorities through cooperation with family and community networks. The program has experienced some initial success in treating alcoholic members of a Navajo subpopulation in New Mexico who had not responded to previous alcoholism treatment approaches. An integral part of the program was the inclusion of American Indian spiritual traditions to encourage abstinence. However, no randomized, controlled studies have been performed to prove that incorporating traditional cultural and spiritual beliefs and practices would enhance treatment in other AI/AN cultures. In particular, the growing urban AI/AN population tends to be highly acculturated with little or no knowledge of reservation or native village cultural traditions.

Chapter 12

Alcohol and Aging

Anyone at any age can have a drinking problem. Great Uncle George may have always liked his liquor, so his family may not see that his drinking behavior is getting worse as he gets older. Grandma Betty was a teetotaler all her life—she started having a drink each night to help her get to sleep after her husband died. Now no one realizes that she needs a couple of drinks to get through each day.

These are common stories. The fact is that families, friends, and health care professionals often overlook their concerns about older people's drinking. Sometimes trouble with alcohol in older people is mistaken for other conditions that happen with age. But alcohol use deserves special attention. Because the aging process affects how the body handles alcohol, the same amount of alcohol can have a greater effect as a person grows older. Over time, someone whose drinking habits haven't changed may find she or he has a problem.

Facts about Alcohol and Aging

* Some research has shown that as people age they become more sensitive to alcohol's effects. In other words, the same amount of

"Alcohol Use and Abuse" is an AgePage by the National Institute on Aging, part of the National Institutes of Health, September 2002, updated January 6, 2006.

alcohol can have a greater effect on an older person than on someone who is younger.

- Some medical conditions, such as high blood pressure, ulcers, and diabetes, can worsen with alcohol use.

- Many medicines—prescription, over-the-counter, or herbal remedies—can be dangerous or even deadly when mixed with alcohol. This is a special worry for older people because the average person over age 65 takes at least two medicines a day. If you take any medicines, ask your doctor or pharmacist if you can safely drink alcohol. Here are some examples:

  - Aspirin can cause bleeding in the stomach and intestines; the risk of bleeding is higher if you take aspirin while drinking alcohol.

  - Cold and allergy medicines (antihistamines) often make people sleepy; when combined with alcohol this drowsiness can be worse.

  - Alcohol used with large doses of the painkiller acetaminophen can raise the risk of liver damage.

  - Some medicine, such as cough syrups and laxatives, have a high alcohol content.

Effects of Alcohol

Even drinking a small amount of alcohol can impair judgment, coordination, and reaction time. It can increase the risk of work and household accidents, including falls and hip fractures. It also adds to the risk of car crashes.

Heavy drinking over time also can cause certain cancers, liver cirrhosis, immune system disorders, and brain damage. Alcohol can make some medical concerns hard for doctors to find and treat. For example, alcohol causes changes in the heart and blood vessels. These changes can dull pain that might be a warning sign of a heart attack. Drinking also can make older people forgetful and confused. These symptoms could be mistaken for signs of Alzheimer's disease. For people with diabetes, drinking affects blood sugar levels.

People who abuse alcohol also may be putting themselves at risk for serious conflicts with family, friends, and coworkers. The more heavily they drink, the greater the chance for trouble at home, at work, with friends, and even with strangers.

How to Know if Someone Has a Drinking Problem

There are two patterns of drinking: early and late onset. Some people have been heavy drinkers for many years. But, as with great Uncle George, over time the same amount of liquor packs a more powerful punch. Other people, like Grandma Betty, develop a drinking problem later in life. Sometimes this is due to major life changes like shifts in employment, failing health, or the death of friends or loved ones. Often these life changes can bring loneliness, boredom, anxiety, and depression. In fact, depression in older adults often goes along with alcohol misuse. At first, a drink seems to bring relief from stressful situations. Later on, drinking can start to cause trouble.

Not everyone who drinks regularly has a drinking problem, and not all problem drinkers drink every day. You might want to get help if you or a loved one:

- drink to calm your nerves, forget your worries, or reduce depression;

- gulp down drinks;

- frequently have more than one drink a day (a standard drink is one 12-ounce bottle or can of beer or a wine cooler, one 5-ounce glass of wine, or 1.5 ounces of 80-proof distilled spirits);

- lie about or try to hide drinking habits;

- hurt yourself, or someone else, while drinking;

- need more alcohol to get high;

- feel irritable, resentful, or unreasonable when not drinking; or

- have medical, social, or financial worries caused by drinking.

Getting Help

Studies show that older problem drinkers are as able to benefit from treatment as are younger alcohol abusers. To get help, talk to your doctor. He or she can give you advice about your health, drinking, and treatment options. Your local health department or social services agencies can also help.

There are many types of treatments available. Some, such as 12-step help programs, have been around a long time. Others include getting alcohol out of the body (detoxification); taking prescription medicines to help prevent a return to drinking once you have stopped; and individual and/or group counseling. Newer programs teach people with drinking problems to learn which situations or feelings trigger the urge to drink as well as ways to cope without alcohol. Because the support of family members is important, many programs also counsel married couples and family members as part of the treatment process. Programs may also link individuals with important community resources.

Scientists continue to study alcohol's effects on people and to look for new ways to treat alcoholism. This research will increase the chance for recovery and improve the lives of problem drinkers.

The National Institute on Alcohol Abuse and Alcoholism, part of the National Institutes of Health, recommends that people over age 65 who choose to drink have no more than one drink a day. Drinking at this level usually is not associated with health risks.

Chapter 13

Other Factors Associated with Alcohol Consumption

Chapter Contents

Section 13.1—Delayed Alcohol Use
          Linked to Fewer Problems with
          Abuse or Dependence as Adults 96

Section 13.2—Alcohol Use Patterns
          Associated with Body Mass Index 98

Section 13.3—Alcohol's Sight and
          Smell Cues Increase Consumption 100

Section 13.1

Delayed Alcohol Use Linked to Fewer Problems with Abuse or Dependence as Adults

From a press release by the Substance Abuse and Mental Health Services Administration (SAMHSA), October 22, 2004.

Persons reporting they first used alcohol before age 15 are more than five times as likely to report past year alcohol dependence or abuse as adults than persons who first used alcohol at age 21 or older. These are the conclusions of a special analysis of the 2003 National Survey on Drug Use and Health.

Substance dependence and abuse is defined in the annual SAMHSA survey of almost 70,000 persons according to definitions of the American Psychiatric Association, and include symptoms such as recurrent use resulting in physical danger; trouble with the law due to alcohol use; increased alcohol tolerance; and giving up or reducing other important activities in favor of alcohol use.

"We now know the passage to alcohol abuse and dependence often begins during childhood and adolescence," SAMHSA Administrator Charles Curie said. "Research has shown that alcohol dependence, while once thought to be an adult-onset disease, is actually developmental in nature. That is why underage drinking prevention programs are a priority at SAMHSA."

The special report, entitled "Alcohol Dependence or Abuse and Age of First Use" clearly found that among the 14 million adults aged 21 or older who were classified as having past year alcohol dependence or abuse, over 13 million (95 percent) had started using alcohol before age 21. The survey found that 74 percent of adults aged 21 or older reported that they had started using alcohol before the current legal drinking age of 21. About 14 percent reported that they had first used alcohol after they had reached age 21.

The study found that among adults aged 21 or older who initiated alcohol use before age 21, the rate of past year alcohol dependence or abuse was nine percent. But only three percent of persons who first used alcohol at age 21 or older were classified as having past year alcohol dependence or abuse. Among those who first used alcohol before age 15, 16 percent were classified with alcohol dependence or abuse.

Alcohol abuse and dependence was higher for those who started drinking earlier, and lowest for those who first used at age 21 or older. Sixteen percent of those who began drinking alcohol before age 12 were classified with alcohol abuse or dependence, while the rate was 15.5 percent for those who began between ages 12 and 14. The rate of alcohol dependence or abuse was nine percent for persons who began drinking between ages 15 and 17, and 4.2 percent for those who began drinking alcohol between ages 18 and 20.

The data show that males aged 21 or older were more likely than females to report having first used alcohol before the age of 15. The survey also found that whites had the lowest rate of never having used alcohol (nine percent) compared to blacks, Asians or Hispanics, and also the highest rate of initiating alcohol use before age 21 (79 percent) and the highest rate of alcohol use before age 15 (20 percent).

Section 13.2

Alcohol Use Patterns Associated with Body Mass Index

From "Study Associates Alcohol Use Patterns With Body Mass Index," a press release by the National Institute on Alcohol Abuse and Alcoholism (www.niaaa.nih.gov), February 15, 2005.

The body mass index (BMI) of individuals who drink alcohol may be related to how much, and how often, they drink, according to a study by researchers at the National Institutes of Health's National Institute on Alcohol Abuse and Alcoholism (NIAAA). In an analysis of data collected from more than 37,000 people who had never smoked, researchers found that BMI was associated with the number of drinks individuals consumed on the days they drank. Calculated as an individual's weight in kilograms divided by height in meters squared, BMI measures whether a person is at a healthy weight—low BMI values generally indicate leanness and higher BMI values indicate being overweight.

"In our study, men and women who drank the smallest quantity of alcohol—one drink per drinking day—with the greatest frequency— three to seven days per week—had the lowest BMIs," said author Rosalind A. Breslow, Ph.D., "while those who infrequently consumed the greatest quantity had the highest BMIs." A report of the study by Dr. Breslow, an epidemiologist in NIAAA's Division of Epidemiology and Prevention Research and colleague Barbara A. Smothers, Ph.D., appeared in the February 15, 2005, issue of the *American Journal of Epidemiology*.

"This is an important issue," said NIAAA Director Ting-Kai Li, M.D. "Obesity is prevalent in the United States and is a risk factor for numerous chronic illnesses and early death. Since alcohol use also is prevalent in this country, it is important to examine the relationship of quantity and frequency of consumption to body weight."

The researchers examined data collected from 1997 through 2001 in the National Health Interview Survey (NHIS), a nationally representative survey of the U.S. population conducted each year by the

National Center for Health Statistics. Drs. Breslow and Smothers compared survey respondents' alcohol drinking patterns with their BMI scores. Since previous studies have shown that smoking and drinking interact to influence body weight, the current study looked only at current drinkers who had never smoked.

Results of previous examinations of the relationship between drinking alcohol and body weight have been inconsistent. The authors noted that one possible reason for this is that prior studies used a different way of assessing alcohol consumption than did the current study.

"Alcohol consumption consists of two components," explained Dr. Breslow, "the amount consumed on drinking days (quantity), and how often drinking days occur (frequency). Previous studies generally examined drinking based only on average volume consumed over time. However, average volume provides a limited description of alcohol consumption as it does not account for drinking patterns. For example, an average volume of 7 drinks per week could be achieved by consuming 1 drink each day or 7 drinks on a single day. Average volume may not fully explain important relations between quantity and frequency of drinking and health outcomes such as obesity."

The authors suggested several possible reasons for the observed associations of both quantity and frequency of alcohol use with BMI.

"Alcohol is a significant source of calories, and drinking may stimulate eating, particularly in social settings," said Dr. Breslow. "However, calories in liquids may fail to trigger the physiologic mechanism that produces the feeling of fullness. It is possible that, in the long-term, frequent drinkers may compensate for energy derived from alcohol by eating less, but even infrequent alcohol-related overeating could lead to weight gain over time."

Dr. Breslow cautioned against inferring cause-and-effect relationships regarding drinking frequency, quantity, and body weight from this study. The study points to the need for prospectively designed studies to determine whether certain drinking patterns constitute risk factors for overweight and obesity.

Section 13.3

Alcohol's Sight and Smell Cues Increase Consumption

Kersting, K. (2003). Alcohol's sight and smell cues increase consumption. *Monitor on Psychology, 34,* p. 14. Copyright © 2003 by the American Psychological Association. Reprinted with permission.

The scent and sight cues generated from a mug of beer increase a drinker's likelihood of wanting more beer, according to a study published in *Experimental and Clinical Psychopharmacology* (Vol. 11, No. 4).

Given a glass of beer to taste and then the option of drinking more, a set of beer drinkers who were prevented from seeing or smelling the beer consumed less than a group whose senses were not blocked, says psychologist Kenneth Perkins, Ph.D., of the University of Pittsburgh School of Medicine.

Eighty young beer drinkers from a university community were asked to drink a 3-ounce beer sample in either an opaque glass—which prevented them from seeing the beer—or a clear glass. And, because taste is highly dependent on smell, half of the participants wore a nose plug that blocked both their ability to smell and taste the beer, Perkins says.

Before and during the alcohol consumption, the researchers also asked participants to evaluate the quality of the beer, indicate their desire for more beer, and measure their mood. The group whose perceptions of sight and smell were blocked rated the quality of the beer much lower than the other group.

After the 3-ounce sample, Perkins and his colleagues gave participants 12 ounces of beer in the same glass and the option of having it refilled twice. They were asked to drink as much of it as they liked, and the researchers measured whatever remained. Those with blocked senses consumed 15 percent less beer—significantly less than the control group, Perkins says.

"The study shows that removing these stimuli can reduce subjective and reinforcing effects of an alcoholic beverage, demonstrating that factors other than the pharmacological effects of alcohol are important for understanding alcohol consumption," Perkins says.

The study found a weaker link to sensory cues than previous sensory research on cocaine and tobacco use, Perkins notes. That finding indicates that, although significant, sight and smell cues for alcohol may not be particularly salient in comparison, he adds.

"Virtually everyone, even alcoholics, consumes many beverages that do not contain alcohol—perhaps limiting the direct association between beverage drinking and alcohol effects," Perkins says. "By contrast, many of the stimuli accompanying cigarette smoking may be narrowly associated with the intake of nicotine and not linked to any other, more regular, behavior."

Despite the indirect link, Perkins says teaching abusers the visual and olfactory impacts of alcohol might be a way to contribute to treatment of alcohol addiction.

"In addition to those implications for treatment, the possibility of a strong role for sensory stimuli in preventing the onset of alcohol consumption in teens warrants some research attention," he adds. "It could help in developing improved alcohol prevention efforts."

Part Two

Preventing Alcohol Abuse, Dependence, and Alcohol-Related Injuries

Chapter 14

How to Cut
Down on Your Drinking

If you are drinking too much, you can improve your life and health by cutting down. How do you know if you drink too much? Read these questions and answer **yes** or **no**:

- Do you drink alone when you feel angry or sad?
- Does your drinking ever make you late for work?
- Does your drinking worry your family?
- Do you ever drink after telling yourself you won't?
- Do you ever forget what you did while you were drinking?
- Do you get headaches or have a hangover after you have been drinking?

If you answered **yes** to any of these questions, you may have a drinking problem. Check with your doctor to be sure. Your doctor will be able to tell you whether you should cut down or abstain. If you are alcoholic or have other medical problems, you should not just cut down on your drinking—you should stop drinking completely. Your doctor will advise you about what is right for you.

"How to Cut Down on Your Drinking," is a handout from the National Institute on Alcohol Abuse and Alcoholism; National Institutes of Health Publication No. 96-3770-1996, updated May 28, 2001. Reviewed by David A. Cooke, MD, on March 13, 2006.

If your doctor tells you to cut down on your drinking, these steps can help you:

#1. *Write your reasons for cutting down or stopping.*

Why do you want to drink less? There are many reasons why you may want to cut down or stop drinking. You may want to improve your health, sleep better, or get along better with your family or friends. Make a list of the reasons you want to drink less.

#2. *Set a drinking goal.*

Choose a limit for how much you will drink. You may choose to cut down or not to drink at all. If you are cutting down, keep below these limits:

- **Women:** No more than one drink a day
- **Men:** No more than two drinks a day

A drink is:

- a 12-ounce bottle of beer;
- a 5-ounce glass of wine; or
- a 1 1/2-ounce shot of liquor.

These limits may be too high for some people who have certain medical problems or who are older. Talk with your doctor about the limit that is right for you.

Now, write your drinking goal on a piece of paper. Put it where you can see it, such as on your refrigerator or bathroom mirror. Your paper might look like this:

My drinking goal

I will start on this day____.

I will not drink more than____drinks in 1 day.

I will not drink more than____drinks in 1 week.

or

I will stop drinking alcohol.

#3. Keep a diary of your drinking.

To help you reach your goal, keep a diary of your drinking. For example, write down every time you have a drink for 1 week. Try to keep your diary for 3 or 4 weeks. This will show you how much you drink and when. You may be surprised. How different is your goal from the amount you drink now?

Now you know why you want to drink less and you have a goal. There are many ways you can help yourself to cut down. Try these tips:

- **Watch it at home.** Keep a small amount or no alcohol at home. Don't keep temptations around.

- **Drink slowly.** When you drink, sip your drink slowly. Take a break of 1 hour between drinks. Drink soda, water, or juice after a drink with alcohol. Do not drink on an empty stomach. Eat food when you are drinking.

- **Take a break from alcohol.** Pick a day or two each week when you will not drink at all. Then, try to stop drinking for 1 week. Think about how you feel physically and emotionally on these days. When you succeed and feel better, you may find it easier to cut down for good.

- **Learn how to say no.** You do not have to drink when other people drink. You do not have to take a drink that is given to you. Practice ways to say no politely. For example, you can tell people you feel better when you drink less. Stay away from people who give you a hard time about not drinking.

- **Stay active.** What would you like to do instead of drinking? Use the time and money spent on drinking to do something fun with your family or friends. Go out to eat, see a movie, or play sports or a game.

- **Get support.** Cutting down on your drinking may be difficult at times. Ask your family and friends for support to help you reach your goal. Talk to your doctor if you are having trouble cutting down. Get the help you need to reach your goal.

- **Watch out for temptations.** Watch out for people, places, or times that make you drink, even if you do not want to. Stay away from people who drink a lot or bars where you used to go.

Plan ahead of time what you will do to avoid drinking when you are tempted. Do not drink when you are angry or upset or have a bad day. These are habits you need to break if you want to drink less.

- **Do not give up.** Most people do not cut down or give up drinking all at once. Just like a diet, it is not easy to change. That is okay. If you do not reach your goal the first time, try again. Remember, get support from people who care about you and want to help.

Chapter 15

Talking to Your Child about Alcohol

- Kids who drink are more likely to be victims of violent crime, to be involved in alcohol-related traffic crashes, and to have serious school-related problems.

- You have more influence on your child's values and decisions about drinking before he or she begins to use alcohol.

- Parents can have a major impact on their children's drinking, especially during the preteen and early teen years.

Introduction

With so many drugs available to young people these days, you may wonder, "Why warn parents about helping kids avoid alcohol?" Alcohol is a drug, as surely as cocaine and marijuana are. It's also illegal to drink under the age of 21. And it's dangerous. Kids who drink are more likely to:

- be victims of violent crime;

- have serious problems in school; and

- be involved in drinking-related traffic crashes.

From the brochure "Make a Difference: Talk to Your Child about Alcohol" by the National Institute on Alcohol Abuse and Alcoholism (NIAAA), NIH Publication 03-4314, 2002.

This information is geared to parents and guardians of young people ages 10 to 14. Keep in mind that the suggestions on the following pages are just that—suggestions. Trust your instincts. Choose ideas you are comfortable with, and use your own style in carrying out the approaches you find useful. Your child looks to you for guidance and support in making life decisions—including the decision not to use alcohol.

"But my child isn't drinking yet," you may think. "Isn't it a little early to be concerned about drinking?" Not at all. This is the age at which some children begin experimenting with alcohol. Even if your child is not yet drinking, he or she may be receiving pressure to drink. Act now. Keeping quiet about how you feel about your child's alcohol use may give him or her the impression that alcohol use is OK for kids.

It's not easy. As children approach adolescence, friends exert a lot of influence. Fitting in is a chief priority for teens, and parents often feel shoved aside. Kids will listen, however. Study after study shows that even during the teen years, parents have enormous influence on their children's behavior.

The bottom line is that most young teens don't yet drink. And parents' disapproval of youthful alcohol use is the key reason children choose not to drink. So make no mistake: You can make a difference.

Young Teens and Alcohol: The Risks

For young people, alcohol is the number one drug of choice. In fact, teens use alcohol more frequently and heavily than all other illicit drugs combined. Although most children under age 14 have not yet begun to drink, early adolescence is a time of special risk for beginning to experiment with alcohol.

Although some parents and guardians may feel relieved that their teen is "only" drinking, it is important to remember that alcohol is a powerful, mood-altering drug. Not only does alcohol affect the mind and body in often unpredictable ways, but teens lack the judgment and coping skills to handle alcohol wisely. As a result:

- Alcohol-related traffic crashes are a major cause of death among teens. Alcohol use also is linked with youthful deaths by drowning, suicide, and homicide.

- Teens who use alcohol are more likely to become sexually active at earlier ages, to have sexual intercourse more often, and to have unprotected sex than teens who do not drink.

- Young people who drink are more likely than others to be victims of violent crime, including rape, aggravated assault, and robbery.

- Teens who drink are more likely to have problems with school-work and school conduct.

- An individual who begins drinking as a young teen is four times more likely to develop alcohol dependence than someone who waits until adulthood to use alcohol.

The message is clear: Alcohol use is very risky business for young people. And the longer children delay alcohol use, the less likely they are to develop any problems associated with it. That's why it is so important to help your child avoid any alcohol use.

Your Young Teen's World

Early adolescence is a time of enormous and often confusing changes for your child, which makes it a challenging time for both your youngster and you. Being tuned in to what it's like to be a teen can help you stay closer to your child and have more influence on the choices he or she makes—including decisions about using alcohol.

Physical changes. Most 10- to 14-year-olds experience rapid increases in height and weight as well as the beginnings of sexual development. As a result, many kids feel more self-conscious about their bodies than they did when they were younger and begin to question whether they are "good enough"—tall enough, slender enough, strong enough, attractive enough—compared with others. A young teen who feels he or she doesn't measure up in some way is more likely to do things to try to please friends, including experimenting with alcohol. During this vulnerable time, it is particularly important to let your children know that in your eyes, they do measure up—and that you care about them deeply.

Thinking skills. Most young teens are still very "now" oriented and are just beginning to understand that their actions—such as drinking—have consequences. They also tend to believe that bad things won't happen to them, which helps to explain why they often take risks. Therefore, it is very important for adults to invest time in helping kids understand how and why alcohol-related risks do apply to them.

Social and emotional changes. As children approach adolescence, friends and "fitting in" become extremely important. Young teens increasingly look to friends and the media for clues on how to behave and begin to question adults' values and rules. Given these normal developments, it is perhaps not surprising that parents often experience conflict with their kids as they go through early adolescence. During this sometimes stormy time, perhaps your toughest challenge is to try to respect your child's growing drive for independence while still providing support and appropriate limits.

Did you know:

- that according to a national survey, one in five eighth graders reports drinking alcohol within the past month?

- that 17 percent of eighth graders say they have gotten drunk at least once in the past year?

- that 71 percent of young teens say that alcohol is easy to get?

The Bottom Line: A Strong Parent-Child Relationship

You may wonder why a chapter about preventing teen alcohol use is putting so much emphasis on parents' need to understand and support their children. But the fact is, the best way to influence your child to avoid drinking is to have a strong, trusting relationship with him or her. Research shows that teens are much more likely to delay drinking when they feel they have a close, supportive tie with a parent or guardian. Moreover, if your son or daughter eventually does begin to drink, a good relationship with you will help protect him or her from developing alcohol-related problems.

The opposite is also true: When the relationship between a parent and teen is full of conflict or is very distant, the teen is more likely to use alcohol and to develop drinking-related problems. This connection between the parent-child relationship and a child's drinking habits makes a lot of sense when you think about it. First, when children have a strong bond with a parent, they are apt to feel good about themselves and therefore be less likely to cave in to peer pressure to use alcohol. Second, a good relationship with you is likely to influence your children to try to live up to your expectations, because they want to maintain their close tie with you. Here are some ways to build a strong, supportive bond with your child:

- **Establish open communication.** Make it easy for your teen to talk honestly with you.

- **Show you care.** Even though young teens may not always show it, they still need to know they are important to their parents. Make it a point to regularly spend one-on-one time with your child—time when you can give him or her your loving, undivided attention. Some activities to share: a walk, a bike ride, a quiet dinner out, or a cookie-baking session.

- **Draw the line.** Set clear, realistic expectations for your child's behavior. Establish appropriate consequences for breaking rules and consistently enforce them.

- **Offer acceptance.** Make sure your teen knows that you appreciate his or her efforts as well as accomplishments. Avoid hurtful teasing or criticism.

- **Understand that your child is growing up.** This doesn't mean a hands-off attitude. But as you guide your child's behavior, also make an effort to respect his or her growing need for independence and privacy.

Tips for Communicating with Your Teen

Developing open, trusting communication between you and your child is essential to helping your child avoid alcohol use. If your child feels comfortable talking openly with you, you'll have a greater chance of guiding him or her toward healthy decision making. Some ways to begin:

- **Encourage conversation.** Encourage your child to talk about whatever interests him or her. Listen without interruption and give your child a chance to teach you something new. Your active listening to your child's enthusiasm paves the way for conversations about topics that concern you.

- **Ask open-ended questions.** Encourage your teen to tell you how he or she thinks and feels about the issue you're discussing. Avoid questions that have a simple "yes" or "no" answer.

- **Control your emotions.** If you hear something you don't like, try not to respond with anger. Instead, take a few deep breaths and acknowledge your feelings in a constructive way.

- **Make every conversation a "win-win" experience.** Don't lecture or try to "score points" by showing how your teen is wrong. If you show respect for your child's viewpoint, he or she will be more likely to listen to and respect yours.

Talking with Your Teen about Alcohol

For many parents, bringing up the subject of alcohol is no easy matter. Your young teen may try to dodge the discussion, and you may feel unsure about how to proceed. To boost your chances for a productive conversation, take some time to think through the issues you want to discuss before you talk with your child. Also, think about how your child might react and ways you might respond to your youngster's questions and feelings. Then choose a time to talk when both you and your child have some down time and are feeling relaxed.

Keep in mind, too, that you don't need to cover everything at once. In fact, you're likely to have a greater impact on your child's drinking by having a number of talks about alcohol use throughout his or her adolescence. Think of this discussion with your child as the first part of an ongoing conversation.

And remember, do make it a conversation, not a lecture! Following are some topics for discussion:

- **Your child's views about alcohol.** Ask your young teen what he or she knows about alcohol and what he or she thinks about teen drinking. Ask your child why he or she thinks kids drink. Listen carefully without interrupting. Not only will this approach help your child to feel heard and respected, but it can serve as a natural "lead-in" to discussing alcohol topics.

- **Important facts about alcohol.** Although many kids believe they already know everything about alcohol, myths and misinformation abound. Here are some important facts to share:

  - Alcohol is a powerful drug that slows down the body and mind. It impairs coordination; slows reaction time; and impairs vision, clear thinking, and judgment.

  - Beer and wine are not safer than hard liquor. A 12-ounce can of beer, a 5-ounce glass of wine, and 1.5 ounces of hard liquor all contain the same amount of alcohol and have the same effects on the body and mind.

  - On average, it takes 2 to 3 hours for a single drink to leave the body's system. Nothing can speed up this process, including drinking coffee, taking a cold shower, or walking it off.

  - People tend to be very bad at judging how seriously alcohol has affected them. That means many individuals who drive after drinking think they can control a car—but actually cannot.

- Anyone can develop a serious alcohol problem, including a teenager.

- **The "magic potion" myth.** The media's glamorous portrayal of alcohol encourages many teens to believe that drinking will make them popular, attractive, happy, and cool. Research shows that teens who expect such positive effects are more likely to drink at early ages. However, you can help to combat these dangerous myths by watching TV shows and movie videos with your child and discussing how alcohol is portrayed in them. For example, television advertisements for beer often show young people having an uproariously good time, as though drinking always puts people in a terrific mood. Watching such a commercial with your child can be an opportunity to discuss the many ways that alcohol can affect people—in some cases bringing on feelings of sadness or anger rather than carefree high spirits.

- **Good reasons not to drink.** In talking with your child about reasons to avoid alcohol, stay away from scare tactics. Most young teens are aware that many people drink without problems, so it is important to discuss the consequences of alcohol use without overstating the case. For example, you can talk about the dangers of riding in a car with a driver who has been drinking without insisting that "all kids who ride with drinkers get into crashes." Some good reasons that teens shouldn't drink:

  - *You want your child to avoid alcohol.* Be sure to clearly state your own expectations regarding your child's drinking and to establish consequences for breaking rules. Your values and attitudes count with your child, even though he or she may not always show it.

  - *To maintain self-respect.* In a series of focus groups, teens reported that the best way to persuade them to avoid alcohol is to appeal to their self-respect—letting them know that they are too smart and have too much going for them to need the crutch of alcohol. Teens also pay attention to ways in which alcohol might cause them to do something embarrassing that might damage their self-respect and important relationships.

- *Drinking is illegal.* Because alcohol use under the age of 21 is illegal, getting caught may mean trouble with the authorities. Even if getting caught doesn't lead to police action, the parents of your child's friends may no longer permit them to associate with your child. If drinking occurs on school grounds, your child could be suspended.

- *Drinking can be dangerous.* One of the leading causes of teen deaths is motor vehicle crashes involving alcohol. Drinking also makes a young person more vulnerable to sexual assault and unprotected sex. And while your teen may believe he or she wouldn't engage in hazardous activities after drinking, point out that because alcohol impairs judgment, a drinker is very likely to think such activities won't be dangerous.

- *You have a family history of alcoholism.* If one or more members of your immediate or extended family has suffered from alcoholism, your child may be somewhat more vulnerable to developing a drinking problem. Your child needs to know that for him or her, drinking may carry special risks.

- **How to handle peer pressure.** It's not enough to tell your young teen that he or she should avoid alcohol—you also need to help your child figure out how. What can your daughter say when she goes to a party and a friend offers her a beer? Or what should your son do if he finds himself in a home where kids are passing around a bottle of wine and parents are nowhere in sight? What should their response be if they are offered a ride home with an older friend who has been drinking? Brainstorm with your teen ways that he or she might handle these and other difficult situations, and make clear how you are willing to support your child. An example: "If you find yourself at a home where kids are drinking, call me and I'll pick you up—and there will be no scolding or punishment." The more prepared your child is, the better able he or she will be to handle high-pressure situations that involve drinking.

Six Ways to Say No to a Drink

At some point, your child will be offered alcohol. To resist such pressure, teens say they prefer quick "one-liners" that allow them to dodge a drink without making a big scene. It will probably work best for your teen to take the lead in thinking up comebacks to drink offers so that he or she will feel comfortable saying them. But to get the brainstorming started, here are some simple pressure busters—from the mildest to the most assertive.

1. No thanks.
2. I don't feel like it—do you have any soda?
3. Alcohol's not my thing.
4. Are you talking to me? Forget it.
5. Why do you keep pressuring me when I've said no?
6. Back off!

Mom, Dad, Did You Drink When You Were a Kid?

This is the question many parents dread—yet it is highly likely to come up in any family discussion of alcohol. The reality is that many parents did drink before they were old enough to legally do so. So how can one be honest with a child without sounding like a hypocrite who advises, "Do as I say, not as I did"?

This is a judgment call. If you believe that your drinking or drug use history should not be part of the discussion, you can simply tell your child that you choose not to share it. Another approach is to admit that you did do some drinking as a teenager, but that it was a mistake—and give your teen an example of an embarrassing or painful moment that occurred because of your drinking. This approach may help your child better understand that youthful alcohol use does have negative consequences.

How to Host a Teen Party

- Agree on a guest list—and don't admit party crashers.
- Discuss ground rules with your child before the party.
- Encourage your teen to plan the party with a responsible friend so that he or she will have support if problems arise.
- Brainstorm fun activities for the party.
- If a guest brings alcohol into your house, ask him or her to leave.
- Serve plenty of snacks and nonalcoholic drinks.
- Be visible and available—but don't join the party!

Taking Action: Prevention Strategies for Parents

Although parent-child conversations about drinking are essential, talking isn't enough—you also need to take concrete action to help your child resist alcohol. Research strongly shows that active, supportive involvement by parents and guardians can help teens avoid underage drinking and prevent later alcohol misuse.

In a recent national survey, 71 percent of eighth graders said alcohol was "fairly easy" or "very easy" to get. The message is clear: Young teens still need plenty of adult supervision. Some ways to provide it:

Monitor alcohol use in your home. If you keep alcohol in your home, keep track of the supply. Make it clear to your child that you don't allow unchaperoned parties or other teen gatherings in your home. If possible, however, encourage him or her to invite friends over when you are at home. The more entertaining your child does in your home, the more you will know about your child's friends and activities.

Connect with other parents. Getting to know other parents and guardians can help you keep closer tabs on your child. Friendly relations can make it easier for you to call the parent of a teen who is having a party to be sure that a responsible adult will be present and that alcohol will not be available. You're likely to find out that you're not the only adult who wants to prevent teen alcohol use—many other parents share your concern.

Keep track of your child's activities. Be aware of your teen's plans and whereabouts. Generally, your child will be more open to your supervision if he or she feels you are keeping tabs because you care, not because you distrust him or her.

Develop family rules about teen drinking. When parents establish clear "no alcohol" rules and expectations, their children are less likely to begin drinking. While each family should develop agreements about teen alcohol use that reflect their own beliefs and values, some possible family rules about drinking are:

- Kids will not drink alcohol until they are 21.
- Older siblings will not encourage younger brothers or sisters to drink and will not give them alcohol.
- Kids will not stay at teen parties where alcohol is served.
- Kids will not ride in a car with a driver who has been drinking.

Once you have chosen rules for your family, you will need to establish appropriate consequences for breaking those rules. Be sure to choose a penalty that you are willing to carry out. Also, don't make the consequences so harsh that they become a barrier to open communication between you and your teen. The idea is to make the penalty "sting" just enough to make your child think twice about breaking the rule. A possible consequence might be temporary restrictions on your child's socializing.

Finally, you must be prepared to consistently enforce the consequences you have established. If your children know that they will lose certain privileges each and every time an alcohol use rule is broken, they will be more likely to keep their agreements.

Set a good example. Parents and guardians are important role models for their children—even children who are fast becoming teenagers. Studies indicate that if a parent uses alcohol, his or her children are more likely to drink themselves. But even if you use alcohol, there may be ways to lessen the likelihood that your child will drink. Some suggestions:

- Use alcohol moderately.

- Don't communicate to your child that alcohol is a good way to handle problems. For example, don't come home from work and say, "I had a rotten day. I need a drink."

- Instead, let your child see that you have other, healthier ways to cope with stress, such as exercise; listening to music; or talking things over with your spouse, partner, or friend.

- Don't tell your kids stories about your own drinking in a way that conveys the message that alcohol use is funny or glamorous.

- Never drink and drive or ride in a car with a driver who has been drinking.

- When you entertain other adults, make available alcohol-free beverages and plenty of food. If anyone drinks too much at your party, make arrangements for them to get home safely.

Don't support teen drinking. Your attitudes and behavior toward teen drinking also influence your child. Avoid making jokes about underage drinking or drunkenness, or otherwise showing acceptance of teen alcohol use. In addition, never serve alcohol to your child's underage friends. Research shows that kids whose parents or friends' parents provide alcohol for teen get-togethers are more likely to engage in heavier drinking, to drink more often, and to get into traffic crashes. Remember, too, that it is illegal in most states to provide alcohol to minors who are not family members.

You can also join school and community efforts to discourage alcohol use by teens. By working with school officials and other members of your community, you can help to develop policies to reduce alcohol availability to teens and to enforce consequences for underage drinking.

Help your child build healthy friendships. If your child's friends use alcohol, your child is more likely to drink too. So it makes sense to try to encourage your young teen to develop friendships with kids who do not drink and who are otherwise healthy influences on your child. A good first step is to simply get to know your child's friends better. You can then invite the kids you feel good about to family get-togethers and outings and find other ways to encourage your child to spend time with those teens. Also, talk directly with your youngster about the qualities in a friend that really count, such as trustworthiness and kindness, rather than popularity or a cool style.

When you disapprove of one of your child's friends, the situation can be tougher to handle. While it may be tempting to simply forbid your child to see that friend, such a move may make your child even more determined to hang out with him or her. Instead, you might try pointing out your reservations about the friend in a caring, supportive way. You can also limit your child's time with that friend through your family rules, such as how after-school time can be spent or how late your child can stay out in the evening.

Encourage healthy alternatives to alcohol. One reason kids drink is to beat boredom. Therefore, it makes sense to encourage your child to participate in supervised after-school and weekend activities that are challenging and fun. According to a recent survey of preteens, the availability of enjoyable, alcohol-free activities is a big reason for deciding not to use alcohol.

If your community doesn't offer many supervised activities, consider getting together with other parents and young teens to help create some. Start by asking your child and other kids what they want to do, since they will be most likely to participate in activities that truly interest them. Find out whether your church, school, or community organization can help you sponsor a project.

Could Your Child Develop a Drinking Problem?

Although this chapter is mainly concerned with preventing teen alcohol use, we also need to pay attention to the possibility of youthful alcohol abuse. Certain children are more likely than others to drink heavily and encounter alcohol-related difficulties, including health, school, legal, family, and emotional problems. Kids at highest risk for alcohol-related problems are those who:

- begin using alcohol or other drugs before the age of 15;
- have a parent who is a problem drinker or an alcoholic;
- have close friends who use alcohol and/or other drugs;
- have been aggressive, antisocial, or hard to control from an early age;
- have experienced childhood abuse and/or other major traumas;
- have current behavioral problems and/or are failing at school;
- have parents who do not support them, do not communicate openly with them, and do not keep track of their behavior or whereabouts; and/or
- experience ongoing hostility or rejection from parents and/or harsh, inconsistent discipline.

The more of these experiences a child has had, the greater the chances that he or she will develop problems with alcohol. Having one or more risk factors does not mean that your child definitely will develop a drinking problem. It does suggest, however, that you may need to act now to help protect your youngster from later problems. For example, if you have not been openly communicating with your child, it will be important to develop new ways of talking and listening to each other. Or, if your child has serious behavioral difficulties, you may want to seek help from your child's school counselor, physician, and/or a mental health professional.

Some parents may suspect that their child already has a drinking problem. Although it can be hard to know for sure, certain behaviors can alert you to the possibility of an alcohol problem. If you think your child may be in trouble with drinking, consider getting advice from a health care professional specializing in alcohol problems before talking with your teen. To find a professional, contact your family doctor or a local hospital. Other sources of information and guidance may be found in your local Yellow Pages under "Alcoholism."

Warning Signs of a Drinking Problem

Although the following behaviors may indicate an alcohol or other drug problem, some also reflect normal teenage growing pains. Experts believe that a drinking problem is more likely if you notice several of these signs at the same time, if they occur suddenly, and if some of them are extreme in nature.

- mood changes: flare-ups of temper, irritability, and defensiveness
- school problems: poor attendance, low grades, and/or recent disciplinary action
- rebelling against family rules
- switching friends, along with a reluctance to have you get to know the new friends
- a "nothing matters" attitude: sloppy appearance, a lack of involvement in former interests, and general low energy
- finding alcohol in your child's room or backpack or smelling alcohol on his or her breath
- physical or mental problems: memory lapses, poor concentration, bloodshot eyes, lack of coordination, or slurred speech

Action Checklist

- Establish a loving, trusting relationship with your child.
- Make it easy for your teen to talk honestly with you.
- Talk with your child about alcohol facts, reasons not to drink, and ways to avoid drinking in difficult situations.
- Keep tabs on your young teen's activities, and join with other parents in making common policies about teen alcohol use.
- Develop family rules about teen drinking and establish consequences.
- Set a good example regarding your own alcohol use and your response to teen drinking.
- Encourage your child to develop healthy friendships and fun alternatives to drinking.
- Know whether your child is at high risk for a drinking problem; if so, take steps to lessen that risk.
- Know the warning signs of a teen drinking problem and act promptly to get help for your child.
- Believe in your own power to help your child avoid alcohol use.

Chapter 16

For Teens: Organizing a Substance-Free Party

Getting Started

Why wait for your school or parents to organize activities for you and your friends? Show adults that you are responsible and take the lead yourself. Organizing a substance-free party is a great idea, one that you shouldn't have a hard time selling to your friends, parents, or teachers. Here are a few tips on getting started:

- **Start Early**—Get a jump on the planning as soon as possible in the school year. Gather a small, but diverse group of student planners to help you work out the details. It's best to include at least one or two members from key support group's teachers, parents, law enforcement, and even local businesses that can help you plan and assist with resources.

- **Develop a Plan**—Make an agenda for the first meeting. Include topics to figure out how many committees you may need and who will participate; how much money you will need to raise through donations, fundraisers, and ticket sales; and how to spread the word.

- **Choose a Chairperson**—This should be someone who has the time and expertise to take the lead in planning the party. It

"Make Your Parties Rock: A Guide to Safe and Sober Event Planning," is produced by the National Highway Traffic Safety Administration (NHTSA), 2001. Reviewed by David A. Cooke, MD, on March 13, 2006.

may be a good idea to enlist class leaders or your student government. Chairing is a big job and it's not always easy. The good news is that it's also rewarding. Just think of all of the new people you'll meet! Plus, you'll be playing a role in saving lives, which is more important than all of the headaches that come from being the boss.

- **Set the Hours**—Decide when the party will begin and end. It is important that your party lasts late into the night. Often when events end while people still want to party, a few might be tempted to continue celebrating in ways that are not safe.

Partnerships

Generating support for your event is a key factor in making it a success. Partners not only help you spread the word about your event, but they can provide credibility, financial support, necessary resources, and give your group any other support it may need. If your group already has established partnerships, then you're aware of their value to the program and its efforts. If not, locate groups in your school or community such as SADD [Students Against Destructive Decisions]. You can begin to build and cultivate partnerships with a host of local businesses, organizations, advocacy groups, and others you think can help make your party the best event in town.

Friends are invaluable partners. They can contribute to the event planning, as well as to seeing that the party's ideas are properly executed. Friends also help your group maintain enthusiasm toward the event, through proper promotion and word of mouth. In addition, friends can help in planning and preparing for future events and providing new ideas and resources for your group. Here are some ways friends can help:

- Chart out activities for the entire year that incorporate as many themes and ideas as possible.
- Create new ideas for parties and activities.
- Promote activities through posters, fliers, invitations, and e-mails.
- Arrange event logistics.
- Recruit help.
- Make sure everyone is included.

Your friends should help your group stress that the event is meant to be an alternative to those where alcohol is present. The theme should be at the forefront of every meeting and prominently featured on advertising to encourage the generation of creative ideas on alternatives to parties with alcohol.

Clean-Up

Ideally, everyone would pick up after themselves throughout the night. Realistically, that usually doesn't happen. There are a few ways to keep the mess to a minimum, while keeping the fun at a maximum.

- **Trash Cans**—Have a lot of them. Make sure trash receptacles are evenly distributed throughout the space and are lined with strong plastic bags to prevent leaks and rips.

- **Plates, Cups, and Utensils**—Use the disposable kind. Mom's fine china may add an air of class to your event, but breaking it will add serious problems. Plastic cups, plates, and utensils are inexpensive and can simply be thrown away after use.

- **Mops, Brooms, and Cleaning Supplies**—Accidents will happen. When they do, these items can help prevent a small spill from becoming a big concern.

- **Your Effort**—It's your party. You and your friends have shown how responsible you are by putting together a great event without alcohol. But as the host, you should also keep an eye on the mess, or anything that might potentially interfere with your guests' enjoyment. If there is trash, throw it out. If someone is dancing dangerously close to the punch bowl, kindly ask him or her to move a few feet away. Small acts like these can go a long way toward making the party fun for you and all your guests.

Chapter 17

Changing the Culture of Campus Drinking

Drinking on college campuses is more pervasive and destructive than many people realize. Alcohol consumption is linked to at least 1,400 student deaths and 500,000 unintentional injuries annually. Alcohol consumption by college students is associated with drinking and driving, diminished academic performance, and medical and legal problems. Nondrinking students, as well as members of the surrounding community, also may experience alcohol-related consequences, such as increased rates of crime, traffic crashes, rapes and assaults, and property damage. For example, each year, more than 600,000 students are assaulted by other students who have been drinking. Yet efforts to reduce student drinking have largely been unsuccessful, in part because proven, research-based prevention strategies have not been consistently applied.

The Culture of College Drinking

Alcohol consumption on many campuses has evolved into a rite of passage. Traditions and beliefs handed down through generations of college drinkers serve to reinforce students' expectations that alcohol is a necessary component of social success. The role of alcohol in college life is evident in the advertising and sale of alcoholic beverages on or near campuses. This combination of social and environmental influences

Excerpted from "Changing the Culture of Campus Drinking," *Alcohol Alert* No. 58, published by the National Institute on Alcohol Abuse and Alcoholism (NIAAA), October 2002. For a complete list of references, see www.niaaa.nih.gov.

creates a culture of drinking that passively or actively promotes the use of alcohol. In a recent survey that questioned students about patterns and consequences of their alcohol use during the past year, 31 percent of participants reported symptoms associated with alcohol abuse (e.g., drinking in hazardous situations and alcohol-related school problems), and 6 percent reported 3 or more symptoms of alcohol dependence (e.g., drinking more or longer than initially planned and experiencing increased tolerance to alcohol's effects). Although it is true that most high-risk student drinkers reduce their consumption of alcohol after leaving college, others may continue frequent, excessive drinking, leading to alcoholism or medical problems associated with chronic alcohol abuse.

Factors Influencing College Drinking

Students' drinking habits are influenced by a combination of personal and environmental factors. Relevant personal factors include family influences, personality, and a person's biological or genetic susceptibility to alcohol abuse. In addition, many students arrive at college with preexisting positive expectations about alcohol's effects and often with a history of alcohol consumption. Thirty percent of 12th graders, for example, report heavy episodic drinking in high school, slightly more report having "been drunk," and almost three quarters report drinking in the past year. Certain campus characteristics also reinforce the culture of college drinking. Rates of excessive alcohol use are highest at colleges and universities where Greek systems (i.e., fraternities and sororities) dominate, at those where sports teams have a prominent role, and at schools located in the Northeast. In the local community, tolerance of student drinking may permit alcoholic beverage outlets and advertising to be located near campus. Likewise, there may be lax enforcement of the laws prohibiting alcohol sales to persons below the minimum legal drinking age and penalizing underage students who use fake IDs to obtain alcohol.

Prevention Strategies

Before launching prevention strategies to address the problem of college drinking, it is necessary to define the patterns of alcohol consumption that may occur on campus. Surveys show that approximately 70 percent of college students consumed some alcohol in the past month. Although some of these students can be considered problem drinkers (e.g., frequent heavy episodic drinkers or those who display symptoms of dependence), others may drink moderately or may misuse alcohol only occasionally (e.g., drinking and driving infrequently). Surveys of drinking patterns show that college students are more likely than their age-mates who are not in college to consume any alcohol, to drink heavily, and to engage in heavy episodic drinking. However, young people who are not in college are more likely to consume alcohol every day.

Evidence supporting the effectiveness of alcohol prevention strategies is incomplete and often inconsistent. In addition, many strategies have not been evaluated specifically for application to college-age drinkers. Some potentially useful preventive interventions include.

Strategies effective among college students. Strong evidence supports the effectiveness of the following strategies: (1) simultaneously addressing alcohol-related attitudes and behaviors (e.g., refuting false beliefs about alcohol's effects while teaching students how to cope with stress without resorting to alcohol); (2) using survey data to counter students' misperceptions about their fellow students' drinking practices and attitudes toward excessive drinking; and (3) increasing students' motivation to change their drinking habits, for example by providing nonjudgmental advice and evaluations of the students' progress. Programs that combine these three strategies have proven effective in reducing alcohol consumption.

Strategies effective among the general population that could be applied to college environments. These strategies have proven successful in populations similar to those found on college campuses. Measures include (1) increasing enforcement of minimum legal drinking age laws; (2) implementing, enforcing, and publicizing other laws to reduce alcohol-impaired driving, such as zero-tolerance laws that reduce the legal blood alcohol concentration for underage drivers to near zero; (3) increasing the prices or taxes on alcoholic beverages; and (4) instituting policies and training for servers of alcoholic beverages to prevent sales to underage or intoxicated patrons.

Promising strategies that require research. These strategies make sense intuitively or show theoretical promise, but more comprehensive evaluation is needed to test their usefulness in reducing the consequences of student drinking. They include more consistent enforcement of campus alcohol regulations and increasing the severity of penalties for violating them, regulating happy hours, enhancing awareness of personal liability for alcohol-related harm to others, establishing alcohol-free dormitories, restricting or eliminating alcohol-industry sponsorship of student events while promoting alcohol-free student activities, and conducting social norms campaigns to correct exaggerated estimates of the overall level of drinking among the student body.

The Role of Campus Administration

The leadership of college presidents and school administrators is crucial to develop appropriate plans, supervise the integration of policies pertaining to different aspects of student life, and ensure consistent enforcement of drinking-related policies. Because the effectiveness of a particular strategy depends on individual campus characteristics, school administrators must determine the nature and scope of drinking and related problems on their campuses before undertaking prevention planning. A strong research base also is necessary to define realistic program objectives and maximize the use of resources, thereby increasing the likelihood of program effectiveness. Progress should be evaluated with the help of the research community, and the results should be publicized to ensure the continuation of successful programs and to add to the existing knowledge base.

Chapter 18

Preventing
Impaired or Drunk Driving

Chapter Contents

Section 18.1—Understanding Blood Alcohol
             Concentration and Alcohol Impairment 132

Section 18.2—Alcohol and Transportation Safety 135

Section 18.3—Lowered National Blood Alcohol
             Concentration Limit for Impaired Driving 140

Section 18.4—Tips for Preventing Drunk Driving 144

Section 18.5—Get the Keys: How You Can Intervene 146

Section 18.6—Strict Licensing Laws Associated with
             Less Teen Drinking and Driving 147

Section 18.1

Understanding Blood Alcohol Concentration and Alcohol Impairment

From the brochure "The ABCs of BAC: A Guide to Understanding Blood Alcohol Concentration and Blood Alcohol Impairment," by the National Highway Traffic Safety Administration (NHTSA), part of the U.S. Department of Transportation, February 2005.

What is BAC?

The amount of alcohol in a person's body is measured by the weight of the alcohol in a certain volume of blood. This is called the blood alcohol concentration, or BAC.

Alcohol is absorbed directly through the walls of the stomach and the small intestine, goes into the bloodstream, and travels throughout the body and to the brain.

Alcohol is quickly absorbed and can be measured within 30 to 70 minutes after a person has had a drink.

Does the type of alcohol I drink affect my BAC?

No. A drink is a drink, is a drink.

A typical drink equals about half an ounce of alcohol (.54 ounces, to be exact). This is the approximate amount of alcohol found in:

- one shot of distilled spirits; or
- one 5-ounce glass of wine; or
- one 12-ounce beer.

What affects my BAC?

How fast a person's BAC rises varies with a number of factors:

- **the number of drinks.** The more you drink, the higher the BAC.

- **how fast you drink.** When alcohol is consumed quickly, you will reach a higher BAC than when it is consumed over a longer period of time.

- **your gender.** Women generally have less water and more body fat per pound of body weight than men. Alcohol does not go into fat cells as easily as other cells, so more alcohol remains in the blood of women.

- **your weight.** The more you weigh, the more water is present in your body. This water dilutes the alcohol and lowers the BAC.

- **food in your stomach.** Absorption will be slowed if you've had something to eat.

What about other medications or drugs?

Medications or drugs will not change your BAC. However, if you drink alcohol while taking certain medications, you may feel—and be—more impaired, which can affect your ability to perform driving-related tasks.

When am I impaired?

Because of the multitude of factors that affect BAC, it is very difficult to assess your own BAC or impairment. Though small amounts of alcohol affect one's brain and the ability to drive, people often swear they are fine after several drinks—but in fact, the failure to recognize alcohol impairment is often a symptom of impairment.

While the lower stages of alcohol impairment are undetectable to others, the drinker knows vaguely when the "buzz" begins. A person will likely be too impaired to drive before looking—or maybe even feeling—drunk.

How will I know I'm impaired, and why should I care?

Alcohol steadily decreases a person's ability to drive a motor vehicle safely. The more you drink, the greater the effect. As with BAC, the signs of impairment differ with the individual.

In single-vehicle crashes, the relative risk of a driver with BAC between .08 and .10 is at least 11 times greater than for drivers with a BAC of zero, and 52 times greater for young males. Further, many studies have shown that even small amounts of alcohol can impair a person's ability to drive.

Table 18.1. Blood Alcohol Concentration Levels and Effects on Driving.

BAC*	Typical Effects	Predictable Effects on Driving
.02%	Some loss of judgment; relaxation; slight body warmth; and altered mood	Decline in visual functions (rapid tracking of a moving target) and decline in ability to perform two tasks at the same time (divided attention)
.05%	Exaggerated behavior; may have loss of small-muscle control (e.g., focusing your eyes); impaired judgment; usually good feeling; lowered alertness; and release of inhibition	Reduced coordination; reduced ability to track moving objects; difficulty steering; and reduced response to emergency driving situations
.08%	Muscle coordination becomes poor (e.g., balance, speech, vision, reaction time, and hearing); harder to detect danger; judgment, self-control, reasoning, and memory are impaired	Concentration; short-term memory loss; speed control; reduced information processing capability (e.g., signal detection, visual search); and impaired perception
.10%	Clear deterioration of reaction time and control; slurred speech, poor coordination, and slowed thinking	Reduced ability to maintain lane position and brake appropriately
.15%	Far less muscle control than normal; vomiting may occur (unless this level is reached slowly or a person has developed a tolerance for alcohol); major loss of balance	Substantial impairment in vehicle control, attention to driving task, and in necessary visual and audi tory information processing

Blood Alcohol Concentration

Note: *Information in this table shows the BAC level at which the effect usually is first observed, and has been gathered from a variety of sources including the National Highway Traffic Safety Administration, the National Institute on Alcohol Abuse and Alcoholism, the American Medical Association, the National Commission Against Drunk Driving, and www.webMD.com.*

Every state has passed a law making it illegal to drive with a BAC of .08 or higher. A driver also can be arrested with a BAC below .08 when a law enforcement officer has probable cause, based on the driver's behavior.

Table 18.1 contains some of the more common symptoms people exhibit at various BAC levels, and the probable effects on driving ability.

What can I do to stay safe when I plan on drinking?

If you plan on drinking, plan not to drive. You should always:

- choose a nondrinking friend as a designated driver; or
- ask ahead of time if you can stay over at your host's house; or
- take a taxi (your community may have a Safe Rides program for a free ride home); and
- always wear your safety belt—it's your best defense against impaired drivers.

Section 18.2

Alcohol and Transportation Safety

Excerpted from *Alcohol Alert* No. 52, a publication of the National Institute on Alcohol Abuse and Alcoholism (NIAAA), April 2001. For a complete list of references, see, www.niaaa.nih.gov. Reviewed by David A. Cooke, M.D., on March 30, 2006.

Research has shown that even low blood alcohol concentration (BAC) impairs driving skills and increases crash risk. BAC is the proportion of alcohol to blood in the body. In the field of traffic safety, BAC is expressed as a percentage reflecting grams of alcohol per deciliter of blood for example, 0.10 percent is equivalent to 0.10 grams per deciliter.

New information about BAC and impairment has led to policy changes, which have contributed to declines in alcohol-related crashes and fatalities. This document examines some aspects of alcohol-induced impairment and reviews selected strategies designed to reduce alcohol-related crashes and repeat drinking-and-driving offenses.

BAC and Impairment

A review of 112 studies concluded that certain skills required to operate essentially any type of motorized vehicle become impaired at even modest departures from zero BAC. At 0.05 percent BAC, most studies reported significant impairment. By 0.08 percent BAC, 94 percent of the studies reported impairment. Some skills are significantly impaired at 0.01 percent BAC, although other skills do not show impairment until 0.06 percent BAC. At BACs of 0.02 percent or lower, the ability to divide attention between two or more sources of visual information can be impaired. Starting at BACs of 0.05 percent, drivers show other types of impairment, including eye movement, glare resistance, visual perception, and reaction time. In one study, researchers reported that alcohol significantly impaired driving simulator performance at all BACs starting at 0.02 percent.

The risk of a fatal crash for drivers with positive BACs compared with other drivers (i.e., the relative risk) increases with increasing BAC, and the risks increase more steeply for drivers younger than age 21 than for older drivers. Between 0.08 and 0.10 percent BACs, the relative risk of a fatal single-vehicle crash varies between 11 percent (for drivers age 35 and older) and 52 percent (for male drivers ages 16 to 20).

Other forms of transportation also have been investigated. Studies using an automated device that simulates actual flight conditions have shown pilot performance to be impaired at BACs as low as 0.04 percent and to remain impaired for as long as 14 hours after pilots reached BACs between 0.10 percent and 0.12 percent. Another experiment using a simulated environment showed that experienced maritime academy students with BACs of 0.05 needed significantly more time than did other students to solve a problem related to power plant operation on board a merchant ship and were not aware of their impairment.

Factors That Influence Alcohol-Induced Impairment

Alcohol Tolerance. Research suggests that the repeated performance of certain tasks while under the influence of alcohol can make a person less sensitive to impairment at a given BAC. However, although impairment from alcohol may not be evident during routine tasks, performance would worsen in novel or unexpected situations.

Age. Based on miles driven, the highest driver fatality rates are found among the youngest and oldest drivers. Compared with the fatality rate for drivers ages 25 to 69, the rate for 16- to 19-year-old drivers is about four times as high, and the rate for drivers age 85 and older is nine times as high. Among male drivers younger than age 21, a BAC increase of 0.02 percent more than doubles the relative risk for a single-vehicle fatal crash. Women in this age group, however, have lower relative risk than do men at every BAC. Young drivers' greater crash risk is attributed, in part, to lack of driving experience coupled with overconfidence. The presence of other teenagers in the car may encourage risky driving and is associated with increased fatal crash risk among young drivers.

Alcohol is less often a factor in crashes involving older drivers. In 1999 drivers age 65 and older killed in crashes were the least likely of any adult age group to have positive BACs. Nevertheless, a person's crash risk per mile increases starting at age 55 and exceeds that of a young, beginning driver by age 80. Factors associated with unsafe driving include problems with vision, attention, perception, and cognition. Older drivers with alcoholism also are more vulnerable than are other elderly drivers to impairment and have greater crash risks.

Sleep Deprivation. Drowsiness increases crash risk, and research shows that BACs as low as 0.01 percent increase susceptibility to sleepiness. Alcohol consumption also increases the adverse effects of sleep deprivation. Subjects given low doses of alcohol following a night of reduced sleep perform poorly in a driving simulator, even with no detectable alcohol in the blood.

Recent Declines in Drinking and Driving

Research shows that drinking and driving in the United States has decreased over the past decade, especially among young drivers. The proportion of all traffic fatalities that are alcohol related has decreased. The overall percentage of drivers with positive BACs among all drivers surveyed on weekend nights also has decreased. In addition, crash statistics and driver surveys both show decreases in the proportion of drivers with BACs of 0.10 percent or higher, with the largest decreases among drivers younger than age 21.

Prevention Strategies

Raising the Minimum Legal Drinking Age (MLDA). The National Highway Traffic Safety Administration (NHTSA) estimates that raising the MLDA to 21 has reduced traffic fatalities involving 18- to 20-year-old drivers by 13 percent and has saved an estimated 19,121 lives since 1975. Twenty of 29 studies conducted between 1981 and 1992 reported significant decreases in traffic crashes and crash fatalities following an increase in MLDA. Three studies found no change in traffic crashes involving youth in various age groups, and six studies had mixed results. Laws that prohibit selling or providing alcohol to minors generally are not well enforced, but community efforts to increase MLDA enforcement can be effective.

Zero-Tolerance Laws. These laws, which set the legal BAC limit for drivers younger than age 21 at 0.00 or 0.02 percent, have been associated with 20 percent declines in the proportion of drinking drivers involved in fatal crashes who are younger than age 21 and in the proportion of single-vehicle, nighttime fatal crashes among drivers younger than age 21. Based on driver surveys, researchers have reported that young drivers may be more successful than are older drivers in separating drinking from driving, and these researchers have suggested that this difference could be attributable to zero-tolerance laws.

BAC Laws That Lower Limits to 0.08 percent. The majority of states are now considering lowering the legal BAC limit for non-commercial drivers age 21 and older to 0.08 percent. In fact, according to NHTSA, 27 states have now approved legislation to lower BAC limits to 0.08 percent. Laws lowering the legal BAC limit for adult drivers to 0.08 percent are associated with declines in alcohol-related fatal crashes. One national study reported that states with 0.08 laws had smaller proportions of adult drivers in fatal crashes with BACs of 0.01 to 0.09 percent and with BACs of 0.10 percent and higher.

Lower BAC Limits for DUI Offenders and Transportation Workers. In Maine, a law lowering the legal BAC limit to 0.05 percent for anyone convicted of driving under the influence (DUI) has been found to reduce significantly the number of fatal crashes among this population. Because drinking and driving by transportation workers threatens public safety, the federal government prohibits commercial truck drivers, railroad and mass transit workers, maritime employees, and aircraft pilots from operating their vehicles with BACs of 0.04 percent or higher.

Community-Wide Prevention. Comprehensive community initiatives to reduce drinking and driving combine the efforts of public agencies and private citizens in implementing strategies, including media campaigns, police training, high school and college prevention programs, and increased liquor outlet surveillance. Such strategies have been found to reduce fatal crashes, alcohol-related fatal crashes, and traffic injuries.

A community program in San Diego was implemented to reduce the binge drinking and impaired driving that result when young people cross the U.S.-Mexico border to drink in Tijuana, where the legal drinking age is 18 and beverage prices are lower. Researchers estimated that more than 250 drivers with BACs of 0.08 percent or higher on U.S. roads every Friday and Saturday night are border-crossers. Targeted enforcement was found to reduce the number of late-night crossers by 26 percent.

Alcohol Screening and Brief Intervention for Emergency Room Patients. Emergency room patients injured in alcohol-related crashes may have an increased motivation to change their drinking behavior. Emergency room interventions have been shown to reduce future drinking and trauma readmission as well as drinking and driving, traffic violations, alcohol-related injuries, and alcohol-related problems among 18- and 19-year-olds.

Reducing Repeated DUI Offenses

License Suspension. Laws that allow for administrative license suspension (ALS) at the time of arrest have been found to reduce both alcohol-related fatal crashes and repeat DUI offenses. A study of an Ohio ALS law found that first-time and repeat DUI offenders who had their licenses immediately confiscated had significantly lower rates of DUI offenses, moving violations, and crashes during the next 2 years compared with DUI offenders convicted before the ALS law went into effect.

Although research shows that license suspension reduces repeat DUI offenses, there is also evidence that up to 75 percent of suspended drivers continue to drive. Evaluation of Oregon's "zebra sticker" law suggests that marking the license plates of vehicles driven by unlicensed drivers deters both driving while suspended (DWS) and DUI by suspended drivers. A similar law in Washington State was enforced differently and had no effect.

Vehicle Impoundment/Immobilization. Two studies of an Ohio law that allowed for vehicle immobilization or impoundment for multiple DUI offenders both found that offenders whose vehicles were immobilized or impounded had lower recidivism rates compared with other offenders while their vehicles were not available and after they were returned.

Other Prevention Strategies. Alcohol ignition interlocks—breath-testing devices designed to prevent operation of a vehicle if the driver's BAC is above a predetermined low level—are used in some jurisdictions as an alternative to full license suspension. Research suggests that offenders who have interlocks installed have lower recidivism rates while the device is in use, but that recidivism rates rise after interlock removal. Conversely, a few studies have reported that recidivism was significantly reduced both during interlock installation and after removal.

At victim impact panels, drinking-and-driving offenders must listen to persons who were injured or who lost a loved one in an alcohol-related crash recount the event's impact on their lives. The effects of victim impact panels on recidivism have been mixed.

Section 18.3

Lowered National Blood Alcohol Concentration Limit for Impaired Driving

Excerpted from ".08 BAC Illegal per se Level" in *Traffic Safety Facts*, Volume 2, Number 1, produced by the National Highway Traffic Safety Administration (NHTSA), March 2004. For a complete list of references, see www.nhtsa.dot.gov.

It is illegal *per se* (in itself) to drive a motor vehicle with a blood alcohol concentration (BAC) at or above a specified level in all states. The previous level in most states had been .10 BAC for drivers 21 and older, but now 45 states, the District of Columbia, and Puerto Rico have enacted laws that set a lower level of .08 BAC. In a 1992 Report to Congress, NHTSA recommended that all states lower the illegal per se level to .08 for all drivers 21 and older.

In 1998, as part of the Transportation Equity Act for the 21st Century (TEA-21), a new Federal incentive grant was created to encourage States to adopt a .08 BAC illegal per se level.

In 2000, Congress passed the DOT Appropriations Act of FY 2001, adopting .08 BAC as the national illegal limit for impaired driving.

The statute provides that states that do not adopt a conforming .08 BAC law by October 1, 2003, will be subject to a withholding 2 percent of certain highway construction funds. Each year, the withholding percentage increases by 2 percent, up to 8 percent in FY 2007 and later. Those states that adopt a conforming .08 BAC law within 4 years of any withholding will be reimbursed for those withheld funds. If a state has not adopted a conforming .08 BAC law by October 1, 2007, portions of its withheld funds shall begin to lapse and will no longer be available to the State

Key Facts about Alcohol-Related Motor Vehicle Deaths

- In 2002, 41 percent of the 42,815 motor vehicle deaths were alcohol-related. This translates to 17,419 alcohol-related motor vehicle deaths during that year, accounting for an average of one alcohol-related fatality every 30 minutes.

- The National Highway Traffic Safety Administration's (NHTSA) position on the relationship between blood alcohol concentration and driving is that driving performance degrades with every drink.

- A comprehensive NHTSA study provides what is perhaps clear evidence of the significant impairment that occurs in the driving-related skills of all drivers with .08 BAC, regardless of age, gender, or drinking history.

- .08 BAC laws are effective in reducing alcohol-related fatal crashes. At least 10 studies, covering many of the states that have enacted .08 BAC laws, have consistently shown that .08 BAC laws are associated with reductions in alcohol-related fatalities, particularly in conjunction with the administrative license revocation (ALR) laws that are present in 41 states.

- NHTSA has published several comprehensive studies on the effectiveness of .08 BAC laws. These studies found consistent and persuasive evidence that .08 BAC laws are associated with reduced incidence of alcohol-related fatal crashes. A study of the effectiveness of a .08 BAC law implemented in Illinois in 1997, found that the .08 BAC law was associated with a 13.7 percent decline in the number of drinking drivers involved in fatal crashes. The reduction included drivers at both high and low BAC levels. This is significant because critics of .08 BAC laws have often claimed that these laws do not affect the behavior of high BAC drivers. The study also found that there were no major problems reported by local law enforcement or court systems due to the change in the law. An updated analysis of Illinois's law estimated that 105 lives were saved in the first two calendar years since its implementation.

- In a comprehensive study of drivers involved in fatal crashes in all 50 states and DC from 1982–1997, it was estimated that .08 BAC laws reduced driver alcohol-related fatal crashes by 8 percent.

- A 1999 report by the U.S. General Accounting Office (GAO) reviewed the studies available at that time and found strong indications that .08 BAC laws, in combination with other drunk driving laws (particularly license revocation laws), sustained public education and information efforts, and vigorous and consistent enforcement, can save lives. The GAO report also concluded that a .08 (BAC) law can be an important component of a state's overall highway safety program.

Why .08?

The research is clear. Virtually all drivers, even those who are experienced drinkers, are significantly impaired at a .08 BAC. As early as 1988, a NHTSA review of 177 studies clearly documented this impairment. NHTSA released a later review of 112 more recent studies, providing additional evidence of impairment at .08 BAC and below. The results of the nearly 300 studies reviewed have shown that, at a .08 BAC level, virtually all drivers are impaired in the performance of critical driving tasks such as divided attention, complex reaction time, steering, lane changing, and judgment.

The risk of being in a crash gradually increases as a driver's BAC increases, but rises more rapidly once a driver reaches or exceeds .08 BAC compared to drivers with no alcohol in their bloodstream. A recent study estimated that drivers at .08 to .09 BACs are anywhere from 11 to 52 times more likely to be involved in a fatal crash than drivers at .00 BAC, depending upon their age and gender.

Lowering the per se limit is an effective countermeasure that will reduce alcohol-related traffic fatalities, especially when combined with an ALR law. There was a 12 percent reduction in alcohol-related fatalities in California in 1990 after a .08 and an ALR law went into effect. The decrease in alcohol-related fatalities occurred at both high and low BAC levels, including drivers with BAC levels of .20 or greater.

A 1996 study at Boston University showed that states adopting .08 laws experienced 16 percent and 18 percent post-law declines in the proportions of fatal crashes involving fatally injured drivers whose BAC levels were .08 or higher and .15 or higher, respectively. The Centers for Disease Control (CDC) and Prevention concluded that .08 BAC laws are associated with a median 7 percent reduction in alcohol-related traffic fatalities in states that adopt them.

The .08 BAC limit is reasonable and has the potential for saving hundreds of lives and reducing thousands of serious injuries each year, if implemented by all States. The public supports a .08 BAC level. A survey conducted in 2001 indicated that 88% of the people in States with .08 laws support the law.

.05 BAC Limit in Other Countries

The international trend continues to be to reduce illegal per se limits to .05 BAC or lower. The illegal limit is .05 BAC in numerous countries, including Australia, Belgium, Bulgaria, Denmark, Finland, France, Germany, Greece, Ireland, Israel, The Netherlands, Portugal, Russia, South Africa, Spain, and Turkey. Russia, Sweden, and Norway have a limit of .02 BAC and Poland recently went to .03 BAC. Several countries have reported studies indicating that lowering the illegal per se limit from .08 BAC to .05 BAC reduces alcohol-related fatalities (e.g., Australia, Austria, Belgium, The Netherlands, and France).

Laboratory studies from these countries indicate that impairment in critical driving functions begins at low BACs. Most subjects in these studies were significantly impaired at .05 BAC with regard to visual acuity, vigilance, drowsiness, psychomotor skills, and information processing, compared to their performance at .00 BAC.

Leading medical, crash prevention, public health and traffic safety organizations in the world support BAC limits at .05 or lower, including: the World Medical Association, the American and British Medical Associations, the European Commission, the European Transport Safety Council, the World Health Organization, and the American College of Emergency Physicians.

Section 18.4

Tips for Preventing Drunk Driving

According to the National Highway Traffic Safety Administration (NHTSA), three out of 10 Americans will be involved in an alcohol-related crash in their lifetime.

Did you know that in 2003, there were more than 17,000 preventable deaths in the United States? Did you also know that you could have helped to prevent one of those deaths?

Sadly, the number of people killed by drunk drivers has continued to increase over the past two years. Today, there is an average of one alcohol-related fatality every 32 minutes, and one alcohol-related injury every 2 minutes, resulting in an average of 310,000 alcohol-related injuries each year (NHTSA, 2002).

Alarmingly, younger drivers are especially at risk. The highest rates of intoxication in fatal crashes during 1999 were recorded for drivers 21 to 24 years old (27%), followed by drivers 25 to 34 (24%) and drivers 35 to 44 (21%).

It is never OK to drive after drinking. A person who gets behind the wheel after consuming alcohol is not only endangering the lives of himself or herself as well as any passengers, but also the lives of everyone else on the road at the time. But there is hope: Impaired driving is 100% preventable.

What can you do to help prevent more drunk driving fatalities? The answer is simple—anything you have to do. Whether you are trying to stop someone else from getting behind the wheel or making a decision yourself about whether to drink and drive, there is always an alternative.

Here are some steps you can take in preventing more impaired driving fatalities:

- Be calm, but firm. Let the impaired person know it is not OK to drive, and that you won't allow it.

- Be a designated driver.
- Take keys away from intoxicated people.
- Make arrangements to spend the night where you are.
- Arrange for taxis or safe rides if you are having a party.
- Offer non-alcoholic beverage alternatives.
- Participate in safe ride and designated driver programs (which are alternative methods of transportation that provide people who have consumed alcohol with safe rides home), either by being a sober driver or by calling one.

How can you tell if someone is too drunk to drive? Ideally, no one should drive after consuming even a small amount of alcohol. But in some cases, a person is clearly impaired and has no business getting behind the wheel.

What to look out for:

- Loss of coordination
- Use of loud or profane language
- Frequent trips to the restroom
- Slow reflexes and reaction time

Though it is often difficult and awkward to reason with someone who has been drinking, the alternative—the loss of a friend or loved one—is much worse. Don't be fooled: It could happen to you or someone you love. So get involved. Friends don't let friends drive drunk.

Section 18.5

Get the Keys: How You Can Intervene

From the National Highway Traffic Safety Administration (NHTSA), part of the U.S. Department of Transportation. This document is undated.

Here are some helpful tips and advice from focus group research on how people can get the keys away from a drunk driver:

1. If it is a close friend, try to use a soft, calm approach at first. Suggest that he or she has had too much to drink and it would be better if someone else drove or if he or he took a cab.

2. Be calm. Joke about it. Make light of it.

3. Try to make it sound like you are doing the person a favor.

4. If it is somebody you don't know well, speak to his or her friends and have them make an attempt to persuade the person to hand over the keys. Usually the person will listen.

5. If it's a good friend, spouse, or significant other, tell him or her that if he or she insists on driving, you are not going with him or her. Suggest that you will call someone else for a ride, take a cab, or walk.

6. Locate his or her keys while he or she is preoccupied and take them away. Most likely, the person will think they've lost them and will be forced to find another mode of transportation.

7. If possible, avoid embarrassing the person or being confrontational, particularly when dealing with men. This makes them appear vulnerable to alcohol and its effects.

Section 18.6

Strict Licensing Laws Associated with Less Teen Drinking and Driving

From "Strict Graduated Driver Licensing Laws Associated With Less Teen Drinking and Driving," a press release by the Substance Abuse and Mental Health Services Administration (SAMHSA), April 30, 2004.

Young drivers in states with more restrictive driver-licensing laws had lower rates of heavy drinking and driving under the influence of alcohol than those in states with less restrictive laws. That is the finding in a report that utilizes data analysis of 1999, 2000, and 2001 Substance Abuse and Mental Health Services Administration (SAMHSA) National Household Surveys.

Although nationwide, one in ten drivers aged 15 to 17 reported driving under the influence of alcohol, the drinking and driving increased as the restrictiveness of graduated drivers' license laws decreased. In the most restrictive states, 8.2 percent of 15- to 17-year-old drivers reported driving under the influence of alcohol in the past year, whereas 11.5 percent of young drivers drove under the influence of alcohol in the least restrictive states.

The report, "Graduated Driver Licensing and Drinking among Young Drivers," released by SAMHSA, showed that although six percent of young drivers nationally were heavy drinkers, young drivers in states with the most restrictive graduated licensing laws had lower rates (5.4 percent) of heavy drinking than did young drivers in states with the least restrictive licensing provisions (7.0 percent).

"This data show us an association between teens who value their driving privileges and states' actions to restrict driving privileges," SAMHSA Administrator Charles Curie said. "We need to protect our young drivers by making it clear that drinking and driving are never acceptable, and that there is no safe level of alcohol for inexperienced drivers."

The report was developed from three years of SAMHSA's National Household Survey on Drug Abuse. The survey was modified in 2002 and is now called the National Survey on Drug Use and Health. The data reflects interviews with 75,000 youth aged 12 to 17. The report is available online at www.drugabusestatistics.samhsa.gov.

Chapter 19

Approaching Alcohol Problems through Community-Based Prevention Programs

One approach for reducing alcohol and other drug problems is community-based prevention programs. These programs focus on changing the environment in which a person consumes alcohol rather than the behavior of the individual drinker. Several international and U.S. programs have assessed the effectiveness of such approaches in reducing alcohol-related problems. Some of those analyses have had inconclusive results. Others, however, found reductions in alcohol-related problems such as drunk driving, alcohol-related car crashes and their consequences, the sale of alcohol to underage drinkers, and assault injuries. Nevertheless, several aspects of community-based prevention programs require further study.

For some chronic health problems, such as cardiovascular disease (CVD), community-based prevention programs have been effective in reducing those problems. Accordingly, researchers, community organizers, and funding agencies are examining the potential of community prevention programs for reducing alcohol and other drug (AOD)-related problems. However, several important differences exist between programs aimed at reducing chronic health problems and those designed for addressing AOD problems. These differences

Excerpted from "Approaching Alcohol Problems Through Local Environmental Interventions," by Andrew J. Treno, Ph.D., and Juliet P. Lee, Ph.D., *Alcohol Research & Health*, Vol. 26, No. 1, published by the National Institute on Alcohol Abuse and Alcoholism (NIAAA), 2002. For a complete list of references, see www.niaaa.nih.gov.

concern philosophies and motivational strategies used in the programs and/or the characteristics of the target problems.

Comparing programs to reduce AOD and CVD as an example, the following four differences arise. First, interventions for high-risk medical conditions, such as changing dietary habits for CVD, operate under the assumption that people suffering from this condition have the power to control their behavior rationally. Conversely, efforts to reduce alcohol-related problems do not necessarily operate under this assumption.

Second, both greater needs and greater opportunities exist for regulating behaviors associated with alcohol-related problems than for regulating behaviors associated with CVD. For example, unlike poor dietary habits and smoking, which primarily affect the person exhibiting these behaviors (with the notable exception of secondhand smoke), alcohol consumption impacts the broader community system through traffic and other injuries. At the same time, alcohol consumption occurs within a highly regulatable distribution system of bars, restaurants, and other establishments.

Third, the consumption of alcohol often is more closely linked in time and space to the resulting alcohol-related problems (e.g., drunk driving and car crashes that occur shortly after drinking at a party) than are poor dietary habits (e.g., consumption of high-fat-content foods) and the resulting CVD, which may develop only after years of unhealthy eating. And fourth, societal norms associated with drinking differ dramatically from those associated with problematic dietary patterns. For example, because the decisions made by drinking drivers have consequences beyond the drinker him- or herself, the drinker's behaviors are perceived as legitimate targets for social control and regulation.

Thus, although much may be learned from the experiences of CVD prevention programs, the specific methods that effectively reduce chronic health problems may be somewhat less applicable to the reduction of alcohol-related problems. The circumstances that surround alcohol consumption and the generation of alcohol-related problems may present unique challenges and strategic opportunities for the development of community prevention programs. In fact, with these differences in mind, researchers, community stakeholders, and funding agencies have increasingly turned to so-called environmental approaches for reducing alcohol-related problems. This text reviews current research on the effectiveness of such approaches. After briefly describing the theoretical framework of community-based environmental approaches, it presents programs that have been implemented in the United States and in other countries and discusses future directions in the study of environmental approaches. The prevention projects included were selected using criteria that, in the absence of random assignment to treatment and control conditions, represent the following scientifically minimal conditions for determining program efficacy:

- The studies include a careful collection of baseline data during the period preceding the intervention.

- They target well-defined community-level alcohol-related problems (e.g., trauma, alcohol-related violence, and initiation of drinking).

- They have a long-term implementation and monitoring period.

- They are followed by a final evaluation of changes in target problems.

- They involve empirically documented, successful or at least promising results in the target problem that are attributable to the intervention.

Characterization of Community-Based Environmental Prevention Programs

In general, community-based environmental prevention programs as described here (subsequently referred to as environmental programs) focus not so much on changing the behavior of the individual drinker but on changing the environment in which a person consumes alcohol. The difference between environmental approaches and other approaches can best be clarified by considering the difference between "problem drinking" and "drinking-related problems." The term "problem drinking" describes the behavior of an individual, and the treatment and prevention of problem drinking address the personal costs of drinking to the individual drinker, such as jeopardizing health, work, and family life. Conversely, "drinking-related problems" refers to consequences of alcohol consumption that affect many other people besides the individual drinker, including family, colleagues, neighbors, and other members of the community. These consequences include the health, social, and economic costs of drinking to the larger community, such as alcohol-related traffic crashes, alcohol-involved violence (e.g., assaults, homicides, rapes, and domestic abuse), and school dropout rates.

On the individual level, problem drinkers disproportionately contribute to drinking problems (i.e., each problem drinker generates more drinking-related problems than each nonproblem drinker). Nevertheless, because most people who consume alcohol cannot be classified as problem drinkers, the majority of drinking-related problems arise from nonproblem drinkers. As a result, community-based environmental prevention efforts seek to address these wider-scale problems caused by nonproblem drinkers rather than those caused by problem drinkers.

Because of this broader scope, environmental approaches to the prevention of alcohol-related problems operate differently than do individual treatment and prevention approaches. For example, environmental approaches focus on the community as a system involving numerous components, including the following:

- Individual drinkers
- Vendors of alcohol, including both places where alcohol is consumed (e.g., bars and restaurants) and places where alcohol is sold (e.g., liquor stores and other shops)
- Social events where alcoholic beverages are sold and consumed
- Local laws, regulations, and enforcement agencies
- Local medical clinics and treatment facilities
- Social organizations that may support and promote public health campaigns, including schools and PTAs, churches, business organizations, and social clubs

Other, less obvious components of the community system affecting and affected by alcohol problems include the social networks and family connections through which people "learn" drinking attitudes and behaviors. These social networks may play a particularly important role with underage drinkers, who most likely obtain alcohol through friends and family networks.

Although various applications of such a comprehensive environmental approach to the reduction of alcohol problems differ in terms of specific targets and tactics, they are all characterized by several strategies that distinguish them from more traditional information-based approaches that aim to change the alcohol use practices of individuals. First, environmental approaches use the media to target policymakers, as opposed to the general public, in support of program goals. Second, environmental approaches focus on mobilizing the community to make structural and system changes rather than on persuading individuals to change their behaviors. Third, environmental approaches generally target the supply of alcohol through social and market systems as opposed to the demand for alcohol by individuals. In sum, environmentally based community prevention programs represent an important and promising approach to the reduction of alcohol problems.

Community-Based Environmental Intervention outside the United States

Several interventions conducted outside the United States have provided useful guidelines for environmental prevention efforts. Together with efforts to evaluate so-called natural experiments, such as increases in the minimum legal drinking age, these interventions provide much of the scientific support for the design of current U.S. programs.

The Community Action Project, conducted during the early 1980s in six New Zealand communities, aimed to increase public support for alcohol regulation policies as well as induce changes in attitudes and behavior. The project involved a mass media campaign conducted in two communities, an intensive intervention media campaign and a community organizer in two other communities, and no intervention in two comparison communities. The project was designed to simultaneously effect change at the individual level by supporting healthy behaviors; at the community level by increasing support for policy change; and at the policy level by reducing both advertising and alcohol availability. Project outcomes, measured in a survey of respondents' attitudes toward various alcohol control measures, included increased support for restrictions on alcohol sales in supermarkets as well as increased age limits in those communities that received the intensive intervention.

The Lahti Project, conducted in Lahti, Finland, from 1992 to 1995, aimed to prevent alcohol-related problems through community action. The project included two intervention communities and two comparison communities. The interventions consisted of several modules: public educational activities conducted through media campaigns and community organizations; brief interventions in primary health care; media activities, community organizing, and training related to responsible beverage service; youth outreach and education utilizing school, community, and family channels as well as theater and video activities; and family counseling sessions. Although the project demonstrated efficacy in mobilizing community-level efforts, it was less effective in reaching the targeted program outcomes, such as achieving changes in public knowledge and perceptions of alcohol problems and changes in drinking and drinking-related problems. Thus, the investigators found no clear differences in drinking patterns or drinking-related problems that could be attributed to the project.

The Community Mobilization for the Prevention of Alcohol-Related Injury (COMPARI) project, conducted in the Australian city of Geraldton between 1992 and 1995, was designed to reduce alcohol-related injuries by focusing not on heavy drinkers or alcoholics but on the general context of use in the community. Specific interventions included networking and support among community activists, community development, alternative options and health education, non-alcoholic youth activities, and policy interventions. However, the results of this project in terms of such outcomes as alcohol sales, assaults and traffic crashes, and hospital morbidity were inconclusive.

Despite their sometimes inconclusive results, these three international studies suggest that environmental approaches may be effective in reducing alcohol-related problems. At the same time, the ambiguous outcomes emphasize the importance of continued research in this area—for example, determining whether more intensive programs or different approaches would result in better outcomes.

Community-Based Environmental Interventions in the United States

Three major U.S. environmental prevention projects have shown significant efficacy. These include the Saving Lives Project, Communities Mobilizing for Change on Alcohol (CMCA), and the Community Trials project.

The Saving Lives Project

The Saving Lives Project, conducted in six Massachusetts communities with the rest of Massachusetts serving as a statistical control, aimed to reduce alcohol-impaired driving and related problems. The specific programs implemented in each community were designed locally and involved such activities as media campaigns, business information programs, speeding and drunk-driving awareness days, speed-watch telephone hotlines, police training, high school peer-led education, Students Against Drunk Driving chapters, and college prevention programs. Over the 5 years of the program, the Saving Lives communities experienced a 33-percent decline in year period. Furthermore, this decline was 42 percent greater than that observed in the rest of Massachusetts. Additionally there was a 47-percent reduction in the number of fatally injured drivers who tested positive for alcohol and a 39-percent decline in fatal crash injuries among 16- to 25-year olds relative to the rest of Massachusetts. Finally, self-reported driving after drinking declined in the experimental communities, particularly among youth.

The CMCA Project

This project, which included 15 communities in Minnesota and western Wisconsin, aimed to reduce access to alcohol among underage youth. The randomized trial was conducted in seven intervention communities, with eight communities serving as controls. The five core components of the project addressed the following issues: (1) community policies, (2) community practices, (3) youth alcohol access, (4) youth alcohol consumption, and (5) youth alcohol problems. Local organizers assisted community members in selecting interventions from an array of programs that affected youth access to alcohol. These measures included underage decoy operations with alcohol outlets, citizen monitoring of outlets selling to youth, keg registration, alcohol-free events for youth, policy action to shorten hours of sale for alcohol, responsible beverage service training programs, and educational programs for youth and adults. The experimental sites were free to modify and shape these intervention activities to address local conditions.

Analyses of the results of the project showed that merchants increased checks for age identification, reduced sales to minors, and reported more care in controlling sales to youth in the experimental communities. Attempts by underage youth to purchase alcohol as well as levels of alcohol use and the propensity to provide alcohol to other teens were reduced among the youth. Furthermore, the results demonstrated a decline in drinking-and-driving arrests among 18- to 20-year-olds and disorderly conduct violations among 15- to 17-year-olds.

The Community Trials Project

The Community Trials Project was a five-component community-level intervention conducted in three experimental communities that were matched with three comparison sites. The goal of the project, broadly defined, was to reduce alcohol-related harm among all residents of the three experimental communities. The project implemented the following five intervention components:

- A media and mobilization component to develop community organization and support for the goals and strategies of the project and to increase local news to raise public support for the goals and strategies of the project
- A responsible beverage service component to reduce service to intoxicated patrons at bars and restaurants
- A sales to youth component to reduce underage access to alcohol
- A drinking and driving component to increase local driving-while-intoxicated enforcement activity
- An access component to reduce the availability of alcohol

Postintervention analysis demonstrated several important improvements in the experimental communities versus the comparison communities. For example, nighttime crashes resulting in injuries were 10 percent lower and crashes in which the driver was found by police to have been drinking were 6 percent lower in the experimental communities than in the comparison communities. Moreover, assault injuries observed in emergency departments declined by 43 percent, and assault injuries requiring hospitalization declined by 2 percent in the intervention communities versus the comparison communities. In addition, as indicated in a random-digit dialed telephone survey of community residents, self-reports of driving after having had "too much to drink" declined by 49 percent and self-reports of driving when "over the legal limit" declined by 51 percent in the experimental communities compared with the comparison communities. And although the drinking population increased slightly in the experimental communities over the course of the study, problematic alcohol use was significantly reduced in those communities. Finally, cost-benefit analyses estimated that the trial resulted in savings of $2.88 for every $1 spent on program implementation based upon reductions in automobile crashes alone. And this estimate is rather conservative because it does not take into consideration savings resulting from the prevention of other injuries, savings accruing over time after completion of the project as a result of the continuation of the intervention measures, or incalculable savings in terms of human suffering.

Future Directions in Environmental Approaches

Although the studies reviewed above support the efficacy of community-based environmental prevention approaches, further research is needed to determine which aspects of this approach are the most promising or effective. Four key areas of such research are described below.

First, the relative efficacy of different preventive interventions must be assessed so that communities with limited resources can choose between alternative intervention strategies and select the most effective programs for their specific needs. To date, however, the efficacy of individual strategies must be inferred primarily from the programs' effects on intermediary variables (e.g., reductions in alcohol access to youth or alcohol service to intoxicated patrons) because any distal effects (e.g. reductions in alcohol-related crashes or injuries) reflect the contribution of all interventions working in concert. For example, the combination of increased enforcement of laws against drinking and driving and increased coverage of that enforcement has been linked to increases in perceived risk of arrest for drinking and driving (i.e., the intermediary variable). This increased perception of risk has, in turn, been linked to decreases in drinking and driving and subsequent automobile crashes (i.e., the distal effect, which is also affected by other measures).

Similarly, merchant training, enforcement, and media advocacy, when used in combination, can be effective in reducing underage purchases of alcohol; training and enforcement would appear to be promising in terms of reducing service to intoxicated patrons; and decreases in alcohol outlet densities have been linked to decreases in automobile crashes. All of these measures ultimately affect a distal variable, or major outcome of interest, such as alcohol-involved car crashes and the resulting injuries and deaths. These various pieces of information provide little conclusive information, however, on the individual contributions of these various interventions to changes in the outcome of interest.

Second, little information exists regarding the effectiveness of environmental programs from a cost-benefit perspective. For example, investigators still must determine the return on funds spent on such programs in terms of costs saved for treatment of alcohol-related injuries or lives saved. Communities facing the allocation of scarce resources will be very interested in the answers to such questions.

Third, the appropriate geographic focus of specific interventions remains unclear. Thus, future analyses must clarify whether interventions are best implemented at the community level or more locally, at the neighborhood level. One can argue that certain problems (e.g., drunk driving) are of a community-wide nature whereas others (e.g., drinking in public

157

parks) are of a more local nature. The questions of who "owns" such problems or who is best equipped to address them are far from resolved.

Fourth, more research must be directed toward establishing the efficacy of local prevention programs in racial/ethnic minority neighborhoods, which typically experience different alcohol problems from those of non-minority communities. Toward this end, the National Institute on Alcohol Abuse and Alcoholism is currently sponsoring a project conducted by the Prevention Research Center, based in Berkeley, California, in two largely Hispanic, low-income neighborhoods in northern California to reduce underage alcohol access, youth drinking, and related problems. This action project, to be conducted over a 5-year period, will include the following components:

- A community awareness component disseminating information about youth and young adult alcohol access and use

- A responsible beverage service program focusing on service to minors and intoxicated patrons at on- and off-sale establishments

- An underage access component providing support for increased police enforcement of underage sales laws and laws regarding provision of alcohol to minors by social hosts

- An enforcement component focusing on laws regulating sales to intoxicated people both in establishments and at special events where alcohol is served

- A community mobilization effort providing neighborhood support for the other components.

This project, though similar to the Community Trials project in terms of its environmental approach, differs from that project in three important regards. First, project interventions are to be implemented at the neighborhood level as opposed to the community level. Second, project interventions have been tailored to address the unique drinking problems and patterns characteristic of neighborhoods with large proportions of low-income ethnic minorities, such as high density of alcohol outlets and associated high levels of youth violence and intensive alcohol advertising targeting ethnic minorities. Third, the focus of project interventions is on youth and young adults (ages 15 to 29), who disproportionately experience alcohol-related problems in these neighborhoods. With this approach, this project will address many of the areas noted above as requiring further exploration and should thereby help to establish the efficacy of community-based environmental interventions in preventing alcohol-related problems in a variety of settings.

Part Three

The Physical
Effects of Alcohol

Chapter 20

How Alcohol Affects the Body

By Gail Gleason Milgram, Ed.D., a professor and director of the Education and Training Division at the Rutgers University Center of Alcohol Studies

Ethyl alcohol, or ethanol, is a clear, thin, odorless liquid that boils at 173 degrees Fahrenheit (78 degrees Celsius). It can burn, it can be mixed with water in any proportion, and it is one of the few alcohols that is made for consumption; however, it never exists full strength in any alcoholic beverage. Ethyl alcohol is the subject of this chapter, and from now on will be referred to simply as alcohol.

Alcohol is produced during a natural process called fermentation, which occurs when yeast, a microscopic plant that floats freely in the air, reacts with the sugar in fruit or vegetable juice, creating alcohol and releasing carbon dioxide. The process stops naturally when about 11% to 14% of the juice is alcohol; the product of this fermentation is wine. A similar process is used to make beer.

Distillation is the process used to make beverages with a higher alcohol content. In this process the fermented liquid is heated until it vaporizes, and then the vapor is cooled until it condenses into a liquid again. Distilled alcoholic beverages (e.g., whiskey, gin, vodka, and rum) contain 40% to 50% alcohol. They are sometimes referred to as spirits or hard liquor.

"Online Facts: The Effects of Alcohol" is reproduced by permission from the Rutgers University Center of Alcohol Studies.

When someone drinks an alcoholic beverage it flows into the stomach. While it is in the stomach, the drinker does not feel the effects of the alcohol, but alcohol does not remain in the stomach very long. Some of it is absorbed through the stomach walls into the bloodstream, but most alcohol passes into the small intestine and then into the bloodstream, and this circulates throughout the body. Once alcohol is in the bloodstream it reaches the brain and the drinker begins to feel its effects. The reason that a large person does not feel the effects of a drink as quickly as a small person is because the large person has more blood and other body fluids and will not have as high a level of alcohol in the blood after drinking the same amount of alcohol.

The body disposes of alcohol in two ways: elimination and oxidation. Only about 10% of the alcohol in the body leaves by elimination from the lungs and kidneys. About 90% of the alcohol leaves by oxidation. The liver plays a major role in the body's oxidation of alcohol. When alcohol enters the liver, some of it is changed to a chemical called acetaldehyde. When acetaldehyde is combined with oxygen, acetic acid is formed. When the acetic acid is further combined with oxygen, carbon dioxide and water are formed.

The oxidation of alcohol produces calories. One ounce of pure alcohol contains about 163 calories (or about 105 calories in a 1.5-ounce glass of whiskey or gin), but it does not contain vitamins or other physically beneficial nutrients. The liver can oxidize only a certain amount of alcohol each minute; the oxidation rate of alcohol in a person weighing 150 pounds, for example, is about 7 grams of alcohol per hour. This is equivalent to about .75 of an ounce of distilled spirits, 2.5 ounces of wine, or 7.75 to 8 ounces of beer per hour. If a person drank no more than .75 of an ounce of whiskey or half a bottle of beer every hour, the alcohol would never accumulate in the body, the person would feel little of the effects of the alcohol, and would not become intoxicated.

Oxidation continues until all the alcohol has left the body. Since the body can remove only a small amount of alcohol at a time, those who choose to drink are advised to drink slowly. The effects of alcohol on an individual depend on a variety of factors. These include:

- **How one feels before drinking:** If a person is upset and tense, very excited, sad, nervous, or even extremely happy, he or she may tend to gulp drinks and actually consume more alcohol than planned.

- **What the drinker expects alcohol to do:** Some people expect a drink to help them feel relaxed, happy, angry or sad. Quite naturally, these feelings can be produced by the drink; how you want to feel helps you feel that way.

- **How much one drinks:** A person who has one drink during dinner is not likely to feel the effects of alcohol. But having six drinks before and during dinner means the individual might not make it through dessert.

- **How long one takes to drink:** This is a critical factor. Four drinks in one hour will have an obvious effect on the drinker, but the same four drinks over a four-hour period will probably have a very slight, if any, effect.

- **Type of alcoholic beverage:** Some beverages have more alcohol in them than others. Beer has about 4.5% alcohol, "table wines" average from 11% to 14%, "fortified" or "dessert wines" (such as sherry or port) have 16% to 20%, and distilled spirits range from 40% to 50%. However, in normal size, each drink (i.e., 12 ounces of beer, 5 ounces of wine, and 1.5 ounces of distilled spirits) contains approximately the same amount of alcohol.

- **Size of the drinker:** Because of the way alcohol circulates in the body, the size of the drinker also relates to the effects of alcohol. A person weighing 220 pounds will not feel the effects of a drink as much as a person weighing 120 pounds.

- **Food in the stomach:** The alcohol consumed does not affect the drinker until it has been absorbed into the bloodstream. Food in the stomach slows the alcohol's absorption, so that a person who has a drink after eating a meal will feel less effect than a person who has a drink on an empty stomach.

- **Experience in using alcoholic beverages:** Someone drinking a glass of wine may experience lightheadedness the first time, but will probably not experience that effect on subsequent occasions. However, most individuals who drink know what to expect from various amounts of alcohol because of their prior experience with drinking.

Alcohol acts directly on the brain and affects its ability to work. The effects of alcohol on the brain are quite complex, but alcohol is usually classified as a depressant. Judgment is the first function of the brain to be affected; the ability to think and make decisions becomes impaired. As more alcohol is consumed, the motor functions of the body are affected.

The effects of alcohol are directly related to the concentration (percentage) of alcohol in the blood; however, the effects vary among individuals and even in the same individual at different times. In the following description, the blood alcohol concentrations (BAC) are those that would probably be found in a person weighing about 150 pounds:

- At a BAC of 0.03% (after about one cocktail, one glass of wine, or one bottle of beer), the drinker will feel relaxed and experience a slight feeling of exhilaration.

- At 0.06% (after two cocktails, two glasses of wine, or two bottles of beer), the drinker will experience a feeling of warmth and relaxation; there will be a decrease of fine motor skills and he or she will be less concerned with minor irritations.

- At 0.09% (after three cocktails, three glasses of wine, or three bottles of beer), reaction time will be slowed, muscle control will be poor, speech will be slurred and the legs will feel wobbly.

- At 0.12% (after four cocktails, four glasses of wine, or four bottles of beer), his or her judgment will be clouded, inhibitions and self-restraint lessened, and the ability to reason and make logical decisions will be impaired.

- At 0.15% (after five cocktails, five glasses of wine, or five bottles of beer), vision will be blurred, speech unclear, walking will be unsteady, and coordination impaired.

- At 0.18% (after six cocktails, six glasses of wine, or six bottles of beer), all of the drinker's behavior will be impaired, and he or she will find it difficult to stay awake.

- At a BAC of about 0.30% alcohol in the blood (after 10 to 12 drinks), the drinker will be in a semi-stupor or deep sleep. Most people are not able to stay awake to reach a BAC higher than 0.30%.

- If the BAC reaches 0.50% the drinker is in a deep coma and in danger of death. As the alcohol level reaches 1% in the blood, the breathing center in the brain becomes paralyzed and death occurs.

In many states a BAC of 0.10% is considered legal evidence that a driver is intoxicated; some states use a BAC of 0.08%. In some European countries the legal BAC is as low as 0.05%.

Suggestions for Further Reading

Johnston, L.D., O'Malley, P.M., & Bachman, J.G. (2003). *Monitoring the future: national survey results on drug use, 1975-2002. Volume I: Secondary school students. Volume II: College students & adults.* (NIH Publication Nos. 03-5375; 03-5376). Bethesda, MD: National Institute on Drug Abuse.

Kinney, J. (2003). *Loosening the grip: a handbook of alcohol information.* (7th ed.) Boston: McGraw-Hill.

Milgram, G. G. (1990). *The facts about drinking: Coping with alcohol use, abuse, and alcoholics.* Mt. Vernon, NY: Consumers Union.

National Institute on Alcohol Abuse and Alcoholism. (2000). *Tenth special report to the U.S. Congress on alcohol and health from the Secretary of Health and Human Services.* (NIH Publication No. 00-1583). Bethesda, MD: National Institutes of Health.

Chapter 21

Hangovers

Definition

Hangover is the collection of physical and mental symptoms that occur after a person drinks excessive amounts of alcohol.

Description

Hangovers have probably been experienced since prehistoric time when alcohol was first discovered. A survey found that about 75% of the persons who drank enough to be intoxicated (drunk) sometimes experienced hangover. Although very prevalent, hangovers have not been extensively studied. It is known that ethanol is the primary chemical component of alcohol to produce the effects associated with drinking.

Whether hangover affects complex mental tasks and the performance of simple tasks is unclear. Studies on these areas have yielded conflicting results, presumably due to differences in methods. Clearly, alcohol consumption can affect sleep, and sleep deprivation is known to affect performance.

Causes and Symptoms

The cause of hangover is believed to be multifactorial. Hangover is likely caused by a combination of direct effects of ethanol, effects of ethanol removal, effects of ethanol breakdown products, effects of other components of the alcoholic beverage, personal characteristics, and behaviors associated with alcohol use.

Direct Effects of Ethanol

Ethanol can directly affect the body by causing dehydration (loss of fluids), electrolyte (body chemicals), imbalance, stomach and intestinal irritation, low blood sugar, and sleep disruption. In addition, alcohol directly affects the circadian rhythm (internal 24-hour clock) causing a feeling similar to jet lag. Ethanol causes vasodilation (enlarged blood vessels) and affects body chemicals, like serotonin and histamine, which may contribute to the headache associated with hangover.

Effects of Ethanol Removal

Because hangover symptoms peak at around the same time that the blood alcohol concentration falls to zero, some researchers propose that hangover is actually a mild form of withdrawal. Excessive drinking causes changes in the chemical messenger system of the brain and, when the alcohol is removed, the system becomes unbalanced. Many of the symptoms of hangover are similar to those associated with mild withdrawal. Some differences exist, however, between hangover and withdrawal; specifically, hangover symptoms do not include the hallucinations, seizures, and the lengthy impairment of withdrawal.

Effects of Ethanol Breakdown Products

In the body, ethanol is first broken down to acetaldehyde and then to acetate. Acetaldehyde is a reactive chemical that, at high concentration, can cause sweating, rapid pulse, skin flushing, nausea, and vomiting. Some researchers believe that acetaldehyde causes hangover. Although there is no acetaldehyde in the blood when the blood alcohol concentration reaches zero, the toxic effects of acetaldehyde on the body may still persist.

Other Factors

Most alcoholic beverages contain small amounts of other active compounds besides ethanol. These compounds add to the smell, taste, and appearance of the beverage. Gin or vodka, which contain almost pure ethanol, produce fewer hangover symptoms than alcoholic beverages that contain other alcohol compounds (such as red wine, brandy, or whiskey). For example, methanol is implicated in contributing to hangover. Red wine, whiskey, and brandy all contain high levels of methanol.

Some inherent personal traits place persons at risk of experiencing hangover. In some persons, high levels of acetaldehyde accumulate (because of a deficient enzyme) which causes them to experience more severe hangovers. Persons who are neurotic, angry, or defensive, feel guilty about drinking, experience negative life events, or have a family history of alcoholism have increased hangover symptoms.

Certain behaviors associated with drinking increase the chance of experiencing hangover. These include drug use, disruption of normal sleep patterns, restricted food intake, and cigarette use.

Hangover symptoms begin within several hours after a person has stopped drinking and may last up to 24 hours. The specific symptoms experienced may vary depending upon the individual, the occasion, and the type and amount of alcohol consumed. The physical symptoms of hangover include headache, fatigue, light and sound sensitivity, muscle aches, eye redness, thirst, nausea, vomiting, and stomach pain. Hangover can cause rapid heartbeat, tremor, increased blood pressure, and sweating. Mental symptoms associated with hangover are decreased sleep, changes in sleep stages, decreased attention, decreased concentration, depression, dizziness, anxiety, irritability, and a sense that the room is spinning (vertigo).

Treatment

Eating balanced meals, drinking extra water, and limiting total alcohol help to reduce or avoid hangover. There are also many alternative treatments to prevent or reduce hangover symptoms. Drinking additional alcohol to relieve hangover, although it reduces short-term symptoms, is not recommended. Some experts believe that drinking alcohol to relieve hangover is a sign of impending alcoholism. The primary measure to fight hangover is to drink plenty of water while drinking alcoholic beverages, before going to bed, and the day after. Sweating from exertion, exercise, sauna, or massage may also help.

Food Therapy

Hangover symptoms may be reduced by taking in lots of extra water and fluids and by eating foods that are high in vitamin C and the B vitamins, which are believed to speed the removal of alcohol from the body. Oranges, guava, grapefruit, and strawberries are rich in vitamin C and beans, fish, and whole grains are rich in the B vitamins. A cocktail prepared from orange juice (1 cup), pineapple juice (1 cup), kiwifruit (one), vitamin-B enriched nutritional yeast (1 tablespoon), and honey (1 tablespoon) provides important nutrients which the body needs to recover from hangover. Juice therapists recommend drinking a mixture of carrot juice (8 oz), beet juice (1 oz), celery juice (4 oz), and parsley juice (1 oz) twice during hangover. The Chinese drink fresh tangerine juice and eat 10 strawberries to treat hangover.

Eating bland complex carbohydrates, such as crackers or toast, is easy on the stomach and helps to raise blood sugar levels. Drinking tea or coffee can relieve fatigue and possible the headache. Throughout the world, traditional food remedies for hangover have certain things in common. These include eggs, tripe, hot spices, hearty soups, and fruit and vegetable juices. These foods all serve to replenish vitamins, minerals, and other nutrients lost by the body as it detoxifies alcohol.

Ayurveda

Ayurvedic practitioners believe that hangover reflects the symptoms of excess pitta. Immediate relief may be found after drinking water containing lime juice (1 teaspoon), sugar (one half teaspoon), salt (pinch), and baking soda (one half teaspoon). Orange juice containing cumin (pinch) and lime juice (1 teaspoon) helps hangover. Drinking cool lassi, water containing yogurt (1 tablespoon), and cumin powder (pinch) three or four times daily may relieve nausea, headache, and drowsiness.

Herbals

The following herbal remedies are useful in treating hangover symptoms:

- An Ayurvedic remedy is to take one half teaspoon of a mixture of *shatavari* (5 parts), *shanka bhasma* (one eighth part), *kama dudha* (one eighth part), and *jata-mamsi* (3 parts) with water two to three times daily.

- An Ayurvedic antidote for alcohol toxicity is one half teaspoon of *tikta* (or myrrh, aloe vera, or *sudharshan*) with warm water three times during the day.

- Barberry (*Barberis vulgaris*) tea reduces hangover symptoms.

- Dandelion (*Taraxacum officinale*) and burdock (*Arctium lappa*) tea (with gentian extract, powdered ginger, and honey) can ease the nausea.

- Evening primrose (*Oenothera biennis*) oil helps to replenish lost gamma-linoleic acid.

- Milk thistle (*Silybum marinum*) reduces alcohol toxicity on the liver.

- Nux vomica (*Strychnos nux vomica*) is a homeopathic antidote for alcohol overconsumption.

- Elutherian ginseng (*Eleutherococcus senticosus*) helps the body adjust to the stress of alcohol toxicity.

- Wintergreen (*Gaultheria procumbens*) tea with hot pepper (*Capsicum*) sauce relieves the headache.

Other Hangover Remedies

Various other remedies for hangover include:

- **Acupressure.** Point LI 4 (between the thumb and index finger) relieves headache and stomach ailments and the B2 points (upper edge of the eye socket) relieve headache accompanied by light sensitivity.

- **Aromatherapy.** The nausea of hangover may be relieved by drinking an aromatic cocktail of water, lemon juice, and a drop of fennel essential oil before breakfast.

- **Imagery.** The hangover sufferer may visualize being on a ship in a stormy ocean. The ocean gradually becomes calm until the ship is gently bobbing in the water.

- **Probiotics.** The bacteria *Bifidobacterium bifidus* is able to remove alcohol breakdown products. To fight hangover, naturopaths recommend taking *B. bifidus* before going to bed and again the following day.

- **Supplements.** Taking 50 mg of vitamin B3 before going to bed may relieve hangover.

- **Hydrotherapy.** Drinking a glass of water containing activated charcoal powder before going to bed may absorb alcohol in the stomach and reduce hangover symptoms.

Allopathic Treatment

Hangover symptoms may be relieved by taking antacids for nausea and stomach pain and aspirin or a nonsteroidal anti-inflammatory drugs (ibuprofen or naproxen) for headache and muscle pains. Acetaminophen (Tylenol) should be avoided while drinking or during hangover because alcohol enhances acetaminophen's toxic effects on the liver. Caffeine, usually taken as coffee, is historically used to treat hangover, although this has not been studied.

Expected Results

There is no cure for hangover. Left untreated, hangover will resolve within several hours. Treatments may reduce the severity of certain symptoms.

Prevention

Hangover may be prevented by limiting the intake of alcohol, or drinking alcoholic beverages with a lesser incidence of causing hangover such as gin, vodka, or pure ethanol.

Chapter 22

Alcohol Overdose

Alcohol Has Changed

Alcohol is a clear, relatively odorless chemical made up of three common molecules: carbon, hydrogen, and oxygen. Alcohol is also a psychoactive drug that changes brain chemistry and is lethal in high doses. Despite general knowledge about alcohol intoxication, drinking and driving, and some of the long term medical consequences of alcohol abuse, few people realize that deaths from alcohol overdoses occur about as often as for other drugs.

When airborne yeast combines with water and sugar from any number of sources, such as potato, grains, or fruits, a process called fermentation occurs and ethyl alcohol is made. Tens of thousands of years ago when the first thirsty person accidentally stumbled onto some puddle of naturally fermented water, the effect must have been quite a shock. Most likely, that first encounter was probably not fatal because of the low alcohol content produced by natural fermentation, the small quantity of beverage available or both.

Today, first-time and even experienced alcohol users may not be as lucky because alcohol is readily available in large volumes, high concentrations, or both. Does everyone who drinks alcohol die from a toxic overdose? Of course not, but let's take a look at why alcohol poisoning kills people every year, the signs and symptoms of alcohol poisoning, and what you can do if confronted by this problem.

How Does Alcohol Kill?

Alcohol can cause death directly by acting on those brain areas that control consciousness, respiration, and heart rate. As a central nervous system depressant, alcohol can "turn off" these vital brain areas, resulting first in coma and then death.

In many cases, drinking too much alcohol will make you sick and you will stop drinking. Contrary to folk tales, getting sick is not from mixing drinks or drinking on an empty stomach, it is because specialized poison control cells in your brain detect danger—too much alcohol—and send a signal to your stomach to vomit. This is the brain's way of dealing with poisoning. Vomiting is an attempt to eliminate any unabsorbed alcohol. The logic is, if you can prevent any alcohol that's still in the stomach from getting into the blood supply, it may save your life. Eating before you drink will slow down the speed of intoxication but it is no guarantee that you won't get sick or die if you consume enough alcohol.

Whereas some people only vomit when they have consumed too much alcohol, other people just fall asleep (with or without vomiting) after they have consumed too much alcohol. In these people, death can follow in one of two ways: you may fall into a deep sleep and vomit while sleeping. What's the result? You choke on your own vomit because you are too intoxicated to wake up and clear out your airway. In other instances, you simply fall asleep and never wake up, because the concentration of alcohol is so high that the areas of your brain controlling life functions are so depressed they stop functioning, and so do you.

How Much Alcohol Is "Lethal"?

The "lethal dose" (LD) of alcohol is clinically defined as the amount that would kill half the population (the LD50). Most authorities place the LD50 at about .40% or about five times the current legal limit in most states. However, there are many cases in which death occurred from alcohol poisoning at much lower, and in some cases, much higher levels. For a 100 lb. man or woman drinking very quickly, it would only require about 8-10 drinks in an hour to reach the lethal level.

Can You Tell If You're Too Intoxicated?

Generally, you can't tell. First of all, alcohol impairs judgment, making your ability to reason difficult, especially at high doses. Second, it takes a while for all the alcohol in the stomach to travel out of the gastrointestinal system and into the blood supply, where it then reaches the brain and other organs. Depending upon how much you drink, how quickly you drink, and what else is in your stomach, it may take anywhere from about 30-90 minutes after you stop drinking, before you reach your highest level of intoxication. Although some drinking scenarios may require less or more time to reach the maximum level of intoxication, you can see that when you decide you have consumed enough alcohol and stop drinking, you will most probably continue to become even more intoxicated. Sweetly flavored alcoholic concoctions such as Jell-O shots, flavored brandies, schnapps, or other drinks can go down easily and quickly but surprise you later on when they get into your brain. Similarly, drinking "games" can be quickly fatal because large quantities of alcohol are often consumed over very short periods of time. Almost-straight alcohol drinks, such as EverClear, are especially dangerous and should not be used at all.

Symptoms of Alcohol Poisoning

If you have any of the following symptoms, you are experiencing an overdose reaction:

- Vomiting
- Passed out
- Difficult to awaken
- Slow, shallow breathing

What You Should Do

Don't let a person who has been drinking heavily "sleep it off." If they persist in falling asleep, wake them up. If they don't respond, it's time to call the police emergency number (911) and tell them you need an ambulance for a possible alcohol overdose. Do not assume your friend will simply sleep it off. When in doubt, call for help. Don't take a chance with your friend's life. If you know or suspect that other drugs may have been taken, be sure to notify at least one or more ambulance personnel. Alcohol in combination with other drugs accounts for about 30% of all drug overdose deaths.

Remember, the word is in**toxic**ation.

Dr. John Brick, PhD, MA, FAPA, Executive Director of Intoxikon International, is a biological psychologist in Yardley, Pennsylvania.

Intoxikon International

Alcohol and Drug Studies: Research and Educational Consulting
1006 Floral Vale
Yardley, PA 19067
www.Intoxikon.com

Chapter 23

Alcohol and Nutrition

Chapter Contents

Section 23.1—The Role of Alcohol in the Diet 178

Section 23.2—Diet Quality Linked to Alcohol
Drinking Patterns 180

Section 23.1

The Role of Alcohol in the Diet

© 2006 A.D.A.M., Inc. Reprinted with permission.

Definition

Alcohol comes from fermenting starches and sugars. When consumed, alcohol depresses your nervous system and acts as a mild anesthetic and tranquilizer. It is toxic in large quantities.

Function

Alcohol has about 7 calories per gram. These are considered empty calories because alcohol contains no beneficial nutrients, such as vitamins and minerals.

A 12-ounce beer contains about 150 calories. Carbonated beverages or fruit juices contribute additional calories when mixed with alcohol in a cocktail.

Beers, wines, and liquors all contain different amounts of alcohol. In general, a 12-ounce beer, a 5-ounce glass of wine, and 1.5-ounce shot of liquor have about the same amount of alcohol.

Beer is between 3% to 8% alcohol. "Light" or lower-calorie beers are closer to 3% alcohol. Liqueurs, such as sherry and dessert liqueurs, contain 40% to 50% alcohol and tend to be higher in calories. White wines average 12%, and red wines are around 14%.

The proof is the alcohol content of distilled liquors. It is the percentage of alcohol multiplied by two. For example:

- 50% alcohol = 100-proof alcohol
- 100% alcohol = 200-proof alcohol

Side Effects

Alcohol is an addictive substance.

Alcohol is a leading cause of traffic accidents in the United States because it slows reaction time and impairs your judgment.

The liver detoxifies (or metabolizes) alcohol. Continued, excessive use of alcohol can damage the liver. You can develop alcoholic hepatitis and then a fatty liver. A fatty liver can progress to cirrhosis of the liver, a potentially fatal condition.

Alcohol is a risk factor for development of cancer of the esophagus, throat, larynx, mouth, and breast.

The presence of alcohol impairs the absorption of essential nutrients because it can damage the lining of the small intestine and the stomach where most nutrients are digested. Alcohol also requires some vitamins in its metabolism, and it interferes with the absorption and storage of some specific vitamins.

Alcohol can impair sexual function, even though it may increase your interest in sexual activity.

Alcohol intake during pregnancy has been identified as the cause of fetal alcohol syndrome.

Recommendations

If you drink it is best to do so **only** in moderation. This means no more than one beer, one glass of wine, or one shot of liquor per day if you are a woman and no more than two if you are a man. Drinking more than that can substantially harm your health. Long-term or excessive use of alcohol may lead to alcoholism. And "problem drinking" (such as drinking and driving) is very risky and can endanger you and others.

Harmful Effects during Pregnancy

For the safety of your baby, **never drink alcohol during pregnancy**. Alcohol in the bloodstream of the mother crosses the placenta and reaches the fetus. This can cause a condition called fetal alcohol syndrome—growth failure after birth, reduced IQ, and malformed facial features.

Responsible Drinking

Here are some ways to drink responsibly, assuming that you **do not** have a drinking problem:

- Only drink if you are of legal age to do so.

- Never drink alcohol and drive a car. Have someone designated to drive if you're going to drink, or plan an alternative way home, such as a taxi or bus.

- Do not drink on an empty stomach. Snack before and during alcohol consumption.

- Drink slowly to avoid becoming intoxicated and only in moderation.

- If you are take medication, including over-the-counter medications, check with your pharmacist before drinking alcohol. Alcohol can intensify the effects of many medications and drugs and can interact with others, making them ineffective.

- Do not drink at all if you have a history of alcohol abuse.

Section 23.2

Diet Quality Linked to Alcohol Drinking Patterns

From "Study Links Diet Quality with Alcohol Drinking Patterns," a press release by the National Institutes of Health and the National Institute on Alcohol Abuse and Alcoholism (NIAAA), February 13, 2006.

Unhealthy alcohol drinking patterns may go hand in hand with unhealthy eating habits, according to a new study by researchers at the National Institute on Alcohol Abuse and Alcoholism (NIAAA), part of the National Institutes of Health (NIH), and the U.S. Department of Agriculture (USDA). Examining diet quality of individuals who drink any kind of alcoholic beverage, researchers found that people who drink the largest quantities of alcohol—even infrequently—have the poorest quality diets. Conversely, people who drink the least amount of alcohol—regardless of drinking frequency—have the best quality diets. A report of the findings appears in the February 15, 2006 issue of the *American Journal of Epidemiology*.

"This is a very useful finding that refines our understanding of the relationship between patterns of alcohol consumption and other aspects of health behavior," said NIAAA Director Ting-Kai Li, M.D.

Previous studies have shown that moderate alcohol consumption is associated with a reduced risk for cardiovascular disease and death, notes first author Rosalind A. Breslow, Ph.D., an epidemiologist in NIAAA's Division of Epidemiology and Prevention Research. However, diet could be partly responsible for these findings, since a healthy diet has been associated with the same outcome.

"Clarifying the relationship between alcohol consumption and diet quality is an important step in determining the extent to which diet influences studies of alcohol and cardiovascular outcomes," explains Dr. Breslow. To that end, the purpose of our study was to determine the association between drinking patterns and diet quality in the U.S. population. It's important to note that determining the cause or causes of any such association was not part of our current study."

Dr. Breslow and her colleagues analyzed data collected from more than 3,000 participants in the National Health and Nutrition Examination Survey (NHANES), an ongoing survey of representative cross-sectional samples of the U.S. population conducted by the U.S. Department of Health and Human Services' Centers for Disease Control and Prevention. Data included alcohol consumption information as well as Healthy Eating Index (HEI) scores, a widely used measure of total diet quality. Created by the USDA [U.S. Department of Agriculture], the HEI measures how closely an individual's diet conforms to USDA recommendations regarding vegetables, fruit, grains, meat, and milk as well as total fat, cholesterol, and sodium consumption.

Total alcohol—the sum of individuals' wine, beer, and liquor consumption—was characterized by three variables: the amount consumed on drinking days (quantity); how often consumption occurs (frequency); and average daily volume (quantity multiplied by frequency). As alcohol quantity increased, HEI scores declined. As alcohol frequency increased, HEI scores improved. Diet quality was poorest among the highest quantity, least frequent drinkers and best among the lowest quantity, more frequent drinkers. The researchers also found that HEI scores were not significantly different between those who drank the highest average daily volume compared with those who drank the lowest average daily volume. They therefore suggest that alcohol drinking patterns—as measured by quantity and frequency—rather than average daily consumption, should be considered in future studies of the relationship between alcohol consumption and health outcomes.

"In our study, healthier diets were associated with healthier drinking patterns," says Dr. Breslow. "In that regard, I think it's important that women have not more than 1 drink per day and that men have not more than 2 drinks per day—the alcohol consumption recommendations set forth in the sixth edition of Dietary Guidelines for Americans, the federal government's science-based advice to promote health and reduce risk of chronic diseases through nutrition and physical activity."

Chapter 24

What Are the Myths and Facts about Alcohol and the Liver?

- Many victims of liver disease are not alcoholics.

- Even moderate social drinkers may risk liver damage.

- People who never drink alcoholic beverages may still get serious liver problems.

Answer: All statements are true. How many did you get right? If you were surprised by the answers, don't be discouraged. You are not alone. Most people are confused about the relationship between alcohol and the liver. Because myths can be harmful, here are straight answers to some of the most common questions about alcohol and the liver.

Does alcohol cause liver disease?

Yes, but it is only one of the many causes, and the risk depends on how much you drink and over how long a period. There are more than 100 liver diseases. Known causes include viruses, hereditary defects, and reactions to drugs and chemicals. Scientists are still investigating the causes for the most serious liver diseases.

How much alcohol can I safely drink?

Because some people are much more sensitive to alcohol than others, there is no single right answer that will fit everyone. Based on current dietary guidelines, moderate drinking for women is defined as an average of 1 drink or less per day. Moderate drinking for men is defined as an average of 2 drinks or less per day (United States Department of Agriculture, 2000). A standard drink is one 12-ounce beer, one 5-ounce glass of wine, or one 1.5-ounce shot of distilled spirits. Each of these drinks contains about half an ounce of alcohol.

Are there dangers from alcohol besides the amount that is consumed?

Yes. Even moderate amounts of alcohol can have toxic effects when taken with over-the-counter drugs containing acetaminophen. If you are taking over-the-counter drugs, be especially careful about drinking and don't use an alcoholic beverage to take your medication. Ask your doctor about precautions for prescription drugs.

Can social drinkers get alcoholic hepatitis?

Yes. Alcoholic hepatitis is frequently discovered in alcoholics, but it also occurs in people who are not alcoholics. People vary greatly in the way their livers react to alcohol.

What kinds of liver diseases are caused by too much alcohol?

Alcoholic hepatitis is an inflammation of the liver. Symptoms include loss of appetite, nausea, vomiting, abdominal pain and tenderness, fever, and jaundice. It is believed to lead to alcoholic cirrhosis over a period of years. Cirrhosis involves permanent damage to the liver cells. Fatty liver is the earliest stage of alcoholic liver disease. If the patient stops drinking at this point, the liver can heal itself.

How can alcoholic hepatitis be diagnosed?

Alcoholic hepatitis is not easy to diagnose. Sometimes symptoms are worse for a time after drinking has stopped than they were during the drinking episode. Although the disease usually comes on after a period of fairly heavy drinking, it may also be seen in people who are moderate drinkers. Blood tests may help in diagnosis. Proof is established best by liver biopsy. This involves taking a tiny specimen of liver tissue with a needle and examining it under a microscope. The biopsy is usually done under local anesthesia.

Are men or women more likely to get alcoholic hepatitis?

Women appear to be more likely to suffer liver damage from alcohol; a woman's body handles alcohol differently than a man's body.

Do all alcoholics get alcoholic hepatitis and eventually cirrhosis?

No. Some alcoholics may suffer seriously from the many physical and psychological symptoms of alcoholism but escape serious liver damage. Alcoholic cirrhosis is found among alcoholics about 10% to 25% of the time.

Is alcoholic hepatitis different from fatty liver?

Yes. Anyone who drinks alcohol heavily, even for a few days, may develop a condition in which liver cells are swollen with fat globules and water. This condition is called fatty liver. It may also result from diabetes, obesity, certain drugs, or severe protein malnutrition. Fatty liver caused by alcohol is reversible when drinking of alcohol is stopped.

Does alcoholic hepatitis always lead to cirrhosis?

No. It usually takes many years for alcoholic hepatitis to produce enough liver damage to result in cirrhosis. If alcoholic hepatitis is detected and treated early, cirrhosis can be prevented.

Is alcoholic hepatitis dangerous?

Yes. It may be fatal, especially if the patient has had previous liver damage. Those who have had nutritional deficiencies because of heavy drinking may have other ailments. These medical complications may affect almost every system in the body. It is important to recognize and treat alcoholic cirrhosis early, so that these life-threatening consequences are prevented.

How can alcoholic hepatitis be prevented?

The best treatment is to stop drinking. Treatment may also include prescribed medication, good nutrition, and rest. The patient may be instructed to avoid various drugs and chemicals. Since the liver has considerable ability to heal and regenerate, the prognosis for a patient with alcoholic hepatitis is very hopeful—if he or she totally abstains from drinking alcohol.

Is cirrhosis different from alcoholic hepatitis?

Yes. Hepatitis is an inflammation of the liver. In cirrhosis, normal liver cells are damaged and replaced by scar tissue. This scarring keeps the liver from performing many of its vital functions.

What causes cirrhosis?

There are many causes for cirrhosis. Long-term alcohol abuse is one. Chronic hepatitis is another major cause. In children, the most frequent causes are biliary atresia, a disease that damages the bile ducts, and neonatal hepatitis. Children with these diseases often receive liver transplants.

Many adult patients who require liver transplants suffer from primary biliary cirrhosis. We do not yet know what causes this illness, but it is not in any way related to alcohol consumption.

Cirrhosis can also be caused by hereditary defects in iron or copper metabolism or prolonged exposure to toxins.

Should alcoholics receive a liver transplant?

Some medical centers will not perform liver transplants on alcoholics because they believe a substantial percentage of these patients will return to drinking. Other centers require abstinence from drinking at least six months before and after surgery, plus enrollment in a counseling program.

Chapter 25

Alcoholic Liver Disease

The liver is one of the largest and most complex organs in the body. It stores vital energy and nutrients, manufactures proteins and enzymes necessary for good health, protects the body from disease, and breaks down (or metabolizes) and helps remove harmful toxins, like alcohol, from the body.

Because the liver is the chief organ responsible for metabolizing alcohol, it is especially vulnerable to alcohol-related injury. Even as few as three drinks at one time may have toxic effects on the liver when combined with certain over-the-counter medications, such as those containing acetaminophen.

This chapter examines the diagnosis and treatment of alcoholic liver disease (ALD), a serious and potentially fatal consequence of drinking alcohol. Another disorder, hepatitis C, also featured here, often is found in patients with ALD.

ALD—From Steatosis to Cirrhosis

ALD includes three conditions: fatty liver, alcoholic hepatitis, and cirrhosis. Heavy drinking for as little as a few days can lead to "fatty" liver, or steatosis—the earliest stage of alcoholic liver disease and the most common alcohol-induced liver disorder. Steatosis is marked by

Excerpted from *Alcohol Alert* No. 64, a publication by the National Institute on Alcohol Abuse and Alcoholism (NIAAA), January 2005. For a complete list of references, visit www.niaaa.nih.gov.

an excessive buildup of fat inside liver cells. This condition can be reversed, however, when drinking stops.

Drinking heavily for longer periods may lead to a more severe, and potentially fatal condition, alcoholic hepatitis—an inflammation of the liver. Symptoms include nausea, lack of appetite, vomiting, fever, abdominal pain and tenderness, jaundice, and, sometimes, mental confusion. Scientists believe that if drinking continues, in some patients this inflammation eventually leads to alcoholic cirrhosis, in which healthy liver cells are replaced by scar tissue (fibrosis), leaving the liver unable to perform its vital functions.

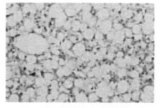

Fatty Liver

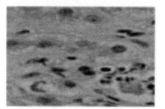

Alcoholic Hepatitis

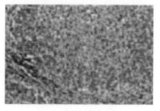

Cirrhosis

Figure 25.1. Biopsies of alcoholic liver disease showing how the cells of the liver change as a patient progresses from fatty liver and alcoholic hepatitis to cirrhosis. Source: NIAAA.

The presence of alcoholic hepatitis is a red flag that cirrhosis may soon follow: Up to 70 percent of all alcoholic hepatitis patients eventually may go on to develop cirrhosis. Patients with alcoholic hepatitis who stop drinking may have a complete recovery from liver disease, or they still may develop cirrhosis.

Liver cirrhosis is a major cause of death in the United States. In 2000, it was the 12th leading cause of death. Cirrhosis mortality rates vary substantially among age groups: They are very low among young people but increase considerably in middle age. In fact, cirrhosis is the fourth leading cause of death in people ages 45 to 54.

Other factors besides alcohol also may influence ALD development, including demographic and biological factors such as ethnic and racial background, gender, age, education, income, employment, and a family history of drinking problems.

Women are at higher risk than men for developing cirrhosis. This higher risk may be the result of differences in the way alcohol is absorbed and broken down. When a woman drinks, the alcohol in her bloodstream reaches a higher level than a man's even if both are drinking the same amount. The chemicals involved in breaking down alcohol also differ between men and women. For example, women's stomachs may contain less of a key enzyme (alcohol dehydrogenase) needed for the initial breakdown of alcohol. This means that a woman breaks down alcohol at a slower rate, exposing her liver to higher blood alcohol concentrations for longer periods of time—a situation that is potentially toxic to the liver. Differences in how a woman's body breaks down and removes alcohol also may be linked to how much and how often she drinks, the fact that estrogen is present in her body, and even her liver size.

Diagnosis

Diagnosing ALD is a challenge. A history of heavy alcohol use along with certain physical signs and positive laboratory tests for liver disease are the best indicators of disease. Alcohol dependence is not necessarily a prerequisite for ALD, and ALD can be difficult to diagnose because patients often minimize or deny their alcohol abuse. Even more confounding is the fact that physical exams and lab findings may not specifically point to ALD.

Diagnosis typically relies on laboratory tests of three liver enzymes: gamma-glutamyltransferase (GGT), aspartate aminotransferase (AST), and alanine aminotransferase (ALT). Liver disease is the most likely diagnosis if the AST level is more than twice that of ALT, a ratio some studies have found in more than 80 percent of alcoholic liver disease patients. An elevated level of the liver enzyme GGT is another gauge of heavy alcohol use and liver injury. Of the three enzymes, GGT is the best indicator of excessive alcohol consumption, but GGT is present in many organs and is increased by other drugs as well, so high GGT levels do not necessarily mean the patient is abusing alcohol.

Treatment

Treatment strategies for ALD include lifestyle changes to reduce alcohol consumption, cigarette smoking, and obesity; nutritional therapy; pharmacological therapy; and possibly liver transplantation (in case of cirrhosis).

Lifestyle Changes

Abstinence from alcohol is vital to prevent further liver injury, scarring, and possibly liver cancer; it appears to benefit patients at each stage of the disease. Although only a few studies have looked specifically at the effects of abstinence on the progression of ALD, virtually every one has shown that abstaining from alcohol is beneficial.

Many people who drink alcohol also smoke cigarettes, and European studies have found scarring of the liver occurs more rapidly in ALD patients who smoked. Obesity is another factor associated with liver disease—specifically, the development of fatty liver and nonalcoholic steatohepatitis, a disorder similar to alcoholic hepatitis. Thus, stopping smoking and maintaining a healthy weight are two more measures patients can take to reduce or prevent further liver injury.

Nutritional Treatment

Although alcoholic beverages contain calories, research suggests that under certain conditions these calories do not have as much value for the body as those derived from other nutrients. In addition, many alcoholics suffer from malnutrition, which can lead to liver damage and impaired liver function. Many drinkers take in less than the recommended daily amount of carbohydrates, proteins, fats, vitamins (A, C, and B, especially thiamine [B1]), and minerals (such as calcium and iron).

To prevent these deficiencies, clinicians should provide alcoholics with a balanced diet. Dietary supplements may prevent or relieve some of alcohol's harmful effects. For example, brain damage resulting from a lack of vitamin B1, which can lead to conditions such as

Wernicke-Korsakoff syndrome, can be reversed to some extent. Because vitamin B1 generally can be administered safely, clinicians often recommend that all alcoholics undergoing treatment receive 50 milligrams of thiamine per day (either by injection if the patients are hospitalized or by mouth). Alcoholics also should receive supplements of vitamins B2 (riboflavin) and B6 (pyridoxine) in dosages found in standard multivitamins. Vitamin A, however, can be toxic when combined with alcohol and should be given only to those alcoholics who have a well–documented deficiency and who can stop or significantly reduce their drinking.

In addition to dietary supplements, alcoholics with moderate malnutrition might benefit from treatment with anabolic steroids. These compounds, which are derived from the male hormone testosterone, can be used in the short term to promote overall body "buildup" and, therefore, may help the alcoholic better recover from malnutrition.

Emerging Therapies

Studies using animals are helping researchers find other dietary supplements that may help in the treatment of liver disease. For example, eating certain healthy fats (called medium-chain triglycerides, or MCTs) may help to reduce the buildup of harmful fats in the liver. MCTs generally are available only in health food stores as a dietary supplement.

Oxidative stress plays a major role in the development of alcoholic liver disease. Oxidative stress occurs when harmful oxygen molecules, or free radicals, form in the body. These molecules are highly charged and very unstable. They cause cellular changes in their effort to pair with the nearest available molecule, injuring cells and modifying their function. Antioxidants can help prevent this free radical damage.

An important antioxidant, glutathione, or GSH, cannot be used as a supplement because this substance cannot directly enter the cells threatened by oxidative stress. However, researchers are using a precursor compound, the molecule S-adenosylmethionine (SAMe), which can enter the cells and then break down to form the helpful antioxidant. When SAMe was given to patients with alcoholic cirrhosis in a clinical trial, they were significantly less likely to die or require a liver transplant within the next 2 years, compared with patients who had received an inactive substance (that is, a placebo). Moreover, the study detected virtually no harmful side effects of SAMe treatment. Thus, this approach appears to hold promise for the treatment of patients with ALD.

Pharmacological Therapy

No FDA-approved therapy exists for either alcoholic cirrhosis or alcoholic hepatitis. However, several drugs have been used "off label," including pentoxifylline (PTX) and corticosteroids. PTX was shown to be effective in patients with severe alcoholic hepatitis. In one study, researchers treated 49 patients with PTX and 52 patients with placebo (vitamin B12) for 4 weeks and found that PTX improved survival: 12 PTX patients died (24.5 percent), compared with 24 placebo patients (46 percent).

Although corticosteroids are the most extensively studied form of therapy for alcoholic hepatitis, their usefulness may be only short-term. Mathurin and colleagues reported significantly improved survival at 28 days (85 percent vs. 65 percent) in severely ill alcoholic hepatitis patients, but this survival advantage did not extend much longer than a year. Most investigators agree that if corticosteroids are used, they should be reserved for patients with the most severe liver disease. In addition, steroids have well-documented side effects, including increasing the risk of infection, which already is substantial in patients with alcoholic hepatitis.

Transplantation

Liver transplantation currently is the only definitive treatment for severe (end stage) liver failure. A total of 41,734 liver transplants using organs from cadavers were performed in the United States between 1992 and 2001. Of these, 12.5 percent were performed in patients with ALD, and 5.8 percent were performed in patients with ALD and a concurrent infection with the hepatitis C virus (HCV), making ALD the second most frequent reason (after HCV infection alone) for transplantation.

ALD patients must undergo a thorough evaluation to determine whether they are suitable candidates for transplant. This screening addresses any coexisting medical problems, such as heart damage, cancer, pancreatitis, and osteoporosis, which might influence the outcome of the transplant. It includes a psychological evaluation to identify those patients who are most likely to remain abstinent and comply with the strict medical regimen that follows the procedure.

For transplantation to be successful in alcoholic patients it is essential that they remain abstinent after the surgery and comply with a demanding medical regimen (e.g., consistently take the necessary antirejection medications). Routinely conducting psychiatric evaluations before patients are included on the list of candidates for transplantation helps to identify those who may not be able to meet these criteria.

Because of the shortage of donated organs, transplantation to patients with alcoholic liver disease remains controversial, mainly out of concern that the transplanted liver could be "wasted" if a patient relapses to drinking and damages the new liver as well. Yet the relapse rates in patients following transplant are lower than in patients undergoing alcoholism treatment, and serious relapses that adversely affect the transplanted liver or the patient are uncommon. In contrast, patients who receive a transplant because of an infection with hepatitis B or C viruses typically experience disease recurrence and are more likely to lose the transplanted liver because of recurrence of these infections.

Another concern is that patients with ALD will not be able to comply with the antirejection medication regimen, but this has not been supported by research. Liver rejection rates are similar for patients transplanted for ALD and those transplanted for other types of liver disease, indicating comparable rates of compliance with the antirejection medications. Finally, it was believed that ALD patients would use more resources, thereby incurring higher costs than non-ALD patients, but again this assumption has not been corroborated by research evidence.

In contrast to these negative assumptions on the use of liver transplants in ALD patients, many clinicians contend that ALD is, in fact, an excellent reason for liver transplantation. The overall improvement in patients with ALD after transplant, including higher productivity and better quality of life, supports considering these patients for liver transplants. Moreover, the long-term costs of transplantation and subsequent management of the alcoholic patient may well be lower than the costs of managing alcoholism and ALD without transplantation.

Hepatitis C and Alcohol

Hepatitis C is a liver disease caused by the hepatitis C virus (HCV). People usually become infected after coming in contact with blood from an infected person. Sharing needles or other equipment for injecting drugs is the most common way of spreading HCV. The disease also can be spread by sexual contact. About 4 million people in the United States have HCV, and between 10,000 and 12,000 die each year. HCV infection is particularly common in alcoholics with liver disease.

Heavy alcohol consumption accelerates patients' progression from chronic HCV to cirrhosis (a condition in which fibrous scar tissue replaces healthy liver tissue) and liver cancer (specifically, hepatocellular carcinoma, the most common form of liver cancer).

Although fewer studies have examined the effects of moderate drinking on the course of liver disease in HCV patients, there is some indication that alcohol consumption in the moderate-to-heavy range may increase HCV-infected patients' risk of developing liver fibrosis and cirrhosis. Research on whether gender has any effect on the connection between alcohol consumption and liver disease progression in HCV patients is very limited.

Blood tests can diagnose HCV infection, either by detecting antibodies to the virus or by detecting the presence and quantity of the virus's genetic material itself. There currently is no vaccine for hepatitis C. The standard treatment includes the use of antiviral treatment (interferon-alfa with ribavirin).

Strict abstinence from alcohol is important during treatment, as heavy drinking during treatment has been shown to hinder patients' responses to therapy. In addition, depression, irritability, and anxiety—side effects that occur in 20 to 30 percent of patients who receive interferon treatment—may be especially difficult to manage in patients with a history of alcoholism, perhaps putting them at greater risk for relapsing to drinking. Thus, for treatment to be most successful, clinicians recommend that alcoholic patients abstain from drinking alcohol at least 6 months prior to beginning interferon therapy. Light-to-moderate drinkers can begin treatment immediately and do not need a period of abstinence before starting therapy.

Summary

The liver is one of the largest organs in the body. It performs many of the vital functions necessary for maintaining good health. The liver is remarkably resilient in responding to disease and infection and, in fact, under certain circumstances, can even generate whole new sections of itself to replace those that are diseased.

Alcohol is a toxin that is especially harmful to the liver, and alcoholic liver disease—particularly cirrhosis—is one of the leading causes of alcohol–related death. Not everyone who drinks heavily will develop ALD. Other factors besides alcohol also influence development of the disease, including demographic, biological, and environmental factors. Nevertheless, stopping drinking can help to alleviate or even reverse ALD, especially in the early stages of disease.

Treatment for ALD includes making lifestyle changes, such as stopping or decreasing alcohol use, stopping smoking, and maintaining a healthy weight. Health care providers may prescribe medications, such as pentoxifylline or prednisone, in cases of alcoholic hepatitis. And patients may want to seek nutritional supplements or complementary and alternative medicine, such as SAMe for cirrhosis. Severe ALD is best treated with transplantation in selected abstinent patients.

Chapter 26

What You Need to Know about Cirrhosis of the Liver

What is cirrhosis of the liver?

Cirrhosis refers to scarring of the liver. Scar tissue forms because of injury or long-term disease. It replaces healthy tissue.

Scar tissue cannot do what healthy liver tissue does—make protein, help fight infections, clean the blood, help digest food, and store energy for when you need it. Scar tissue also blocks the normal flow of blood through the liver. Too much scar tissue means that your liver cannot work properly. To live, you need a liver that works.

Cirrhosis can be life threatening, but it can also be controlled if treated early.

What are the symptoms of cirrhosis?

You may have no symptoms at all in the early stages. As cirrhosis progresses you may:

- feel tired or weak;
- lose your appetite;
- feel sick to your stomach; or
- lose weight.

"What I Need to Know about Cirrhosis of the Liver," from the National Digestive Diseases Information Clearinghouse (NDDIC) of the National Institute of Diabetes and Digestive and Kidney Diseases (NIDDK), October 2005.

Cirrhosis can also lead to other problems.

- You may bruise or bleed easily or have nosebleeds.

- Bloating or swelling may occur as fluid builds up in the abdomen or legs. Fluid build up in the abdomen is called ascites and in the legs is called edema.

- Medications may have a stronger effect on you because your liver does not break them down as quickly.

- Waste materials from food may build up in the blood or brain and may cause confusion or difficulty thinking. For example, protein that you eat breaks down into chemicals like ammonia. When red blood cells get old, they break down and leave a substance called bilirubin. A healthy liver removes these byproducts, but a diseased liver leaves them in the body.

- Blood pressure may increase in the vein entering the liver, a condition called portal hypertension.

- Enlarged veins, called varices, may develop in the esophagus and stomach. Varices can bleed suddenly, causing vomiting of blood or passing of blood in a bowel movement.

- The kidneys may not work properly or may fail.

As cirrhosis progresses, your skin and the whites of your eyes may turn yellow, a condition called jaundice. You may also develop severe itching or gallstones.

In the early stages, cirrhosis causes your liver to swell. Then, as more scar tissue replaces normal tissue, the liver shrinks.

About 5 percent of patients with cirrhosis also get cancer of the liver.

What causes cirrhosis?

Cirrhosis has many causes, including:

- alcohol abuse (alcoholic liver disease);

- chronic viral hepatitis (hepatitis B, C, or D);

- autoimmune hepatitis, which is destruction of liver cells by the body's immune system;

- nonalcoholic fatty liver disease or nonalcoholic steatohepatitis (NASH), which is fat deposits and inflammation in the liver;

- some drugs, toxins, and infections;
- blocked bile ducts, the tubes that carry bile from the liver; and
- some inherited diseases such as:
    - hemochromatosis, a disease that occurs when the body absorbs too much iron and stores the excess iron in the liver, pancreas, and other organs;
    - Wilson's disease, which is caused by the buildup of too much copper in the liver; and
    - protoporphyria, a disorder that affects the skin, bone marrow, and liver.

Sometimes the cause of cirrhosis remains unknown even after a thorough medical examination.

How is cirrhosis diagnosed?

Your symptoms, a physical examination, and certain tests can help your doctor diagnose cirrhosis. Some tests are:

- blood tests to see whether your liver is working properly. Routine blood tests may be normal in cirrhosis. However, with advanced cirrhosis, blood tests may reveal abnormal levels of bilirubin and other substances.
- x-rays, magnetic resonance imaging, or ultrasound images, which are pictures developed from sound waves, may show an enlarged or shrunken liver.
- liver biopsy, an examination of a piece of your liver under a microscope, to look for scar tissue. This is the most accurate way to diagnose cirrhosis.

In a liver biopsy, a needle is used to take a small piece of liver tissue. That sample is then examined under a microscope.

How is cirrhosis treated?

Once you have cirrhosis, nothing can make the scar tissue go away completely. However, treating the cause will keep cirrhosis from getting worse. For example, if cirrhosis is due to alcoholic liver disease, the treatment is to completely stop drinking alcohol. If cirrhosis is caused by hepatitis C, then that disease may be treated with medication.

Your doctor will suggest treatment based on the cause of your cirrhosis and your symptoms. Early diagnosis and carefully following an appropriate treatment plan can help many people with cirrhosis. In very advanced cirrhosis, however, certain treatments may not be possible. In that situation, your doctors will work with you to prevent or manage the complications that cirrhosis can cause.

What if the treatment doesn't work?

If too much scar tissue forms, your liver could fail. Then you may need to consider a liver transplant. A liver transplant can return you to good health.

How can I prevent cirrhosis if I already have liver disease?

See your doctor for treatment of your liver disease. Many of the causes of cirrhosis are treatable, and early treatment may prevent cirrhosis.

- Follow a healthy lifestyle, eat a healthy diet, and stay active.

- Try to keep your weight in the normal range. Being overweight can make several liver diseases worse.

- Do not drink alcohol. Alcohol can harm liver cells, and chronic alcohol use is one of the major causes of cirrhosis.

- Stay away from illegal (street) drugs, which can increase your chances of getting hepatitis B or hepatitis C.

- See your doctor if you have chronic viral hepatitis. Effective treatments for both hepatitis B and hepatitis C are available. If you are on treatment, follow your treatment directions exactly.

- If you have autoimmune hepatitis, take medications and have regular checkups as recommended by your doctor or a liver specialist (hepatologist).

What can I do to keep cirrhosis from getting worse?

- Stop drinking alcohol completely.

- Do not take any medications, including those you can buy without a prescription such as vitamins and herbal supplements, without discussing them with your doctor. Cirrhosis makes your liver sensitive to certain medications.

- Get vaccinated against hepatitis A and hepatitis B. These forms of liver disease are preventable. Also, ask your doctor about getting a flu shot and being vaccinated against pneumonia.

- Avoid eating raw oysters or other raw shellfish. Raw shellfish can harbor bacteria (*Vibrio vulnificus*) that cause severe infections in people with cirrhosis.

Chapter 27

Testing the Liver for Signs of Damage or Disease

In a liver biopsy, the physician examines a small piece of tissue from your liver for signs of damage or disease. A special needle is used to remove the tissue from the liver. The physician decides to do a liver biopsy after tests suggest that the liver does not work properly. For example, a blood test might show that your blood contains higher than normal levels of liver enzymes or too much iron or copper. An x ray could suggest that the liver is swollen. Looking at liver tissue itself is the best way to determine whether the liver is healthy or what is causing it to be damaged.

Preparation

Before scheduling your biopsy, the physician will take blood samples to make sure your blood clots properly. Be sure to mention any medications you take, especially those that affect blood clotting, like blood thinners. One week before the procedure, you will have to stop taking aspirin, ibuprofen, and anticoagulants.

You must not eat or drink anything for 8 hours before the biopsy, and you should plan to arrive at the hospital about an hour before the scheduled time of the procedure. Your physician will tell you whether to take your regular medications during the fasting period and may give you other special instructions.

"Liver Biopsy" is from the National Digestive Diseases Information Clearinghouse (NDDIC) of the National Institute of Diabetes and Digestive and Kidney Diseases (NIDDK), November 2004.

Procedure

Liver biopsy is considered minor surgery, so it is done at the hospital. For the biopsy, you will lie on a hospital bed on your back with your right hand above your head. After marking the outline of your liver and injecting a local anesthetic to numb the area, the physician will make a small incision in your right side near your rib cage, then insert the biopsy needle and retrieve a sample of liver tissue. In some cases, the physician may use an ultrasound image of the liver to help guide the needle to a specific spot.

You will need to hold very still so that the physician does not nick the lung or gallbladder, which are close to the liver. The physician will ask you to hold your breath for 5 to 10 seconds while he or she puts the needle in your liver. You may feel pressure and a dull pain. The entire procedure takes about 20 minutes.

Two other methods of liver biopsy are also available. For a laparoscopic biopsy, the physician inserts a special tube called a laparoscope through an incision in the abdomen. The laparoscope sends images of the liver to a monitor. The physician watches the monitor and uses instruments in the laparoscope to remove tissue samples from one or more parts of the liver. Physicians use this type of biopsy when they need tissue samples from specific parts of the liver.

Transvenous biopsy involves inserting a tube called a catheter into a vein in the neck and guiding it to the liver. The physician puts a biopsy needle into the catheter and then into the liver. Physicians use this procedure when patients have blood-clotting problems or fluid in the abdomen.

Recovery

After the biopsy, the physician will put a bandage over the incision and have you lie on your right side, pressed against a towel, for 1 to 2 hours. The nurse will monitor your vital signs and level of pain.

You will need to arrange for someone to take you home from the hospital since you will not be allowed to drive after having the sedative. You must go directly home and remain in bed (except to use the bathroom) for 8 to 12 hours, depending on your physician's instructions. Also, avoid exertion for the next week so that the incision and liver can heal. You can expect a little soreness at the incision site and possibly some pain in your right shoulder. This pain is caused by irritation of the diaphragm muscle (the pain usually radiates to the shoulder) and should disappear within a few hours or days. Your physician may recommend that you take Tylenol for pain, but you must not take aspirin or ibuprofen for the first week after surgery. These medicines decrease blood clotting, which is crucial for healing.

Like any surgery, liver biopsy does have some risks, such as puncture of the lung or gallbladder, infection, bleeding, and pain, but these complications are rare.

Chapter 28

Alcoholism: A Common Cause of Pancreatitis

Pancreatitis is an inflammation of the pancreas. The pancreas is a large gland behind the stomach and close to the duodenum. The duodenum is the upper part of the small intestine. The pancreas secretes digestive enzymes into the small intestine through a tube called the pancreatic duct. These enzymes help digest fats, proteins, and carbohydrates in food. The pancreas also releases the hormones insulin and glucagon into the bloodstream. These hormones help the body use the glucose it takes from food for energy.

Normally, digestive enzymes do not become active until they reach the small intestine, where they begin digesting food. But if these enzymes become active inside the pancreas, they start "digesting" the pancreas itself.

Acute pancreatitis occurs suddenly and lasts for a short period of time and usually resolves. Chronic pancreatitis does not resolve itself and results in a slow destruction of the pancreas. Either form can cause serious complications. In severe cases, bleeding, tissue damage, and infection may occur. Pseudocysts, accumulations of fluid and tissue debris, may also develop. And enzymes and toxins may enter the bloodstream, injuring the heart, lungs, and kidneys, or other organs.

Excerpted from the document by National Digestive Diseases Information Clearinghouse (NDDIC) of the National Institute of Diabetes and Digestive and Kidney Diseases (NIDDK), February 2004.

Acute Pancreatitis

Some people have more than one attack and recover completely after each, but acute pancreatitis can be a severe, life-threatening illness with many complications. About 80,000 cases occur in the United States each year; some 20 percent of them are severe. Acute pancreatitis occurs more often in men than women.

Acute pancreatitis is usually caused by gallstones or by drinking too much alcohol, but these aren't the only causes. If alcohol use and gallstones are ruled out, other possible causes of pancreatitis should be carefully examined so that appropriate treatment—if available—can begin.

Symptoms

Acute pancreatitis usually begins with pain in the upper abdomen that may last for a few days. The pain may be severe and may become constant—just in the abdomen—or it may reach to the back and other areas. It may be sudden and intense or begin as a mild pain that gets worse when food is eaten. Someone with acute pancreatitis often looks and feels very sick. Other symptoms may include:

- swollen and tender abdomen;
- nausea;
- vomiting;
- fever; or
- rapid pulse.

Severe cases may cause dehydration and low blood pressure. The heart, lungs, or kidneys may fail. If bleeding occurs in the pancreas, shock and sometimes even death follow.

Diagnosis

Besides asking about a person's medical history and doing a physical exam, a doctor will order a blood test to diagnose acute pancreatitis. During acute attacks, the blood contains at least three times more amylase and lipase than usual. Amylase and lipase are digestive enzymes formed in the pancreas. Changes may also occur in blood levels of glucose, calcium, magnesium, sodium, potassium, and bicarbonate. After the pancreas improves, these levels usually return to normal.

A doctor may also order an abdominal ultrasound to look for gallstones and a CAT (computerized axial tomography) scan to look for inflammation or destruction of the pancreas. CAT scans are also useful in locating pseudocysts.

Treatment

Treatment depends on the severity of the attack. If no kidney or lung complications occur, acute pancreatitis usually improves on its own. Treatment, in general, is designed to support vital bodily functions and prevent complications. A hospital stay will be necessary so that fluids can be replaced intravenously.

If pancreatic pseudocysts occur and are considered large enough to interfere with the pancreas's healing, your doctor may drain or surgically remove them.

Unless the pancreatic duct or bile duct is blocked by gallstones, an acute attack usually lasts only a few days. In severe cases, a person may require intravenous feeding for 3 to 6 weeks while the pancreas slowly heals. This process is called total parenteral nutrition. However, for mild cases of the disease, total parenteral nutrition offers no benefit.

Before leaving the hospital, a person will be advised not to drink alcohol and not to eat large meals. After all signs of acute pancreatitis are gone, the doctor will try to decide what caused it in order to prevent future attacks. In some people, the cause of the attack is clear, but in others, more tests are needed.

Complications

Acute pancreatitis can cause breathing problems. Many people develop hypoxia, which means that cells and tissues are not receiving enough oxygen. Doctors treat hypoxia by giving oxygen through a face mask. Despite receiving oxygen, some people still experience lung failure and require a ventilator.

Sometimes a person cannot stop vomiting and needs to have a tube placed in the stomach to remove fluid and air. In mild cases, a person may not eat for 3 or 4 days and instead may receive fluids and pain relievers through an intravenous line.

If an infection develops, the doctor may prescribe antibiotics. Surgery may be needed for extensive infections. Surgery may also be necessary to find the source of bleeding, to rule out problems that resemble pancreatitis, or to remove severely damaged pancreatic tissue.

Acute pancreatitis can sometimes cause kidney failure. If your kidneys fail, you will need dialysis to help your kidneys remove wastes from your blood.

Gallstones and Pancreatitis

Gallstones can cause pancreatitis and they usually require surgical removal. Ultrasound or a CAT scan can detect gallstones and can sometimes give an idea of the severity of the pancreatitis. When gallstone surgery can be scheduled depends on how severe the pancreatitis is. If the pancreatitis is mild, gallstone surgery may proceed within about a week. More severe cases may mean gallstone surgery is delayed for a month or more.

After the gallstones are removed and inflammation goes away, the pancreas usually returns to normal.

Chronic Pancreatitis

If injury to the pancreas continues, chronic pancreatitis may develop. Chronic pancreatitis occurs when digestive enzymes attack and destroy the pancreas and nearby tissues, causing scarring and pain. The usual cause of chronic pancreatitis is many years of alcohol abuse, but the chronic form may also be triggered by only one acute attack, especially if the pancreatic ducts are damaged. The damaged ducts cause the pancreas to become inflamed, tissue to be destroyed, and scar tissue to develop.

While common, alcoholism is not the only cause of chronic pancreatitis. The main causes of chronic pancreatitis are:

- alcoholism;
- blocked or narrowed pancreatic duct because of trauma or because pseudocysts have formed;
- heredity; and
- unknown cause (idiopathic).

Damage from alcohol abuse may not appear for many years, and then a person may have a sudden attack of pancreatitis. In up to 70 percent of adult patients, chronic pancreatitis appears to be caused by alcoholism. This form is more common in men than in women and often develops between the ages of 30 and 40.

Hereditary pancreatitis usually begins in childhood but may not be diagnosed for several years. A person with hereditary pancreatitis usually has the typical symptoms that come and go over time. Episodes last from 2 days to 2 weeks. A determining factor in the diagnosis of hereditary pancreatitis is two or more family members with pancreatitis in more than one generation. Treatment for individual attacks is usually the same as it is for acute pancreatitis. Any pain or nutrition problems are treated just as they are for acute pancreatitis. Surgery can often ease pain and help manage complications.

Other causes of chronic pancreatitis are:

- congenital conditions such as pancreas divisum;
- cystic fibrosis;
- high levels of calcium in the blood (hypercalcemia);
- high levels of blood fats (hyperlipidemia or hypertriglyceridemia);
- some drugs; and
- certain autoimmune conditions.

Symptoms

Most people with chronic pancreatitis have abdominal pain, although some people have no pain at all. The pain may get worse when eating or drinking, spread to the back, or become constant and disabling.

In certain cases, abdominal pain goes away as the condition advances, probably because the pancreas is no longer making digestive enzymes. Other symptoms include nausea, vomiting, weight loss, and fatty stools.

People with chronic disease often lose weight, even when their appetite and eating habits are normal. The weight loss occurs because the body does not secrete enough pancreatic enzymes to break down food, so nutrients are not absorbed normally. Poor digestion leads to excretion of fat, protein, and sugar into the stool. If the insulin-producing cells of the pancreas (islet cells) have been damaged, diabetes may also develop at this stage.

Diagnosis

Diagnosis may be difficult, but new techniques can help. Pancreatic function tests help a doctor decide whether the pancreas is still making enough digestive enzymes. Using ultrasonic imaging, endoscopic retrograde cholangiopancreatography (ERCP), and CAT scans, a doctor can see problems indicating chronic pancreatitis.

Such problems include calcification of the pancreas, in which tissue hardens from deposits of insoluble calcium salts. In more advanced stages of the disease, when diabetes and malabsorption occur, a doctor can use a number of blood, urine, and stool tests to help diagnose chronic pancreatitis and to monitor its progression.

Treatment

Relieving pain is the first step in treating chronic pancreatitis. The next step is to plan a diet that is high in carbohydrates and low in fat.

A doctor may prescribe pancreatic enzymes to take with meals if the pancreas does not secrete enough of its own. The enzymes should be taken with every meal to help the body digest food and regain some weight. Sometimes insulin or other drugs are needed to control blood glucose.

In some cases, surgery is needed to relieve pain. The surgery may involve draining an enlarged pancreatic duct or removing part of the pancreas.

For fewer and milder attacks, people with pancreatitis must stop drinking alcohol, stick to their prescribed diet, and take the proper medications.

Chapter 29

What You Need to Know about Cancer of the Pancreas

Introduction

In the United States, cancer of the pancreas is diagnosed in more than 29,000 people every year. It is the fifth leading cause of cancer death.

This chapter discusses possible causes of cancer of the pancreas. It also describes symptoms, diagnosis, treatment, and followup care. This information can help patients and their families better understand and cope with this disease.

Scientists are studying cancer of the pancreas to learn more about this disease. They are finding out more about its causes. Doctors are exploring new ways to treat it. Research already has led to better quality of life for people with cancer of the pancreas.

The Pancreas

The pancreas is a gland located deep in the abdomen between the stomach and the spine (backbone). The liver, intestine, and other organs surround the pancreas.

The pancreas is about 6 inches long and is shaped like a flat pear. The widest part of the pancreas is the head, the middle section is the body, and the thinnest part is the tail.

Excerpted from the document by the National Cancer Institute (www.cancer.gov), NIH Publication No. 01-1560, updated September 16, 2002.

The pancreas makes insulin and other hormones. These hormones enter the bloodstream and travel throughout the body. They help the body use or store the energy that comes from food. For example, insulin helps control the amount of sugar in the blood.

The pancreas also makes pancreatic juices. These juices contain enzymes that help digest food. The pancreas releases the juices into a system of ducts leading to the common bile duct. The common bile duct empties into the duodenum, the first section of the small intestine.

Most pancreatic cancers begin in the ducts that carry pancreatic juices. Cancer of the pancreas may be called pancreatic cancer or carcinoma of the pancreas.

A rare type of pancreatic cancer begins in the cells that make insulin and other hormones. Cancer that begins in these cells is called islet cell cancer.

When cancer of the pancreas spreads (metastasizes) outside the pancreas, cancer cells are often found in nearby lymph nodes. If the cancer has reached these nodes, it means that cancer cells may have spread to other lymph nodes or other tissues, such as the liver or lungs. Sometimes cancer of the pancreas spreads to the peritoneum, the tissue that lines the abdomen.

When cancer spreads from its original place to another part of the body, the new tumor has the same kind of abnormal cells and the same name as the primary tumor. For example, if cancer of the pancreas spreads to the liver, the cancer cells in the liver are pancreatic cancer cells. The disease is metastatic pancreatic cancer, not liver cancer. It is treated as pancreatic cancer, not liver cancer.

Pancreatic Cancer: Who's at Risk?

No one knows the exact causes of pancreatic cancer. Doctors can seldom explain why one person gets pancreatic cancer and another does not. However, it is clear that this disease is not contagious. No one can "catch" cancer from another person.

Research has shown that people with certain risk factors are more likely than others to develop pancreatic cancer. A risk factor is anything that increases a person's chance of developing a disease.

Studies have found the following risk factors:

- **Age**—The likelihood of developing pancreatic cancer increases with age. Most pancreatic cancers occur in people over the age of 60.

- **Smoking**—Cigarette smokers are two or three times more likely than nonsmokers to develop pancreatic cancer.

- **Diabetes**—Pancreatic cancer occurs more often in people who have diabetes than in people who do not.

- **Being male**—More men than women are diagnosed with pancreatic cancer.

- **Being African American**—African Americans are more likely than Asians, Hispanics, or whites to get pancreatic cancer.

- **Family history**—The risk for developing pancreatic cancer triples if a person's mother, father, sister, or brother had the disease. Also, a family history of colon or ovarian cancer increases the risk of pancreatic cancer.

- **Chronic pancreatitis**—Chronic pancreatitis is a painful condition of the pancreas. Some evidence suggests that chronic pancreatitis may increase the risk of pancreatic cancer.

Other studies suggest that exposure to certain chemicals in the workplace or a diet high in fat may increase the chance of getting pancreatic cancer.

Most people with known risk factors do not get pancreatic cancer. On the other hand, many who do get the disease have none of these factors. People who think they may be at risk for pancreatic cancer should discuss this concern with their doctor. The doctor may suggest ways to reduce the risk and can plan an appropriate schedule for checkups.

Symptoms

Pancreatic cancer is sometimes called a "silent disease" because early pancreatic cancer often does not cause symptoms. But, as the cancer grows, symptoms may include:

- pain in the upper abdomen or upper back;
- yellow skin and eyes, and dark urine from jaundice;
- weakness;
- loss of appetite;
- nausea and vomiting; and
- weight loss.

These symptoms are not sure signs of pancreatic cancer. An infection or other problem could also cause these symptoms. Only a doctor can diagnose the cause of a person's symptoms. Anyone with these symptoms should see a doctor so that the doctor can treat any problem as early as possible.

Treatment

Many people with pancreatic cancer want to take an active part in making decisions about their medical care. They want to learn all they can about their disease and their treatment choices. However, the shock and stress that people may feel after a diagnosis of cancer can make it hard for them to think of everything they want to ask the doctor. Often it helps to make a list of questions before an appointment. To help remember what the doctor says, patients may take notes or ask whether they may use a tape recorder. Some patients also want to have a family member or friend with them when they talk to the doctor—to take part in the discussion, to take notes, or just to listen.

Cancer of the pancreas is very hard to control with current treatments. For that reason, many doctors encourage patients with this disease to consider taking part in a clinical trial. Clinical trials are an important option for people with all stages of pancreatic cancer.

At this time, pancreatic cancer can be cured only when it is found at an early stage, before it has spread. However, other treatments may be able to control the disease and help patients live longer and feel better. When a cure or control of the disease is not possible, some patients and their doctors choose palliative therapy. Palliative therapy aims to improve quality of life by controlling pain and other problems caused by this disease.

The doctor may refer patients to an oncologist, a doctor who specializes in treating cancer, or patients may ask for a referral. Specialists who treat pancreatic cancer include surgeons, medical oncologists, and radiation oncologists. Treatment generally begins within a few weeks after the diagnosis. There will be time for patients to talk with the doctor about treatment choices, get a second opinion, and learn more about the disease.

Methods of Treatment

People with pancreatic cancer may have several treatment options. Depending on the type and stage, pancreatic cancer may be treated with surgery, radiation therapy, or chemotherapy. Some patients have a combination of therapies.

Surgery may be used alone or in combination with radiation therapy and chemotherapy.

The surgeon may remove all or part of the pancreas. The extent of surgery depends on the location and size of the tumor, the stage of the disease, and the patient's general health.

- **Whipple procedure:** If the tumor is in the head (the widest part) of the pancreas, the surgeon removes the head of the pancreas and part of the small intestine, bile duct, and stomach. The surgeon may also remove other nearby tissues.

- **Distal pancreatectomy:** The surgeon removes the body and tail of the pancreas if the tumor is in either of these parts. The surgeon also removes the spleen.

- **Total pancreatectomy:** The surgeon removes the entire pancreas, part of the small intestine, a portion of the stomach, the common bile duct, the gallbladder, the spleen, and nearby lymph nodes.

Sometimes the cancer cannot be completely removed. But if the tumor is blocking the common bile duct or duodenum, the surgeon can create a bypass. A bypass allows fluids to flow through the digestive tract. It can help relieve jaundice and pain resulting from a blockage.

The doctor sometimes can relieve blockage without doing bypass surgery. The doctor uses an endoscope to place a stent in the blocked area. A stent is a tiny plastic or metal mesh tube that helps keep the duct or duodenum open.

After surgery, some patients are fed liquids intravenously (by IV) and through feeding tubes placed into the abdomen. Patients slowly return to eating solid foods by mouth. A few weeks after surgery, the feeding tubes are removed.

Radiation therapy (also called radiotherapy) uses high-energy rays to kill cancer cells. A large machine directs radiation at the abdomen. Radiation therapy may be given alone, or with surgery, chemotherapy, or both.

Radiation therapy is local therapy. It affects cancer cells only in the treated area. For radiation therapy, patients go to the hospital or clinic, often 5 days a week for several weeks.

Doctors may use radiation to destroy cancer cells that remain in the area after surgery. They also use radiation to relieve pain and other problems caused by the cancer.

Chemotherapy is the use of drugs to kill cancer cells. Doctors also give chemotherapy to help reduce pain and other problems caused by pancreatic cancer. It may be given alone, with radiation, or with surgery and radiation.

Chemotherapy is systemic therapy. The doctor usually gives the drugs by injection. Once in the bloodstream, the drugs travel throughout the body.

Usually chemotherapy is an outpatient treatment given at the hospital, clinic, doctor's office, or home. However, depending on which drugs are given and the patient's general health, the patient may need to stay in the hospital.

The Promise of Cancer Research

Laboratory scientists are studying the pancreas to learn more about it. They are studying the possible causes of pancreatic cancer and are researching new ways to detect tumors. They also are looking for new therapies that may kill cancer cells.

Doctors in clinics and hospitals are conducting many types of clinical trials. These are research studies in which people take part voluntarily. In these trials, researchers are studying ways to treat pancreatic cancer. Research already has led to advances in treatment methods, and researchers continue to search for more effective approaches to treat this disease.

Patients who join clinical trials have the first chance to benefit from new treatments that have shown promise in earlier research. They also make an important contribution to medical science by helping doctors learn more about the disease. Although clinical trials may pose some risks, researchers take very careful steps to protect their patients.

In trials with people who have pancreatic cancer, doctors are studying new drugs, new combinations of chemotherapy, and combinations of chemotherapy and radiation before and after surgery.

Biological therapy is also under investigation. Scientists are studying several cancer vaccines to help the immune system fight cancer. Other studies use monoclonal antibodies to slow or stop the growth of cancer.

Patients who are interested in joining a clinical study should talk with their doctor.

Chapter 30

Alcohol's Role in Gastrointestinal Tract Disorders

When alcohol is consumed, the alcoholic beverages first pass through the various segments of the gastrointestinal (GI) tract. Accordingly, alcohol may interfere with the structure as well as the function of GI-tract segments. For example, alcohol can impair the function of the muscles separating the esophagus from the stomach, thereby favoring the occurrence of heartburn. Alcohol-induced damage to the mucosal lining of the esophagus also increases the risk of esophageal cancer. In the stomach, alcohol interferes with gastric acid secretion and with the activity of the muscles surrounding the stomach. Similarly, alcohol may impair the muscle movement in the small and large intestines, contributing to the diarrhea frequently observed in alcoholics. Moreover, alcohol inhibits the absorption of nutrients in the small intestine and increases the transport of toxins across the intestinal walls, effects that may contribute to the development of alcohol-related damage to the liver and other organs.

The GI Tract—An Overview

The GI tract's functions are to physically and chemically break down ingested food, allow the absorption of nutrients into the bloodstream, and excrete the waste products generated. The GI tract can

Excerpted from the article by Christiane Bode and J. Christian Bode, *Alcohol Research & Health*, Vol. 21, No. 1, 1997, pp. 76–83. For a complete list of references, see www.niaaa.nih.gov. Revised by David A. Cooke, M.D., on March 13, 2006.

be viewed as one continuous tube extending from the mouth to the anus, which is subdivided into different segments with specific functions.

In the mouth, or oral cavity, the teeth mechanically grind the food into small pieces. Moreover, saliva excreted by the salivary glands initiates the food's chemical degradation. From the oral cavity, the food passes through the throat (i.e., pharynx) into the esophagus. The coordinated contraction and relaxation of the muscles surrounding the esophagus propels the food into the stomach.

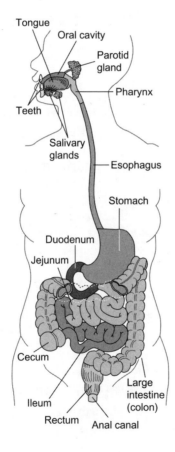

Figure 30.1. *The human gastrointestinal tract. The small intestine comprises the duodenum, the ileum, and the jejunum.*

In the stomach, the chemical degradation of the food continues with the help of gastric acid and various digestive enzymes. Damage to the stomach's naturally acid-resistant lining, the mucosa, may cause gastric pain and result in the development of gastric ulcers. Two bands of muscle fibers (i.e., sphincters) close off the stomach to the esophagus and the intestine. Weakness of the sphincter separating the stomach from the esophagus allows the stomach content to flow back into the esophagus. This process, which is called gastroesophageal reflux, can lead to heartburn as well as inflammation (i.e., reflux esophagitis) and even to the development of ulcers in the lower part of the esophagus.

From the stomach, the food enters the small intestine, which is divided into three segments: the duodenum, the jejunum, and the ileum. Like the esophagus and stomach, the intestine is surrounded by layers of muscles, the rhythmic movements of which help mix the food mass and push it along the GI tract. The intestine's inner mucosal surface is covered with small projections called villi, which increase the intestinal surface area. As the food mass moves through the small intestine, digestive enzymes secreted by the intestinal cells complete the chemical degradation of nutrients into simple molecules that can be absorbed through the intestinal wall into the bloodstream. What finally remains in the intestine are primarily indigestible waste products.

These products progress into the large intestine, where the waste is compacted and prepared for excretion through the anus. Like the small intestine, the large intestine can be divided into three segments: the cecum; the colon, which constitutes about 80 percent of the large intestine; and the rectum. The following sections review alcohol's effect on the different regions of the GI tract.

The Oral Cavity and the Esophagus

The oral cavity, pharynx, esophagus, and stomach are exposed to alcohol immediately after its ingestion. Thus, alcoholic beverages are almost undiluted when they come in contact with the mucosa of these structures. It is therefore not surprising that mucosal injuries (i.e., lesions) occur quite frequently in people who drink large amounts of alcohol.

Chronic alcohol abuse damages the salivary glands and thus interferes with saliva secretion. In alcoholics this damage commonly manifests itself as an enlargement (i.e., hypertrophy) of the parotid gland, although the mechanisms leading to this condition are unknown. Moreover, alcoholics may suffer from inflammation of the tongue (i.e., glossitis) and the mouth (i.e., stomatitis). It is unclear, however, whether these changes result from poor nutrition or reflect alcohol's direct effect on the mucosa. Finally, chronic alcohol abuse increases the incidence of tooth decay, gum disease, and loss of teeth.

Alcohol consumption can affect the esophagus in several ways. For example, alcohol distinctly impairs esophageal motility, and even a single drinking episode (i.e., acute alcohol consumption) significantly weakens the lower esophageal sphincter. As a result, gastroesophageal reflux may occur, and the esophagus' ability to clear the refluxed gastric acid may be reduced.

Both of these factors promote the occurrence of heartburn. Moreover, some alcoholics exhibit an abnormality of esophageal motility known as a "nutcracker esophagus," which mimics symptoms of coronary heart disease.

Chronic alcohol abuse leads to an increased incidence not only of heartburn but also of esophageal mucosal inflammation (i.e., esophagitis) and other injuries that may induce mucosal defects (i.e., esophagitis with or without erosions). In addition, alcoholics make up a significant proportion of patients with Barrett's esophagus. This condition, which occurs in 10 to 20 percent of patients with symptomatic gastroesophageal reflux disease, is characterized by changes in the cell layer lining the esophagus (i.e., the epithelium) that lead to abnormal acid production. A diagnosis of Barrett's esophagus is an important indicator of an increased risk of esophageal cancer, because in some patients the altered epithelial cells become cancerous.

Another condition affecting alcoholics is Mallory-Weiss syndrome, which is characterized by massive bleeding caused by tears in the mucosa at the junction of the esophagus and the stomach. The syndrome accounts for 5 to 15 percent of all cases of bleeding in the upper GI tract. In 20 to 50 percent of all patients, the disorder is caused by increased gastric pressure resulting from repeated retching and vomiting following excessive acute alcohol consumption.

The Stomach

Both acute and chronic alcohol consumption can interfere with stomach functioning in several ways. For example, alcohol—even in relatively small doses—can alter gastric acid secretion, induce acute gastric mucosal injury, and interfere with gastric and intestinal motility.

Gastric Acid Secretion

The resulting decrease in acid production reduces the stomach's ability to destroy the bacteria that enter with food and thus favors the colonization of the upper small intestine with potentially harmful microorganisms. Abstinence, however, can at least partly reverse these changes.

Acute Gastric Mucosal Injury

Researchers have known for more than 100 years that alcohol abuse can cause mucosal inflammation. In addition, alcohol abuse is an important cause of bleeding (i.e., hemorrhagic) gastric lesions that can destroy parts of the mucosa. Although low or moderate alcohol doses do not cause such damage in healthy subjects, even a single episode of heavy drinking can induce mucosal inflammation and hemorrhagic lesions. Nonsteroidal anti-inflammatory drugs (e.g., aspirin and ibuprofen) may aggravate the development of alcohol-induced acute gastric lesions.

Alcoholic beverages with a low alcohol content (e.g., beer and wine) strongly increase gastric acid secretion and the release of gastrin, the gastric hormone that induces acid secretion. In contrast, beverages with a higher alcohol content (e.g., whisky and cognac) stimulate neither gastric acid secretion nor gastrin release.

The mechanisms underlying the effects of alcoholic beverages on gastric acid secretion have not yet been identified. Alcohol may interact directly with the gastric mucosa (i.e., topical stimulation); or, it may act through a more general mechanism affecting the release of hormones and the regulation of nerve functions involved in acid secretion. Moreover, researchers have shown that after beer consumption, gastric acid secretion also is stimulated by byproducts of the fermentation process other than alcohol.

Inflammatory reactions also might contribute to the development of alcohol-induced mucosal injury.

Gastric and Intestinal Motility

Alcohol can interfere with the activity of the muscles surrounding the stomach and the small intestine and thus alter the transit time of food through these organs. In humans, alcohol's effect on gastric motility depends on the alcohol concentration and accompanying meals. In general, beverages with high alcohol concentrations (i.e., above 15 percent) appear to inhibit gastric motility and thus delay the emptying of the stomach. As a result of the increased gastric transit time, bacterial degradation of the food may begin; the resulting gases may lead to feelings of fullness and abdominal discomfort.

In the small intestine, alcohol decreases the muscle movements that help retain the food for further digestion (i.e., the impeding wave motility).

In contrast, alcohol does not affect the movements that propel food through the intestine (i.e., the propulsive wave motility) in either alcoholics or healthy subjects. These effects may contribute to the increased sensitivity to foods with a high sugar content (e.g., candy and sweetened juices), shortened transit time, and diarrhea frequently observed in alcoholics.

The Small Intestine

The small intestine is the organ in which most nutrients are absorbed into the bloodstream. Studies in humans and animals as well as in tissue culture have demonstrated that alcohol can interfere with the absorption of several nutrients. The importance of these absorption disorders in the development of nutritional disturbances in alcoholics, however, is unclear. In alcoholics with limited pancreatic function or advanced liver disease, digestion of nutrients may be a more significant problem than impaired absorption disorders.

Intestinal Enzymes

Alcohol can interfere with the activity of many enzymes that are essential for intestinal functioning. One of these enzymes is lactase, which breaks down the milk sugar lactose; lactase deficiency results in lactose intolerance.

Alcohol also interferes with some of the enzymes involved in transporting nutrients from the intestine into the bloodstream and inhibits important enzymes that participate in the metabolism of drugs and other foreign organic substances in the gut.

Intestinal Mucosal Injury

Excessive alcohol consumption frequently causes mucosal damage in the upper region of the duodenum. Even in healthy people, a single episode of heavy drinking can result in duodenal erosions and bleeding.

Intestinal Permeability

In animal studies, alcohol administration increased the permeability of the intestinal mucosa, allowing large molecules that normally cannot cross the intestinal wall intact (e.g., hemoglobin) to travel between the gut and the bloodstream.

Similarly, intestinal permeability was enhanced in nonintoxicated alcoholics. The enhanced permeability induced by acute and chronic alcohol ingestion could allow toxic compounds, such as endotoxin and other bacterial toxins, to enter the bloodstream and subsequently reach the liver. The presence of endotoxin in the blood has been documented in patients with early stages of alcohol-related liver damage and transiently, after excessive alcohol consumption, in people with no evidence of liver disease.

Intestinal Bacterial Microflora

Certain bacteria that are a major source of endotoxin may overgrow the normal bacterial flora in the jejunum of alcoholics. Together with the altered permeability of the gut induced by alcohol, this process may allow an increased escape of endotoxin from the intestine into the blood vessels leading to the liver, thus increasing the liver's exposure to these toxins and, consequently, the risk of liver injury.

The Large Intestine

Until recently, alcohol's effects on the large intestine had received only minor attention. Studies in dogs found that acute alcohol administration depressed the colon's impeding motility but enhanced its propulsive motility. In healthy humans, alcohol administration also significantly reduced the frequency and strength (i.e., amplitude) of the muscle contractions in a segment of the rectum. These effects could reduce the transit time—and thus the compaction—of the intestinal contents and thereby contribute to the diarrhea frequently observed in alcoholics.

Medical Consequences

Alcohol-induced digestive disorders and mucosal damage in the GI tract can cause a variety of medical problems. These include a loss of appetite and a multitude of abdominal complaints, such as nausea, vomiting, feelings of fullness, flatulence, and abdominal pain. Diseases of the liver and pancreas may contribute to and aggravate these complaints. Thus, about 50 percent of alcoholics with an initial stage of liver damage (i.e., fatty liver) and 30 to 80 percent of patients with an advanced stage of alcohol-induced liver injury (i.e., alcoholic hepatitis) report some symptoms of abdominal discomfort. These abdominal complaints can lead to reduced food intake, thereby causing the weight loss and malnutrition commonly observed in alcoholics.

In addition to causing abdominal complaints, alcohol plays a role in the development of cancers of the GI tract. It is likely, however, that alcohol does not cause GI-tract cancers by itself but acts in concert with other cancer-inducing agents (i.e., as a cocarcinogen). Alcohol abuse, like smoking, is associated with the development of cancers of the tongue, larynx (i.e., the organ of voice), and pharynx; both alcohol consumption and smoking independently increase the risk for these tumors.

Epidemiological studies also strongly indicate that chronic alcohol consumption, especially of distilled spirits, markedly contributes to the development of esophageal cancer. Thus, after adjusting for smoking habits, heavy beer drinkers have a 10 times greater risk and heavy whiskey drinkers a 25 times greater risk of developing esophageal cancer, compared with people who consume less than 30 g of alcohol (i.e., about 2 standard drinks) daily. The differences between beer and whisky drinkers remain even if they consume the same amount of pure alcohol. In drinkers who also smoke 20 cigarettes or more daily, the risk of esophageal cancer increases about 45-fold.

Heavy alcohol consumption also is associated with the development of tumors in the colon and rectum. However, the relative risk of cancer is higher for rectal cancer than for colon cancer. Moreover, the increased risk of rectal cancer appears to result mainly from heavy beer consumption, whereas distilled spirits appear to have no effect.

Summary

Alcohol consumption can interfere with the function of all parts of the gastrointestinal tract. Acute alcohol ingestion induces changes in the motility of the esophagus and stomach that favor gastroesophageal reflux and, probably, the development of reflux esophagitis.

Alcohol abuse may lead to damage of the gastric mucosa, including hemorrhagic lesions. Beverages with a low alcohol content stimulate gastric acid secretion, whereas beverages with a high alcohol content do not.

Motility disorders, maldigestion, and malabsorption in alcoholics can result in digestive problems, such as anorexia, nausea, and abdominal pain.

Alcohol abuse also promotes the development of cancers of the tongue, larynx, pharynx, and esophagus. Finally, the results of recent epidemiological studies indicate an association between alcohol consumption and the development of colorectal cancer.

Chapter 31

Alcohol's Damaging Effects on the Brain

Difficulty walking, blurred vision, slurred speech, slowed reaction times, impaired memory: Clearly, alcohol affects the brain. Some of these impairments are detectable after only one or two drinks and quickly resolve when drinking stops. On the other hand, a person who drinks heavily over a long period of time may have brain deficits that persist well after he or she achieves sobriety. Exactly how alcohol affects the brain and the likelihood of reversing the impact of heavy drinking on the brain remain hot topics in alcohol research today.

We do know that heavy drinking may have extensive and far-reaching effects on the brain, ranging from simple "slips" in memory to permanent and debilitating conditions that require lifetime custodial care. And even moderate drinking leads to short-term impairment, as shown by extensive research on the impact of drinking on driving.

A number of factors influence how and to what extent alcohol affects the brain, including:

- how much and how often a person drinks;
- the age at which he or she first began drinking, and how long he or she has been drinking;
- the person's age, level of education, gender, genetic background, and family history of alcoholism;

Excerpted from *Alcohol Alert,* Number 63, by the National Institute for Alcohol Abuse and Alcoholism (NIAAA), October 2004. For a complete list of references, see www.niaaa.nih.gov.

- whether he or she is at risk as a result of prenatal alcohol exposure; and

- his or her general health status.

This chapter reviews some common disorders associated with alcohol-related brain damage and the people at greatest risk for impairment. It looks at traditional as well as emerging therapies for the treatment and prevention of alcohol-related disorders and includes a brief look at the high-tech tools that are helping scientists to better understand the effects of alcohol on the brain.

Blackouts and Memory Lapses

Alcohol can produce detectable impairments in memory after only a few drinks and, as the amount of alcohol increases, so does the degree of impairment. Large quantities of alcohol, especially when consumed quickly and on an empty stomach, can produce a blackout, or an interval of time for which the intoxicated person cannot recall key details of events, or even entire events.

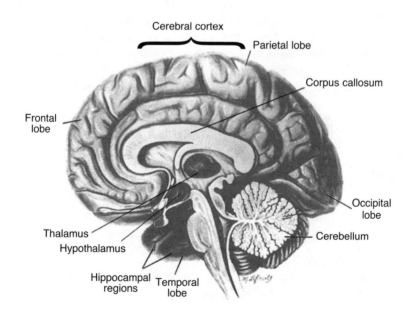

Figure 31.1. Areas of the human brain vulnerable to damage by alcohol. Source: NIAAA.

Blackouts are much more common among social drinkers than previously assumed and should be viewed as a potential consequence of acute intoxication regardless of age or whether the drinker is clinically dependent on alcohol. Researchers surveyed 772 college undergraduates about their experiences with blackouts and asked, "Have you ever awoken after a night of drinking not able to remember things that you did or places that you went?" Of the students who had ever consumed alcohol, 51 percent reported blacking out at some point in their lives, and 40 percent reported experiencing a blackout in the year before the survey. Of those who reported drinking in the 2 weeks before the survey, 9.4 percent said they blacked out during that time. The students reported learning later that they had participated in a wide range of potentially dangerous events they could not remember, including vandalism, unprotected sex, and driving.

Equal numbers of men and women reported experiencing blackouts, despite the fact that the men drank significantly more often and more heavily than the women. This outcome suggests that regardless of the amount of alcohol consumption, females—a group infrequently studied in the literature on blackouts—are at greater risk than males for experiencing blackouts. A woman's tendency to black out more easily probably results from differences in how men and women metabolize alcohol. Females also may be more susceptible than males to milder forms of alcohol-induced memory impairments, even when men and women consume comparable amounts of alcohol.

Binge Drinking and Blackouts

Drinkers who experience blackouts typically drink too much and too quickly, which causes their blood alcohol levels to rise very rapidly. College students may be at particular risk for experiencing a blackout, as an alarming number of college students engage in binge drinking. Binge drinking, for a typical adult, is defined as consuming five or more drinks in about 2 hours for men, or four or more drinks for women.

Are Women More Vulnerable to Alcohol's Effects on the Brain?

Women are more vulnerable than men to many of the medical consequences of alcohol use. For example, alcoholic women develop cirrhosis, alcohol-induced damage of the heart muscle (i.e., cardiomyopathy), and nerve damage (i.e., peripheral neuropathy) after fewer years of heavy drinking than do alcoholic men. Studies comparing men and women's sensitivity to alcohol-induced brain damage, however, have not been as conclusive.

Using imaging with computerized tomography, two studies compared brain shrinkage, a common indicator of brain damage, in alcoholic men and women and reported that male and female alcoholics both showed significantly greater brain shrinkage than control subjects. Studies also showed that both men and women have similar learning and memory problems as a result of heavy drinking. The difference is that alcoholic women reported that they had been drinking excessively for only about half as long as the alcoholic men in these studies. This indicates that women's brains, like their other organs, are more vulnerable to alcohol-induced damage than men's.

Yet other studies have not shown such definitive findings. In fact, two reports appearing side by side in the *American Journal of Psychiatry* contradicted each other on the question of gender-related vulnerability to brain shrinkage in alcoholism. Clearly, more research is needed on this topic, especially because alcoholic women have received less research attention than alcoholic men despite good evidence that women may be particularly vulnerable to alcohol's effects on many key organ systems.

Brain Damage from Other Causes

People who have been drinking large amounts of alcohol for long periods of time run the risk of developing serious and persistent changes in the brain. Damage may be a result of the direct effects of alcohol on the brain or may result indirectly, from a poor general health status or from severe liver disease.

For example, thiamine deficiency is a common occurrence in people with alcoholism and results from poor overall nutrition. Thiamine, also known as vitamin B1, is an essential nutrient required by all tissues, including the brain. Thiamine is found in foods such as meat and poultry; whole grain cereals; nuts; and dried beans, peas, and soybeans. Many foods in the United States commonly are fortified with thiamine, including breads and cereals. As a result, most people consume sufficient amounts of thiamine in their diets. The typical intake for most Americans is 2 mg/day; the Recommended Daily Allowance is 1.2 mg/day for men and 1.1 mg/day for women.

Wernicke-Korsakoff Syndrome

Up to 80 percent of alcoholics, however, have a deficiency in thiamine, and some of these people will go on to develop serious brain disorders such as Wernicke-Korsakoff syndrome (WKS). WKS is a disease that consists of two separate syndromes, a short-lived and severe condition called Wernicke encephalopathy and a long-lasting and debilitating condition known as Korsakoff psychosis.

The symptoms of Wernicke encephalopathy include mental confusion, paralysis of the nerves that move the eyes (i.e., oculomotor disturbances), and difficulty with muscle coordination. For example, patients with Wernicke encephalopathy may be too confused to find their way out of a room or may not even be able to walk. Many Wernicke encephalopathy patients, however, do not exhibit all three of these signs and symptoms, and clinicians working with alcoholics must be aware that this disorder may be present even if the patient shows only one or two of them. In fact, studies performed after death indicate that many cases of thiamine deficiency-related encephalopathy may not be diagnosed in life because not all the "classic" signs and symptoms were present or recognized.

Approximately 80 to 90 percent of alcoholics with Wernicke encephalopathy also develop Korsakoff psychosis, a chronic and debilitating syndrome characterized by persistent learning and memory problems. Patients with Korsakoff's psychosis are forgetful and quickly frustrated and have difficulty with walking and coordination. Although these patients have problems remembering old information (i.e., retrograde amnesia), it is their difficulty in "laying down" new information (i.e., anterograde amnesia) that is the most striking. For example, these patients can discuss in detail an event in their lives, but an hour later might not remember ever having the conversation.

Treatment

The cerebellum, an area of the brain responsible for coordinating movement and perhaps even some forms of learning, appears to be particularly sensitive to the effects of thiamine deficiency and is the region most frequently damaged in association with chronic alcohol consumption. Administering thiamine helps to improve brain function, especially in patients in the early stages of WKS. When damage to the brain is more severe, the course of care shifts from treatment to providing support to the patient and his or her family. Custodial care may be necessary for the 25 percent of patients who have permanent brain damage and significant loss of cognitive skills.

Scientists believe that a genetic variation could be one explanation for why only some alcoholics with thiamine deficiency go on to develop severe conditions such as WKS, but additional studies are necessary to clarify how genetic variants might cause some people to be more vulnerable to WKS than others.

Liver Disease

Most people realize that heavy, long-term drinking can damage the liver, the organ chiefly responsible for breaking down alcohol into harmless byproducts and clearing it from the body. But people may not be aware that prolonged liver dysfunction, such as liver cirrhosis resulting from excessive alcohol consumption, can harm the brain, leading to a serious and potentially fatal brain disorder known as hepatic encephalopathy.

Hepatic encephalopathy can cause changes in sleep patterns, mood, and personality; psychiatric conditions such as anxiety and depression; severe cognitive effects such as shortened attention span; and problems with coordination such as a flapping or shaking of the hands (called asterixis). In the most serious cases, patients may slip into a coma (i.e., hepatic coma), which can be fatal.

New imaging techniques have enabled researchers to study specific brain regions in patients with alcoholic liver disease, giving them a better understanding of how hepatic encephalopathy develops. These studies have confirmed that at least two toxic substances, ammonia and manganese, have a role in the development of hepatic encephalopathy. Alcohol-damaged liver cells allow excess amounts of these harmful byproducts to enter the brain, thus harming brain cells.

Treatment

Physicians typically use the following strategies to prevent or treat the development of hepatic encephalopathy.

- Treatment that lowers blood ammonia concentrations, such as administering L-ornithine L-aspartate.

- Techniques such as liver-assist devices, or "artificial livers," that clear the patients' blood of harmful toxins. In initial studies, patients using these devices showed lower amounts of ammonia circulating in their blood, and their encephalopathy became less severe.

- Liver transplantation, an approach that is widely used in alcoholic cirrhotic patients with severe (i.e., end-stage) chronic liver failure. In general, implantation of a new liver results in significant improvements in cognitive function in these patients and lowers their levels of ammonia and manganese.

Alcohol and the Developing Brain

Drinking during pregnancy can lead to a range of physical, learning, and behavioral effects in the developing brain, the most serious of which is a collection of symptoms known as fetal alcohol syndrome (FAS). Children with FAS may have distinct facial features. FAS infants also are markedly smaller than average. Their brains may have less volume (i.e., microencephaly). And they may have fewer numbers of brain cells (i.e., neurons) or fewer neurons that are able to function correctly, leading to long-term problems in learning and behavior.

Treatment

Scientists are investigating the use of complex motor training and medications to prevent or reverse the alcohol-related brain damage found in people prenatally exposed to alcohol. In a study using rats, researchers used an obstacle course to teach complex motor skills, and this skills training led to a reorganization in the adult rats' brains (i.e., cerebellum), enabling them to overcome the effects of the prenatal alcohol exposure. These findings have important therapeutic implications, suggesting that complex rehabilitative motor training can improve motor performance of children, or even adults, with FAS.

Scientists also are looking at the possibility of developing medications that can help alleviate or prevent brain damage, such as that associated with FAS. Studies using animals have yielded encouraging results for treatments using antioxidant therapy and vitamin E. Other preventive therapies showing promise in animal studies include 1-octanol, which ironically is an alcohol itself. Treatment with l-octanol significantly reduced the severity of alcohol's effects on developing mouse embryos. Two molecules associated with normal development (i.e., NAP and SAL) have been found to protect nerve cells against a variety of toxins in much the same way that octanol does. And a compound (MK-801) that blocks a key brain chemical associated with alcohol withdrawal (i.e., glutamate) also is being studied. MK-801 reversed a specific learning impairment that resulted from early postnatal alcohol exposure.

Though these compounds were effective in animals, the positive results cited here may or may not translate to humans. Not drinking during pregnancy is the best form of prevention; FAS remains the leading preventable birth defect in the United States today.

Growing New Brain Cells

For decades scientists believed that the number of nerve cells in the adult brain was fixed early in life. If brain damage occurred, then, the best way to treat it was by strengthening the existing neurons, as new ones could not be added. In the 1960s, however, researchers found that new neurons are indeed generated in adulthood—a process called neurogenesis. These new cells originate from stem cells, which are cells that can divide indefinitely, renew themselves, and give rise to a variety of cell types. The discovery of brain stem cells and adult neurogenesis provides a new way of approaching the problem of alcohol-related changes in the brain and may lead to a clearer understanding of how best to treat and cure alcoholism.

For example, studies with animals show that high doses of alcohol lead to a disruption in the growth of new brain cells; scientists believe it may be this lack of new growth that results in the long-term deficits found in key areas of the brain (such as hippocampal structure and function). Understanding how alcohol interacts with brain stem cells and what happens to these cells in alcoholics is the first step in establishing whether the use of stem cell therapies is an option for treatment.

Using High-Tech Tools to Assess Alcoholic Brain Damage

Researchers studying the effects of alcohol use on the brain are aided by advanced technology such as magnetic resonance imaging (MRI), diffusion tensor imaging (DTI), positron emission tomography (PET), and electrophysiological brain mapping. These tools are providing valuable insight into how alcohol affects the brain's structure and function.

Long-term heavy drinking may lead to shrinking of the brain and deficiencies in the fibers (white matter) that carry information between brain cells (gray matter). MRI and DTI are being used together to assess the brains of patients when they first stop chronic heavy drinking and again after long periods of sobriety, to monitor for possible relapse to drinking.

Memory formation and retrieval are highly influenced by factors such as attention and motivation. Studies using MRI are helping scientists to determine how memory and attention improve with long-time abstinence from alcohol, as well as what changes take place when a patient begins drinking again. The goal of these studies is to determine which alcohol-induced effects on the brain are permanent and which ones can be reversed with abstinence.

PET imaging is allowing researchers to visualize, in the living brain, the damage that results from heavy alcohol consumption. This "snapshot" of the brain's function enables scientists to analyze alcohol's effects on various nerve cell communication systems (i.e., neurotransmitter systems) as well as on brain cell metabolism and blood flow within the brain. These studies have detected deficits in alcoholics, particularly in the frontal lobes, which are responsible for numerous functions associated with learning and memory, as well as in the cerebellum, which controls movement and coordination. PET also is a promising tool for monitoring the effects of alcoholism treatment and abstinence on damaged portions of the brain and may help in developing new medications to correct the chemical deficits found in the brains of people with alcohol dependence.

Another high-tech tool, electroencephalography (EEG), records the brain's electrical signals. Small electrodes are placed on the scalp to detect this electrical activity, which then is magnified and graphed as brain waves (i.e., neural oscillations). These brain waves show real-time activity as it happens in the brain.

Many male alcoholics have a distinctive electrophysiological profile—that is, a low amplitude of their P3 components. P3 amplitudes in women alcoholics also are reduced, although to a lesser extent than in men. For many years it was assumed that the P3 deficit observed in alcoholics was the result of alcohol's damage to the brain.

Then it was determined that while many of the clinical symptoms and electrophysiological measures associated with alcoholism return to normal after abstinence, the P3 amplitude abnormality persists. The P3 component is reduced in alcoholics compared with control subjects.

This continued deficit in long-term abstinent alcoholics suggests that P3 deficits may be a marker of risk for alcohol dependence, rather than a result of alcohol use. In fact, a number of studies have since reported low P3 amplitudes in young people who have not started drinking alcohol but who are at high risk for developing alcoholism, such as young sons of alcoholic fathers. Markers such as the P3 can help identify people who may be at greatest risk for developing problems with alcohol.

Summary

Alcoholics are not all alike. They experience different degrees of impairment, and the disease has different origins for different people. Consequently, researchers have not found conclusive evidence that any one variable is solely responsible for the brain deficits found in alcoholics. Characterizing what makes some alcoholics vulnerable to brain damage whereas others are not remains the subject of active research.

The good news is that most alcoholics with cognitive impairment show at least some improvement in brain structure and functioning within a year of abstinence, though some people take much longer. Clinicians must consider a variety of treatment methods to help people stop drinking and to recover from alcohol-related brain impairments, and tailor these treatments to the individual patient.

Advanced technology will have an important role in developing these therapies. Clinicians can use brain-imaging techniques to monitor the course and success of treatment, because imaging can reveal structural, functional, and biochemical changes in living patients over time. Promising new medications also are in the early stages of development, as researchers strive to design therapies that can help prevent alcohol's harmful effects and promote the growth of new brain cells to take the place of those that have been damaged by alcohol.

Chapter 32

Alcohol and Heart Disease

Are there cardiovascular risks associated with drinking alcohol?

Drinking too much alcohol can raise the levels of some fats in the blood (triglycerides) (tri-GLIS'er-idz). It can also lead to high blood pressure, heart failure, and an increased calorie intake. (Consuming too many calories can lead to obesity and a higher risk of developing diabetes.) Excessive drinking and binge drinking can lead to stroke. Other serious problems include fetal alcohol syndrome, cardiomyopathy (kar"de-o-mi-OP'ah-the), cardiac arrhythmia (ah-RITH'me-ah) and sudden cardiac death.

AHA Recommendation: If you drink alcohol, do so in moderation. This means an average of one to two drinks per day for men and one drink per day for women. (A drink is one 12-oz. beer, 4 oz. of wine, 1.5 oz. of 80-proof spirits, or 1 oz. of 100-proof spirits.) Drinking more alcohol increases such dangers as alcoholism, high blood pressure, obesity, stroke, breast cancer, suicide, and accidents. Also, it's not possible to predict in which people alcoholism will become a problem. Given these and other risks, the American Heart Association cautions people **not** to start drinking if they do not already drink alcohol. Consult your doctor on the benefits and risks of consuming alcohol in moderation.

"Alcohol, Wine and Cardiovascular Disease" is reproduced with permission from www.americanheart.org. © 2005, American Heart Association.

What about red wine and heart disease?

Over the past several decades, many studies have been published in science journals about how drinking alcohol may be associated with reduced mortality due to heart disease in some populations. Some researchers have suggested that the benefit may be due to wine, especially red wine. Others are examining the potential benefits of components in red wine such as flavonoids (FLAV'oh-noidz) and other antioxidants (an"tih-OK'sih-dants) in reducing heart disease risk. Some of these components may be found in other foods such as grapes or red grape juice. The linkage reported in many of these studies may be due to other lifestyle factors rather than alcohol. Such factors may include increased physical activity and a diet high in fruits and vegetables and lower in saturated fats. No direct comparison trials have been done to determine the specific effect of wine or other alcohol on the risk of developing heart disease or stroke.

Are there potential benefits of drinking wine or other alcoholic beverages?

Research is being done to find out what the apparent benefits of drinking wine or alcohol in some populations may be due to, including the role of antioxidants, an increase in HDL ("good") cholesterol or anti-clotting properties. Clinical trials of other antioxidants such as vitamin E have not shown any cardio-protective effect. Also, even if they were protective, antioxidants can be obtained from many fruits and vegetables, including red grape juice.

The best-known effect of alcohol is a small increase in HDL cholesterol. However, regular physical activity is another effective way to raise HDL cholesterol, and niacin can be prescribed to raise it to a greater degree. Alcohol or some substances such as resveratrol (res-VAIR'ah-trol) found in alcoholic beverages may prevent platelets in the blood from sticking together. That may reduce clot formation and reduce the risk of heart attack or stroke. (Aspirin may help reduce blood clotting in a similar way.) How alcohol or wine affects cardiovascular risk merits further research, but right now the American Heart Association does not recommend drinking wine or any other form of alcohol to gain these potential benefits. The AHA does recommend that to reduce your risk you should talk to your doctor about lowering your cholesterol and blood pressure, controlling your weight, getting enough exercise, and following a healthy diet. There is no scientific proof that drinking wine or any other alcoholic beverage can replace these conventional measures.

What about alcohol and pregnancy?

Pregnant women shouldn't drink alcohol in any form. It can harm the baby seriously, including causing birth defects.

What about alcohol and aspirin?

The U.S. Food and Drug Administration warns that people who take aspirin regularly should not drink alcohol. Heart disease patients should stop drinking and keep taking aspirin if their doctor prescribed it for their heart condition. Patients should not stop taking aspirin without first talking to their doctor.

Detailed Research

AHA Scientific Statement: AHA Dietary Guidelines: Revision 2000, #71-0193 *Circulation.* 2000;102:2284–2299; *Stroke.* 2000;31:2751–2766.

AHA Science Advisory: Alcohol and Heart Disease, #71-0097 *Circulation.* 1996;94:3023–3025.

AHA Science Advisory: Wine and Your Heart, #71-0199 *Circulation.* 2001;103:472–475.

Chapter 33

Alcoholic Cardiomyopathy

Definition

Alcoholic cardiomyopathy is a disorder in which excessive, habitual use of alcohol weakens the heart muscle. The heart cannot pump blood efficiently, and this in turn affects the lungs, liver, brain, and other body systems.

Causes, Incidence, and Risk Factors

Drinking alcohol in large quantities has a directly toxic effect on heart muscle cells. Alcoholic cardiomyopathy is a form of dilated cardiomyopathy caused by habitual alcohol abuse.

Alcoholic cardiomyopathy causes the weakened heart muscle to pump inefficiently, leading to heart failure. Lack of blood flow affects all parts of the body, resulting in damage to multiple tissues and organ systems.

The disorder is most commonly seen in males ages 35 to 55 years old, but it may develop in anyone who consumes too much alcohol over a long period of time.

Alcoholic cardiomyopathy may be identified as idiopathic dilated cardiomyopathy if the person's drinking history is not known.

Symptoms

Symptoms are usually absent until the disease is in an advanced stage. At that point, the symptoms occur because of heart failure.

Possible symptoms include:

- ankle, feet, and leg swelling;
- overall swelling;
- loss of appetite;
- shortness of breath, especially with activity;
- breathing difficulty while lying down;
- fatigue, weakness, faintness;
- decreased alertness or concentration;
- cough containing mucus or pink, frothy material;
- decreased urine output (oliguria);
- need to urinate at night (nocturia);
- sensation of feeling the heart beat (palpitations); and
- irregular or rapid pulse.

Signs and Tests

A health care provider will conduct a physical examination, which may reveal:

- abnormal heart sounds;
- abnormal lung sounds;
- murmurs;
- irregular or rapid heartbeat;
- weight gain;
- swollen neck veins;
- enlarged liver;
- ankle swelling; and
- low blood pressure.

Alcoholic cardiomyopathy is usually diagnosed when chronic heavy drinking is discovered as a cause of the heart failure.

The following tests may reveal signs of heart failure:

- An echocardiogram may show enlarged heart chambers, leaking valves, or reduced pumping efficiency.
- An ECG may show signs of enlarged heart chambers or rhythm abnormalities (arrhythmias).

- A chest x-ray or chest CT may show heart enlargement, fluid accumulation in the lungs and valves, and reduced pumping function.

- A complete routine laboratory study is performed to measure the hormone B-type natriuretic peptide (BNP).

- Cardiac catheterization and coronary angiography may be done to rule out coronary artery blockages as the cause for dilated heart chambers and decreased pumping function.

Treatment

You may be placed on a low-salt diet. The amount of fluids you drink may be restricted. Heart failure may be treated with diuretics (furosemide and spironolactone) to remove excessive fluid from your body, ACE inhibitors, and beta-blockers.

People with congestive heart failure and severely weakened pumping functions may receive an implantable defibrillator (ICD) to help them live longer. In some cases, a biventricular pacemaker improves the symptoms and quality of life. A single device that combines a biventricular pacemaker and an ICD may be recommended.

A heart transplant may be considered when the cardiomyopathy is not reversible. Eventually, associated nutritional deficiencies (thiamine deficiency) and abnormalities in phosphorus, potassium, or magnesium levels may require treatment.

Expectations (Prognosis)

Total abstinence from alcohol may stop the disease and improve the heart's functioning, although people with severe heart damage may not return to normal.

Once the heart damage and heart failure is irreversible, the outlook is poor.

Complications

- congestive heart failure
- heart arrhythmias, including lethal arrhythmias

Calling Your Health Care Provider

- Call your provider if you have any symptoms of heart failure or cardiomyopathy.

- Call your provider if alcoholic cardiomyopathy has been diagnosed and symptoms do not improve with treatment.

- Go to the emergency room or call 911 if severe chest pain, palpitations, or fainting occur in a person with alcoholic cardiomyopathy.

Prevention

Alcoholic cardiomyopathy is a consequence of years of excessive alcohol use. Do not use alcohol in excess. If you drink heavily and find that you cannot cut down or stop drinking, seek help.

Control other risk factors for heart disease by maintaining a healthy weight and exercising regularly. Eat a generally well-balanced, nutritious diet and avoid or minimize smoking.

Chapter 34

Alcohol and the Immune System

Chapter Contents

Section 34.1—How Does the Immune System Work? 246

Section 34.2—The Influence of Alcohol and Gender
on the Immune Response 254

Section 34.1

How Does the Immune System Work?

Excerpted from the brochure "Understanding the Immune System: How
It Works" by the National Institute of Allergy and Infectious Diseases
(NIAID, www.niaid.nih.gov), September 2003.

Introduction

The immune system is a network of cells, tissues, and organs that
work together to defend the body against attacks by "foreign" invaders. These are primarily microbes (germs)—tiny, infection-causing
organisms such as bacteria, viruses, parasites, and fungi. Because the
human body provides an ideal environment for many microbes, they
try to break in. It is the immune system's job to keep them out or, failing that, to seek out and destroy them.

When the immune system hits the wrong target or is crippled,
however, it can unleash a torrent of diseases, including allergy, arthritis, or AIDS.

The immune system is amazingly complex. It can recognize and
remember millions of different enemies, and it can produce secretions
and cells to match up with and wipe out each one of them.

The secret to its success is an elaborate and dynamic communica-
tions network. Millions and millions of cells, organized into sets and
subsets, gather like clouds of bees swarming around a hive and pass
information back and forth. Once immune cells receive the alarm, they
undergo tactical changes and begin to produce powerful chemicals.
These substances allow the cells to regulate their own growth and
behavior, enlist their fellows, and direct new recruits to trouble spots.

Self and Nonself

The key to a healthy immune system is its remarkable ability to
distinguish between the body's own cells—self—and foreign cells—
nonself. The body's immune defenses normally coexist peacefully with
cells that carry distinctive "self" marker molecules. But when immune

defenders encounter cells or organisms carrying markers that say "foreign," they quickly launch an attack.

Anything that can trigger this immune response is called an antigen. An antigen can be a microbe such as a virus, or even a part of a microbe. Tissues or cells from another person (except an identical twin) also carry nonself markers and act as antigens. This explains why tissue transplants may be rejected.

In abnormal situations, the immune system can mistake self for nonself and launch an attack against the body's own cells or tissues. The result is called an autoimmune disease. Some forms of arthritis and diabetes are autoimmune diseases. In other cases, the immune system responds to a seemingly harmless foreign substance such as ragweed pollen. The result is allergy, and this kind of antigen is called an allergen.

The Structure of the Immune System

The organs of the immune system are positioned throughout the body. They are called lymphoid organs because they are home to lymphocytes, small white blood cells that are the key players in the immune system.

Bone marrow, the soft tissue in the hollow center of bones, is the ultimate source of all blood cells, including white blood cells destined to become immune cells. The thymus is an organ that lies behind the breastbone; lymphocytes known as T lymphocytes, or just "T cells," mature in the thymus.

Lymphocytes can travel throughout the body using the blood vessels. The cells can also travel through a system of lymphatic vessels that closely parallels the body's veins and arteries. Cells and fluids are exchanged between blood and lymphatic vessels, enabling the lymphatic system to monitor the body for invading microbes. The lymphatic vessels carry lymph, a clear fluid that bathes the body's tissues.

Small, bean-shaped lymph nodes are laced along the lymphatic vessels, with clusters in the neck, armpits, abdomen, and groin. Each lymph node contains specialized compartments where immune cells congregate, and where they can encounter antigens.

Immune cells and foreign particles enter the lymph nodes via incoming lymphatic vessels or the lymph nodes' tiny blood vessels. All lymphocytes exit lymph nodes through outgoing lymphatic vessels. Once in the bloodstream, they are transported to tissues throughout the body. They patrol everywhere for foreign antigens, then gradually drift back into the lymphatic system, to begin the cycle all over again.

The spleen is a flattened organ at the upper left of the abdomen. Like the lymph nodes, the spleen contains specialized compartments where immune cells gather and work, and serves as a meeting ground where immune defenses confront antigens.

Clumps of lymphoid tissue are found in many parts of the body, especially in the linings of the digestive tract and the airways and lungs—territories that serve as gateways to the body. These tissues include the tonsils, adenoids, and appendix.

Immune Cells and Their Products

The immune system stockpiles a huge arsenal of cells, not only lymphocytes but also cell-devouring phagocytes and their relatives. Some immune cells take on all comers, while others are trained on highly specific targets. To work effectively, most immune cells need the cooperation of their comrades. Sometimes immune cells communicate by direct physical contact, sometimes by releasing chemical messengers.

The immune system stores just a few of each kind of the different cells needed to recognize millions of possible enemies. When an antigen appears, those few matching cells multiply into a full-scale army. After their job is done, they fade away, leaving sentries behind to watch for future attacks.

All immune cells begin as immature stem cells in the bone marrow. They respond to different cytokines and other signals to grow into specific immune cell types, such as T cells, B cells, or phagocytes. Because stem cells have not yet committed to a particular future, they are an interesting possibility for treating some immune system disorders. Researchers currently are investigating if a person's own stem cells can be used to regenerate damaged immune responses in autoimmune diseases and immune deficiency diseases.

B Lymphocytes

B cells and T cells are the main types of lymphocytes.

B cells work chiefly by secreting substances called antibodies into the body's fluids. Antibodies ambush antigens circulating the bloodstream. They are powerless, however, to penetrate cells. The job of attacking target cells—either cells that have been infected by viruses or cells that have been distorted by cancer—is left to T cells or other immune cells.

Each B cell is programmed to make one specific antibody. For example, one B cell will make an antibody that blocks a virus that causes the common cold, while another produces an antibody that attacks a bacterium that causes pneumonia.

When a B cell encounters its triggering antigen, it gives rise to many large cells known as plasma cells. Every plasma cell is essentially a factory for producing an antibody. Each of the plasma cells descended from a given B cell manufactures millions of identical antibody molecules and pours them into the bloodstream.

An antigen matches an antibody much as a key matches a lock. Some match exactly; others fit more like a skeleton key. But whenever antigen and antibody interlock, the antibody marks the antigen for destruction.

Antibodies belong to a family of large molecules known as immunoglobulins. Different types play different roles in the immune defense strategy.

- Immunoglobulin G, or IgG, works efficiently to coat microbes, speeding their uptake by other cells in the immune system.

- IgM is very effective at killing bacteria.

- IgA concentrates in body fluids—tears, saliva, the secretions of the respiratory tract and the digestive tract—guarding the entrances to the body.

- IgE, whose natural job probably is to protect against parasitic infections, is the villain responsible for the symptoms of allergy.

- IgD remains attached to B cells and plays a key role in initiating early B-cell response.

T Cells

Unlike B cells, T cells do not recognize free-floating antigens. Rather, their surfaces contain specialized antibody-like receptors that see fragments of antigens on the surfaces of infected or cancerous cells. T cells contribute to immune defenses in two major ways: some direct and regulate immune responses; others directly attack infected or cancerous cells.

Helper T cells, or Th cells, coordinate immune responses by communicating with other cells. Some stimulate nearby B cells to produce antibody, others call in microbe-gobbling cells called phagocytes, still others activate other T cells.

Killer T cells—also called cytotoxic T lymphocytes or CTLs—perform a different function. These cells directly attack other cells carrying certain foreign or abnormal molecules on their surfaces. CTLs are especially useful for attacking viruses because viruses often hide from other parts of the immune system while they grow inside infected cells. CTLs recognize small fragments of these viruses peeking out from the cell membrane and launch an attack to kill the cell.

In most cases, T cells only recognize an antigen if it is carried on the surface of a cell by one of the body's own MHC, or major histo-compatibility complex, molecules. MHC molecules are proteins recognized by T cells when distinguishing between self and nonself. A self MHC molecule provides a recognizable scaffolding to present a foreign antigen to the T cell.

Although MHC molecules are required for T-cell responses against foreign invaders, they also pose a difficulty during organ transplantations. Virtually every cell in the body is covered with MHC proteins, but each person has a different set of these proteins on his or her cells. If a T cell recognizes a nonself MHC molecule on another cell, it will destroy the cell. Therefore, doctors must match organ recipients with donors who have the closest MHC makeup. Otherwise the recipient's T cells will likely attack the transplanted organ, leading to graft rejection.

Natural killer (NK) cells are another kind of lethal white cell, or lymphocyte. Like killer T cells, NK cells are armed with granules filled with potent chemicals. But while killer T cells look for antigen fragments bound to self-MHC molecules, NK cells recognize cells lacking self-MHC molecules. Thus NK cells have the potential to attack many types of foreign cells.

Both kinds of killer cells slay on contact. The deadly assassins bind to their targets, aim their weapons, and then deliver a lethal burst of chemicals.

Phagocytes and Their Relatives

Phagocytes are large white cells that can swallow and digest microbes and other foreign particles. Monocytes are phagocytes that circulate in the blood. When monocytes migrate into tissues, they develop into macrophages. Specialized types of macrophages can be found in many organs, including lungs, kidneys, brain, and liver.

Macrophages play many roles. As scavengers, they rid the body of worn-out cells and other debris. They display bits of foreign antigen in a way that draws the attention of matching lymphocytes. And they churn out an amazing variety of powerful chemical signals, known as monokines, which are vital to the immune responses.

Granulocytes are another kind of immune cell. They contain granules filled with potent chemicals, which allow the granulocytes to destroy microorganisms. Some of these chemicals, such as histamine, also contribute to inflammation and allergy.

One type of granulocyte, the neutrophil, is also a phagocyte; it uses its prepackaged chemicals to break down the microbes it ingests. Eosinophils and basophils are granulocytes that "degranulate," spraying their chemicals onto harmful cells or microbes nearby.

The mast cell is a twin of the basophil, except that it is not a blood cell. Rather, it is found in the lungs, skin, tongue, and linings of the nose and intestinal tract, where it is responsible for the symptoms of allergy.

A related structure, the blood platelet, is a cell fragment. Platelets, too, contain granules. In addition to promoting blood clotting and wound repair, platelets activate some of the immune defenses.

Cytokines

Components of the immune system communicate with one another by exchanging chemical messengers called cytokines. These proteins are secreted by cells and act on other cells to coordinate an appropriate immune response. Cytokines include a diverse assortment of interleukins, interferons, and growth factors.

Some cytokines are chemical switches that turn certain immune cell types on and off.

One cytokine, interleukin 2 (IL-2), triggers the immune system to produce T cells. IL-2's immunity-boosting properties have traditionally made it a promising treatment for several illnesses. Clinical studies are ongoing to test its benefits in other diseases such as cancer, hepatitis C, and HIV infection and AIDS. Other cytokines also are being studied for their potential clinical benefit.

Other cytokines chemically attract specific cell types. These so-called chemokines are released by cells at a site of injury or infection and call other immune cells to the region to help repair the damage or fight off the invader. Chemokines often play a key role in inflammation and are a promising target for new drugs to help regulate immune responses.

Complement

The complement system is made up of about 25 proteins that work together to "complement" the action of antibodies in destroying bacteria. Complement also helps to rid the body of antibody-coated antigens (antigen-antibody complexes). Complement proteins, which cause blood vessels to become dilated and then leaky, contribute to the redness, warmth, swelling, pain, and loss of function that characterize an inflammatory response.

Complement proteins circulate in the blood in an inactive form. When the first protein in the complement series is activated—typically by antibody that has locked onto an antigen—it sets in motion a domino effect. Each component takes its turn in a precise chain of steps known as the complement cascade. The end product is a cylinder inserted into—and puncturing a hole in—the cell's wall. With fluids and molecules flowing in and out, the cell swells and bursts. Other components of the complement system make bacteria more susceptible to phagocytosis or beckon other cells to the area.

Mounting an Immune Response

Infections are the most common cause of human disease. They range from the common cold to debilitating conditions like chronic hepatitis to life-threatening diseases such as AIDS. Disease-causing microbes (pathogens) attempting to get into the body must first move past the body's external armor, usually the skin or cells lining the body's internal passageways.

The skin provides an imposing barrier to invading microbes. It is generally penetrable only through cuts or tiny abrasions. The digestive and respiratory tracts—both portals of entry for a number of microbes—also have their own levels of protection. Microbes entering the nose often cause the nasal surfaces to secrete more protective mucus, and attempts to enter the nose or lungs can trigger a sneeze or cough reflex to force microbial invaders out of the respiratory passageways. The stomach contains a strong acid that destroys many pathogens that are swallowed with food.

If microbes survive the body's front-line defenses, they still have to find a way through the walls of the digestive, respiratory, or urogenital passageways to the underlying cells. These passageways are lined with tightly packed epithelial cells covered in a layer of mucus, effectively blocking the transport of many organisms. Mucosal surfaces also secrete a special class of antibody called IgA, which in many cases is the first type of antibody to encounter an invading microbe. Underneath the epithelial layer a number of cells, including macrophages, B cells, and T cells, lie in wait for any germ that might bypass the barriers at the surface.

Next, invaders must escape a series of general defenses, which are ready to attack, without regard for specific antigen markers. These include patrolling phagocytes, NK cells, and complement.

Microbes that cross the general barriers then confront specific weapons tailored just for them. Specific weapons, which include both antibodies and T cells, are equipped with singular receptor structures that allow them to recognize and interact with their designated targets.

Bacteria, Viruses, and Parasites

The most common disease-causing microbes are bacteria, viruses, and parasites. Each uses a different tactic to infect a person, and, therefore, each is thwarted by a different part of the immune system.

Most bacteria live in the spaces between cells and are readily attacked by antibodies. When antibodies attach to a bacterium, they send signals to complement proteins and phagocytic cells to destroy the bound microbes. Some bacteria are eaten directly by phagocytes, which signal to certain T cells to join the attack. All viruses, plus a few types of bacteria and parasites, must enter cells to survive, requiring a different approach. Infected cells use their MHC molecules to put pieces of the invading microbes on the cell's surface, flagging down cytotoxic T lymphocytes to destroy the infected cell. Antibodies also can assist in the immune response, attaching to and clearing viruses before they have a chance to enter the cell.

Parasites live either inside or outside cells. Intracellular parasites such as the organism that causes malaria can trigger T-cell responses. Extracellular parasites are often much larger than bacteria or viruses and require a much broader immune attack. Parasitic infections often trigger an inflammatory response when eosinophils, basophils, and other specialized granular cells rush to the scene and release their stores of toxic chemicals in an attempt to destroy the invader. Antibodies also play a role in this attack, attracting the granular cells to the site of infection.

Section 34.2

The Influence of Alcohol and Gender on the Immune Response

Excerpted from "Influence of Alcohol and Gender on Immune Response," by Elizabeth J. Kovacs, Ph.D., and Kelly A.N. Messingham, Ph.D., *Alcohol Research & Health,* Vol. 26, No. 4, published by the National Institute on Alcohol Abuse and Alcoholism (NIAAA), 2002. For a complete list of references, see www.niaaa.nih.gov.

Clinical and experimental research has demonstrated naturally occurring gender differences in immune response, but the reasons for these differences have yet to be determined. This text examines alcohol's effects on the immune systems of both genders and the differential effects of alcohol on males' and females' immune responses. It then discusses whether alcohol-induced changes in stress hormones and in gonadal steroid hormones such as estrogen and testosterone are sufficient to trigger the observed defects in immune response and to explain gender differences in alcohol-induced immune suppression. Finally, the text considers the reasons why women are at higher risk than men of developing liver disease at any given level of alcohol intake.

Alcohol and Immune Responses

An overwhelming amount of evidence reveals that both acute and chronic alcohol exposure suppresses all branches of the immune system, including early responses to infection and the tumor surveillance system. For example, there is a decrease in the ability to recruit and activate germ-killing white blood cells and an increase in the incidence of breast cancer in people who consume alcohol.

Some experts suspect that alcohol exerts an "all-or-none" effect on immune response—that is, the presence or absence of alcohol, rather than its amount, dictates the immune response. Other researchers believe that low doses of alcohol—the amount equivalent to a glass of wine—can confer health benefits, including protection against damage to the cardiovascular and immune systems. Such benefits, if they are present, may be attributable to antioxidants in alcoholic beverages such as red wine. In any case, health experts agree that the beneficial effects of antioxidants in some alcoholic beverages are lost if the level of alcohol consumption is elevated.

There are several mechanisms by which alcohol impedes immune function. First, alcohol impairs the ability of white blood cells known as neutrophils to migrate to sites of injury and infection, a process called chemotaxis. In addition, removing germ-fighting white blood cells (macrophages) and proteins that act as messengers between immune cells (cytokines) from an animal that has not been given alcohol and culturing them in the presence of alcohol, or isolating these cells from humans or animals after administering alcohol, has been shown to alter production of these macrophages and cytokines.

Rodent studies also show that animals are more vulnerable to infection after chronic or acute exposure to alcohol. This increase in susceptibility is equally dramatic in human patients who sustain traumatic injury. Those who have consumed alcohol prior to their injury are six times more likely to die than are alcohol-free patients with comparable injuries. The mechanisms responsible for this increased mortality are unknown, but it is thought that alcohol compromises the immune system's ability to quickly fight infection by unidentified invaders—a function of the innate immune system.

Gender Differences in Immune Response Following Alcohol Exposure

To date, only a handful of studies have directly examined gender differences in the effects of alcohol on inflammatory and immune responses. These studies were conducted in rodents and employed different methods, including varying the quantity and duration of alcohol exposure. These reports show that in the absence of alcohol exposure, inflammatory and immune responses are stronger in females than in males. However, the increased immunity in females is nullified by alcohol exposure. For example, in one study, proliferation of white blood cells was suppressed in alcohol-exposed female rats; however, investigation also showed that alcohol induced an increase in antibody production. In two other studies, female rats were less able to fight infection when intoxicated. The mechanisms driving these effects remain uncertain. One possibility is that gender differences in inflammatory and immune responses following alcohol exposure stem from alcohol-induced changes in the production of gonadal steroid hormones, such as estrogen and testosterone.

In general, estrogen stimulates immune responses and testosterone is immunosuppressive. During their reproductive years, females have more vigorous cellular and humoral immune responses than do males. This heightened immunity in females is evidenced by a more developed thymus, higher antibody concentrations, and a greater ability to reject tumors and transplanted tissues. Ironically, the enhanced immune function in women of reproductive age is associated with a higher prevalence of autoimmune disorders than is found in postmenopausal women or in men.

The effects of alcohol on production of the gonadal steroid hormones are well documented. In women, chronic alcohol exposure causes an initial increase in estrogen levels, followed by a marked decrease. In men, chronic alcohol consumption causes a decrease in testosterone. The alcohol-induced decrease in testosterone levels is significant enough to cause shrinkage (atrophy) of the testes, impotence, and loss of secondary sex characteristics.

Estrogen and Cytokines

From the limited information available, it is thought that fluctuations in estrogen may alter immune cell function, in part, by increasing or decreasing the production of cytokines. There are several pieces of evidence for this idea. First, researchers found that removing the ovaries of adult rodents (eliminating the primary source of estrogen) lowered the level of cytokine production by certain types of white blood cells. This lower level of cytokine production was comparable to that of males and could be restored by administering estrogen.

In other studies, drugs known as estrogen receptor antagonists inhibited the effect of estrogen on immune cells in animals. While receptor antagonists are bound to the same receptors that normally interact with estrogen, they block the binding of the hormone. Thus, it is possible to alter immune responses by blocking estrogen at one of its sites of action in white blood cells.

Further evidence that estrogen affects immune cell function, in part, by altering production of cytokines comes from cell-culture studies in which estrogen was added to a culture of white blood cells. The effects of estrogen on cytokine production by immune target cells may involve direct interaction (binding) of the hormone and hormone receptors within those cells. The idea of direct effects of estrogen on target cells is supported by the existence of estrogen receptors not only in reproductive tissues, including the uterus, ovaries, and testes, where one would expect the hormone's actions to occur, but also in white blood cells.

Alcohol, Stress Responses, and Immunity

Like other stressors, alcohol stimulates a neuroendocrine network known as the hypothalamic–pituitary–adrenal (HPA) axis, resulting in a dampening of the immune response. This process begins with activation of the hypothalamus (near the base of the brain), which produces a molecule called corticotropin-releasing hormone (CRH). This triggers the pituitary gland (below the hypothalamus) to secrete adrenal corticotropic hormone (ACTH). Finally, ACTH stimulates the adrenal glands (above the kidneys) to release glucocorticoids (cortisol in humans and corticosterone in rodents). These steroid hormones, which direct the activity of many cell types, are transmitted throughout the body in the blood. At high levels, they suppress inflammatory and immune responses. Several studies have documented that under resting (baseline) conditions and in response to stress, females have higher levels of glucocorticoids than do men. Furthermore, estrogen stimulates glucocorticoid production in females, whereas testosterone suppresses its production in both male and female subjects. Alcohol exposure stimulates glucocorticoid production in both males and females. Thus, there are two possible pathways by which alcohol-induced changes in steroid hormones could suppress immune responses in females, whereas there is only one such potential pathway in males. Further study will be required to determine if and how the two pathways interact to mediate alcohol-induced effects on immune function in females.

Gender, Alcohol, and Liver Damage

Epidemiologic evidence clearly indicates that the adverse consequences of alcohol consumption, including severe liver disease, such as alcoholic cirrhosis, develop more quickly and require lower levels of alcohol exposure for females than for males. At any given level of alcohol intake, women are at higher risk than men of developing liver disease. It has been shown that a daily alcohol ingestion of as low as two drinks per day increases the risk of developing cirrhosis in women, although at least four drinks per day are required to increase this risk in men. These observations were made taking into account differences in body weight, fat distribution, body water, and other potentially confounding variables.

The mechanisms responsible for the gender difference in alcohol-related liver injury are currently under intense investigation and have been better described in animal studies. Performing studies in animals allows the investigator to include experiments involving hormone manipulations that would not be feasible in human experimentation. These experiments could include removing ovaries (the primary site of estrogen production) or giving a hormone receptor antagonist (i.e., a molecule that blocks the hormone from binding to its receptor).

It is possible that gender differences in alcohol-related liver disease could be explained by gender differences in:

- The breakdown and elimination of alcohol and its byproducts, including the resulting differences in acetaldehyde levels within the liver.

- The level of activation of inflammatory and immune cells within the liver in response to alcohol ingestion, including Kupffer cells. Upon stimulation, these cells produce free oxygen radicals and cytokines, which damage and destroy liver cells.

- The amount of alcohol that is metabolized in the stomach (first-pass metabolism). Some research has indicated that women break down less alcohol in the stomach than men do, leading to higher blood alcohol levels—and hence greater risk to the liver—for a given dose of alcohol.

Summary

Taken together, these studies show clearly that there are dramatic suppressive effects of both acute and chronic alcohol exposure on inflammation and immunity, regardless of gender. This results in decreased ability of the immune system to fight infections and tumors. The decrease in immunity after consumption of larger quantities of alcohol is in marked contrast to the effects of very low levels of some alcoholic beverages (such as a single glass of red wine), which contain immunoprotective antioxidants. By depressing estrogen levels, chronic or acute alcohol exposure may cause females to lose the important boost to the immune system that estrogen normally provides. This could act additively or synergistically with an elevation in immunosuppressive glucocorticoids (through activation of the HPA axis) to attenuate immune response, thus leading to a weakened ability to fight infections and tumors. Finally, although chronic alcohol exposure causes liver damage in both males and females, it takes less alcohol and shorter periods of consumption to raise the risk of liver damage for females than for males. Like the observed gender differences in alcohol-induced immune suppression, this effect may involve the combined effect of stimulating glucocorticoid production and inhibiting estrogen production.

Further studies will be required to determine whether the alcohol-induced changes in gonadal steroid hormone production are sufficient to explain the observed gender differences in immune function. These will require using a similar model system in which both males and females are given alcohol at doses designed to raise blood alcohol levels to the same extent, after which immune responses can be examined. Because of the complexity of studying these parameters in humans, it may be necessary to conduct these studies in animal models of alcohol exposure. By using animal models, it will also be possible to manipulate the levels of estrogen, testosterone, and glucocorticoids by removing organs (ovaries, testes, and adrenal glands, respectively) and administering hormones and hormone antagonists to determine the role of those hormones in regulating inflammatory and immune responses after alcohol exposure.

Chapter 35

Alcohol Consumption, Kidney Disease, and High Blood Pressure

For many adults, minimal alcohol intake usually causes no problems. Some studies have shown that one to two drinks a day may help to prevent heart disease. Excess drinking can cause many medical problems. It can cause heart disease, liver disease, and even kidney disease. It can also cause high blood pressure (HBP). HBP may lead to stroke, heart disease, and kidney disease. Medical problems from drinking happen more rapidly in women than in men. Drinking is also more dangerous for older people than for younger people. In one study, African-American men who only had one to two drinks a day were more likely to have HBP.[1,2]

Safe Alcohol Consumption

Men should not have more than two drinks a day. Women and older adults should not have more than one drink a day. One drink can be a 12-ounce bottle of beer, one glass of wine, or one ounce (one shot) of whiskey. Some people should not drink at all. These are people advised by their doctor not to drink at all. Most people taking medications should not drink. Drinking can complicate how medications work. You should check with your doctor about drinking alcohol while

"What is the impact of alcohol consumption for someone with kidney disease and high blood pressure?" is reprinted with permission from http://www .aakp.org. This article originally appeared in *Kidney Beginnings: The Magazine*, Vol. 3, No. 3, September/October 2004. © 2004 American Association of Kidney Patients.

on medication. Even if you are only using over-the-counter (OTC) medications, check with your doctor. Also, pregnant women should not drink.

Drinking Alcohol and HBP

More than two drinks a day can increase your chance of developing HBP.[3] HBP is the number two cause of kidney failure. If you have HBP, alcohol can make it harder for you to keep your blood pressure controlled. People with HBP should be extra careful about drinking alcohol. It may interfere with their medications and increase their blood pressure.

Drinking Alcohol and Your Heart

People who only drink a little are less likely to have heart disease. They are less likely to die from heart disease than people who do not drink any alcohol or those who drink a lot. Small amounts of alcohol help to protect against heart disease. Heart disease can lead to kidney problems. If you do not drink, you should not start drinking just to try to help your heart. You can help your heart by exercising and following a healthy diet. If you do drink, keep it to less than two drinks a day.

Drinking Alcohol and Your Kidneys

More than 20 million Americans have kidney disease. Kidney disease is often "silent" in its early stages. This means that you may not see or feel any symptoms. For many people, kidney disease can often be treated when detected early. People who have an increased risk of developing kidney disease should have a test for protein in their urine and a blood test to check their level of kidney function.

Drinking alcohol can hurt your kidneys in many ways and can increase the chance of needing dialysis.[4,5,6] It may damage the kidney cells. It increases your chance of developing HBP, a leading cause of kidney disease. Drinking alcohol can interfere with your medicines and make it harder to control your pressure.

Drinking alcohol can cause the kidneys to increase urinary output. This can lead to dehydration. More than two drinks a day can cause a rise in blood pressure.[7,8] The carbohydrate load from drinking can cause obesity. This could increase the risk of diabetes and diabetic kidney disease. Drinking can interfere with the blood chemistries and increase the ability of the body to protect the kidneys.[9] Many people who drink are more likely to smoke. Smoking also causes kidney disease.

Other Medical Problems from Drinking Alcohol

Drinking alcohol can interfere with your sleep. It also lowers the body's immune system, which makes it easier for a person to get sick. There are other problems drinking causes for men. Drinking alcohol decreases the male hormone testosterone, which leads to decreased sexual function. Drinking also causes damage to unborn children.

Alcohol moves quickly into the brain and can impair thinking. It can increase the chance of a person mixing up or even missing medications. Alcohol also goes to the liver and can affect how the liver handles different medications. This can also affect blood levels of medications. It can cause the levels to be too high or too low and this can be dangerous. Alcohol can irritate your stomach, causing heartburn and eventually ulcers. People who drink are more likely to have cancer of the mouth, esophagus, stomach, and intestines. Drinking leads to destruction of liver cells, called cirrhosis. This can lead to liver failure, which is a fatal condition.

Heavy alcohol drinking may cause some of the following medical problems:

- heart disease
- high blood pressure
- stroke
- liver disease
- kidney disease
- heartburn and stomach ulcers
- lowered immune system
- sexual dysfunction
- sleep disorders
- cancer

Summary

Drinking alcohol can be dangerous for your kidneys. This is especially true if you have HBP or kidney disease. Always check with your doctor to make sure it is safe for you to drink. Even if it is safe, it is important to drink in moderation. One to two drinks a day for men and one drink a day for women and elderly. Being smart about drinking alcohol is another way to take care of your body.

References

1. National Kidney Foundation. Alcohol and Your Health. [Web document: www.kidney.org/atoz/atozItem.cfm?id=46—accessed 7-6-04].

2. Fuchs FD, Chambless LE, Whelton PK, Nieto FJ, Heiss G. Alcohol consumption and the incidence of hypertension: The Atherosclerosis Risk in Communities Study. *Hypertension.* 2001; 37(5): 1242–1250.

3. Cushman WC. Alcohol consumption and hypertension. *J Clin Hypertens.* 2001 3(3): 166–170.

4. Cecchin E, De Marchi S. Alcohol misuse and renal damage. *Addict Biol.* 1996; 1(1): 7–17.

5. Heidland A, Horl WH, Schaefer RM, Teschner M, Weipert J, Heidbreder E. Role of alcohol in clinical nephrology. *Klin Wochenschr.* 1985; 63(18): 948–958.

6. Perneger TV, Whelton PK, Puddey IB, Klag MJ. Risk of end-stage renal disease associated with alcohol consumption. *Am J Epidemiol.* 1999; 150(12): 1275–1281.

7. Puddey IB, Beilin LJ, Vandongen R, et al. Evidence for a direct effect of alcohol consumption on blood pressure in normotensive men. A randomised controlled trial. *Hypertension* 1985; 7: 707–713.

8. Smith RM, Spargo RM, King RA, et al. Risk factors for hypertension in Kimberley Aborigines. *Med J Aust* 1992; 156: 562–566.

9. Vamvakas S, Teschner M, Bahner U, Heidland A. Alcohol abuse: potential role in electrolyte disturbances and kidney diseases. *Clin Nephrol.* 1998; 49(4): 205–213.

Chapter 36

Alcohol Consumption and Nerve Damage

Definition

Alcoholic neuropathy is a disorder involving decreased nerve functioning caused by damage that results from excessive drinking of alcohol.

Causes, Incidence, and Risk Factors

The cause of alcoholic neuropathy is controversial but may be the toxic effect of alcohol on nerve tissue. It is likely also associated with nutritional deficiencies and may be indistinguishable from nutrition-related neuropathies such as beriberi.

The most common symptoms are numbness, tingling, burning feet, or weakness. In severe cases, however, the autonomic nerves (those that regulate internal body functions) may be involved.

Prolonged heavy use of alcohol, or alcoholism that is present for 10 years or more indicates high risk for alcoholic neuropathy.

Symptoms

- numbness
- abnormal sensations (paresthesia)—"pins and needles"
- painful sensations

"Alcoholic neuropathy" © 2006 A.D.A.M., Inc. Reprinted with permission.

- muscle weakness
- muscle cramps or muscle aches
- heat intolerance, especially after exercise
- impotence (in men)
- difficulty urinating
  - incontinence (leaking urine)
  - feeling of incomplete bladder emptying
  - difficulty beginning to urinate
- constipation
- diarrhea
- nausea, vomiting

Additional symptoms that may be associated with this disease:

- swallowing difficulty
- speech impairment
- loss of muscle function or feeling
- muscle contractions or spasm
- muscle atrophy
- dysfunctional movement
- hoarseness or changing voice
- eyelid drooping (ptosis)

Note: Changes in muscle strength and/or sensation usually occur on both sides of the body and are more common in the legs than in the arms. Symptoms may develop gradually and progressively become worse over time.

Signs and Tests

Results of a neurological exam may be abnormal. Reflexes may be reduced and localized nerve abnormalities may be present. Neurologic deficits are usually symmetrical (affecting both sides of the body).

Signs of autonomic nervous system dysfunction may be present. Eye inspection may show decreased pupil response or other abnormality. Blood pressure may show orthostatic changes (a fall in blood pressure when the person rises to a standing position).

Lab tests may be performed as indicated by the history, signs, and symptoms to rule out other possible causes of neuropathy.

- Nutritional studies may show deficiencies of thiamine (vitamin B-1), pyridoxine (vitamin B-6), pantothenic acid and biotin, vitamin B-12, folic acid, niacin (vitamin B-3), vitamin A, or other deficiencies. Alcoholism is a risk factor for nutritional deficiency.

- Serum chemistries may show abnormalities.

- Nerve conduction tests and EMG (a test of electrical activity in muscles) may be used to determine the extent of neurologic damage. Nerve biopsy may be used to rule out other possible causes of the signs and symptoms.

- An upper GI and small bowel series may show decreased motility (movement), delayed emptying of the stomach, or other abnormalities. This study may be used to rule out physical obstruction as a cause of vomiting or other GI (gastrointestinal) symptoms.

- EGD (esophagogastroduodenoscopy) is used to rule out physical obstruction as a cause of gastrointestinal (GI) symptoms.

- Isotope studies may indicate gastroparesis (decreased gastric motility).

- VCUG (voiding cystourethrogram) may show decreased bladder emptying caused by damage to the nerves controlling the bladder.

Other tests may be performed to determine the presence and extent of other neurologic losses.

Treatment

Treatment goals (assuming the immediate alcohol problem has been addressed) include controlling symptoms, maximizing ability to function independently, and preventing injury. It is important to supplement the diet with vitamins including thiamine and folic acid.

Physical therapy and/or use of orthopedic appliances such as splints may be necessary to maximize muscle function and to maintain useful positioning of the limbs.

Medication may be used if necessary to treat pain or uncomfortable sensations. Response to medications varies. The least amount of medication needed to reduce symptoms is advised, to reduce dependence and other side effects of chronic use.

Common medications may include over-the-counter analgesics such as aspirin, ibuprofen, or acetaminophen to reduce pain. Stabbing pains may respond to tricyclic antidepressants or anticonvulsant medications such as phenytoin, gabapentin, or carbamazepine.

Positioning, or the use of a bed frame that keeps the covers off the legs, may reduce pain for some people.

Treatment of autonomic dysfunction (such as blood pressure problems, difficulty with urination, and slow gastrointestinal movement) may be necessary. Treatment may be chronic and long term, and response to treatment varies.

Many treatments may be tried before finding one that is successful in reducing symptoms. Wearing elastic stockings, eating extra salt, sleeping with the head elevated, or using medications such as fludrocortisone may reduce postural blood pressure changes (orthostatic hypotension).

Manual expression of urine, intermittent catheterization, or medications such as bethanechol may be necessary to treat bladder dysfunction.

Impotence, diarrhea, constipation, or other symptoms are treated when necessary. These symptoms may respond poorly to treatment.

It is important to protect arms and legs with reduced sensation from being injured. This may include checking the temperature of bath water to prevent burns, change in footwear, frequent inspection of shoes to reduce injury caused by pressure or objects in the shoes, or other measures. Extremities should be guarded to prevent injury from pressure.

Use of alcohol should be stopped to reduce progression of the damage. Treatment of alcoholism may include psychiatric interventions, social support such as AA (Alcoholics Anonymous), medications, and behavior modification.

Expectations (Prognosis)

Damage to nerves from alcoholic neuropathy is usually permanent and may be progressive if alcohol use continues. Symptoms vary from mild discomfort to severe disability. The disorder is usually not life threatening, but may severely compromise the quality of life.

Complications

- disability
- chronic discomfort or pain
- injury to extremities

Calling Your Health Care Provider

Call for an appointment with your health care provider if symptoms indicate alcoholic neuropathy may be present.

Prevention

Avoid or minimize alcohol use. Total abstinence from alcohol may be necessary for persons with alcoholism.

Chapter 37

Alcohol and Sleep

Many people think of alcohol as a substance that can help them relax after a long day at the office or even act as a sleeping aid after a stressful or active day.

But a drink before bed can have a serious effect on sleep, often aggravating insomnia rather than eliminating it. And for those people at risk for alcohol dependence, drinking regularly before bed, over time, could lead to dependency.

In fact, ongoing research at the Addiction Research Center at the University of Michigan (U-M) Health System shows a strong relationship between alcohol dependence and insomnia, defined as trouble falling asleep, staying asleep, or feeling dissatisfied with sleep. The study revealed that up to 75 percent of people surveyed who were alcohol dependent had difficulty with insomnia. However, alcohol's effect on sleep is not limited to those who are alcohol dependent.

"Alcohol disrupts sleep," says Kirk Brower, M.D., a U-M addiction psychiatrist who leads the research. "It may help people initially fall asleep, but as it wears off when blood alcohol levels drop during sleep, it will cause a person to wake up or have restless sleep."

Alcohol dependence also affects other areas of a person's life. When a person is alcohol dependent, he or she may drink more than intended, even though there may be a desire to stop or cut down. Due to an impaired control over alcohol, a person who is alcohol dependent

"Alcohol before bed: No Rx for insomnia" is reprinted with permission from the University of Michigan Health System, www.med.umich.edu. Copyright © 2002 Regents of the University of Michigan.

will continue to drink despite adverse consequences. Alcoholism often refers to a severe, chronic, and progressive form of alcohol dependence, which worsens over time without treatment.

A vicious cycle can develop when people become dependent on alcohol to help them sleep. The alcohol may work initially, but over time, it can disrupt sleep, causing a person to feel the need to drink even more before bed to fall asleep. Ultimately, Brower says, this cycle leads to an increased use of alcohol.

"There's really a spectrum of drinking before bed," says Brower. "Some people have one drink, the so-called 'nightcap,' while other may drink more heavily, causing an even greater disruption to sleep. But sleep laboratory tests have also shown that even one drink before bed can be disruptive to sleep."

Taking an even closer look at the effect of alcohol on sleep, Brower and his colleagues at U-M have studied the sleeping patterns of people who had been diagnosed as alcohol dependent. The study was based on the patients' self-reporting of their sleep patterns and overnight stays at a U-M sleep laboratory.

The study followed the patients for about five months after they began treatment for alcohol dependence. The researchers found that those people who complained the most about sleep, experienced the most insomnia, and had the most disruptive sleep while at the sleep laboratory, were more likely to relapse to alcohol use and dependence then those who did not complain of insomnia.

Following the study, Brower says he and his colleagues decided to explore ways to help alcohol dependent people with their sleep problems to prevent them from using an alcoholic "nightcap" as a solution.

Alcohol dependence is often a matter of life and death, says Brower. In many cases, it can lead to automobile accidents, liver and brain disease, and some forms of cancer. It can also impair relationships and job performance, taking a toll on a person's entire life.

"We are always looking for ways to help people with sleep and other problems without resorting to sleeping pills that have some abuse potential because they are habit forming," says Brower. "There are a variety of other medications out on the market that are not necessarily designed for sleep, but are used to treat other disorders such as depression or epilepsy. We've found that some of those medications work quite well in people with alcohol dependence."

Sometimes, however, the first and most difficult step for a person facing alcohol dependence is to admit they have a problem. Often, Brower says, it is the people surrounding that person that initially recognize there is a problem.

"For people who don't think they have a problem, we may ask them to demonstrate that by abstaining completely from alcohol for several weeks or longer. People who can abstain readily at will are unlikely to have alcohol dependence. People who cannot are candidates for treatment.

But there is treatment for alcohol dependence such as various forms of counseling and medications like disulfiram and naltrexone. Brower is the executive director of Chelsea Arbor Treatment Center, which provides these treatments.

"Treatment works," Brower says. "Studies have shown that about two thirds of people who undergo treatment for the condition either significantly reduce their drinking or are able to abstain from alcohol completely."

Facts about the effect of alcohol on sleep:

- For one in ten Americans who are alcohol dependent, a drink before bed can have a serious effect on their sleep, in most cases creating insomnia rather than eliminating it.

- A recent study conducted by the Addiction Research Center at the U-M Health System showed that up to 75 percent of people who are alcohol dependent experience insomnia.

- Drinking before bed can develop into a vicious cycle. When one drink isn't enough to avoid sleeplessness or restless sleep, most often alcohol consumption is increased before bed to aid with sleep.

- About two thirds of people who undergo treatment for alcohol dependency either significantly reduce their drinking or are able to abstain from its use. Often it's necessary to correct other problems, such as sleep disorders, that may result in alcohol use to treat the dependence successfully.

Chapter 38

Alcohol and Cancer

Chapter Contents

Section 38.1—Overview of Alcohol Consumption and
the Risk of Cancer 276

Section 38.2—Confusion Regarding the
Alcohol-Cancer Link 278

Section 38.3—Ingredient in Alcohol Related to the
Formation of Cancer 282

Section 38.1

Overview of Alcohol Consumption and the Risk of Cancer

"PLWC Feature: Alcohol and Cancer," from Knowledge and News Section of www.plwc.org. Reprinted with permission from the American Society of Clinical Oncology. © 2005 American Society of Clinical Oncology. All rights reserved.

Drinking alcohol has long been an accepted part of social activities in many cultures. But increasing research is showing that regular use of alcohol can increase chances of developing cancer. Most cancer experts recommend that those who do not already drink not start, and that others drink only occasionally and in moderation, if at all.

Drinking Alcohol Regularly Raises the Risk of Developing Cancer

Breast cancer. New research shows that regular drinking, even amounts averaging around one drink a day, can raise a woman's lifetime risk of breast cancer by about 7%. The risk appears to increase with the amount of alcohol a woman drinks.

Oral cancers. Regular use of alcohol greatly increases the risk of cancers of the inside of the mouth. Those who drink are six times more likely to develop such cancers than nondrinkers. Using tobacco in any form raises risk as well, and those who both drink and use are at even higher risk.

Esophageal cancer. Heavy drinking over a long period of time raises the risk of developing cancer of the esophagus, the tube that connects the throat to the stomach. Tobacco use raises risk by itself, and the combination of alcohol use further raises risk.

Laryngeal cancer. Frequent drinking raises the risk of cancer of the larynx, the "voice box" at the upper end of the windpipe in the throat. Using tobacco products of any kind raises risk as well, and the use of both alcohol and tobacco raises the risk even more.

Liver cancer. In the United States, heavy use of alcohol is the main cause of cirrhosis of the liver, which increases the risk of liver cancer more than any other single risk factor.

Colon cancer. Most studies suggest heavy drinking raises colon cancer risk. Some evidence suggests very small amounts of red wine—one or two servings weekly—may reduce risk. Most experts believe more research is needed to understand how alcohol affects a person's risk of developing colon cancer.

How Alcohol May Influence Cancer Risk

Scientists do not fully know how alcohol raises a person's risk of cancer. There are several ideas.

- Alcohol can increase production of estrogen, a naturally occurring hormone known to increase risk of several cancers, including breast, ovarian, and uterine cancer.

- In the liver, alcohol can change substances known as procarcinogens into carcinogens (cancer-causing substances). An excess of carcinogens may contribute to cirrhosis of the liver, the major risk factor of liver cancer.

- In the colon, alcohol can interfere with folate, a B vitamin protective against cancer. And alcohol contains nitrosamines, chemicals known to raise cancer risk.

Is It "Safer" to Drink Beer or Wine, Compared to Hard Liquor?

Drinks with a lower percentage of alcohol—such as beer—are usually served in larger amounts than wine or liquor, so the amount of alcohol consumed per serving is usually about the same. A 12-ounce glass of beer, a 5-ounce glass of wine, and a 1.5-ounce shot of whiskey all contain the same amount of alcohol—about 17 grams.

Alcohol and the Heart

Research suggests very moderate amounts of red wine may reduce the risk of heart disease. But such protection is absent among some groups, such as blacks, and even small amounts raise the risk of some kinds of cancer. And the more any person drinks, the greater the risk of high blood pressure, obesity, stroke, and other diseases. The American Heart Association does not recommend alcohol use to reduce heart disease risk.

Section 38.2

Confusion Regarding the Alcohol-Cancer Link

"Cancer Experts Call for 'Alcohol Facts' Labels: Troubling Survey Shows Confusion About Alcohol-Cancer Link is Rising Sharply," September 20, 2005, is reprinted with permission from the American Institute for Cancer Research.

The American Institute for Cancer Research (AICR) has urged the federal government to add basic health information to labels of beer, wine, and distilled spirits products.

The proposed "Alcohol Facts" panel would carry information about health risks and calorie content, a step the cancer experts say is needed to combat a striking drop in public awareness of the connection between alcohol consumption and chronic diseases like cancer.

"Recent headlines associating possible health benefits with moderate consumption of alcohol in general and red wine in particular have confused Americans about the real risks involved with drinking," said AICR Nutrition Advisor Karen Collins, R.D.

"Labels on food packages help people make their own informed decisions about what they eat," Collins said. "We think it's time for similar labels on alcoholic beverages to help people sort through the confusion and weigh possible benefits against proven risks."

In a letter to the Chief of the Regulations and Procedures Division of the U.S. Alcohol and Tobacco Tax and Trade Bureau, AICR Executive Vice President Kelly Browning said: "At a time when the aging American population is recognizing that diet and physical activity are directly connected to chronic disease and overweight and obesity, having standardized information about the alcohol and calorie content on the labels of beer, wine, and distilled spirits products will be an in important way for all of us to make better informed decisions about how much beverage alcohol we consume."

The cancer experts point to research showing a convincing link between excessive alcohol consumption and cancers of the mouth, pharynx, larynx, esophagus, and liver. Evidence linking alcohol to colorectal and breast cancers is slightly less strong, but the experts judge the link probable, while evidence linking alcohol to lung cancer is considered possible.

Apart from this direct evidence, AICR also suggested that alcohol's high caloric load can contribute to obesity, which is itself a separate risk factor for many cancers and other chronic health conditions.

Awareness of Cancer Link Dropping, Survey Shows

According to a new survey, the number of Americans who correctly identify alcohol as a risk factor for cancer has dropped from 42 percent in 2001 to 33 percent today.

"It is very troubling that only 1 in 3 Americans recognizes that alcohol consumption has been convincingly linked to cancer," said Collins. "Between 2001 and 2003 the number dropped from 42 percent to 38 percent, and this latest, further drop suggests that we're looking at a trend that will ultimately have serious repercussions on public health."

In this year's survey, 1,010 adult Americans were telephoned at random and read a list of 28 factors, including actual risk factors (such as tobacco, obesity, and diets low in vegetables and fruits) and many others that have no proven cancer link (such as cell phones and stress). The list of factors was based on the most commonly asked questions about cancer risk received by AICR's Nutrition Hotline. Survey respondents were asked whether they believed these factors are linked to increased cancer risk. [Note: The complete Facts vs. Fears Survey Table at www.aicr.org/survey contains year-by-year breakdowns of survey responses, with each potential risk factor ranked by popularity. The scientific evidence for each potential cancer link, graded as "convincing," "probable," "possible" or "insufficient evidence/no proven link," is also provided.]

The drop in awareness of the alcohol-cancer link is the one of the only observable changes that has taken place in American attitudes about cancer risk, according to the survey. More importantly, the downward trend shows no sign of leveling off.

Red Wine Studies Likely Source of Confusion, Experts Say

Recent studies on alcohol and heart health and on specific components of red wine that display cancer-fighting potential in vitro have clouded the issue in the public's mind, Collins said.

Some of these studies have suggested that alcohol itself inhibits the formation of blood platelets, reducing undesirable clotting; it may also raise HDL ("good") cholesterol. Red wine contains substances called polyphenols (such as the much-studied resveratrol) that are potent antioxidants and anti-inflammatory agents, which may also benefit heart health. Resveratrol has also been shown to exhibit a range of potential cancer-fighting activities in laboratory studies.

But the key issue, Collins said, is that all of these possible health benefits are associated with moderate drinking. And many Americans who consider their drinking "moderate" might be surprised to learn how AICR, the U.S. Department of Agriculture, and other health organizations define the term.

"AICR Guidelines recommend that those who wish to consume alcohol not exceed one drink a day for women, and two drinks a day for men," said Collins. (One drink is defined as 12 ounces of beer, 5 ounces of wine, or 1.5 ounces of 80-proof liquor.)

Although the possible benefits of moderate consumption demand further study, there is a wealth of clear and convincing evidence that excessive consumption of alcohol is associated with increases in blood pressure, triglyceride levels, and stroke risk, as well as with cancers of the mouth, pharynx, larynx, and esophagus (especially among those who drink and smoke simultaneously), liver, colon, and rectum.

Collins stressed that even moderate alcohol consumption has been shown to increase risk for breast cancer by a small but significant amount.

The effect of alcohol consumption on weight management also concerns AICR experts. Collins said that alcoholic drinks are a significant source of calories without nutrients.

"Even a glass or two of wine makes it more likely that you'll unthinkingly exceed your caloric needs for the day. Over time, that means weight gain, and that means increased risk for cancer, heart disease, diabetes, and a host of other chronic conditions."

It's important to remember that there are healthier, more comprehensive ways to get the cancer-preventive, heart-protective benefits that may be associated with moderate alcohol consumption.

"A diet that's high in a variety of fruits, vegetables, whole grains, and beans provides an arsenal of polyphenols and other disease-preventive substances and nutrients," Collins said. Combining such a power-packed diet with increased physical activity bestows pervasive health benefits that come without any of the clear risks associated with excessive alcohol consumption.

The Facts on the Proposed Alcohol Facts Panel on beverage alcohol products that AICR is suggesting to the U.S. Alcohol and Tobacco Tax and Trade Bureau would contain the following information in a standardized format:

- serving size

- amount of alcohol in fluid ounces/serving

- percentage alcohol by volume

- number of calories/serving

- definition of a "standard drink" (12 fluid ounces of beer, 5 fluid ounces for wine, and 1.5 fluid ounces for distilled spirits)

- number of standard drinks/container

- an admonition to drink moderately (1 drink/day for women, 2/day for men)—if drinking at all—with reference to the *Dietary Guidelines for Americans 2005*

In the letter to the Chief of the Regulations and Procedures Division, AICR's Browning concluded by urging the Bureau to permit bottlers to provide this health information immediately, on a voluntary basis, until changes to the Bureau's regulations can be enacted.

"[The voluntary labeling] will be a valuable first step in promoting healthy and informed purchasing and consumption decisions," Browning said.

Section 38.3

Ingredient in Alcohol
Related to the Formation of Cancer

"Finding May Explain Link Between Alcohol and Certain Cancers," from a press release by the National Institute on Alcohol Abuse and Alcoholism (NIAAA, www.niaaa.nih.gov) and the National Institutes of Health (NIH), August 3, 2005.

Drinking alcoholic beverages has been linked to an increased risk of upper gastrointestinal cancer and other types of cancer. Researchers looking for the potential biochemical basis for this link have focused on acetaldehyde, a suspected carcinogen formed as the body metabolizes alcohol. In the journal *Nucleic Acids Research* (vol. 33, num. 11), scientists from the National Institute on Alcohol Abuse and Alcoholism (NIAAA) and the National Institute of Standards and Technology (NIST) report that polyamines—natural compounds essential for cell growth—react with acetaldehyde to trigger a series of reactions that damage DNA, an event that can lead to the formation of cancer.

"We've long suspected acetaldehyde's role in the carcinogenicity of alcohol beverage consumption, but this study gives us important new clues about its involvement," says Ting-Kai Li, M.D., director of the NIAAA, which is part of the National Institutes of Health (NIH). "This work provides an important framework for understanding the underlying chemical pathway that could explain the association between drinking and certain types of cancer."

The research team, led by P.J. Brooks, Ph.D., of NIAAA and Miral Dizdaroglu, Ph.D., of NIST, examined acetaldehyde's reaction with polyamines, small molecules found in all cells. "Polyamines are usually considered 'good guys,' because they have been shown to protect DNA from oxidative damage," says Dr. Brooks. Yet the researchers found the polyamines facilitated the conversion of acetaldehyde into crotonaldehyde (CrA), an environmental pollutant that has been shown to cause cancer in animals. This chemical in turn altered DNA, generating an abnormal, mutagenic DNA base called a Cr-PdG adduct.

Dr. Brooks says, "We concluded that polyamines stimulated the formation of Cr-PdG adducts from acetaldehyde, and this may provide a mechanism to explain how alcohol consumption increases the risk of some types of cancer."

Previous studies had shown acetaldehyde could be converted to mutagenic Cr-PdG, but those studies used very high acetaldehyde concentrations. "We were able to demonstrate that these reactions can take place with acetaldehyde concentrations that have been measured in human saliva during alcohol consumption," says Dr. Brooks.

An important part of this research was a new chemical analysis method developed at NIST. According to Dr. Dizdaroglu, "This novel chemical assay is a powerful method that accurately measures the Cr-PdG adduct."

George Kunos, M.D., Ph.D., director of NIAAA's Division of Intramural Clinical and Biological Research, says, "These findings also have significant implications for researchers seeking to understand how genes affect the risk for cancer." Many studies have shown that certain genetic variants that affect alcohol and acetaldehyde metabolism can also affect individual susceptibility to alcohol-related gastrointestinal cancer. Dr. Kunos adds, "This work could serve as a roadmap for future studies to investigate other genetic factors, particularly those that influence DNA repair pathways, in relation to alcohol consumption and cancer."

Chapter 39

Alcohol's Long-Term Effects on Bone

Alcoholism and Recovery

According to the National Institute of Alcohol Abuse and Alcoholism (NIAAA), nearly 14 million Americans—or 1 in 13 adults—abuse alcohol or are alcoholic. Alcoholism is a disease characterized by a dependency on alcohol. Since alcohol affects almost every organ in the body, chronic heavy drinking is associated with many serious health problems, including pancreatitis, liver disease, heart disease, cancer, and osteoporosis. In fact, the NIAAA estimates that the economic costs of alcohol abuse approach $185 billion per year.

Maintaining sobriety is undoubtedly the most important health goal for an individual recovering from alcoholism. However, attention to other aspects of health, including bone health, can help increase the likelihood of a healthy future, free from the devastating consequences of osteoporosis and fracture.

Facts about Osteoporosis

Osteoporosis is a condition in which bones become less dense and more likely to fracture. Fractures from osteoporosis can result in significant pain and disability. It is a major health threat for an estimated 44 million American men and women.

"What People Recovering from Alcoholism Need to Know About Osteoporosis" is from the National Institute of Arthritis and Musculoskeletal and Skin Diseases (NIAMS, www.niams.nih.gov), August 2005.

Risk factors for developing osteoporosis include:

- being thin or having a small frame;

- having a family history of the disease;

- for women, being postmenopausal, having an early menopause, or not having menstrual periods (amenorrhea);

- using certain medications, such as glucocorticoids;

- not getting enough calcium;

- not getting enough physical activity;

- smoking; and

- drinking too much alcohol.

Osteoporosis is a silent disease that can often be prevented. However, if undetected, it can progress for many years without symptoms until a fracture occurs. It has been called "a pediatric disease with geriatric consequences," because building healthy bones in one's youth is important to help prevent osteoporosis and fractures later in life.

The Alcohol-Osteoporosis Link

Alcohol negatively impacts bone health for several reasons. To begin with, excessive alcohol interferes with the balance of calcium, an essential nutrient for healthy bones. It also increases parathyroid hormone (PTH) levels, which in turn reduce the body's calcium reserves. Calcium balance is further disrupted by alcohol's ability to interfere with the production of vitamin D, a vitamin essential for calcium absorption.

In addition, chronic heavy drinking can cause hormone deficiencies in men and women. Men with alcoholism tend to produce less testosterone, a hormone linked to the production of osteoblasts (the cells that stimulate bone formation). In women, chronic alcohol exposure often produces irregular menstrual cycles, a factor that reduces estrogen levels, increasing osteoporosis risk. Also, cortisol levels tend to be elevated in people with alcoholism. Cortisol is known to decrease bone formation and increase bone breakdown.

Due to the effects of alcohol on balance and gait, people with alcoholism tend to fall more frequently than those without the disorder. Heavy alcohol consumption has been linked to an increase in the risk of fracture, including the most serious kind: hip fracture. Vertebral fractures are also more common in those who abuse alcohol.

Osteoporosis Management Strategies

The most effective strategy for alcohol-induced bone loss is abstinence. People with alcoholism who abstain from drinking tend to have a rapid recovery of osteoblastic (bone building) activity. Some studies have even found that lost bone can be partially restored when alcohol abuse ends.

Nutrition. Due to the negative nutritional effects of chronic alcohol use, people recovering from alcoholism should make healthy nutritional habits a top priority. As far as bone health is concerned, a well-balanced diet rich in calcium and vitamin D is critical. Good sources of calcium include low-fat dairy products; dark green, leafy vegetables; and calcium-fortified foods and beverages. Also, supplements can help ensure that the calcium requirement is met each day. The Institute of Medicine recommends a daily calcium intake of 1,000 mg (milligrams) for men and women, increasing to 1,200 mg for those over age 50.

Vitamin D plays an important role in calcium absorption and bone health. It is synthesized in the skin through exposure to sunlight. Food sources of vitamin D include egg yolks, saltwater fish, and liver. Some individuals may require vitamin D supplements in order to achieve the recommended intake of 400 to 800 IU (International Units) each day.

Exercise. Like muscle, bone is living tissue that responds to exercise by becoming stronger. The best exercise for bones is weight-bearing exercise that forces you to work against gravity. Some examples include walking, climbing stairs, lifting weights, and dancing. Regular exercises such as walking may help prevent bone loss and provide many other health benefits.

Healthy lifestyle. Smoking is bad for bones as well as the heart and lungs. In addition, smokers may absorb less calcium from their diets. Studies suggest that in people recovering from alcoholism, smoking cessation may actually enhance abstinence from drinking. Since many suspect that smokers who abuse alcohol tend to be more dependent on nicotine than those who don't, a formal smoking cessation program may be a worthwhile investment for individuals in recovery.

Bone density test. Specialized tests known as bone mineral density (BMD) tests measure bone density in various sites of the body. These tests can detect osteoporosis before a fracture occurs and predict one's chances of fracturing in the future. Individuals in recovery are encouraged to talk to their health care providers about whether they might be candidates for a bone density test.

Medication. There is no cure for osteoporosis. However, there are medications available to prevent and treat the disease in postmenopausal women and in men.

Chapter 40

Alcohol and HIV/AIDS

People with alcohol use disorders are more likely than the general population to contract HIV (human immunodeficiency virus). Similarly, people with HIV are more likely to abuse alcohol at some time during their lives. Alcohol use is associated with high-risk sexual behaviors and injection drug use, two major modes of HIV transmission. Concerns about HIV have increased as recent trends suggest a resurgence of the epidemic among men who have sex with men, as well as dramatic increases in the proportion of cases transmitted heterosexually. In persons already infected, the combination of heavy drinking and HIV has been associated with increased medical and psychiatric complications, delays in seeking treatment, difficulties with HIV medication compliance, and poorer HIV treatment outcomes. Decreasing alcohol use in people who have HIV or who are at risk for becoming infected reduces the spread of HIV and the diseases associated with it.

This chapter briefly examines the changing patterns of HIV transmission in the United States; the role of alcohol in the transmission of HIV within, and potentially beyond, high-risk populations; the potential influence of alcohol abuse on the progression and treatment of HIV-related illness; and the benefits of making alcoholism treatment an integral part of HIV prevention programs.

Excerpted from *Alcohol Alert* No. 57, a publication of the National Institute on Alcohol Abuse and Alcoholism (NIAAA), a part of the National Institutes of Health, September 2002. A complete list of references is available at www.niaaa.nih.gov.

Trends in HIV Transmission in the United States

HIV is most commonly transmitted by sexual contact and the sharing of contaminated needles by injection drug users. By the end of 2000, an estimated 900,000 Americans were living with HIV. Approximately 40,000 new cases of active AIDS [acquired immunodeficiency syndrome] disease are diagnosed annually. Historically, HIV has been most prevalent among men who have sex with men, whereas most new HIV infections are reported among men who have sex with men and among injection drug users. Recently, however, the proportion of HIV cases acquired through heterosexual contact has increased and almost equals the proportion of cases attributable to injection drug use. The proportion of all AIDS cases reported among women has tripled since the mid-1980s, primarily as a result of heterosexual exposure and secondarily through injection drug use. Minority groups are the most heavily affected by HIV associated with drug injection, and Blacks and Hispanics now account for an estimated 70 percent of all new AIDS cases.

Alcohol and HIV Transmission

People who abuse alcohol are more likely to engage in behaviors that place them at risk for contracting HIV. For example, rates of injection drug use are high among alcoholics in treatment, and increasing levels of alcohol ingestion are associated with greater injection drug-related risk behaviors, including needle sharing.

A history of heavy alcohol use has been correlated with a lifetime tendency toward high-risk sexual behaviors, including multiple sex partners, unprotected intercourse, sex with high-risk partners (e.g., injection drug users, prostitutes), and the exchange of sex for money or drugs. There may be many reasons for this association. For example, alcohol can act directly on the brain to reduce inhibitions and diminish risk perception. However, expectations about alcohol's effects may exert a more powerful influence on alcohol-involved sexual behavior. Studies consistently demonstrate that people who strongly believe that alcohol enhances sexual arousal and performance are more likely to practice risky sex after drinking.

Some people report deliberately using alcohol during sexual encounters to provide an excuse for socially unacceptable behavior or to reduce their conscious awareness of risk. According to researchers, this practice may be especially common among men who have sex with men. This finding is consistent with the observation that men who drink prior to or during homosexual contact are more likely than heterosexuals to engage in high-risk sexual practices.

Finally, the association between drinking levels and high-risk sexual behavior does not imply that alcohol necessarily plays a direct role in such behavior or that it causes high-risk behavior on every occasion. For example, bars and drinking parties serve as convenient social settings for meeting potential sexual partners. In addition, alcohol abuse occurs frequently among people whose lifestyle or personality predisposes them to high-risk behaviors in general.

Alcohol and Medical Aspects of AIDS

Alcohol increases susceptibility to some infections that can occur as complications of AIDS. Infections associated with both alcohol and AIDS include tuberculosis; pneumonia caused by the bacterium *Streptococcus pneumoniae*; and the viral disease hepatitis C, a leading cause of death among people with HIV. Alcohol may also increase the severity of AIDS-related brain damage, which is characterized in its severest form by profound dementia and a high death rate.

The progression of HIV and the development of AIDS-associated infections may be controlled by highly active antiretroviral therapy (HAART), a combination of powerful antiviral medications. Despite markedly increased survival rates, HAART is associated with several disadvantages, including the emergence of medication-resistant HIV strains and the occurrence of adverse interactions with other medications, some of which are prescribed for AIDS-related infections. In addition, many patients fail to comply with the complex medication regimen. Studies have associated heavy alcohol use with decreased medication compliance as well as with poorer response to HIV therapy in general. The outcome of HIV therapy improved significantly among alcoholics who stopped drinking.

Alcoholism Treatment as HIV Prevention

Studies show that decreasing alcohol use among HIV patients not only reduces the medical and psychiatric consequences associated with alcohol consumption but also decreases other drug use and HIV transmission. Thus, alcohol and other drug abuse treatment can be considered primary HIV prevention as well. For example, researchers found a 58 percent reduction in injection drug use, with similar decreases in high-risk sexual behaviors, among heterosexual patients one year after treatment. Participants who remained abstinent showed substantially greater improvement in both outcomes compared with those who continued to drink.

Research also suggests that for heterosexual alcoholics, the focus of screening and prevention for HIV risk factors should be on people with more severe alcohol dependence. For male alcoholics who have sex with men, the focus should be on those who socialize primarily in bars.

Alcoholism prevention among youth is of particular importance. AIDS is a leading cause of death among people ages 15 to 24, and new injection drug users who contract HIV or viral hepatitis often become infected within 2 years after beginning to inject drugs. Researchers have found that:

- the prevalence of current, binge, and heavy drinking peaks between the ages of 18 and 24 (36), which is a high-risk period for initiating injection drug use;

- drug injection is usually associated with prior use of alcohol in conjunction with non-injection drugs, especially among adolescents with alcohol use disorders;

- and high rates of risky sexual practices have been reported among adolescents and may be correlated with alcohol consumption.

Therefore, it has been suggested that HIV prevention programs for youth should target alcohol consumption in addition to injection drug use and sexual risk reduction.

Treatment Access and Integration

Analyses of HIV surveillance data collected by the national Centers for Disease Control and Prevention, urban and rural health departments, and health maintenance organizations revealed that Blacks, Hispanics, women, the chronically mentally ill, and the poor are less likely to obtain appropriate HIV therapy compared with the general population. HIV-infected people in rural areas report reduced access to medical and mental health care services relative to their urban counterparts.

Timeliness is an essential aspect of effective HIV treatment and prevention. Early detection of HIV infection facilitates the prompt initiation of behavioral changes aimed at reducing transmission and also may enhance treatment effectiveness. Unfortunately, many facilities for the treatment of alcohol or other drug use disorders do not routinely or consistently screen their patients for HIV. In addition, many people who test positive for HIV fail to seek medical care until the disease has reached an advanced stage. Alcohol abuse has been associated with longer delays in seeking treatment.

Some evidence suggests that such problems may be ameliorated in part by designing programs that link primary medical care with treatment for abuse of alcohol and other drugs, HIV risk-reduction education, and psychiatric care when appropriate. In drug treatment programs, for example, both patients and clinicians may focus on what is perceived as the main problem (typically heroin or cocaine use), and neglect or minimize the use of other drugs, including alcohol. Yet in one study, a large proportion of patients in a residential drug treatment program reported daily consumption of large quantities of alcohol.

In a randomized controlled trial, researchers demonstrated the feasibility of incorporating a multidisciplinary medical clinic within a detoxification unit designed to treat alcohol, heroin, and cocaine dependence. Because the integration of different services at a single site can be expensive, the researchers recommended that efforts be made to facilitate information transfer or patient transportation among programs based at multiple locations.

Chapter 41

The Interactions between Alcohol and Medicines

Chapter Contents

Section 41.1—Harmful Interactions:
        Mixing Alcohol with Medicines 296
Section 41.2—Aging, Medicines, and Alcohol 300

Section 41.1

Harmful Interactions: Mixing Alcohol with Medicines

From the brochure produced by the National Institute on Alcohol Abuse and Alcoholism (NIAAA), NIH Publication No. 03-5329, August 2005.

May cause DROWSINESS.
ALCOHOL may intensify this effect.
USE CARE when operating a car or dangerous machinery.

You've probably seen these warnings on medicines you've taken. The danger is real. Mixing alcohol with certain medications can cause nausea and vomiting; headaches; drowsiness; fainting; loss of coordination; and can put you at risk for internal bleeding, heart problems, and difficulties in breathing. Alcohol also can decrease the effectiveness of a medication or make it totally ineffective.

Many of these medications can be purchased over the counter without a prescription, including herbal remedies and others you may never have suspected of reacting with alcohol. This text describes the harmful effects of drinking while taking certain medicines. Brand names are used only to help you recognize a medicine you may be taking. **The table presented here does not include all the medications that may react with alcohol. Most important, the list does *not* include all the ingredients in every medication.** Medications are safe and effective when used appropriately. Your pharmacist or health care provider can help you determine which medicines interact harmfully with alcohol.

Did You Know? Facts about Alcohol and Medications

- Many types of medication can make you sleepy. Taking these medicines while drinking can make you even more drowsy, dizzy, and lightheaded. You may have trouble concentrating or performing mechanical skills. Mixing alcohol with certain medicines

296

makes it dangerous for you to drive. Combining alcohol with some medicines can lead to falls and serious injuries, especially among older people.

- Some medications, including many popular painkillers and cough, cold, and allergy remedies, contain more than one ingredient that can react with alcohol. Read the label on your medication bottle to find out exactly what ingredients it contains.

- Certain medicines contain up to 10 percent alcohol. Cough syrup and laxatives have some of the highest alcohol concentrations.

- Women and older people are at higher risk for harmful alcohol medication reactions.

- Alcohol and medicines can interact harmfully even if they are not taken at the same time.

Mixing alcohol and a medication puts you at risk for dangerous reactions. Protect yourself by avoiding alcohol if you are taking a medication and don't know its effect. To learn more about a medicine and whether it will interact with alcohol, talk to your pharmacist or health care provider.

Table 41.1. Common Medications That May Interact with Alcohol

Symptoms/Disorders	Common medications and selected brand names	Some possible reactions with alcohol
Angina (chest pain), coronary heart disease	Isordil® (isosorbide), nitroglycerine	Rapid heartbeat, sudden changes in blood pressure
Anxiety	Xanax® (alprazolam); Klonopin® (clonazepam); Valium® (diazepam); Ativan® (lorazepam)	Drowsiness, dizziness; increased risk for overdose
Blood clots	Coumadin ® (warfarin)	Occasional drinking may lead to internal bleeding; heavier drinking may have the opposite effect, resulting in possible blood clots, strokes, or heart attacks
Colds, coughs, flu, allergies	Benadryl® (diphenhydramine); Tylenol® Cold and Flu (chlorpheniramine); Robitussin A-C® (codeine)	Drowsiness, dizziness; increased risk for overdose
Depression	Elavil® (amitriptyline); Anafranil® (clomipramine); Norpramin® (desipramine); Serzone® (nefazodone); Desyrel® (trazodone)	Drowsiness, dizziness; increased risk for overdose
Diabetes	Micronase® (glyburide); Glucophage® (metformin); Orinase® (tolbutamide)	Rapid heartbeat, sudden changes in blood pressure; convulsions, coma, death
Heartburn, indigestion, sour stomach	Tagamet® (cimetidine); Axid® (nizatidine); Zantac® (ranitidine); Reglan® (metoclopramide)	Rapid heartbeat, sudden changes in blood pressure (metoclopramide); increased alcohol effect

Condition	Medicines	Interactions
Infections	Grisactin® (griseofulvin); Flagyl® (metronidazole); Macrodantin® (nitrofurantoin); Septra® (sulfamethoxazole); Nydrazid® (isoniazid); Seromycin® (cycloserine)	Rapid heartbeat, sudden changes in blood pressure; liver damage (isoniazid)
Muscle pain	Soma® (carisoprodol); Flexeril® (cyclobenzaprine)	Drowsiness, dizziness; increased risk of seizures; increased risk for overdose
Nausea, motion sickness	Antivert® (meclizine); Atarax® (hydroxyzine); Phenergan® (promethazine)	Drowsiness, dizziness; increased risk for overdose
Pain such as that from headache, fever, muscle ache, arthritis; inflammation	Aspirin (salicylates); Advil®, Motrin® (ibuprofen); Tylenol®, Excedrin® (acetaminophen); Vioxx® (rofecoxib); Celebrex® (celecoxib); Naprosyn® (naproxen)	Stomach upset, bleeding, and ulcers; liver damage (acetaminophen); rapid heartbeat
Seizures	Klonopin® (clonazepam); phenobarbital; Dilantin® (phenytoin)	Drowsiness, dizziness; increased risk of seizures
Severe pain from injury; postsurgical care; oral surgery; migraines	Fiorinal® with codeine (butalbital and codeine); Darvocet-N® (propoxyphene); Vicodin® (hydrocodone); Percocet® (oxycodone)	Drowsiness, dizziness; increased risk for overdose
Sleep problems	Restoril® (temazepam); ProSom™ (estazolam); Sominex® (diphenhydramine) Herbal preparations (Chamomile, Valerian, Lavender)	Drowsiness, dizziness Increased drowsiness

299

Section 41.2

Aging, Medicines, and Alcohol

From "As You Age: A Guide to Aging, Medicines, and Alcohol," a
brochure produced by the Substance Abuse and Mental Health Services
Administration (SAMHSA), 2004.

As we age, the need to take more and different kinds of medications tends to increase. Also, growing older means that our bodies respond differently to alcohol and to medication than when we were younger.

You should be aware that:

- Some of your medicines won't mix well with other medications, including over-the-counter medications and herbal remedies.

- Many medications do not mix well with alcohol.

- Changes in body weight can influence the amount of medicine you need to take and how long it stays in your body. Body circulation may slow down, which can affect how quickly drugs get to the liver and kidneys. In addition, the liver and kidneys may work slower, which can affect how a drug breaks down and is eliminated from the body. Due to these changes, medicine may remain in your body longer and create a greater chance of interaction.

To guard against potential problems with medicines, become knowledgeable about your medication and how it makes you feel.

Take Steps on Your Own

- Read the labels of your medications carefully, and follow the directions.

- Look for pictures or statements on your prescriptions and pill bottles that tell you not to drink alcohol while taking the particular medication. If you are taking medications for sleeping, pain, anxiety, or depression, it is unsafe to drink alcohol.

- One alcoholic drink a day is the recommended limit for anyone over the age of 65 who has not been diagnosed with a drinking problem. That's 12 ounces of beer, 1.5 ounces of distilled spirits, or 5 ounces of wine.

- Talk to your health care professional about all medicines you take, including prescription; over-the-counter (OTC) medications; and dietary supplements, vitamins, and herbals.

- Tell your doctor about any food or medicine allergies you have.

- Keep track of side effects, and let your doctor know immediately about any unexpected symptoms or changes in the way you feel.

- Go through your medicine cabinet at least once a year to get rid of old or expired medicines.

- Have all of your medicine reviewed by your doctor at least once a year.

Medicine and alcohol misuse can happen unintentionally. Here are some signals that may indicate an alcohol- or medication-related problem:

- Memory trouble after having a drink or taking medicine
- Loss of coordination (walking unsteadily, frequent falls)
- Changes in sleeping habits
- Unexplained bruises
- Being unsure of yourself
- Irritability, sadness, depression
- Unexplained chronic pain
- Changes in eating habits
- Wanting to stay alone a lot of the time
- Failing to bathe or keep clean
- Having trouble finishing sentences
- Having trouble concentrating
- Difficulty staying in touch with family or friends
- Lack of interest in usual activities

Do you think you may be having trouble with alcohol or medications? Do you want to avoid a problem? Here are some things you can do.

Talk to Someone You Trust

- Talk with your doctor or other health care professional. They can check for any problems you may be having and discuss treatment options with you.

- Ask for advice from a staff member at a senior center or other program in which you participate.

- Share your concerns with a friend, family member, or spiritual advisor.

Share the Right Information with Your Health Care Professional

- Make a list for your doctor of all your medications.

- Remind your doctor or pharmacist about any previous conditions that might affect your ability to take certain medicines, such as allergies, a stroke, hypertension, serious heart disease, liver problems, or lung disease.

- Don't be afraid to ask questions if you want more information.

- Whenever possible, have your doctor or a member of the medical staff give you written advice or instructions.

Part Four

Alcohol Use during Pregnancy and Its Effect on Fetal Development

Chapter 42

Drinking Alcohol during Pregnancy

Drinking alcohol during pregnancy can cause physical and mental birth defects. Each year, up to 40,000 babies are born with some degree of alcohol-related damage.[1,2] Although many women are aware that heavy drinking during pregnancy can cause birth defects, many do not realize that moderate—or even light—drinking also may harm the fetus.

In fact, no level of alcohol use during pregnancy has been proven safe. Therefore, the March of Dimes recommends that pregnant women do not drink any alcohol—including beer, wine, wine coolers, and hard liquor—throughout their pregnancy and while nursing. In addition, because women often do not know they are pregnant for a few months, women who may be pregnant or those who are attempting to become pregnant should abstain from drinking alcoholic beverages.

Recent government surveys indicate that about 13 percent of pregnant women drink during pregnancy.[3] About 3 percent of pregnant women report binge drinking (five or more drinks on any one occasion) or frequent drinking (seven or more drinks per week).[3] Women who binge drink or drink frequently greatly increase the risk of alcohol-related damage to their babies.

When a pregnant woman drinks, alcohol passes swiftly through the placenta to her fetus. In the unborn baby's immature body, alcohol is broken down much more slowly than in an adult's body. As a result, the alcohol level of the baby's blood can be even higher and can remain elevated longer than the level in the mother's blood. This sometimes causes the baby to suffer lifelong damage.

In February 2005, Dr. Richard H. Carmona, surgeon general of the United States, warned pregnant women and women who may become pregnant about the risks of alcohol during pregnancy.

What are the hazards of drinking alcohol during pregnancy?

Drinking alcohol during pregnancy can cause a number of birth defects, ranging from mild to severe. These include mental retardation; learning, emotional and behavioral problems; and defects involving the heart, face and other organs. The term "fetal alcohol spectrum disorder" is used to describe the many problems associated with exposure to alcohol before birth. The most severe of these is fetal alcohol syndrome (FAS), a combination of physical and mental birth defects.

Consuming alcohol during pregnancy also increases the risk of miscarriage, low birthweight (less than 5½ pounds), and stillbirth. A 2002 Danish study found that women who drank five or more drinks a week were three times more likely to have a stillborn baby than women who had less than one drink a week.[4]

What is fetal alcohol syndrome (FAS)?

FAS is one of the most common known causes of mental retardation, and the only cause that is entirely preventable. Studies by the Centers for Disease Control and Prevention (CDC) suggest that between 1,000 and 6,000 babies in the United States are born yearly with FAS.[3]

Babies with FAS are abnormally small at birth and usually do not catch up on growth as they get older. They have characteristic facial features, including small eyes, a thin upper lip and smooth skin in place of the normal groove between the nose and upper lip. Their organs, especially the heart, may not form properly. Many babies with FAS also have a brain that is small and abnormally formed, and most have some degree of mental disability. Many have poor coordination, a short attention span and emotional and behavioral problems.

The effects of FAS last a lifetime. Even if not mentally retarded, adolescents and adults with FAS have varying degrees of psychological and behavioral problems and often find it difficult to hold down a job and live independently.[3]

What are fetal alcohol effects (FAE)?

The CDC estimates that about three times the number of babies born with FAS are born with lesser degrees of alcohol-related damage.[5] This condition is sometimes referred to as fetal alcohol effects (FAE). These children have some of the physical or mental birth defects associated with FAS. The Institute of Medicine uses more specific diagnostic categories for FAE, referring to the physical birth defects (such as heart defects) as alcohol-related birth defects (ARBD), and to the mental and behavioral abnormalities as alcohol-related neurodevelopmental disorders (ARND).[6]

In general, alcohol-related birth defects (such as heart and facial defects) are more likely to result from drinking during the first trimester. Drinking at any stage of pregnancy can affect the brain as well as growth.[5]

During pregnancy, how much alcohol is too much?

No level of drinking alcohol has been proven safe during pregnancy. The full pattern of FAS usually occurs in offspring of women who are alcoholics or chronic alcohol abusers. These women either drink heavily (about four or five or more drinks daily) throughout pregnancy or have repeated episodes of binge drinking. However, FAS can occur in women who drink less. ARBD and ARND can occur in babies of women who drink moderately or lightly during pregnancy.

Researchers are taking a closer look at the more subtle effects of moderate and light drinking during pregnancy. A 2002 study found that 14-year-old children whose mothers drank as little as one drink a week were significantly shorter and leaner and had a smaller head circumference (a possible indicator of brain size) than children of women who did not drink at all.[7] A 2001 study found that 6- and 7-year-old children of mothers who had as little as one drink a week during pregnancy were more likely than children of nondrinkers to have behavior problems, such as aggressive and delinquent behaviors. These researchers found that children whose mothers drank any alcohol during pregnancy were more than three times as likely as unexposed children to demonstrate delinquent behaviors.[8]

Other researchers report behavioral and learning problems in children exposed to moderate drinking during pregnancy, including attention and memory problems, hyperactivity, impulsivity, poor social and communication skills, psychiatric problems (including mood disorders), and alcohol and drug use.[1]

Is there a cure for FAS?

There is no cure for FAS. However, a recent study found that early diagnosis (before 6 years of age) and being raised in a stable, nurturing environment can improve the long-term outlook for individuals with FAS.[9] Those who experienced these protective factors during their school years were two to four times more likely to avoid serious behavioral problems resulting in trouble with the law or confinement in a psychiatric institution.

If a pregnant woman has one or two drinks before she realizes she is pregnant, can it harm the baby?

It is unlikely that the occasional drink a woman takes before she realizes she is pregnant will harm her baby. The baby's brain and other organs begin developing around the third week of pregnancy, however, and are vulnerable to damage in these early weeks. Because no amount of alcohol is proven safe, a woman should stop drinking immediately if she even suspects she could be pregnant, and she should abstain from drinking all alcohol if attempting to become pregnant.

Is it safe to drink alcohol while breastfeeding?

Small amounts of alcohol do get into breast milk and are passed on to the baby. One study found that breastfed babies of women who had one or more drinks a day were a little slower in acquiring motor skills (such as crawling and walking) than babies who had not been exposed to alcohol.[10] Large amounts of alcohol also may interfere with ejection of milk from the breast. For these reasons, the March of Dimes recommends that women abstain from drinking alcohol while they are nursing. Similarly, the American Academy of Pediatrics (AAP) recommends that breastfeeding mothers avoid regular use of alcohol. However, according to the AAP, an occasional alcoholic drink probably won't hurt the baby, but a mother who chooses to have a drink should wait at least two hours before breastfeeding her baby.[11]

Can heavy drinking by the father contribute to FAS?

To date, there is no proof that heavy drinking by the father can cause FAS. But men can help their partner avoid alcohol by not drinking during their partner's pregnancy.

What is the March of Dimes doing to prevent and treat FAS and FAE?

March of Dimes-supported researchers are investigating the influence of alcohol on pregnancy. One grantee is seeking to identify genes that are disregulated by alcohol during fetal development as a step toward learning how to prevent alcohol-related birth defects in babies of mothers who continue to drink during pregnancy. Another is examining differences in the structure and function of the brain in children who were heavily exposed to alcohol before birth in order to develop intervention strategies to optimize development in children with FAS and FAE.

The March of Dimes also works to prevent FAS and FAE by educating the general public, teenagers, adults of childbearing age, and expectant mothers about the dangers of alcohol and other drugs to their unborn children. Because there currently is no way to predict which babies will be damaged by alcohol, the safest course is not to drink at all during pregnancy and to avoid heavy drinking during childbearing years (because at least 50 percent of pregnancies are unplanned). All women who drink alcohol should stop as soon as they think they are pregnant. Heavy drinkers should avoid pregnancy until they believe they can abstain from alcohol throughout pregnancy.

References

1. Sokol, R.J., et al. Fetal Alcohol Spectrum Disorder. *Journal of the American Medical Association*, volume 290, number 22, December 10, 2003, pages 2996–2999.

2. National Organization on Fetal Alcohol Syndrome. Frequently Asked Questions: What are the Statistics and Facts about FAS and FASD? Accessed 8/17/04.

3. Bertrand, J., et al., National Task Force on FAS/FAE. Fetal Alcohol Syndrome: Guidelines for Referral and Diagnosis. Atlanta, GA: Centers for Disease Control and Prevention, July 2004.

4. Kesmodel, U., et al. Moderate Alcohol Intake During Pregnancy and the Risk of Stillbirth and Death in the First Year of Life. *American Journal of Epidemiology*, volume 155, number 4, February 15, 2002, pages 305–312.

5. Centers for Disease Control and Prevention. Frequently Asked Questions: Fetal Alcohol Syndrome. Updated 8/5/04, accessed 8/17/04.

6. Institute of Medicine. *Fetal Alcohol Syndrome: Diagnosis, Epidemiology, Prevention, and Treatment.* Washington, D.C., National Academy Press, 1996.

7. Day, N.L., et al. Prenatal Alcohol Exposure Predicts Continued Deficits in Offspring Size at 14 Years of Age. *Alcoholism: Clinical and Experimental Research*, volume 26, number 10, 2002, pages 1584–1591.

8. Sood, B., et al. Prenatal Alcohol Exposure and Childhood Behavior at Age 6 to 7. *Pediatrics*, volume 108, number 2, August 2001, e34.

9. Streissguth, A.P., et al. Risk Factors for Adverse Life Outcomes in Fetal Alcohol Syndrome and Fetal Alcohol Effects. *Journal of Developmental and Behavioral Pediatrics*, volume 25, number 4, August 2004, pages 228–238.

10. Little, R.E., et al. Maternal Alcohol Use During Breast-Feeding and Infant Mental and Motor Development at One Year. *New England Journal of Medicine*, volume 321, number 7, August 17, 1989, pages 425–430.

11. Meek, J.Y. American Academy of Pediatrics: *New Mother's Guide to Breastfeeding*. New York, NY: Bantam Books and the American Academy of Pediatrics. 09-404-00, January 2005.

Chapter 43

Understanding Fetal Alcohol Spectrum Disorders

What does the term fetal alcohol spectrum disorder (FASD) mean?

The term FASD indicates that there are a variety of effects of prenatal alcohol exposure. FASD is not a diagnosis.

Although the various fetal alcohol spectrum disorders are permanent conditions, specific symptoms may be treatable or manageable. Thus, the definition notes possible lifelong implications, depending on the specific nature of the disorder and the individual affected.

FASD is one of the newer terms introduced to this field, and there is not universal agreement on how or when to use it. Canada uses the singular term "fetal alcohol spectrum disorder," and the United States uses the plural "disorders." However, both view FASD as a descriptive term and not a diagnostic term.

This definition of FASD was agreed on in April 2004 by a group of national experts representing the Centers for Disease Control and Prevention (CDC); the National Institute on Alcohol Abuse and Alcoholism (NIAAA); the Substance Abuse and Mental Health Services Administration (SAMHSA); Health Canada; and the fields of research, psychiatry, and justice. The meeting was facilitated by the National Organization on Fetal Alcohol Syndrome (NOFAS).

Excerpted from "Fetal Alcohol Spectrum Disorders: The Basics," by the FASD Center for Excellence, part of the Substance Abuse and Mental Health Services Administration (SAMHSA), January 2006.

311

What are some overall difficulties for persons with an FASD?

People with FASD may have difficulty:

- taking in information;
- storing information;
- recalling information when necessary; and
- using information appropriately in a specific situation.

Individuals with an FASD experience difficulties in all these areas. They may not be able to take all the information given to them into their brain. If they take it in (i.e., can repeat what they were told), they may have difficulty storing it, so they forget it after a short time. If they store it, they might have difficulty recalling it when they need it. They may have learned the rules that include doing their chores on Thursdays, but on Thursday, they do not recall that they need to do chores. Even if they can recall the information, they may have difficulty recognizing how to use the information in a given situation.

These problems are not unique to FASD and may occur with other disabilities. There is no established checklist of behaviors unique to fetal alcohol spectrum disorders. These problems can occur in individuals whose mothers did not drink while pregnant.

What are the primary disabilities of persons with an FASD?

People with an FASD may have:

- lower IQ;
- impaired ability in reading, spelling, and arithmetic; and
- lower level of adaptive functioning (more significantly impaired than IQ).

Primary disabilities are characteristics or behaviors that reflect differences in brain structure and function, such as mental retardation, attention deficits, and sensory integration dysfunction. Secondary disabilities are disabilities that the individual is not born with. These disabilities and behaviors develop over time because of a poor fit between the person and the environment.

A study identified a number of primary disabilities in persons with an FASD. For example, in the study, persons with FAS had an average IQ of 79. Persons with FAE [fetal alcohol effects] had an average IQ of 90. The average IQ in persons without neurologic disorders or brain damage is 100.

Adaptive functioning is defined as the ability of an individual to independently cope with common life demands in areas such as communication, self-care, home living, social/interpersonal skills, use of community resources, self-direction, academic skills, work, leisure, health, and safety.

What are some typical difficulties for persons with an FASD?

People with FASD may have sensory integration issues. They may be:

- overly sensitive to sensory input;
- upset by bright lights or loud noises;
- annoyed by tags in shirts or seams in socks;
- bothered by certain textures of food; and
- have problems sensing where their body is in space (i.e., clumsy).

Sensory integration refers to the way the body responds to external stimuli to the senses (sight, hearing, smell, touch, taste). Persons with an FASD may have sensory integration problems, making them over- or understimulated. They may flinch at the slightest touch or perceive it as an attack and lash out. They may refuse to eat certain foods or wear certain clothes. Conversely, they may hurt themselves because they do not feel pain, such as when touching a hot stove, or dress inappropriately for the weather because they do not feel cold.

Persons with sensory integration issues can also be clumsy because they have problems sensing where they are in space. They may bump into other people or into objects.

Persons with an FASD may have problems with tasks that involve recalling information, such as using multiplication tables. They also may have trouble with tasks that require use of working memory, such as following a sequence of events. They may forget the first event by the time they get to the last.

People with an FASD may also have problems with information processing. They may:

- not complete tasks or chores and may appear to be oppositional;
- have trouble determining what to do in a given situation; and
- not ask questions because they want to fit in.

Information processing refers to the way the brain stores, organizes, recalls, and uses information.

A person with an FASD may refuse to do something or simply not do it, especially if given multiple tasks. For example, a child may be told, "Go to your room, put your dirty clothes in the hamper, fold the clean clothes and put them away, and make your bed." The child does not follow through, because he or she cannot remember what to do.

Persons with an FASD have problems applying information. For example, Jimmy has an FASD and learns not to talk to strangers. He then refuses to talk to his substitute teacher because he does not know her. Another example is that people with an FASD know that when they are with their friends on the weekends, they can dress casually and talk in slang. Then they do the same when they are in school or on the job.

Persons with an FASD recognize that there is something different about them but do not want others to know, so they do not ask for help when they need it. The reasons include:

- They want to fit in.
- They do not want people to know there is something wrong with them.
- They do not know what questions to ask.

People with FASD may also:

- say they understand when they do not;
- have verbal expressive skills that often exceed their level of understanding;
- misinterpret others' words, actions, or body movements; and
- have trouble following multiple directions.

People, especially adolescents, want to be like everyone else and not be seen as different. They may not want to let on that they have difficulty with what is being told to them, so they will say that they understand. Thus, they can feel that they are doing things by choice and are in control, rather than saying that they do not know what to do. In addition, they may think that they understand at the moment, but later on do not know or remember what they were told.

Individuals with an FASD are often very talkative. They have more difficulty accurately taking in verbal information and processing it accurately than they do expressing themselves. Much of education is auditory learning, which can be particularly difficult for those with an FASD.

People with an FASD may see someone staring at them and think that the person is planning to attack them. Someone might be having a bad day, and they might think the person is mad at them. Also, idiomatic expressions, metaphors, and similes can be misinterpreted when people process information very literally. For example, someone says, "We are all in the same boat," and the person with an FASD responds, "I don't see any boats."

Individuals with an FASD typically have difficulty following multiple directions, but people commonly give more than one direction at a time.

What are some typical executive function difficulties for persons with an FASD?

Executive function refers to areas such as planning and problem solving that enable people to cope with the tasks and demands of everyday life.

Young children with an FASD lack stranger anxiety. As children, adolescents, and adults, persons with an FASD may go with people they do not know and get hurt.

Individuals with an FASD often do not know the rules or do not remember the rules when they need to. Most often, persons are given a list of rules, which people with an FASD will often have difficulty following. They lack the ability to apply rules to various situations.

Individuals with an FASD often have difficulty understanding cause and effect. Therefore, they may repeat behaviors that have gotten them into trouble. The natural consequences of some mistakes, such as eviction for not paying rent, could place the individual in dangerous situations.

People with FASD may not respond to point or level systems. Most programs in various systems of care use some type of point, level, or sticker system. Individuals with an FASD will often be on the lowest level or have the fewest points, yet they will frequently be the ones to say that they want to do well.

People with FASD may also have problems with the concept of time. Historical time and future time are abstract concepts that are difficult to grasp due to the effects of prenatal alcohol exposure. Persons with an FASD have problems understanding concepts such as the idea of a future consequence for a present behavior or a present consequence for an earlier act. They also may not understand that if an appointment is at 2:00 and is 1 hour away, they need to leave at 1:00.

Also, individuals with FASD may have trouble with the concept of money. It is difficult for individuals with an FASD to understand that if they spend all their money when they get it, they will not be able to pay their rent or buy food in a week or two. They may spend whatever money they have without being able to consider what they might need a day or a week later.

Peer pressure can also be a problem for people with FASD. Persons with an FASD are very naive and gullible. They believe what others tell them and often do what others tell them to do. In addition, since they want so much to have friends, they will often follow others.

What are some typical difficulties with self-esteem and personal issues for people with an FASD?

It is not unusual for an individual with a fetal alcohol spectrum disorder to do well one day and poorly the next or to remember to do something one day and not the next.

All individuals with an FASD have experienced losses in their lives. The fact that they are not like their peers is a loss of the ability to be like everyone else. Some have the loss of the hopes and dreams of what they wanted to be. Others lose their family or a secure future. These losses can affect people in many ways and need to be addressed.

In addition, persons with an FASD have difficulty maintaining good hygiene. They may not know how to keep themselves clean. They may not recognize when they are wearing dirty or stained clothes. They may take a shower or bath and then put dirty clothes back on. They may take off dirty clothes, put them in the pile with their clean clothes, and then pick up clothes to wear from that pile. The natural consequences approach is to tell them that if they go out looking or smelling dirty, people will not want to be their friends. However, saying this will just make them feel worse about themselves.

People with FASD may also have social difficulties because they:

- cannot entertain themselves;
- have trouble changing tasks; and
- do not accurately pick up social cues.

Persons with an FASD are easily bored. They have difficulty choosing something to do on their own and sticking to it. As children, they can go to their room filled with toys and come back 5 or 10 minutes later saying that they are bored and have nothing to do.

It is difficult for many people with an FASD to change tasks, especially often. Changing tasks is something that often occurs at home, at school, and in job settings.

It is difficult for individuals with an FASD to correctly assess social situations. If they misread a social interaction, they could be perceived as being different, rude, intrusive, or uninterested.

What are some secondary disabilities of persons with an FASD?

Secondary disabilities are problems that result from the primary disability but are not directly caused by it. For example, prenatal alcohol exposure can cause attention deficits that interfere with schoolwork. The attention deficits are a primary disability. The academic problem is a secondary disability.

Researchers from the University of Washington conducted a secondary disabilities study with funding from the CDC. The 4-year study examined 415 individuals with FAS or FAE who had been through the university's clinic. They ranged in age from 6 to 51 years. In addition to having primary disabilities (FAS or FAE), a significant proportion of these individuals experienced secondary disabilities. There might be many reasons for these disabilities, including environment and how the individual processes information. This is only one study, and it did not include a control group. More research is needed on secondary disabilities.

Of the individuals identified with secondary disabilities:

- 94 percent had mental health issues.
- 43 percent had disrupted school experiences.
- 60 percent of those age 12 and older had trouble with the law.
- 50 percent experienced confinement in jail or treatment facilities.
- 45 percent engaged in inappropriate sexual behavior.
- 24 percent of adolescents, 46 percent of adults, and 35 percent overall had alcohol and drug problems.
- 83 percent of adults experienced dependent living.
- 79 percent of adults had employment problems.

What is the link between FASD and mental health disorders?

Prenatal alcohol exposure may lead to severe behavioral, cognitive, and psychiatric problems, however, fetal alcohol spectrum disorders are not identified as specific diagnoses in the *Diagnostic and Statistical Manual of Mental Disorders, Fourth Edition (DSM-IV)*. This manual is used by mental health clinicians to diagnose mental illnesses.

An FASD may co-occur with mental illness or substance use disorders. The mental illness may be a misdiagnosis or a co-occurring disorder.

Because of the possibility of misdiagnosis and co-occurrence, it is essential to conduct a thorough diagnostic evaluation that includes medical, neuropsychological, and adaptive functioning testing; a psychiatric exam; and a family history.

Often a person with a fetal alcohol spectrum disorder may have a mental illness or substance use disorder. It is very important to determine exactly what is affecting the person's functioning. Otherwise, the proposed treatment may not help. Therefore, a thorough diagnostic evaluation is imperative.

Chapter 44

Frequently Asked Questions about Prenatal Alcohol-Related Conditions

What is FAS?

FAS stands for fetal alcohol syndrome. It is one of the leading known preventable causes of mental retardation and birth defects. FAS represents the severe end of a spectrum of effects that can occur when a woman drinks alcohol during pregnancy. Fetal death is the most extreme outcome. FAS is characterized by abnormal facial features, growth deficiency, and central nervous system (CNS) problems. People with FAS can have problems with learning, memory, attention span, communication, vision, hearing, or a combination of these things. These problems often lead to difficulties in school and problems getting along with others. FAS is a permanent condition. It affects every aspect of an individual's life and the lives of his or her family. However, FAS is 100% preventable—if a woman does not drink alcohol while she is pregnant.

What are FAE, ARND, and ARBD?

Prenatal exposure to alcohol can cause a spectrum of disorders. Many terms have been used to describe children who have some, but not all, of the clinical signs of FAS. Three terms are fetal alcohol effects (FAE), alcohol-related neurodevelopmental disorder (ARND), and

From the Centers for Disease Control and Prevention, National Center on Birth Defects and Developmental Disabilities (www.cdc.gov/ncbddd), September 29, 2005.

alcohol-related birth defects (ARBD). The term FAE has been used to describe behavioral and cognitive problems in children who were prenatally exposed to alcohol, but who do not have all of the typical diagnostic features of FAS. In 1996, the Institute of Medicine (IOM) replaced FAE with the terms ARND and ARBD. People with ARND can have functional or mental problems linked to prenatal alcohol exposure. These include behavioral or cognitive deficits, or both. Examples are learning difficulties, poor school performance, and poor impulse control. They can have difficulties with mathematical skills, memory, attention, judgment, or a combination of these. People with ARBD can have problems with the heart, kidneys, bones, hearing, or a combination of these.

Facial features of FAS

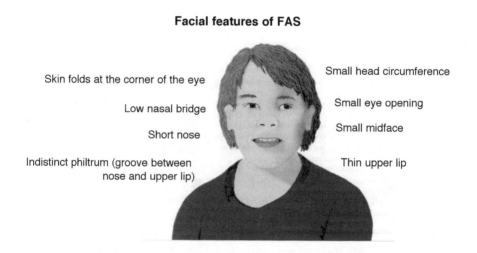

Skin folds at the corner of the eye

Low nasal bridge

Short nose

Indistinct philtrum (groove between nose and upper lip)

Small head circumference

Small eye opening

Small midface

Thin upper lip

Figure 44.1. Craniofacial features associated with fetal alcohol syndrome. Source: National Institute for Alcohol Abuse and Alcoholism (NIAAA).

What are FASDs?

The term fetal alcohol spectrum disorders (FASDs) has emerged to address the need to describe the spectrum of disorders related to fetal alcohol exposure. It is an umbrella term describing the range of effects that can occur in an individual whose mother drank alcohol during pregnancy. These effects can include physical, mental, behavioral, learning disabilities, or a combination of these, with possible lifelong implications. The term FASDs is not intended for use as a clinical diagnosis. Unlike people with FAS, those with other prenatal alcohol-related conditions under the umbrella of FASDs do not show the identifying physical characteristics of FAS and, as a result, they often go undiagnosed.

How common are fetal alcohol syndrome (FAS) and other prenatal alcohol-related conditions (known collectively as FASDs)?

The reported rates of FAS vary widely. These different rates depend on the population studied and the surveillance methods used. CDC studies show FAS rates ranging from 0.2 to 1.5 cases per 1,000 live births in different areas of the United States. Other prenatal alcohol-related conditions, such as ARND and ARBD, are believed to occur about three times as often as FAS.

How do I know if my child has been affected by maternal alcohol use?

Children with FAS have evidence of growth deficiency, CNS problems, and a distinct pattern of facial characteristics such as a thin upper lip, smooth philtrum (the groove running vertically between the nose and lips), and small eye openings. Children with different FASDs have CNS problems like children with FAS and/or a pattern of behavior or cognitive abnormalities such as learning difficulties and poor school performance. People with FASDs can have poor coordination or hyperactive behavior. They can have developmental disabilities such as speech and language delays, learning disabilities, mental retardation, or low IQ. They can have problems with self-care such as tying shoes or organizing one's day. People with FASDs can have poor reasoning and judgment skills. Infants with FASDs have sleep and sucking disturbances. People with FASDs often have problems as they get older. These might include mental health problems, disrupted school experiences, trouble with the law, unemployment, inappropriate sexual behavior, or a combination of these.

I suspect my child, or a child in my care, might have FAS. What should I do?

If you think a child might have FAS or another prenatal alcohol-related disorder, contact the National Organization on Fetal Alcohol

Syndrome (NOFAS). NOFAS has a directory of national and state services such as diagnostic and treatment services and family support groups. Go to http://www.nofas.org. At the home page, click on Resources. From there, click on National & State Resource Directory. From the map, click on your state for a list of services near you.

Can FASDs be treated?

FASDs are permanent conditions. They last a lifetime and affect every aspect of a child's life and the lives of his or her family members. There is no cure for these conditions. However, FASDs can be completely prevented—if a woman does not drink alcohol while she is pregnant. With early identification and diagnosis, a child with an FASD can get services that can help him or her lead a more productive life.

If a woman has an FASD, but does not drink during pregnancy, can her child have an FASD? Are FASDs hereditary?

FASDs are not genetic or hereditary. If a woman drinks alcohol during her pregnancy, her baby can be born with an FASD. But if a woman has an FASD, her own child cannot have an FASD, unless she drinks alcohol during pregnancy.

What are the economic consequences of FAS?

The 10th Special Report to the U.S. Congress on Alcohol and Health estimated the annual cost of FAS in 1998 to be $2.8 billion. A recent report estimates that the lifetime cost for one individual with FAS in 2002 was $2 million. This is an average for all people with FAS. People with severe problems, such as profound mental retardation, have much higher costs. [Source: Lupton C, Burd L, Harwood R. Cost of fetal alcohol spectrum disorders. *American Journal of Medical Genetics* Part C (Seminars in Medical Genetics) 2004;127C:42–50.]

Is there any safe amount of alcohol to drink during pregnancy? Is there a safe time during pregnancy to drink alcohol?

When a pregnant woman drinks alcohol, so does her unborn baby. There is no known safe amount of alcohol that a woman can drink during pregnancy. There is also no safe time during pregnancy to drink alcohol. Alcohol can have negative effects on a fetus in every trimester of pregnancy. Therefore, women should not drink if they are pregnant, planning to become pregnant, or could become pregnant (that is, sexually active and not using an effective form of birth control).

What is a "drink"? What if I drink only beer or wine coolers?

All drinks containing alcohol can hurt an unborn baby. A standard 12-ounce can of beer has the same amount of alcohol as a 4-ounce glass of wine or a 1-ounce shot of straight liquor. Some alcoholic drinks such as malt beverages, wine coolers, and mixed drinks often contain more alcohol than a 12-ounce can of beer. There is no safe kind of alcohol.

How does alcohol cause these problems?

Alcohol in the mother's blood crosses the placenta freely and enters the embryo or fetus through the umbilical cord. Alcohol exposure in the first 3 months of pregnancy can cause structural defects (e.g., facial changes). Growth and CNS problems can occur from drinking alcohol any time during pregnancy. The brain is developing throughout pregnancy. It can be damaged at any time. It is unlikely that one mechanism can explain the harmful effects of alcohol on the developing fetus. For example, brain images of some people with FAS show that certain areas have not developed normally. The images show that certain cells are not in their proper place and tissues have died in some areas.

Is there anything I can do now to decrease the chances of having a child with an FASD?

- If a woman is drinking during pregnancy, it is never too late for her to stop. The sooner a woman stops drinking, the better it will be for her baby. A woman should use an effective form of birth control until her drinking is under control. If a woman is not able to stop drinking, she should contact her physician, local Alcoholics Anonymous chapters, or a local alcohol treatment center, if needed.

- If a woman is sexually active and not using an effective form of birth control, she should not drink alcohol. She could be pregnant and not know it for several weeks or more.

- Mothers are not the only ones who can prevent FASDs. Spouses, partners, family members, friends, schools, health and social service organizations, and communities can help prevent FASDs through education and support.

I just found out I am pregnant. I have stopped drinking now, but I was drinking in the first few weeks of my pregnancy, before I knew I was pregnant. Could my baby have an FASD? What should I do now?

The most important thing is that you have completely stopped drinking after learning of your pregnancy. It is never too late to stop drinking. The sooner you stop, the better the chances for your baby's health. It is not possible to know what harm might have been done already. Some women can drink heavily during pregnancy and their babies do not seem to have any problems. Others drink less and their babies show various signs of alcohol exposure. Many body parts and organs are developing in the embryonic stage (weeks 3 to 8 of the pregnancy). This is the time when most women do not know they are pregnant. There is no known safe amount of alcohol or safe time to drink alcohol during pregnancy. It is recommended not to drink at all if one is pregnant or planning to become pregnant. Also, if a woman is sexually active and not using an effective form of birth control, she should avoid alcohol. The best advice is to try not to be alarmed, talk to your doctor about this, and be sure to receive routine prenatal care throughout your pregnancy.

Can a father's drinking cause FASDs?

How alcohol affects the male sperm is currently being studied. Whatever the effects are found to be, they are not FASDs. FASDs are caused specifically by the mother's alcohol use during pregnancy. However, the father's role is important. He can help the woman avoid drinking alcohol during pregnancy. He can encourage her abstinence from alcohol by avoiding social situations that involve drinking. He can also help her by avoiding alcohol himself.

Chapter 45

Caring for a Child Diagnosed with Fetal Alcohol Syndrome (FAS)

Chapter Contents

Section 45.1—If Your Child Has FAS 326

Section 45.2—Diagnosing FAS 332

Section 45.3—Health Concerns of Children with FAS 333

Section 45.4—FAS through the Years 336

Section 45.1

If Your Child Has FAS

Excerpted from "Guidelines of Care for Children With Special Health Care Needs: Fetal Alcohol Syndrome and Fetal Alcohol Effects," 1999. Minnesota Department of Health, Minnesota Children With Special Health Needs. This Minnesota Children with Special Health Care Needs program 'Guideline' accurately reflected the consensus of the health care community at the time of its publication in 1999, though readers should note that the understanding of Fetal Alcohol Spectrum Disorders is continuing to evolve rapidly. Revised by David A. Cooke, M.D., April 2006.

What Are Fetal Alcohol Syndrome (FAS) and Fetal Alcohol Effects (FAE)?

Fetal alcohol syndrome (FAS) is an alcohol-related birth disability. The condition occurs from alcohol use during pregnancy. When a pregnant woman drinks alcohol, it passes through the placenta and is absorbed by the unborn baby. The alcohol can harm the embryo and fetus even if the mother feels no effects.

FAS is a condition which includes physical, mental, and behavioral abnormalities. Most children with FAS will have different facial features. Most will have problems with growth. Permanent brain injury frequently occurs.

Not all children with FAS are alike. The effects of alcohol use during pregnancy will vary. Some children are more severely affected than others. Some show more of the reasoning and behavioral problems than the physical features. Some have a normal IQ while others do not. Many will have learning disabilities. Each child will have his or her own special needs, problems, and potential.

Some children are affected by alcohol but do not have all the features of FAS. These children may be diagnosed with fetal alcohol effects (FAE). They may have normal growth and a more normal appearance. They are more likely to have a normal IQ than a child with FAS. Like children with FAS, those with FAE can have mild to severe problems. These may involve problems with reasoning, behavior, and learning.

The Danger of Alcohol Use in Pregnancy

It is clear that alcohol use during pregnancy can injure the developing fetus, and may cause permanent damage. However, no one knows how much alcohol it takes to cause problems, or whether there are certain times during pregnancy when it is especially harmful. As a result, there is no known safe amount of alcohol use during pregnancy. Alcohol can do more damage to the developing embryo and fetus than illegal or legal drugs. Pregnant women should not drink alcohol at all. No alcoholic beverage is safe during pregnancy.

Alcohol use in the first trimester may:

- cause the greatest brain damage;
- impair cell development;
- affect major organs such as the heart, liver, and kidneys;
- cause facial malformations; and
- cause miscarriage.

Alcohol use in the second trimester may:

- impair brain development;
- cause miscarriage which may be life threatening for the mother; and
- damage muscles, skin, teeth, glands, and bones.

Alcohol use in the third trimester may:

- impair brain and lung development;
- prevent adequate weight gain for the fetus; and
- cause early labor and delivery.

How Common Is FAS/FAE?

It is believed that 3 to 19 in 10,000 children are born with FAS each year in the United States. It is not known how many are born with FAE.

Alcohol can affect a pregnancy as early as the first month. Many women discontinue drinking alcohol during pregnancy. However, some may not know they are pregnant until the second or third month.

The annual cost of FAS to the United States has been estimated to be $2.7 billion. These do not include hard-to-measure FAS costs such as special education, welfare, and residential care. They also do not include the costs of FAE.

What Are the Characteristics of FAS/FAE?

Not all children with FAS/FAE are alike. The effects range from mild to severe. They depend on the amount of alcohol used and the time in which it is used. They also depend on the mother's diet, age, and drinking history. Typically, children with FAS/FAE have more physical, developmental and behavioral problems than other children. Early identification is the first step to an improved prognosis.

The following are the most common characteristics found in children affected by alcohol use during pregnancy. Remember, not all children with FAS/FAE have all the characteristics.

Physical Characteristics Related to FAS/FAE

Growth deficiencies may include:

- low birth weight;
- small size for age in weight and length;
- small head for age; and
- failure to thrive.

Facial malformations may include:

- short eye slits;
- droopy eyelids;
- widely spaced eyes;
- nearsightedness;
- crossed eyes;
- short upturned nose;
- low and/or wide bridge of the nose;
- flat or smooth area between the nose and lip;
- thin upper lip;
- flat midface; and
- small underdeveloped jaw.

Other effects may include:

- large or malformed ears;
- underdeveloped fingernails or toenails;
- short neck;
- poor eye-hand coordination;
- hearing problems; and
- joint and bone abnormalities.

Behavioral Characteristics Related to FAS/FAE

Children with FAS/FAE often have behavior problems due to brain injury. Some have more behavioral problems than others. Some are so severely affected that they cannot function independently in the community. Behavior problems will vary. They include:

- hyperactivity;
- stubbornness;
- impulsiveness;
- passiveness;
- fearlessness;
- irritability;
- sleep difficulties; and
- teasing or bullying of others.

Other effects may include:

- hypersensitivity to sound and touch;
- difficulty with change;
- organizational difficulties;
- poor self-image;
- overstimulation difficulties;
- depression or withdrawal;
- problems with truancy; and
- problems with sexuality.

Learning Difficulties Related to FAS/FAE

Children with FAS/FAE frequently have learning difficulties. These difficulties result from poor thinking and processing skills. Information may be known, but cannot be applied to different situations. Learning may occur in spurts. Easy learning periods may be followed by harder ones. During difficult periods, children may have trouble remembering and using their learned information. Because of inconsistent learning, teachers may think they are just not trying. They may label them as lazy or stubborn.

Difficulties may include:

- developmental delays;
- attention deficit;
- poor organization skills;
- problems with memory;
- poor mathematical skills;
- difficulty with abstract concepts;
- difficulty learning from past experiences;
- difficulty understanding cause and effect; and
- speech delays, stuttering, and stammering.

Inappropriate Social Skills Related to FAS/FAE

Children with FAS/FAE often show socially inappropriate behavior due to impaired practical reasoning skills. They also may be unable to consider results of their actions. They may miss cues used as subtle messages like gestures and facial expressions. They may be socially and emotionally immature and have difficulty getting along with peers.

Children with FAS/FAE can easily be influenced by others. Due to their trusting nature and eagerness to please, random attraction to strangers may occur. They may be vulnerable to manipulation and victimization. This can cause concern for caregivers. Constant supervision may be required.

Developmental Skills Related to FAS/FAE

There is a great difference between physical maturity and emotional and social development. An individual of 18 years of age with

FAS/FAE may have a much lower developmental age. Problems can occur if age-appropriate behavior is expected but cannot be met. Gradual catch-up may occur in adulthood.

Positive Characteristics of Children with FAS/FAE

Children with FAS/FAE have many valuable qualities and talents. With early identification, intervention and family support many can develop their best qualities. These children may be:

- cuddly, cheerful, and tactile;
- friendly and happy;
- caring, kind, loyal, nurturing, and compassionate;
- trusting and loving;
- determined, committed, and persistent;
- curious and involved;
- energetic, hard working, and athletic;
- artistic, musical, and creatively intelligent;
- fair and cooperative;
- highly verbal;
- kind with younger children and animals;
- able to have long-term visual memory; and
- able to participate in problem solving.

Section 45.2

Diagnosing FAS

Excerpted from "Guidelines of Care for Children With Special Health Care Needs: Fetal Alcohol Syndrome and Fetal Alcohol Effects," 1999. Minnesota Department of Health, Minnesota Children With Special Health Needs. This Minnesota Children with Special Health Care Needs program 'Guideline' accurately reflected the consensus of the health care community at the time of its publication in 1999, though readers should note that the understanding of Fetal Alcohol Spectrum Disorders is continuing to evolve rapidly. Revised by David A. Cooke, M.D., April 2006.

How Is FAS/FAE Diagnosed?

FAS/FAE is diagnosed after completion of a medical examination and psychological, occupational therapy, and speech/language evaluations.

- Medical examination—this includes:
  - evaluation of the prenatal and birth history and previous medical history;
  - general physical examination;
  - evaluation of early and current growth patterns; and
  - measurement of facial features.
- Psychological evaluation including developmental tests to determine abilities and deficits.
- Occupational therapy evaluation to determine motor functions and adaptive abilities.
- Speech and language evaluation to determine abilities to understand and communicate.

Think about your child's medical history. Write down what you know. Try to collect photos of your child taken between the ages of two and ten. Photos should be straight on, not smiling and without glasses. This may help your health provider or professional to obtain a diagnosis.

Once the diagnosis is made, specific deficits will be identified. Recommendations for intervention and treatment services will then be made.

Discussing the Diagnosis with Your Child

Some parents and caretakers are hesitant to discuss the diagnosis with their child. By school age, children with FAS/FAE usually recognize that they are not like others. They may have suffered teasing, frustration, and humiliation in the classroom or on the playground. Self-esteem may be bruised by the time the diagnosis is made.

Having a medical diagnosis is often a relief to children with FAS/FAE. A diagnosis provides a reason for their problems. They understand it is not their fault. They can begin to understand that their mother did not intentionally hurt them by drinking during pregnancy. Parents may also feel a sense of relief. A diagnosis provides a medical reason for their child's behavior. They can understand that behaviors may not be intentional or due to poor parenting skills.

Section 45.3

Health Concerns of Children with FAS

Excerpted from "Guidelines of Care for Children With Special Health Care Needs: Fetal Alcohol Syndrome and Fetal Alcohol Effects," 1999. Minnesota Department of Health, Minnesota Children With Special Health Needs. This Minnesota Children with Special Health Care Needs program 'Guideline' accurately reflected the consensus of the health care community at the time of its publication in 1999, though readers should note that the understanding of Fetal Alcohol Spectrum Disorders is continuing to evolve rapidly. Revised by David A. Cooke, M.D., April 2006.

The most important concern for children with FAS/FAE is the altered brain function. Physical health problems related to the central nervous system (CNS) are frequent. These may include visual problems, seizures, tremors, and incoordination. CNS problems may also cause a wide variety of behavior and learning difficulties.

Children with FAS/FAE sometimes also have congenital anomalies. These may include abnormalities of the ears or eyes, cleft lip, and palate and heart defects. Heart defects occur in about one third of the children. Skeletal problems such as scoliosis may also occur. Children born with heart murmurs or other defects may need monitoring, medical management, or surgery. Medical management difficulties can occur if the child is unable to cooperate with the treatment plan.

Early intervention is the first step to an improved prognosis. Discuss a plan for early intervention with your health providers and professionals.

These health problems need medical attention between regular visits. Ask your health providers or professionals when to call or bring your child in for medical care. Call for advice if you have a health concern or are unsure if medical attention is needed. Always call if your child has:

- high fever or fever unusual for the child;

- difficulty breathing or swallowing;

- signs of depression, withdrawal, anxiety, sudden change in school performance, or school attendance;

- urges to harm him or herself or others; or

- noncompliance with the treatment plan.

Periodic Health Care

Regular health care visits are important to the well-being of all children. The visits are necessary to check FAS/FAE-related problems as well as growth and development. The schedule of visits will depend on the child's age and needs. Children are individuals and their needs will vary. Periodic health care may include any of the following health issues:

- physical examinations

- immunizations including *Haemophilus influenzae* type B (HIB)

- influenza (flu) shots

- height and weight measuring and graphing

- nutritional assessments

- vision, hearing, and scoliosis screening

- discussion of the treatment plan

- discussion of the medication plan, medication effectiveness, possible side effects, and adjustments

- discussion of dental and other specialty care
- discussion of development since the last visit
- discussion of emotional adaption and self-esteem
- discussion of performance at school
- discussion of problems, questions, and concerns

Record Keeping

Record keeping is an important part of coordinating health care. Some parents find it helpful to keep their own records. Others prefer to rely on their health provider's records. If you keep your own records, you can use a loose-leaf notebook, which can be divided into sections to fit your needs. Calendars or expandable pocket files can also be used. Section topics may include:

- names, titles, addresses, and phone numbers of health care team members;
- immunization records;
- growth charts and development records;
- dates of developmental milestones such as walking and saying first words;
- results of vision, hearing, and scoliosis screenings;
- nutritional information such as food intake;
- results of tests;
- dates of illnesses and complications;
- daily care plans if any;
- medication plans and medication side effects;
- reports from hospitalizations and surgeries;
- appointment dates;
- school records including assessments, performance reports and copies of the Individual Family Service Plan (IFSP), Individual Education Plan (IEP) and Individual Health Plan (IHP);
- resource information such as financial assistance and support systems; and
- copies of financial information such as bills and payments, insurance policies, and applications for financial assistance.

Write down questions before visits to health care team members. It is easy to forget what you want to ask during a busy clinic visit. Some parents tape record instructions from health providers and professionals. The tape can be replayed later to review the instructions. It can also be shared with others working with the child.

Section 45.4

FAS through the Years

Excerpted from "Guidelines of Care for Children With Special Health Care Needs: Fetal Alcohol Syndrome and Fetal Alcohol Effects," 1999. Minnesota Department of Health, Minnesota Children With Special Health Needs. This Minnesota Children with Special Health Care Needs program 'Guideline' accurately reflected the consensus of the health care community at the time of its publication in 1999, though readers should note that the understanding of Fetal Alcohol Spectrum Disorders is continuing to evolve rapidly. Revised by David A. Cooke, M.D., April 2006.

Infants and Toddlers with FAS/FAE—Ages 0 to 3

Infants born with FAS/FAE may have a difficult first few months. Some infants show behaviors related to withdrawal symptoms from alcohol. These symptoms can include seizures, sleeping disorders, stomach upsets, and extreme fussiness. Some infants are unable to screen out unwanted noise and distractions. This may cause overstimulation, frustration, and irritability.

Many infants with FAS/FAE are born with low birth weight. Some have difficulty getting adequate nourishment due to poor sucking and swallowing abilities or mouth abnormalities. There may be failure to thrive or height and weight growth deficiencies. Nutritional assessments and monitoring may be needed.

Most infants with FAS/FAE show:

- irritability, jitteriness, and nervousness;
- sucking or feeding difficulties;

- poor muscle tone;
- sleep disorders;
- sensitivity to sound and light;
- excessive crying; and
- decreased alertness.

Older infants with FAS/FAE tend to:

- be easily upset;
- be easily distractible;
- be hyperactive;
- have short attention spans;
- have developmental delays; and
- have problems using muscles.

Health care team members need to be aware of the infant's physical, mental, emotional, and behavioral development. This will help determine special needs related to FAS/FAE. It also helps health providers and professionals understand family strengths and resources. Early intervention is the first step to an improved prognosis. Ongoing followup will also be required.

Helpful suggestions for interventions include the following:

- It is important to learn what your infant is trying to tell you. Understanding cues helps parents meet their child's needs and lessen stress.
- Because of hypersensitivity to sound and touch, sensory stimulation should be decreased. Try to:
  - Keep lights low.
  - Keep noise levels to a minimum.
  - Gradually introduce stimuli one at a time.
  - Use calming techniques when overstimulation occurs. A warm bath or shower, listening to quiet music, swaddling, or rocking may help.
  - Provide consistent bedtime routines. Darken the bedroom at night and at nap times. Provide soft snug clothing. Try to discover which textures are comforting. Lessen distractions

in the bedroom. Avoid mobiles. Use plain bumper pads. Simplify room decorations. Avoid clutter and busyness. Use white noise such as a fan or soft relaxing music.

- Healthy eating should be a daily goal. Try to make mealtime a positive experience. Suggestions for feeding include:

  - Learn hunger signs and serve food when signs are first shown.

  - Serve small frequent high calorie meals and snacks. Four to six meals per day may be needed for adequate nourishment.

  - Reduce distractions while feeding. This helps an infant focus on eating. Feed in a quiet and slightly darkened room. Do not rock or talk while feeding. Do not turn on a radio or television.

  - Never prop a bottle or leave a child unattended while eating.

  - Allow ample time for eating. Have reasonable expectations on portion size. Serve food warm. Avoid hot or cold foods. It may be helpful to reduce the texture of foods offered.

  - Limit choices.

  - Seek help from a nutrition professional.

Health Care

Continue regular health care. Concerns for this age group include vision, hearing, and dental screening, cognitive, motor and language development. Social skills, nutrition, and special needs related to FAS/FAE also need consideration. The following may be included:

- Height and weight need to be obtained and graphed.

- Infants and toddlers with FAS/FAE often have growth problems. Diets need to be monitored. The diet will have many changes during this period. Contact your health provider or dietitian if you have questions.

- Some feeding practices seem to reduce the development of allergies. Breastfeeding is usually best. Avoid alcohol while breastfeeding. Avoid cow's milk during the first year. Your health care provider or professional can suggest an infant formula if needed. Wait until your infant is 6 months old to slowly introduce solid foods.

- Flu shots may be given to prevent influenza.

- Medication dosages may need to be changed frequently.

- Upper respiratory and ear infections may occur frequently due to an impaired immune system. Antibiotics may be given to treat some infections.

- Parents should be present as much as possible for comfort and support if hospitalization occurs.

- Remember that all children need well-baby checkups and immunizations.

Development

- Children develop faster as infants and toddlers than at any other time in life. Enjoy watching your child grow and develop. Note the dates your infant or toddler reaches milestones. Examples of developmental milestones are crawling, standing, and walking. Language milestones include saying the first word, using several words and connecting two words. Remember, infants with FAS/FAE may show some delays in reaching these milestones.

- Provide an environment where your child can play safely with the least restriction. Provide toys and activities which are right for your child's age and development. Children with FAS/FAE may need some safety restrictions. Gates on stairways, crib nets, and door alerting systems may be necessary.

- Infants with FAS/FAE may have eating problems. Some infants and toddlers fail to gain weight even when eating enough. Growth deficiency may continue throughout childhood. Watch your child's food intake and weight gain. Talk to your health provider or professional if you have concerns. Children with FAS/FAE are less likely to develop regular sleep cycles than other children. They may also experience more interruptions in their sleep.

Helpful Hints to Manage Hyperactivity

- Limit activities which cause overstimulation. Activities such as pillow fighting, wrestling, television, video games, or rock music may overstimulate. Alternate activities requiring attention with those requiring physical exercise. Quiet and focused activities such as finger painting or coloring may help children slow down.

- Have a place where your toddler can go when overstimulated or overwhelmed. It should be a comfortable and calm area. It should not be treated as a punishment.

- Teach self-calming techniques. Soft music can be calming and may also help to develop listening skills. If one technique is not working, try something different.

Helpful Hints for Discipline Issues

- Set both expectations and limitations. Consistent direction and discipline are important for a child who has trouble learning and remembering rules. Your child may not learn from past mistakes. Mistakes may be repeated over and over again. Consistency helps all children develop self-control.

- Develop a system of rewards and discipline. Try to use the same system for all your children. Children may notice if one child receives special privileges.

- Discipline should be immediate. Do not delay. Your child may have trouble connecting cause and effect. This means there may be difficulty in seeing a connection between the behavior and the punishment. Discipline should be viewed as an opportunity to teach appropriate behavior. A reward system may work best. Sometimes praise and hugs can be just as effective. Change rewards often to keep interest high. To avoid frustration, make sure there are more successes than failures.

- Do not debate rules. Be brief. Avoid lecturing and threats. Review and repeat consequences of negative behavior. Take time to teach and encourage positive behavior.

- Avoid statements which place a value on behavior. For example, do not say "that is a bad word." Say "you may not use that word." Offer a different word that is acceptable.

- Children with FAS/FAE may copy behavior they have experienced or observed. For this reason, never use physical punishments. Avoid all forms of violence. Monitor television, movies, and radio programs.

Helpful Hints to Provide Structure

- Establish a few simple rules. Use picture cues. Use the same language repetitively. Avoid using words with more than one

340

meaning. Be specific when telling your child what to do. Repeat directions as needed.

- Speak slowly. Pause between sentences to allow time for understanding.

- Daily routine is very important. Daily routine helps your child predict coming events. Before bedtime, prepare for the next day. For example, lay out clothing and shoes.

- Clearly define your child's space. Children with FAS/FAE may benefit from a comfortable area they can call their own. Avoid clutter and distractions.

Helpful Hints to Encourage Self-Esteem

- All children are better able to manage life if they feel good about themselves. Praise your child often to build self-esteem. Praise accomplishments. Reward rather than punish. Offer support, not criticism. Praise the behavior rather than the child. For example, say "good work" rather than "good boy" or "girl." Separate your child from the behavior. Do not make your child feel as if he or she is a bad person. Encourage positive self-talk.

- Children with FAS/FAE may need to be reminded that you like them. Notice good qualities and behaviors. Thank them for their efforts.

Helpful Hints for Behavior Issues

- Behavior may be changed by redirecting activities. Try to engage your child into positive play. Learn how to read and respond to emotional cues. This may help avoid behavior problems.

- Infants and toddlers with FAS/FAE often have problems with attachment. They may not show a preference for parents over others. They may not be able to differ between a friend and someone they just met. These problems may get worse as the child gets older. This can be very difficult for parents. Caregivers may need to be alert 24 hours a day to keep their child safe.

- Sometimes, children who are not feeling well may regress in behavior. They want parents to help them do things they previously did themselves. Usually this is temporary and will end when they are feeling better.

Child Care

- If you use child care, choose a provider who is willing to learn about caring for a child with FAS/FAE. Be sure you feel confident in your provider's ability to understand and carry out your instructions. Teach the provider about FAS/FAE and how to manage the condition.

- Children with FAS/FAE may need extra supervision to keep them safe. Choose child care where this can be provided. Often, children with FAS/FAE do better in small groups. Consistency with caregivers and routines is important. Centers which value attachment, predictability, flexibility, nurturing, and provide various ways of coping are best.

- Develop an emergency plan for your child care provider. Write a list of the reasons to contact you. Include phone numbers for yourself, your doctor, and several family members.

- Be sure your child care provider and helpers do not smoke if your child has allergies, asthma, or frequent ear infections.

- Colds and other infections are common in large child care centers. Children with FAS/FAE often have more ear infections. Child care with fewer children will reduce exposure to infections. It is not necessary nor are you likely to prevent all illnesses. Having an occasional illness will help develop your child's immune system.

- The Americans with Disabilities Act (ADA) provides that child care may not refuse a child because of a special health need. This is regardless of child care size or whether they receive public funds.

School

Part C of the Individuals with Disabilities Education Act (IDEA) requires schools to provide Early Intervention services. Services are provided to children who have special health needs which affect learning or who have developmental delays. Children from birth to age 3 are entitled to these services. Parents are partners on a multidisciplinary team that develops an Individual Family Service Plan (IFSP) for their child. Contact your local school district to find out how this program works in your area. Ask to speak to the Early Childhood Intervention Coordinator.

Preschool Children with FAS/FAE—Ages 3 to 6

Preschool children with FAS/FAE are usually friendly, outgoing, highly social, and talkative. Verbal skills are often better than thinking skills. However, cognitive, motor, and complex speech development are usually slow.

Signs of hyperactivity are seen in many children with FAS/FAE. Sensitivity to sensory stimulation like touch and sound may continue. There may be difficulty making a transition from one activity to another. There may be difficulty adjusting to change in routines. Frustration and temper tantrums often occur, especially as children get older.

Children with FAS/FAE often have no real sense of "stranger danger." They may not be able to differ between a friend and someone they just met. They may respond to strangers the same way they respond to their parents. Close supervision is usually required. Parents may need to be alert 24 hours a day to keep their child safe. This can cause stress and frustration which increases as the child gets older.

The entire family may need support from others to help with coping. Family members can benefit from venting frustrations without feeling blamed. Parent support groups may be helpful.

Health Care

Continue regular health care. Concerns for this age group include promoting optimal growth and development and activities of daily living (ADL) skills. A preschool evaluation and determining special needs related to FAS/FAE also need consideration. The following may be included:

- Height and weight need to be obtained and graphed. Children with FAS/FAE may tend to grow slower than other children. They may be small for their age. They may not catch up later.

- A nutritious and balanced diet is important. A nutritional assessment may be done.

- Poor gross motor coordination can lead to injury. Frequently the child does not recall how he or she got hurt. Suspicion may fall unjustly upon the caregiver. The child may not be able to identify pain or know how to tell you about it. Children with FAS/FAE may also have a high tolerance for pain. They may not complain. Injuries can go untreated. Teach children what to do when their body hurts.

- Extra care may be needed to treat ear infections, which can lead to hearing loss.

- An impaired immune system may continue. It places the child with FAS/FAE at greater risk for opportunistic infections.

- Flu shots are usually given to prevent influenza. They are given in the fall to provide protection during the flu season.

Development

- Provide your child with simple information about FAS/FAE. Help them tell their own story and identify feelings.

- Provide your child with opportunities to:
  - play with other children the same age. However, some children with FAS/FAE are more comfortable playing with children one to two years younger.
  - learn to start and complete activities during play.
  - play outdoors in a safe area.
  - succeed and gain self-confidence.
  - maintain a balance between structured activities and free time.

- Offer assistance or aids to help your child overcome difficulties which may hinder progress. For example, a computer may help a child who has difficulty writing.

- Irregular sleep patterns may continue. Stay with an established evening routine and bedtime. Routines help children who have difficulty predicting and organizing. Music, singing, or reading can help to calm or soothe. Naps may be needed, however, many children with FAS/FAE will not nap at all.

- Mealtime is an opportunity for socialization. It helps in bonding and developing relationships. A positive mealtime should be a priority. Children with FAS/FAE may lose interest in eating before completing a meal. They may need to be reminded to eat. Often, they need to move about while eating.

- Children with FAS/FAE may have difficulty making and keeping friends. Plan brief play periods with one or two friends. Teach friendship and sharing. Friends may be the same age or younger. Supervise and structure activities. Lack of friendships may result in increased dependency on caregivers.

- Parents may need a break from caregiving. Try to arrange re-spite care. Family and friends may be of assistance. Respite care may also be obtained through county services or parent organizations for children with disabilities. Sometimes trained volunteers can provide babysitting for a few hours or days.

- Most children this age love to pretend. They may act out things they have seen or that have happened to them. Usually this type of play, with friends or stuffed animals, can help the child learn. Parents can help children understand experiences through this type of play. Sometimes parents will need to teach the child how to play and how to separate fact from fiction.

- Children with FAS/FAE often must be taught some of the most basic skills. This may include recognizing the difference between friends and strangers. Lessons should be related to needs. Provide real-life examples. Role play may help teach these skills.

For helpful hints about managing hyperactivity and behavior, fostering self-esteem, disciplining a child with FAS, and arranging child care, see information under the portion of text labeled "Infants and Toddlers with FAS/FAE—Ages 0 to 3" above.

School

- Part C of the Individuals with Disabilities Education Act (IDEA) requires schools to provide Early Intervention services. Services are provided to children who have special health needs that affect learning or who have developmental delays. Children ages 3 to 5 are entitled to these services. Parents are partners on a multidisciplinary team that develops an Individual Family Service Plan (IFSP) for their child. Contact your local school district to find out how this program works in your area. Ask to speak to the Early Childhood Intervention Coordinator.

- At the beginning of each school year, meet with your child's teacher and school nurse. Inform them of your child's development and any special needs related to FAS/FAE. Keep them informed of changes throughout the year.

- If your child has asthma or allergies, ask about pets and plants in the classroom.

- Make sure the school has instructions from your health provider about use of medication if needed. The school nurse will need a pharmacy label on all medications given at school. Contact your child's school for policies on medication given at school.

- Encourage your child to be involved in activities appropriate for his or her abilities.

- Medical appointments may conflict with family and school schedules. Decide on priorities and then arrange appointments. This may not be as important during preschool years as it is when the child is older. Try to arrange appointments during slow times at school.

- If your child is absent from school, request that schoolwork be sent home. If schoolwork causes too much conflict at home, work with teachers to develop alternatives.

- If possible, get to know your child's teachers and let them know you. If you have time, volunteer. Develop relationships with school staff. This helps to promote sharing of information and understanding of your child's needs.

- Try to take another parent or friend along with you to important school meetings. Their support may be helpful.

School-Age Children with FAS/FAE—Ages 6 to 13

School-age children with FAS/FAE may continue to grow slowly. They may appear thin and malnourished even though the diet is adequate. Their slow-growing head size is related to slow brain growth and development.

The elementary school years mark the time when additional problems may begin to show. Children with FAS/FAE may have difficulty "fitting in" and making friends. They may want to play with younger children or adults. It is important to teach your child social skills. Skills must be taught early and repetitively to become habits.

Children with FAS/FAE may not be able to learn from experience. They may also have difficulty following rules. Rules may be known, but cannot be applied. They may lack understanding of action and consequence.

The complex school environment can be especially challenging. Children may feel overwhelmed, which can result in problems with learning. Anger, frustration, temper tantrums, and refusals can be signs your child is having difficulty. Listen to your child's complaints. The school environment may need to be modified to suit special needs. It is important to work closely with the school to assure that your child's needs are being met.

Due to problems with short-term memory, skills must be taught over and over again. This can be frustrating for parents and teachers. However, repetition and practice help in learning.

Health Care

Continue regular health care. Concerns for this age group include promoting optimal growth and development and activities of daily living (ADL) skills. Special needs related to FAS/FAE also need consideration. The following may be included:

- Height and weight need to be obtained and graphed. Children with FAS/FAE tend to grow slower than other children. They may not catch up later.

- A nutritious and balanced diet is important. A nutritional assessment may be done.

- Exercise is important for all children. Exercise helps increase and maintain muscle strength. Exercise also builds stamina. Releasing energy through activity may help a child focus on learning. Find activities, sports or exercise which fit your child's physical abilities. Discuss any concerns with your health provider or professional.

Development

- Provide your child with specific information about FAS/FAE and related conditions. Encourage questions. Remind him or her that concerns can be discussed with parents, health providers, and other professionals.

- Provide your child with opportunities to:
  - play with other children the same age. However, some children with FAS/FAE are more comfortable playing with children one to two years younger.
  - learn to start and complete activities during play.
  - play outdoors in a safe area.
  - succeed and gain self-confidence.

347

- - maintain a balance between structured activities and free time.

- Offer assistance or aids to help your child overcome difficulties that may hinder progress. For example, a computer may help a child who has difficulty writing.

- Difficulty making and keeping friendships may continue. This can result in an increased dependency on caregivers.

- Parents may need a break from caregiving. Try to arrange respite care. Family and friends may be of assistance. Respite care may also be obtained through county services or parent organizations for children with disabilities. Sometimes trained volunteers can provide babysitting for a few hours or days.

- Children with FAS/FAE may have difficulty with abstract concepts such as time, money, and math. They may not be able to tell time even by the age of 12. Problems understanding the concept of time may continue after mastering the skill. The value of money is also a difficult concept to grasp. Your child may not associate value to items. For example, $5.00 for a piece of candy or for a television may seem acceptable. Monitor your child's money. Limit access to money when you cannot directly supervise its use. Give your child money only in small amounts. Do not expect understanding of equal values such as four quarters being the same as a dollar.

- Teach your child about ownership. A child with FAS/FAE will often take something which catches his or her eye. The concept of stealing may not be understood. Teach your child to ask before taking anything that does not belong to him or her.

- Teach your child visual and verbal gestures to help understand directions. Limit directions to 5 to 10 seconds. Use eye contact. Direct one task at a time. Avoid using words with more than one meaning. Be specific when telling your child what to do. Repeat directions as needed.

For helpful hints about managing hyperactivity and behavior, fostering self-esteem, disciplining a child with FAS, arranging child care, and working with school personnel, see information under the portions of text labeled "Infants and Toddlers with FAS/FAE—Ages 0 to 3" and "School-Age Children with FAS/FAE—Ages 6 to 13" above.

Adolescents with FAS/FAE—Ages 13 to 18

Typically, the thin build of children with FAS/FAE begins to change during adolescence. Girls tend to become obese. After puberty, the facial features of FAS/FAE are more difficult to recognize.

Teenagers with FAS/FAE may display problem behaviors such as lying and stealing. They may have poor judgment. They may have difficulty with peer relationships. Alcohol and drug abuse are common. There is also a greater risk for depression and suicide.

Teenagers with FAS/FAE usually look like typical adolescents. However, their developmental level may only be that of a six year old. Extra guidance and protection may be needed.

In guiding adolescents with FAS/FAE, stress the following:

- Structure—create a structured environment that includes limited choices. Have clear and set routines. Adjust the environment for slower development and understanding.
- Supervision—carefully supervise adolescents so they do not place themselves in dangerous situations.

- Simplicity—state instructions briefly and clearly. Use simple directions and orders.

- Steps—break tasks down into small steps. Teach each step through repetition. Lists may be helpful. Use rewards as incentives.

- Setting—teach desired skills in the way in which they will be used. Adolescents with FAS/FAE may not have the ability to transfer skills from one setting to another.

Health Care

Continue regular health care. Routine health visits should address both the medical and psychosocial aspects of health. Adolescence is a time of significant change in development and behavior. There may be new needs that relate to special issues of this age. Concerns include screening for health risk behaviors and promoting optimal growth and development and activities of daily living (ADL) skills. Special needs related to FAS/FAE also need consideration. The following may be included:

- A discussion of health prevention topics such as:
  - use of tobacco products and use and abuse of alcohol or other drugs;

- severe or recurrent depression and suicide attempts;
- physical, sexual, and emotional abuse;
- high blood pressure;
- high cholesterol;
- infectious diseases; and
- learning problems.

- A discussion of health promotion topics such as:
  - adjustment to puberty and adolescence;
  - healthy eating habits, proper nutrition, and prevention of eating disorders or obesity;
  - safety and injury prevention;
  - physical fitness; and
  - parent's ability to respond to health needs of their adolescent.

- A discussion of mental health issues such as:
  - anger and violence management;
  - ruling out other diagnoses such as personality disorders and depression;
  - self-esteem; and
  - emotional abuse.

- A discussion of sexual health topics such as:
  - birth control;
  - victimizing others and becoming victims;
  - sexually transmitted diseases (STDs); and
  - inappropriate sexual behavior.

- Health services should meet the needs of the individual teenager. Information shared with health providers is personal and confidential.

- Health care for teenagers with FAS/FAE may be difficult for health providers and professionals. They need to be aware that teenagers with FAS/FAE may not be able to provide accurate information. Due to memory gaps, they may be unable to report symptoms or take medication.

- Exercise is important for all teenagers. Exercise helps increase and maintain muscle strength. Exercise also builds stamina. Releasing energy through activity may help a teen focus on learning. Find activities, sports, or exercise that fit your teen's physical abilities. Discuss any concerns with your health provider or professional.

Development

- Teenagers understand factual information about FAS/FAE. Give them specific information about their condition. The information can be more detailed than for younger children. Encourage your teen to read about FAS/FAE.

- Teenagers may need encouragement to ask questions. Remind them that concerns can be discussed with parents, health providers, and professionals.

- Allow your teenager increasing control over when to take medication or do other treatments. Encourage him or her to be responsible for remembering these things. Mastering self-care skills gives all teens a feeling of control and accomplishment. It may still be necessary to remind a teen to take his or her medication. Many teens with FAS/FAE are not able to manage their medication or treatments.

- Provide opportunities for your teenager to be faced with opinions, values, and beliefs which differ from his or her own. Peers are of increasing importance to teens. Teenagers with high self-esteem can better resist peer pressure. They will also be less concerned about being different from their friends.

- Some teenagers may be vulnerable to pressure to be sexually active or to use alcohol and drugs. They may seek acceptance from their peers through these activities. Parents can help prevent these behaviors by discussing concerns with their teen. Ask a health professional for ideas on how to deal with specific problems and promote self-esteem.

- Independence is necessary for teenagers to develop responsible behavior. They will need encouragement to increase their independence and make the transition to adult life.

- It is important to remember that teenagers will not outgrow the effects of FAS/FAE. It lasts a lifetime. Regardless of age, mental and emotional functioning may be much lower. Teens may continue to require supervision to keep out of trouble or dangerous situations.

For helpful hints about managing hyperactivity and behavior, fostering self-esteem, disciplining a child with FAS, arranging child care, and working with school personnel, see information under the portions of text labeled "Infants and Toddlers with FAS/FAE—Ages 0 to 3" and "School-Age Children with FAS/FAE—Ages 6 to 13" above.

Chapter 46

Behavioral Issues and Other Conditions Associated with FAS

Chapter Contents

Section 46.1—Understanding FAS and Behavior 354

Section 46.2—Secondary Conditions Associated with FAS 358

Section 46.1

Understanding FAS and Behavior

Excerpted from "Ain't Misbehavin': Understanding the Behaviors of
Children and Adolescents with Fetal Alcohol Syndrome" by Deb
Evensen. Copyright 2005 Deb Evensen. Reprinted with permission.

Fetal Alcohol Syndrome

Fetal Alcohol Syndrome (FAS) and other alcohol-related birth defects refer to a group of physical and mental birth defects resulting from a woman drinking alcohol during pregnancy.

Four primary diagnostic criteria indicate full fetal alcohol syndrome:

- growth deficiencies—stunted prenatal and/or postnatal growth;

- permanent brain damage—resulting in neurological abnormalities, delay in development, intellectual impairment, and learning/behavior disorders;

- abnormal facial features—short eye openings, short nose, flat mid-face, thin upper lip, and small chin; and

- maternal alcohol use during pregnancy.

Some but not all of the primary diagnostic criteria for FAS can lead to such diagnoses as:

- Fetal Alcohol Effect (FAE)
- Alcohol Related Neurodevelopmental Disorder (ARND)
- Fetal Alcohol Related Conditions (FARC)
- Alcohol Related Birth Defects (ARBD)

Alcohol is a teratogen that affects whatever is developing in her fetus when a pregnant woman drinks. Whether a child has the specific physical characteristics of FAS simply depends on when and how much the mother drank alcohol. However, the brain is developing throughout gestation, and prenatal exposure to alcohol at any time during pregnancy can alter the development of the baby's brain.

Prenatal exposure to alcohol causes an "invisible disability" that manifests behaviorally. Many children have the brain damage without all of the physical dysmorphology of full FAS, which reminds others of their disability.

Without an understanding of the physically based cognitive challenges faced by people with fetal alcohol related conditions, typical, normal behaviors can be misinterpreted as willful misconduct or deliberate disobedience, when it is often just the opposite.

Information Processing Differences

Due to the way the brain prenatally exposed to alcohol works, people with fetal alcohol related conditions have difficulty with the following:

- input, or taking in of information
- integration of new information with previous learning
- memory, especially short-term memory
- output, or ability to use information

Children and adolescents prenatally exposed to alcohol have difficulty with:

- Abstract Reasoning—Abstract concepts are the invisible foundation that structures our world.

- Cause and Effect Reasoning—Imagination. People with fetal alcohol related conditions often can't imagine something they haven't experienced.

- Generalization—They don't have moveable parts in the thinking process; so when you change a piece of the routine for the child, you have created an entirely new routine.

- Time—Telling time, feeling the passage of time, associating specific activities to numbers on a clock, cyclical nature of events.

- Memory—Especially short-term memory. They often talk better than they think. They can "talk the talk" but can't "walk the walk."

They have difficulty with socialization and skills of independence.

Fetal alcohol syndrome is a lifelong disability, but secondary characteristics may occur, such as:

- fatigue and tantrums
- irritability, frustration, anger, and aggression
- fear, anxiety, avoidance, withdrawal, shutdown, lying, and running away
- trouble at home and/or school
- legal trouble and drug/alcohol abuse
- mental health problems

These secondary conditions are preventable when parents and professionals understand the cognitive challenges associated with a child's history of prenatal exposure to alcohol.

Behavioral Expectations of Children and Adolescents with FAS/E:

Age-Appropriate Versus Developmental Age-Appropriate Expectations

Typical 5-year-olds:

- go to school;
- follow three instructions;
- participate in interactive, cooperative play;
- share; and
- take turns.

Five-year-olds with FAS/E:

- take naps;
- follow one instruction;
- help a parent;
- sit still for 5 to 10 minutes;
- participate in parallel play;
- are active; and
- act as if it's "My way or no way."

Typical 10-year-olds:

- answer abstract questions;
- get along with others and solve problems;
- learn inferentially;
- are academic and social;
- have physical stamina; and
- generalize information learned from worksheets.

Ten-year-olds with FAS/E:

- learn by doing (experientially);
- mirror and echo words and behaviors;
- participate in supervised play and structured play;
- learn from modeled problem solving; and
- are easily fatigued by mental work.

Typical 18-year-olds:

- are on the verge of independence;
- maintain a job and graduate from school;
- have a plan for life;
- budget their own money; and
- organize.

Eighteen-year-olds with FAS/E:

- need structure and guidance;
- have limited choices of activities;
- are in the "here and now";
- experience giggles, curiosity, and frustration;
- get an allowance; and
- get organized with help of adults.

FAS in a Nutshell

- FAS is the leading known cause of mental retardation.

- Most individuals with FAS have normal intelligence.
- FAS causes serious social and behavior problems.
- Each year in the United States 5,000 babies are born with FAS.
- Ten times as many are born with alcohol-related disorders.
- No amount of alcohol is known to be safe during pregnancy.
- Alcohol causes more damage to a baby than any other drug.
- FAS and related conditions are 100% preventable.

Section 46.2

Secondary Conditions Associated with FAS

From the Centers for Disease Control and Prevention, National Center on Birth Defects and Developmental Disabilities (www.cdc.gov/ncbddd), April 13, 2005.

Secondary conditions are problems that a person is not born with, but might acquire as a result of fetal alcohol syndrome (FAS). These conditions can be lessened or prevented through better understanding of and appropriate interventions for children and adults with FAS and their families.

The following are some of the secondary conditions that have been found to be associated with FAS.

Mental Health Problems. Several studies have shown an increased risk for cognitive disorders, psychiatric illness, or psychological dysfunction among individuals with FAS. The most frequently diagnosed disorders are attention problems, including attention deficit/hyperactivity disorder (ADHD); conduct disorder; alcohol or drug dependence; depression; or psychotic episodes. Other psychiatric problems, such as anxiety disorders, depression, eating disorders, and posttraumatic stress disorder, have also been reported for some patients.

Disrupted School Experience. Children with FAS are more likely than most children to be suspended, expelled, or drop out of school. Difficulty getting along with other children, poor relationships with teachers, and truancy are some of the reasons that lead to their removal from the school setting. Many children with FAS remain in school but have negative experiences because of their behavioral challenges.

Trouble with the Law. Teenagers and adults with FAS are more likely than those who do not have FAS to have interactions with police, authorities, or the judicial system. Difficulty controlling anger and frustration, combined with problems understanding the motives of others, result in many individuals with FAS being involved in violent or explosive situations. People with FAS can be very easy to persuade and manipulate, which can lead to their taking part in illegal acts without being aware of it.

Inappropriate Sexual Behavior. Individuals with FAS are more likely than individuals who do not have FAS to exhibit inappropriate sexual behavior, such as inappropriate advances and inappropriate touching. Being a victim of violence increases the risk of participating in sexually inappropriate behavior.

Alcohol and Drug Problems. Studies suggest that more than a third of individuals with FAS have had problems with alcohol or drugs, with more than half requiring inpatient treatment.

Dependent Living and Problems with Employment over 21 Years. Adults with FAS generally have difficulty sustaining employment or living independently as productive members of their communities.

Problems with Parenting. Individuals with FAS who experience some of the other problems described here are more likely to become parents compared to individuals who do not have FAS. For example, an individual who has FAS may have poor judgment and poor impulse control as a result of primary brain dysfunction. These factors, combined with a secondary condition of alcohol dependence, may result in unprotected sex and pregnancy. This can possibly lead to another generation of babies at risk of prenatal alcohol exposure. Individuals with FAS who become parents are more likely to have a history of having lived in unstable homes, more likely to have been homeless, more likely to have run away from home, and more likely to have experienced domestic violence compared to individuals with FAS who do not become parents.

Source: Streissguth, A.P., Barr, H.M., Kogan, J. & Bookstein, F. L., "Understanding the Occurrence of Secondary Disabilities in Clients with Fetal Alcohol Syndrome (FAS) and Fetal Alcohol Effects (FAE)," Final Report to the Centers for Disease Control and Prevention (CDC), August, 1996, Seattle: University of Washington, Fetal Alcohol & Drug Unit, Tech. Rep. No. 96-06, (1996).

Part Five

Mental Health
Problems Associated with
Alcohol Use

Chapter 47

Alcohol and Mental Health

Chapter Contents

Section 47.1—Mental Illness and Problem Drinking 364

Section 47.2—The Prevalence and Co-Occurrence of
Alcohol, Drug, Mood, and Anxiety Disorders 370

Section 47.1

Mental Illness and Problem Drinking

"Alcohol and Mental Health," © 2004 Institute of Alcohol Studies.
Reprinted with permission.

There is a close relationship between alcohol problems and mental health. People with mental health problems are at raised risk of alcohol problems and vice versa.

There is thus more than one kind of relationship involved:

- Mental health problems may be a cause of problem drinking.

- Problem drinking may be a cause of mental ill-health problems.

- There may be a factor in common, in the genes, or in the early family environment, which later contributes to both a mental health problem and an alcohol problem.

- Some studies suggest that that light to moderate drinking may have some beneficial effects on mental health for some people, although the science basis for this is somewhat weak.

- Sometimes heavy drinkers start to misuse prescribed drugs, or illegal drugs, causing harm to mental health.

Mental Ill Health and Problem Drinking

American research suggests that overall, the prevalence of alcohol dependence is almost twice as high in those with psychiatric disorders as in the general population. One U.S. study[1] found that 19.9% of the general population had one or more psychiatric disorders, but in those with alcohol abuse or dependence the figure rose to 36.6%.

Another U.S.[2] study found that around half of those with a lifetime addictive disorder also had lifetime mental disorders, and vice versa.

Similar findings have been reported for the U.K. Less than 1% of the general U.K. household population report being moderately or severely dependent on alcohol, but this figure rises to 2% for people with any neurotic disorder, 5% among those with a phobia, and 6% in those with two or more neurotic disorders.

Conditions in which people may try to use alcohol to cope, with resulting problems include:

- depression—resulting from, for example, bereavement, retirement or arising out of the blue;

- anxiety—social anxiety, claustrophobia, agoraphobia;

- obsessive-compulsive disorders;

- manic-depressive illness—the elation phase is associated with drinking bouts; and/or

- schizophrenia.

The risk of alcohol problems is also known to be raised in those with a history of sexual abuse in childhood.

The condition most clearly associated with alcohol abuse and dependence is antisocial personality disorder (ASPD)—people with ASPD have 21 times the average population risk of experiencing alcohol abuse or dependence. In the U.K., drinking at hazardous levels has also been shown to be more likely in those with ASPD. In one survey, 59% of those (men and women combined) with ASPD were classified as hazardous drinkers, compared with 25% of those without.

This compares with:

- schizophrenia—3 times the population average risk of alcohol dependence;

- depression and affective disorders—1.9 times the average population risk of alcohol dependence; and

- anxiety—1.5 times the average population risk of experiencing alcohol dependence.

Alcohol, Anxiety, and Depression

Alcohol is the most widely consumed psychoactive drug in the world, and some of the most frequently cited reasons for drinking involve bringing about a change of mood in order to feel better—drinking 'to relieve stress,' cheer oneself up, etc. Equally, drinkers may complain that alcohol makes them feel depressed or has some other adverse effect on their mental state. Stress has also been identified as a cause of relapse in alcohol dependence.

There is a range of reasons why alcohol could have both positive and negative effects on mental state. These reasons are not restricted to its pharmacological action but also include the ways in which this interacts with other factors such as the pre-existing mood and personality of the drinker; the drinker's beliefs and expectations about the effects of alcohol, and the circumstances in which it is consumed. Further differences can arise from the quantities involved and the pattern of consumption. Small quantities have different effects from large ones; binge drinking can have different effects from the same quantity of alcohol consumed over a longer period; alcohol dependence is often characterized by the vicious circle of short-term psychological benefits from drinking, at the expense of long-term deterioration and increasing depression and sense of hopelessness.

While studies have found that small quantities of alcohol may reduce feelings of tension or being under pressure, alcohol can also, in some individuals, actually induce rather than reduce the body's stress response by stimulating the release of certain hormones.[3]

Alcohol and the Brain

Acute Intoxication

As alcohol has a high initial concentration in the brain, neurological effects are seen almost immediately leading, if enough alcohol is consumed, to all the well-known signs and symptoms of intoxication and the consequent deterioration of behavior. The effects of alcohol intoxication at various dosage levels are, however, influenced by a range of factors, genetic, psychological, cultural, and environmental.[4]

At blood alcohol levels around 50 mg% [0.05 mg/ml blood alcohol concentration] (the U.K. legal limit for driving is 80 mg% [0.08 mg/ml blood alcohol concentration]), cognitive impairment is normally evident, with adverse effects on learning, memory and the ability to process complex information. The ability to undertake novel tasks is significantly impaired, the ability to undertake routine, well-rehearsed ones less so. Psychomotor performance is also degraded. The higher the blood alcohol level, the greater the impairment. At blood alcohol levels around 300 mg% [0.3 mg/ml blood alcohol concentration], amnesia for the drinking episode is likely.[4]

Long-Term Effects

There is evidence to suggest that regular consumption of alcohol may have either beneficial or harmful effects on brain functioning and on cognitive competence depending on the quantities involved.

However, the studies were not wholly consistent in regard to quantity.

One study found that in elderly populations, consumption of 1 to 9 (U.K.) standard drinks per week may improve cognitive functioning and reduce the risk of dementia, while consuming 21 or more drinks per week may increase the risk of dementia.[5]

A British study found that in middle-aged subjects, alcohol consumption was associated with better function regarding some aspects of cognition. Those who drank at least one drink per week were significantly less likely to have poor cognitive function compared with non-drinkers. The beneficial effect extended to those drinking more than 30 drinks per week. The effect was stronger for women than men.[6]

However, previous studies had found that in all populations, consumption of more than 40 grams of alcohol per day, equal to 5 standard U.K. drinks, is associated with measurable declines in brain functioning and cognitive efficiency, possibly with tissue damage. Such impairment is likely at a consumption level of 84 grams per day, equal to 10.5 standard U.K. drinks.[4]

Chronic alcohol dependence is associated with extensive brain damage and cognitive deficits leading in extreme cases to alcoholic dementia, a loss of intellectual functioning combined with amnesia. Alcohol-induced brain damage appears to be partially reversible with abstinence.[4]

Alcohol and Depression

Alcohol consumption may be either a cause or a consequence of depression. In relation to its causal role, some have suggested that alcohol is biphasic in its effects, initially producing a sense of euphoria, which turns to feelings of depression as the blood alcohol levels falls. Problem drinking and dependence can cause a range of problems such as family conflict and disruption, job loss and financial problems that are likely in themselves to result in increased levels of anxiety and depression. Alcohol dependence is one of the main risk factors for suicide.

However, these strong relationships between drinking, depression, and suicide may be restricted to extreme patterns of consumption, which tend to characterize clinical populations, and are much less in evidence in the general population. One Canadian study found no significant relationship between alcohol consumption and depression in a general population sample, apart from binge drinking being associated with raised risk of depression in women.[7]

Benefits for Mental Health of Alcohol Consumption

It has been suggested that light to moderate drinking can improve mood and social adjustment and help non-problem drinkers cope with stress or other negative emotional states.

However, the evidence for this is mainly anecdotal. Scientific studies apparently showing alcohol to have mental health benefits have often lacked control groups; failed to take into account other confounding factors such as individuals' sociability and the extent of their supporting social network, or have been unable to eliminate the factor of psychological expectancy, leaving open the possibility that apparent benefits were actually the result of a placebo effect.[8]

There is scant evidence that light to moderate drinking has any beneficial effects in relation to psychiatric disorders. Alcohol dependence delays recovery from coexisting psychiatric conditions.[9]

Other Drugs

Drinking alcohol is also closely linked with use of other drugs, legal and illegal. Smoking, drinking, and drug taking often coexist. Nearly one in four (24%) of smokers state that they have used drugs, cannabis being the commonest, in the last year, compared to only one in twenty (5%) of non-smokers.

Only 6% of non-smoking, non-alcohol users report ever trying drugs, whereas 77% of smokers who also misuse alcohol report trying drugs.

References

1. Epidemiologic Catchment Area Study, in Regier et al (1990). Co-morbidity of mental disorder with alcohol and other drug abuse: results from the Epidemiological Catchment Area (ECA) study. *Journal of the American Medical Association*, vol. 264, pp. 2511–2518 [quoted in chapter 32 of Heather N, Peter TJ, Stockwell T (eds) *International Handbook Alcohol Dependence and Problems*. Wiley 2001. Mueser KT and Kavanagh D, Treating comorbidity of alcohol problems and psychiatric disorder].

2. Kessler et al (1996). The epidemiology of co-occurring addictive and mental disorders: implications for prevention and service utilization. *American Journal of Orthopsychiatry*, vol. 66 (1) pp. 17–31. [quoted in chapter 32 of Heather N, Peter TJ,

Stockwell T (eds) *International Handbook Alcohol Dependence and Problems.* Wiley 2001. Mueser KT and Kavanagh D, Treating co-morbidity of alcohol problems and psychiatric disorder].

3. Alcohol and Stress, National Institute of Alcohol Abuse and Alcoholism (NIAAA), *Alcohol Alert*, April 1996, No. 32, p. 363.

4. Knight, Robert G. Neurological Consequences of Alcohol Use, Chapter 7, *International Handbook of Alcohol Dependence,* 2001, ed. Heather N, Peters T J, Stockwell.

5. Mukami KJ, Kuller LH, Fitzpatrick AL, Longstreth WT, Mittleman MA, Siscovick DS. Prospective Study of Alcohol Consumption and Risk of Dementia in Older Adults, *Journal of the American Medical Association*, 2003, no. 289, pp. 1405–1415.

6. Britton A, Singh-Manoux A, and Marmot M. Alcohol Consumption and Cognitive Function in the Whitehall 2 Study. *American Journal of Epidemiology*, vol. 160, no. 3, 2004, pp. 240–247.

7. Wang JL, Patten SB. Alcohol Consumption and Major Depression: Findings from a Follow-Up Study, *Canadian Journal of Psychiatry*, 2001, no. 46, pp. 632–638.

8. Chick J. Can Light or Moderate Drinking Benefit Mental Health, *European Addiction Research*, 1999, no. 5, pp. 74–81.

9. Greenfield TK. Individual Risk of Alcohol-Related Disease and Problems, in Heather N, Peter TJ, Stockwell T (eds) *International Handbook Alcohol Dependence and Problems.* Wiley 2001.

10. Coulthard M, Farrell M, Simpson N, Meltzer H. Tobacco, alcohol and use and mental health, Office for National Statistics, based on ONS Survey of Psychiatric Morbidity among Adults in Great Britain, carried out in 2000 for the Department of Health, the Scottish Executive Health Department and the National Assembly for Wales.

Section 47.2

The Prevalence and Co-Occurrence of
Alcohol, Drug, Mood, and Anxiety Disorders

This information is from "Largest Ever Comorbidity Study Reports
Prevalence and Co-Occurrence of Alcohol, Drug, Mood and Anxiety Dis-
orders," by the National Institute on Alcohol Abuse and Alcoholism
(NIAAA) and the National Institutes of Health, August 2, 2004.

An estimated 17.6 million American adults (8.5 percent) meet standard diagnostic criteria for an alcohol use disorder and approximately
4.2 million (2 percent) meet criteria for a drug use disorder. Overall,
about one tenth (9.4 percent) of American adults, or 19.4 million persons, meet clinical criteria for a substance use disorder—either an alcohol or drug use disorder or both—according to results from the
2001–2002 National Epidemiologic Survey on Alcohol and Related
Conditions (NESARC) reported in the *Archives of General Psychiatry*, Volume 61, August 2004.

Alcohol use disorders include (1) alcohol abuse, a condition characterized by recurrent drinking resulting in failure to fulfill major role
obligations at work, school, or home; persistent or recurrent alcohol-
related interpersonal, social, or legal problems; and/or recurrent drinking in hazardous situations, and (2) alcohol dependence (also known
as alcoholism), a condition characterized by impaired control over
drinking, compulsive drinking, preoccupation with drinking, withdrawal symptoms, and/or tolerance to alcohol.

Conducted by the National Institute on Alcohol Abuse and Alcoholism, National Institutes of Health, the NESARC is a representative survey of the U.S. civilian non-institutionalized population aged
18 years and older. With more than 43,000 adult Americans participating, the NESARC is the largest study ever conducted of the co-
occurrence of psychiatric disorders among U.S. adults.

Results from the NESARC show that 19.2 million adults (9.2 percent) meet diagnostic criteria for independent mood disorders (including major depression, dysthymia, manic disorder, and hypomania)
and 23 million (11.08 percent) meet criteria for independent anxiety

disorders (including panic disorder, generalized anxiety disorder, and specific and social phobias).

The NESARC is the first national epidemiologic survey to use the *Diagnostic and Statistical Manual of Mental Disorders—Fourth Edition* (*DSM-IV*) definitions of independent mood and anxiety disorders to examine the comorbidity, or co-occurrence, of mental health disorders. Independent mood and anxiety disorders exclude transient cases of these disorders that result from alcohol and/or drug withdrawal or intoxication, conditions that usually improve rapidly without treatment once substance use ceases. The distinction is important because the diagnosis of current mood and anxiety disorders among active substance abusers is complicated by the fact that many symptoms of intoxication and withdrawal from alcohol and other substances resemble the symptoms of mood and anxiety disorders and thus, the additional psychiatric disorder may be overlooked.

The NESARC results show substantial comorbidity between substance use disorders and independent mood and anxiety disorders is pervasive in the U.S. general population: About 20 percent of persons with a current (at the time of the survey or within the past year) substance use disorder experience a mood or anxiety disorder within the same time period. Similarly, about 20 percent of persons with a current mood or anxiety disorder experience a current substance use disorder.

NESARC results also indicate high rates of comorbidity among persons who sought treatment for mood, anxiety, or substance use disorders. The high rates of comorbidity among treated persons suggest that primary care physicians, mental health specialists, and alcohol and drug abuse specialists should assess patients for multiple mental health disorders, the authors conclude.

"It would be incorrect for health care professionals to assume that the majority of mood and anxiety disorders are due to substance intoxication or withdrawal and will remit when the patients stops drinking," said Ting-Kai Li, M.D., Director, National Institute on Alcohol Abuse and Alcoholism. "These findings suggest that treatment professionals should be prepared to treat or refer patients in stable remission from substance use for comorbid mood and anxiety disorders. Earlier research has demonstrated that, left untreated, such disorders may lead to substance use relapse and other negative outcomes."

"This study does not resolve questions about causal mechanisms that may underlie relationships between *DSM-IV* substance use and mood and anxiety disorders," according to Bridget Grant, Ph.D., Ph.D.,

Chief of the Laboratory of Epidemiology and Biometry, Division of Intramural Clinical and Biological Research. "Analyses of data from NESARC's 'second wave' in 2004–2005 will help to form a foundation for future etiologic research."

Chapter 48

Alcohol Use and Depression

Chapter Contents

Section 48.1—Depression Linked to Alcohol Dependence 374

Section 48.2—Suicide, Depression, and Youth Drinking 377

Section 48.1

Depression Linked to Alcohol Dependence

From "National Survey Sharpens Picture of Major Depression Among U.S. Adults," a press release by the National Institutes of Health, October 3, 2005.

Findings from the largest survey ever mounted on the co-occurrence of psychiatric disorders among U.S. adults afford a sharper picture than previously available of major depressive disorder (MDD) in specific population subgroups and of MDD's relationship to alcohol use disorders (AUDs) and other mental health conditions.

The NESARC [National Epidemiologic Survey of Alcohol and Related Conditions] defined lifetime MDD as having had at least one major depressive episode (at least 2 weeks of persistent depressed mood accompanied by at least five symptoms of *DSM-IV* [*Diagnostic and Statistical Manual of Mental Disorders*] major depression without history of a bipolar disorder) over the life course. Current MDD was defined as having had at least one major depressive episode during the 12 months preceding the survey among persons classified with lifetime MDD. The AUDs alcohol dependence and alcohol abuse (together with nicotine and illicit drug use disorders) comprise *DSM-IV* substance use disorders. Alcohol dependence, also known as alcoholism, is characterized by impaired control over drinking, compulsive drinking, preoccupation with drinking, withdrawal symptoms, and/or tolerance to alcohol. Alcohol abuse is characterized by recurrent drinking resulting in failure to fulfill major role obligations at work, school, or home; persistent or recurrent alcohol-related interpersonal, social, or legal problems; and/or recurrent drinking in hazardous situations.

The new analysis of data from the 2001-2002 National Epidemiologic Survey of Alcohol and Related Conditions (NESARC) shows for the first time that middle age and Native American race increase the likelihood of current or lifetime MDD, along with female gender, low income, and separation, divorce, or widowhood. Asian, Hispanic, and black race-ethnicity reduce that risk. Conducted by the NIH's National Institute on Alcohol Abuse and Alcoholism (NIAAA), the analysis appears in the Monday, October 3, 2005 *Archives of General Psychiatry*.

The NESARC involved face-to-face interviews with more than 43,000 non-institutionalized individuals aged 18 years and older and questions that reflect diagnostic criteria established by the American Psychiatric Association's *DSM-IV*. Its principal foci were alcohol dependence (alcoholism) and alcohol abuse and the psychiatric conditions that most frequently co-occur with those AUDs. Because of its size and scrutiny of multiple sociodemographic factors, the NESARC provides more precise information than previously available on between-group differences that influence risk.

For example, the analysis indicates that 5.28 percent of U.S. adults experienced MDD during the 12 months preceding the survey and 13.23 percent had experienced MDD at some time during their lives. The highest lifetime risk was among middle-aged adults, a shift from the younger adult population shown to be at highest risk by surveys conducted during the 1980s and 1990s. "This marks an important transformation in the distribution of MDD in the general population and specific risk for baby-boomers aged 45 to 64 years," note the authors.

Risk for the onset of MDD increases sharply between age 12 and age 16 and more gradually up to the early 40s when it begins to decline, with mean age of onset about age 30. Women are twice as likely as men to experience MDD and somewhat more likely to receive treatment. About 60 percent of persons with MDD received treatment specifically for the disorder, with mean treatment age at 33.5 years—a lag time of about 3 years between onset and treatment. Of all persons who experienced MDD, nearly one half wanted to die, one third considered suicide, and 8.8 percent reported a suicide attempt.

Among race-ethnic groups, Native Americans showed the highest (19.17 percent) lifetime MDD prevalence, followed by whites (14.58 percent), Hispanics (9.64 percent), Blacks (8.93 percent), and Asian or Pacific Islanders (8.77 percent). Since information is scarce on diagnosed mental disorders among Native Americans, this finding appears to warrant increased attention to the mental health needs of that group, the authors maintain.

Among persons with current MDD, 14.1 percent also have an AUD, 4.6 percent have a drug use disorder, and 26 percent have nicotine dependence. More than 37 percent have a personality disorder and more than 36 percent have at least one anxiety disorder. Among persons with lifetime MDD, 40.3 percent had experienced an AUD, 17.2 percent had experienced a drug use disorder, and 30 percent had experienced nicotine dependence.

"Major depression is a prevalent psychiatric disorder and a pressing public health problem. That it so often accompanies alcohol dependence raises questions about when and how to treat each diagnosis," says NIAAA Director Ting-Kai Li, M.D. "Today's results both inform clinical practice and provide researchers with information to advance hypotheses about common biobehavioral factors that may underlie both conditions."

The NESARC results demonstrate a strong relationship of MDD to substance dependence and a weak relationship to substance abuse, a finding that suggests focusing on dependence when studying the relationship of depression to substance use disorders. This research direction is supported by earlier genetic studies that identified factors common to MDD and alcohol dependence and at least one epidemiologic study that demonstrated excess MDD among long-abstinent former alcoholics, state the authors.

Coexisting substance dependence disorder and MDD predict poor outcome among clinic patients. A decade ago, many treatment leaders discouraged treating MDD in patients with substance dependence on the grounds that arresting substance dependence was the more immediate need and that its resolution well might also resolve MDD. Results from foregoing epidemiologic surveys and several clinical trials over time altered that picture, so that treating both disorders simultaneously is today common practice.

The NESARC also found strong relationships between MDD and anxiety disorders, with the strongest comorbidity for current diagnoses. In addition, MDD was strongly associated with personality disorders, but the magnitude of the association varied considerably among discrete personality disorder types. "Given the seriousness of MDD, the importance of information on its prevalence, demographic correlates, and psychiatric comorbidity cannot be overstated," note the authors. "This study provides the grounds for further investigation in a number of areas."

The NESARC data set, interview, descriptive materials, and citations are available at http://niaaa.census.gov. News releases based on NESARC data and additional alcohol research information and publications are available at www.niaaa.nih.gov.

Section 48.2

Suicide, Depression, and Youth Drinking

Excerpted from *Prevention Alert*, Volume 5, Number 17, by the Substance Abuse and Mental Health Services Administration, National Clearinghouse for Alcohol and Drug Information, December 13, 2002.

Alcohol used in adolescence is associated with psychological distress and depression.

- Among 12- to 17-year-olds who were current drinkers, 31 percent exhibited extreme levels of psychological distress and 39 percent exhibited serious behavioral problems.[1]

- Twelve- to 16-year-old girls who were current drinkers were four times more likely than their nondrinking peers to suffer depression.[2]

- In a recent Center for Substance Abuse Treatment (CSAT) study, 48 percent of women in treatment for substance abuse had been sexually abused.[3]

The severity of behavioral problems in adolescents is significantly associated with increased likelihood of adolescent alcohol use.

- Past-month alcohol use was reported by approximately 14 percent of adolescents with low levels of behavioral problems, by 23 percent of those with intermediate problem scores, and by 38 percent of those with significant behavioral problems.[4]

- Adolescents with serious behavioral problems were nearly three times more likely to use alcohol than those with low levels of behavioral problems.[5]

There is a link between suicide and alcohol use in adolescents.

- Twenty-eight percent of suicides by children ages 9 to 15 could be attributed to alcohol.[6]

- Using a national school sample, a study reported that suicide attempts among heavy-drinking adolescents were three to four times greater than among abstainers.[7]

Adolescents struggling with serious emotional disturbances (SED) face even greater challenges when they use alcohol.

- Adolescents with high levels of SED were nearly twice as likely as adolescents with low levels of SED to have used alcohol in the past month.[8]

- Adolescents with high levels of SED were five times as likely as those with low levels of SED to report alcohol dependence.[9]

References

1. Substance Abuse and Mental Health Services Administration (SAMHSA), Office of Applied Studies. The Relationship Between Mental Health and Substance Abuse Among Adolescents. (SMA) 99-3286. Rockville, MD: SAMHSA, 1999.

2. Hanna EZ, Hsiao-ye Y, Dufour MC, et al. The relationship of drinking and other substance use alone and in combination to health and behavior problems among youth ages 12-16: Findings from the Third National Health and Nutrition Survey (NHANES III). Paper presented at the 23rd Annual Scientific Meeting of the Research Society on Alcoholism, June 24-29, 2000, Denver, CO.

3. Burgdorf K, Chen X, Herrell J. The prevalence and prognostic significance of sexual abuse in substance abuse treatment of women. Center for Substance Abuse Treatment (CSAT), 2001.

4. SAMHSA. The Relationship Between Mental Health and Substance Abuse Among Adolescents.

5. Ibid.

6. Unpublished data extrapolated by National Institute on Alcohol Abuse and Alcoholism from *State Trends in Alcohol Mortality, 1979-1992; U.S. Alcohol Epidemiologic Data Reference Manual,* Volume 5. Rockville, MD: National Institute on Alcohol Abuse and Alcoholism, 1996.

7. Windle M, Miller-Tutzauer C, Domenico D. Alcohol use, suicidal behavior, and risky activities among adolescents. *J Res Adolesc* 2(4):317–330, 1992.

8. SAMHSA. The Relationship Between Mental Health and Substance Abuse Among Adolescents.

9. Ibid.

Chapter 49

Anxiety and Alcohol Use

Chapter Contents

Section 49.1—Researchers Shed Light on Anxiety and
    Alcohol Intake 382

Section 49.2—Social Anxiety Disorder and Alcohol Use 384

Section 49.1

Researchers Shed Light on Anxiety and Alcohol Intake

From the National Institute on Alcohol Abuse and Alcoholism (NIAAA),
October 3, 2005.

Scientists have identified a brain mechanism in rats that may play a central role in regulating anxiety and alcohol-drinking. The finding, by researchers supported by the National Institute on Alcohol Abuse and Alcoholism (NIAAA), part of the National Institutes of Health (NIH), could provide important clues about the neurobiology of alcohol-drinking behaviors in humans. A report of the study appears in the October 3, 2005 issue of the *Journal of Clinical Investigation*.

"This is an intriguing finding," notes NIAAA Director Ting-Kai Li, M.D. "These experiments, conducted in rats selectively bred to have a high affinity for alcohol, help us address questions about the potential role that anxiety might play in human alcoholism. These molecular studies also may reveal potential targets for therapy of anxiety and alcoholism."

Some researchers have suggested that high levels of anxiety may predispose some individuals to becoming alcoholic.

Researchers led by Subhash C. Pandey, Ph.D., associate professor and director of neuroscience alcoholism research in the Department of Psychiatry at the University of Illinois and Jesse Brown VA Medical Center in Chicago, found that "P" rats, a strain bred to prefer alcohol, showed more anxiety-like behaviors and drank more alcohol, than non alcohol-preferring "NP" rats. They measured anxiety in the rats with an apparatus known as an elevated plus-maze, which consists of two open arms and two closed arms connected to a central platform. Anxiety is gauged as a function of the amount of time a rat spends in the closed versus the open arms of the maze during a 5-minute testing period—the greater an animal's level of anxiety, the less open-arm activity it displays.

Dr. Pandey and his colleagues also found that levels of CREB, a protein involved in a variety of brain functions, were lower in certain brain areas of P rats compared with NP rats. Levels of neuropeptide Y (NPY), a molecule that regulates the function of several neurotransmitters and is known to play a role in anxiety and alcohol-drinking behaviors, also were lower in P rats. One function of CREB is to regulate the production of NPY.

"Compared to NP rats, levels of CREB and NPY were innately lower in the central amygdala and medial amygdala of P rats," explains Dr. Pandey, "brain areas which play a crucial role in anxiety behaviors and which have been shown previously to be involved in rewarding, reinforcing, and motivational aspects of alcohol drinking behaviors. And turning off CREB function in the central amygdala of NP rats makes them look like P rats—more anxious and thus more likely to drink."

Alcohol intake reduced anxiety-like behaviors in the P rats, an effect that was associated with increased CREB function and NPY production in the central and medial amygdala. And by administering compounds that promote CREB function and NPY production in the central amygdala, researchers were able to reduce anxiety—and alcohol intake—in P rats. On the other hand, by disrupting CREB function (and the concomitant NPY production) in the central amygdala of NP rats, the researchers were able to provoke anxiety-like behavior and promote alcohol intake in those animals.

Dr. Pandey and his colleagues proposed that decreased CREB-dependent NPY production in the central amygdala might be a pre-existing condition for anxiety and alcohol-drinking behaviors.

"Our findings implicate this pathway in genetic predisposition to high anxiety and alcohol-drinking behaviors of P rats," says Dr. Pandey. "Future studies should explore the relationship of other CREB-related compounds to these phenomena in P rats or other animal models."

Section 49.2

Social Anxiety Disorder and Alcohol Use

Excerpted the article by Sarah W. Book, M.D., and Carrie L. Randall,
Ph.D., published in *Alcohol Research & Health,* Vol. 26, No. 2, 2002. For
a complete list of references, see www.niaaa.nih.gov.

Many people experience social anxiety—that is, they feel uncomfortable or even anxious in social situations, such as talking with strangers (or even friends) or speaking in front of a group of people. In the general population, levels of social anxiety exist on a continuum from mild to severe. A clinical diagnosis of social anxiety disorder, also referred to as social phobia,[1] is assigned only when the social anxiety results in significant fear when faced with the situation, impairment of performance, or avoidance of anxiety-provoking situations. People with high levels of social anxiety typically report that alcohol helps them feel more comfortable in social situations. Thus, it is not surprising that individuals with clinically diagnosed social anxiety disorder have a higher incidence of alcohol-related problems than does the general population.

Social Anxiety Disorder

According to the American Psychiatric Association's *Diagnostic and Statistical Manual of Mental Disorders, Fourth Edition (DSM–IV)* (1994), social anxiety disorder is defined as excessive fear in social situations in which the person believes he or she will do something embarrassing or have anxiety symptoms (e.g., blushing or sweating) that will be humiliating. The feared situations can vary from interpersonal social interactions in small groups to talking to strangers. Performance fears, such as speaking in public, also are common. People with social anxiety disorder either avoid feared situations or experience them with extreme anxiety. Most individuals with the disorder have the more severe, generalized type, in which the person has other social fears in addition to the common fear of public speaking.

Typically, social anxiety disorder begins in the teenage years and does not improve without treatment. The mechanisms or causes underlying the disease are unknown but may involve multiple predisposing factors. These potential factors include genetic background, traumatic early emotional learning experiences, observation and modeling of parental behaviors, and biological irregularities in brain chemical systems. People with the disorder often report having been shy or behaviorally inhibited as small children and, in severe cases, a child with social anxiety may not want to go to school.

As young adults, people with social anxiety disorder tend to make life choices based on their fears, such as avoiding classes requiring oral presentations or accepting jobs beneath their ability because they can work alone. Because these life choices circumvent their underlying social fears, many people with social anxiety disorder may be able to function adequately for extended periods of time. Once the contrived situation changes (e.g., when a promotion is offered), however, the social anxiety fears may resurface. Many people with social anxiety disorder will turn down a promotion rather than encounter the social demands required for the new job. Thus, for many of these people, life is orchestrated around social fears, even if this results in social isolation or less financial independence and academic achievement.

The Prevalence of Social Anxiety Disorder

Prevalence estimates of social anxiety disorder vary considerably, both for social anxiety alone and concurrently with alcohol use disorders (AUDs). This variability results in large part from methodological differences among studies. For example, an analysis of data from the Epidemiologic Catchment Area study, a door-to-door survey conducted in four communities across the United States in the 1970s, found the prevalence of social anxiety disorder to be only 2 percent. In this analysis, a diagnosis of social phobia was given to respondents who admitted to extreme anxiety while eating in front of others, speaking to a small group of people they knew, or speaking to a large group of strangers. In contrast, a later community study, the National Comorbidity Survey, found the prevalence of social anxiety disorder to be as high as 13 percent. In this study, respondents acknowledging anxiety in a wider range of social situations were considered to have social anxiety disorder. This higher prevalence rate of social anxiety disorder would make it the third most prevalent psychiatric disorder after alcohol dependence and depression.

Conservative estimates of the prevalence of co-occurring, or comorbid, social anxiety disorder and AUDs found that approximately 20 percent of patients treated for social anxiety disorder and 15 percent of people receiving alcoholism treatment have both disorders. Despite a paucity of controlled research in the area, many researchers have written about the high comorbidity between social anxiety disorder and alcohol use problems. One viable hypothesis to explain this high comorbidity is that people with social anxiety use alcohol as self-medication for social fears.

The Tension Reduction Hypothesis

Clinical reports indicate that people use alcohol as a means of coping with social fears as well as with stress. One standard theory of why people drink—the tension reduction hypothesis—implies that alcohol acts as a negative reinforcer to reduce stress and anxiety. A negative reinforcer is something that eliminates an unpleasant experience. In this case, anxiety or stress is the unpleasant experience and alcohol consumption, which reduces these feelings, would be considered the negative reinforcer. Once a person experiences stress relief after consuming alcohol, he or she is likely to continue to use alcohol for its stress-reducing properties. Whether alcohol actually reduces stress is debatable. In fact, some researchers have argued that based on its pharmacological properties, alcohol actually should increase stress and that therefore negative reinforcement using alcohol would be ineffective.

Nevertheless, people with social anxiety disorder report that aside from totally avoiding anxiety-inducing situations, alcohol use is one of their primary means of coping. It is possible that positive expectancies—beliefs that alcohol will relieve social anxiety, whether supported in fact or not—play a role in the relationship between social anxiety and alcohol use. For example, people with social anxiety may drink excessively because they strongly expect alcohol to reduce their anxious feelings in social situations. The role of alcohol expectancies and their relation to alcohol consumption and behavior has been studied extensively in young adults. These experiments demonstrated that both positive and negative expectations can be powerful behavioral moderators. Differences in expectancies might in fact explain why not all people with social anxiety drink alcohol to cope with their fears. People with negative expectancies about alcohol's effects probably do not consume alcohol because it increases their fear of appearing even more foolish.

Positive expectancies that alcohol can relieve social fears may explain why some people experiment with alcohol as a coping strategy in the first place. If a person's expectancy that alcohol reduces stress is left unchallenged (i.e., if the person is not shown by a clinician or researcher that alcohol consumption does not actually reduce stress either behaviorally or physiologically), it may be a powerful enough belief system to explain why a person continues to use alcohol to relieve stress. Alternatively, one can argue that for a subgroup of socially anxious people alcohol may have a genuine pharmacological effect that results in decreased social anxiety. These individuals may have started drinking as a coping mechanism because of their positive expectancies, but they may continue to use alcohol because they associate alcohol consumption with symptom relief. Unfortunately, few experimental studies have investigated expectancies about alcohol's ability to reduce social fears, determined how expectancies translate into actual alcohol consumption, or demonstrated that alcohol reduces social fears in a laboratory setting.

Much of what is known about the association between social anxiety and alcohol consumption comes from research with college students who did not have clinical diagnoses of social anxiety disorder, rather than from research with patients diagnosed as having the disorder. In one study examining the effects of alcohol expectancies on drinking, researchers divided a sample of college students into two groups according to their anxiety level (i.e., high or low) and assessed their expectancies about alcohol's ability to relieve social anxiety as well as their alcohol consumption. The study found that among those respondents who believed that alcohol would definitely reduce social fears, the level of social anxiety did not affect the level of alcohol consumption. Thus, although the investigators had expected the high-anxiety group to consume more alcohol than the low-anxiety group when alcohol was being used to cope with social fears, no such difference existed, at least in these non-treatment-seeking college students. This lack of a difference might, however, be, in part, the result of the social context of college student drinking. That is, for both groups baseline drinking levels would be expected to be relatively high, to be defined by drinking binges, and to occur in the context of peer pressure and social situations.

Another way to examine the relationship between alcohol expectancies and alcohol consumption is to ask whether people with high expectations of reduced social anxiety actually experience less anxiety when they are drinking. In a sample of 72 female college-age social drinkers, women who expected positive results from alcohol did, in fact, report less anxiety after drinking alcohol than did women with negative or neutral beliefs. One can assume that the greater reduction in anxiety after alcohol consumption would result in more drinking in the group with the positive alcohol expectancies. However, the study did not examine drinking behavior, nor did it compare results for women with high or low levels of social anxiety.

Another study assessed drinking in a sample of male college students with high social anxiety and failed to find evidence of increased alcohol consumption compared with students with lower levels of anxiety. In fact, severity of social anxiety was a negative predictor of alcohol quantity consumed—that is, participants with higher levels of anxiety consumed less alcohol than did those with lower levels of anxiety. Unfortunately, however, this study did not examine alcohol expectancies and only sampled males.

Taken together, the results from these last two studies suggest that the interaction of gender and alcohol expectancies may be an important factor in determining who will report that alcohol benefits them and who might drink alcohol to cope with their anxiety.

Whether alcohol reduces social anxiety in a controlled laboratory environment is still open to debate. Several studies have addressed this issue in college students, and one study was conducted in a clinical sample of clients with a formal diagnosis of social anxiety disorder. This latter study did not find that alcohol had any effect in reducing social fears. The conclusions from this study are limited, however, because the investigators excluded patients with a diagnosis of alcohol abuse or dependence and did not evaluate alcohol expectancies. Thus, researchers do not yet know whether alcohol reduces social anxiety in people who believe it is effective or in people who consume it to the point that they meet the criteria for an AUD. The specific alcohol effects observed may also depend on how anxiety is measured (e.g., by behavioral or psychophysiological measures or by self-report).

Regardless of whether researchers can demonstrate in the laboratory that alcohol reduces social fears, many people with social anxiety report that they expect alcohol to have that effect and that they use it to cope with their social anxiety. Because of their alcohol consumption, some of these individuals will eventually develop alcohol use problems in addition to their preexisting social anxiety disorder. For other people, alcohol use as a coping mechanism could still lead to alcohol-related risks, such as automobile crashes, interpersonal conflicts, or medical risks, even if they do not meet the criteria for an AUD. Treatment of social anxiety therefore is warranted to prevent the development of alcohol-related problems and AUDs.

Chapter 50

Post-Traumatic Stress Disorder and Problems with Alcohol Use

Post-traumatic stress disorder (PTSD) does not automatically cause problems with alcohol use; there are many people with PTSD who do not have problems with alcohol. However, PTSD and alcohol together can be serious trouble for the trauma survivor and his or her family.

How Do PTSD and Alcohol Use Affect Each Other and Make Problems Worse?

PTSD and alcohol problems often occur together. People with PTSD are more likely than others with similar backgrounds to have alcohol use disorders both before and after being diagnosed with PTSD, and people with alcohol use disorders often also have PTSD.

Being diagnosed with PTSD increases the risk of developing an alcohol use disorder.

Women exposed to trauma show an increased risk for an alcohol use disorder even if they are not experiencing PTSD. Women with problematic alcohol use are more likely than other women to have been sexually abused at some point in their lives.

Men and women reporting sexual abuse have higher rates of alcohol and drug use disorders than other men and women.

From "PTSD and Problems with Alcohol Use," a fact sheet by the National Center for Post-Traumatic Stress Disorder, U.S. Department of Veterans Affairs (www.va.gov), February 8, 2005.

Twenty-five to seventy-five percent of those who have survived abusive or violent trauma also report problems with alcohol use.

Ten to thirty-three percent of survivors of accidental, illness, or disaster trauma report problematic alcohol use, especially if they are troubled by persistent health problems or pain.

Sixty to eighty percent of Vietnam veterans seeking PTSD treatment have alcohol use disorders. Veterans over the age of 65 with PTSD are at increased risk for attempted suicide if they also experience problematic alcohol use or depression. War veterans diagnosed with PTSD and alcohol use tend to be binge drinkers. Binges may be in reaction to memories or reminders of trauma.

Alcohol Problems Often Lead to Trauma and Disrupt Relationships

Persons with alcohol use disorders are more likely than others with similar backgrounds to experience psychological trauma. They also experience problems with conflict and intimacy in relationships.

Problematic alcohol use is associated with a chaotic lifestyle, which reduces family emotional closeness, increases family conflict, and reduces parenting abilities.

PTSD Symptoms Often Are Worsened by Alcohol Use

Although alcohol can provide a temporary feeling of distraction and relief, it also reduces the ability to concentrate, enjoy life, and be productive.

Excessive alcohol use can impair one's ability to sleep restfully and to cope with trauma memories and stress.

Alcohol use and intoxication also increase emotional numbing, social isolation, anger and irritability, depression, and the feeling of needing to be on guard (hyper-vigilance).

Alcohol use disorders reduce the effectiveness of PTSD treatment.

Many individuals with PTSD experience sleep disturbances (trouble falling asleep or problems with waking up frequently after falling asleep). When a person with PTSD experiences sleep disturbances, using alcohol as a way to self-medicate becomes a double-edged sword. Alcohol use may appear to help symptoms of PTSD because the alcohol may decrease the severity and number of frightening nightmares commonly experienced in PTSD. However, alcohol use may, on the other hand, continue the cycle of avoidance found in

PTSD, making it ultimately much more difficult to treat PTSD because the client's avoidance behavior prolongs the problems being addressed in treatment. Also, when a person withdraws from alcohol, nightmares often increase.

Individuals with a Combination of PTSD and Alcohol Use Problems Often Have Additional Mental or Physical Health Problems

As many as 10% to 50% of adults with alcohol use disorders and PTSD also have one or more of the following serious disorders:

- anxiety disorders (such as panic attacks, phobias, incapacitating worry, or compulsions)

- mood disorders (such as major depression or a dysthymic disorder)

- disruptive behavior disorders (such as attention deficit or anti-social personality disorder)

- addictive disorders (such as addiction to or abuse of street or prescription drugs)

- chronic physical illness (such as diabetes, heart disease, or liver disease)

- chronic physical pain due to physical injury/illness or due to no clear physical cause

What Are the Most Effective Treatment Patterns?

Because the existence of both PTSD and an alcohol use disorder in an individual makes both problems worse, alcohol use problems often must be addressed in PTSD treatment. When alcohol use is (or has been) a problem in addition to PTSD, it is best to seek treatment from a PTSD specialist who also has expertise in treating alcohol (addictive) disorders. In any PTSD treatment, several precautions related to alcohol use and alcohol disorders are advised.

The initial interview and questionnaire assessment should include questions that sensitively and thoroughly identify patterns of past and current alcohol and drug use.

Treatment planning should include a discussion between the professional and the client about the possible effects of alcohol use problems on PTSD, sleep, anger and irritability, anxiety, depression, and work or relationship difficulties.

Treatment should include education, therapy, and support groups that help the client address alcohol use problems in a manner acceptable to the client.

Treatment for PTSD and alcohol use problems should be designed as a single consistent plan that addresses both sources of difficulty together. Although there may be separate meetings or clinicians devoted primarily to PTSD or to alcohol problems, PTSD issues should be included in alcohol treatment, and alcohol use ("addiction" or "sobriety") issues should be included in PTSD treatment.

Relapse prevention must prepare the newly sober individual to cope with PTSD symptoms, which often seem to worsen or become more pronounced with abstinence.

Where Can You Get Help?

For a listing of professionals in the USA and Canada who treat alcohol disorders and PTSD, consult the membership directories of the International Society for Traumatic Stress Studies or the Association of Traumatic Stress Specialists. For veterans experiencing problems with PTSD and alcohol use, the Department of Veterans Affairs has a network of specialized PTSD and substance use treatment programs. For information on these programs, contact the local VA Vet Center or the Psychiatry Service at a VA Medical Center. (For addresses and telephone numbers, look under the "United States Government" listings in the telephone directory.)

Chapter 51

Childhood Attention Deficit Hyperactivity Disorder and Alcoholism during the Teen Years

Scientists tracking the progress of children diagnosed with attention-deficit/hyperactivity disorder (ADHD) as they became teenagers have shed new light on the link between ADHD and the risk of developing alcohol and substance use problems. The researchers found that individuals with severe problems of inattention as children were more likely than their peers to report alcohol-related problems, a greater frequency of getting drunk, and heavier and earlier use of tobacco and other drugs.

The findings, published in the August [2003] issue of *the Journal of Abnormal Psychology*, indicate that childhood ADHD may be as important for the risk of later substance use problems as having a history of family members with alcoholism and other substance use disorders.

ADHD is one of the most commonly diagnosed pediatric mental health disorders. It occurs in 3 percent to 5 percent of school-age children. While previous research has indicated that ADHD together with a variety of other childhood behavior disorders may predispose children to drug, alcohol, and tobacco use earlier than children without ADHD, this study explores more closely specific aspects of that association.

"This is one of the first studies to focus on the severity of inattention problems in childhood ADHD as distinct from impulsivity and hyperactivity," says Ting-Kai Li, M.D., director of the National Institute on Alcohol Abuse and Alcoholism (NIAAA). "It demonstrates the

From "Severe Childhood ADHD May Predict Alcohol, Substance Use in Teen Years," *FDA Consumer* Magazine, U.S. Food and Drug Administration (www.fda.gov), September-October 2003.

usefulness of distinguishing ADHD's effects from the effects of childhood behavior disorders, such as aggression and defiance."

NIAAA supported the study together with the National Institute on Drug Abuse, the National Institute of Mental Health, and the National Institute of Environmental Health Sciences, all components of the Department of Health and Human Services' National Institutes of Health.

Brooke Molina, Ph.D., at the University of Pittsburgh School of Medicine and University of Pittsburgh Medical Center, and William Pelham Jr., Ph.D., at the State University of New York at Buffalo conducted the research. The scientists recruited 142 teens between 13 and 18 years old who had received treatment for childhood ADHD an average of five years earlier at the Attention Deficit Disorder Clinic at the University of Pittsburgh School of Medicine. The researchers interviewed the teens along with their parents and teachers.

The scientists also recruited a control group of 100 similar teens not diagnosed with childhood ADHD. They asked both groups about their alcohol and substance use, including whether they had ever tried a substance during their lifetime, how old they were when they first tried tobacco, alcohol, or drugs, and the type, frequency, and quantity of substances used during the past six months.

The researchers found that significantly more of the participants diagnosed with ADHD as children reported episodes of drunkenness than their counterparts in the non-ADHD group. Nearly twice as many of the ADHD group reported having been drunk more than once in the past six months.

Both groups gave similar responses when asked if they had ever tried alcohol, cigarettes, or marijuana at least once; however, the ADHD group was three times more likely to have tried some other illegal drug besides marijuana. The teens with childhood ADHD also reported having used tobacco and having tried an illegal drug other than marijuana at younger ages than their non-ADHD peers. Additionally, about 11 percent of the teens diagnosed with ADHD reported having used two or more different illegal drugs more often, compared with 3 percent of the control group. The researchers analyzed distinctions within the ADHD group, focusing on responses from youngsters with more severe symptoms of inattention in childhood, something not routinely done previously.

The researchers found that the teenagers who reported more frequent episodes of drunkenness, higher alcohol problem scores, and a greater likelihood of substance abuse were those diagnosed with more severe inattention problems in childhood. The youngsters with severe inattention were about five times more likely than others to use an illegal drug other than alcohol and marijuana at an early age.

Although impulsivity/hyperactivity was not associated with teenage substance abuse, the authors say that better measurement of this behavior in future studies will be important. "The presence of ADHD during childhood appears to be as strong a risk factor for substance use and abuse as having a positive family history of substance use disorder. It is not specific to only one substance but cuts across alcohol, marijuana, and other drugs," says Molina.

Chapter 52

Alcohol Use and Its Association with Other Dangerous Substances

Chapter Contents

Section 52.1—Almost Half of People in Addiction
Treatment Had Both Drug and
Alcohol Abuse 398

Section 52.2—Alcohol and Nicotine Abuse May Be
Influenced by Same Genes 400

Section 52.3—Alcohol and Tobacco Use 402

Section 52.1

Almost Half of People in Addiction Treatment Had Both Drug and Alcohol Abuse

From the Substance Abuse and Mental Health Services Administration (SAMHSA), November 9, 2005.

Of the 1.1 million people in drug and alcohol treatment on a typical day in 2003, 47 percent were treated for both drug and alcohol abuse. The *National Survey of Substance Abuse Treatment Services (N-SSATS): 2003*, released by the Substance Abuse and Mental Health Services Administration (SAMHSA), showed that 33 percent were being treated for drug abuse only, while 20 percent were being treated for alcohol abuse only.

The survey showed that on March 31, 2003, 1,092,546 people were enrolled in substance abuse treatment. Most of them, 87 percent, were in outpatient treatment. Of the remainder, 11 percent were in non-hospital residential treatment while 2 percent were in inpatient hospital treatment. The survey also showed that 92,251 clients, 8 percent of the total, were under the age of 18.

"*N-SSATS* is a snapshot of the substance abuse treatment service delivery system in the United States," said SAMHSA Administrator Charles G. Curie. "This data will assist SAMHSA and state and local governments assess the nature and extent of services provided in state-supported and other treatment facilities, and forecast treatment resource requirements. *N-SSATS* also gives us tools to analyze treatment services trends and conduct comparative analyses for the nation, regions and states."

N-SSATS: 2003 contains data on the location, characteristics, and use of alcoholism and drug abuse treatment facilities and services throughout the United States and its territories. A total of 13,623 facilities responded to the 2003 survey, a response rate of 96 percent.

The 2003 national survey reported that the number and proportion of clients receiving methadone/LAAM [levo-alpha-acetyl-methadol] increased from 138,009 (15 percent of all clients) in 1997 to 229,567, 21 percent of all clients. It also indicated that opioid treatment programs were available in 8 percent of all substance abuse treatment programs surveyed.

The median number of clients in substance abuse treatment at a facility at the time of the survey was 40. Government-operated facilities were generally larger than private for-profit or private non-profit facilities. The survey also showed that 94 percent of all non-residential beds and 80 percent of all hospital inpatient beds designated for substance abuse treatment were in use.

N-SSATS:2003 points out that the great majority of facilities—84 percent—offered specially designed programs or groups directed toward specific client types.

- 35 percent of facilities offered special programs or groups for women.

- 35 percent of facilities offered special programs or groups for persons with co-occurring mental health and substance abuse disorders.

- 33 percent of facilities offered special programs for driving under the influence (DUI)/driving while intoxicated (DWI) offenders.

- 32 percent of facilities offered special programs for adolescents.

- 27 percent of facilities offered special programs or groups for men and for criminal justice clients.

Special programs or groups offered less frequently included those designed specifically to treat pregnant and postpartum women (14 percent), persons with HIV or AIDS (11 percent), seniors or older adults (7 percent), and gays or lesbians (6 percent).

Substance abuse treatment services were offered in languages other than English in 44 percent of all facilities. Most often this was in Spanish, offered in 40 percent of the facilities.

N-SSATS is also used to update SAMHSA's Substance Abuse Treatment Facility Locator, available at http://findtreatment.samhsa.gov. The locator service provides the phone numbers and locations of the nearest state-approved treatment facilities.

Section 52.2

Alcohol and Nicotine Abuse
May Be Influenced by Same Genes

From "Same Genes May Underlie Alcohol and Nicotine Co-Abuse," a press release by the National Institute on Alcohol Abuse and Alcoholism (NIAAA), part of the National Institutes of Health (NIH), March 17, 2006.

Vulnerability to both alcohol and nicotine abuse may be influenced by the same genetic factor, according to a recent study supported by the National Institute on Alcohol Abuse and Alcoholism (NIAAA), part of the National Institutes of Health (NIH).

In the study, two genetically distinct kinds of rat—one an innately heavy-drinking strain bred to prefer alcohol ("P" rats), the other strain bred to not prefer alcohol ("NP" rats)—learned to give themselves nicotine injections by pressing a lever. Researchers found that P rats took more than twice as much nicotine as NP rats. Their findings were reported recently in the *Journal of Neuroscience.*

"Our findings suggest that the genetic factor underlying the high alcohol consumption seen in P rats may also contribute to their affinity for nicotine," said lead author A.D. Lê, Ph.D., a NIAAA-supported researcher at Toronto's Centre for Addiction and Mental Health and University of Toronto.

Researchers have known for some time that people who smoke are more likely to drink alcohol than non-smokers. Similarly, smoking is three times more common in people with alcoholism than in the general population. Since previous studies have also determined that genetics plays an important role in both alcohol and nicotine addictions, researchers have hypothesized that the same gene or genes may influence the co-abuse of these substances.

Investigating this hypothesis in human studies is stymied by the possibility that alcohol use leads to nicotine use, and vice versa. However, in the current study, researchers showed that the P rats' affinity for nicotine could be demonstrated before the animals were ever exposed to alcohol.

P rats were also found to be more vulnerable to nicotine relapse than NP rats. Researchers withheld nicotine from the rats until their lever pressing occurred infrequently. Then, both P and NP rats were given a single nicotine injection. P rats, but not NP rats, resumed pressing the lever previously associated with nicotine infusions.

The researchers also showed that the P rats' apparent genetic vulnerability to alcohol and nicotine does not appear to extend to other drugs of abuse. When P and NP rats learned to press a lever to receive cocaine, each group took about the same amount of that drug. The authors note that the lack of a difference in cocaine self-_____ference between P and NP rats _____ due to a general "reward defi-

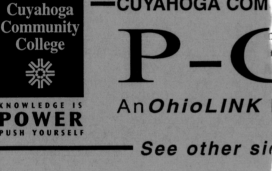

_____ a reliable and useful animal _____ and physiological character- _____ Director and study co-author _____gest that they may be as use- _____d by expanding our knowledge _____hol and nicotine co-morbidity _____s to address those important

Section 52.3

Alcohol and Tobacco Use

From *Alcohol Alert* No. 39, a publication of the National Institute on Alcohol Abuse and Alcoholism (NIAAA), January 1998, updated October 2000. For a complete list of references, see www.niaaa.nih.gov. Reviewed by David A. Cooke, MD, on March 13, 2006.

Extensive research supports the popular observation that "smokers drink and drinkers smoke." Moreover, the heaviest alcohol consumers are also the heaviest consumers of tobacco. Concurrent use of these drugs poses a significant public health threat. A survey of persons treated for alcoholism and other drug addictions revealed that 222 of 845 subjects had died over a 12-year period; one third of these deaths were attributed to alcohol-related causes, and one-half were related to smoking. This chapter explores the association between alcohol and tobacco use, possible mechanisms of their combined health effects, and some implications for alcoholism treatment.

The Co-Occurrence of Alcoholism and Smoking

Between 80 and 95 percent of alcoholics smoke cigarettes, a rate that is three times higher than among the population as a whole. Approximately 70 percent of alcoholics are heavy smokers (i.e., smoke more than one pack of cigarettes per day), compared with 10 percent of the general population. Drinking influences smoking more than smoking influences drinking. Nevertheless, smokers are 1.32 times as likely to consume alcohol as are nonsmokers.

Most adult users of alcohol or tobacco first tried these drugs during their early teens. Among smoking alcoholics, the initiation of regular cigarette smoking typically precedes the onset of alcoholism by many years, although data are inconsistent. Adolescents who begin smoking are 3 times more likely to begin using alcohol, and smokers are 10 times more likely to develop alcoholism than are nonsmokers.

Why Are Alcohol and Tobacco Used Together?

Postulated mechanisms for the concurrent use of alcohol and tobacco fall into two broad, nonexclusive categories: Either drug may increase the desired (rewarding) effects of the other, or either may decrease the toxic or unpleasant (aversive) effects of the other. These interactions involve processes of reinforcement or tolerance, as described below. (A third possibility—that one drug may alter the metabolism of the other, thereby affecting its absorption, distribution, or elimination from the body—has not been convincingly established.)

Reinforcement. Reinforcement refers to the physiological processes by which a behavior—such as consumption of a drug—becomes habitual. A key process in reinforcement for some drugs occurs when nerve cells release the chemical messenger dopamine into a small area of the brain called the nucleus accumbens following consumption of the drug. Nicotine is the primary ingredient of tobacco that triggers reinforcement. After reaching the brain, nicotine activates a group of proteins called nicotinic receptors. These proteins, located on the surface of certain brain cells, normally regulate a host of physiological functions, some of which may contribute to aspects of reinforcement. Ultimately, nicotine brings about the release of dopamine in the nucleus accumbens. Alcohol consumption also leads to dopamine release, although the mechanism by which alcohol produces this effect is incompletely understood.

Tolerance. Tolerance is decreased sensitivity to a given effect of a drug such that increased doses are needed to achieve the same effect. Long-term administration of nicotine in animals can induce tolerance to some of alcohol's reinforcing effects, and chronic alcohol administration induces tolerance to some effects of nicotine. Such cross-tolerance might lead to increased consumption of both drugs in an attempt to regain former levels of reward. In addition, cross-tolerance can develop to the aversive effects of drugs. For example, smokers may reduce their tobacco intake when they begin to feel its aversive effects (e.g., increased heart rate and nervousness). Alcohol's sedating effects may mitigate these effects of nicotine, facilitating continued tobacco use. Conversely, nicotine's stimulating effects can mitigate alcohol-induced loss of mental alertness.

Animal studies provide support for these interactions. For example, alcohol appears to induce loss of physical coordination in mice by inhibiting nicotinic receptors in the cerebellum, a part of the brain that is active in coordinating movement and balance. Administration of nicotine appears to remove this inhibition and restore coordination. In addition, alcohol interferes with the normal functioning of the chemical messenger vasopressin, which may play a role in memory processes. Vasopressin is also associated with the development of tolerance to alcohol. Nicotine helps normalize vasopressin function in the brain, reducing alcohol-induced impairment of memory and other intellectual abilities.

What Is the Risk of Cancer from Alcohol and Tobacco?

Smoking and excessive alcohol use are risk factors for cardiovascular and lung diseases and for some forms of cancer. The risks of cancer of the mouth, throat, or esophagus for the smoking drinker are more than the sum of the risks posed by these drugs individually. For example, compared with the risk for nonsmoking nondrinkers, the approximate relative risks for developing mouth and throat cancer are 7 times greater for those who use tobacco, 6 times greater for those who use alcohol, and 38 times greater for those who use both tobacco and alcohol.

How Do Alcohol and Tobacco Increase Cancer Risk?

Approximately 4,000 chemical substances are generated by the chemical reactions that occur in the intense heat of a burning cigarette. A group of these chemicals, collectively known as tar, is carried into the lungs on inhaled smoke. The bloodstream then distributes the components of tar throughout the body. Certain enzymes found mainly in the liver (i.e., microsomal enzymes) convert some ingredients of tar into chemicals that can cause cancer. Long-term alcohol consumption can activate some such microsomal enzymes, greatly increasing their activity and contributing to smoking-related cancers.

Microsomal enzymes are found not only in the liver but also in the lungs and digestive tract, which are major portals of entry for tobacco smoke. The esophagus may be particularly susceptible, because it lacks an efficient mechanism for removing toxic substances produced by activated microsomal enzymes. Consistent with these observations, alcohol has been shown to promote esophageal tumors in laboratory animals exposed simultaneously to specific components of tar.

Finally, alcoholics frequently exhibit deficiencies of zinc and vitamin A, substances that confer some protection against cancer.

Addictions Treatment for Smoking Alcoholics

Until recently, alcoholism treatment professionals have generally not addressed the issue of smoking cessation, largely because of the belief that the added stress of quitting smoking would jeopardize an alcoholic's recovery.

Research has not confirmed this belief. One study evaluated the progress of residents in an alcoholism treatment facility who were concurrently undergoing a standard smoking cessation program (i.e., experimental group). A comparison group of smoking alcoholics participated in the same alcoholism program but without undergoing the smoking cessation program. One year after treatment, results indicated that the smoking cessation program had no effect on abstinence from alcohol or other drugs. In addition, 12 percent of the subjects in the experimental group, but none of the subjects in the comparison group, had stopped smoking.

Some data suggest that alcoholism recovery may facilitate nicotine abstinence. In one study, patients participating in concurrent treatment for nicotine addiction during residential treatment for alcohol and other drug abuse achieved at least a temporary reduction in smoking and an increased motivation to quit smoking. Similarly, persons who achieve abstinence from alcohol without formal treatment often stop smoking at the same time.

Following the lead of other health facilities, many addictions treatment facilities are becoming smoke-free, providing a "natural experiment" on the effectiveness of dual recovery programs. Initial evaluations suggest that no-smoking policies are feasible in this setting. However, no outcome studies have been performed, and additional research is needed.

Problems encountered in smoke-free alcoholism treatment programs include surreptitious smoking by patients as well as by staff. Further, researchers have suggested modifying smoking cessation programs to conform with the structure and language of concurrent alcoholism programs (e.g., use of a 12-step approach). Nicotine patch therapy for smoking alcoholics may require higher doses of nicotine than are usually applied, because of alcohol-induced tolerance to some of nicotine's effects. Smoking alcoholics with a history of depressive disorders are generally less successful at smoking cessation than are subjects without such a history. Smoking may diminish the chances of recurring depression in some people, and a major depressive episode may follow smoking cessation in these subjects. An additional clinical consideration is that activation of microsomal enzymes by alcohol and tobacco tar may reduce the effectiveness of antidepressant medications. Therefore, medication levels should be carefully monitored in patients undergoing treatment for depression and addiction to alcohol and tobacco.

Part Six

The Effects of Alcohol on Family, Work, and Society

Chapter 53

How Alcohol Affects the Family: The Impact of Substance Abuse on Families

Family structures in America have become more complex—growing from the traditional nuclear family to single-parent families, stepfamilies, foster families, and multigenerational families. Therefore, when a family member abuses substances, the effect on the family may differ according to family structure.

A growing body of literature suggests that substance abuse has distinct effects on different family structures. For example, the parent of small children may attempt to compensate for deficiencies that his or her substance-abusing spouse has developed as a consequence of that substance abuse. Frequently, children may act as surrogate spouses for the parent who abuses substances. For example, children may develop elaborate systems of denial to protect themselves against the reality of the parent's addiction. Because that option does not exist in a single-parent household with a parent who abuses substances, children are likely to behave in a manner that is not age-appropriate to compensate for the parental deficiency. Alternately, the aging parents of adults with substance use disorders may maintain inappropriately dependent relationships with their grown offspring, missing the necessary "launching phase" in their relationship, so vital to the maturational processes of all family members involved.

Excerpted from "Substance Abuse Treatment and Family Therapy," from the Health Services/Technology Assessment Text, Treatment Impact Protocol (TIP) 39, by the Substance Abuse and Mental Health Services Administration (SAMHSA), 2004.

The effects of substance abuse frequently extend beyond the nuclear family. Extended family members may experience feelings of abandonment, anxiety, fear, anger, concern, embarrassment, or guilt; they may wish to ignore or cut ties with the person abusing substances. Some family members even may feel the need for legal protection from the person abusing substances. Moreover, the effects on families may continue for generations. Intergenerational effects of substance abuse can have a negative impact on role modeling, trust, and concepts of normative behavior, which can damage the relationships between generations. For example, a child with a parent who abuses substances may grow up to be an overprotective and controlling parent who does not allow his or her children sufficient autonomy.

Neighbors, friends, and coworkers also experience the effects of substance abuse because a person who abuses substances often is unreliable. Friends may be asked to help financially or in other ways. Coworkers may be forced to compensate for decreased productivity or carry a disproportionate share of the workload. As a consequence, they may resent the person abusing substances.

People who abuse substances are likely to find themselves increasingly isolated from their families. Often they prefer associating with others who abuse substances or participate in some other form of antisocial activity. These associates support and reinforce each other's behavior.

Different treatment issues emerge based on the age and role of the person who uses substances in the family and on whether small children or adolescents are present. In some cases, a family might present a healthy face to the community while substance abuse issues lie just below the surface.

Researchers describe several characteristic patterns of interaction, one or more of which are likely to be present in a family that includes parents or children abusing alcohol or illicit drugs:

- **Negativism.** Any communication that occurs among family members is negative, taking the form of complaints, criticism, and other expressions of displeasure. The overall mood of the household is decidedly downbeat, and positive behavior is ignored. In such families, the only way to get attention or enliven the situation is to create a crisis. This negativity may serve to reinforce the substance abuse.

- **Parental inconsistency.** Rule setting is erratic, enforcement is inconsistent, and family structure is inadequate. Children are confused because they cannot figure out the boundaries of right and wrong. As a result, they may behave badly in the hope of getting their parents to set clearly defined boundaries. Without known limits, children cannot predict parental responses and adjust their behavior accordingly. These inconsistencies tend to be present regardless of whether the person abusing substances is a parent or child and they create a sense of confusion a key factor in the children.

- **Parental denial.** Despite obvious warning signs, the parental stance is: (1) "What drug/alcohol problem? We don't see any drug problem!" or (2) after authorities intervene: "You are wrong! My child does not have a drug problem!"

- **Miscarried expression of anger.** Children or parents who resent their emotionally deprived home and are afraid to express their outrage use drug abuse as one way to manage their repressed anger.

- **Self-medication.** Either a parent or child will use drugs or alcohol to cope with intolerable thoughts or feelings, such as severe anxiety or depression.

- **Unrealistic parental expectations.** If parental expectations are unrealistic, children can excuse themselves from all future expectations by saying, in essence, "You can't expect anything of me, I'm just a pothead/speed freak/junkie." Alternatively, they may work obsessively to overachieve, all the while feeling that no matter what they do it is never good enough, or they may joke and clown to deflect the pain or may withdraw to sidestep the pain. If expectations are too low, and children are told throughout youth that they will certainly fail, they tend to conform their behavior to their parents' predictions, unless meaningful adults intervene with healthy, positive, and supportive messages.

In all of these cases, what is needed is a restructuring of the entire family system, including the relationship between the parents and the relationships between the parents and the children.

Families with a Member Who Abuses Substances

Substance Abuser Lives Alone or with Partner

The consequences of an adult who abuses substances and lives alone or with a partner are likely to be economic and psychological. Money may be spent for drug use; the partner who is not using substances often assumes the provider role. Psychological consequences may include denial or protection of the person with the substance abuse problem, chronic anger, stress, anxiety, hopelessness, inappropriate sexual behavior, neglected health, shame, stigma, and isolation.

In this situation, it is important to realize that both partners need help. The treatment for either partner will affect both, and substance abuse treatment programs should make both partners feel welcome. If a person has no immediate family, family therapy should not automatically be ruled out. Issues regarding a person's lost family, estranged family, or family of origin may still be relevant in treatment. A single person who abuses substances may continue to have an impact on distant family members who may be willing to take part in family therapy. If family members come from a distance, intensive sessions (more than 2 hours) may be needed and helpful. What is important is not how many family members are present, but how they interact with each other.

In situations where one person is substance dependent and the other is not, questions of codependency arise. Codependency has become a popular topic in the substance abuse field. Separate 12-step groups such as Al-Anon and Alateen, Co-Dependents Anonymous (CoDA), Adult Children of Alcoholics, Adult Children Anonymous, Families Anonymous, and Co-Anon have formed for family members.

CoDA describes codependency as being overly concerned with the problems of another to the detriment of attending to one's own wants and needs. Codependent people are thought to have several patterns of behavior:

- They are controlling because they believe that others are incapable of taking care of themselves.

- They typically have low self-esteem and a tendency to deny their own feelings.

- They are excessively compliant, compromising their own values and integrity to avoid rejection or anger.

- They often react in an oversensitive manner, as they are often hypervigilant to disruption, troubles, or disappointments.

- They remain loyal to people who do nothing to deserve their loyalty.

Substance Abuser Lives with Spouse (or Partner) and Minor Children

Similar to maltreatment victims, who believe the abuse is their fault, children of those with alcohol abuse disorders feel guilty and responsible for the parent's drinking problem. Children whose parents abuse illicit drugs live with the knowledge that their parents' actions are illegal and that they may have been forced to engage in illegal activity on their parents' behalf. Trust is a key child development issue and can be a constant struggle for those from family systems with a member who has a substance use disorder.

Most available data on the enduring effects of parental substance abuse on children suggest that a parent's drinking problem often has a detrimental effect on children. These data show that a parent's alcohol problem can have cognitive, behavioral, psychosocial, and emotional consequences for children. Among the lifelong problems documented are impaired learning capacity; a propensity to develop a substance use disorder; adjustment problems, including increased rates of divorce, violence, and the need for control in relationships; and other mental disorders such as depression, anxiety, and low self-esteem.

The children of women who abuse substances during pregnancy are at risk for the effects of fetal alcohol syndrome, low birth weight (associated with maternal addiction), and sexually transmitted diseases. Latency age children (age 5 to the onset of puberty) frequently have school-related problems, such as truancy. Older children may be forced prematurely to accept adult responsibilities, especially the care of younger siblings. In adolescence, drug experimentation may begin. Adult children of those with alcohol abuse disorders may exhibit problems such as unsatisfactory relationships, inability to manage finances, and an increased risk of substance use disorders.

Although, in general, children with parents who abuse substances are at increased risk for negative consequences, positive outcomes have also been described. Resiliency is one example of a positive outcome. Some children seem better able to cope than others; the same is true of spouses. Because of their early exposure to the adversity of a family member who abuses substances, children develop tools to respond to extreme stress, disruption, and change, including mature judgment, capacity to tolerate ambiguity, autonomy, willingness to shoulder responsibility, and moral certitude. Nonetheless, substance abuse can lead to inappropriate family subsystems and role taking. For instance, in a family in which a mother uses substances, a young daughter may be expected to take on the role of mother. When a child assumes adult roles and the adult abusing substances plays the role of a child, the boundaries essential to family functioning are blurred. The developmentally inappropriate role taken on by the child robs her of a childhood, unless there is the intervention by healthy, supportive adults.

The spouse of a person abusing substances is likely to protect the children and assume parenting duties that are not fulfilled by the parent abusing substances. If both parents abuse alcohol or illicit drugs, the effect on children worsens. Extended family members may have to provide care as well as financial and psychological support. Grandparents frequently assume a primary caregiving role. Friends and neighbors may also be involved in caring for the young children. In cultures with a community approach to family care, neighbors may step in to provide whatever care is needed. Sometimes it is a neighbor who brings a child abuse or neglect situation to the attention of child welfare officials. Most of the time, however, these situations go unreported and neglected.

Substance Abuser Is Part of a Blended Family

Researchers note that many people who abuse substances belong to stepfamilies. Even under ordinary circumstances, stepfamilies present special challenges. Children often live in two households in which different boundaries and ambiguous roles can be confusing. Effective coparenting requires good communication and careful attention to possible areas of conflict, not only between biological parents, but also with their new partners. The difficulty of coordinating boundaries, roles, expectations, and the need for cooperation places children raised in blended households at far greater risk of social, emotional, and behavioral problems. Children from stepfamilies may develop substance abuse problems to cope with their confusion about family rules and boundaries.

Substance abuse can intensify problems and become an impediment to a stepfamily's integration and stability. When substance abuse is part of the family, unique issues can arise. Such issues might include parental authority disputes, sexual or physical abuse, and self-esteem problems for children.

Substance abuse by stepparents may further undermine their authority, lead to difficulty in forming bonds, and impair a family's ability to address problems and sensitive issues. If the noncustodial parent abuses drugs or alcohol, visitation may have to be supervised. (Even so, visitation is important. If contact stops, children often blame themselves or the drug problem for a parent's absence.)

If a child or adolescent abuses substances, any household can experience conflict and continual crisis. In a study, researchers found that increased adolescent marijuana use occurs more frequently when an adolescent living with a divorced parent and stepparent becomes less attached to the family. With fewer ties to the family, the likelihood increases that the adolescent will form attachments to peers who abuse substances. Weaker ties to the family and stronger ones to peers using drugs increase the chances of the adolescent starting to use marijuana or increasing marijuana use.

Stepparents living in a household in which an adolescent abuses substances may feel they have gotten more than they bargained for and resent the time and attention the adolescent requires from the biological parent. Stepparents may demand that the adolescent leave the household and live with the other parent. In fact, a child who is acting out and abusing substances is not likely to be welcomed in either household.

Clinicians treating substance abuse should know that the family dynamics of blended families differ somewhat from those of nuclear families and require some additional considerations.

Older Substance Abuser Has Grown Children

When an adult, age 65 or older, abuses a substance it is most likely to be alcohol and/or prescription medication. The 2002 National Household Survey on Drug Abuse found that 7.5 percent of older adults reported binge and 1.4 percent reported heavy drinking within the past month of the survey. Veterans hospital data indicate that, in many cases, older adults may be receiving excessive amounts of one class of addictive tranquilizer (benzodiazepines), even though they should receive lower doses. Further, older adults take these drugs longer than other age groups. Older adults consume three times the number of prescription medicine as the general population, and this trend is expected to grow as children of the Baby Boom (born 1946–1958) become senior citizens.

As people retire, become less active, and develop health problems, they use (and sometimes misuse) an increasing number of prescription and over-the-counter drugs. Among older adults, the diagnosis of this (or any other) type of substance use disorder often is difficult because the symptoms of substance abuse can be similar to the symptoms of other medical and behavioral problems that are found in older adults, such as dementia, diabetes, and depression. In addition, many health care providers underestimate the extent of substance abuse problems among older adults, and, therefore, do not screen older adults for these problems.

Older adults often live with or are supported by their adult children because of financial necessity. An older adult with a substance abuse problem can affect everyone in the household. If the older adult's spouse is present, that person is likely to be an older adult as well and may be bewildered by new and upsetting behaviors. Therefore, a spouse may not be in a position to help combat the substance abuse problem. Additional family resources may need to be mobilized in the service of treating the older adult's substance use disorder.

Whether grown children and their parents live together or apart, the children must take on a parental, caretaking role. Adjustment to this role reversal can be stressful, painful, and embarrassing. In some cases, grown children may stop providing financial support because it is the only influence they have over the parent. Adult children often will say to "let them have their little pleasure." In other instances, children may cut ties with the parent because it is too painful to have to watch the parent's deterioration. Cutting ties only increases the parent's isolation and may worsen his predicament.

Substance Abuser Is an Adolescent and Lives with Family of Origin

Substance use and abuse among adolescents continues to be a serious condition that impacts cognitive and affective growth, school and work relationships, and all family members. In the National Household Survey on Drug Abuse, of adolescents ages 12 to 17, 10.7 percent reported binge use of alcohol (five drinks on one occasion in the last month before the survey) and 2.5 percent reported heavy alcohol use (at least five binges in the previous month). In addition, two trends are increasing rates of substance use by youth and first onset of substance use at younger ages.

In a general population sample of 10- to 20-year-olds, roughly 12.4 percent (96 of 776) met criteria for a substance use disorder. Alcohol and other psychoactive drugs play a prominent role in violent death for teenagers, including homicide, suicide, traffic accidents, and other injuries. Aside from death, drug use can lead to a range of possible detrimental consequences:

- Violent behavior
- Delinquency
- Psychiatric disorders

- Risky sexual behavior, possibly leading to unwanted pregnancy or sexually transmitted diseases

- Impulsivity

- Neurological impairment

- Developmental impairment

As youth abuse alcohol and illicit drugs, they may establish a continuing pattern of behavior that damages their legal record, educational options, psychological stability, and social development. Drug use (particularly inhalants and solvents) may lead to cognitive deficits and perhaps irreversible brain damage. Adolescents who use drugs are likely to interact primarily with peers who use drugs, so relationships with friends, including relationships with the opposite sex, may be unhealthy, and the adolescent may develop a limited repertoire of social skills.

When an adolescent uses alcohol or drugs, siblings in the family may find their needs and concerns ignored or minimized while their parents react to constant crises involving the adolescent who abuses drugs. The neglected siblings and peers may look after themselves in ways that are not age-appropriate, or they might behave as if the only way to get attention is to act out.

Clinicians should not miss opportunities to include siblings, who are often as influential as parents, in the family therapy sessions treating substance abuse. Whether they are adults or children, siblings can be an invaluable resource. Sibling relationships characterized by mutual attachment, nurturance, and lack of conflict can protect adolescents against substance abuse.

Another concern often overlooked is the case of the substance-using adolescent whose parents are immigrants and cannot speak English. Immigrant parents often are perplexed by their child's behavior. Degrees of acculturation between family members create greater challenges for the family to address substance abuse issues and exacerbate intergenerational conflict.

In many families that include adolescents who abuse substances, at least one parent also abuses substances. This unfortunate modeling can set in motion a dangerous combination of physical and emotional problems. If adolescent substance use is met with calm, consistent, rational, and firm responses from a responsible adult, the effect on adolescent learning is positive. If, however, the responses come from an impaired parent, the hypocrisy will be obvious to the adolescent, and the result is likely to be negative. In some instances, an impaired parent might form an alliance with an adolescent using substances to keep secrets from the parent who does not use substances. Even worse, sometimes in families with multigenerational patterns of substance abuse, an attitude among extended family members may be that the adolescent is just conforming to the family history.

Since the early 1980s, treating adolescents who abuse substances has proven to be effective. Nevertheless, most adolescents will deny that alcohol or illicit drug use is a problem and do not enter treatment unless parents, often with the help of school-based student assistant programs or the criminal justice system, require them to do so. Often, a youngster's substance abuse is hidden from members of the extended family. Adolescents who are completing treatment need to be prepared for going back to an actively addicted family system. Alateen, along with Alcoholics Anonymous, can be a part of adolescents' continuing care, and participating in a recovery support group at school (through student assistance) also will help to reinforce recovery.

Other Treatment Issues

In any form of family therapy for substance abuse treatment, consideration should be given to the range of social problems connected to substance abuse. Problems such as criminal activity, joblessness, domestic violence, and child abuse or neglect may also be present in families experiencing substance abuse. To address these issues, treatment providers need to collaborate with professionals in other fields. This is also known as concurrent treatment.

Whenever family therapy and substance abuse treatment take place concurrently, communication between clinicians is vital. In addition to family therapy and substance abuse treatment, multifamily group therapy, individual therapy, and psychological consultation might be necessary. With these different approaches, coordination, communication, collaboration, and exchange of the necessary releases of confidential information are required.

Chapter 54

Coping with an Alcoholic Parent

Anthony is already in bed when he hears the front door slam. He covers his head with his pillow to drown out the predictable sounds of his parents arguing. Anthony is all too aware that his father has been drinking and his mother is angry.

Many teens like Anthony live with a parent who is an alcoholic, a person physically and emotionally addicted to alcohol. Alcoholism has been around for centuries, yet no one has discovered how to prevent or stop it. Alcoholism continues to cause anguish not only for the person who drinks, but for everyone who is involved with that person.

According to the National Council on Alcoholism and Drug Dependence (NCADD), there are nearly 14 million Americans who are considered problem drinkers (including 8 million who have alcoholism) and 76 million people who are exposed to alcoholism in family settings. Although these numbers show a huge number of problem drinkers, they also show that people who live with alcoholic family members are not alone.

Why Does My Parent Drink?

Alcoholism is a disease. Like any disease, it needs to be treated. Without professional help, an alcoholic will probably continue to drink and may become worse over time.

This information was provided by TeensHealth, one of the largest resources online for medically reviewed health information written for parents, kids, and teens. For more articles like this one, visit www.TeensHealth.org, or www.Kids Health.org. © 2004 The Nemours Center for Children's Health Media, a division of The Nemours Foundation. Reviewed in January 2004 by D'Arcy Lyness, Ph.D.

Just like any other disease, alcoholism is no one's fault. Some people who live with alcoholics blame themselves for their loved one's drinking. But the truth is, that person would drink anyway. If your parent drinks, it won't change anything if you do better in school, help more around the house, or do any of the other things you may believe your parent wants you to do.

Other people may tell themselves that their parents drink because of some other problem, such as having a rough time at work or being out of work altogether. Parents may be having marital problems, financial problems, or someone may be sick. But even if an alcoholic parent has other problems, nothing you can do will make things better. No one else can help an alcoholic get well.

Why Won't My Parent Stop Drinking?

Denial can play a big role in an alcoholic's life. A person in denial is one who refuses to believe the truth about a situation. A problem drinker may blame another person for the drinking because it is easier than taking responsibility for it. Some alcoholic parents make their kids feel bad by saying things like, "You're driving me crazy!" or "I can't take this anymore." An alcoholic parent may become enraged at the slightest suggestion that drinking is a problem. Those who acknowledge their drinking may show their denial by saying, "I can stop any time I want to," "Everyone drinks to unwind sometimes," or "My drinking is not a problem."

Why Do I Feel So Bad?

If you're like most teens, your life is probably filled with emotional ups and downs, regardless of what's happening at home. Add an alcoholic parent to this tumultuous time and a person's bound to feel overwhelmed. Some of the emotions teens with alcoholic parents report feeling are anger, sadness, embarrassment, loneliness, helplessness, and a lack of self-esteem.

These emotions can be triggered by the added burdens of living with an alcoholic parent. For example, many alcoholics behave unpredictably, and kids growing up with alcoholic parents may spend a lot of energy trying to feel out a parent's mood or guess what he or she wants. One day you might walk on eggshells to avoid an outburst because the dishes aren't done or the lawn mowed; the next day, you may find yourself comforting a parent who promises that things will be better. The pressure to manage these situations in addition to your own life—and maybe take care of younger siblings, too—can leave you exhausted and drained.

Although alcoholism causes similar patterns of damage to many families, each situation is unique. Some alcoholics abuse their children emotionally or physically. Others neglect their children by not providing sufficient nurturing and guidance. Drugs may be involved. Your family may have money troubles. And although each family is different, teens with alcoholic parents almost always report feeling alone, unloved, depressed, or burdened by the secret life they lead at home. Because it's not possible to control the behavior of an alcoholic, what can a person do to feel better?

What Can I Do?

Teenage children of alcoholics are at a higher risk of becoming alcoholics themselves. Acknowledging the problem and reaching out for support can help ensure that your future does not repeat your parent's past.

Acknowledge the problem. An alcoholic parent is never the child's fault. Many children of alcoholics try to hide the problem or find themselves telling lies to cover up for a parent's drinking. Admitting that your parent has a problem—even if he or she won't—is the first step in taking control.

Being aware of how your parent's drinking affects you can help put things in perspective. For example, some teens who live with alcoholic adults become afraid to speak out or show any normal anger or emotion because they worry it may trigger a parent's drinking binge. This can erode self-esteem. Acknowledging feelings of anger or resentment—even if it's just to yourself or a close friend—can help protect against this. Recognizing the emotions that go with the problem can also help you from suppressing your feelings and pretending that everything's OK.

Likewise, realizing that you are not the cause of a parent's drinking problem can help you feel better about yourself.

Find support. It's good to share your feelings with a friend, but it's equally important to talk to an adult you trust. A school counselor, favorite teacher, or coach may be able to help. Some teens turn to their school D.A.R.E. (Drug and Alcohol Resistance Education) officer, whereas others find a sympathetic uncle or aunt.

Because alcoholism is such a widespread problem, several organizations offer confidential support groups and meetings for people living with alcoholics. Al-Anon, an organization designed to help the families and friends of alcoholics, has a group called Alateen that is specifically geared to young people living with adults who have drinking problems. Alateen is not only for children of alcoholics, it can also help teens whose parents may already be in recovery. Another group called Alcoholics Anonymous (AA) also offers a variety of programs and resources for people living with alcoholics.

You're not betraying your parent by seeking help. Keeping "the secret" is part of the disease of alcoholism—and it allows the problems to get worse. As with any disease, it's still possible to love a parent while recognizing that he or she has alcoholism. And it's not disloyal to seek help in dealing with the problems your parent's drinking create for you.

Find a safe environment. If you find yourself avoiding your house as much as possible, or if you're thinking about running away, consider whether you feel in danger at home. If you feel that the situation at home is becoming dangerous, you can call the National Domestic Violence Hotline at (800) 799-SAFE. And never hesitate to dial 911 if you think you or another family member is in immediate danger.

Because alcoholism is a disease and not a behavior, chances are that you won't be able to change your parent's actions. But you can show your love and support—and, above all, take care of yourself.

Chapter 55

Alcohol and Substance Use in the Workplace

Alcohol Abuse and Dependence

Alcohol abuse and dependence are the most prevalent substance use disorders in our society and in the workplace, representing enormous, often unrecognized social, health, safety, and productivity costs. Yet, because alcohol use is widely accepted in our society and nearly three quarters of the adult population drink, employers may be ambivalent about addressing its use by employees, and often view illegal drug use as a much more serious workplace issue. This chapter identifies the impact on the workplace of alcohol abuse, looking at the economic, health, productivity, and family costs associated with alcohol abuse. It also points out the adverse impact that excessive, but non-dependent drinking has on employee productivity, offering important evidence that workplace policies and practices significantly affect employee behavior toward alcohol use. Lastly, the chapter suggests successful approaches employers can utilize in working to address prevention and treatment of alcohol abuse.

The Economic Burden of Alcohol Abuse

Alcohol abuse imposes major economic costs on American society, including illness, deaths, medical costs, and other related costs

Apgar, Kristen Reasoner, and Burgess, Angela Glover. Alcohol Use to Alcohol Abuse: The Economic Burden, Health Consequences, and Impact on the Workplace. In *Working Solutions to Substance Abuse,* Washington Business Group on Health, April 2001. © 2001 National Business Group on Health. Reprinted with permission. Revised by David A. Cooke, M.D., April 2006.

amounting to nearly $166.5 billion annually.[1] As the vast majority of individuals whose health and performance are adversely affected by their alcohol use are employed, these costs directly affect employers. Indeed 85 percent of heavy drinkers (those who consume five or more drinks at one time each week) in the United States are employed.[2] Companies bear the direct and indirect costs associated with alcohol abuse through health care costs sustained by employees and their families, disability costs, and workers' compensation claims. Misuse of alcohol also adversely impacts workplace safety and employee morale, resulting in overall productivity losses from employees with impaired performance and from affected fellow workers.

Health Care Costs. The cost of illness in the United States associated with alcohol abuse has been well documented. Estimates for 1998 amounted to approximately $683 for every man, woman, and child living in the United States.[3] The health care costs of alcohol abuse are estimated at $26.3 billion for 1998 (14.3 percent) of the total estimated cost ($184.6 billion) of alcohol abuse. This includes the cost of treating alcohol abuse and dependence (in a variety of private and public settings, support, research, and administrative costs), as well as the considerably larger costs of treating the adverse medical consequences of alcohol consumption.[3]

Productivity Losses. Nationally, productivity losses resulting from alcohol abuse are estimated at $134.2 billion (almost 73 percent of the total cost of alcohol abuse), including losses due to premature deaths, alcohol-related illness, and alcohol-related crime. Alcohol abuse also impairs worker productivity, and is represented in reduced earnings, job absences, and lost employment.[3] Further, the adverse impact that alcohol use and abuse patterns have in the workplace and on work performance can result from a broad range of alcohol consumption patterns including binge drinking; drinking prior to work due to the "hangover effect" during work; and heavy, as well as addictive, drinking.[8]

Costs to Families. Alcohol abuse also affects the financial and psychological stability of families. Alcohol abuse is characterized by continued alcohol consumption despite adverse impacts on health, family, or work. The most extreme condition of alcohol abuse is "alcoholism," a disease caused by chronic alcohol consumption. Excessive drinking poses a financial strain on a family budget, diverting vital family resources to the cost of alcohol consumption.

Further, one of the most damaging effects of excessive use of alcohol is the connection between heavy drinking and marital violence. Indeed, 57 percent of the victims of domestic violence report that the partner perpetrators were under the influence of alcohol at the time of the assault.[1]

The children of families with substance abusing parents also are at much higher risk of suffering neglect and abuse, are more likely to have problems with delinquency, do poorly in school, and suffer a range of emotional disturbances. Such risk factors predispose them to becoming alcohol abusers themselves. In 1996, six million children lived with a parent who was dependent on alcohol.[1]

The Health Consequences of Alcohol Abuse

Neurological Effects. Advances in neurobiological research in the last decade have begun to identify the brain processes that cause individuals to abuse alcohol and to become alcohol dependent. These advances in knowledge of the biology underlying drinking behavior reveal that multiple chemical messenger systems in the brain—neurotransmitter systems—are involved in problem drinking. Some neurotransmitter systems are known to produce pleasurable effects that occur in the use of alcohol and other drugs, while other neurotransmitter systems are involved in maintaining dependence.[5] In alcoholics, tolerance occurs when, after prolonged alcohol consumption, the brain becomes less sensitive to the acute actions of alcohol. More and more alcohol consumption is required to "get drunk," resulting in dependence with physical withdrawal symptoms, such as tremors and seizures or psychological symptoms, such as a negative emotional state, when drinking stops. The brains of such individuals experience permanent injury, with shrinkage in the deeper brain regions, including brain structures associated with memory, as well as in the cerebellum, which helps regulate coordination and balance.[4] Current research and development in alcohol treatment focuses on producing medications that will block these effects, thereby reducing cravings and addiction.[5]

Other Health Risks. Chronic alcohol use also puts individuals at risk for developing other serious health problems, such as liver disease (manifested in three phases), heart disease (high blood pressure, cardiovascular disease, certain kinds of stroke), cancer (esophagus, mouth, throat, voice box, colon and rectum), pancreatitis (inflammation of the pancreas)[6], head trauma, and depression. Although light to moderate (1 to 2 drinks per day maximum) alcohol consumption appears to have positive benefits on the heart, larger amounts are definitely harmful. For example, for those who have coronary heart disease, studies have shown that binge drinking increases episodes of angina (heart pain), with six times the risk of a fatal heart attack than moderate drinkers.[7] Individuals who abuse alcohol use four times as many hospital days as nondrinkers. Alcohol use is also closely associated with higher incidence of injury from accident related trauma, with alcohol taken in tandem with other drugs contributing to a rising incidence of emergency room visits.[1] Excessive use of alcohol is also associated with untreated depression or other mental illnesses, as individuals turn to alcohol in place of appropriate treatment for their illness. Indeed studies of individuals with mental illnesses suggest that as many as half also experience alcohol and other drug abuse problems.[17]

Further, use of alcohol in amounts that can be tolerated in males without significant adverse health effects—as little as seven to 13 drinks per week—can cause serious harm to women.[5] Studies have found that much lower intakes of alcohol in women can result in liver disease, degenerative myopathy, and cardiomyopathy. And, mortality rates are higher for women who drink heavily than they are for men. In addition, women who drink three or more alcoholic beverages per day have a 69 percent higher risk of developing breast cancer than their non-drinking peers.

Lastly, even moderate alcohol use by women during pregnancy poses serious health risks to their babies. Fetal alcohol syndrome is known to cause significant prenatal neurological injuries, resulting in mental retardation and other serious learning disabilities, as well as facial and other physical abnormalities. Significantly, the most serious harm to the child occurs in the first month of pregnancy, even before a woman may be aware that she is pregnant. Indeed, ten percent of all health care costs associated with alcohol abuse result from the costs of care associated with fetal alcohol syndrome.[1]

Impact on the Workplace

Health Care Costs. Under company-sponsored health plans, employers bear a significant portion of the costs associated with the adverse health impacts of employee and family members' alcohol abuse. It is important to note that the direct costs for employer-funded alcohol and other drug abuse treatment are themselves rather modest when compared to overall health care expenditures of companies, averaging one half of one percent of overall health care costs.[18] Rather, the greatest share of the costs are for treatment for alcohol-related medical conditions and for trauma and injury connected to alcohol use. Prevention of alcohol abuse could also provide significant reduction in health care costs, in the costs associated with the trauma and injury resulting from alcohol-related accidents and family violence, and in treatment required by children who suffer the effects of family stress or fetal alcohol syndrome.

Productivity Losses. Excessive alcohol use also impacts the bottom line through indirect costs. Productivity losses related to alcohol use have been estimated at $135 billion annually—the costs of lost productivity, medical claims, and accidents related to alcohol use.[1] A 1999 study of the connection between employee drinking practices and productivity at work showed that drinking at work, problem drinking, and getting drunk—both on and off the job—were positively associated with:

- frequency of absenteeism;
- late arrival to or early departure from work;
- poor quality of work and poor performance; and
- argumentative attitudes toward coworkers.[8]

Further, a study conducted for the Substance Abuse and Mental Health Services Administration of the U.S. Department of Health and Human Services, in 1999, found that one out of five employees who were heavy drinkers voluntarily left their jobs in the last year and eleven percent reported skipping work within the past 30 days.[16] When employees with alcoholism are unable to continue working, the direct costs related to alcohol abuse treatment are shifted to the cost of disability benefits.

Safety Concerns and Federal Worksite Requirements. Impaired performance through heavy alcohol use creates hazards, for employees, coworkers and, for the general public, and results in cost attendant on employee injuries and liability for injuries to the public. For this reason, the federal government has established a range of worksite regulations aimed at eliminating the consumption of alcohol and illegal substances in the workplace (the Drug-Free Workplace Act), and at preventing employees who are using alcohol or drugs from engaging in work activities that would create safety hazards (the

Omnibus Transportation Employee Testing Act of 1991). The Department of Transportation (DOT) regulations, which implement the Employee Testing Act, require random drug testing, as well as substance abuse awareness education for supervisors and employees including flight, aircraft, air traffic control personnel in commercial aviation; certain operators of commercial motor vehicles in interstate commerce; certain railroad services personnel; workers operating on pipelines or liquid natural gas facilities; or crew members on a commercial vessel licensed, certified or documented by the U.S. Coast Guard.

Impact of Workplace Policies and Practices on Alcohol Abuse

Workplace Culture. The culture of the workplace can accept and encourage drinking or discourage and inhibit it. In addition, studies have suggested that work environment and peers also influence individual behavior outside the workplace. The influence on drinking behavior persists even after controlling for age, gender, education levels, marital status, race, religion, family income, managerial status, functional work area, and region of country.[11]

Studies of the workplace culture in so-called "male-dominated" occupations have found that those worksites become places where workers use drinking to build solidarity and show conformity to the group. These workplaces tend to have high rates of heavy drinking and alcohol-related problems, including instances of employees engaging in drinking at the worksite. In contrast, both males and females in "predominately female occupations" are less likely to drink and to have fewer alcohol-related problems than employees of either sex in the male-dominated occupations.[11] Such studies suggest that employer attitudes and worksite culture can be important factors in discouraging and preventing alcohol misuse and abuse.

Lack of Clarity about Alcohol Policies. There is also considerable variation in company policies on alcohol use, as well as a variation in manager and employee knowledge of their existence, or enforcement. Even when there are written company guidelines, employees are often unaware of their workplace policies about alcohol use. A recent study showed 15 percent of managers and 25 percent of employees did not know what their company's policies were regarding alcohol at on-site events, and 20 percent did not know their company's policies about alcohol use generally or when driving a company car. Indeed, many companies did not even have policies related to driving. Many employees also did not know whether their company had policies on drinking during lunch or whether it was acceptable to have alcohol on one's breath at work.[8]

Where company policies are not well communicated or disseminated, employees may be unclear about what the standards or rules are for their company. A recent survey of managers and supervisors of companies representing various industries illustrates the inconsistencies and mixed messages that employees receive with regard to alcohol use and abuse. Of the managers and supervisors surveyed:

- 58 percent indicated their company is tough on illicit drug use but soft on alcohol use;

- 49 percent indicated they "pay a price" for confronting a worker who has an alcohol problem;

- 43 percent felt their employee union protects problem drinkers; and

- 73 percent stated that employees who are abusing alcohol are often still able to do an adequate job.[9]

Lack of Supervision and Workplace Alienation. Limited work supervision, often a problem on evening shifts, has also been associated with employee alcohol problems. In one study of 832 workers at a large manufacturing plant, workers on evening shifts, during which supervision was reduced, were more likely than those on other shifts to report drinking at work.[15] In addition, work that is boring, stressful, or isolating can also contribute to employees' drinking. Employee drinking has been associated with:

- low job autonomy;

- lack of job complexity;

- lack of control over work conditions and products;

- boredom;

- sexual harassment;

- verbal and physical aggression; and

- disrespectful behavior toward coworkers.[12]

Alcohol Availability. The availability and accessibility of alcohol also influences employee drinking. In a survey of 6,540 employees at 16 worksites representing a range of industries, 23 percent of upper-level managers reported easy access to alcohol and drinking during working hours in the previous month.[13] Restricting workers' access to alcohol may reduce their drinking. Another example highlights the influence of cultural prohibition against alcohol. U.S. military personnel serving in the Middle East during Desert Shield and Desert Storm were surveyed regarding their alcohol consumption. An estimated 80 percent of the personnel surveyed reported decreased drinking while serving in those operations.[14]

Fragmented Approaches. Further, even when alcohol use is identified as a problem and the employer becomes involved, it is likely to be addressed by a range of uncoordinated systems within the company, including behavioral health care under employer-sponsored health plans, employee assistance programs (EAPs), disability programs, employee education programs, work/life benefits, as well as company workplace personnel policies on alcohol use at the worksite or company functions. Frequently, different personnel administer these benefits and employee policies, and the multiplicity of programs prevents the implementation of a coordinated approach to addressing alcohol use and abuse.

Employees, as well as supervisors and managers, may be unsure of the rules they should follow, or unaware of the tools available to assist an employee in need of information or treatment. For example, in the study cited above, 80 percent of the managers and supervisors indicated they did not have enough training to know how to properly confront employees with alcohol-related performance problems.[7] Communication among those administering various programs within a company is often poor. Individual programs address a small audience. Further, because the overall productivity costs of alcohol abuse are not easily recognized or identified and the expenditures on each program are relatively low, the problem of alcohol abuse throughout the workplace may be minimized.

Recognition and Treatment Availability. Employees may not recognize that they are engaging in alcohol use patterns that pose health risks or risk of dependence. They may not be aware of the programs and services available to them through their employee assistance and health care benefits. EAPs can offer an excellent source of information and referral to appropriate treatment, however, access to EAPs varies by company size, with a majority of large employers at 83 percent; mid-size and small companies have access of 59 percent and 24 percent, respectively. In a recent national study, half of all full-time employees age 18 to 49 reported access to an EAP or other types of counseling programs for substance abuse-related problems.[2]

Further, when employees seek help for alcohol abuse, they may encounter barriers to accessing appropriate care. Employer-sponsored health coverage for substance abuse treatment is often more limited than benefits for treatment of other medical conditions.[21] These limitations often reflect concerns about cost of care, but they also reflect concerns that employees will fail to complete full courses of treatment for addiction, including outpatient aftercare, and about the frequency of relapse. Experts in the field of addiction argue that the course of treatment and the phenomenon of relapse for substance abuse are similar to that of other chronic conditions such as hypertension or diabetes, and that the standards for evaluating effectiveness of treatment, as well as disease management approaches should be similar as well.[20]

Stigma. The societal stigma attached to drug and alcohol addiction is a pervasive and continuing barrier to early identification and appropriate treatment. In the workplace, employees may be reluctant to seek treatment for alcohol abuse even when employee assistance and health care benefits are available. They fear exposure to their supervisors or coworkers that could result in losing their job, interfere with their workplace relationships, or result in other adverse consequences. It is not uncommon for employees to avoid taking steps that could result in a diagnosis, or to pay for treatment at their own expense to assure that their condition is not made known to their employer and coworkers. Even beyond this, the stigma attached to alcohol abuse and dependence can lead employees and their dependents to avoid disclosing treatment information to their primary care physicians, because they fear that such disclosure could negatively impact an otherwise amiable patient-physician relationship, or that their spouse may learn of the problem.[10] Similarly, many primary care physicians are reluctant to screen for or discuss excessive drinking with their patients because of concerns about raising a potentially embarrassing subject or general uncertainty about what to do with the information if received.[19]

Approaches to Managing Alcohol Abuse

For all the reasons cited above, employers have strong financial, employee health, and productivity interests in taking proactive steps to provide clear standards on alcohol use, to assist employees in taking steps to prevent its abuse, and to offer employees appropriate treatment. The following recommendations describe some of the successful approaches employers can use to encourage prevention of alcohol abuse and to promote access to appropriate treatment.

The Workplace Environment, Policies, and Practice

Health Promotion. Employers are increasingly developing innovative approaches to employee education and health promotion, taking advantage of the new tools made available through Internet technology. Employers have successfully taken on smoking and other wellness issues (e.g., diabetes, cholesterol screening) to improve individual employee health, recognizing that good health positively affects productivity. Employers should equally engage in health promotion activities aimed at prevention of alcohol use disorders through advocacy for moderate and safe drinking habits and increased employee awareness of potential health risks (especially during pregnancy) even from non-dependent use of alcohol. Such health promotion efforts also encourage healthy behaviors that maintain employees' personal safety and the safety of others. Successful employee education and communication efforts also offer employees a mechanism to become familiar with company policies and procedures on use of alcohol. Awareness programs can set forth company expectations for policy compliance and testing procedures and inform employees of the consequences attendant on use at work, at work-related functions, and on the employee's own time.

Early Intervention. Incorporating brief interventions at the primary care level is one such approach. Brief interventions are time-limited counseling techniques in individuals with alcohol use disorders, with a goal of helping individuals reduce alcohol consumption. Such interventions may also help those with alcohol dependence seek specialized alcohol treatment.

Employee Assistance Programs and Employee Advocacy. In addition, employers recognize that employees may need assistance in accessing and navigating the health care and behavioral health care systems. Most large employers offer around the clock, seven days a week telephone access to information and referral systems for employees seeking information and access to treatment for alcohol and other behavioral health concerns. These referral systems may be operated by the company's behavioral health vendor, by work/life benefits programs, or by the company's employee assistance programs (EAPs).[10] EAPs offer a valuable and cost-effective resource in dealing with substance abuse as they aid in the reduction of employee accidents, absenteeism, and raise productivity. The utilization of EAPs is an important avenue to improve employee access to appropriate treatment for alcohol problems as well as dependence. Further, under the Drug-Free Workplace Act as well as the DOT workplace regulations for safety sensitive industries, companies must offer employee access to employee assistance programs.

Substance Abuse Benefits and Treatment. Effective, evidence-based treatments for alcohol abuse are available. Further, treatment should be regarded as a continuum of care that includes behavioral therapies (including counseling, psychotherapy, support groups, or family therapy) as well as treatment medications. Some employees may need short-term (and in some cases long-term) outpatient or residential treatments. More positive outcomes are realized when individuals in treatment can remain for several months so that short-term and long-term reduction and abstinence goals can be achieved and maintained.[5] Employers, particularly large employers, are increasingly providing generous substance abuse treatment benefits to assure that employees access appropriate care, and they are beginning to recognize that providing high quality care to employees makes good business sense through increasing employee productivity and safety, and reducing drug and alcohol-related health care costs.[10]

Employee Education and Communication. Increasingly, large employers are engaging in extensive efforts to assure that employees are aware of and make good use of their substance abuse treatment benefits. These efforts have been significantly advanced by the availability of the Internet to deliver information on benefit plans, and on the steps needed to access behavioral health care. Programs for employee education and communication can encourage early identification of risk, as well as offer greater access and utilization of available health benefits. New web-based employee decision-support tools are being introduced to employees that offer confidential, personalized access to relevant health and substance abuse information, risk assessments, as well as information needed to encourage them to seek early intervention and treatment.

References

1. Horgan, C., et al, *Substance Abuse: The Nation's Number One Health Problem,* Schneider Institute for Health Policy, Brandeis University, 2001.

2. Worker Drug Use and Workplace Policies and Programs: Results from the National Household Survey on Drug Abuse, Substance Abuse and Mental Health Services Administration, 1999.

3. Harwood, H., D. Fountain, G. Livermore, The Economic Costs of Alcohol and Drug Abuse in the United States, Rockville, MD: National Institute on Drug Abuse, 1998.

4. Imaging and Alcoholism: A Window on the Brain, *Alcohol Alert*, National Institute on Alcohol Abuse and Alcoholism, 47, 2000.

5. 10th Special Report to the U.S. Congress on Alcohol and Health (2000), National Institute on Alcohol Abuse and Alcoholism, Bethesda, MD.

6. Alcoholism: Getting the Facts (1996), National Institute on Alcohol Abuse and Alcoholism, Bethesda, MD.

7. Walitzer, K, Conners, G, "Treating problem drinking", *Alcohol Research & Health*, 23: 138–143, 1999.

8. Mangione, T, Howland, J et. al., Employee drinking practices and work performance, *Journal of Studies on Alcohol*, 60(2):261–269, 1999.

9. Kauhanen, J, Kaplan, G, Goldberg D, Salonen, J. Beer binging and mortality: Results from the Kuopio ischemic heart disease risk factor study, a prospective population-based study, *BMJ* 315(7112):, 1997.

10. Apgar, K, *Large Employer Experiences and Best Practices in Design, Administration, and Evaluation of Mental Health and Substance Abuse Benefits—A Look at Parity in Employer-Sponsored Health Benefit Programs.*

11. Kraft, J, Blum, T, Martin, J, Roman, P, "Drinking patterns and the gender mix of occupations: Evidence from a national survey of American workers," *Journal of Substance Abuse* 5(2): 157–174, 1993.

12. Alcohol and the Workplace, *Alcohol Alert*, National Institute on Alcohol Abuse and Alcoholism, 44, 1999.

13. Mangione, T., J. Howland, & M. Lee, New Perspectives for Worksite Alcohol Strategies: Results From a Corporate Drinking Study. Boston, MA JSI Research and Training Institute, 1998.

14. Bray, R, L. Kroutil, et. al., Highlights: 1992 Worldwide Survey of Substance Abuse and Health Behaviors Among Military Personnel. Research Triangle Park, NC: Research Triangle Institute, 1992.

15. Ames, G, J. Gruba, R. Moore, "The relationship of drinking and hangovers to workplace problems: An empirical study," *Journal of Studies on Alcohol* 58:137–47, 1997.

16. Zhang Z, Huang LX, Brittingham, AM, Worker Drug Use and Workplace Policies and Programs: Results from 1994 and 1997, NHSDA, SAMHSA, Rockville, MD, 1999.

17. Mental Health: A Report of the Surgeon General, U.S. Dept. of Health and Human Services, 288, 1999.

18. Sturm, R., Effects of Substance Abuse Parity in Private Insurance Plans under Managed Care, Testimony submitted to the U.S. House of Representatives Subcommittee on Criminal Justice, Drug Policy and Human Resources, October 1999.

19. CASA, Missed Opportunity: National Survey of Primary Care Physicians and Patients in Substance Abuse, Chicago: Survey Research Laboratory, University of Illinois, 2000.

20. McLellan, A.T., D. Lewis, P. O'Brien, H.D. Kleber, "Is Drug Dependence a Chronic Medical Illness: Implications for Treatment, Insurance and Outcome Evaluation?" *Journal of the American Medical Society*, 285 (4), 1689–95, 2000.

21. Sturm, R. & C.D. Sherbourne, Are Barriers to Mental Health and Substance Abuse Care Still Rising?, Working Paper No. H-156, RAND, 1999.

Other resources include: Alcohol: What You Don't Know Can Harm You (1999), Bethesda, MD. Employer Leadership Forum on Substance Abuse, Washington Business Group on Health, 2000.

Chapter 56

Alcohol and Violence

Chapter Contents

Section 56.1—Alcohol Use and Violence in Youth 438
Section 56.2—Domestic Violence and Alcohol Use 442

Section 56.1

Alcohol Use and Violence in Youth

"Youth Violence and Alcohol/Drug Abuse," Research Update, January 2002. Copyright 2002 Hazelden Foundation. Reprinted by permission of Hazelden Foundation, Center City, MN.

Although homicides committed by youth have dropped since the early 1990s, arrests and self-reports for other violent behaviors are on the rise.[1] In 1999, five million youth aged 12 to 17 reported serious fights with others at school or work and almost two million youth reported attacking others with the intent to harm.[2]

Often violence and substance abuse occur together. As drug abuse violations have increased in recent years, so too have arrests for assault and disorderly conduct.[1] Several studies have examined the relationship between substance abuse and violence and developing effective prevention programs has become a priority.

Violent Behavior

According to a recent National Household Survey on Drug Abuse (NHSDA), adolescents who used alcohol in the month prior to the survey were significantly more likely to have behaved violently in the previous year.[3] Youth ages 12 to 17 were divided into groups based on their alcohol use patterns in the past month: heavy drinkers drank five or more drinks per occasion on five or more days, binge drinking was defined as fiver or more drinks on one to five occasions, and light drinking was defined as one to four drinks on any occasion. Heavy drinkers were much more likely than binge or light drinkers to report destroying property and threatening or physically attacking others. Non-drinkers were the least likely to engage in these behaviors.

Drinking levels are associated with severe criminal behavior, as well. Heavy- and binge-drinking youth were significantly more likely to report shoplifting, drunken driving, drug trafficking, and having been arrested or booked for legal violations at least once in their lifetimes compared to non-drinking peers.[3]

The NHSDA also found significant differences among drinking groups in terms of violence directed toward the self. Heavy- and binge-drinking youth were twice as likely to think about killing themselves and three times more likely to try to hurt or kill themselves compared to non-drinking peers.[3]

Handguns and Substance Abuse

Substance abuse is also associated with the possession of firearms. Youths who used illegal drugs in the year prior to the NHSDA survey were three times more likely to have carried a handgun than youth who did not use drugs. Binge-drinking and heavy alcohol use were also highly associated with handgun possession, with youth being four and five times more likely, respectively, to have carried a handgun in the past year compared to non-drinking peers.[4]

Are Substance Abuse and Victimization Related?

A survey of over 11,000 youth ages 11 to 17 found significant correlations between alcohol and drug abuse, risky behavior (i.e., walking alone at night) and victimization.[5] Illicit drug abuse, combined with risky behavior, was associated with victimization among females. Among eighth-grade boys, risky behavior and alcohol abuse was associated with victimization.

Which Comes First: Violence or Substance Abuse?

Violent behavior appears to be both a risk factor for and a consequence of alcohol and drug abuse in this population. Aggression and impulsivity in young children is predictive of later chemical abuse in adolescence.[6,7] Conversely, studies have shown that substance use decreases inhibitions and self-control, which, in turn, increases the likelihood of violent behavior.[8,9]

Preventing Violence among Youth

Treatment for substance dependence decreases violent and criminal behavior among youth. According to a large-scale study conducted by the National Institute on Drug Abuse, the number of 11- to 18-year-olds engaging in criminal activities dropped from 75.6% to 52.8% in the year following treatment.[10] The more time spent in treatment, the greater the improvements. Specifically, youth who stayed in treatment at least 90 days, whether residential or outpatient, were 1.45 times less likely to be arrested in the year following treatment compared to peers with shorter treatment stays.

A comprehensive review prepared by the office of the U.S. Surgeon General found that the most effective violence prevention programs for youth are multi-modal, behavioral, and include social, moral reasoning, and thinking skills training.[11] Such programs significantly reduce the number of reoffenses, the level of substance abuse, and aggressive behaviors among youth. School participation, achievement, and avoidance of individuals with antisocial tendencies also work to inhibit the development of later behavior problems and substance use among aggressive boys.[12]

Summary

Although violence and chemical abuse commonly co-occur, it is important to remember that not all youth who use substances act violently and not all violent youth use substances. Nonetheless, the association between violence and chemical abuse warrants specific and effective interventions for this population. Youth who struggle with both substance use and violent behaviors can be helped and effectively treated.

How to Use This Information

Parents: If your teenager is having difficulties with substance abuse and violent behavior, remember that substance abuse treatment can help. The longer your teen is engaged in treatment, the better the outcome in reducing violent behavior and substance abuse.

Educators: Support the implementation of effective, empirically based violence and substance abuse prevention programs in your school.

Treatment Providers: Work to keep young people engaged in the alcohol/drug treatment process. Longer treatment stays and using structured skills-based approaches effectively reduce violence among youth.

References

1. OJJDP. (2000). *Office of Juvenile Justice and Delinquency Prevention Statistical Briefing Book* [On-line]. Available: http://ojjdp.ncfrs.org/ojstatbb/html/qa253.html.

2. SAMHSA. (2001). The NHSDA report: Youth violence linked to substance use [On-line]. Available: www.samhsa.gov/oas/facts.cfm.

3. Greenblatt, J. C. (2000). Patterns of alcohol use among adolescents and associations with emotional and behavioral problems [On-line]. Available: www.samhsa.gov/oas.

4. SAMHSA. (2002). The NHSDA report: Youths who carry handguns [On-line]. Available: www.DrugAbuseStatistics.samhsa.gov.

5. Windle. M. (1994). Substance use, risky behaviors, and victimization among a U.S. national adolescent sample. *Addiction,* 89, 175–182.

6. Berman, S. M., Whipple, S. C., Fitch, R. J., & Noble, E. P. (1993). P3 in young boys as a predictor of adolescent substance use. *Alcohol,* 10, 69–76.

7. Caspi, A., Moffitt, T. E., Newman, D. L., & Silva, P. A. (1996). Behavioral observations at age 3 years predict adult psychiatric disorders: Longitudinal evidence from a birth cohort. *Archives of General Psychiatry,* 53, 1033–1039.

8. Bushman, B. J. & Cooper, H. M. (1990). Effects of alcohol on human aggression: An integrative research review. *Psychological Bulletin,* 107, 341–354.

9. Ito, T. A. Miller, N., & Pollock, V. E. (1996). Alcohol and aggression: A meta-analysis on the moderating effects of inhibitory cues, triggering events, and self-focused attention. *Psychological Bulletin,* 120, 60–82.

10. National Institute on Drug Abuse. (2001). Study of teens in four cities finds drug treatment effective [On-line]. Available: www.nida.nih.gov.

11. Surgeon General of the Public Health Service. (2002). Youth violence: A report of the Surgeon General [On-line}. Available: www.surgeongeneral.gov/library/youthviolence.

12. O'Donnell, J. O., Hawkins, J. D., & Abbott, R. D. (1995). Predicting serious delinquency and substance use among aggressive boys. *Journal of Consulting and Clinical Psychology,* 63, 529–537.

Section 56.2

Domestic Violence and Alcohol Use

"The first time he hit me he was drunk. He used to call me names and was always really jealous but after we had our son he started drinking more and more and his behavior got worse. I always blamed the abuse on his drinking and begged him to stop. It wasn't until he got a DUI and gave up drinking that I began to realize I couldn't blame it all on the alcohol. Sure, things were different in my home but my kids and I were still scared of him. The last time he threatened me with a knife and he had been sober for 13 months."

Drugs and Alcohol Don't Cause Abuse

Domestic violence and drug and alcohol addiction frequently occur together but are two separate and distinct problems. One does not cause the other. Domestic violence is a pattern of controlling behavior that is learned and is not the result of alcohol or drug abuse. Not all alcoholics or drug addicts are abusers and most abusers are not addicted to drugs and alcohol. Abusers frequently blame alcohol and drug use for their violence so they don't have to take responsibility for their problem.

Drugs, Alcohol, and Domestic Violence Don't Mix

Victims of domestic violence experience worse injuries and are more likely to be killed when drugs and alcohol are involved. Drugs and alcohol interfere with your judgment and make you less prepared to keep you and your family safe.

Similarities and Differences between Domestic Violence and Drug and Alcohol Addiction

Domestic violence and drug and alcohol addiction have many similarities. Both problems hurt the whole family, get worse over time, have the potential to be deadly, and involve denying and minimizing and blaming others for the problem. However, both problems are different and need different types of treatment. Domestic violence is a pattern of assaulting and controlling behavior that is used to control another person. However, addiction is a disease that is characterized by loss of control, poor judgment, and increasing tolerance.

Women, Addiction, and Domestic Violence

While most victims of domestic violence are not addicted to drugs and alcohol, some women use and abuse alcohol and drugs to cope with abusive relationships. It is extremely painful to live with domestic violence. Abused women use alcohol and drugs for a variety of reasons: because they are forced to by their abusive partner, because they are addicted to drugs and alcohol, because their doctors over prescribe addictive medications, because of societal oppression, and because abusive partners interfere with victims' attempts to be sober.

Help for Drugs and Alcohol Abuse

If you abuse alcohol and/or drugs, get help. Your life may depend on it. See Chapters 72 and 73 on pages 577 and 589 for more information about agencies that can help you.

Chapter 57

Substance Use and Risky Sexual Activity

In recent years, researchers have begun to explore the intersection of alcohol or drug use and sexual "risk behaviors"—activities that put people at increased risk for STDs, unintended pregnancy, and sexual violence. Risky sexual activities include using condoms inconsistently, having multiple sexual partners over one's lifetime, or having intercourse with a casual partner. Studies conducted to date indicate that drinking and illicit drug use often occur in association with risky sexual activity. Still, a direct link between substance use and these sexual behaviors can be difficult to document.

Public health experts hope that creating a greater awareness of the potential relationship between substance use and risky sexual activity can influence individuals who rely on drinking or drugs to help reduce inhibitions, increase sociability, or enhance sexual arousal. Some people may drink or use drugs to gain courage, relieve pressure, or justify behavior they might otherwise feel is uncomfortable or unwise—without considering the potential consequences. In addition, determining how the use of alcohol or other substances influence sexual risk-taking can help to inform efforts by health care providers, educators, social workers, and policy makers to create effective

"Substance Use and Risky Sexual Activity," (#3214), The Henry J. Kaiser Family Foundation, February 2002. This information was reprinted with permission from the Henry J. Kaiser Family Foundation. The Kaiser Family Foundation, based in Menlo Park, California, is a nonprofit, independent national health care philanthropy and is not associated with Kaiser Permanente or Kaiser Industries.

programs for substance abuse prevention and treatment, STD and HIV prevention, and sexual health education.

This section examines the current available data concerning drinking, drug use, and risky sexual activity—including the degree to which these behaviors may be related. It also outlines the ways in which these behaviors can lead to potentially harmful health consequences.

Sex, Drinking, and Drug Use: How Common?

A national survey of Americans aged 18 to 59 found that 90 percent of men and 86 percent of women had sex in the year prior to the survey.[1] More than 80 percent of adults have ever used alcohol and more than half have had a drink in the past month.[2] Illicit drug use is less common, particularly among adults aged 35 and older. About half of adults aged 18-35 say they have ever tried an illicit drug, as have about a third of those 35 and older.[2]

Fifty-two percent of boys and 48 percent of girls in 9th-12th grades report having ever had sex and 36 percent of high school students say they have had sex recently.[3] Seventy-nine percent of high school students say they have tried alcohol and more than half of all high school students in 1997 reported having used at least one illicit drug and a quarter reported frequent drug use.[4,5]

Researching the Links: Substance Use and Risky Sexual Activity

Drinking and Sex

Increased alcohol use seems to be associated with an increased likelihood of sexual activity. When men aged 18 to 30 were asked to report their episode of heaviest drinking in the last year, 35 percent said that they had sex after consuming five to eight drinks and 45 percent had sex after consuming eight or more drinks, compared with 17 percent of those who had one or two drinks. Among women aged 18 to 30, 39 percent had sex while consuming five to eight drinks and 57 percent had sex when consuming eight or more drinks, compared with 14 percent of women who had one or two drinks.[6]

There is some evidence that heavy alcohol use[7] is associated with having multiple sex partners, which is a primary risk factor for transmission of STDs, including HIV. Seven percent of adults who report never drinking or drinking less than once a month say that they have had two or more sex partners in the last year, compared with fifteen percent of those who say they drink monthly, and 24 percent of those who drink weekly.[8]

Among adults aged 18 to 30, binge drinkers[9] are twice as likely as those who do not binge drink to have had two or more sex partners in the previous year. (That is, seven percent of those who never binge drink compared with 40 percent of those who report monthly binge drinking.)[8] This is true even after controlling for other factors—including age, sex, marital status, and drug use—that can affect a person's likelihood of having multiple sex partners.[2,8] Heavy drinkers[7] are five times as likely as non-heavy drinkers to have at least ten sex partners in a year.

Drugs and Sex

About two million adults—one man in 100 and one woman in 200—admit to using drugs before having sex in the past year.[4,10] Illicit drug users are also more likely than non-users to have multiple sex partners. One study found that 52 percent of those who used marijuana in the previous year had two or more sex partners during the same period, compared with sixteen percent of those who had not smoked pot.[6] There is even more extensive research documenting the relationship between the use of crack or injection drugs and an increased number of sexual partners.[4,11] And, people who are receiving treatment for alcohol and drug use or who use multiple drugs are more likely than others to engage in risky sexual activity. A study of alcoholics found that those who also have drug problems are more likely than those who do not to have multiple sex partners.[4,12]

Alcohol, Drugs, and Condom Use

Results from research about how drinking might influence condom use have been contradictory.[4] An analysis of thirty studies on the interplay between alcohol use and failure to use condoms found that ten showed an association between the two behaviors, fifteen demonstrated no such association, and five had mixed results.[4] At the same time, studies of "high risk" groups—such as users of crack cocaine[4] and injection drug users[4]—have tended to more consistently suggest links between illicit drug use and reduced use of condoms.[4]

As researchers gather more data, they may be able to refine their understanding of the relationship between substance abuse and condom use. It is possible that drinking or drug use by themselves, for instance, may not sufficiently explain inconsistent condom use. However, studying people who use multiple substances over the course of their lifetimes—or who use of multiple substances within a given time period—may yield more useful information. One recent analysis of data about young adults aged 18 to 30 found that the more different substances a person had ever used, the less likely he or she is to have used a condom at last sex.[13] Similarly, people who use multiple substances—such as alcoholics who also use drugs—do appear to be less likely to use condoms.[4,12]

Unintended Consequences

Sexually Transmitted Diseases (STDs)

Approximately fifteen million new cases of sexually transmitted diseases (STDs) occur annually in the United States.[14] By age 24, one in three sexually active people will have contracted an STD—and many may not realize when they become infected.[14] Of the 900,000 people currently living with HIV in the United States, up to a third remain unaware of their HIV status.[15] STDs and substance use are associated in several ways.

To the extent that alcohol and drug users are more likely than others to have sex with multiple partners, their risk of being exposed to STDs—and thus becoming infected—increases. For HIV, in particular, the current profile of someone considered at "high risk" for infection involves multiple and simultaneous risk-taking behaviors, including having multiple sex partners as well as using illicit drugs and trading sex for drugs or money.[16]

In addition to the potential for increased STD exposure, substance use may make a person biologically more susceptible to infection. Alcohol, for instance, can have a substantial impact on the immune system of a heavy drinker, interfering with the body's mechanisms for destroying viruses. This process, in turn, enhances a person's vulnerability to HIV infection or the development of AIDS-related illnesses.[4] Drug use can indirectly result in other types of physical vulnerability. For example, it has been theorized that because drugs like crack cocaine, amphetamines, and nitrates can delay ejaculation, they may be associated with longer or particularly vigorous sexual activity—thus increasing the potential for physical trauma during sex that makes it easier to transmit HIV.[4] The spread of other blood-borne and sexually transmitted infections, such as hepatitis, have previously been associated with both decreased immunity and genital trauma.

STDs among Risk Takers

There is significant research on STDs among alcoholics and crack cocaine users. Rates of STDs are high in geographic areas where rates of substance use are high.[17] STD prevalence rates in these communities range from 30 to 87 percent, compared with about 1.6 percent of all adults.[4] Adults who report having gotten drunk in the last year are almost twice as likely as those who did not to have ever had an STD.[18] Problem drinkers[19] are three times more likely than nondrinkers to have ever contracted an STD.[18] Heterosexual men and women who abuse alcohol (and not injection drugs) are six and twenty times more likely, respectively, to be HIV positive than individuals in the general population.[20] Alcohol use has also been found to be associated with risky sexual behaviors in vulnerable populations, including the mentally ill, runaway youth, and the HIV-negative female partners of men with HIV.[17]

Adults who use illicit drugs have almost three times the risk of nonusers of contracting an STD.[18] Non-injection drug use, particularly of crack cocaine, has proven to be a significant risk factor for HIV and other STDs, with drug-for-sex exchanges and unprotected sex with multiple partners among crack users accounting for the rapid spread of HIV through drug and sex networks.[18] Use of multiple substances—such as having alcohol and drug problems at the same time—is also associated with a higher likelihood of having had an STD and being HIV positive.[4,12]

Injection Drugs and HIV/AIDS

Because of the AIDS epidemic, researchers have extensively studied the connections between injection drug abuse and HIV transmission. Sharing drug needles is known to be a primary route of HIV transmission. Drug use also contributes to the spread of HIV to people who have sex with a drug user and to children born to HIV-infected mothers who acquired the infection from sharing needles or having sex with an infected drug user.

Injection drug use or sex with partners who inject drugs account for a larger proportion of female than male AIDS cases in the U.S. (59 percent and 31 percent of all cases, respectively, since the epidemic began). Today, more than 48,000 women in the United States have been diagnosed with AIDS attributed to injection drug use, and more than a third of AIDS cases in adult and adolescent women diagnosed from July 1998 through June 1999 reported injection drug use as their risk exposure.[22]

Unintended Pregnancy

More than 3 million unintended pregnancies occur every year in the United States, nearly half—47 percent—among women who were not using a regular method of birth control. [23] While there is no explicit data linking unintended pregnancy and substance use, the two may be related to the extent that drinking or drug use is associated with a lesser likelihood of using condoms and/or a greater likelihood of having "casual" sexual encounters—intercourse taking place outside the context of an ongoing relationship, during which contraceptives of any kind are less likely to be used. [24]

The ability to conduct research in this area is complicated by the fact that the use of contraceptives, including condoms, is inconsistent in the general population. Of the 9.8 million women using barrier contraceptives such as the male condom, the female condom, and the diaphragm, one-third report not using their method every time they have intercourse. [25] And, whether a woman uses contraception—and which method she chooses—is known to change over time, influenced by a host of personal and lifestyle factors. For example, while more than one-third (37%) of teenage women using contraceptives choose condoms as their primary method, these numbers decline as women grow older and marry. [26]

Sexual Assault and Violence

Substance use, particularly drinking alcohol, appears to play a role in a significant number of crimes of sexual violence—whether it is the victim or the perpetrator who uses. Substance use during instances of sexual violence and rape is estimated to range from 30 to 90 percent for alcohol use, and from 13 to 42 percent for the use of illicit substances. [4] These statistics, however, are difficult to gather and track. A study of arrested sex offenders found that 42 percent of them tested positive for drugs at the time of their arrest. [4]

When it comes to date rapes among college students, alcohol use by the victim, perpetrator, or both, has been implicated in 46 to 75 percent of the incidents. [4] Other drugs that disable a potential sexual assault victim, particularly Rohypnol and gamma hydroxybutyrate (GHB), have been anecdotally implicated in date rape scenarios. [4] In addition to the immediate physical and emotional damage caused by sexual assault, women and girls who experience sexual violence may be unable to implement practices to protect themselves against unintended pregnancy or STDs.

Trading Sex for Money or Drugs

Research examining rates of substance abuse among prostitutes finds that from 40 to 86 percent of prostitutes use drugs and that some also drink while working.[4] Meanwhile, 43 percent of women and 10 percent of men in alcohol treatment programs say they have traded sex for money or drugs.[4] Risk behaviors other than substance abuse are also implicated among people who engage in prostitution or sex trade. Studies have shown that condom use is highly inconsistent in cases of sex for drug or money exchanges: One of the many small studies of non-injecting, crack-using women who traded sex for money found that only 38 percent said that they always used a condom with their paying partners.[4] Prostitutes tend to have higher rates of infection with HIV and other STDs than the general population, and are more likely to report having been sexually victimized.[4]

Making the Connections: Implications for the Future

Researchers believe that the association between substance use and risky sexual activities could stem from a host of personal factors, including a reduction in sexual inhibitions because of the actual pharmacological effect of alcohol or drugs and cognitive impairment caused by drinking or drug use. A particular individual's personality or risk-taking tendencies may also influence which, if any, risk behaviors they engage in. And assumptions that alcohol or drugs will enhance a person's sexual attraction, behavior, or performance can also have an impact. For example, adolescents who expect alcohol to lead them to be less inhibited sexually are more likely to participate in risky sexual behavior when they drink.[27]

Similarly, the social context of drinking or alcohol use may be an important factor. Social environments that support the use of alcohol and other drugs may also support the meeting of new sexual partners,[28] which may help to explain the relationship between recent substance use and the likelihood of having multiple partners.[13]

The ability of researchers to determine how substance abuse and sexual risk-taking are connected also has important implications for education and treatment efforts. If sexual risk taking is caused by lessened inhibitions due to substance use, then education might warn about the impact of alcohol and drugs on one's judgment and the potential consequences of such situations, such as the increased risk of STD and HIV transmission. On the other hand, if personality or other unique factors of individuals influence sexual-risk taking and substance use, then prevention efforts might be better focused on particular groups of people with more specific messages to help them channel potentially destructive risk-taking impulses into healthier activities.[29]

References

1. Laumann EO et al., *The Social Organization of Sexuality: Sexual Practices in the United States*, Chicago, IL: The University of Chicago Press, 1994.

2. Department of Health and Human Services, SAMHSA, Office of Applied Studies, Summary of Findings from the 1998 National Household Survey on Drug Abuse, Rockville, MD: Department of Health and Human Services, 1999.

3. Centers for Disease Control and Prevention, Youth Risk Behavior Surveillance, 1999. "Recently" was defined as having intercourse in the three months prior to being surveyed.

4. The National Center of Addiction and Substance Abuse (CASA) at Columbia University. (1999). *Dangerous liaisons: Substance abuse and sex.* New York, The National Center on Addiction and Substance Abuse (CASA) at Columbia University.

5. "Heavy drug use" was defined as using any drug at least 20 times in one's lifetime.

6. Graves KL, Risky sexual behavior and alcohol use among young adults: Results from a national survey, *American Journal of Health Promotion*, 1995, vol. 10.

7. "Heavy drinkers" were defined as those who have ever had twenty or more drinks in one day; or who reported drinking at least seven drinks each day for two weeks; or who reported drinking seven or more drinks at least once a week for two months.

8. Leigh BC et al., The relationship of alcohol use to sexual activity in a U.S. national sample, *Social Science and Medicine*, 1994, vol. 39.

9. "Binge drinkers" were defined as those who consume five or more drinks at one sitting.

10. Michael RT et al., *Sex in America: A Definitive Survey*, Boston: Little Brown, 1994.

11. National Institute on Drug Abuse and National Institutes of Health, A Collection of NIDA Notes: Articles on Drugs and AIDS, 1996.

12. Scheidt DM and M Windle, A comparison of alcohol typologies using HIV risk behaviors among alcoholic inpatients, *Psychology of Addictive Behaviors*, 1997, vol. 11.

13. Santelli JS et al., Timing of alcohol and other drug use and sexual risk behaviors among unmarried adolescents and young adults, *Family Planning Perspectives*, 2001, vol. 33.

14. American Social Health Association/Kaiser Family Foundation, Sexually Transmitted Diseases in America: How Many Cases and At What Cost? Menlo Park, CA: The Henry J Kaiser Family Foundation, 1998, and the Centers for Disease Control and Prevention (CDC), Tracking the Hidden Epidemics: Trends in STDs in the United States 2000, Atlanta, GA: CDC, 2001.

15. Kaiser Family Foundation, Critical Policy Brief: Challenges in the Third Decade of the AIDS Epidemic, Menlo Park, CA: The Henry J Kaiser Family Foundation, 2001.

16. http://grants.nih.gov/grants/guide/pa-files/PA-01-023.html

17. Eng TR and WT Butler, eds., The Hidden Epidemic: Confronting Sexually Transmitted Diseases, Washington D.C.: National Academy Press, 1997.

18. Eriksen KP and KF Trocki, Sex, alcohol, and sexually transmitted diseases: a national survey, *Family Planning Perspectives*, 1994, vol. 26.

19. "Problem drinkers" were defined as ever having had three of eight major symptoms indicating an increased tolerance or desire for alcohol; impaired control over drinking; symptoms of withdrawal; or increased social disruption.

20. Avins AL et al., HIV infection and risk behaviors among heterosexuals in alcohol treatment, *JAMA*, 1994, vol. 271.

21. Scheidt DM and M Windle, A comparison of alcohol typologies using HIV risk behaviors among alcoholic inpatients, *Psychology of Addictive Behaviors*, 1997, vol. 11.

22. Centers for Disease Control and Prevention (CDC), HIV/AIDS Surveillance in Women, L264 Slide Series, 1999, which draws on information from various HIV/AIDS Surveillance Reports. See also http://grants.nih.gov/grants/guide/pa-files/PA-01-023.html.

23. The Alan Guttmacher Institutes, Facts in Brief: Induced Abortion, New York, NY: AGI, 2000.

24. Anderson JE et al., Condom use and HIV risk behaviors among U.S. adults: Data from a national survey, *Family Planning Perspectives*, 1999, vol. 31. (National Household Survey of Drug Abuse).

25. Piccinino LJ and Mosher WD, Trends in contraceptive use in the US: 1982-1995, *Family Planning Perspectives*, 1998, vol. 30.

26. National Center for Health Statistics, Fertility, family planning, and women's health: New data from the 1995 NSFG, Vital and Health Statistics, 1997, series 23.

27. Dermen KH et al., Sex-related alcohol expectancies as moderators of the relationship between alcohol use and risky sex in adolescents, *Journal of Studies on Alcohol*, 1998, vol. 59.

28. Fergusson DM and Lynskey MT, Alcohol misuse and adolescent sexual behaviors and risk taking, *Pediatrics*, 1996, vol. 98.

29. Kim N et al., Effectiveness of the 40 adolescent AIDS-risk reeducation interventions; quantitative review, *Journal of Adolescent Health*, 1997, vol. 20.

For additional free copies of this publication (#3214), please contact the Henry J. Kaiser Family Foundation Publication Request Line at (800) 656-4533.

Chapter 58

Alcohol and Sexual Assault

Conservative estimates of sexual assault prevalence suggest that 25 percent of American women have experienced sexual assault, including rape. Approximately one half of those cases involve alcohol consumption by the perpetrator, victim, or both. Alcohol contributes to sexual assault through multiple pathways, often exacerbating existing risk factors. Beliefs about alcohol's effects on sexual and aggressive behavior, stereotypes about drinking women, and alcohol's effects on cognitive and motor skills contribute to alcohol-involved sexual assault. Despite advances in researchers' understanding of the relationships between alcohol consumption and sexual assault, many questions still need to be addressed in future studies.

Sexual assault of adolescent and adult women has been called a silent epidemic, because it occurs at high rates yet is rarely reported to the authorities. Several reasons contribute to the underreporting of sexual assault cases. Many victims do not tell others about the assault, because they fear that they will not be believed or will be derogated, which, according to research findings, is a valid concern. Other victims may not realize that they have actually experienced legally defined rape or sexual assault, because the incident does not fit the prototypic scenario of "stranger rape." For example, in one study, a

Excerpted from the article by Antonia Abbey, Ph.D., Tina Zawacki, M.A., Philip O. Buck, M.A., A. Monique Clinton, M.A., and Pam McAuslan, Ph.D., published in *Alcohol Research & Health*, Vol. 25, No. 1, pp. 43–51. 2001. For a complete list of references, see, www.niaaa.nih.gov. Reviewed by David A. Cooke, M.D., on March 13, 2006.

woman wrote, "For years I believed it was my fault for being too drunk. I never called it 'rape' until much more recently, even though I repeatedly told him 'no'."

The Prevalence of Sexual Assault and Alcohol-Involved Sexual Assault

The prevalence of sexual assault, both involving and not involving alcohol use, cannot be accurately determined, because it is usually unreported. Estimates of sexual assault prevalence have been based on a variety of sources, including police reports, national random samples of crime victims, interviews with incarcerated rapists, interviews with victims who seek hospital treatment, general population surveys of women, and surveys of male and female college students. In such studies, the estimates' adequacy varies with the sources of information used.

Conservative estimates suggest that at least 25 percent of American women have been sexually assaulted in adolescence or adulthood and that 18 percent have been raped. Furthermore, at least 20 percent of American men report having perpetrated sexual assault and 5 percent report having committed rape. Due to their accessibility, college student surveys tend to employ the most thorough measures of sexual assault by including the largest number of behaviorally specific questions. These studies suggest that approximately 50 percent of college women have been sexually assaulted, and 27 percent have experienced rape or attempted rape; in contrast, 25 percent of college men have committed sexual assault, and 8 percent have committed rape or attempted rape.

At least one half of all violent crimes involve alcohol consumption by the perpetrator, the victim, or both. Sexual assault fits this pattern. Thus, across the disparate populations studied, researchers consistently have found that approximately one half of all sexual assaults are committed by men who have been drinking alcohol. The estimates for alcohol use among perpetrators have ranged from 34 to 74 percent. Similarly, approximately one half of all sexual assault victims report that they were drinking alcohol at the time of the assault, with estimates ranging from 30 to 79 percent. It is important to emphasize, however, that although a woman's alcohol consumption may place her at increased risk of sexual assault, she is in no way responsible for the assault. The perpetrators are legally and morally responsible for their behavior.

Finally, alcohol consumption by perpetrators and victims tends to co-occur—that is, when one of them is drinking, the other one is generally drinking as well. Rarely is only the victim drinking alcohol. This finding is not surprising, because in social situations (e.g., in bars or at parties), drinking tends to be a shared activity. However, this finding complicates researchers' efforts to disentangle the unique effects of alcohol consumption on the perpetrators' versus the victims' behavior.

Common Characteristics of Non-Alcohol-Involved and Alcohol-Involved Sexual Assaults

Sexual assault occurs most commonly among women in late adolescence and early adulthood, although infants, as well as women in their 80s, have been raped. Most sexual assaults that are reported to the police occur between strangers. These assaults, however, represent only a small proportion of all sexual assaults. At least 80 percent of sexual assaults occur among persons who know each other.

Several studies in various populations have attempted to identify "typical" characteristics of sexual assault. Among college students, a typical sexual assault occurs on a date, at either the man's or the woman's home, and is preceded by consensual kissing. In addition, the assault involves a single assailant who uses no weapon, but twists the woman's arm or holds her down. The woman, who believes that she has clearly emphasized her nonconsent, tries to resist through reasoning and by physically struggling.

Although alcohol-involved and non-alcohol-involved sexual assaults share many characteristics, some differences exist. For example, sexual assaults involving alcohol consumption are more likely than other sexual assaults to occur between men and women who do not know each other well (e.g., strangers, acquaintances, or casual dates as opposed to steady dates or spouses). Furthermore, alcohol-involved sexual assaults tend to occur at parties or in bars, rather than in either person's home.

Investigating the Relationship Between Alcohol Consumption and Sexual Assault

Although alcohol consumption and sexual assault frequently co-occur, this phenomenon does not prove that alcohol use causes sexual assault. Thus, in some cases, the desire to commit a sexual assault may actually cause alcohol consumption (e.g., when a man drinks alcohol before committing a sexual assault in order to justify his behavior). Moreover, certain factors may lead to both alcohol consumption and sexual assault. For example, some fraternities encourage both heavy drinking and sexual exploitation of women. In fact, many pathways can prompt a man to commit sexual assault, and not all perpetrators are motivated by the same factors.

Perpetrators' Personality Characteristics, Attitudes, and Experiences

Several studies that compared the characteristics of men who had committed sexual assault with those who had not noted the following differences:

- With respect to personality traits, men who had committed sexual assault were more hostile toward women and lower in empathy compared with other men.

- With respect to attitudes, men who had committed sexual assault were more likely than other men to endorse traditional stereotypes about gender roles—for example, that men are responsible for initiating sex and women are responsible for setting the limits. Perpetrators of sexual assault also were more likely to endorse statements that have been used to justify rape—for example, "women say 'no' when they mean 'yes' " and "women enjoy forced sex." Finally, men who had committed sexual assaults were more likely to hold adversarial beliefs about relationships between men and women (e.g., "all's fair in love and war") and to consider the use of force in interpersonal relationships acceptable.

- With respect to their personal experiences, sexual assaulters were more likely than other men to have experienced abuse or violence as a child, to have been delinquent in adolescence, to have peers who viewed forced sex as acceptable, and to have had early and frequent dating and sexual experiences.

Heavy alcohol consumption also has been linked to sexual assault perpetration. Men who reported that they drank heavily were more likely than other men to report having committed sexual assault. General alcohol consumption could be related to sexual assault through multiple pathways. First, men who often drink heavily also likely do so in social situations that frequently lead to sexual assault (e.g., on a casual or spontaneous date at a party or bar). Second, heavy drinkers may routinely use intoxication as an excuse for engaging in socially unacceptable behavior, including sexual assault. Third, certain personality characteristics (e.g., impulsivity and antisocial behavior) may increase men's propensity both to drink heavily and to commit sexual assault.

Certain alcohol expectancies have also been linked to sexual assault. For example, alcohol is commonly viewed as an aphrodisiac that increases sexual desire and capacity. Many men expect to feel more powerful, disinhibited, and aggressive after drinking alcohol. To assess the influence of such expectancies on perceptions of sexual behavior, researchers asked sober college men to read a story about a man forcing a date to have sex. Study participants reported that they would be more likely to behave like the man in the story when they were drunk, rather than when they were sober, suggesting that they could imagine forcing sex when intoxicated. Furthermore, college men who had perpetrated sexual assault when intoxicated expected alcohol to increase male and female sexuality more than did college men who perpetrated sexual assault when sober. Men with these expectancies may feel more comfortable forcing sex when they are drinking, because they can later justify to themselves that the alcohol made them act accordingly.

Attitudes about women's alcohol consumption also influence a perpetrator's actions and may be used to excuse sexual assaults of intoxicated women. Despite the liberalization of gender roles during the past few decades, most people do not readily approve of alcohol consumption and sexual behavior among women, yet view these same behaviors among men with far more leniency. Thus, women who drink alcohol are frequently perceived as being more sexually available and promiscuous compared with women who do not drink. Sexually assaultive men often describe women who drink in bars as "loose," immoral women who are appropriate targets for sexual aggression. In fact, date rapists frequently report intentionally getting the woman drunk in order to have sexual intercourse with her.

Victims' Personality Characteristics, Attitudes, and Experiences

Numerous studies have compared the personality characteristics, attitudes, and life experiences of women who were sexually assaulted with those of other women. Overall, those analyses found only few significant effects and explain only small amounts of variance, indicating that women's personal characteristics are not strong predictors of victimization.

Some differences exist, however, among women who have been victims of sexual assault and those who have not. Women who have been sexually assaulted are more likely than are other women to have experienced childhood sexual abuse, to have frequent sexual relationships, and to be heavy drinkers. Explanations of these findings focus on the long-term effects of childhood victimization. Some victims of childhood sexual abuse cope with the resulting stress and negative emotions through early and frequent sexual relations and heavy drinking. These women may also be more likely to drink alcohol in potential sexual situations as a means of coping with their ambivalent feelings about sex. In turn, drinking in potential sexual situations increases women's risk of being sexually assaulted, both because sexually assaultive men may view them as easy targets and because the women may be less able to resist effectively.

Situational Factors

Sexual assault involves both sexual behavior and aggression; accordingly, researchers must consider situational influences (i.e., cues) relevant to both behaviors, such as the location or social situation in which the assault occurs. These cues may differ somewhat depending on the type of sexual assault (i.e., stranger sexual assault versus date sexual assault). In the case of sexual assaults that occur among strangers or people who have just met, men who drink heavily may frequent settings, such as bars and parties, where women also tend to drink heavily and where a man can easily find an intoxicated woman to target for a possible sexual assault. In these situations, alcohol may give men the "liquid courage" required to act on their desires and may reinforce their stereotypes about drinking women.

Alcohol consumption is also used by date rapists to excuse their behavior. For example, 62 percent of the college date rapists interviewed by one researcher felt that they had committed rape because of their alcohol consumption. These rapists did not see themselves as "real criminals," because real criminals used weapons to assault strangers. In fact, some men may purposely get drunk when they want to act sexually aggressive, knowing that intoxication will provide them with an excuse for their socially inappropriate behavior.

As described earlier, at least 80 percent of all sexual assaults occur during social interaction, typically on a date. The fact that sexual assault often happens in situations in which consensual sex is a possible outcome means that a man's interpretation of the situation can influence his responses. Consequently, additional situational factors are relevant to these types of sexual assaults. For example, American men are socialized to be the initiators of sexual interactions. Consequently, if a man is interested in having sex with a woman, he is likely to feel that he should make the first move. Initial sexual moves are usually subtle in order to reduce the embarrassment associated with potential rejection. Both men and women are used to this indirect form of establishing sexual interest and usually manage to make their intentions clear and save face if the other person is not interested. However, because the cues are subtle and sometimes vague, miscommunication can occur, particularly if communication skills are impaired by alcohol use.

As male-female interaction progresses, a woman who has been misperceived as being interested in sex may realize that her companion is reading more into her friendliness than she intended. However, she may not feel comfortable giving a direct message of sexual disinterest, because traditional female gender roles emphasize the importance of being nice and "letting men down easy." The man, in turn, may not take an indirect approach to expressing sexual disinterest seriously. Research on the power of stereotypes, expectancies, and self-fulfilling prophecies demonstrate that when people have an expectation about a situation or another person, they tend to observe and recall primarily the cues that fit their hypothesis and to minimize or ignore the cues that contradict their hypothesis. Consequently, when a man hopes that a woman is interested in having sex with him, he will pay most attention to the cues that fit his expectation and disregard cues that do not support his expectation. Studies with both perpetrators and victims have confirmed that the man's misperception of the woman's degree of sexual interest is a significant predictor of sexual assault.

General Research on Alcohol's Effects on Aggressive and Sexual Behavior

Most investigators agree that alcohol's effects on aggressive behavior are mediated by alcohol-induced cognitive deficits. Alcohol consumption disrupts higher order cognitive processes—including abstraction, conceptualization, planning, and problem-solving—making it difficult for the drinker to interpret complex stimuli. Thus, when under the influence of alcohol, people have a narrower perceptual field and can attend only to the most obvious (i.e., salient) cues in a given situation. In aggression-inducing situations, the cues that usually inhibit aggressive behavior (e.g., concerns about future consequences or a sense of morality) are typically less salient than feelings of anger and frustration. Therefore, when a person is intoxicated, inhibitory cues are ignored or minimized, making aggression seem like the most reasonable response.

In contrast, studies of alcohol's influence on sexual behavior have found more psychological effects. In men, high alcohol doses generally reduce physiological sexual responding, whereas low and moderate alcohol doses increase subjective sexual arousal. Many studies have demonstrated that men who believe they have consumed alcohol experience greater physiological and subjective sexual arousal in response to erotic materials depicting consensual and forced sex than do men who believe they have consumed a non-alcoholic beverage, regardless of what they actually drank.

Fewer studies have examined alcohol's effects on sexual behavior in women, and the results have been inconsistent. This finding is generally explained in terms of society's negative messages regarding women's alcohol consumption and sexuality. Thus, sexual behavior and drunken excess are considered less acceptable in women than in men, and unlike men, women must be concerned about being labeled as loose, or promiscuous. In addition, women are concerned about their increased vulnerability to sexual and nonsexual aggression when intoxicated. Consequently, women's expectancies about alcohol's sexual effects are less positive than men's expectancies, because the social costs associated with alcohol use and sexual behavior are greater for women.

In summary, research suggests that alcohol exerts its effects on aggressive behavior principally through its pharmacological effects on cognitive processing, whereas alcohol's effects on sexual behavior occur through pharmacological processes as well as psychological expectancies.

Chapter 59

Driving under the Influence

"Have one [drink] for the road" was, until recently, a commonly used phrase in American culture. It has only been within the past 20 years that as a nation, we have begun to recognize the dangers associated with drunk driving. Through a multipronged and concerted effort involving many stakeholders, including educators, media, legislators, law enforcement, and community organizations, such as Mothers Against Drunk Driving (MADD), the nation has seen a decline in the numbers of people killed or injured due to drunk driving. It is now time that we recognize and address the similar dangers that can occur with drugged driving.

In 12 states (Arizona, Georgia, Indiana, Illinois, Iowa, Michigan, Minnesota, Nevada, Pennsylvania, Rhode Island, Utah, and Wisconsin), it is illegal to operate a motor vehicle with any detectable level of a prohibited drug, or its metabolites, in the driver's blood. Other state laws define "drugged driving" as driving when a drug "renders the driver incapable of driving safely," or "causes the driver to be impaired."

In reality, the principal concern regarding drugged driving is that driving under the influence of any drug that acts on the brain could impair one's motor skills, reaction time, and judgment. Drugged driving is a public health concern because it puts not only the driver at risk, but passengers and others who share the road.

"Drugged Driving" is a fact sheet produced by the National Institute on Drug Abuse (NIDA), August 2005. For a complete list of references, visit www.nida.nih.gov.

Statistics on Driving under the Influence of Drugs and Alcohol

The National Highway Traffic Safety Administration (NHTSA) reports that 16,000 people are killed annually due to drunk and drugged driving. Furthermore, NHTSA estimates that drugs are used by approximately 10 to 22 percent of drivers involved in crashes, often in combination with alcohol. According to the 2003 National Survey on Drug Use and Health, an estimated 10.9 million people reported driving under the influence of an illicit drug during the year prior to being surveyed. This corresponds to 4.8 percent of the population aged 15 or older, but 14.1 percent among young adults aged 18 to 25. In addition:

- Younger adult drivers were more likely to have driven under the influence of alcohol or illicit drugs than older adult drivers, with more than one in three drivers aged 21 to 25 (33.8 percent) and nearly one in four drivers aged 26 to 34 (24.3 percent) having driven under the influence of drugs or alcohol during the previous year. These percentages go down further in drivers over age 35.

- Male drivers were nearly twice as likely as female drivers to have driven under the influence of alcohol or drugs during the previous year (22 percent compared with 11.4 percent).

In recent years, drugs that act on the brain other than alcohol have increasingly been recognized as hazards to road traffic safety. Research examining these drugs indicates that marijuana is the most prevalent illegal drug detected in impaired drivers, fatally injured drivers, and motor vehicle crash victims. A variety of other drugs, such as benzodiazepines, cocaine, opiates, and amphetamines, have also been reported in fatal and nonfatal motor vehicle crashes.

A number of studies have examined illicit drug use in drivers involved in motor vehicle crashes, reckless driving, or in fatal accidents. For example:

- A recent study found that 34 percent of drivers admitted to a Maryland trauma center tested positive for drugs only, while 16 percent tested positive for alcohol only; 50 percent of those under 18 tested positive for alcohol and/or drugs. While it is interesting that more people in this study tested positive for drugs-only compared to alcohol-only, it should be noted that this represents one geographic location, so findings cannot be generalized. In fact, many studies among similar populations have found higher prevalence rates of alcohol compared with drug use.

- In one study of 168 fatally injured truck drivers in eight states, 33 percent tested positive for psychoactive drugs or alcohol.

- Studies conducted in a number of localities have found that approximately 4 to 14 percent of drivers who sustained injury or death in traffic accidents tested positive for delta-9-tetrahydro-cannabinol (THC), the active ingredient in marijuana.

- In a large study of almost 3,400 fatally injured drivers from three Australian states (Victoria, New South Wales, and Western Australia) between 1990 and 1999, drugs other than alcohol were present in 26.7 percent of the cases. These included cannabis (13.5 percent), opioids (4.9 percent), stimulants (4.1 percent), benzodiazepines (4.1 percent), and other psychotropic drugs (2.7 percent). Almost 10 percent of the cases involved both alcohol and drugs.

Teens and Driving under the Influence

According to NHTSA, vehicle accidents are the leading cause of death among those aged 15 to 20. It is generally accepted that because teens are the least experienced drivers as a group, they have a higher risk of being involved in an accident compared with more experienced drivers. When this lack of experience is combined with the use of marijuana or other substances that impact cognitive and motor abilities, the results can be tragic.

The National Institute on Drug Abuse (NIDA)'s Monitoring the Future survey indicated that in 2004, 12.7 percent of high school seniors reported driving under the influence of marijuana, and 13.2 percent reported driving under the influence of alcohol in the two weeks prior to completing the survey.

The State of Maryland's Adolescent Survey indicates that 26.8 percent of the state's licensed, 12th-grade drivers reported driving under the influence of marijuana during 2001.

Why Is Driving under the Influence Hazardous?

Drugs act on the brain and can alter perception, cognition, attention, balance, coordination, and other faculties required for safe driving. The effects of specific drugs of abuse differ depending on their mechanisms of action, the amount consumed, the history of the user, and other factors.

Marijuana

THC affects areas of the brain that control the body's movements, balance, coordination, memory, and judgment abilities, as well as sensations. Because these effects are multifaceted, more research is required to understand marijuana's impact on the ability of drivers to react to complex and unpredictable situations. However, we do know that:

- A meta-analysis of approximately 60 experimental studies, including laboratory, driving simulator, and on-road experiments, found that behavioral and cognitive skills related to driving performance were impaired in a dose-dependent fashion with increasing THC blood levels.

- Evidence from both real and simulated driving studies indicates that marijuana can negatively impact a driver's attentiveness, perception of time and speed, and the ability to draw on information obtained through past experiences.

- Research shows that impairment increases significantly when marijuana use is combined with alcohol.

- Studies have found that many drivers who test positive for alcohol also test positive for THC, making it clear that drinking and drugged driving are often linked behaviors.

Other Drugs

- Prescription drugs: Many medications (e.g., benzodiazepines and opiate analgesics) act on systems in the brain that could impair driving ability. In fact, many prescription drugs come with warnings against the operation of machinery—including vehicles—for a specified period of time after use. When prescription drugs are taken without medical supervision (i.e., when abused), impaired driving and other harmful reactions can also result.

In short, drugged driving is a dangerous activity that puts us all at risk.

Part Seven

Treatment and Recovery from Alcohol Dependence

Chapter 60

Recognizing and Helping Someone Who Might Have a Drug or Alcohol Problem

Are you worried that someone you care about has a drug or alcohol problem? Or do you feel your own use is out of control?

You or your loved one can get better, and there are many ways to get help. This chapter will provide important facts about addiction and ways to get started on a path to recovery.

Act now. First steps are often the most difficult, but when it comes to addiction, you cannot wait. Addiction is a disease—a serious health problem like heart disease, cancer, or diabetes—that can happen to anyone who uses drugs or alcohol. If left untreated, it can progress and may even be fatal.

You Are Not Alone

Don't wait until something really bad happens. Get help now.

Addiction can affect anyone. It afflicts 22 million Americans; men and women, teens and adults, poor, middle class and affluent, in rural towns, suburbs, and cities. Because it has a strong genetic component, addiction tends to run in families. However, families just like yours have successfully intervened when loved ones are in trouble with drugs or alcohol and helped them get well.

"Hope, Help, & Healing: A Guide to Helping Someone Who Might Have a Drug or Alcohol Problem" © Partnership for a Drug-Free America, 2005. Used with permission.

You are not alone. You may feel that no one can help you—that you and those you care about have to suffer alone. But there are people who have been there and many resources to help you understand and cope with drug and alcohol addiction.

Families can thrive with hope, help, and healing. Drug and alcohol addiction can change family relationships in profound ways. You and members of your family may feel guilty, frustrated, confused, angry, or powerless. Attending Al-Anon or Alateen meetings, which provide support to families and friends of people with addictions, may be helpful.

Signs to Look For

The most obvious sign of addiction is using drugs or alcohol uncontrollably, despite the fact that use is causing problems. Addicted people's behavior can change dramatically, and they can act out of character, which is confusing and upsetting to friends and family members. If you've noticed any of the warning signs listed below, investigate as soon as possible.

Physical Signs to Look For

- Bloodshot eyes
- Slurred or agitated speech
- Sudden or dramatic weight loss
- Skin abrasions/bruises
- Neglected appearance/poor hygiene
- Frequently sick
- Accidents or injuries
- Unusual odors on breath; stains and odors on clothing

Behavioral Signs to Look For

- Hyperactivity or unusual aggression
- Secretive behavior, including lying and locked doors
- Hidden stashes of alcohol, drugs, or drug paraphernalia
- Missing alcohol or prescription medicine

- Not fulfilling responsibilities or missing school or work
- Avoiding eye contact

Emotional Signs to Look For

- Sudden shifts or changes in mood and personality
- Emotional instability
- Depression
- No interest in previously enjoyed hobbies or activities

Where to Start

Learn the facts. Educating yourself about drug or alcohol addiction is the first step. For more information about addiction and types of treatment, visit www.drugfree.org.

Friends and family members can influence and motivate addicted people to get well. However, people sometimes feel powerless to help, because they accept myths like the ones below:

Myth: She can stop using drugs if she really wants to.

Reality: A person can control his or her alcohol or drug use at first. But long-term use actually changes some people's brain and body functions so they crave alcohol or the drug, and feel bad and sick without it. They find it difficult to stop on their own using willpower.

Myth: People don't go for help until they hit rock bottom.

Reality: Your loved one does not have to lose everything before taking the first step. Pressure from family members and employers, the legal system, healthcare professionals, and clergy can motivate an addicted person to seek treatment earlier. And that may save his or her life.

Myth: Treatment won't work for him.

Reality: No matter how compulsive the addiction, treatment can work, especially when a person is committed to working on recovery and has a strong support system. In fact, the success rate for such treatment is similar to other chronic illnesses like diabetes, asthma, and hypertension.

If you're concerned about your own drug or alcohol use, you don't have to deal with it alone. Consider talking to your doctor, therapist, teacher, or a family member who can lend support. Or attend a meeting of Alcoholics Anonymous (AA), Narcotics Anonymous (NA), Smart Recovery, or another anonymous self-help group devoted to helping members recover and lead healthy lives.

How to Intervene

Before you intervene. Much is now known about how to intervene effectively. The goal of a group intervention is for an addicted person to get a professional evaluation and begin treatment. You may want to consult with a professional interventionist before intervening, because the intervention may be more effective when led by a health professional.

The family's role. To be effective, an intervention needs to include an addicted person's loved ones. Often they reach "rock bottom" before the person who needs help does, and can team up to push him or her to seek professional help. Family members and friends need to educate themselves about addiction and change their own behavior if their loved one's recovery is to succeed.

Locate resources—near and far. People get well through a variety—and sometimes a combination—of approaches, so it's essential to find out what help is available before you intervene. Call 1-800-662-HELP, or go to www.drugfree.org to identify appropriate alcohol or drug treatment programs.

Treatment has many forms, but effective treatment will address physical, psychological, emotional, and social problems and will involve family members. Make an appointment at a treatment center and attend meetings of local self-help groups to better understand what your loved one is going through. Recovery is much more effective with support from family members and friends.

Intervene as soon as possible. Whether you are a friend, family member, concerned employer, or coworker, you can encourage an addicted person to get the help he or she needs. Interventions do not have to be angry or dramatic, and effective ones can be loving, but firm, expressions of concern. But do intervene, either immediately or as soon as possible. It's never too late, although the earlier you act, the greater the likelihood of successful treatment and recovery.

When You Intervene

- Talk when the person has not been using drugs or alcohol.

- Stay calm.

- Express your comments with nonjudgmental caring and concern.

- Avoid labeling the person an "alcoholic" or "addict."

- List specific incidents resulting from the person's drug or alcohol problem (for example, "You were recently arrested for DWI [driving while intoxicated].").

- Stick to what you know firsthand, not hearsay.

- Talk in "I" statements, explaining how the person's behavior has affected you ("I felt scared when you came home high last night . . .").

- Be prepared for denial, resentment, and rejection.

- Be supportive and hopeful about change. Recovery is much more effective when family members are involved and have realistic, yet optimistic, expectations about the process.

People with drug and alcohol problems can get well; they can regain their physical health and well-being and improve their relationships with others. This happens when the person has stopped using drugs or alcohol and is in recovery.

Recovery is not instantaneous. It's a process that requires work to maintain, but it can lead to a profound life transformation with enormous personal growth. Some people experience it as a spiritual awakening, but recovery is also possible through therapy and non-spiritual self-help groups.

If you are worried that you or someone you care about may have a drug or alcohol problem, it's important to intervene now.

Chapter 61

Screening for Alcohol Use and Alcohol-Related Problems

Screening for disease has become a mainstay of today's preventive health care, with roots in medical practice that extend back to the 1930s and 1940s. As screening's effectiveness continues to be demonstrated, the demand for these assessments also has increased. The result is double-edged. Increased screening enables clinicians to step in early to prevent and treat a wide range of public health problems before they become too serious. But the time available for conducting those screens has steadily declined. Deciding whether a particular screen is warranted, choosing the best one for an individual patient, and administering it in a cost-effective way are key issues for clinicians to address.

Routine screening for problems with alcohol is a relatively recent practice, but has a solid base of support. In 1990, the Institute of Medicine's landmark report on broadening the base of alcohol and

Excerpted from "Screening for Alcohol Use and Alcohol-Related Problems," *Alcohol Alert* No. 65, a publication of the National Institute for Alcohol Abuse and Alcoholism (NIAAA), April 2005. For a complete list of references, see www.niaaa.nih.gov. The CAGE Questionnaire is from Ewing, J. A. (1984). Detecting alcoholism: The CAGE questionnaire. *Journal of the American Medical Association*, 252 (14), 1905–1907. Copyright © 1984 American Medical Association. All rights reserved. The AUDIT Screening Test and the information in the section titled "Screening for Alcohol Use Disorders with the AUDIT" is excerpted with permission from Babor, T. F.; Higgins-Biddle, J. C.; Saunders, J. B.; and Monteiro, M. G. AUDIT: The Alcohol Use Disorders Test. Guidelines for use in primary health care. Second Edition. Geneva, Switzerland: World Health Organization. © 2001 World Health Organization.

other drug abuse treatment recommended that patients in all medical settings be screened for the full spectrum of problems that can accompany alcohol use and, when necessary, be offered brief intervention or referral to treatment services.

What Is Screening?

Doctors routinely screen patients for an increasing number of conditions. The term "screening" refers to the testing of members of a certain population (such as all the patients in a physician's practice) to estimate the likelihood that they have a specific disorder, such as alcohol abuse or dependence.

Screening is not the same as diagnostic testing, which establishes a definite diagnosis of a disorder. Instead, screening is used to identify people who are likely to have a disorder, as determined by their responses to certain key questions. People with positive screening results may be advised to undergo more detailed diagnostic testing to definitively confirm or rule out the disorder. A clinician might initiate further assessment, provide a brief intervention, and/or arrange for clinical followup when a screening test indicates that a patient may have a problem with alcohol. There is good evidence that even patients who do not meet the criteria for alcohol dependence or abuse, but who are drinking at levels that place them at risk for increased problems, can be helped through screening and brief intervention.

Screening in Different Settings

In Primary Care

Screening for alcohol disorders in primary care can vary from one simple question to an extensive assessment using a standardized questionnaire. The level of screening used by a clinician typically depends on the patient's characteristics, whether he or she has other medical or psychiatric problems, the physician's skills and interest, and the amount of time available.

Clinicians under strict time constraints may have time to ask a patient only one screening question about his or her alcohol consumption. One study has shown that a positive response to the question "On any single occasion during the past 3 months, have you had more than 5 drinks containing alcohol?" accurately identifies patients who meet either criteria for at-risk drinking or the criteria for alcohol abuse or dependence specified in the *Diagnostic and Statistical Manual of Mental Disorders, Fourth Edition (DSM–IV)*.

Whenever possible, questions about alcohol use should be asked of all patients on an annual basis or in response to problems that may be alcohol related. The questions can be included in a pre-exam interview and conducted as part of the patient's check-in process. If the patient appears to be at risk for alcohol-related medical problems, or if the clinician suspects that the patient is minimizing his or her alcohol use, more qualitative questions should be asked to better determine the nature and extent of the problem.

The CAGE questionnaire is popular for screening in the primary care setting because it is short, simple, easy to remember, and because it has been proven effective for detecting a range of alcohol problems.

CAGE

C—Have you ever felt you should cut down on your drinking?
A—Have people annoyed you by criticizing your drinking?
G—Have you ever felt bad or guilty about your drinking?
E—Eye opener: Have you ever had a drink first thing in the morning to steady your nerves or to get rid of a hangover?

The CAGE can identify alcohol problems over the lifetime. Two positive responses are considered a positive test and indicate further assessment is warranted.

Longer tests, such as the 25-question Michigan Alcoholism Screening Test (MAST) or the 10-question Alcohol Use Disorders Identification Test (AUDIT), may be used to obtain more qualitative information about a patient's alcohol consumption.

The MAST includes questions about drinking behavior and alcohol-related problems; it is particularly useful for identifying alcohol dependence. The AUDIT includes questions about the quantity and frequency of alcohol use, as well as binge drinking, dependence symptoms, and alcohol-related problems. Its strength lies in its ability to identify people who have problems with alcohol but who may not be dependent.

Research shows that the AUDIT may be especially useful when screening women and minorities. This screening tool also has shown promising results when tested in adolescents and young adults; it is less accurate in older patients, though further research is needed with these populations.

Computerized versions of the AUDIT and other screening instruments now are available and can be used in conjunction with other health assessment questionnaires.

Table 61.1. The Alcohol Use Disorders Identification Test (AUDIT): Self-Report Version

Patient: Because alcohol use can affect your health and can interfere with certain medications and treatments, it is important that we ask some questions about your use of alcohol. Your answers will remain confidential so please be honest. Place an X in one box that best describes your answer to each question.

Questions	0	1	2	3	4
1. How often do you have a drink containing alcohol?	Never	Monthly or less	2-4 times a month	2-3 times a week	4 or more times a week
2. How many drinks containing alcohol do you have on a typical day when you are drinking?	1 or 2	3 or 4	5 or 6	7 to 9	10 or more
3. How often do you have six or more drinks on one occasion?	Never	Less than monthly	Monthly	Weekly	Daily or almost daily
4. How often during the last year have you found that you were not able to stop drinking once you had started?	Never	Less than monthly	Monthly	Weekly	Daily or almost daily
5. How often during the last year have you failed to do what was normally expected of you because of drinking?	Never	Less than monthly	Monthly	Weekly	Daily or almost daily
6. How often during the last year have you needed a first drink in the morning to get yourself going after a heavy drinking session?	Never	Less than monthly	Monthly	Weekly	Daily or almost daily
7. How often during the last year have you had a feeling of guilt or remorse after drinking?	Never	Less than monthly	Monthly	Weekly	Daily or almost daily
8. How often during the last year have you been unable to remember what happened the night before because of your drinking?	Never	Less than monthly	Monthly	Weekly	Daily or almost daily
9. Have you or someone else been injured because of your drinking?	No		Yes, but not in the last year		Yes, during the last year
10. Has a relative, friend, doctor, or other health care worker been concerned about your drinking or suggested you cut down?	No		Yes, but not in the last year		Yes, during the last year
				Total	

Screening for Alcohol Use Disorders with the AUDIT

The AUDIT is easy to score. Each of the questions has a set of responses to choose from, and each response has a score ranging from 0 to 4. In the self-report questionnaire format, the number in the column of each response checked by the patient should be entered beside the extreme right-hand column. All the response scores should then be added and recorded in the box labeled "Total."

Total scores of 8 or more are recommended as indicators of hazardous and harmful alcohol use, as well as possible alcohol dependence. (A cut-off score of 10 will provide greater specificity but at the expense of sensitivity.) Since the effects of alcohol vary with average body weight and differences in metabolism, establishing the cut-off point for all women and men over age 65 one point at a score of 7 will increase sensitivity for these population groups. Selection of the cut-off point should be influenced by national and cultural standards and by clinician judgment, which also determine recommended maximum consumption allowances. Technically speaking, higher scores simply indicate greater likelihood of hazardous and harmful drinking. However, such scores may also reflect greater severity of alcohol problems and dependence, as well as a greater need for more intensive treatment.

More detailed interpretation of a patient's total score may be obtained by determining on which questions points were scored. In general, a score of 1 or more on Question 2 or Question 3 indicates consumption at a hazardous level. Points scored above 0 on questions 4-6 (especially weekly or daily symptoms) imply the presence or incipience of alcohol dependence. Points scored on questions 7-10 indicate that alcohol-related harm is already being experienced. The total score, consumption level, signs of dependence, and present harm all should play a role in determining how to manage a patient. The final two questions should also be reviewed to determine whether patients give evidence of a past problem (i.e., "yes, but not in the past year"). Even in the absence of current hazardous drinking, positive responses on these items should be used to discuss the need for vigilance by the patient.

In most cases, the total AUDIT score will reflect the patient's level of risk related to alcohol. In general health care settings and in community surveys, most patients will score under the cut-offs and may be considered to have low risk of alcohol-related problems. A smaller, but still significant, portion of the population is likely to score above the cut-offs but record most of their points on the first three questions.

A much smaller proportion can be expected to score very high, with points recorded on the dependence-related questions as well as exhibiting alcohol-related problems. As yet there has been insufficient research to establish precisely a cut-off point to distinguish hazardous and harmful drinkers (who would benefit from a brief intervention) from alcohol dependent drinkers (who should be referred for diagnostic evaluation and more intensive treatment). This is an important question because screening programs designed to identify cases of alcohol dependence are likely to find a large number of hazardous and harmful drinkers if the cut-off of 8 is used. These patients need to be managed with less intensive interventions. In general, the higher the total score on the AUDIT, the greater the sensitivity in finding persons with alcohol dependence.

Based on experience gained in a study of treatment matching with persons who had a wide range of alcohol problem severity, AUDIT scores were compared with diagnostic data reflecting low, medium, and high degrees of alcohol dependence. It was found that AUDIT scores in the range of 8-15 represented a medium level of alcohol problems whereas scores of 16 and above represented a high level of alcohol problems. On the basis of experience gained from the use of the AUDIT in this and other research, it is suggested that the following interpretation be given to AUDIT scores:

- Scores between 8 and 15 are most appropriate for simple advice focused on the reduction of hazardous drinking.

- Scores between 16 and 19 suggest brief counseling and continued monitoring.

- AUDIT scores of 20 or above clearly warrant further diagnostic evaluation for alcohol dependence.

In the absence of better research these guidelines should be considered tentative, subject to clinical judgment that takes into account the patient's medical condition, family history of alcohol problems, and perceived honesty in responding to the AUDIT questions.

While use of the 10-question AUDIT questionnaire will be sufficient for the vast majority of patients, special circumstances may require a clinical screening procedure. For example, a patient may be resistant, uncooperative, or unable to respond to the AUDIT questions. If further confirmation of possible dependence is warranted, a physical examination procedure and laboratory tests may be used.

Screening in the Emergency Department

Many of the estimated 110 million emergency department (ED) visits in the United States each year are related to alcohol use. Up to 31 percent of patients treated in EDs and 50 percent of severely injured trauma patients (i.e., those requiring hospital admission, usually to an intensive care unit) screen positive for alcohol problems. Patients treated in EDs also are 1.5 to 3 times more likely than those treated in primary care clinics to report heavy drinking, to experience the adverse effects of drinking (e.g., alcohol-related injuries, illnesses, and legal or social problems), and to have been treated previously for an alcohol problem.

Researchers demonstrated that screening using such tools as quantity/frequency questions and the four-item CAGE questionnaire is feasible in a real-world ED setting. Likewise, in another study researchers screened a sample of young adults ages 18 to 39 while they were waiting for treatment in the ED. Most of these patients (87 percent) consented to the screening. Of these, a large portion (43 percent) screened positive for alcohol problems on the AUDIT. (In this study, a score of 6 or more points was considered a positive screen) and of those with positive screens, 94 percent received counseling. The high prevalence of alcohol problems and the broad acceptance of screening and brief intervention in this sample show that screening is indeed feasible in an ED setting.

Yet barriers to screening in an ED setting are clear. This environment typically is chaotic and time is precious. Emergency practitioners and trauma physicians may believe that interventions for alcoholism are ineffective, or they may lack confidence in their ability or the ability of their staffs to screen patients effectively. And resources may not be available for conducting screening and brief interventions in the ED.

In some cases, ethical and insurance issues also present obstacles to screening. For example, because of existing laws, third-party payers (i.e., insurers) may deny reimbursement for medical services if a patient has a positive blood alcohol level at the time of the ED visit. This can place a large financial burden on the patient or on the treating hospital (if it does not receive payment from the patient or the insurance company).

Another legal issue related to screening for alcohol use in the ED is the possible denial of benefits because the patient was injured while committing a crime. In many states, driving while impaired (DWI) is a felony, especially if a crash is severe enough to result in the need for medical attention. (The classification of DWI offenses depends entirely on the law of each state. Many states classify them as misdemeanors. A number of states, however, classify DWI offenses as felonies under the following circumstances: when they are repeat offenses, when they cause death or serious bodily injury, or when they involve a blood alcohol concentration over 0.15 percent, or when there is a combination of previous traffic offenses.) Many insurance policies will not pay benefits for injuries sustained during the commission of a felony (but will provide for injuries sustained in the commission of a lesser crime). Other policies, however, exclude benefits for injuries sustained in the commission of any criminal act; in these cases, lesser offenses such as public intoxication or illegal consumption of an alcoholic beverage could be used as justification to deny benefits.

An increase in screening has occurred in trauma centers in recent years, but the practice still is not routine.

Screening in Prenatal Care Settings

Women who drink during pregnancy come from all walks of life. Anywhere from 14 to 22.5 percent of women report drinking some alcohol while pregnant. The U.S. Surgeon General recently issued an advisory warning pregnant women and women who might become pregnant to abstain from any alcohol use to eliminate the chance of giving birth to a baby with Fetal Alcohol Spectrum Disorders (FASD)—a range of preventable birth defects caused by prenatal alcohol exposure. This current advisory is an update of the 1981 Surgeon General's Advisory.

Identifying women who are drinking during pregnancy clearly is important. Yet determining a woman's prenatal alcohol consumption can be difficult. Many women alter their drinking once they learn they are pregnant. But a woman may have been drinking harmful levels of alcohol prior to learning about her pregnancy, and some injury already could have been done to the fetus. The standard questions about a woman's current quantity and frequency of alcohol use may not show her true risk for problems. Asking her about her drinking patterns before she became pregnant would solicit more accurate measures of her first-trimester consumption.

A woman also may not report her alcohol consumption accurately because she is embarrassed or afraid to admit to drinking while pregnant. And popular screening instruments, such as the CAGE, although effective in other populations, may not identify harmful drinking by pregnant women. The T-ACE, a four-item questionnaire based on the

CAGE, is a simple screening instrument that can identify women's prenatal consumption. Women who screen positive using the T-ACE or another screening questionnaire, such as the AUDIT, should receive further assessment and brief intervention to help reduce the risk to the developing fetus and to maximize pregnancy outcome.

Screening in the Criminal Justice System

By the end of 2003, about 1.47 million people were incarcerated in U.S. federal and state prisons, and an additional 4.85 million were on probation or parole. Approximately 18 percent of federal prison inmates and about 25 percent of state prison inmates reported having experienced problems consistent with a history of alcohol abuse or dependence. Alcohol misuse plays a particularly large role in domestic violence and DWI offenses ("DWI" is used generically as a reference to the impaired driving offense and includes impairment by alcohol and/or other drugs.)—29 percent of federal and 40 percent of state prisoners reported a previous domestic violence dispute involving alcohol, and almost two-thirds of convicted DWI offenders are alcohol dependent. Routine alcohol screening of all offenders in the criminal justice system would help to identify people at greatest risk for problems with alcohol.

Most States mandate screening and assessment of DWI offenders to evaluate the extent of their problem with alcohol and their need for treatment. Current sentencing guidelines also recommend that all DWI offenders be screened for alcohol use problems and recidivism risk, but the existing screening programs for DWI offenders differ in how they evaluate clients. Some programs conduct a simple screening—typically, a brief questionnaire—to determine whether the client should be transferred either to an education program or to treatment. Other programs combine screening with assessment and provide referral guidelines and specific treatment recommendations.

Screening for alcohol disorders in the criminal justice setting poses specific challenges. One factor that may limit the effectiveness of current screening procedures is that most instruments, such as the commonly used MAST, were developed in populations other than DWI offenders or other criminal justice populations and were not designed specifically for use in court-mandated screening. These instruments rely on the offenders' reports of their own alcohol use (that is, self-reports), without considering other information (such as court records for previous alcohol-related offenses, statements from the offender's family or others, or data obtained from biochemical tests to detect alcohol consumption), making it more difficult to truly gauge alcohol consumption.

Offenders also may feel coerced into screening and treatment, fearing that they may be penalized if they admit to alcohol use, perhaps losing custody of their children or receiving unfavorable probation conditions. Issues of confidentiality also may come into play.

These factors can make it difficult to assess the true nature and severity of an offender's alcohol problems and underscore the need for adequately trained personnel to conduct screening in criminal justice populations so that any under-reporting of problems can be avoided. Many programs, however, cannot afford specially trained staff to conduct these evaluations.

Financial constraints are an issue in community and State criminal justice systems. Yet the costs to society of failing to properly identify and treat alcohol abusers in the criminal justice system also are substantial. Appropriately delivered treatment can be effective in changing behavior and reducing re-arrests—the result is a cost that's much less than incarceration.

Screening in College Populations

Alcohol use among college students is a serious cause for concern. Many students are under the legal drinking age. Moreover, many engage in heavy episodic, or binge, drinking. NIAAA defines binge drinking as consuming enough alcohol to result in a blood alcohol content (BAC) of .08, which, for most adults, would be five drinks for men or four for women over a 2-hour period.

Approximately 39 to 44 percent of college students reported binge drinking at least once in the 2 weeks prior to taking a survey. Additionally, according to one study, nearly one third of college students met *DSM–IV* criteria for alcohol abuse, and 6 percent met *DSM–IV* criteria for alcohol dependence.

Identifying those students at greatest risk for alcohol problems is the first step in prevention. Screening instruments must be selected that will accurately detect the problem within the population of interest, and be feasible to implement.

A number of screening tests have been evaluated. The CAGE has been used in college student populations but has been criticized for its inability to detect the full range of drinking problems experienced by people in this age group. Another test, the MAST, includes 9 to 25 questions; the longest version takes less than 10 minutes to complete. The MAST is particularly useful in detecting more advanced problems with alcohol (such as dependence), but this may limit its usefulness within a college population. The Young Adult Alcohol Problems Screening Test (YAAPST), which consists of 27 items, takes less than 10 minutes to complete and has demonstrated good sensitivity. Other screening tools—the College Alcohol Problems Scale–revised (CAPS-r), the Rutgers Alcohol Problem Index (RAPI), and the AUDIT—can be used to detect alcohol problems experienced in the past year, making them good candidates for use with students.

With the AUDIT, the proper cutoff score to use for screening college students has been disputed, however. A recent study using high-risk drinking as the criterion suggests that a cutoff score of 8 results in levels of sensitivity and specificity comparable to those of earlier studies. (High-risk drinking was defined, for men, as consuming 5 or more consecutive drinks on 4 or more occasions, or 57 or more drinks total during the preceding 28-day period; and for women, consuming 4 or more consecutive drinks on 4 or more occasions, or 29 or more drinks total during the preceding 28-day period.)

Screening may occur in the campus health center, counseling center, or local hospital emergency department (for example, students may answer questions as part of normal intake procedures). Incorporating screening into campus judicial systems has several advantages. Many campuses already have policies in place that mandate students cited for alcohol policy violations to complete assessment and interventions, and trained staff typically are available to respond to these policy violators.

Researchers suggest that administrators also consider retaining an on-campus specialist—that is, a health care or counseling professional responsible for direct access to services—to reduce the need for off-campus providers. This specialist could coordinate the full range of alcohol-screening services, including those in the health or counseling center and mandated or campus judicial settings, as well as any universal screening efforts, thus solving some of the confidentiality issues raised by the involvement of academic affairs offices in screening.

Summary

Screening tests are a first-line defense in the prevention of disease. Screening for alcohol problems can take place in a wide variety of populations and settings. Research shows that a number of good screening instruments are available that can be tailored to specific audiences and needs. Detecting alcohol abuse and dependence early in the course of disease enables clinicians to get people the help they

Chapter 62

Barriers to Alcoholism Treatment

Millions of Americans suffer from alcohol and drug use disorders, which include misuse, dependence, or addiction to alcohol and/or legal or illegal drugs. In 2002, an estimated 22 million Americans met the criteria for substance dependence or abuse.[1] Alcohol and drug use disorders also have a significant impact on spouses and others who are close to people with such disorders. Family members may experience increased family conflict; emotional or physical violence; and increased family stress, including work problems, illness, marital strain, and financial problems.[2]

Many people in need of recovery have difficulty obtaining the treatment that can help them rejoin their families, their jobs, and their lives in their communities. Yet many others have overcome the numerous barriers to recovery, and as a result are leading healthy and productive lives.

The statistics surrounding those who face barriers to being treated for alcohol and drug use disorders are startling. In 2002:

- Only 10.3 percent of Americans age 12 or older who needed treatment for an alcohol or drug use disorder actually received treatment.[3]

- More than 95 percent of people with an alcohol use disorder who did not receive treatment did not believe treatment was

"Overview: Access to Recovery from Alcohol and Drug Use Disorders" is from the Substance Abuse and Mental Health Services Administration (SAMHSA), 2004.

necessary; more than 94 percent of people with untreated drug use disorders held the same belief.[4]

- Of those who recognized that they needed treatment, 35 percent (266,000) of Americans suffering from alcohol use disorder—and an estimated 88,000 people suffering from a drug use disorder (24.4 percent)—tried but were unable to obtain treatment.[5]

Clearly, barriers must be overcome to improve Americans' access to recovery.

What Are the Barriers to Treatment?

Many barriers keep people from the treatment they need, including:

- a system-wide failure to identify affected people and their families and direct them to treatment and recovery resources;

- the cost of treatment;

- treatment systems that do not have the facilities or staff to accommodate the needs of some individuals (such as the disabled and those with childcare issues that make it difficult to access treatment); and

- denial and stigma associated with alcohol and drug use disorders.[6]

Even when people recognize that they are having problems with alcohol or drugs, many say they do not seek treatment because they are not prepared to face the challenges of treatment and recovery. Another reason is that they do not believe they can afford to obtain treatment.[7]

Public and private insurers do not cover treatment at the same level as they cover other health programs, leaving states and local governments to shoulder a large share of the costs for treatment programs. As state budgets tighten, the money available to fund treatment programs is shrinking, making it more difficult for Americans to obtain access to local treatment programs.[8]

Access to Recovery: A New Federal Initiative

To overcome some of these barriers, the Substance Abuse and Mental Health Services Administration (SAMHSA) has launched the Access to Recovery grant program, a centerpiece of the initiative announced by President Bush in 2003 to help people who want to get off drugs secure the best treatment options available to meet their specific needs. The competitive grant program gives recipient states, territories, the District of Columbia, and tribal organizations broad discretion to design and implement federally supported voucher programs to pay for a range of effective, community-based, substance abuse clinical treatment and recovery support services. By providing vouchers to people in need of treatment, the grant program promotes individual choice for substance abuse treatment and recovery services. It also expands access to care, including access to faith- and community-based programs, and increases substance abuse treatment capacity.

Access to Recovery provides people seeking treatment with vouchers to pay for a range of community-based services. The state-run program is built on three principles:

- **Consumer Choice.** The process of recovery is a personal one. Achieving recovery can take many pathways: physical, mental, emotional, and/or spiritual. With vouchers, people in need of treatment can select the programs and providers that best suit their personal needs.

- **Measured Results.** Programs must demonstrate that their treatment is effective and leads to recovery, as measured by treatment outcomes such as abstinence from drugs and alcohol, no involvement with the criminal justice system, attainment of employment or enrollment in school, and stable housing.

- **Increased Capacity.** The initial phase of Access to Recovery expands the array of treatment services available, including medical detoxification, inpatient and outpatient treatment programs, residential services, peer support, relapse prevention, case management, and other recovery-promoting services.

More information about the Access to Recovery initiative and grant program is available from SAMHSA at www.samhsa.gov.

Sources

1. *Results from the 2002 National Survey on Drug Use and Health: National Findings.* DHHS Publication No. (SMA) 03-3774. Rockville, MD: U.S. Department of Health and Human Services, Substance Abuse and Mental Health Services Administration, Office of Applied Studies, September 2003, p. 4.

2. El Guebaly, N. & Offord, D.R., 1997. "The offspring of alcoholics: a critical review," *American Journal of Psychiatry,* 134:4, pp. 357–365.

3. *The NSDUH Report: Reasons for Not Receiving Substance Abuse Treatment.* Rockville, MD: U.S. Department of Health and Human Services, Substance Abuse and Mental Health Services Administration, Office of Applied Studies, November 7, 2003, sections entitled "Illicit Drug Treatment Need" and "Alcohol Treatment Need."

4. Ibid.

5. Ibid.

6. *Improving Substance Abuse Treatment: The National Treatment Plan Initiative,* Changing the Conversation. DHHS Publication No. (SMA) 00-3479. Rockville, MD: U.S. Department of Health and Human Services, Substance Abuse and Mental Health Services Administration, 2000, p. iii.

7. *The NSDUH Report: Reasons for Not Receiving Substance Abuse Treatment,* section entitled "Reasons for not Receiving Treatment."

8. Scanlon A. *State Spending on Substance Abuse Treatment.* National Conference of State Legislators, Forum for State Health Policy Leadership, December 2002, p. 1.

Chapter 63

Brief Interventions for Alcohol Use

Unlike traditional alcoholism treatment, which focuses on helping people who are dependent on alcohol, brief interventions—or short, one-on-one counseling sessions—are ideally suited for people who drink in ways that are harmful or abusive. Unlike traditional alcoholism treatment, which lasts many weeks or months, brief interventions can be given in a matter of minutes, and they require minimal followup.

The goals of brief interventions differ from formal alcoholism treatment. Brief interventions generally aim to moderate a person's alcohol consumption to sensible levels and to eliminate harmful drinking practices (such as binge drinking), rather than to insist on complete abstinence from drinking—although abstinence may be encouraged, if appropriate. (A "binge" is a pattern of drinking alcohol that brings blood alcohol concentration [BAC] to 0.08 gram percent or above. For a typical adult this pattern corresponds with consuming five or more drinks [male], or four or more drinks [female] in about 2 hours.) Reducing levels of drinking or changing patterns of harmful alcohol use helps to reduce the negative outcomes of drinking, such as alcohol-related medical problems, injuries, domestic violence, motor vehicle crashes, arrests, or damage to a developing fetus.

Exactly what constitutes a brief intervention remains a source of debate. Brief interventions typically consist of one to four short

Excerpted from *Alcohol Alert* No. 66, a publication of the National Institute on Alcohol Abuse and Alcoholism (NIAAA), July 2005. For a complete list of references, see www.niaaa.nih.gov.

counseling sessions with a trained interventionist (e.g., physician, psychologist, social worker). Researchers looked at 34 different studies and found that people who received brief interventions when they were being treated for other conditions consistently showed greater reductions in alcohol use than comparable groups who did not receive an intervention. People seeking treatment specifically for alcohol abuse appeared to reduce their alcohol use about the same amount, whether they received brief interventions or extended treatments (five or more sessions). These findings show that brief interventions can be an effective way to reduce drinking, especially among people who do not have severe drinking problems requiring more intensive treatment.

The appropriate intervention depends on the patient—that is, on the severity of his or her problems with alcohol and whether he or she uses tobacco or other drugs, or has a co-occurring medical or psychiatric problem. The choice of intervention also is based on the clinical setting, the clinician's skills and interest, and time constraints. A brief intervention usually includes personalized feedback and counseling based on the patient's risk for harmful drinking. Often, simply providing this feedback is enough to encourage those at risk to reduce their alcohol intake.

Brief interventions may include approaches—such as motivational interviewing—that are designed to persuade people who are resistant to moderating their alcohol intake or who do not believe they are drinking in a harmful or hazardous way. Motivational interviewing encourages patients to decide to change for themselves by using empathy and warmth rather than confrontation. Clinicians also can assist patients by helping them establish specific goals and build skills for modifying their drinking behavior.

Screening: The First Step

People who would benefit from brief interventions may be identified through routine medical screenings, such as during a visit to a primary care physician. Standardized screening instruments exist that are specifically designed to identify alcohol use disorders. Though not as common, a person also might be identified during a hospital stay when lab tests reveal he or she has an alcohol-related health problem (such as liver disease). Screening might take place after an arrest for driving under the influence or during a visit to an emergency department (ED) as a result of alcohol-related injuries. Or screening might identify a woman who could benefit from a brief intervention during a prenatal visit to her obstetrician. All of these settings represent opportunities for clinicians and others who offer brief interventions to work with people who may be particularly receptive to advice to alter their drinking.

Administering the Intervention

Seeking treatment for problems with alcohol can be potentially embarrassing, stigmatizing, and inconvenient, taking time away from work or family responsibilities. Brief interventions give patients a simple way to receive care in a comfortable and familiar setting. Because they are brief, they can be easily incorporated into a variety of medical practices. Moreover, these approaches offer a lower cost alternative to more formal, specialist-led, alcoholism treatment.

Typically a nonspecialist authority figure who the patient may already trust or feel comfortable being treated by—such as a physician, a nurse, or physician's assistant in a primary care setting, or nurse or physician's assistant on a medical unit—delivers the brief intervention.

Supplemental handouts may be provided to patients during the intervention, including pamphlets, manuals, or workbooks to reinforce the strategies offered during the session. Clinicians also can follow up at a later date, either in person or through the mail, to provide additional assessment and further motivate the patient to achieve the goals set during the initial meeting. If the brief intervention does not motivate the patient to reduce alcohol consumption, clinicians can recommend more intensive treatment.

Many of the challenges involved in administering brief interventions—such as finding the time to administer them in busy doctors' offices, obtaining the extra training that helps staff become comfortable providing interventions, and managing the cost of using interventions—may be overcome through the use of technology. Patients may be encouraged to use computer programs in the doctor's waiting room or at home, or to access the intervention through the Internet, which offers privacy and the ability to complete the program at any time of day.

Another potential tool for administering interventions is "video doctor technology," in which an actor–doctor asks health questions in an interactive computer program. Pilot results of this program indicate that although users reported they would be most comfortable consulting with a doctor in person, they responded positively to the "virtual" doctor intervention, which was accessible even to those with little computer experience.

Putting Research into Practice

Research shows that brief interventions can decrease alcohol consumption, and they work in a variety of populations—younger and older adults, men and women. Interventions that involve repeated contact generally are more effective than single-contact interventions. A review of studies reported that intervention participants reduced their alcohol consumption an average of 13 percent to 34 percent compared with a control group. In addition, a recent analysis concluded that brief interventions may reduce mortality rates among problem drinkers by an estimated 23 to 26 percent.

The following sections examine the use of brief interventions in a variety of settings. Although the basic interventions may be similar, there are specific things to keep in mind when tailoring interventions to specific audiences and settings.

Primary Care Settings

In one study, about 20 percent of primary care patients reported levels of consumption that exceeded the limits recommended by the National Institute on Alcohol Abuse and Alcoholism. Simple interventions offer clinicians an ideal strategy for getting these patients the help they need.

Brief intervention in primary care can be simple and short—ranging from only a few questions (with appropriate responses)—or more extensive, including referral to a substance abuse specialist. Clinicians with limited time may want to use a basic intervention for all patients who use alcohol above the recommended limits; patients who do not respond to the basic intervention can be referred to an alcohol treatment specialist at the followup visit.

The most basic level of brief intervention consists of a simple statement or two. The clinician states that he or she is concerned about the patient's drinking, that it exceeds recommended limits and could lead to alcohol-related problems, and the clinician advises the patient to cut down or stop drinking.

Another brief intervention, which was studied extensively in Project TrEAT (Trial for Early Alcohol Treatment, a large-scale clinical trial conducted in primary care practices), involves two brief face-to-face sessions scheduled 1 month apart, with a followup telephone call 2 weeks after each session. Patients participating in this intervention reported reduced alcohol use, fewer days of hospitalization, and fewer emergency department visits compared with control-group patients. This intervention may be especially useful with patients who are experiencing alcohol-related problems but who do not necessarily need to be referred to an addiction treatment specialist and may not need to stop drinking completely. This intervention was found to be effective up to 4 years later.

Patients who have clear symptoms of alcohol abuse or dependence also may benefit from brief interventions in the primary care setting. Referral to a specialist for alcoholism treatment is a key component of this type of intervention. These interventions typically are more intense; the goal is abstinence from alcohol, not merely cutting down on drinking.

Despite evidence that brief interventions are useful in primary care settings, these short counseling sessions are not routine practice. One survey of primary care physicians found that although most (88 percent) reported asking their patients about alcohol use, only 13 percent used standard screening instruments. A survey of primary care patients revealed that more than 50 percent said their primary care physician did nothing about their substance abuse; 43 percent said their physician never diagnosed their condition.

A number of strategies have been suggested to help physicians make use of screening and brief interventions in their practices, including using group education strategies to hone clinicians' skills with role-playing and other counseling tactics; providing performance feedback; offering training to all clinic members; providing financial incentives to staff; and offering training using credible experts.

The Emergency Department

Up to 31 percent of all patients who are treated in an ED and as many as 50 percent of severely injured trauma patients (i.e., patients who require hospital admission, usually to an intensive care unit) test positive when screened for alcohol problems.

Younger people, in particular, are more likely to seek treatment in an ED. These patients tend to be uninsured and to use the ED as their primary source of medical care. (The terms "older" and "younger" are defined differently among various studies. Most commonly, "younger people" are defined as those age 25 and younger.) Young adults also have the highest prevalence of binge or hazardous drinking in the United States, putting them at particular risk for alcohol-related injuries, often in conjunction with driving. According to the 2001 National Household Survey on Drug Abuse, 3 million people ages 16 to 20 had driven under the influence of alcohol at least once in the previous year, including 600,000 16- and 17-year-olds. Motor vehicle crashes are the number one cause of death for people ages 1 to 35.

Researchers reported on the use of brief interventions in the ED, demonstrating that the interventions could motivate alcohol-dependent patients to begin alcoholism treatment. In a recent survey, ED practitioners reported that they considered performing a brief intervention for harmful and hazardous drinkers feasible and acceptable in their everyday practice. Other investigators have demonstrated that ED residents who receive training in screening and brief intervention in a skills-based workshop increase their knowledge and practice of these procedures. Fifty-eight percent of medical records of patients treated by trained residents contained evidence of screening and intervention, compared with 17 percent of records of patients treated by a control group of similar residents who did not receive training.

Many clinicians consider situations in which a patient receives acute medical care for an alcohol-related injury to be "teachable moments"—situations in which the patient may be particularly open to an alcohol intervention. Brief interventions delivered while patients are receiving trauma care may reduce those patients' alcohol consumption and risk of subsequent alcohol-related injuries. In a study, patients receiving emergency care who screened positive for harmful drinking were given a brief intervention, a brief intervention plus a booster session 7 to 10 days later, or standard ED care. The booster session was designed to help overcome time limitations and distractions, such as pain, treatment for injuries, waiting family members, or the influence of alcohol, all of which could affect the patients' ability to benefit from the intervention.

One year later, patients who received the booster session along with the brief intervention, but not the brief intervention alone, had fewer alcohol-related problems and alcohol-related injuries compared with patients who received standard ED care. The booster sessions particularly may be useful for ED patients, as people being treated in EDs tend to leave quickly after they are treated for their injuries.

Patients who are admitted to medical wards for longer term care may have an even better outcome from brief interventions and, because they already are admitted to the hospital, they do not need to return for additional booster sessions.

Lack of time has been cited as the main obstacle to screening and intervention in the ED. As a result, a brief intervention that can be performed in less than 10 minutes has been developed specifically for emergency practitioners.

Innovative methods for screening and intervention are being developed for use in the ED, including the use of computer-based approaches. These interventions are intended to help physicians use the patients' waiting time for health promotion and to target patients at risk for various health problems.

Prenatal Care Settings

Approximately 14 to 22.5 percent of women report drinking some alcohol during pregnancy, and an estimated 1 percent of all newborns experience some prenatal alcohol-related damage. Routine screening in obstetrical offices may prove to be vital in preventing drinking during pregnancy—the leading cause of preventable birth defects.

Brief interventions have been recommended as the first step in approaching people with mild-to-moderate alcohol problems. Because pregnant women generally are motivated to change their behaviors and only infrequently have severe alcohol problems, they may be especially receptive to brief interventions. In addition, studies show that the people who change their drinking behavior do so within 6 months of receiving the brief intervention. Because most pregnant women seek prenatal care during their first trimester, this is an opportune time to help them to make the changes necessary for a healthy pregnancy.

Research also shows that these interventions are effective. In a recent study, 304 pregnant women were assigned to receive an intervention or to be in a control group. Some of these women tested positive for prenatal alcohol use, whereas others were selected randomly to participate in the study. A unique twist to this investigation was that women received the intervention along with their partners (usually their husbands or the fathers of their unborn children). Results indicated that the women with the highest levels of drinking had the greatest reductions in drinking when they received the brief intervention. The effects of the brief intervention were much greater when a partner participated.

An innovative approach in the prenatal setting, the Protecting the Next Pregnancy Project involves intervening with women who have been identified as drinking during their last pregnancy. The goal of this approach is to reduce alcohol use during the women's future pregnancies. Following the intervention, these women not only drank significantly less than those in a control group during their later pregnancies, they also had fewer low-birth-weight babies and fewer premature deliveries. Moreover, children born to women in the brief intervention group had better neurobehavioral performance at 13 months when compared with control group children.

The Criminal Justice System

Alcohol use is closely linked to crime. According to the 2002 National Crime Victimization Survey, 21.6 percent of victims of violent crimes thought or knew the offender had consumed alcohol. Approximately 40 percent of offenders on probation reported that they had been using alcohol at the time of their offense. In 2001, 1.4 million driving-while-impaired (DWI) arrests were made, making this the number one crime related to alcohol and other drug (AOD) use other than drug possession. ("DWI," or driving while impaired, is used generically to refer to the impaired driving offense and includes impairment by alcohol and/or other drugs.)

Few studies have evaluated the impact of brief interventions in criminal justice populations. Researchers examined whether brief motivational feedback helped to increase offenders' participation in treatment after they completed their jail sentences. They found that offenders receiving feedback were more likely to schedule and keep appointments for followup treatment than were offenders in a control group. However, a study of DWI offenders found that brief individual interventions reduced recidivism only among offenders who showed evidence of depression, but not among offenders who were not depressed. This study suggests that brief interventions may be particularly useful in certain subgroups of DWI offenders. More research is needed to evaluate the effectiveness of brief interventions within the criminal justice system, especially considering the large number of people arrested each year for AOD-related offenses and the high recidivism rates among them.

College Settings

Alcohol use and the resulting problems among young adults have been widely documented. Of particular concern is the pattern of alcohol use among college students; in one survey, approximately 39 to 44 percent of students reported binge drinking within the previous 2 weeks.

Researchers reviewed individual intervention efforts among college students between 1984 and 1999 and found strong evidence to support the use of brief motivational interventions. These interventions are especially useful in college settings because they often focus on moderating a person's alcohol consumption to sensible levels and eliminating harmful drinking practices (such as binge drinking). Brief interventions may be used in campus health centers, counseling centers, or local hospital emergency rooms. Incorporating these interventions into campus judicial systems has several advantages: Many campuses already have policies in place that require students cited for alcohol policy violations to complete an assessment and intervention, and trained staff usually is available to respond to policy violators.

Two key questions to consider when implementing brief interventions in college populations are: Who should deliver the interventions— peer or professional counselors? And how can students be encouraged to participate in the interventions?

Peer counseling has a long history on college campuses and generally has been found to be effective for solving both academic and health problems. Although few studies have looked at the effectiveness of brief interventions for alcohol problems, research indicates that trained peer counselors (i.e., college undergraduates) are as effective as professionals in encouraging drinking changes among college students. A disadvantage is that peer providers require considerable training and supervision; most research protocols recommend weekly individual or group supervision by a trained therapist.

Studies have found that students who most need alcohol-related interventions may be least likely to participate in these sessions. So motivating students to receive brief interventions, especially interventions delivered outside the health center and mandated contexts, is key to reducing alcohol consumption on campus. One solution may be to treat students as consumers of brief intervention services and then to market the intervention "product" accordingly. Researchers reviewed research suggesting that social marketing techniques may improve recruitment of students to alcoholism prevention and intervention services. Calling students when they miss appointments and using other program reminders may increase participation by heavier drinkers.

Support also is emerging for the use of mailed or computerized feedback in place of personalized, individual feedback. Such approaches have been successful in producing at least short-term reductions in students' alcohol consumption.

Another approach to implementing brief interventions is to use different levels or steps of care, perhaps starting with assessing and providing feedback through the Internet, then moving to in-person interventions for those students who have more severe alcohol-related problems or those who do not respond to the initial intervention.

Conclusion

Brief interventions can be useful in a variety of settings and are potentially cost-effective in reducing hazardous or harmful alcohol consumption. Medical settings such as emergency departments or trauma centers also may provide opportunities, or teachable moments, when people may be open to making changes in their alcohol consumption. New technology, such as computerized interventions, may offer an effective means for implementing brief interventions, especially in settings in which time constraints or lack of resources or training in intervention techniques are issues.

Research is yielding new information on the efficacy of various brief interventions at a rapid pace; practitioners, clinicians, college administrators, and others responsible for initiating screening and brief interventions should consider this new scientific evidence when deciding which strategies best fit their situations.

Chapter 64

Inpatient and Outpatient Treatment for Alcoholism or Substance Abuse

Millions of Americans abuse or are dependent on alcohol or drugs. All of these people have families—so remember, you are not alone. The fact that you or your family member is in treatment is a good sign and a big step in the right direction. People with alcohol or drug dependence problems can and do recover.

What Is Substance Abuse?

Alcoholism and drug dependence and addiction, known as substance use disorders, are complex problems. People with these disorders once were thought to have a character defect or moral weakness; some people mistakenly still believe that. However, most scientists and medical researchers now consider dependence on alcohol or drugs to be a long-term illness, like asthma, hypertension (high blood pressure), or diabetes. Most people who drink alcohol drink very little, and many people can stop taking drugs without a struggle. However, some people develop a substance use disorder—use of alcohol or drugs that is compulsive or dangerous (or both).

Excerpted from the brochure "What Is Substance Abuse Treatment? A Booklet for Families," by the Substance Abuse and Mental Health Services Administration (SAMHSA), Center for Substance Abuse Treatment, 2004. DHHS Publication No. SMA 04-3955.

Why Do Some People Develop a Problem But Others Don't?

Substance use disorder is an illness that can affect anyone: rich or poor, male or female, employed or unemployed, young or old, and any race or ethnicity. Nobody knows for sure exactly what causes it, but the chance of developing a substance use disorder depends partly on genetics—biological traits passed down through families. A person's environment, psychological traits, and stress level also play major roles by contributing to the use of alcohol or drugs. Researchers have found that using drugs for a long time changes the brain in important, long-lasting ways. It is as if a switch in the brain turned on at some point. This point is different for every person, but when this switch turns on, the person crosses an invisible line and becomes dependent on the substance. People who start using drugs or alcohol early in life run a greater risk of crossing this line and becoming dependent. These changes in the brain remain long after a person stops using drugs or drinking alcohol.

Even though your family member has an illness, it does not excuse the bad behavior that often accompanies it. Your loved one is not at fault for having a disease, but he or she is responsible for getting treatment.

What Are the Symptoms of Substance Use Disorders?

One of the most important signs of substance addiction or dependence is continued use of drugs or alcohol despite experiencing the serious negative consequences of heavy drug or alcohol use. Often, a person will blame other people or circumstances for his or her problems instead of realizing that the difficulties result from use of drugs or alcohol. For example, your partner may believe he was fired from jobs because his bosses didn't know how to run a business. Or your daughter may believe she got a ticket for driving under the influence of alcohol because the police were targeting her. Perhaps your loved one has even blamed you. People with this illness really may believe that they drink normally or that everyone takes drugs. These false beliefs are called denial, and denial is part of the illness.

Other important symptoms of substance use disorders include:

- **Tolerance**—A person will need increasingly larger amounts of alcohol or drugs to get high.

- **Craving**—A person will feel a strong need, desire, or urge to use alcohol or drugs, will use alcohol or a drug despite negative consequences, and will feel anxious and irritable if he or she can't use them. Craving is a primary symptom of addiction.

- **Loss of control**—A person often will drink more alcohol or take more drugs than he or she meant to, or may use alcohol or drugs at a time or place he or she had not planned. A person also may try to reduce or stop drinking or using drugs many times, but may fail.

- **Physical dependence or withdrawal symptoms**—In some cases when alcohol or drug use is stopped, a person may experience withdrawal symptoms from a physical need for the substance.

Withdrawal symptoms differ depending on the drug, but they may include nausea, sweating, shakiness, and extreme anxiety. The person may try to relieve these symptoms by taking either more of the same or a similar substance.

What Is Substance Abuse Treatment?

Who Provides Treatment?

Many different kinds of professionals provide treatment for substance use disorders. In most treatment programs, the main caregivers are specially trained individuals certified or licensed as substance abuse treatment counselors. About half these counselors are people who are in recovery themselves. Many programs have staff from several different ethnic or cultural groups.

Most treatment programs assign patients to a treatment team of professionals. Depending on the type of treatment, teams can be made up of social workers, counselors, doctors, nurses, psychologists, psychiatrists, or other professionals.

What Will Happen First?

Everyone entering treatment receives a clinical assessment. A complete assessment of an individual is needed to help treatment professionals offer the type of treatment that best suits him or her. The assessment also helps program counselors work with the person to design an effective treatment plan. Although clinical assessment continues throughout a person's treatment, it starts at or just before a person's admission to a treatment program. The counselor will begin by gathering information about the person, asking many questions such as those about:

- kinds, amount, and length of time of substance or alcohol use;
- cultural issues around use of alcohol or drugs;
- effects of drug or alcohol use on the person's life;
- medical history;
- current medical problems or needs;
- current medications (including pain medication);
- mental health issues or behavioral problems;
- family and social issues and needs;
- legal or financial problems;
- educational background and needs;
- current living situation and environment;
- employment history, stability, problems, and needs;
- school performance, problems, and needs, if relevant; and
- previous treatment experiences or attempts to quit drug or alcohol use.

The counselor may invite you, as a family member, to answer questions and express your own concerns as well. Be honest—this is not the time to cover up your loved one's behavior. The counselor needs to get a full picture of the problem to plan and help implement the most effective treatment. It is particularly important for the counselor to know whether your family member has any serious medical problems or whether you suspect that he or she may have an emotional problem. You may feel embarrassed answering some of these questions or have difficulty completing the interview, but remember: the counselor is there to help you and your loved one. The treatment team uses the information gathered to recommend the best type of treatment. No one type of treatment is right for everyone; to work, the treatment needs to meet your family member's individual needs.

After the assessment, a counselor or case manager is assigned to your family member. The counselor works with the person (and possibly his or her family) to develop a treatment plan. This plan lists problems, treatment goals, and ways to meet those goals.

Based on the assessment, the counselor may refer your family member to a physician to decide whether he or she needs medical supervision to stop alcohol or drug use safely.

Medically supervised withdrawal (often called detoxification or detox) uses medication to help people withdraw from alcohol or drugs. People who have been taking large amounts of opioids (e.g., heroin, OxyContin®, or codeine), barbiturates or sedatives ("downers"), pain medications, or alcohol—either alone or together—may need medically monitored or managed withdrawal services. Sometimes, alcohol withdrawal can be so severe that people hallucinate, have convulsions, or develop other dangerous conditions. Medication can help prevent or treat such conditions. Anyone who has once had hallucinations or seizures from alcohol withdrawal or who has another serious illness or (in some cases) a mental disorder that could complicate detoxification may need medical supervision to detoxify safely. Medically supervised withdrawal can take place on a regular medical ward of a hospital, in a specialized inpatient detoxification unit, or on an outpatient basis with close medical supervision. Detoxification may take several days to a week or more. During that time, the person will receive medical care and may begin to receive education about his or her disease.

Not everyone needs inpatient medically supervised detox. People with mild withdrawal symptoms from alcohol or drugs and people using cocaine, marijuana, opioids, or methamphetamine do not generally need to be hospitalized for detoxification. However, they may need outpatient medical care, a lot of support, and someone to ensure their well-being.

Social detoxification can meet this need. Sometimes social detoxification centers are part of a residential treatment program; other times they are separate facilities. Social detoxification centers are not hospitals and seldom use medication, but the person does stay there from several days to 1 week. The social detoxification staff includes nurses and counselors. The staff watches each person's medical condition closely, and counselors are available to help him or her through the most difficult part of withdrawing from alcohol and drugs.

It is important to know that detoxification is not treatment; it is a first step that can prepare a person for treatment.

What Types of Treatment Programs Are Available?

Several types of treatment programs are available:

- Inpatient treatment
- Residential programs

- Partial hospitalization or day treatment

- Outpatient and intensive outpatient programs

- Methadone clinics (also called opioid treatment programs)

Inpatient treatment, provided in special units of hospitals or medical clinics, offers both detoxification and rehabilitation services. Several years ago, many hospital-based treatment programs existed. Today, because of changes in insurance coverage, inpatient treatment is no longer as common as it used to be. People who have a mental disorder or serious medical problems as well as a substance use disorder are the ones most likely to receive inpatient treatment. Adolescents may also need the structure of inpatient treatment to make sure a full assessment of their substance use and mental disorders can be done.

Residential programs provide a living environment with treatment services. Several models of residential treatment (such as the therapeutic community) exist, and treatment in these programs lasts from a month to a year or more. The programs differ in some ways, but they are similar in many ways.

Residential programs often have phases of treatment, with different expectations and activities during each phase. For example, in the first phase, an adult's contact with family, friends, and job may be restricted. An adolescent may be able to have contact with his or her parents but not with friends or with school. This restriction helps the person become part of the treatment community and adjust to the treatment setting. In a later phase, a person may be able to start working again, going "home" to the facility every evening. If your loved one is in a residential treatment program, it is important that you know and understand the program rules and expectations. Often residential programs last long enough to offer general equivalency diploma (GED) preparation classes, training in job-seeking skills, and even career training. In residential programs for adolescents, the participants attend school as a part of the program. Some residential programs are designed to enable women who need treatment to bring their children with them. These programs offer child care and parenting classes.

Residential programs are best for people who do not have stable living or employment situations and/or have limited or no family support. Residential treatment may help people with very serious substance use disorders who have been unable to get and stay sober or drug free in other treatment.

Partial hospitalization or day treatment programs also may be provided in hospitals or free-standing clinics. In these programs, the person attends treatment for 4 to 8 hours per day but lives at home. These programs usually last for at least 3 months and work best for people who have a stable, supportive home environment.

Outpatient and intensive outpatient programs provide treatment at a program site, but the person lives elsewhere (usually at home). Outpatient treatment is offered in a variety of places: health clinics, community mental health clinics, counselors' offices, hospital clinics, local health department offices, or residential programs with outpatient clinics. Many meet in the evenings and on weekends so participants can go to school or work. Outpatient treatment programs have different requirements for attendance. Some programs require daily attendance; others meet only one to three times per week.

Intensive outpatient treatment programs require a person to attend 9 to 20 hours of treatment activities per week. Outpatient programs last from about 2 months to 1 year.

People who do best in an outpatient program are willing to attend counseling sessions regularly, have supportive friends or family members, have a place to live, and have some form of transportation to get to treatment sessions

Opioid treatment programs (OTPs), sometimes known as methadone clinics, offer medication-assisted outpatient treatment for people who are dependent on opioid drugs (such as heroin, OxyContin, or Vicodin). These programs use a medication, such as methadone or LAAM, to help a person not use illicit opioids. OTPs provide counseling and other services along with the medication.

What Actually Happens in Treatment Programs?

Although treatment programs differ, the basic ingredients of treatment are similar. Most programs include many or all elements presented below.

Assessment

As discussed earlier, all treatment programs begin with a clinical assessment of a person's individual treatment needs. This assessment helps in the development of an effective treatment plan.

Medical Care

Programs in hospitals can provide this care on site. Other outpatient or residential programs may have doctors and nurses come to the program site for a few days each week, or a person may be referred to other places for medical care. Medical care typically includes screening and treatment for HIV/AIDS, hepatitis, tuberculosis, and women's health issues.

A Treatment Plan

The treatment team, along with the person in treatment, develops a treatment plan based on the assessment. A treatment plan is a written guide to treatment that includes the person's goals, treatment activities designed to help him or her meet those goals, ways to tell whether a goal has been met, and a timeframe for meeting goals. The treatment plan helps both the person in treatment and treatment program staff stay focused and on track. The treatment plan is adjusted over time to meet changing needs and ensure that it stays relevant.

Group and Individual Counseling

At first, individual counseling generally focuses on motivating the person to stop using drugs or alcohol. Treatment then shifts to helping the person stay drug and alcohol free. The counselor attempts to help the person:

- see the problem and become motivated to change;
- change his or her behavior;
- repair damaged relationships with family and friends;
- build new friendships with people who don't use alcohol or drugs; and
- create a recovery lifestyle.

Group counseling is different in each program, but group members usually support and try to help one another cope with life without using drugs or alcohol. They share their experiences, talk about their feelings and problems, and find out that others have similar problems. Groups also may explore spirituality and its role in recovery.

Individual Assignments

People in treatment may be asked to read certain things (or listen to audiotapes), to complete written assignments (or record them on audiotapes), or to try new behaviors.

Education about Substance Use Disorders

People learn about the symptoms and the effects of alcohol and drug use on their brains and bodies. Education groups use videotapes or audiotapes, lectures, or activities to help people learn about their illness and how to manage it.

Life Skills Training

This training can include learning and practicing employment skills, leisure activities, social skills, communication skills, anger management, stress management, goal setting, and money and time management.

Testing for Alcohol or Drug Use

Program staff members regularly take urine samples from people for drug testing. Some programs are starting to test saliva instead of urine. They also may use a Breathalyzer™ to test people for alcohol use.

Relapse Prevention Training

Relapse prevention training teaches people how to identify their relapse triggers, how to cope with cravings, how to develop plans for handling stressful situations, and what to do if they relapse. A trigger is anything that makes a person crave a drug. Triggers often are connected to the person's past use, such as a person he or she used drugs with, a time or place, drug use paraphernalia (such as syringes, a pipe, or a bong), or a particular situation or emotion.

Orientation to Self-Help Groups

Participants in self-help groups support and encourage one another to become or stay drug and alcohol free. Twelve-Step programs are perhaps the best known of the self-help groups. These programs include Alcoholics Anonymous (AA), Narcotics Anonymous (NA), Cocaine Anonymous, and Marijuana Anonymous. Other self-help groups include SMART (Self Management and Recovery Training) Recovery® and Women for Sobriety.

Members themselves, not treatment facilities, run self-help groups. In many places, self-help groups offer meetings for people with particular needs. You may find special meetings for young people; women;

lesbian, gay, and bisexual people; newcomers; and those who need meetings in languages other than English. Internet chat groups and online meetings are also available for some groups.

Many treatment programs recommend or require attendance at self-help groups. By attending, many people make new friends who help them stay in recovery. The number of meetings required varies by treatment program; many programs require participants to attend "90 meetings in 90 days," as AA and NA recommend. Some treatment programs encourage people to find a "sponsor," that is, someone who has been in the group for a while and can offer personal support and advice.

Self-help groups are very important in most people's recovery. It is important to understand, however, that these groups are not the same as treatment.

There are self-help groups for family members, too, such as Al-Anon and Alateen.

Treatment for Mental Disorders

Many people with a substance use disorder also have emotional problems such as depression, anxiety, or posttraumatic stress disorder. Adolescents in treatment also may have behavior problems, conduct disorder, or attention deficit/hyperactivity disorder. Treating both the substance use and mental disorders increases the chances that the person will recover. Some counselors think people should be alcohol and drug free for at least 3 to 4 weeks before a treatment professional can identify emotional illness correctly. The program may provide mental health care, or it may refer a person to other sites for this care. Mental health care often includes the use of medications, such as antidepressants.

Family Education and Counseling Services

This education can help you understand the disease and its causes, effects, and treatment. Programs provide this education in many ways: lectures, discussions, activities, and group meetings. Some programs provide counseling for families or couples. Family counseling is especially critical in treatment for adolescents. Parents need to be involved in treatment planning and followup care decisions for the adolescent. Family members also need to participate as fully as possible in the family counseling the program offers.

Medication

Many programs use medications to help in the treatment process. Although no medications cure dependence on drugs or alcohol, some do help people stay abstinent and can be lifesaving.

Medication is the primary focus of some programs, such as the medication-assisted OTPs discussed earlier. Methadone is a medication that prevents opioid withdrawal symptoms for about 24 hours, so the person must take it daily. Taken as directed, it does not make a person high but allows him or her to function normally. In fact, methadone blocks the high a person gets from an opioid drug.

Some people stay on methadone for only 6 months to 1 year and then gradually stop taking it; most of these people relapse and begin to use opioids again. However, others stay on methadone for long periods of time or for life, which is called methadone maintenance treatment. People receiving this treatment often have good jobs and lead happy, productive lives.

If your family member is taking medications for HIV infection or AIDS or for any other medical condition, it is important that OTP staff members know exactly what he or she is taking. Mixing some medications with methadone or LAAM may mean that your family member will need special medical supervision.

Buprenorphine is another medication that may be used to treat opioid dependence and is sometimes used by OTPs. Buprenorphine recently was approved for treatment by primary care doctors in their offices. A doctor treating a patient with buprenorphine generally will provide or refer the patient for counseling, also.

Disulfiram (Antabuse®) is a medication that causes a bad reaction if people drink alcohol while taking it. The reaction is flushing, nausea, vomiting, and anxiety. Because people know the medication will make them very ill if they drink alcohol, it helps them not to drink it. Antabuse is taken daily.

Another medication, naltrexone (ReVia®), reduces the craving for alcohol. This medication can help keep people who drink a small amount of alcohol from drinking more of it. Programs also sometimes use naltrexone to treat heroin or other opioid dependence because it blocks the drug's effects. It is important for people who use heroin to go through detox first, so they are heroin free before starting to take naltrexone.

Because it is very difficult for a person to detoxify from opioid drugs, many people don't make it that far; buprenorphine is sometimes used to help people make that transition. If a person does detoxify

511

from opioids and begins to take naltrexone, it still will not work well for this purpose unless a person has a strong social support system, including someone who will make sure that he or she continues to take the medication regularly. When an adolescent is taking naltrexone to treat opioid dependence, it is particularly important that parents provide strong support and supervision.

Followup Care (Also Called Continuing Care)

Even when a person has successfully completed a treatment program, the danger of returning to alcohol or drug use (called a "slip" or relapse) remains. The longer a person stays in treatment, including followup, the more likely he or she is to stay in recovery. Once a person has completed basic treatment, a program will offer a followup care program at the treatment facility or will refer him or her to another site. Most programs recommend that a person stay in followup care for at least 1 year. Adolescents often need followup care for a longer period.

Followup care is very important to successful treatment. Once a person is back in his or her community, back in school, or back at work, he or she will experience many temptations and cravings for alcohol or drugs. In followup care, your family member will meet periodically with a counselor or a group to determine how he or she is coping and to help him or her deal with the challenges of recovery.

For some people, particularly those who have been in residential treatment or prison-based programs, more intensive forms of followup care may be helpful. Halfway houses or sober houses are alcohol- and drug-free places to live for people coming from a prison-based or residential program. People usually stay from 3 months to 1 year, and counseling is provided at the site or at an outpatient facility.

Supportive living or transitional apartments provide small group living arrangements for those who need a sober and drug-free living environment. The residents support one another, and involvement in outpatient counseling and self-help groups is expected.

Why Does Treatment Take So Long?

Substance use disorders affect every part of a person's life. For that reason, treatment needs to affect every part of a person's life as well.

Treatment involves more than helping someone stop drinking alcohol or using drugs. Actually, stopping alcohol use or drug use is just the beginning of the recovery process. Your family member will need to learn new ways to cope with daily life. He or she will need to re-learn how to deal with stress, anger, or social situations and how to have fun without using drugs or drinking. Learning these new skills is a lot of work. Many people enter treatment only because of pressure from the legal system, employers, parents, spouses, or other family members. The first step in treatment then is to help them see that they do have a problem and to become motivated to change for themselves. This process often takes time.

Your family member also will need time to understand and begin to use the support of the self-help groups mentioned before. These groups will be important to his or her recovery for many years to come.

Remember: It can take a long time for the disease to develop and it is often chronic; therefore, it can take a long time to treat it.

Just for You

Now that your family member is in treatment, things are starting to change. Some of the tension and turmoil that probably were part of your life may be starting to ease. But the first weeks of treatment are stressful. Each family member is adjusting to changes, starting to deal with past conflicts, and establishing new routines. Amid all these changes, it is important that you take good care of yourself—get enough sleep, eat right, rest, exercise, and talk to supportive friends and relatives. Your church, mosque, synagogue, temple, or other spiritual organization also may be a good source of support.

Recovery is not just an adjustment for the person in treatment—it also is an adjustment for you. For the past few years, you may have assumed roles or taken care of tasks that were your loved one's responsibilities. Now, as time passes, you and he or she may need to learn new ways of relating to each other and learn different ways of sharing activities and chores. If you are the parent of an adolescent in treatment, you will need to be closely involved in treatment planning and treatment activities. You may need to adjust your life and family relationships to allow for the extra time this involvement will take.

You may have many questions about how your family member will behave in these early stages of recovery. Everyone acts differently. Some people are very happy to be getting treatment at last; others suffer a great deal while they adjust to a new life and attempt to live it without alcohol and drugs. They may be sad, angry, or confused. It is important for you to realize that these are normal reactions and to get support for yourself.

Al-Anon is the best-known and most available resource for family members and friends of alcoholics. Al-Anon was founded 50 years ago to provide support for those living with someone with alcoholism. Alateen, for older children and adolescents, was founded somewhat later on. Today, many family members of people who use drugs also participate in Al-Anon or Alateen. These meetings are free and available in most communities.

Your community also may have Nar-Anon meetings. This group was founded for families and friends of those using drugs. Other groups also may be helpful, such as Co-Dependents Anonymous and Adult Children of Alcoholics. The treatment program should be able to give you schedules of local meetings of all these groups.

Many treatment professionals consider substance use disorders family diseases. To help the whole family recover and cope with the many changes going on, you may be asked to take part in treatment. This approach may involve going to a family education program or to counseling for families or couples.

It is important to remember the following points as you and your family member recover:

- You are participating in treatment for yourself, not just for the sake of the person who used substances.

- Your loved one's recovery, sobriety, or abstinence does not depend on you.

- Your family's recovery does not depend on the recovery of the person who used substances.

- You did not cause your family member's substance use disorder. It is not your fault.

You still may have hurt feelings and anger from the past that need to be resolved. You need support to understand and deal with these feelings, and you need to support your loved one's efforts to get well.

Remember: Help is always there for you, too. Ask the counselor for some suggestions.

What If I Need Help with Basic Living Issues?

You may need very practical help while your family member is in treatment. If your family member is the sole financial provider and unable to work because he or she is in treatment, how will the bills get paid? If your family member is the primary caregiver for children or an elderly adult, how will these needs be met? The treatment program may be able to help you arrange disability leave or insurance through your loved one's employer. Ask the counselor about different types of assistance that may be available to help you meet various needs. Most treatment programs work with other community programs. These programs may include food pantries, clothing programs, transportation assistance, child care, adult day care, legal assistance, financial counseling, and health care services. Your family may be eligible for help from programs that help those in recovery.

I'm Afraid It Won't Work

Treatment is just the first step to recovery. During this process family members sometimes have mixed feelings. You may feel exhausted, angry, relieved, worried, and afraid that, if this doesn't work, nothing will. You may feel as if you are walking on eggshells and that, if you do something wrong, you may cause your loved one to relapse. It is important for you to remember that you cannot cause a relapse—only the person who takes a drug or picks up a drink is responsible for that.

No one can predict whether your family member will recover, or for how long, but many people who receive treatment do get better. The longer people stay in treatment the more likely they will remain drug and alcohol free. About half the people who complete treatment for the first time continue to recover. Of course, this means that about half will return to drinking alcohol and using drugs (called relapse) before they finally give them up for good. Adolescents are even more likely to use drugs or alcohol or both again. It is not uncommon for a person to need to go through treatment more than one time. Often the person needs to return to treatment quickly to prevent a slip or relapse from leading to a chronic problem.

It is important for you to understand that relapse is often a part of the recovery process. Do not be discouraged if your family member uses alcohol or drugs again. Many times relapses are short and the person continues to recover.

A treatment program may involve you in relapse prevention planning and may help you learn what to do if your family member relapses. Your family member will benefit if you do not drink or use drugs around him or her, especially in the first months after his or her treatment begins. When you choose not to use drugs or alcohol, you help your loved one avoid triggers. As you both begin to understand and accept the illness, the risk of relapse decreases. The changes in attitudes, behaviors, and values that you both are learning and practicing will become part of your new recovering lifestyle.

Especially for Young People

You may be having difficulty handling some of your concerns about living with a person who abuses alcohol or drugs. Whether this person is your mom, dad, grandparent, brother, or sister, it is important that you talk about your problems, fears, and concerns with people who are understanding and sympathetic.

You may feel that you caused your family member's substance use disorder or that it is somehow your fault. You may think that if you had behaved better, done better in school, or been different in some way your mom or dad or the person you care about would not drink so much alcohol or take drugs. You did not in any way cause their disease. No one ever causes another person's substance use disorder. It is nobody's fault that someone you care about has become ill.

Your family member may have embarrassed you in front of friends, teachers, or another person. You may have stopped bringing friends home or stopped telling your parents about school activities. Now that your relative is in treatment, his or her behavior should improve.

You may have lived with fighting and stress, and you may have been abused or witnessed other kinds of violence. You may feel very angry and sad because of these experiences. Now you can talk about this and other feelings with your family or the staff at the treatment program. It will be important for you to share your thoughts and feelings about what has happened. You may want to go to self-help groups such as Al-Anon or Alateen. Some young people find these meetings to be helpful. These groups talk about the three C's: You didn't Cause it, you can't Control it, and you can't Cure it. Remembering the three C's can help.

It is important to know that substance use disorders run in families. People who have a blood relative with a substance use disorder are about four times more likely to develop the same disorder than those who do not. This means that you may have inherited a tendency to develop a problem yourself, and you should be careful about drinking alcohol or taking drugs. This information is meant to educate you, not to scare you.

The situation at home will probably improve because your relative is in treatment. Like treatment for people with other illnesses, treatment for substance use disorders is helpful, but not everyone knows or believes it is. A great deal of stigma and shame are still associated with substance use disorders. What and how much you tell your friends or teachers is your decision and your family's. You may just want to say something like, "My mom is ill, but she will get better and come home soon. Thank you for asking."

You may choose to help educate some of your close friends about your relative's illness and his or her progress in treatment. Or, you may decide not to share this information with them. It's your choice.

Remember, you didn't create this problem, but you can play an important role in helping everyone heal. Hang in there.

Chapter 65

Substance Abuse Treatment for Children and Adolescents

It's hard for most parents to believe that their child might be caught up in substance abuse and in need of professional help. Don't feel bad if you didn't see the warning signs until your child was in trouble or until someone told you about a drug problem in your family. When most parents find out about their child's drug abuse, they feel shocked and stunned and wonder where they went wrong.

Many children and teens feel great pressure to try alcohol, tobacco, and drugs (ATD). They are flooded with pro-use messages from their friends; from alcohol and tobacco advertising and marketing; and from movies, music, music videos, and websites that appeal to youth. Parents often have less time to spend with their equally busy kids and fewer chances to keep track of their activities, friendships, and other influences. Parents feel like they are not ready to guide children on serious matters like alcohol and drug abuse.

Try not to blame yourself or your child if he or she has a substance abuse problem. The important thing is to act now to find the best available services to help your child stop using drugs and alcohol and begin building a drug-free future.

Your child's school may suggest a good substance abuse treatment program. If not, the school district is likely to have a substance abuse prevention and counseling program. Contact them for help. Local

"When Your Child Needs Substance Abuse Treatment" is from the Center for Substance Abuse Prevention, Substance Abuse and Mental Health Services Administration (SAMHSA), part of the U.S. Department of Health and Human Resources, April 28, 2004.

519

substance abuse or antidrug coalitions also can refer you to treatment services. To find a coalition in your neighborhood, check out http://www.helpyourcommunity.org. Your county's health department probably has substance abuse services and is another good source for information. The county agency may be called "alcohol and drug programs" or "behavioral health" or may be within a "mental health services" division. A call to the county health agency's general information number should point you in the right direction.

Unfortunately, the demand for services to meet the treatment needs of teens and children is greater than the treatment options available. So, there are a few questions you should ask of any program before placing your child in their care:

- How does the program meet the needs of people under age 18?

- How does the program assess a teen's problems?

- Does the program offer medication as part of the treatment plan, if needed?

- How does the program review/update its treatment plan in light of a client's progress?

- How is the family part of the treatment experience and process?

- What does the program do to help children stay in treatment?

- What are the staff's qualifications? Is the program run by state-accredited, licensed, or trained professionals? What clinical supervision is given?

- Is the facility clean, organized, and well-run?

- Does the program encompass the full range of needs of the child (medical, including infectious diseases; psychological, including co-occurring mental illness; social; vocational; legal; etc.)?

- Does the treatment program also address sexual orientation and physical disabilities as well as provide age, gender, and culturally appropriate treatment services?

- Does the program offer counseling (individual or group) and other behavioral therapies to enhance the child's ability to function in the family/community? Are single-sex groups, as well as mixed groups, offered? Are there male and female counselors?

- What followup care is given after treatment is over? Does the program employ strategies to engage and keep the child in longer-term treatment, increasing the likelihood of success?

- What evidence is there to show that the program works?

- What are all of the costs involved in enrolling a child in the program?

- What types of insurance coverage are allowed? Are scholarships or sliding-scale fees given?

As with any illness or medical problem, early intervention and treatment of your child's substance abuse raises the chances of successful results. The sooner your child gets help, the less harm his or her drug or alcohol problem may cause and the better his or her chances are of developing a healthy, safe, and drug-free lifestyle. With your encouragement and support and an effective treatment plan, what is now a painful family experience can become a positive step toward a happy and fulfilling future.

You Can Help Your Child Make Healthy Choices

- **Talk with your child**—It's important to establish and maintain good communication with your child. Get into the habit of talking with your child every day.

- **Get involved**—It really can make a difference when you get involved in your child's life. Young people are much less likely to have mental health and substance use problems when they have positive activities to do and when caring adults are involved in their lives.

- **Set rules**—Make clear, sensible rules for your child and enforce them with consistency and appropriate consequences.

- **Be a role model**—Set a good example for your child. Think about what you say and how you act in front of him or her.

- **Teach kids to choose friends wisely**—Support your child's social development. Teach your child how to form positive relationships.

- **Monitor your child's activities**—Do you know what your child listens to and reads and how he or she spends time with friends?

Chapter 66

Physical Symptoms of Alcoholism Recovery

Chapter Contents

Section 66.1—Alcohol Withdrawal 524

Section 66.2—Delirium Tremens 528

Section 66.1

Alcohol Withdrawal

© 2006 A.D.A.M., Inc. Reprinted with permission.

Definition

Alcohol withdrawal refers to symptoms that may occur when a person who has been drinking too much alcohol every day suddenly stops drinking alcohol.

Causes, Incidence, and Risk Factors

Alcohol withdrawal usually occurs in adults, but it may happen in teenagers or children as well. It can occur when a person who uses alcohol excessively suddenly stops drinking alcohol. The withdrawal usually occurs within 5–10 hours after the last drink, but it may occur up to 7–10 days later.

Excessive alcohol use is generally considered the equivalent of 2–6 pints of beer (or 4 ounces of "hard" alcohol) per day for 1 week or habitual use of alcohol that disrupts a person's life and routines.

The more heavily a person had been drinking every day, the more likely that person will develop alcohol withdrawal symptoms when they stop. The likelihood of developing severe withdrawal symptoms also increases if a person has other medical problems.

Symptoms

Mild-to-moderate psychological symptoms:

- jumpiness or nervousness
- shakiness
- anxiety
- irritability or easy excitability
- rapid emotional changes

- depression
- fatigue
- difficulty thinking clearly
- bad dreams

Mild-to-moderate physical symptoms:

- headache—general, pulsating
- sweating—especially the palms of the hands or the face
- nausea and vomiting
- loss of appetite
- insomnia (sleeping difficulty)
- pallor
- rapid heart rate
- eye pupils enlarged (dilated pupils)
- clammy skin
- tremor of the hands
- involuntary, abnormal movements of the eyelids

Severe symptoms:

- delirium tremens—a state of confusion and visual hallucinations
- agitation
- fever
- convulsions
- black outs—when the person forgets what happened during the drinking episode

Signs and Tests

The health care provider will check for:

- rapid heartbeat (tachycardia);
- rapid breathing (tachypnea);
- elevated temperature;

- abnormal eye movements;
- shaky hands;
- general body shaking;
- abnormal heart rhythms;
- internal bleeding;
- liver failure; and
- dehydration.

A toxicology screen may be performed as well as other blood tests.

Treatment

The goals are to treat the immediate withdrawal symptoms, prevent complications, and begin long-term preventative therapy.

The person will probably have to stay at the hospital for constant observation. Heart rate, breathing, body temperature, and blood pressure are monitored, as well as fluids and electrolytes (chemicals in the body such as sodium and potassium).

The patient's symptoms may progress rapidly and may quickly become life threatening. Drugs that depress the central nervous system (such as sedatives) may be required to reduce symptoms, often in moderately large doses.

Treatment may require maintenance of a moderately sedated state for a week or more until withdrawal is complete. A class of medications known as the benzodiazepines is often useful in reducing a range of symptoms.

A drying-out period may be appropriate. No alcohol is allowed during this time. The health care provider will watch closely for signs of delirium tremens. Hallucinations that occur without other symptoms or complications are uncommon.

They are treated with hospitalization and antipsychotic medications as needed. Testing and treatment for other medical problems associated with use of alcohol is necessary. This may include disorders such as alcoholic liver disease, blood clotting disorders, alcoholic neuropathy, heart disorders (such as alcoholic cardiomyopathy), chronic brain syndromes (such as Wernicke-Korsakoff syndrome), and malnutrition.

Rehabilitation for alcoholism is often recommended. This may include social support such as Alcoholics Anonymous, medications, and behavior therapy.

Expectations (Prognosis)

Alcohol withdrawal may range from a mild and uncomfortable disorder to a serious, life-threatening condition. Symptoms usually begin within 12 hours of the last drink. The symptoms peak in 48–72 hours and may persist for a week or more.

Symptoms such as sleep changes, rapid changes in mood, and fatigue may last for 3–12 months or more. If a person continues to drink excessively, they may develop many medical conditions such as liver and heart disease.

Calling Your Health Care Provider

Call your health care provider or go the emergency room if symptoms indicate alcohol withdrawal, especially in a person who has a history of habitual use of alcohol or a history of stopping use of alcohol after a period of heavy alcohol consumption. Alcohol withdrawal is a serious condition that may rapidly become life threatening.

Call for an appointment with your health care provider if symptoms persist after treatment.

Go to the emergency room or call the local emergency number (such as 911) if potentially lethal symptoms occur, including seizures, fever, delirium or severe confusion, hallucinations, and irregular heart beat.

Prevention

Minimize or avoid the use of alcohol. In people with alcoholism, total abstinence from alcohol may be necessary.

Section 66.2

Delirium Tremens

© 2006 A.D.A.M., Inc. Reprinted with permission.

Definition

Delirium tremens is a disorder involving sudden and severe mental changes (psychosis) or neurologic changes (including seizures) caused by abruptly stopping the use of alcohol. Rapid pulse rate, elevated blood pressure, and temperature elevation also may be present.

Causes, Incidence, and Risk Factors

Delirium tremens can occur after a period of heavy alcohol drinking, especially when the person does not eat enough food.

It may also be triggered by head injury, infection, or illness in people with a history of heavy use of alcohol. It is most common in people who have a history of experiencing alcohol withdrawal when alcohol is stopped, especially in those who drink the equivalent of 7–8 pints of beer (or 1 pint of "hard" alcohol) per day for several months, and in those with a history of habitual alcohol use or alcoholism that has existed for more than 10 years.

Symptoms occur because of the toxic effects of alcohol on the brain and nervous system. They may be severe and progress rapidly.

Symptoms

- Symptoms of alcohol withdrawal
  - feeling jumpy or nervous
  - feeling shaky
  - anxiety
  - irritability or easily excited
  - emotional volatility/rapid emotional changes

- depression
- fatigue
- difficulty thinking clearly
- palpitations (sensation of feeling the heart beat)
- headache—general, pulsating
- sweating, especially the palms of the hands or the face
- nausea
- vomiting
- loss of appetite
- insomnia (difficulty falling and staying asleep)
- pale skin

- Mental status changes

  - mood changes rapidly
  - restlessness, excitement
  - increased activity
  - decreased attention span
  - excitement
  - fear
  - confusion/disorientation
  - agitation/irritability
  - hallucinations (visual hallucinations such as seeing things that are not present are most common)
  - sensory hyperacuity (highly sensitive to light, sound, touch)
  - delirium (severe, acute loss of mental functions)
  - decreased mental status: stupor, sleepiness, lethargy; deep sleep that persists for a day or longer; usually occurs after acute symptoms

- Seizures

  - usually generalized tonic-clonic seizures
  - most common in first 24–48 hours

- most common in people with previous alcohol withdrawal complications

- Body tremors

Additional symptoms that may occur:

- fever

- stomach pain

- chest pain

Symptoms most commonly occur within 72 hours after the last drink, but may occur up to 7–10 days after the last drink. Symptoms may progress rapidly.

Signs and Tests

Delirium tremens is a medical emergency. The health care provider should be consulted promptly.

An examination of the neuromuscular system may show an increased startle reflex, rapid rhythmic muscle tremor, or other changes indicating alcohol withdrawal. Evidence of increased autonomic function—such as profuse sweating—may be present.

There may be symptoms of dehydration or malnutrition, and signs indicating electrolyte disturbances. An eye inspection may show abnormalities of eye muscle movement—such as lid lag. The heart rate may be rapid, and there may be an irregular heartbeat. The blood pressure may be normal, elevated, or low.

A serum toxicology screen is usually positive for alcohol. Serum chemistry (chem-20) may show electrolyte disturbances, especially decreased levels of potassium and magnesium. An ECG (electrocardiogram) may show arrhythmias. An EEG (electroencephalogram) may be performed to rule out other causes of seizures.

Treatment

This is an emergency condition. The goals of treatment are saving the patient's life, treating the immediate symptoms, and preventing complications. Long-term preventive treatment may begin after initial treatment of the acute condition.

Hospitalization is required. Vital signs (temperature, pulse, rate of breathing, blood pressure), and fluid and electrolyte status are monitored, and abnormalities are treated as appropriate.

Seizures and cardiovascular conditions, such as heart arrhythmias, are treated as appropriate. This may include lifesaving or life-support measures, anticonvulsant medications such as phenytoin, or other medications. Clonidine may reduce cardiovascular symptoms, and helps reduce anxiety. Central nervous system depressants and sedatives may be required, often in large doses, to reduce symptoms.

Treatment may require maintenance of a sedated state for a week or more until withdrawal is complete. Benzodiazepine medications such as diazepam are often useful to provide sedation. Diazepam is also useful to treat seizures as well as anxiety and tremors.

Hallucinations are treated similarly to any acute psychotic episode, with hospitalization as needed. Cautious use of antipsychotic medications, such as haloperidol, may be necessary in some cases.

A "drying out" period may be appropriate. No alcohol is allowed during this time. Treatment for alcohol use or alcoholism is recommended. This may include psychologic interventions, social supports such as AA (Alcoholics Anonymous), behavior modification, or other interventions.

Testing and treatment for other medical problems associated with use of alcohol is necessary. This may include disorders such as alcoholic liver disease, blood clotting disorders, alcoholic neuropathy, heart disorders (such as alcoholic cardiomyopathy), and chronic brain syndromes (such as Wernicke-Korsakoff syndrome).

Expectations (Prognosis)

Delirium tremens is serious and may be life threatening. Symptoms such as sleeplessness, feeling tired, and emotional instability may persist for a year or more.

Complications

- seizures

- heart arrhythmias (may be life threatening)

- injury from falls during seizures

- injury to self or others caused by mental state (confusion/ delirium)

531

Calling Your Health Care Provider

Go to the emergency room or call the local emergency number (such as 911) if symptoms develop. Delirium tremens is an emergency condition!

Prevention

Avoid or minimize the use of alcohol. Treat known alcoholism appropriately. Obtain prompt medical treatment for symptoms of alcohol withdrawal. Also, look into alcohol detoxification or detox centers in your area, as well as alcohol rehabilitation centers or rehab facilities.

Chapter 67

Medications for Treating Alcohol Dependence

Chapter Contents

Section 67.1—What Medications Treat Alcoholism? 534

Section 67.2—Drugs to Treat Alcohol Dependence 535

Section 67.1

What Medications Treat Alcoholism?

"Treatment for Alcoholism" © 2006 American Association for Clinical Chemistry. Reprinted with permission. For additional information about clinical lab testing, visit the Lab Tests Online website at www.labtestsonline.org.

Treatment usually consists primarily of counseling and support. Patients must acknowledge that they have a drinking problem and have a strong desire to stop drinking. Once the decision has been made, patients may check into a treatment center for a period of time to rehabilitate as they stop drinking. The treatment center (and/or doctor) counsels patients, gives them support, and helps patients get through their initial symptoms and safely withdraw from the alcohol. In some cases, short-term medications such as benzodiazepines (Valium or similar drugs) are used to help alleviate some of the symptoms of alcohol dependence.

There are three medications that have been FDA approved to help patients remain sober: disulfiram (Antabuse), naltrexone (ReVia), and acamprosate (Campral). They are prescribed for some patients who have indicated their intention to abstain from alcohol but require some reinforcement. Disulfiram causes unpleasant symptoms such as nausea, vomiting, and flushing with any amount of drinking. Naltrexone blocks the "high" feeling a person may get from drinking but can cause severe withdrawal symptoms in patients who are also dependent on opiates. Acamprosate helps reduce the craving for alcohol. All of these medications are meant to be used in combination with counseling.

Just as there is no one test for screening or diagnosing alcoholism, there is not one single therapy or medication that definitively treats alcoholism in all patients. It is not an easy condition to resolve, and many patients will relapse into drinking several times before gaining lasting sobriety. Some of the damage done to the liver and to other organs while drinking may resolve, while some may be permanent. Patients and their doctors will need to work together over the years to maintain sobriety and to address any complications that arise from alcohol damage.

Section 67.2

Drugs to Treat Alcohol Dependence

By Steven H. Williams, Ph.D., Veterans Affairs Medical Center, Lebanon, Pennsylvania

Medications for treating alcohol dependence primarily have been adjunctive interventions, and only three medications—disulfiram, naltrexone, and acamprosate—are approved for this indication by the U.S. Food and Drug Administration. Disulfiram, an aversive agent that has been used for more than 40 years, has significant adverse effects and compliance difficulties with no clear evidence that it increases abstinence rates, decreases relapse rates, or reduces cravings. In contrast, naltrexone, an anticraving agent, reduces relapse rates and cravings and increases abstinence rates. Acamprosate also reduces relapse rates and increases abstinence rates. Serotonergic and anticonvulsant agents promise to play more of a role in the treatment of alcohol dependence. Although not approved by the U.S. Food and Drug Administration for this indication, the anticonvulsant topiramate and several serotonergic agents (e.g., fluoxetine, ondansetron) have been shown in recent studies to increase abstinence rates and decrease drinking.

Almost one third of Americans consume enough alcohol to be considered at risk for alcohol dependence, and alcohol abuse and dependence are associated with more than 100,000 deaths from alcohol-related diseases and injuries each year. The economic cost of alcohol abuse and dependence was estimated at more than $184 billion for 1998.[1] Use of screening tools and brief primary care interventions for alcohol problems significantly reduces drinking levels in "problem drinkers" who are not yet alcohol dependent.[2] Counseling and 12-step structured treatment programs have been the mainstays of alcohol dependence treatment, whereas pharmacologic treatments traditionally have played an adjunctive role.

To date, three medications—disulfiram (Antabuse), naltrexone (Trexan), and acamprosate (Campral)—have been approved by the U.S. Food and Drug Administration (FDA) for the treatment of alcohol dependence, and only about 20 percent of eligible patients receive them. In the past decade, however, there has been a growing body of evidence supporting a more central role for medications in the treatment of alcohol dependence. These medications, the evidence supporting them, and recommended dosages are discussed. Table 67.1[3,4] provides a summary of the medications with prescribing information, adverse effects, contraindications, and costs.

Naltrexone

Naltrexone is an opioid-receptor antagonist approved for use in the treatment of alcohol dependence in conjunction with psychosocial interventions. It is believed that naltrexone works through its blockage of μ-opioid receptors, which reduces the reinforcing effects of alcohol leading to decreased feelings of intoxication and fewer cravings.

In a systematic review[5] of 11 double-blind, placebo-controlled trials, researchers found that naltrexone reduces short-term relapse rates in patients with alcohol dependence when combined with psychosocial treatments. Short-term outcomes in favor of naltrexone included fewer patients relapsing to alcohol dependence (38 versus 60 percent with placebo), fewer patients returning to drinking (61 versus 69 percent), reduced cravings for alcohol, and fewer drinking days.[5] The data showed one relapse was prevented for every five patients treated with naltrexone (i.e., number needed to treat [NNT] = 5).

More recent randomized controlled trials (RCTs) looking at longer-term outcomes report mixed results. In a systematic review[6] of three studies assessing medium-term outcomes (six to 12 months), researchers found no difference between naltrexone and placebo groups. In addition, a large trial[7] comparing outcomes of three therapy groups—12 months of naltrexone therapy, three months of naltrexone followed by nine months of placebo, and 12 months of placebo—found no significant differences among the groups in the number of days to relapse, number of drinking days, or number of drinks per drinking day. Although there is good evidence supporting short-term benefit with naltrexone, the evidence for longer-term use is less compelling.

The recommended dosage of naltrexone is 50 mg per day in a single dose. Long-term opioid therapy for chronic pain or heroin dependence is a contraindication for naltrexone because the drug could precipitate severe withdrawal syndrome. Naltrexone has been shown to have dose-related hepatotoxicity, although generally this occurs at doses higher than those recommended for treatment of alcohol dependence. The drug also is contraindicated in patients with hepatitis or liver failure, and all patients should have hepatic transaminase levels checked monthly for the first three months and every three months thereafter.[8]

Naltrexone generally is well tolerated; nausea is the most common adverse effect (reported by 10 percent of patients), followed by headache, anxiety, and sedation.[9] Naltrexone is FDA pregnancy category C. Good compliance is considered essential for successful treatment.

Disulfiram

Disulfiram inhibits acetaldehyde dehydrogenase. Although it has been used to treat alcohol dependence for more than 40 years, the evidence for its effectiveness is weak. An evidence report from the Agency for Healthcare Research and Quality[6] concluded that studies using the disulfiram implant display serious methodologic weaknesses (most substantively, regarding the question of bioavailability), and that the four placebo-controlled RCTs using oral disulfiram produced mixed results. Although in two trials oral disulfiram was shown to reduce frequency of drinking days, it did not improve relapse rates compared with placebo. Two studies noted patient compliance with oral disulfiram and showed it to be low, and a third study had a 46 percent dropout rate. These methodologic limitations and mixed results make it difficult to state clearly how many patients benefit from disulfiram.

Disulfiram usually is given in a dosage of 250 mg per day with a maximum dosage of 500 mg per day. Consuming alcohol after taking disulfiram results in symptoms such as palpitations, flushing, nausea, vomiting, and headache. More severe reactions could include myocardial infarction, congestive heart failure, respiratory depression, and death. Because of the potential for a severe alcohol-disulfiram interaction, disulfiram is contraindicated in patients who are receiving or have recently received metronidazole or ingested alcohol, have psychosis, or have cardiovascular disease, and is not recommended for patients with severe pulmonary disease, chronic renal failure, or diabetes, or those older than 60 years. It also is not recommended in patients with peripheral neuropathy, seizures, or cirrhosis with portal hypertension. Hepatotoxicity is a rare but potentially fatal adverse effect.[8] Some experts recommend that baseline liver function tests

Table 67.1. Medications for Treatment of Alcohol Dependence

Medication:	Acamprosate (Campral)
FDA approved?	Yes
Dosage:	333-mg enteric coated tablets; Adults > 132 lbs (60 kg): two tablets three times per day; Adults < 132 lbs: two tablets with the morning meal, one with the midday meal, and one with the evening meal
Side effects:	Diarrhea, headache, flatulence, nausea, vomiting, dyspepsia
Contraindications*:	Severe renal impairment (creatinine clearance < 30 mL per minute [0.5 mL per second])
Comments:	To avoid adverse gastrointestinal effects, initial dosing usually is at one half the given dosages with an increase of one tablet to the daily dosage each week.
Cost**:	$25
Medication:	Disulfiram (Antabuse)
FDA approved?	Yes
Dosage:	Begin with 250 mg once per day; increase to 500 mg once per day.
Side effects:	Disulfiram-alcohol interaction: palpitations, flushing, nausea, vomiting, headache
Contraindications*:	Alcohol, metronidazole (Flagyl), or paraldehyde use; psychosis; cardiovascular disease
Comments:	Initiate only after patient has abstained from alcohol for at least 12 hours. Not generally recommended for treating alcohol dependence in the primary care setting. Patient should carry an identification card describing the disulfiram-alcohol interaction. Monitor liver function tests for hepatotoxicity.
Cost**:	$42
Medication:	Fluoxetine (Prozac)
FDA approved?	No
Dosage:	Begin with 20 mg per day; may increase to 60 mg per day as needed.
Side effects:	Nausea, headache, sedation, anxiety, sexual dysfunction
Contraindications*:	Use of an MAOI, mesoridazine (Serentil), or thioridazine (Mellaril)
Comments:	Recommended only in patients with comorbid depression
Cost**:	$127 (79 to 89 generic)

Medications for Treating Alcohol Dependence

Medication:	Nalmefene (Revex)
FDA approved?	No
Dosage:	Available only in an injectable form (outside of research) to treat opiate overdose.
Side effects:	Nausea, tachycardia, vasodilation, dizziness, headache, chills, vomiting
Contraindications*:	None
Cost**:	$62 (for 2 mL [2 mg])
Medication:	Naltrexone (Trexan)
FDA approved?	Yes
Dosage:	50 mg once per day
Side effects:	Nausea, headache, anxiety, sedation
Contraindications*:	Narcotic use, acute opioid withdrawal, acute hepatitis, liver failure
Comments:	Monitor liver function tests for hepatotoxicity.
Cost**:	$205 (128 to 137 generic)
Medication:	Ondansetron (Zofran)
FDA approved?	No
Dosage:	4 mcg per kg twice per day
Side effects:	Malaise, fatigue, headache, dizziness, anxiety
Contraindications*:	None
Cost**:	$661 (for 4 mg daily)
Medication:	Topiramate (Topamax)
FDA approved?	No
Dosage:	Begin with 25 mg morning dose and increase to a total of 300 mg given twice a day in divided doses.
Side effects:	Recent FDA warning of metabolic acidosis, especially with renal or liver disease. Dizziness, somnolence, ataxia, impaired concentration, confusion, fatigue, paresthesias, speech difficulties, diplopia, nausea
Contraindications*:	None
Comments:	Consider interactions with other anticonvulsant drugs.
Cost**:	$53

Notes: FDA = U.S. Food and Drug Administration; MAOI = monoamine oxidase inhibitor. *Other than hypersensitivity to the drug, which is a contraindication for all medications listed. **Estimated cost to the pharmacist based on average wholesale prices (rounded to the nearest dollar) in *Red Book*. Montvale, N.J.: Medical Economics Data, 2005. Cost to the patient will be higher, depending on prescription filling fee. Information from references 3 and 4.

should be obtained, with repeat testing at two weeks, three months, six months, and then every six months thereafter. Because of these significant restrictions and problems with compliance, disulfiram is not recommended for treating alcohol dependence, particularly in the primary care setting.[6] Disulfiram is FDA pregnancy category C.

Acamprosate

Acamprosate (calcium homotaurinate) is believed to block gluta-minergic N-methyl-d-aspartate receptors and activate g-aminobutyric acid type A receptors, and was recently approved by the FDA for the treatment of alcohol dependence. A systematic review[10] of 15 studies showed that acamprosate reduces short-term and long-term (more than six months) relapse rates in patients with alcohol dependence when combined with psychosocial treatments. Outcomes in favor of acamprosate included fewer patients returning to drinking (68 versus 80 percent, NNT = 8) and higher percentage of days of total abstinence (54 versus 38 percent, NNT = 7).[10]

Acamprosate is available in 333-mg enteric, coated tablets; dosing is by weight. It is well tolerated with limited side effects, most commonly transient diarrhea (occurring in approximately 10 percent of patients). There are no interactions with concomitant use of alcohol, diazepam (Valium), disulfiram, or imipramine (Tofranil), so patients with alcohol dependence can continue to use acamprosate during a relapse. Patients with renal insufficiency or advanced cirrhosis should not take acamprosate, but it may be taken safely by patients with liver dysfunction.[11] Like naltrexone and disulfiram, acamprosate is FDA pregnancy category C (adverse effects on the fetus in animal studies but no human trials).

Serotonergic Agents

Research into the use of selective serotonin reuptake inhibitors (SSRIs) to treat patients with alcohol dependence has been under way for the past decade; however, most of this work has used small samples and inconsistent outcome measures. One clinical trial[12] of 101 patients showed that fluoxetine (Prozac) at a dosage of up to 60 mg per day had no significant effect on alcohol consumption in persons who were alcohol dependent without major depression. In a study[13] involving psychiatric patients with major depression and alcohol dependence, those treated with 20 to 40 mg per day of fluoxetine over 12 weeks had fewer drinks, fewer drinking days, and fewer heavy drinking days than those receiving placebo. Other SSRIs have shown similar results.[14] Studies on the effect of SSRIs in patients with more severe alcohol dependence (Type B according to the classification system by Babor and colleagues[15]) show no clear benefit and sometimes show trends toward worse outcomes with SSRIs,[16] and studies involving patients with less severe alcohol dependence (Babor Type A[15]) show no consistent benefit.[17]

The use of selective serotonin antagonists for early-onset alcohol dependence also has been investigated, with positive results. In one RCT,[3] ondansetron (Zofran) was shown to significantly reduce self-reported drinking. Patients who received ondansetron 4 mcg per kg twice per day had fewer drinks per day. They also had a greater percentage of days of abstinence (70 versus 50 percent with placebo) and a greater total number of days abstinent per study week (6.7 versus 5.9 with placebo) in patients with early-onset alcoholism. All patients also received weekly group cognitive behavior therapy.

Serotonergic agents generally are well tolerated.[18] Nausea, headache, sedation, and sexual dysfunction are among the most commonly reported adverse effects. The most significant drug interactions for SSRIs are with monoamine oxidase inhibitors, warfarin (Coumadin), some antipsychotics, tetracyclic antidepressants, some benzodiazepines, St. John's wort, and phenytoin (Dilantin).[18]

Anticonvulsants

Recent research suggests a role for anticonvulsants in the treatment of alcohol dependence beyond their use in withdrawal syndromes.[4] Topiramate (Topamax) inhibits mesocorticolimbic dopamine release, which is believed to be associated with craving for alcohol. It is the best-studied drug in this class, although gabapentin (Neurontin)[19] and valproate (Depacon)[20] have shown some promise in case studies and small trials.

In a 12-week double-blind RCT[4] of actively drinking patients with alcohol dependence, topiramate was more effective than placebo in initiating abstinence (26 percent more abstinent days with topiramate) and in reducing self-reported drinks per day, drinks per drinking day, and heavy drinking days. Compared with placebo, it also significantly reduced craving as measured on an obsessive-compulsive-drinking scale. These findings occurred in patients with early-onset and late-onset alcoholism.

The study[4] used an escalating dose of 25 to 300 mg of topiramate per day. Hypersensitivity to the drug is the only known contraindication.

Adverse effects include dizziness and somnolence (which are not dose related), ataxia, impaired concentration, confusion, fatigue, paresthesias, speech difficulties, diplopia, and nausea. Interactions exist between topiramate and other anticonvulsants, including phenytoin, valproic acid (Depakene), and carbamazepine (Tegretol).

Nalmefene

Nalmefene (Revex), another opioid antagonist, is similar to naltrexone but without FDA approval for treatment of alcohol dependence. Nalmefene at dosages of 20 or 80 mg orally per day has been shown in one RCT[21] to significantly reduce relapse to heavy drinking in outpatients with alcohol dependence. Patients receiving nalmefene had a 37 percent relapse rate compared with 59 percent in the placebo group. However, treatment groups did not differ significantly in the percentage of days abstinent, in the mean number of drinks consumed in a drinking day, or in self-reported craving ratings. This 12-week study[21] also provided weekly cognitive behavior therapy to all groups. Outside of research, nalmefene is available only in an injectable form.

Final Comments

The best choices for prevention of relapse are acamprosate and naltrexone with concurrent counseling through professional or self-help programs. Family physicians also may consider the use of an SSRI in the presence of a comorbid mood disorder. Evidence is lacking for combination pharmacotherapy, but research is under way. Topiramate and ondansetron show promise as treatments to increase abstinence. Because of its lack of effectiveness and problems with adverse effects and compliance, disulfiram is not recommended in the primary care setting.

About the Author

Steven H. Williams, Ph.D., is former director of behavioral medicine at the Harrisburg (Pennsylvania) Family Practice Residency Program and currently is a clinical psychologist with the Psychology Service at the Veterans Affairs Medical Center in Lebanon, Pennsylvania. Dr. Williams received a doctoral degree in counseling psychology from the University of Florida, Gainesville, and a postdoctoral certification in psychopharmacology from Fairleigh Dickinson University, Teaneck, New Jersey.

References

1. Harwood HJ. Updating estimates of the economic costs of alcohol abuse in the United States: estimates, update methods, and data. Bethesda, MD.: U.S. Department of Health and Human Services; National Institute on Alcohol Abuse and Alcoholism, 2000.

2. Beich A, Thorsen T, Rollnick S. Screening in brief intervention trials targeting excessive drinkers in general practice: systematic review and meta-analysis. *BMJ* 2003;327:536–42.

3. Johnson BA, Roache JD, Javors MA, DiClemente CC, Cloninger CR, Prihoda TJ, et al. Ondansetron for reduction of drinking among biologically predisposed alcoholic patients: a randomized controlled trial. *JAMA* 2000;284:963–71.

4. Johnson BA, Ait-Daoud N, Bowden CL, DiClemente CC, Roache JD, Lawson K, et al. Oral topiramate for treatment of alcohol dependence: a randomised controlled trial. *Lancet* 2003;361: 1677–85.

5. Srisurapanont M, Jarusuraisin N. Opioid antagonists for alcohol dependence. *Cochrane Database Syst Rev*;(1):CD001867.

6. West SL, Garbutt JC, Carey TS, Lux LJ, Jackman AM, Tolleson-Rinehart S, et al. Pharmacotherapy for alcohol dependence. Rockville, MD.: U.S. Department of Health and Human Services; Public Health Service; Agency for Health Care Policy and Research, 1999.

7. Krystal JH, Cramer JA, Krol WF, Kirk GF, Rosenheck RA. Naltrexone in the treatment of alcohol dependence. *N Engl J Med* 2001;345:1734–9.

8. Doering PL. Substance-related disorders: alcohol, nicotine, and caffeine. In: DiPiro JT, Talbert RL, Yee GC, Matzke GR, Wells BG, Posey LM, eds. *Pharmacotherapy: a pathophysiologic approach.* 4th ed. Stamford, Conn.: Appleton & Lange, 1999.

9. Croop RS, Faulkner EB, Labriola DF. The safety profile of naltrexone in the treatment of alcoholism: results from a multicenter usage study. *Arch Gen Psychiatry* 1997;54:1130–5.

10. Mason BJ. Treatment of alcohol-dependent outpatients with acamprosate: a clinical review. *J Clin Psychiatry* 2001;62 (suppl 20):42–8.

11. Graham R, Wodak AD, Whelan G. New pharmacotherapies for alcohol dependence. *MJA* 2002;177:103–7.

12. Kranzler HR, Burleson JA, Korner P, Del Boca FK, Bohn MJ, Brown J, et al. Placebo-controlled trial of fluoxetine as an adjunct to relapse prevention in alcoholics. *Am J Psychiatry* 1995;152:391–7.

13. Cornelius JR, Salloum IM, Ehler JG, Jarrett PJ, Cornelius MD, Perel JM, et al. Fluoxetine in depressed alcoholics: a double-blind, placebo-controlled trial. *Arch Gen Psychiatry* 1997;54:700–5.

14. Naranjo CA, Knoke DM. The role of selective serotonin reuptake inhibitors in reducing alcohol consumption. *J Clin Psychiatry* 2001;62(suppl 20):18–25.

15. Babor TF, Dolinsky ZS, Meyer RE, Hesselbrock M, Hofmann M, Tennen H. Types of alcoholics: concurrent and predictive validity of some common classification schemes. *Br J Addict* 1992;87:1415–31.

16. Kranzler HR, Burleson JA, Brown J, Babor TF. Fluoxetine treatment seems to reduce the beneficial effects of cognitive-behavioral therapy in type B alcoholics. *Alcohol Clin Exp Res* 1996;20:1534–41.

17. Pettinati HM, Volpicelli JR, Kranzler HR, Luck G, Rukstalis MR, Cnaan A. Sertraline treatment for alcohol dependence: interactive effects of medication and subtype. *Alcohol Clin Exp Res* 2000;24:1041–9.

18. Bezchlibnyk-Butler KZ, Jeffries JJ, Martin BA. *Clinical handbook of psychotropic drugs.* 10th ed. Seattle: Hogrefe & Huber, 2000.

19. Chatterjee CR, Ringold AL. A case report of reduction in alcohol craving and protection against alcohol withdrawal by gabapentin. *J Clin Psychiatry* 1999;60:617.

20. Brady KT, Myrick H, Henderson S, Coffey SF. The use of divalproex in alcohol relapse prevention: a pilot study. *Drug Alcohol Depend* 2002;67:323–30.

21. Mason BJ, Salvato FR, Williams LD, Ritvo EC, Cutler RB. A double-blind, placebo-controlled study of oral nalmefene for alcohol dependence. *Arch Gen Psychiatry* 1999;56:719–24.

Chapter 68

The Secret of the Twelve Steps: Spirituality's Role in Substance Abuse Prevention and Treatment

Seven of the 12 steps at the heart of Alcoholics Anonymous feature spirituality. For example, participants surrender their will to a higher power, use prayer and meditation to improve their relationship with him, and seek spiritual awakening.

Over the years, researchers have confirmed an association between this kind of spirituality and positive outcomes in alcoholism and substance abuse treatment. Now psychologists and others are trying to figure out what's behind that association—research that's especially timely given the Bush administration's creation of a $600 million voucher program that could allow federal dollars to support faith-based treatment.

Exemplifying the new research interest is a series of exploratory grants given by the National Institute on Alcohol Abuse and Alcoholism (NIAAA) and the Fetzer Institute in 2000. Thanks to these grants and other initiatives, psychologists are finding that spirituality can play a role—sometimes more indirect than once thought—in preventing and treating alcoholism and substance abuse in vulnerable populations such as adolescents and minorities.

"A lot of the research in the past has just been correlative," says psychologist Thomas R. Gentry, Ph.D., a health science administrator at NIAAA, noting that confounding variables and self-selection biases have marred many studies. "To simply say the more often you

Clay, R. (2003). The secret of the 12 steps. *Monitor on Psychology, 34,* p. 50. Copyright © 2003 by the American Psychological Association. Reprinted with permission from the author and the American Psychological Association.

go to a religious service, the less likely you are to be an alcoholic doesn't provide a whole lot of information a clinician can use. We're trying to figure out what part of the spiritual or religious experience is important."

Prevention

Much of the new research focuses on how spirituality or religiosity could help prevent alcoholism and substance abuse in adolescents.

For example, Kathy Goggin, Ph.D., associate professor of psychology at the University of Missouri in Kansas City, says she was pushed into studying spirituality by the very adolescents she studies.

As part of an ongoing study of substance use and sexual risk behavior among urban African-American adolescents, conducted with her co-investigator Vanessa Malcarne, PhD, of San Diego State University, she asked her subjects whether she was asking the right questions.

"They kept saying, 'You're missing God,'" says Goggin, who received a NIAAA/Fetzer grant. "That scared us, since how to measure that has been a problem."

Goggin solved the problem by developing the Alcohol-Related God Locus of Control Scale, which measures whether adolescents believe God controls their drinking behavior. In a not-yet-published study, she used the scale to discover that the more adolescents believe that God plays a role in their lives, the less likely they are to drink.

Although the findings need to be replicated in other populations, Goggin says they have implications for prevention efforts.

"The one-size-fits-all approach to prevention has kept us from thinking about individual differences," she says. "For kids who believe God plays a role in their lives, it may be particularly helpful to incorporate that into prevention messages."

Research by psychologist Thomas Ashby Wills, Ph.D., a professor of epidemiology and population health at Albert Einstein College of Medicine in the Bronx, backs up the finding that spiritual or religious beliefs can be protective.

"With notable consistency, almost everyone who's ever studied religiosity has found it to be a protective factor for adolescents," says Wills, whose work is supported by NIAAA/Fetzer and also by the National Institute on Drug Abuse. "What's not well known is why it's a protective factor and how it works."

Wills thought that one traditional measure of religiosity—congregation membership—was too simple. "There are a lot of people who belong to a church, for instance, but don't go very often," he points out. Instead, Wills used a scale that determines how important religion is to people.

In a study published in *Psychology of Addictive Behaviors* (Vol. 17, No. 1), he administered the scale to a multi-ethnic sample of 1,182 kids in metropolitan New York. In another study, he administered a similar measure to African-American adolescents in rural Iowa and Georgia.

What he found counters the conventional wisdom that adherence to doctrinal do's and don'ts explains religiosity's protective effect. He found that religiosity keeps kids from smoking, drinking, and using marijuana by buffering the impact of life stresses. Religiosity was especially beneficial for kids facing stressful situations, such as illness or an unemployed parent. However, it's not just adolescents' religiosity that helps prevent drinking and drug use. Gene H. Brody, Ph.D., Distinguished Research Professor of Child and Family Development at the University of Georgia in Athens, has found that parental religiosity also plays a role.

In studies published in *Developmental Psychology* (Vol. 32, No. 4), *Child Development* (Vol. 69, No. 3), and the *Journal of Marriage and the Family* (Vol. 56, No. 4), Brody found that African-American parents in the rural South who were more involved in church were more likely to have harmonious marital relationships and better parenting skills. That, in turn, promoted kids' competence, self-regulation, psychological adjustment, and school performance—all factors that keep kids from turning to alcohol and drugs.

"Imagine a series of steps," says Brody. "Religiosity works indirectly through family relationships to promote the factors that protect kids."

Treatment

Other psychologists are focusing on spirituality's role in treating alcoholism and substance abuse, especially among minorities. J. Scott Tonigan, PhD, research professor of psychology at the University of New Mexico in Albuquerque and another of the NIAAA/Fetzer grantees, rejects the common idea that spirituality and religiosity have a direct impact on treatment outcomes. Most of those studies that reach that conclusion are cross-sectional and thus suspect, he notes, and any effect they find is so small it's clinically irrelevant.

Like Brody, Tonigan has found that spirituality affects treatment outcomes indirectly. In a 10-year follow-up of 226 clients—a majority of whom became members of Alcoholics Anonymous—participating in a large NIAAA-funded trial called Project MATCH (Matching Alcoholism

Treatments to Client Heterogeneity), published in *Alcoholism: Clinical and Experimental Research* (Vol. 26, No. 5), Tonigan found that increases in spirituality predicted behaviors such as honesty and responsibility. Those behaviors, in turn, promoted abstinence from alcohol. "Spirituality is one of those variables that's really in the background," says Tonigan.

That's not to say that background effect isn't important. In another study published in the *Journal of Studies on Alcohol* (Vol. 59, No. 3), Tonigan found that spirituality allows Hispanics to derive just as much benefit from Alcoholics Anonymous as their white counterparts despite being less engaged in the program. According to Tonigan, this paradoxical finding is related to a deeper religious faith that makes Hispanics more comfortable with spiritually based programs.

And alcoholics and substance abusers themselves often feel spirituality plays a key role in recovery, say psychologists.

Many Alaska Natives, for example, believe that alienation from their spiritual heritage contributes to their community's high alcoholism rates and that reconnection to those roots helps them on their path to sobriety, says Kelly L. Hazel, Ph.D., an associate professor of psychology at Metropolitan State University in Minneapolis, Minnesota.

Although those beliefs haven't been confirmed by science, Hazel and former colleagues at the University of Alaska in Fairbanks have done research suggesting that spirituality can indeed play a role in prevention and treatment.

In one not-yet-published study, they interviewed more than 100 Alaska Natives who had been sober for at least five years, or who had never had drinking problems, with the hope of identifying protective factors. For many, spiritual reawakenings were the impetus for getting sober, and reconnecting with their spirituality—often a hybrid of native and Western traditions—helped them on their way.

"Leaders in the native sobriety movement had asked us, 'Why does the research always focus on the problems? Why doesn't it focus on the strengths?' " recalls Hazel. "Spirituality is clearly one of those strengths."

—Rebecca A. Clay is a writer in Washington, D.C.

Chapter 69

Alternative and Complementary Medicine Treatments for Alcoholics

Alcoholism is a chronic, often progressive disease in which a person continues to crave alcohol and drink despite repeated alcohol-related problems (like losing a job or getting into trouble with the law). Approximately 18 million people in the United States abuse alcohol. Teen drinking is on the rise with over 4 million adolescents between the ages of 14 and 17 having trouble at school, at home, or even with the law because of alcohol use. This disease contributes to more than 50 percent of car and industrial fatalities, drownings, and child or domestic abuse.

Treatment Approach

The first and most important step in getting appropriate treatment for alcoholism is recognizing that you have a problem. Often, family members and close friends initiate treatment for the person with the addiction.

Treatment must address both existing medical issues and rehabilitation, such as motivational techniques for abstaining from drinking, psychotherapy, and Alcoholics Anonymous (or other support groups). For rehabilitation, referred to as "recovery" or staying sober, there are both outpatient and inpatient programs available. Talk to a health care provider about what is best for you or your loved one.

Excerpted from "Alcoholism" © 2006 A.D.A.M., Inc. Reprinted with permission.

Lifestyle

- Attend Alcoholics Anonymous.
- Family members should attend Al Anon to learn how best to help the person with the addiction and to get help and support themselves.
- Exercise regularly to help reduce cravings.
- Quit smoking.

Nutrition and Dietary Supplements

A well-balanced, nutritionally adequate diet can help stabilize fluctuations in blood sugar due to alcohol and decrease cravings. Follow these tips and work with a nutritionist to evaluate if these steps are helping:

- Eliminate simple sugars.
- Increase complex carbohydrates.
- Consume adequate protein.
- Increase essential fatty acids.
- Decrease saturated fats and fried foods.
- Avoid caffeine.

Because chronic use of alcohol decreases your appetite and interferes with absorption of vital nutrients, taking supplements may be necessary. Potentially beneficial supplements include vitamin B complex, vitamin C, selenium, magnesium, and zinc. A combination of amino acids—namely, carnitine, glutamine, and glutathione—may help reduce cravings, blood sugar fluctuations, and stress related to alcohol use.

Thiamine (vitamin B1) is of particular importance if you drink heavy amounts of alcohol on a regular basis. Thiamine deficiency can lead to a brain disorder called Wernicke-Korsakoff syndrome. Replacing thiamine alleviates the symptoms of this syndrome. Wernicke-Korsakoff is actually two disorders in one: (1) Wernicke's disease which involves damage to nerves in the central and peripheral nervous systems and is generally caused by malnutrition associated with habitual alcohol abuse, and (2) Korsakoff syndrome which is characterized by memory impairment along with symptoms of nerve damage. High doses of thiamine can improve confusion and muscle coordination and confusion associated with this disease, but only rarely improves the memory loss.

Gamma-Aminobutyric Acid (GABA)

Brown rice extracts rich in GABA seem to protect animals from the liver-damaging effects of alcohol. Whether this same benefit would be safe or effective in people requires research.

Herbs

The use of herbs is a time-honored approach to strengthening the body and treating disease. Herbs, however, contain active substances that can trigger side effects and interact with other herbs, supplements, or medications. For these reasons, herbs should be taken with care and only under the supervision of a practitioner knowledgeable in the field of herbal medicine.

Evening Primrose (Oenothera biennis)

Although more conclusive research is needed, there is some evidence to suggest that this herb may lessen cravings for alcohol. Evening primrose is often used as an oil extracted from the seed of this herb. This is commonly called EPO. The main active ingredient of EPO is gamma-linolenic acid (GLA), an omega-6 fatty acid that can also be found in borage and black currant oils.

Ginseng

American and Asian ginseng (*Panax quinquefolium* and *Panax ginseng* respectively) may help treat alcohol intoxication because each of these herbs speed up the metabolism (break down) of alcohol. Faster break down clears alcohol from your body more quickly. In addition, animal research suggests that Asian ginseng may reduce the amount of alcohol that is absorbed from the stomach.

Milk Thistle (Silybum marianum)

Some studies evaluating milk thistle for the treatment of alcoholic liver disease have found significant improvements in liver function with use of this herb. People with the mildest form of alcohol-related liver damage seem to improve the most. Milk thistle is less effective for those with severe liver disease such as cirrhosis. (Cirrhosis is characterized by scarring and permanent, non-reversible damage to the liver. It is often referred to as end-stage liver disease.)

St. John's Wort (**Hypericum perforatum**)

Those with depression and alcoholism share certain similarities in brain chemical activity. In addition, some people (especially men) who are depressed may mask their feelings or try to cope with their low mood by drinking alcohol. For these reasons, researchers have considered whether St. John's Wort, often used to treat depression, may help reduce alcohol consumption. Animal studies suggest that this may prove to be an appropriate use of this herb. St. John's Wort interacts with many different medications. It is particularly important, therefore, that you check with your doctor before using.

Others

Additional herbs that an herbal specialist might consider to support you while undergoing treatment for alcoholism include:

- **Dandelion** *(Taraxacum officinale)*: Traditionally used for liver-related problems and as a nutritional support because it is rich in vitamins and minerals. Tends to work well with milk thistle.

- **Skullcap** *(Scutellaria lateriflora)*: Traditionally used for tension and anxiety, this herb may help ease the withdrawal process.

Homeopathy

There have been few studies examining the effectiveness of specific homeopathic remedies. Professional homeopaths, however, may recommend a treatment for alcoholism based on their knowledge and clinical experience. Before prescribing a remedy, homeopaths take into account a person's constitutional type. In homeopathic terms, a person's constitution is his or her physical, emotional, and intellectual makeup. An experienced homeopath assesses all of these factors when determining the most appropriate remedy for a particular individual. The following are a few examples of remedies that an experienced homeopath might consider for symptoms related to alcohol abuse or withdrawal:

- *Arsenicum album* for anxiety and compulsiveness, with nausea, vomiting, and diarrhea

- *Nux vomica* for irritability and compulsiveness with constipation, nausea, and vomiting

- *Lachesis* for cravings for alcohol, headaches, and difficulty swallowing

- *Staphysagria* for angry individuals who tend to suppress their emotions and may have been abused physically, sexually, or psychologically in the past

Mind/Body Medicine

Cognitive-behavioral therapy with a psychologist or psychiatrist is a very effective treatment approach for alcohol addiction. This type of therapy, which is geared toward restructuring your beliefs and thought process about drinking, can help you cope with stress and control your behavior. Talk to your health care provider about finding a qualified cognitive-behavioral therapist.

Acupuncture

Acupuncture has shown potential as an effective treatment for addiction, according to a 1997 Consensus Statement by the National Institutes of Health. While some but not all studies of acupuncture for the treatment of alcohol abuse have shown benefit, many addiction programs that currently offer acupuncture report that people appear to "like acupuncture" and, in many cases, want to continue with their detox program for longer periods of time when acupuncture is provided as a treatment option. This is very important since attendance is essential for the success of treatment.

Acupuncturists treat people with alcoholism based on an individualized assessment of the excesses and deficiencies of qi located in various meridians. In the case of alcoholism, a qi deficiency is usually detected in the liver meridian, while the gallbladder meridian tends to contain excess qi. In addition to performing needling treatment, acupuncturists may employ other methods such as moxibustion (a technique in which the herb mugwort is burned over specific acupuncture points). Although not all studies agree, auricular acupuncture may be particularly beneficial.

Traditional Chinese Medicine

Kudzu **(Pueraria lobata)**

Although a modern day scientific study suggests that this Chinese herb does not reduce cravings for alcohol or improve one's chances of staying sober, traditional use does include treatment of alcoholism. This one study was quite small; therefore, this traditional use of kudzu requires more thorough research to determine whether it is safe and effective or not.

Chapter 70

Improving Access to Treatment for People with Alcohol Use Disorders

Alcohol and drug problems seep into our communities and surface in the criminal justice system, child welfare system, family and social services agencies, and faith-based and community organizations. Systems of care work to combat and prevent alcohol and drug use disorders on a national, state, and local level, wherever they surface.

Alcohol and drug use disorders—which are defined as misuse, dependence, or addiction to alcohol and/or legal or illegal drugs—affect everyone, from teens and parents to colleagues and neighbors. According to the U.S. Substance Abuse and Mental Health Administration's 2002 National Survey on Drug Use and Health, an estimated 22 million Americans age 12 or older were considered to have an alcohol or drug use disorder. Among youths ages 12 to 17, an estimated 11.6 million were illicit drug users. Research shows the enormous impact of the problem on society:

- Children whose families do not receive appropriate treatment for alcohol and drug use disorders tend to remain in foster care longer than other children and are more likely than other foster children to re-enter foster care once they have returned home. Their siblings also are more likely than other children to end up in foster care.

Excerpted from "Supporting and Integrating Systems of Care," a publication by the National Institute on Alcohol Abuse and Alcoholism (NIAAA) and the Substance Abuse and Mental Health Services Administration, 2004. For a complete list of references, see www.recoverymonth.gov.

- The social cost of alcohol and drug use in the United States is staggering, estimated at more than $294 billion in 1997.

Through federal grants to states for treatment and prevention services, and through programs such as Medicaid, which provides financial assistance for medical care to individuals and families with low incomes, federal and state agencies allocate resources among systems of care to help people who need treatment. But with nearly 10 percent of the population requiring treatment for alcohol or drug problems, mobilization at the local level—including involvement from community organizations and churches—is needed to help more people with alcohol and drug use disorders and their families get the assistance they need.

This chapter examines the various federal, state, and community systems of care, the challenges they face, the benefits of increasing access to recovery, and the steps you can take to help those in need of treatment.

Justice System

Many people with untreated alcohol and drug use disorders end up in the criminal justice system. Nearly 1.7 million of the 2 million adult Americans in prison or jail are seriously involved with drugs or alcohol. Yet most criminal offenders do not receive help for their alcohol and drug use disorders. Only 14 percent of inmates who had been drinking at the time of their offense had been treated for their alcohol problems since they were admitted to prison, and about one in seven prisoners who had used drugs in the month before their offense were treated for their drug problems since their admission. Additionally, up to three fourths of parolees who leave prison without drug treatment for their cocaine or heroin addictions resume drug use within three months of release.

But there are reforms in place to improve this situation and increase access to treatment. Since 1996, more than 150 drug reform laws and ballot measures have been passed at the state level to treat alcohol and drug use disorders with a focus on treatment, rather than as a punishable crime. Voters in 17 states have approved drug reform ballot measures, often to provide treatment rather than incarceration for drug offenders, and 46 states have passed laws to reduce sentences and provide treatment for drug offenders.

However, alcohol and drug use disorders are rarely the only problems an offender faces. Drug courts report that many participants suffer from co-occurring disorders (a combination of alcohol and drug use disorders and mental disorders, which refers to any mental or emotional disorder, including eating, anxiety, mood, and depression disorders, bipolar disorders, and schizophrenia). In fact, 61 percent of drug courts report screening for mental problems.

A successful treatment program must include a comprehensive recovery support system to meet the social, physical, and mental health needs of the individual. For example, among juvenile offenders, treatment options that show the best evidence of effectiveness are behavioral therapies, intensive case management, cognitive-behavioral skills training, family-oriented therapies, and multi-systemic therapy. Research has found that effective treatment saves money, reduces crime, and lowers relapse and recidivism rates. For example, alcohol and drug use disorder treatment cuts drug use in half, reduces criminal activity up to 80 percent, and reduces arrests up to 64 percent.

Child Welfare System

One of the greatest consequences of untreated alcohol and drug use disorders is the negative impact on children—many of whom come to the attention of the child welfare system. Problems with alcohol and drug use disorders are estimated to exist in up to 80 percent of families in the child welfare system. Drug and alcohol problems have an impact on children of all social, economic, and racial groups—but children from families with scant financial and emotional resources are the most severely affected.

Unfortunately, the complex problems faced by families with alcohol and drug use disorders are likely to require intervention beyond what the child welfare system can offer. A 1997 study by the Child Welfare League of America found that state child welfare agencies were only able to provide alcohol and drug use disorder treatment for one third of families who needed it, and the wait for treatment services was up to 12 months. In the interim, according to the National Association for Children of Alcoholics, age-appropriate services should be sought for the children of parents with alcohol and drug use disorders, because a child's brain and emotional development continues regardless of the parent's stage of recovery. Age-appropriate services can be found via educational support groups offered by local schools, faith communities, youth organizations, child welfare agencies, and treatment centers.

Collaborative model programs, including partnerships with community-based family and social services, are showing signs of success because they offer the adequate, integrated treatment and recovery services required for families in need.

Family and Social Services

Evidence from various national studies suggests that families with drug and alcohol problems who are involved in the child welfare system require access to a comprehensive array of services and supports to achieve long-term abstinence from drugs and alcohol, including access to housing, transportation, therapy (including family and trauma recovery services), and child care. In addition, personalized services directed to the individual, their children, and other family members are essential for the recovery of the entire family.

One successful and cost-effective innovation is the use of family drug treatment courts that provide timely and coordinated access to treatment and support services for families. This coordination reduces the trauma that families experience when faced with multiple systems, policies, and competing timelines.

Additionally, "unified family courts" combine all the elements and resources of traditional juvenile and family courts. Within these courts, families can access social services, dispute resolution assistance, and counseling. Such systems can better address the needs of children and families, and minimize the reliance on traditional court procedures, often avoiding costly trials and other direct judicial intervention.

Faith-Based and Community Organizations

Community and faith-based approaches are a key component of building resilience against alcohol and drug use disorders and facilitating recovery. With the help of faith-based and community organizations, people with alcohol and drug use disorders can access treatment and get the support they need.

Faith-based and community organizations can create support systems that successfully guide people through treatment and recovery because they can address the various needs of their constituents. For example:

- Six out of 10 Americans say that religious faith is the most important influence in their lives; for eight out of 10, religious beliefs provide comfort and support.

- Positive peer affiliations, bonding with and involvement in school and after-school activities, relationships with caring adults, opportunities for school success and responsible behavior, and the availability of drug-free activities all have been cited as factors that help students resist drugs.

In particular, the African-American church has a historical role in addressing social and political issues of the community. Equipped with education and training about alcohol and drug use disorders, these churches are in an ideal position to better identify strategies to address these problems within the context of African-American spirituality. Organizations such as African American Family Services provide education and awareness about alcohol and drug use disorders to churches, schools, and community groups.

Making a Difference: What Can I Do?

Reach out to families. Children, spouses, siblings, and parents of people with alcohol and drug use disorders are frequently in need of education and support and may require referrals that can help them understand the recovery process. Family members may need to be directed to social services and counseling professionals to address multiple issues and problems, such as family dynamics and communication in stressful relationships; children's attendance, performance, and behavior in school; and/or economic needs.

Integrate and use all available services. Professionals in the child welfare and criminal and juvenile justice systems should work closely with alcohol and drug use disorder and mental health treatment providers, funding agencies, counselors, local health officials, social service organizations, state alcohol and drug agencies, and others in the community to share information, workforce resources, and recovery materials. Developing and cultivating partnerships can extend a program's reach, impact, and credibility.

Focus on prevention with an emphasis on youth. Young people with alcohol and drug use disorders often experience a variety of accompanying problems, including academic difficulties, a decline in physical and mental health, ineffective communication and poor relationships with their families and friends, social and economic consequences, and delinquency. By conducting a comprehensive assessment of a youth when he or she first enters the justice system, juvenile justice professionals can help youth receive early intervention and treatment that will help in their efforts to become free from drug and alcohol problems.

Educate yourself and the community about treatment. Demonstrating to the community that alcohol and drug use disorders are treatable diseases may encourage other community-based organizations to work aggressively for more community programs. This starts with leaders who truly understand the disease of alcohol and drug use disorders. Seek out people in recovery in your community who are willing to speak openly about their experiences or contact local support groups or religious organizations for spokespeople who might be willing to educate your leaders.

Work with existing channels in your community. Community organizations can work with store owners to enforce a crackdown on alcohol sales to underage youth. You also can support local schools and enlist the help of parents to spread the message that not all children use alcohol or drugs and that treatment is available for those with alcohol and drug use disorders. Most importantly, community organizations and faith communities can support those already working in the treatment field, celebrating the accomplishments of these often hidden heroes.

Create a community anti-drug coalition. Anti-drug coalitions combine existing resources into a single community-wide system of prevention and treatment. These coalitions provide support services and plans for those in need. Each community's coalition will be different due to the available resources and priorities of the community. Information on how to form a coalition and great examples of local coalitions that support community-wide efforts to reduce alcohol and drug use disorders are available from the Community Anti-Drug Coalitions of America (CADCA, www.cadca.org), Join Together (www.join together.org), and the National Commission Against Drunk Driving (NCADD, www.ncadd.com).

Be informed. Make sure your community-based organization and faith community leaders are kept up-to-date on the latest alcohol and drug use disorder and mental health information, such as the newest types of treatments.

Making a Difference: How Can I Raise Awareness within My Community?

Make a public statement. Express your opinion about the importance of alcohol and drug use disorder treatment in the context of the criminal justice or child welfare system by sending an op-ed article—a short written piece that appears opposite the editorial page of a newspaper—to the editor of your local paper. Include relevant statistics, persuasive examples, and a compelling story of a local person in recovery to illustrate the effectiveness of treatment programs.

Spread the word online. Promote your support for alcohol-recovery programs through your organization's website by posting relevant statistics or fact sheet information. Consider linking your site to organizations in your own community.

Form a speakers' bureau. Organize a small group of professionals from one of the systems of care to serve as guest speakers at schools, community events, places of worship, businesses, civic group meetings, and/or other venues to deliver clear messages about the need for effective treatment to help combat alcohol and drug use disorders.

Support existing community efforts. Collaborate with a local alcohol and drug use disorder treatment facility in your community by volunteering time, money, and/or other resources to further the program. You also may consider collaborating with a treatment organization on an event to raise public awareness about alcohol and drug use disorders, treatment, and recovery. For example, reporters could be invited to a press briefing that honors recent drug court graduates or families reunited from the child welfare system (who agree to appear publicly), as well as members of the drug court team and others who have dedicated themselves to helping those in need of treatment.

Be creative. Work with local volunteer performance organizations (e.g., dance troupes, theater companies, choirs) to create shows that help get the message out that alcohol and drug use disorders are treatable diseases. Make sure the show or concert targets both youth and adults, and offer it free to the community. Make information about alcohol and drug use disorder treatment available to those attending. Spokespeople from local treatment centers could hold a question-and-answer session before or after the show. Place advertisements about the upcoming show or concert in your organization's newsletter or church bulletin and in windows of local stores and restaurants.

Integrate your message into activities for the community. Get involved in local sports at the high school or college level. Work with the schools and coaches to educate students on the dangers of steroids and other "performance-enhancing" drugs. Sponsor a night at a local minor league hockey or baseball game and distribute hand-outs with alcohol and drug use disorders information or fun giveaway items, such as key chains or whistles with your organization's name, phone number, and Web site. Help sponsor a run or walk for an alcohol and drug use disorders cause in your community. Donate the money you raise to a local treatment center for new programs, new staff, or a new facility.

Sponsor a health and community fair. If your community does not have a local fair, coordinate one and make it health-focused with education about alcohol and drug use disorders and activities for children. Set up booths for local treatment centers to offer information and speak to their neighbors. Offer treatment materials for those who might be in need. Invite local politicians and celebrities to speak on alcohol and drug use disorder topics. If your community already sponsors a local fair, make sure your organization secures a booth or space.

Part Eight

Additional Help and Information

Chapter 71

Glossary of Terms
Related to Alcoholism

Abstainer: Drinks less than 0.01 fluid ounces of alcohol per day (i.e., fewer than 12 drinks in the past year).

Abstinence: Involves avoiding environmental triggers, recognizing psychosocial and emotional triggers, and developing healthy behaviors to handle life's stresses instead of using substances.

Acetaldehyde: A toxic product that results from the breakdown of alcohol by the enzyme alcohol dehydrogenase.

Acidosis: A condition in which body fluids become too acidic.

Addiction: Uncontrollable craving, seeking, and use of a substance such as a drug or alcohol.

Adenosine triphosphate (ATP): A molecule, generated largely in the mitochondria, that provides the energy needed for many key metabolic reactions.

This glossary contains terms excerpted from glossaries and documents produced by the following government agencies: Centers for Disease Control and Prevention (CDC); National Cancer Institute (NCI); National Heart, Lung, and Blood Institute (NHLBI); National Highway Traffic Safety Administration (NHTSA); National Institute on Alcohol Abuse and Alcoholism (NIAAA); National Institute of Diabetes and Digestive and Kidney Diseases (NIDDK); National Institute on Drug Abuse (NIDA); National Institute of Neurological Disorders and Stroke (NINDS); and the Substance Abuse and Mental Health Services Administration (SAMHSA).

Alanine aminotransferase (ALT)/aspartate aminotransferase (AST): Liver enzymes that indicate excessive alcohol consumption.

Alcohol abuse: Alcohol abuse differs from alcoholism in that it does not include an extremely strong craving for alcohol, loss of control over drinking, or physical dependence. Alcohol abuse is defined as a pattern of drinking that results in one or more of the following situations within a 12-month period: Failure to fulfill major work, school, or home responsibilities; drinking in situations that are physically dangerous, such as while driving a car or operating machinery; having recurring alcohol-related legal problems, such as being arrested for driving under the influence of alcohol or for physically hurting someone while drunk; and continued drinking despite having ongoing relationship problems that are caused or worsened by the drinking.

Alcohol dehydrogenase (ADH): An enzyme that breaks down alcohol by oxidation, converting it to acetaldehyde.

Alcohol ignition interlocks: Breath-testing devices designed to prevent operation of a vehicle if the driver's BAC is above a predetermined low level.

Alcohol poisoning: The result of the acute toxic effects of alcohol consumption, which can range from gastritis and severe gastrointestinal bleeding to respiratory arrest and death.

Alcohol: The colorless, flammable liquid, ethanol, which is the intoxicating agent in whisky, gin, rum, beer, wine coolers, and other fermented or distilled liquors.

Alcoholic cardiomyopathy: Cardiomyopathy is a disease that affects the heart muscle. Because of chronic and excessive use of alcohol, the heart loses its ability to pump blood and in some instances, heart rhythm is disturbed, leading to irregular beats, or arrhythmias.

Alcoholic cirrhosis: When healthy liver cells are replaced by scar tissue (fibrosis), leaving the liver unable to perform its vital functions. Liver cirrhosis is a major cause of death in the United States. In 2000, it was the twelfth leading cause of death.

Alcoholic dementia: Dementia associated with alcoholism consists of global loss of intellectual abilities with an impairment in memory function, together with disturbances of abstract thinking, judgment, other higher cortical functions, or personality change without a clouding of consciousness.

Alcoholic hepatitis: An inflammation of the liver. Symptoms include nausea, lack of appetite, vomiting, fever, abdominal pain and tenderness, jaundice, and, sometimes, mental confusion.

Alcoholic neuropathy: Nerve damage caused by heavy drinking.

Alcoholism: Alcoholism, also known as alcohol dependence, is a disease that includes the following four symptoms: *Craving*—a strong need, or urge, to drink; *loss of control*—not being able to stop drinking once drinking has begun; *physical dependence*—withdrawal symptoms, such as nausea, sweating, shakiness, and anxiety after stopping drinking; and *tolerance*—the need to drink greater amounts of alcohol to get high.

Alkalosis: A condition in which the body fluids become too alkaline.

Allele: Gene variants that alter alcohol metabolism.

Ascites: Accumulation of fluid in the abdomen, one of the most common complications of advanced liver disease. The presence of ascites generally indicates a poor prognosis and high likelihood of death.

Atherosclerosis: A disease of the arteries in which fatty plaques accumulate on the arteries' inner walls, usually leading to narrowing and hardening of the arteries and eventually obstructing blood flow.

Barrett esophagus: A condition in which the esophagus, the muscular tube that carries food and saliva from the mouth to the stomach, changes so that some of its lining is replaced by a type of tissue similar to that normally found in the intestine. This process is called intestinal metaplasia.

Benzodiazepines: Highly addictive medicines to help a person who stops drinking to safely withdraw from alcohol.

Bile: A liquid made by the liver. It contains water, cholesterol, bile salts, fats, proteins, and bilirubin, a bile pigment.

Binge drinking: Drinking five or more drinks on one occasion, meaning in a row or within a short period of time. Among women, binge drinking is often defined as having four or more drinks on one occasion. This lower cut-point is used for women because women are generally of smaller stature than men, and absorb and metabolize alcohol differently than men.

Blood alcohol concentration (BAC): The amount of alcohol in a person's body, which is measured by the weight of the alcohol in a certain volume of blood.

Body mass index (BMI): A number calculated from a person's weight and height. BMI provides a reliable indicator of body fatness for most people and is used to screen for weight categories that may lead to health problems.

Brief intervention: Short, one-on-one counseling sessions that may help people dependent on alcohol. They generally aim to moderate a person's alcohol consumption to sensible levels and to eliminate harmful drinking practices (such as binge drinking), rather than to insist on complete abstinence from drinking—although abstinence may be encouraged, if appropriate.

Carcinogen: Any substance that causes cancer.

Chemotherapy: The use of drugs to kill cancer cells.

Comorbidity: The condition of having two or more diseases at the same time.

Craving: A strong need, or urge, to drink.

Delirium tremens (DTs): DTs are a serious manifestation of alcohol dependence that develops 1 to 4 days after the onset of acute alcohol withdrawal in persons who have been drinking excessively for years. Signs of DTs include extreme hyperactivity of the autonomic nervous system, along with hallucinations.

Denial: The thought process in which a person does not believe he or she has a problem, despite strong evidence to the contrary. It is a way of protecting oneself from painful thoughts and feelings.

Detoxification (detox): A process that helps the body rid itself of substances while the symptoms of withdrawal are treated. It is often a first step in a substance abuse treatment program.

Distal pancreatectomy: A surgical procedure used to treat pancreatic cancer. The surgeon removes the body and tail of the pancreas if the tumor is in either of these parts. The surgeon also removes the spleen.

Disulfiram: A medication that discourages drinking by making the person feel sick if he or she drinks alcohol.

Diuretic: Agent that increases urine production.

Dopamine: An excitatory neurotransmitter that plays a role in the reward system in the brain and possibly also in the reinforcing properties of alcohol use.

Drink: One drink equals one 12-ounce bottle of beer or wine cooler, one 5-ounce glass of wine, or 1.5 ounces of 80-proof distilled spirits.

DUI: Driving under the influence of alcohol or drugs.

DWI: Driving while intoxicated.

Electrolyte: A substance that breaks up into ions (electrically charged particles) when it is dissolved in body fluids or water. Some examples of electrolytes are sodium, potassium, chloride, and calcium. Electrolytes are primarily responsible for the movement of nutrients into cells and the movement of wastes out of cells.

Enzyme: A protein that directs and accelerates (i.e., catalyzes) chemical reactions in the body, such as the breakdown of complex molecules into simpler ones, but does not itself undergo permanent change.

Esophagitis: Inflammation of the esophagus.

Esophagus: The esophagus is a hollow tube that carries food and liquids from the throat to the stomach.

Fatty acids: A building block of fat molecules. Alcohol interferes with the normal metabolism of fatty acids and promotes the deposit of dietary fat in the liver.

Fatty liver (steatosis): The earliest stage of alcoholic liver disease and the most common alcohol-induced liver disorder. Steatosis is marked by an excessive buildup of fat inside liver cells. This condition can be reversed, however, when drinking stops.

Fetal alcohol effects (FAE): The presence of some of the symptoms of FAS, but not enough to be diagnosed as fetal alcohol syndrome (usually the absence of facial characteristics).

Fetal alcohol syndrome (FAS): A full spectrum of mental (central nervous system abnormalities) and physical effects (reduced growth and typical facial features) caused by prenatal alcohol exposure.

Fetus: State of development from the eighth week of pregnancy through birth.

Fibrosis: Buildup of scar tissue.

Followup care: Also called continuing care. Treatment is prescribed after completion of inpatient or outpatient treatment. It can be participation in individual or group counseling, regular contact with a counselor, or other activities designed to help people stay in recovery.

Gamma-aminobutyric acid (GABA): An inhibitory neurotransmitter whose actions are influenced by alcohol; may play a role in alcohol withdrawal.

Gamma-glutamyltransferase (GGT): An elevated level of the liver enzyme GGT is a gauge of heavy alcohol use and liver injury. GGT is the best indicator of excessive alcohol consumption, but GGT is present in many organs and is increased by other drugs as well, so high GGT levels do not necessarily mean the person is abusing alcohol.

Gastritis: Several different conditions that involve inflammation of the stomach lining. It may be caused by drinking too much alcohol.

Gastroesophageal reflux: Weakness of the sphincter separating the stomach from the esophagus allows the stomach content to flow back into the esophagus.

Gestation: Prenatal development.

Glossitis: Inflammation of the tongue.

Halfway house/sober house: A place to live for people recovering from substance use disorders. Usually several people in recovery live together with limited or no supervision by a counselor.

Hangover: A hangover is characterized by the constellation of unpleasant physical and mental symptoms that occur after a bout of heavy alcohol drinking. Physical symptoms of a hangover include fatigue, headache, increased sensitivity to light and sound, redness of the eyes, muscle aches, and thirst. Signs of increased sympathetic nervous system activity can accompany a hangover, including increased systolic blood pressure, rapid heartbeat (i.e., tachycardia), tremor, and sweating. Mental symptoms include dizziness; a sense of the room spinning (i.e., vertigo); and possible cognitive and mood disturbances, especially depression, anxiety, and irritability. The particular set of symptoms experienced and their intensity may vary from person to person and from occasion to occasion.

Heavy drinker: Drinks more than 1.00 fluid ounces of alcohol per day (i.e., more than two drinks per day).

Hepatic: Refers to the liver.

Hepatitis C: A liver disease caused by the hepatitis C virus (HCV). HCV infection is particularly common in alcoholics with liver disease. Heavy alcohol consumption accelerates a person's progression from chronic HCV to cirrhosis.

Hypertension (high blood pressure): A blood pressure of 140/90 or higher. High blood pressure usually has no symptoms. It can harm the arteries and cause an increase in the risk of stroke, heart attack, kidney failure, and blindness.

Hypothalamus: The area of the brain that controls body temperature, hunger, and thirst.

Inflammation: A defensive response to local tissue injury or infection, serving to prevent the spread of injury and activate the immune system; regulated by cytokines. Prolonged or excessive inflammation can damage healthy tissue, as in alcoholic liver disease.

Inpatient treatment: Treatment in a setting that is connected to a hospital or a hospital-type setting where a person stays for a few days or weeks.

Jaundice: A yellowish staining of the skin, whites of the eyes, and deeper tissues produced by an accumulation of metabolic end products in the blood; often a sign of liver disease.

Light drinker: Drinks 0.01 to 0.21 fluid ounces of alcohol per day (i.e., one to 13 drinks per month).

Liver biopsy: When a physician examines a small piece of tissue from the liver for signs of damage or disease. Looking at liver tissue is the best way to determine whether the liver is healthy or what is causing it to be damaged.

Liver: The largest organ in the body. The liver carries out many important functions, such as making bile, changing food into energy, and cleaning alcohol and poisons from the blood.

Minimal legal drinking age (MLDA): All U.S. states and the District of Columbia have enforced 21-year-old minimum drinking age laws, which makes it illegal for people under age 21 to drink alcohol.

Moderate drinker: Drinks 0.22 to 1.00 fluid ounces of alcohol per day (i.e., four to 14 drinks per week).

Morbidity: A disease or the incidence of disease within a population. Morbidity also refers to adverse effects caused by a treatment.

Mortality: The number of deaths during a specific time period.

Mucosal lining: The stomach's naturally acid-resistant lining.

Naltrexone: A medication to help people remain sober. When combined with counseling naltrexone can reduce the craving for alcohol and help prevent a person from returning, or relapsing, to heavy drinking.

Neuron: A nerve cell.

Neurotransmitter: A chemical messenger released by an excited or stimulated neuron. After release, the neurotransmitters travel across a synapse and then bind to a receptor on an adjacent neuron, usually triggering a series of chemical and electrical changes in the second cell.

Oncologist: A doctor who specializes in treating cancer.

Osteoporosis: A skeletal disease characterized by low bone mass, increased bone fragility, and susceptibility to fracture

Outpatient treatment: Treatment provided at a facility. The services vary but do not include overnight accommodation. Sometimes it is prescribed after inpatient treatment.

Oxidative stress: Oxidative stress occurs when harmful oxygen molecules, or free radicals, form in the body. These molecules are highly charged and very unstable. They cause cellular changes in their effort to pair with the nearest available molecule, injuring cells and modifying their function.

Palliative therapy: Medical care that aims to improve quality of life by controlling pain and other problems caused by disease when a cure or control of the disease is not possible.

Pancreas: The pancreas is a large gland behind the stomach and close to the duodenum. The duodenum is the upper part of the small intestine. The pancreas secretes digestive enzymes into the small intestine through a tube called the pancreatic duct. These enzymes help digest fats, proteins, and carbohydrates in food. The pancreas also releases the hormones insulin and glucagon into the bloodstream. These hormones help the body use the glucose it takes from food for energy.

Pancreatitis: Pancreatitis is an inflammation of the pancreas. Acute pancreatitis occurs suddenly and lasts for a short period of time and usually resolves. Chronic pancreatitis does not resolve itself and results in a slow destruction of the pancreas.

Parotid glands: The largest salivary glands, which lie just below and in front of the ears.

Pharynx: The space behind the mouth. Serves as a passage for food from the mouth to the esophagus and for air from the nose and mouth to the larynx.

Physical dependence: Withdrawal symptoms, such as upset stomach, sweating, shakiness, and anxiety after stopping drinking.

Proof: The proof is the alcohol content of distilled liquors. It is the percentage of alcohol multiplied by two. For example: 50% alcohol = 100-proof alcohol and 100% alcohol = 200-proof alcohol.

Radiation therapy (radiotherapy): The use of high-energy rays to kill cancer cells.

Receptor: A protein usually found on the surface of a neuron or other cell that recognizes and binds to neurotransmitters or other chemical messengers.

Relapse prevention: Any strategy or activity that helps keep a person in recovery from drinking alcohol or using drugs again. It may include developing new coping responses; changing beliefs and expectations; and changing personal habits, lifestyles, and schedules.

Relapse: A recurrence of symptoms of a disease after a period of improvement; that is, a person in recovery drinks or uses drugs again after a period of abstinence.

Residential treatment: Treatment in a setting in which both staff and peers can help with treatment. It provides more structure and more intensive services than outpatient treatment. Participants live in the treatment facility. Residential treatment is long term, typically lasting from one month to more than one year.

Self-help/Twelve-step groups: Support groups consisting of people in recovery that offer a safe place where recovering people share their experiences, strengths, and hopes. For example, Alcoholics Anonymous' 12 Steps help the members recover from addiction, addictive behavior, and emotional suffering. These groups are free and are not supported by any particular treatment program.

Serotonin: A neurotransmitter that subtly modifies neuron function, exerting its effects by interacting with receptors on the neuron's surface.

Sphincters: Two bands of muscle fibers that close off the stomach to the esophagus and the intestine.

Stomatitis: Inflammation of the mouth.

Substance use disorders: Alcohol and drug dependence and addiction.

Supportive living: Also called transitional apartments. A setting in which the skills and attitudes needed for independent living can be learned, practiced, and supported. It provides a bridge between supervised care and independent living.

Synapse: A microscopic gap separating adjacent neurons where neurotransmitters and receptors cluster.

Teratogen: A substance that adversely affects embryonic or fetal development.

Therapeutic community: Long-term residential treatment that focuses on behavioral change and personal responsibility in all areas of a person's life, not just substance use.

Tolerance: The need to drink greater amounts of alcohol to get high.

Total pancreatectomy: A surgical procedure used to treat pancreatic cancer. The surgeon removes the entire pancreas, part of the small intestine, a portion of the stomach, the common bile duct, the gallbladder, the spleen, and nearby lymph nodes.

Treatment plan: A plan that provides a blueprint for treatment. It describes the problems being addressed, the treatment's goals, and the specific steps that both the treatment professionals and the person in treatment will take.

Treatment team: A team of professionals (e.g., clinical supervisor, counselor, therapist, and physician) responsible for treating a person and helping his or her family.

Trigger: Any event, place, thing, smell, idea, emotion, or person that sets off a craving to drink alcohol or use drugs.

Trimester: The time period of three months. Three trimesters occur during pregnancy: the first, second, and third.

Wernicke-Korsakoff syndrome: This condition, also known as Wernicke encephalopathy, is a degenerative brain disorder caused by the lack of thiamine (vitamin B1). It may result from alcohol abuse, dietary deficiencies, prolonged vomiting, eating disorders, or the effects of chemotherapy.

Whipple procedure: A surgical procedure used to treat pancreatic cancer. If the tumor is in the head (the widest part) of the pancreas, the surgeon removes the head of the pancreas and part of the small intestine, bile duct, and stomach. The surgeon may also remove other nearby tissues.

Withdrawal: Symptoms, such as nausea, sweating, shakiness, and anxiety, that occur when alcohol use is stopped after a period of heavy drinking.

Zero-tolerance laws: These laws make it illegal for youth under age 21 years to drive with any measurable amount of alcohol in their system (i.e., with a blood alcohol concentration (BAC) more than 0.02 g/dL).

Chapter 72

Directory of Government and Private Resources That Provide Information about Alcoholism

Government Agencies That Provide Information about Alcoholism

Agency for Healthcare Research and Quality (AHRQ)
540 Gaither Road
Rockville, MD 20850
Clearinghouse Toll-Free:
800-358-9295
Clearinghouse TTY: 888-586-6340
Phone: 301-427-1364
Website: www.ahrq.gov
E-mail: info@ahrq.gov

Bureau of Alcohol, Tobacco, Firearms and Explosives
U.S. Department of Justice
Office of Public and
Governmental Affairs
650 Massachusetts Avenue, NW
Room 8290
Washington, DC 20226
Toll-Free: 888-283-8477
Website: www.atf.treas.gov
E-mail: ATFMail@atf.gov

Centers for Disease Control and Prevention
1600 Clifton Road
Atlanta, GA 30333
Toll-Free: 800-311-3435
Phone: 404-639-3311
Website: www.cdc.gov
E-mail: cdcinfo@cdc.gov

Centers for Medicare and Medicaid Services
7500 Security Boulevard
Baltimore, MD 21244-1850
Toll-Free: 877-267-2323
TTY: 866-226-1819
Phone: 410-786-3000
Website: www.cms.hhs.gov

Resources in this chapter were compiled from several sources deemed reliable; all contact information was verified and updated in April 2006.

577

Healthfinder®

U.S. Department of Health and
Human Services
P.O. Box 1133
Washington, DC 20013-1133
Website: www.healthfinder.gov
E-mail: healthfinder@nhic.org

Office of Minority Health

U.S. Department of Health and
Human Services
The Tower Building
1101 Wootton Parkway
Suite 600
Rockville, MD 20852
Toll-Free: 800-444-6472
Phone: 240-453-2882
Fax: 240-453-2883
Website: www.omhrc.gov
E-mail: info@omhrc.gov

National Cancer Institute

Cancer Information Service
6116 Executive Boulevard
Room 3036A
Bethesda, MD 20892-8322
Toll-Free: 800-4-CANCER
(422-6237)
TTY Toll-Free: 800-332-8615
Website: www.cancer.gov
E-mail:
cancergovstaff@mail.nih.gov

National Center for Complementary and Alternative Medicine (NCCAM)

NCCAM Clearinghouse
P.O. Box 7923
Gaithersburg, MD 20898-7923
Toll-Free: 888-644-6226
Phone: 301-519-3153
TTY: 866-464-3615
Fax: 866-464-3616
Website: nccam.nih.gov
E-mail: info@nccam.nih.gov

National Center for Health Statistics

3311 Toledo Road
Hyattsville, MD 20782
Toll-Free: 866-441-NCHS (441-6247)
Phone: 301-458-4000
Website: www.cdc.gov/nchs
E-mail: nchsquery@cdc.gov

National Highway Traffic Safety Administration (NHTSA)

400 Seventh Street, SW
Washington, DC 20590
Toll-Free: 888-327-4236
TTY: 800-424-9153
Website: www.nhtsa.dot.gov

National Institute of Child Health and Human Development (NICHD)
Bldg. 31, Room 2A32, MSC 2425
31 Center Drive
Bethesda, MD 20892-2425
Toll-Free: 800-370-2943
TTY: 888-320-6942
Fax: 301-984-1473
Website: www.nichd.nih.gov
E-mail:
NICHDInformationResourceCenter
@mail.nih.gov

National Institute of Diabetes and Digestive and Kidney Diseases
National Institutes of Health
Building 31, Room 9A04
31 Center Drive, MSC 2560
Bethesda, MD 20892-2560
NIDDK Information
Clearinghouse Toll-Free:
800-891-5390
Website: www.niddk.nih.gov
E-mail:
dkwebmaster@extra.niddk.nih.gov

National Institute of Neurological Disorders and Stroke (NINDS)
P.O. Box 5801
Bethesda, MD 20824
Toll-Free: 800-352-9424
Phone: 301-496-5751
TTY: 301-468-5981
Website: www.ninds.nih.gov
E-mail: braininfo@ninds.nih.gov

National Institute on Aging
Building 31C, Room 5C27
31 Center Drive, MSC 2292
Bethesda, MD 20892
Publications Toll-Free:
800-222-2225
Phone: 301-496-1752
TTY: 800-222-4225
Fax: 301-496-1072
Websites: www.nia.nih.gov,
www.niapublications.org
E-mail: niainfo@nia.nih.gov

National Institute on Alcohol Abuse and Alcoholism (NIAAA)
5635 Fishers Lane, MSC 9304
Bethesda, MD 20892-9304
Websites: www.niaaa.nih.gov,
www.collegedrinkingprevention.gov
E-mail: niaaaweb-
r@exchange.nih.gov

National Institute of Drug Abuse
6001 Executive Boulevard,
Room 5213
Bethesda, MD 20892-9561
Phone: 301-443-1124
Website: www.nida.nih.gov
E-mail:
information@nida.nih.gov

National Women's Health Information Center
8270 Willow Oaks Corporate Dr.
Fairfax, VA 22031
Toll-Free: 800-994-WOMAN
(994-9662)
TTY: 888-220-5446
Website: www.4woman.gov

Substance Abuse and Mental Health Services Administration (SAMHSA)
1 Choke Cherry Road
Rockville, MD 20857
Phone: 240-276-2130
Fax: 240-276-2135
Websites: www.samhsa.gov,
prevention.samhsa.gov,
ncadi.samhsa.gov,
www.findtreatment.samhsa.gov
E-mail: info@samhsa.gov

U.S. Department of Education
Office of Safe and Drug-Free Schools
400 Maryland Avenue, SW
Washington, DC 20202
Toll-Free: 800-USA-LEARN
(872-5327)
TTY: 800-437-0833
Fax: 202-401-0689
Website: www.ed.gov/offices/oese/sdfs

U.S. Food and Drug Administration
5600 Fishers Lane
Rockville, MD 20857-0001
Toll-Free: 888-463-6332
Website: www.fda.gov

U.S. National Library of Medicine
8600 Rockville Pike
Bethesda, MD 20894
Toll-Free: 888-346-3656
Phone: 301-594-5983
Website: www.nlm.nih.gov
E-mail: custserv@nlm.nih.gov

Private Organizations That Provide Information about Alcoholism

Adult Children of Alcoholics World Service Organization, Inc. (ACAWSO)
P.O. Box 3216
Torrance, CA 90510
Phone: 310-534-1815
Website: www.adultchildren.org
E-mail: info@adultchildren.org

Advertising Council
261 Madison Avenue, 11th Floor
New York, NY 10016
Phone: 212-922-1500
Website: www.adcouncil.org

Ala-Anon/Alateen
1600 Corporate Landing
Parkway
Virginia Beach, VA 23454-5617
Toll-Free: 888-4AL-ANON
(888-425-2666)
Phone: 757-563-1600
Fax: 757-563-1655
Website: www.al-
anon.alateen.org
E-mail: wso@al-anon.org

Alcoholics Anonymous (AA)
475 Riverside Drive, 11th Floor
New York, NY 10115
Phone: 212-870-3400
Fax: 212-870-3003
Website: www.aa.org

American Academy of Family Physicians
11400 Tomahawk Creek
Parkway
Leawood, KS 66211-2672
Toll-Free: 800-274-2237
Phone: 913-906-6000
Website: www.aafp.org
E-mail: fp@aafp.org

American Association for Clinical Chemistry
1850 K Street, NW, Suite 625
Washington, DC 20006-2213
Toll-Free: 800-892-1400
Phone: 202-857-0717
Fax: 202-833-4576
Website: www.aacc.org
E-mail: custserv@aacc.org

American Cancer Society
1599 Clifton Road NE
Atlanta, GA 30329
Toll-Free: 800-ACS-2345
(227-2345)
TTY: 866-228-4327
Website: www.cancer.org

American College of Obstetricians and Gynecologists
409 12th Street, SW
P.O. Box 96920
Washington, DC 20090-6920
Phone: 202-638-5577
Website: www.acog.org
E-mail: resources@acog.org

American Council for Drug Education (ACDE)
164 West 74th Street
New York, NY 10023
Toll-Free: 800-488-DRUG
(488-3784)
Website: www.acde.org
E-mail: acde@phoenixhouse.org

American Liver Foundation
75 Maiden Lane, Suite 603
New York, NY 10038
Toll-Free: 800-GOLIVER
(465-4837)
Phone: 212-668-1000
Fax: 212-483-8179
Website:
www.liverfoundation.org
E-mail: info@liverfoundation.org

American Medical Association/Medem
649 Mission Street, 2nd Floor
San Francisco, CA 94105
Toll-Free: 877-926-3336
Phone: 415-644-3800
Fax: 415-644-3950
Website: www.medem.com
E-mail: info@medem.com

American Psychological Association
750 First Street, NE
Washington, DC 20002-4242
Toll-Free: 800-374-2721
Phone: 202-336-5500
TDD/TTY: 202-336-6123
Website: www.apa.org

American Public Health Association
800 I Street Northwest
Washington, DC 20001-3710
Phone: 202-777-APHA
(777-2742)
Fax: 202-777-2534
Website: www.apha.org
E-mail: comments@apha.org

American Society of Addiction Medicine
4601 North Park Ave, Arcade
Suite 101
Chevy Chase, MD 20815
Phone: 301-656-3920
Fax: 301-656-3815
Website: www.asam.org
E-mail: email@asam.org

Association for Medical Education and Research in Substance Abuse
125 Whipple Street, Third Floor,
Suite 300
Providence, RI 02908
Phone: 401-349-0000
Fax: 877-418-8769
Website: www.amersa.org

Canadian Centre on Substance Abuse
75 Albert Street, Suite 300
Ottawa, ON K1P 5E7
Canada
Phone: 613-235-4048
Fax: 613-235-8101
Website: www.ccsa.ca
E-mail: info@ccsa.ca

Caron Foundation
P.O. Box 150
Wernersville, PA 19565
Toll-Free: 800-678-2332
Website: www.caron.org
E-mail: info@caron.org

Center on Alcohol Marketing and Youth
Health Policy Institute
Georgetown University
P.O. Box 571444
3300 Whitehaven Street, NW,
Suite 5000
Washington, DC 20057-1485
Phone: 202-687-1019
Website: www.camy.org
E-mail: info@camy.org

Center for Substance Abuse Research

University of Maryland
4321 Hartwick Road, Suite 501
College Park, MD 20740
Phone: 301-405-9770
Fax: 301-403-8342
Website: www.cesar.umd.edu

Center of Alcohol Studies

Rutgers, the State University
607 Allison Road
Piscataway, NJ 08854-8001
Phone: 732-445-0903
Fax: 732-445-5944
Website:
alcoholstudies.rutgers.edu
E-mail: chrouse@rci.rutgers.edu

Cleveland Clinic

9500 Euclid Avenue
Cleveland, OH 44195
Toll-Free: 800-223-2273
Phone: 216-444-2200
TTY: 216-444-0261
Website: www.clevelandclinic.org

Do It Now Foundation

P.O. Box 27568
Tempe, AZ 85285-7568
Phone: 480-736-0599
Fax: 480-736-0771
Website: www.doitnow.org
E-mail: e-mail@doitnow.org

Dual Recovery Anonymous

P.O. Box 8107
Prairie Village, KS 66208
Toll-Free: 877-883-2332
Fax: 615-297-9346
Website: www.draonline.org
E-mail: draws@draonline.org

Ensuring Solutions to Alcohol Problems

George Washington University
2021 K Street NW, Suite 800
Washington, DC 20006
Phone: 202-530-0272
Fax: 202-296-0025
Website:
www.ensuringsolutions.org
E-mail:
info@ensuringsolutions.org

FACE: Facing Alcohol Concerns Through Education

105 West Fourth Street
Clare, MI 48617
Phone: 888-822-3223
Fax: 989-386-3532
Website: www.faceproject.org
E-mail: face@faceproject.org

Family Empowerment Network

University of Wisconsin Medical School
Department of Family Medicine
777 S. Mills Street
Madison, WI 53715
Toll-Free: 800-462-5254
Phone: 608-262-6590
Fax: 608-263-5813
Website: www.fammed.wisc.edu/fen
E-mail: fen@fammed.wisc.edu

FAS Family Resource Institute
P.O. Box 2525
Lynnwood, WA 98036
Toll-Free: 800-999-3429
Phone: 253-531-2878
Website:
www.fetalalcoholsyndrome.org
E-mail:
vicky@fetalalcoholsyndrome.org

Betty Ford Center
39000 Bob Hope Drive
Rancho Mirage, CA 92270
Toll-Free: 800-434-7365
Phone: 760-773-4100
Website:
www.bettyfordcenter.org

Higher Education Center for Alcohol and Other Drug Abuse and Violence Prevention
Education Development Center, Inc.
55 Chapel Street
Newton, MA 02458-1060
Toll-Free: 800-676-1730
Fax: 617-928-1537
Website: www.edc.org/hec
E-mail: HigherEdCtr@edc.org

Hazelden Foundation
CO3, P.O. Box 11
Center City, MN 55012-0011
Toll-Free: 800-257-7810
Phone: 651-213-4000
Website: www.hazelden.org
E-mail: info@hazelden.org

Institute of Alcohol Studies
Alliance House
12 Caxton Street
London SW1H 0QS
Phone: +44 (0) 207 222 4001
Fax: +44 (0) 207 799 2510
Website: www.ias.org.uk
E-mail: info@ias.org.uk

Intervention Resource Center, Inc.
1028 Barret Avenue
Louisville, KY 40204
Toll-Free: 888-421-4321
Fax: 502-451-1334
Website:
www.interventioninfo.org
E-mail:
help@interventioninfo.org

Jewish Alcoholics, Chemically Dependent Persons and Significant Others
850 Seventh Avenue
New York, NY 10019
Phone: 212-397-4197
Fax: 212-399-3525
Website: www.jacsweb.org
E-mail: jacs@jacsweb.org

Robert Wood Johnson Foundation
P.O. Box 2316
College Road East and Route 1
Princeton, NJ 08543
Toll-Free: 888-631-9989
Website: www.rwjf.org

Johnson Institute
613 Second Street NE
Washington, DC 20002
Phone: 202-662-7104
Website:
www.johnsoninstitute.org
E-mail:
information@johnsoninstitute.org

Join Together
One Appleton Street 4th floor
Boston, MA 02116-5223
Phone: 617-437-1500
Fax: 617-437-9394
Websites: www.jointogether.org,
www.alcoholscreening.org
E-mail: info@jointogether.org

Henry J. Kaiser Family Foundation
2400 Sand Hill Road
Menlo Park, CA 94025
Phone: 650-854-9400
Fax: 650-854-4800
Website: www.kff.org

Leadership to Keep Children Alcohol-Free
c/o The CDM Group, Inc.
7500 Old Georgetown Road,
Suite 900
Bethesda, MD 20814
Phone: 301-654-6740
Fax: 301-656-4012
Website:
www.alcoholfreechildren.org
E-mail:
leadership@alcoholfreechildren.org

Lowe Family Foundation
3339 Stuyvesant Place, NW
Washington, DC 20015
Phone: 202-362-4883
Fax: 202-362-9419
Website: www.lowefamily.org
E-mail: help@lowefamily.org

March of Dimes
1275 Mamaroneck Avenue
White Plains, NY 10605
Website:
www.marchofdimes.com

Marin Institute
24 Belvedere Street
San Rafael, CA 94901
Phone: 415-456-5692
Website:
www.marininstitute.org
E-mail: info@marininstitute.org

Mothers Against Drunk Driving (MADD)
511 E. John Carpenter Freeway,
Suite 700
Irving, TX 75062
Toll-Free: 800-GET-MADD
(438-6233)
Phone: 214-744-6233
Fax: 972-869-2206
Website: www.madd.org
E-mail: info@madd.org

National Association for Children of Alcoholics
11426 Rockville Pike, Suite 301
Rockville, MD 20852
Toll-Free: 888-554-2627
Phone: 301-468-0985
Fax: 301-468-0987
Website: www.nacoa.net
E-mail: nacoa@nacoa.org

National Association of Addiction Treatment Providers
313 W. Liberty Street, Suite 129
Lancaster, PA 17603-2748
Phone: 717-392-8480
Fax: 717-392-8481
Website: www.naatp.org
E-mail: rhunsicker@naatp.org

National Association of Alcoholism and Drug Abuse Counselors
901 N. Washington Street
Suite 600
Alexandria, VA 22314
Toll-Free: 800-548-0497
Phone 703-741-7686
Fax: 703-741-7698
Website: www.naadac.org
E-mail: naadac@naadac.org

National Association of Lesbian and Gay Addiction Professionals (NALGAP)
901 North Washington Street,
Suite 600
Alexandria, VA 22314
Phone: 703-465-0539
Website: www.nalgap.org

National Association of State Alcohol and Drug Abuse Directors
808 17th Street NW
Suite 410
Washington, DC 20006
Phone: 202-293-0090
Fax: 202-293-1250
E-mail: dcoffice@nasadad.org
Website: www.nasadad.org

National Association on Alcohol, Drugs and Disability, Inc. (NAADD)
2165 Bunker Hill Drive
San Mateo, CA 94402-3801
Phone: 650-578-8047
Fax: 650-286-9205
Website: www.naadd.org
E-mail: solanda@sbcglobal.net

National Center on Addiction and Substance Abuse at Columbia University
633 Third Avenue
19th Floor
New York, NY 10017-6706
Phone: 212-841-5200
Website: www.casacolumbia.org

National Commission Against Drunk Driving
Website: www.ncadd.com
E-mail: info@ncadd.com

National Council on Alcoholism and Drug Dependence (NCADD)
22 Cortlandt Street, Suite 801
New York, NY 10007-3128
Toll-Free: 800-NCA-CALL
(622-2255)
Phone: 212-269-7797
Fax: 212-269-7510
Website: www.ncadd.org
E-mail: national@ncadd.org

National Organization on Fetal Alcohol Syndrome
900 17th Street, NW, Suite 910
Washington, DC 20006
Toll-Free: 800-66NOFAS
(666-6327)
Phone: (202) 785-4585
Fax: 202-466-6456
Website: www.nofas.org

Pancreatic Cancer Action Network (PanCAN)
2141 Rosecrans Avenue
Suite 7000
El Segundo, CA 90245
Toll-Free: 877-272-6226
Phone: 310-725-0025
Fax: 310-725-0029
Website: www.pancan.org
E-mail: info@pancan.org

Partnership for a Drug-Free America
405 Lexington Avenue
Suite 1601
New York, NY 10174
Phone: 212-922-1560
Fax: 212-922-1570
Website: www.drugfree.org

Phoenix House
164 West 74th Street
Toll-Free: 800-DRUG HELP
New York, NY 10023
Phone: 212-595-5810 x7800
Website:
www.phoenixhouse.org

Promising Practices
Website:
www.promprac.gmu.edu

RID (Remove Intoxicated Drivers) USA, Inc.
P.O. Box 520
Schenectady, NY 12301
Phone: 518-393-4357
Fax: 518-370-4917
Website: www.rid-usa.org
E-mail: dwi@rid-usa.org

Secular Organizations for Sobriety (SOS)
4773 Hollywood Boulevard
Hollywood, CA 90027
Phone: 323-666-4295
Website:
www.sossobriety.org
E-mail:
SOS@CFIWest.org

Students Against Destructive Decisions (SADD)
255 Main Street
Marlborough, MA 01752
Toll-Free: 877-SADD-INC
(723-3462)
Fax: 508-481-5759
Website: www.sadd.org
E-mail: info@sadd.org

Women for Sobriety, Inc.
P.O. Box 618
Quakertown, PA 18951-0618
Phone: 215-536-8026
Fax: 215-538-9026
Website:
www.womenforsobriety.org
E-mail: NewLife@nni.com

Chapter 73

State Substance Abuse Agencies

Alabama

Substance Abuse Services
Division
Department of Mental Health/
Retardation
100 N. Union Street
Montgomery, AL 36130-1410
Toll-Free: 800-367-0955
Phone: 334-242-3174
Website: www.mh.state.al.us/
services/sa/sa-main.html

Alaska

Office of Alcoholism and Drug
Abuse
Department of Health and
Social Services
249 Main Street
Juneau, AK 99811-0608
Toll-Free: 888-464-8920
Phone: 907-465-8920
Fax: 907-465-4410
Website: www.hss.state.ak.us/
dbh

Arizona

Alcoholism and Drug Abuse,
Office of Community Behavior
Health
Department of Health Services
Department of Health Services
150 North 18th Avenue
Phoenix, AZ 85007-3228
Phone: 602-542-1000
Fax: 602-542-0883
Website: www.azdhs.gov

Resources in this chapter were
compiled from information published
by the U.S. Department of Health and
Human Services Substance Abuse
and Mental Health Services Administration (SAMHSA); all contact information was verified and updated in
April 2006.

Arkansas

Office of Alcohol & Drug Abuse
Prevention
Division of Behavioral Health
Services, DHHS
4313 W. Markham
3rd Floor Administration,
Room 303
Little Rock, AR 72205
Phone: 501-686-9866
Fax: 510-280-4519
Website: www.state.ar.us/dhs/
dmhs

California

Department of Alcohol and Drug
Programs
1700 K Street
Sacramento, CA 95814-4037
Phone: 800-879-2772
Fax: 916-445-0834
Website: www.adp.ca.gov

Colorado

Alcohol and Drug Abuse
Division
Department of Health
4055 S. Lowell Boulevard
Denver, CO 80236-3120
Phone: 303-866-7480
Fax: 303-866-7481
Website: www.cdhs.state.co.us/
ohr/adad/index.html

Connecticut

Department of Mental Health
and Addiction Services
410 Capitol Avenue
P.O. Box 341431
Hartford, CT 06134
Toll-Free: 800-418-7000
Phone: 860-418-7000
TDD Toll-Free: 888-621-3551
TDD: 860-418-6707
Website: www.dmhas.state.ct.us

Delaware

Division of Substance Abuse &
Mental Health
1901 North DuPont Highway,
Main Bldg.
New Castle, DE 19720
Toll-Free Helpline:
800-464-HELP (4357)
Phone: 302-255-9399
Fax: 302-255-4428
Website:
www.dhss.delaware.gov/dhss/
dsamh/index.html

District of Columbia

Addiction Prevention and
Recovery Administration
1300 First Street, NE
Washington, DC 20002
24-Hour Hotline: 888-7WE-HELP
Phone: 202-698-6080
Website: dchealth.dc.gov

Florida
Substance Abuse Program Office
Florida Dept. of Children &
Families
1317 Winewood Boulevard
Building 6 Room 300
Tallahassee, FL 32399-0700
Phone: 850-487-2920
Fax: 850-414-7474
Website: www.dcf.state.fl.us/
mentalhealth/sa

Georgia
MHDDAD
Two Peachtree Street, NW
22nd Floor
Atlanta, GA 30303-3171
Toll-Free Helpline: 800-338-6745
Phone: 404-657-5737
Website: mhddad.dhr.georgia
.gov/portal/site

Hawaii
Alcohol and Drug Abuse
Division
Department of Health
601 Kamokila Blvd. Room 360
Kapolei, HI 96707
Phone: 808-692-7506
Website: www.hawaii.gov/health/
substance-abuse

Idaho
Substance Abuse Program
Department of Health & Welfare
450 West State Street, 5th Floor
Boise, ID 83720-0036
Toll-Free: 800-926-2588
Phone: 208-334-5500
TDD: 208-332-7205
Fax: 208-334-6558
Website:
www.healthandwelfare.idaho.gov

Illinois
Department of Alcoholism and
Substance Abuse
Toll-Free: 800-843-6154
TTY: 800-447-6404
Website: www.dhs.state.il.us/oasa

Indiana
Division of Mental Health and
Addiction
Family and Social Services
Administration
402 West Washington Street
Room W353
Indianapolis, IN 46204-2739
Phone: 317-232-7800
Fax: 317-233-3472
Website: www.in.gov/fssa/
servicemental

Iowa
Department of Public Health
Division of Substance Abuse and
Health Promotion
Lucas State Office Building
321 East 12th Street, 6th Floor
Des Moines, IA 50319-0075
Phone: 515-281-4417
Website: www.idph.state.ia.us/
bhpl/default.asp

Kansas
Alcohol and Drug Abuse
Prevention, Treatment and
Recovery
DSOB
1915 SW Harrison Street, 10th
Floor North
Topeka, KS 66612-1570
Toll-Free: 800-586-3690
Phone: 785-296-6807
Fax: 785-296-7275
Website: www.srskansas.org/
accesspoints/substance.htm

Kentucky
Division of Mental Health &
Substance Abuse
Department for
MH/MR Services
100 Fair Oaks Lane, 4th Floor
Frankfort, KY 40621
Phone: 502-564-2880
Fax: 502-564-7152
Website: mhmr.ky.gov/mhsas

Louisiana
Office for Addictive Disorders
Department of Health and
Hospitals
1201 Capitol Access Road
P.O. Box 2790 Bin #18
Baton Rouge, LA 70821-2790
Phone: 225-342-6717
Fax: 225-342-3875
Website: www.dhh.louisiana.gov/
offices/?ID=23

Maine
Office of Substance Abuse
Department of Health and
Human Services
AMHI Complex, Marquardt
Bldg., 3rd Floor
SHS # 11
Augusta, ME 04333-0011
Toll-Free: 800-499-0027
(Maine only)
Phone: 207-287-2595
TTY: 207-287-4475
Fax: 207-287-8910
Website: www.maine.gov/
dhhs/bds/osa

Maryland
Alcohol and Drug Abuse
Administration
55 Wade Avenue
Catonsville, MD 21228
Phone: 410-402-8600
TTY: 410-528-2258
Fax: 410-402-8601
Website:
www.maryland-adaa.org

Massachusetts
Bureau of Substance Abuse
Services
Department of Public Health
250 Washington Street,
3rd Floor
Boston, MA 02108-4619
Phone: 617-624-5111
Fax: 617-624-5185
Website: www.mass.gov/
dph/bsas

Michigan

Office of Substance
Abuse Services
Department of Public Health
320 S. Walnut
Lansing, MI 48913
Toll-Free: 888-736-0253
Phone: 517-373-4700
Website: www.michigan.gov/
mdch

Minnesota

Chemical Dependency
Program Division,
Department of Human Services
P.O. Box 64977
Saint Paul, MN 55164-0977
Phone: 651-431-2460
Fax: 651-431-7449
Website: www.dhs.state.mn.us

Mississippi

Division of Alcohol &
Drug Abuse
Department of Mental Health
239 North Lamar Street
1101 Robert E. Lee Building,
Suite 901
Jackson, MS 39201
Phone: 601-359-6220
Fax: 601-576-4040
Website: www.dmh.state.ms.us/
alcohol_and_drug_abuse_
services.htm

Missouri

Division of Alcohol and Drug
Abuse
Missouri Department of Mental
Health
1706 East Elm Street
P.O. Box 687
Jefferson City, MO 65102
Toll-Free: 800-364-9687
Phone: 573-751-4942
Fax: 573-751-8224
Website: www.dmh.missouri.gov/
ada/adaindex.htm

Montana

Addictive & Mental Disorders
Division
Department of PH and HS
555 Fuller
Helena, MT 59620-2905
Phone: 406-444-3964
Fax: 406-444-4435
Website: www.dphhs.mt.gov

Nebraska

Division of Behavioral Health
Department of Health & Human
Services Systems
P.O. Box 98925
Lincoln, NE 68509
Information Clearinghouse:
800-648-4444
Phone: 402-479-5583
Website: www.hhss.ne.gov/sua/
suaindex.htm

Nevada

Bureau of Alcohol and
Drug Abuse
Department of Human
Resources
505 E King Street, Room 500
Carson City, NV 89701
Phone: 775-684-4190
Fax: 775-684-4185
Website: health2k.state.nv.us/
BADA

New Hampshire

Office of Alcohol and
Drug Policy
Department of Health and
Human Services
State Office Park South
105 Pleasant Street
Concord, NH 03301
Toll-Free: 800-804-0909
Phone: 603-271-6110
Fax: 603-271-6105
Website: www.dhhs.state.nh.us

New Jersey

Division of Addiction Services
Department of Human Services
120 S Stockton Street, 3rd Floor
P.O. Box 362
Trenton, NJ 08625-0362
Toll-Free: 800-322-5525
(New Jersey only)
Phone: 609-292-7232
Website: www.state.nj.us/
humanservices/das

New Mexico

Behavioral Health Division
Department of Health
1190 Saint Francis Drive
Room 3300 North
P.O. Box 26110
Santa Fe, NM 87502
Toll-Free: 800-962-8936
(outside Albuquerque)
Phone: 505-827-2658
Fax: 505-827-0097
Website:
www.health.state.nm.us

New York

New York State Office of
Alcoholism and Substance
Abuse Services
1450 Western Avenue
Albany, NY 12203-3526
Phone: 518-485-1768
Fax: 518-485-2142
Website: www.oasas.state.ny.us

North Carolina

Alcohol and Drug Abuse Section
Division of MH/MR Services
325 North Salisbury St.
Raleigh, NC 27603
Toll-Free: 800-688-4232
Phone: 919-715-3197
Website: www.dhhs.state.nc.us/
mhddsas

North Dakota

Division of MH and SA Services
1237 West Divide Ave, Suite C
Bismarck, ND 58501-1208
Phone: 701-328-8920
Fax: 701-328-8969
Website: www.nd.gov/human
services/services/mentalhealth

Ohio
Bureau on Alcohol Abuse
and Recovery
280 N. High Street, 12th Floor
Columbus, OH 43215-2550
Phone: 614-466-3445
Fax: 614-752-8645
Website: www.odadas.state.oh.us

Oklahoma
Substance Abuse Program
Department of
MH & SA Services
1200 NE 13th
P.O. Box 53277
Capital Station
Oklahoma City, OK 73152-3277
Toll-Free: 800-522-9054
Toll-Free Teenline: 800-522-8336
Phone: 405-522-3908
Fax: 405-522-3650
Website: www.odmhsas.org

Oregon
Office of Mental Health &
Addiction Services
Department of Human Services
500 Summer Street NE E86
Salem, OR 97301-1118
Phone: 503-945-5763
TTY: 503-945-5895
Fax: 503-378-8467
Website: www.oregon.gov/DHS/
addiction

Pennsylvania
Bureau of Drug and
Alcohol Programs
Pennsylvania Department
of Health
02 Kline Plaza
Harrisburg, PA 17104
Toll-Free: 800-582-7746
Phone: 717-787-2712
Fax: 717-787-6285
Website:
www.health.state.pa.us/bdap

Rhode Island
Council on Alcoholism
Department of Mental Health &
Retardation
500 Prospect Street
Pawtucket, RI 02860
Toll-Free: 866-252-3784
Phone: 401-725-0410
Fax: 401-462-6078
Website: www.mhrh.state.ri.us/
substance_abuse.htm

South Carolina
Commission on Alcohol and
Drug Abuse
101 Executive Center Drive,
Suite 215
Columbia, SC 29210-9498
Phone: 803-896-5555
Fax: 803-896-5557
Website: www.daodas.state.sc.us

South Dakota
Division of Alcohol and
Drug Abuse
East Highway 34,
Hillsview Plaza
C/O 500 East Capitol Avenue
Toll-Free: 800-265-9684
Pierre, SD 57501-5070
Phone: 605-773-3123
Fax: 605-773-7076
Website: www.state.sd.us/dhs/
ada

Tennessee
Bureau of Alcohol & Drug
Abuse Services
William R. Snodgrass Tennessee
Tower, 26th Floor
312 Eighth Avenue North
Nashville, TN 37247-4401
Phone: 615-741-1921
Fax: 615-532-2419
Website: www2.state.tn.us/
health/A&D

Texas
Commission on Alcohol
and Drug Abuse
909 West 45th Street
Austin, TX 78758
Toll-Free: 800-832-9623
Phone: 512-206-5000
Fax: 512-821-4419
Website:
www.dshs.state.tx.us/sa

Utah
Division of Substance Abuse
and Mental Health
Utah Department of Human
Services
120 North 200 West #209
Salt Lake City, UT 84103
Toll-Free: 888-633-4673
Phone: 801-538-3939
Fax: 801-538-9892
Website:
www.dsamh.utah.gov

Vermont
Office of Alcohol and Drug
Abuse Programs
108 Cherry Street
P.O. Box 70
Burlington, VT 05402-0070
Toll-Free: 800-464-4343
Phone: 802-651-1550
Fax: 802-651-1573
Website: healthvermont.gov

Virginia
Office of Substance
Abuse Services
Dept. of MH, MR & SAS
P.O. Box 1797
1220 Bank Street
Richmond, VA 23218-1797
Phone: 804-786-3921
Website:
www.dmhmrsas.virginia.gov

Washington
Division of Alcohol
and Substance Abuse
Department of Social and
Health Services
P.O. Box 45330
Olympia, WA 98504-5330
Toll-Free: 877-301-4557
Phone: 360-725-3700
Fax: 360-438-8057
Website: www1.dshs.wa.gov/
DASA

West Virginia
Division on Alcoholism
and Drug Abuse
Office of Behavioral Health
Services
Department of Health &
Human Resources
350 Capitol Street, Room 350
Charleston, WV 25301-3702
Phone: 304-558-2276
Fax: 304-558-3275
Website: www.wvdhhr.org/
bhhf/ada.asp

Wisconsin
Bureau of Mental Health and
Substance Abuse Services
1 West Wilson Street
Madison, WI 53702
Phone: 608-266-2717
Fax: 608-266-1533
Website: www.dhfs.state.wi.us/
substabuse

Wyoming
Substance Abuse Division
Department of Health
6101 Yellowstone Road
Suite 220
Cheyenne, WY 82002
Phone: 307-777-6494
Fax: 307-777-7006
Website: wdh.state.wy.us/sad

Index

Index

Page numbers followed by 'n' indicate a footnote. Page numbers in *italics* indicate a table or illustration.

A

AA *see* Alcoholics Anonymous
AAFP *see* American Academy of Family Physicians
Abbey, Antonia 455n
"The ABCs of BAC: A Guide to Understanding Blood Alcohol Concentration and Blood Alcohol Impairment" (NIAAA) 132n
abstainer, defined 565
abstinence (alcohol)
    defined 565
    hepatitis C 194
acamprosate 534, 535, *538*, 540, 542
ACAWSO *see* Adult Children of Alcoholics World Service Organization, Inc.
acculturation, drinking patterns 67
ACDE *see* American Council for Drug Education
acetaldehyde
    defined 565
    hangovers 168, 169
    see also alcohol dehydrogenase
acetaminophen
    alcohol interactions 45, *299*
    hangover 172
    liver damage 92, 184
acidosis, defined 565
ACOG *see* American College of Obstetricians and Gynecologists
acquired immune deficiency syndrome (AIDS), alcohol consumption 289–93
acupressure, hangovers 171
acupuncture, alcoholism treatment 553
acute gastric mucosal injury, alcohol consumption 223
acute pancreatitis, described 207, 208–10, 573
A.D.A.M., Inc., publications
    alcoholic neuropathy 265n
    CAM treatment 549n
addiction
    defined 565
    described 77
    domestic violence 443
    gender factor 75
    heredity 30
    nicotine abuse 405–6
    symptoms 470–71
adenosine triphosphate (ATP), defined 565

ADH *see* alcohol dehydrogenase

ADHD *see* attention deficit
hyperactivity disorder

administrative license revocation
(ALR), described 141–42

administrative license suspension
(ALS), described 139

adolescents
alcohol consumption 79–80
alcohol consumption facts 44–47
alcohol consumption statistics
34–35, 47–49, 49–51, 53–54
alcohol sources 49–51
alcohol use discussions 109–22
attention deficit hyperactivity
disorder 393–95
depression 377–79
driving under influence 465
fetal alcohol spectrum disorders 314
fetal alcohol syndrome 349–52,
356–57
parental alcoholism 419–22
substance abuse 416–18
substance abuse treatment 516–17,
519–21
violent behavior 438–41
see also underage drinking

Adult Children of Alcoholics World
Service Organization, Inc.
(ACAWSO), contact information 580

advertisements, alcohol 53–63

Advertising Council
contact information 580
drunk driving prevention
publication 144n

Advil (ibuprofen) *299*

age factor
alcohol abuse 75–76, 96–97
alcohol consumption 23, 91–94
alcohol consumption statistics 9–16
blood alcohol concentration 136–37
legal limit for drinking 6
medications 300–302
pancreatic cancer 214
see also adolescents; children; older
individuals; students

Agency for Healthcare Research and
Quality (AHRQ), contact
information 577

AHRQ *see* Agency for Healthcare
Research and Quality

AIDS *see* acquired immune
deficiency syndrome

"Ain't Misbehavin': Understanding
the Behaviors of Children and
Adolescents with Fetal Alcohol
Syndrome" (Evensen) 354n

Ala-Anon/Alateen, contact
information 581

Alabama, substance abuse agency,
contact information 589

alanine aminotransferase (ALT)
alcoholic liver disease 189
defined 566

Alaska, substance abuse agency,
contact information 589

alcohol
body effects 161–65
defined 566
described 161–62, 178
immune system 254–59
lethal dose, described 174
long-term effects 92
side effects 178–79

"Alcohol, Wine and Cardiovascular
Disease" (American Heart
Association) 237n

alcohol abuse
cirrhosis 199
college drinking 67
defined 566
described 5, 76
overview 17–24

Alcohol Alert (NIAAA) 29n, 34n,
135n, 187n, 227n, 289n, 402n,
491n

"Alcohol and Drug Abuse in Men"
(NWHIC) 75

"Alcohol and Mental Health"
(Institute of Alcohol Studies) 364n

"Alcohol and Minorities: An Update"
(NIAAA) 85n

"Alcohol: An Important Women's
Health Issue" (NIAAA) 79n

"Alcohol before bed: No Rx for
insomnia" (University of Michigan
Health System) 271n

alcohol cirrhosis, defined 566

alcohol consumption
  anxiety 365–66, 370–72, 382–88
  body mass index 98–99
  cancer risk 276–83
  cutting down 105–8
  depression 365–66, 367, 374–79
  ethnic differences 85–86
  HIV/AIDS 289–93
  kidney disorders 261–64
  nerve damage 265–69
  osteoporosis 285–88
  overview 3–8
  post-traumatic stress
    disorder 389–92
  pregnancy 305–10
  sleep patterns 271–73
  workplace 423–35
alcohol dehydrogenase (ADH)
  defined 566
  genetic research 32
  see also acetaldehyde
alcohol dehydrogenase-2 87
alcohol dependence
  age factor 96–97
  college drinking 67
  defined 567
  described 76
  medications 535–44
  statistics 10–11
  treatment access 555–62
  see also alcoholism
alcoholic cardiomyopathy
  alcohol consumption 237
  defined 566
  overview 241–44
alcoholic dementia, defined 566–67
alcoholic hepatitis
  alcoholic liver disease 188–89, 192
  defined 567
  overview 184–86
  see also hepatitis C
alcoholic liver disease (ALD),
  overview 187–95
"Alcoholic Neuropathy" (A.D.A.M.,
  Inc.) 265n
alcoholic neuropathy, defined 567
Alcoholics Anonymous (AA), contact
  information 581
alcohol ignition interlocks, defined 566

alcohol-impaired driving
  college drinking 67, 72–73
  minority groups 86
  overview 132–43
  prevention 144–58
  statistics 12, 54
  see also blood alcohol concentration;
    driving under influence; driving
    while intoxicated
alcoholism
  brief interventions 491–500
  defined 567
  described 4, 25–26, 76
  medications 534
  overview 17–24
  treatment 501–17
  treatment barriers 487–90
  see also alcohol dependence
"Alcoholism" (A.D.A.M., Inc.) 549n
"Alcohol Marketing and Youth"
  (Center on Alcohol Marketing and
  Youth) 53n
alcohol overdose *see* alcohol poisoning
alcohol poisoning
  adolescent alcohol consumption 44
  defined 566
  described 173–76
"Alcohol Poisoning" (Brick) 173n
alcohol prevention programs
  college drinking 128–30
  minority groups 87–89
  see also family-based prevention
    programs; school-based
    prevention programs
Alcohol Research and Health 219n
alcohol taxes, alcohol consumption
  statistics 15–16
alcohol use *see* alcohol consumption
"Alcohol Use and Abuse" (NIA) 91n
Alcohol Use Disorders Identification
  Test (AUDIT) 477–85, *478*
"Alcohol Use to Alcohol Abuse:
  The Economic Burden, Health
  Consequences, and Impact on the
  Workplace" (Apgar; Glover Burgess)
  423n
alcohol withdrawal *see* withdrawal
ALD *see* alcoholic liver disease
aldehyde dehydrogenase-2 (ALDH2) 87

ALDH2 *see* aldehyde dehydrogenase-2
alkalosis, defined 567
allele, defined 567
allergens, described 247
allopathic treatment, hangovers 172
alprazolam *298*
ALR *see* administrative license
  revocation
ALS *see* administrative license
  suspension
ALT *see* alanine aminotransferase
Alzheimer disease, alcohol
  consumption 83
American Academy of Family
  Physicians (AAFP)
  contact information 581
  medications, alcoholism
    publication 535n
American Association for
  Clinical Chemistry
  alcoholism treatment
    publication 534n
  contact information 581
American Association of Kidney
  Patients, hypertension
  publication 261n
American Cancer Society, contact
  information 581
American College of Obstetricians
  and Gynecologists (ACOG),
  contact information 581
American Council for Drug Education
  (ACDE), contact information 581
American Heart Association, alcohol
  use publication 237n
American Institute for Cancer
  Research, alcohol, cancer
  publication 278n
American Liver Foundation
  alcohol use publication 183n
  contact information 581
American Medical Association/
  Medem, contact information 582
American Psychological Association,
  contact information 582
American Public Health Association,
  contact information 582
American Society of Addiction
  Medicine, contact information 582

American Society of Clinical
  Oncology, alcohol, cancer
  publication 276n
amitriptyline *298*
amnesia, alcohol consumption 231
amylase 208
anabolic steroids, alcoholic liver
  disease 191
Anafranil (clomipramine) *298*
animal studies
  alcohol abuse 400–401
  alcoholism 30
  immune system 255
  osteoporosis 83
  tobacco abuse 403–4
Antabuse (disulfiram) 19, 511, 534,
  535, *538*
antibiotic medications,
  pancreatitis 209
antibodies, described 248–49
antigens, described 247–49
antioxidants
  alcoholic liver disease 191
  fetal alcohol syndrome 233
  immune system 255
Antivert (meclizine) *299*
anxiety, alcohol consumption 365–66,
  370–72, 382–88
Apgar, Kristen Reasoner 423n
"Approaching Alcohol Problems
  Through Local Environmental
  Interventions" (Treno; Lee) 149n
Arizona, substance abuse agency,
  contact information 589
Arkansas, substance abuse agency,
  contact information 590
aromatherapy, hangovers 171
Arsenicum album 553
ascites
  cirrhosis 198
  defined 567
Asian ginseng 551
aspartate aminotransferase (AST)
  alcoholic liver disease 189
  defined 566
aspirin
  alcohol consumption 239
  liver biopsy 205
  side effects *299*

Association for Medical Education
and Research in Substance Abuse,
contact information 582
AST *see* aspartate aminotransferase
asterixis, described 232
"As You Age: A Guide to Aging,
Medicines, and Alcohol"
(SAMHSA) 300n
Atarax (hydroxyzine) *299*
atherosclerosis, defined 567
Ativan (lorazepam) *298*
ATP *see* adenosine triphosphate
attention deficit hyperactivity
disorder (ADHD), alcohol
consumption 393–95
AUDIT *see* Alcohol Use Disorders
Identification Test
"Audit: The Alcohol Use Disorders
Test" (WHO) 475n
autoimmune diseases, described 247
autoimmune hepatitis, cirrhosis 199
Axid (nizatidine) *298*
ayurveda, hangovers 170–71

B

Babor, T. F. 475n
BAC *see* blood alcohol concentration
".08 BAC Illegal per se Level"
(NHTSA) 140n
Barrett esophagus
alcohol consumption 222
defined 567
B cells, described 248–49
beer
adolescent alcohol consumption 46
alcohol content 4, 178
described 161
Benadryl (diphenhydramine) *298*
benzodiazepines
alcoholism treatment 18–19
defined 567
bile
defined 567
described 214
bilirubin
cirrhosis 198
described 567

binge drinking
adolescent alcohol consumption 45
alcohol consumption statistics 14
blackouts 229
defined 567–68
described 4
health effects 6
heredity 87
statistics 9–10
biological factors, minority groups 87
biopsy
alcoholic hepatitis 184–85
liver 199, 203–5, 571
blackouts, described 228–29
blood alcohol concentration (BAC)
alcohol ignition interlocks 566
defined 568
described 164
driving effects *134*
overview 132–43
see also alcohol-impaired driving
blood platelets, described 251
BMI *see* body mass index
Bode, Christiane 219n
Bode, J. Christian 219n
body image, adolescents 111
body mass index (BMI)
alcohol effects 163
alcohol use patterns 98–99
defined 568
bone density test, osteoporosis 287–88
bone disease, alcohol consumption
82–83
Book, Sarah W. 384
boys *see* gender factor; men
brain
adolescent alcohol consumption
38, 44
alcohol consumption 80, 83, 227–36,
366–67
alcohol effects 163
fetal alcohol syndrome 233
brain waves, genetic research 32
breast cancer, alcohol consumption
81, 276
breastfeeding, alcohol consumption
308
breath tests, alcohol ignition
interlocks 566

Breslow, Rosalind A. 98–99, 181
Brick, John 173n, 175
brief interventions
  alcohol consumption statistics 16
  alcohol use 491–500
  defined 568
  emergency room patients 139
  see also interventions;
    treatment plans
Brody, Gene H. 547
Brooks, P. J. 282–83
Brower, Kirk 271–73
Browning, Kelly 278, 281
Buck, Philip O. 455n
Burgess, Angela Glover 423n
buprenorphine 511
Bureau of Alcohol, Tobacco,
  Firearms and Explosives,
  contact information 577
butalbital *299*

C

caffeine 550
CAGE questionnaire 477, 483
calcium homotaurinate 540
California
  community intervention
    programs 158
  substance abuse agency, contact
    information 590
Campral (acamprosate) 534, 536, *538*
Canadian Centre on Substance
  Abuse, contact information 582
cancer
  alcohol consumption 81
  alcohol consumption statistics 15
  pancreas 213–18, 568–69, 575
  tobacco use 404
  see also liver cancer
"Cancer Experts Call for 'Alcohol
  Facts' Labels: Troubling Survey
  Shows Confusion About Alcohol-
  Cancer Link is Rising Sharply"
  (American Institute for Cancer
  Research) 278n
carbamazepine 542
carcinogen, defined 568

cardiac arrhythmia, alcohol
  consumption 237
cardiomyopathy
  alcohol consumption 237
  described 566
cardiovascular disease (CVD),
  comprehensive community
  programs 149–51
carisoprodol *299*
carnitine 550
Caron Foundation, contact
  information 582
CAT scan *see* computed tomography
CDC *see* Centers for Disease Control
  and Prevention
Celebrex (celecoxib) *299*
celecoxib *299*
cells, immune system 246
Center for Substance Abuse
  Research, contact information 583
Center of Alcohol Studies, contact
  information 583
Center on Alcohol Marketing and Youth
  alcohol advertising to youths
    publication 53n
  contact information 582
Centers for Disease Control and
  Prevention (CDC)
  contact information 577
  publications
    alcohol consumption 3n
    alcohol statistics 9n
Centers for Medicare and Medicaid
  Services, contact information 577
chamomile *299*
"Changing the Culture of Campus
  Drinking" (NIAAA) 127n
chemokines, described 251
chemotherapy
  defined 568
  pancreatic cancer 218
child care, fetal alcohol syndrome 342
children
  alcohol advertisements 53–63
  alcohol consumption statistics 53
  alcohol use discussions 109–22
  substance abuse treatment 519–21
  treatment access 555, 557
  see also fetal alcohol syndrome

chlorpheniramine *298*
chronic hepatitis, cirrhosis 186
chronic liver disease
    alcohol consumption statistics 15
    minority groups 86
    see also cirrhosis
chronic pancreatitis
    described 207, 210–12, 573
    pancreatic cancer 215
cimetidine *298*
cirrhosis
    alcoholic hepatitis 185–86
    alcoholic liver disease 189
    described 566
    minority groups 86
    overview 197–201
Clay, Rebecca A. 545n, 548
Cleveland Clinic, contact
    information 583
Clinton, A. Monique 455n
clonazepam *298, 299*
CMCA Project (Minnesota;
    Wisconsin) 155
codeine *298, 299*
cognitive behavioral therapy,
    alcoholism treatment 553
college drinking
    alcohol consumption statistics
        72–73
    alcohol use screening 484–85
    brief interventions 498–99
    hidden consequences 71–72
    overview 66–70
    prevention 127–30
Collins, Karen 278–81
colon cancer, alcohol consumption 277
Colorado, substance abuse agency,
    contact information 590
communication
    adolescent alcohol consumption
        112–16
    workplace alcohol abuse 433
Community Action Project (New
    Zealand) 153
Community Mobilization for the
    Prevention of Alcohol-Related
    Injury (COMPARI) 154
Community Reinforcement
    Approach 89

Community Trials Project 155–56
comorbidity, defined 568
COMPARI *see* Community
    Mobilization for the Prevention of
    Alcohol-Related Injury
complementary and alternative
    medicine (CAM)
    alcoholism treatment 549–54
    hangover 170–72
complement system, described
    251–52
comprehensive community programs
    alcohol consumption statistics 16
    blood alcohol concentrations 138–39
    overview 149–58
computed tomography (CAT scan;
    CT scan)
    brain damage 230
    pancreatitis 209, 210, 211
Connecticut, substance abuse agency,
    contact information 590
continuing care, described 570
Cooke, David A. 123n, 135n, 219n,
    326n, 332n, 333n, 336n, 402n,
    423n, 455n
coronary heart disease (CHD), alcohol
    consumption 82
corticosteroids, alcoholic
    hepatitis 192
Coumadin (warfarin) *298*, 541
counseling
    alcoholism treatment 534
    continuing care 570
    substance abuse treatment 508
craving
    alcoholism 17, 25, 76
    defined 568
    described 567
    substance abuse 502–3
CTL *see* cytotoxic T lymphocytes
CT scan *see* computed tomography
Curie, Charles 96, 147, 398
CVD *see* cardiovascular disease
cyclobenzaprine *299*
cycloserine *299*
cytokines
    described 251
    immune system 256
    inflammation 571

cytotoxic T lymphocytes (CTL), described 249–50

D

daily alcohol consumption, excessive drinking 5–6
dandelion, alcoholism treatment 552
Darvocet-N (propoxyphene) *299*
deaths
college drinking 66, 73
excessive alcohol consumption 12–13
minority alcohol consumption 86, 88–89
motor vehicle accidents 141–43, 144
underage drinking 34, 44
see also homicides; suicides
Delaware, substance abuse agency, contact information 590
delirium tremens (DTs)
defined 568
overview 528–32
dementia
alcohol abuse 566–67
alcohol consumption 83
alcoholism 566–67
denial
alcoholism 4
defined 568
Depacon (valproate) 541
Depakene (valproic acid) 542
Department of Education *see* US Department of Education
dependence *see* alcohol dependence; physical dependence
depression, alcohol consumption 365–66, 367, 374–79
desipramine *298*
Desyrel (trazodone) *298*
detoxification
defined 568
treatment plans 505
diabetes mellitus, pancreatic cancer 215
diarrhea, alcohol consumption 219
diary, described 107–8
diazepam *298*

diet and nutrition
alcohol consumption 180–82, 281
alcoholic cardiomyopathy 243
alcoholic liver disease 190–91
alcoholism 267
alcoholism treatment 550–51
hangovers 169–70
osteoporosis 287
Dietary Guidelines for Americans
alcoholic beverages 7
nutrition 182
dietary supplements *see* supplements
diffusion tensor imaging (DTI), alcoholic brain damage 234
Dilantin (phenytoin) *299*, 541
diphenhydramine *298*, *299*
distal pancreatectomy
defined 568–69
described 217
distillation, described 161
District of Columbia (Washington, DC), substance abuse agency, contact information 590
disulfiram
alcoholism treatment 18
defined 569
described 511, 534, 535
FDA approval 535
overview 537–40, *538*
side effects *538*, 542
diuretics
alcoholic cardiomyopathy 243
defined 569
Dizdaroglu, Miral 282
Do It Now Foundation, contact information 583
domestic violence, alcohol consumption 442–43
dopamine, defined 569
DOT Appropriations Act (2001) 140–42
drink
defined 569
described 4, 106, 132
drink diary, described 107–8
drinking *see* alcohol consumption; binge drinking; heavy drinking; moderate drinking
drinking patterns, described 99

drinking problems
  adolescents 121–22
  comprehensive community
    programs 151–53
  described 7, 20, 93
drinking too much, described 5
driving under influence (DUI)
  described 569
  overview 463–66
  prevention 139–40
  see also alcohol-impaired driving;
    blood alcohol concentration
driving while intoxicated (DWI),
  described 569
  see also alcohol-impaired driving;
    blood alcohol concentration
drug abuse
  alcohol consumption 398–99
  driving under influence 466
  gender factor 75
"Drugged Driving" (NIDA) 463n
drunk driving *see* alcohol-impaired
  driving; driving under influence;
  driving while intoxicated
"Drunk Driving Prevention"
  (Advertising Council) 144n
drunkenness, described 5–6
DTI *see* diffusion tensor imaging
DTs *see* delirium tremens
Dual Recovery Anonymous,
  contact information 583
DUI *see* driving under influence
duodenum, described 573
DWI *see* driving while intoxicated

E

ECG *see* electrocardiogram
edema, cirrhosis 198
EEG *see* electroencephalogram
EGD *see*
  esophagogastroduodenoscopy
Elavil (amitriptyline) *298*
electrocardiogram (ECG), delirium
  tremens 530
electroencephalogram (EEG)
  alcoholic brain damage 235
  delirium tremens 530

electrolytes, defined 569
emergency departments
  alcoholism screening 481–82
  brief interventions 495–97
employee assistance programs,
  alcohol abuse 432–33
endocrine effects, adolescent alcohol
  consumption 38–39
endoscopic retrograde
  cholangiopancreatography (ERCP),
  pancreatitis 211
Ensuring Solutions to Alcohol
  Problems, contact information 583
environmental factors
  adolescent alcohol consumption
    37–38
  college drinking 68–69
  comprehensive community
    programs 152–53
  see also family issues
enzymes
  cancer 404
  defined 569
  intestines 224
  liver 566, 570
  pancreas 207, 208, 573
EPO *see* evening primrose
ERCP *see* endoscopic retrograde
  cholangiopancreatography
esophageal cancer, alcohol
  consumption 219, 276
esophageal mucosal inflammation,
  alcohol consumption 222
esophagitis, defined 569
esophagogastroduodenoscopy
  (EGD) 267
esophagus
  alcohol consumption 221–22
  defined 569
  see also gastroesophageal
    reflux disease
estazolam *299*
estrogen, immune system 256
ethanol
  described 161, 566
  hangovers 168
ethnic factors
  alcohol advertisements 61–62
  drinking patterns 85–86

ethyl alcohol, described 161, 173
evening primrose 551
Evensen, Deb 354n
Excedrin (acetaminophen) *299*
excessive drinking
  daily alcohol consumption 5–6
  getting help 24
  providing help 20–22

F

FACE: Facing Alcohol Concerns
  Through Education, contact
  information 583
Faden, Vivian B. 48
FAE *see* fetal alcohol effects
family-based prevention programs
  adolescent alcohol
    consumption 41
  ethnic differences 88
Family Empowerment Network,
  contact information 583
family history *see* heredity
family issues
  adolescent alcohol
    consumption 49–51
  alcoholism 26, 29
  alcohol use discussions 109–22
  interventions 472
  parental alcoholism 419–22
  substance abuse 409–18
  substance abuse treatment
    513–15
  treatment access 558
  see also adolescents; children;
    parents
"FAQs on Alcohol Abuse and
  Alcoholism" (NIAAA) 17n
FAS *see* fetal alcohol syndrome
FASD *see* fetal alcohol spectrum
  disorders
FAS Family Resource Institute,
  contact information 584
fatty acids, defined 569
fatty liver *see* steatosis
Fay, Michael P. 48
FDA *see* US Food and Drug
  Administration

fermentation, described 161, 173
fetal alcohol effects (FAE)
  defined 569
  described 307, 319–20
  overview 326–31
fetal alcohol spectrum disorders
  (FASD)
  overview 311–18
  questions and answers 319–24
"Fetal Alcohol Spectrum Disorders:
  The Basics" (SAMHSA) 311n
fetal alcohol syndrome (FAS)
  alcohol consumption
    statistics 13–14
  behavioral issues 354–58
  defined 570
  described 233, 319–24
  diagnosis 332–33
  health concerns 333–36
  maternal alcohol consumption 81
  overview 306–9, 326–31, 336–52
  secondary conditions 358–60
fetus, defined 570
fibrosis
  alcoholic cirrhosis 188–89, 566
  defined 570
financial considerations
  adolescent alcohol
    consumption 40
  alcohol abuse 423–25, 426–28,
    556
  fetal alcohol syndrome 328
"Finding May Explain Link
  Between Alcohol and Certain
  Cancers" (NIAAA) 282n
Fiorinal (butalbital) *299*
Flagyl (metronidazole) *299*
Flexeril (cyclobenzaprine) *299*
Florida, substance abuse agency,
  contact information 591
fluoxetine 535, *538*, 540
followup care, defined 570
Food and Drug Administration
  (FDA) *see* US Food and Drug
  Administration
food therapy, hangovers 169–70
Betty Ford Center, contact
  information 584
furosemide 243

G

GABA *see* gamma-aminobutyric acid

gabapentin 541

Gale Encyclopedia of Alternative Medicine 167n

gallstones, pancreatitis 208–10

gamma-aminobutyric acid (GABA)
  alcoholic liver disease 189–90
  alcoholism treatment 551
  defined 570
  described 551
  genetic research 31

gamma-glutamyltransferase (GGT), defined 570

gamma-linolenic acid (GLA) 551

gastric acid secretion, alcohol consumption 222–23

gastric motility, alcohol consumption 223–24

gastritis, defined 570

gastroesophageal reflux disease (GERD)
  defined 570
  described 221, 222

gastrointestinal tract
  alcohol consumption 219–26
  depicted *220*

gender factor
  alcohol advertisements 60
  alcohol consumption 75–77, 79–84
  alcohol consumption effects 229–30
  alcohol consumption statistics 9–16
  alcohol effects 23
  alcoholic brain damage 235
  alcoholic hepatitis 185
  alcoholic liver disease 189
  binge drinking 567–68
  blood alcohol concentration 133, 137
  drinking definitions 4
  immune system 254–59
  pancreatic cancer 215
  pancreatitis 208
  see also men; women

"General Alcohol Information" (CDC) 9n

genes
  alcoholism 26, 30
  alcohol metabolism 567
  ALDH2 87

genetic factors *see* heredity

genetic research, alcoholism 31–32

Gentry, Thomas R. 545

Georgia, substance abuse agency, contact information 591

GERD *see* gastroesophageal reflux disease

gestation, defined 570

GGT *see* gamma-glutamyltransferase

ginseng 551

girls *see* gender factor; women

GLA *see* gamma-linolenic acid

glossitis, defined 570

glucagon
  described 573
  pancreas 207

Glucophage (metformin) *298*

glutamine 550

glutathione 550

glyburide *298*

Goggin, Kathy 546

Grant, Bridget 371

granulocytes, described 251

Grisactin (griseofulvin) *299*

griseofulvin *299*

growth effects, adolescent alcohol consumption 38–39

"Guidelines of Care for Children With Special Health Care Needs: Fetal Alcohol Syndrome and Fetal Alcohol Effects" (Minnesota Department of Health) 326n, 332n, 333n, 336n

H

halfway house, defined 570

hallucinations *see* delirium tremens

hangovers
  defined 570–71
  overview 167–72

Hawaii, substance abuse agency, contact information 591

Hazel, Kelly L. 548

Hazelden Foundation
  contact information 584
  youth violence publication 438n
health effects
  adolescent alcohol consumption
    38–39, 44
  alcohol consumption statistics
    12–15
  minority groups 86
Healthfinder, contact
  information 578
health problems, college
  drinking 67
heartburn, alcohol consumption
  222
heart disorders
  alcohol consumption 82, 237–39,
    262, 277–78
  alcoholic cardiomyopathy 237,
    241–44, 566
heart health
  alcohol consumption 23–24
  moderate drinkers 77
heart transplantation, alcoholic
  cardiomyopathy 243
heavy drinker, defined 571
heavy drinking
  described 4
  ethnic differences 85–86
  health effects 6
  memory deficit 83
  men 77
  statistics 10
helper T cells, described 249
hemochromatosis, cirrhosis 199
hepatic, defined 571
hepatic encephalopathy, alcohol
  consumption 232–33
hepatitis, cirrhosis 199
hepatitis C
  alcohol consumption 193–94
  alcohol consumption statistics 15
  defined 571
  see also alcoholic hepatitis
herbal remedies
  alcohol interactions 92
  alcoholism treatment 551–52
  hangovers 170–71
  side effects *299*

heredity
  addiction 469
  adolescent alcohol consumption
    36–37, 116
  alcoholism 18, 25–27, 29–32, 76
  cirrhosis 186
  fetal alcohol spectrum disorders 322
  pancreatic cancer 215
  pancreatitis 210–11
Higgins-Biddle, J. C. 475n
high blood pressure *see* hypertension
Higher Education Center for Alcohol
  and Other Drug Abuse and Violence
  Prevention, contact information 584
Hill, J. Edward 49–51
Hingson, Ralph W. 72–73
HIV *see* human immunodeficiency
  virus
homeopathy, alcoholism treatment
  552–53
homicides
  adolescent alcohol consumption 34
  alcohol consumption statistics 11
hormones
  alcohol consumption 80, 81–82
  immune system 256–57
  pancreas 207, 214
"How to Cut Down on Your Drinking"
  (NIAAA) 105n
human immunodeficiency virus
  (HIV), alcohol consumption 289–93
hydrocodone *299*
hydrotherapy, hangovers 171
hydroxyzine *299*
Hypericum perforatum 552
hypertension (high blood pressure)
  defined 571
  kidney disorders 261–64
hypothalamus, defined 571
hypoxia, pancreatitis 209

I

ibuprofen 172, 205, *299*
Idaho, substance abuse agency,
  contact information 591
Illinois, substance abuse agency,
  contact information 591

imagery, hangovers 171
immune response, described 252–53
immune system
  gender factor 254–59
  overview 246–53
Indiana, substance abuse agency,
  contact information 591
infections, immune response 252–53
inflammation, defined 571
inpatient treatment, defined 571
  see also outpatient treatment;
    residential treatment
insomnia, alcohol consumption 271–73
Institute of Alcohol Studies
  contact information 584
  mental health publication 364n
insulin
  described 573
  pancreas 214
interferon, hepatitis C 194
interleukins, described 251
Internet Web sites, online games
  58–59
Intervention Resource Center, Inc.,
  contact information 584
interventions
  adolescent alcohol consumption 39,
    40–41
  alcohol consumption statistics 16
  alcohol-impaired driving 146
  described 20–22
  emergency room patients 139
  minority alcohol consumption 89
  overview 469–73
  see also brief interventions;
    treatment plans
intestinal bacterial microflora,
  alcohol consumption 224–25
intestinal metaplasia, described 567
  see also Barrett esophagus
intestinal motility, alcohol
  consumption 223–24
intestinal mucosal injury, alcohol
  consumption 224
intestinal permeability, alcohol
  consumption 224–25
intestines, alcohol consumption
  224–26
intoxication, described 174–75

Intoxikon International, contact
  information 176
Iowa, substance abuse agency,
  contact information 591
Iowa Strengthening Families
  Program (ISFP) 41
ISFP *see* Iowa Strengthening
  Families Program
islet cell cancer, described 214
isoniazid *299*
Isordil (isosorbide) *298*
isosorbide *298*

J

jaundice
  cirrhosis 198
  defined 571
Jewish Alcoholics, Chemically
  Dependent Persons and Significant
  Others, contact information 584
Robert Wood Johnson Foundation,
  contact information 584
Johnson Institute, contact
  information 585
Join Together, contact information 585

K

Henry J. Kaiser Family Foundation
  contact information 585
  risky sexual activity publication 445n
Kansas, substance abuse agency,
  contact information 592
Kentucky, substance abuse agency,
  contact information 592
Kersting, K. 100n
kidney disorders
  alcohol consumption 261–64
  pancreatitis 210
killer T cells, described 249–50
Klonopin (clonazepam) *298, 299*
Korsakoff syndrome
  described 231
  thiamine 550–51
  see also Wernicke-Korsakoff
    syndrome
Kovacs, Elizabeth J. 254n

Kudzu, alcoholism treatment 554
Kunos, George 283

L

Lachesis 553
Lahti Project (Finland) 153–54
"Largest Ever Comorbidity Study
  Reports Prevalence and Co-
  Occurrence of Alcohol, Drug, Mood
  and Anxiety Disorders" (NIAAA) 370n
laryngeal cancer, alcohol consumption
  276–77
lavender *299*
Lê, A. D. 400
Leadership to Keep Children Alcohol-
  Free, contact information 585
Lee, Juliet P. 149n
legal limit for drinking, described 6
legislation
  adolescent alcohol consumption 45,
    116
  blood alcohol levels 140–41
  minimal legal drinking age 16, 40,
    137–38, 572
  underage drinking prevention 62–63
  zero tolerance laws 6, 11, 40–41,
    138, 575
Li, Ting-Kai 47, 72, 98, 180, 282, 371,
  376, 382, 393, 401
Librium 18
Life Skills Training (LST) 88
lifestyle factors
  alcoholic liver disease 190
  alcoholism 18, 76
  alcoholism treatment 550
  cirrhosis 200
  older women 83
  osteoporosis 287
light drinker, defined 571
lipase 208
liver
  alcohol consumption
    adolescents 38
    older individuals 92
    overview 183–86
  defined 572
  described 187

liver biopsy
  alcoholic hepatitis 184–85
  cirrhosis 199
  defined 571
  described 203–5
"Liver Biopsy" (NIDDK) 203n
liver cancer
  alcohol consumption 277
  cirrhosis 198
  hepatitis C 194
liver disorders
  alcohol consumption statistics 15
  alcoholic cirrhosis 184, 566
  alcoholic hepatitis 184, 567
  ascites 567
  fatty liver 184, 185
  hepatitis C 571
  jaundice 571
liver enzymes
  alcohol consumption 566, 570
  alcoholic liver disease 189–90
liver transplantation
  alcoholic liver disease 190, 192–93
  alcoholism 186, 232–33
  cirrhosis 200
  hepatic encephalopathy 232–33
lorazepam *298*
loss of control
  alcoholism 17, 25, 76
  described 567
  substance abuse 503
Louisiana, substance abuse agency,
  contact information 592
Lowe Family Foundation, contact
  information 585
LST *see* Life Skills Training
lymph nodes, described 247–48
lymphocytes, described 247, 248–50
lymphoid organs, described 247–48
Lyness, D'Arcy 419n

M

Macrodantin (nitrofurantoin) *299*
MADD *see* Mothers Against Drunk
  Driving
magazine advertisements *see*
  advertisements

magnesium 550
magnetic resonance imaging (MRI),
    alcoholic brain damage 234
Maine, substance abuse agency,
    contact information 592
major histocompatibility complex
    (MHC) 250
"Make a Difference: Talk to Your
    Child about Alcohol" (NIAAA) 109n
"Make Your Parties Rock: A Guide to
    Safe and Sober Event Planning"
    (NHTSA) 123n
Malcarne, Vanessa 546
Mallory-Weiss syndrome, alcohol
    consumption 222
malnutrition, alcoholic liver
    disease 191
March of Dimes, contact
    information 585
marijuana, driving under influence 466
Marin Institute, contact information
    585
marketing *see* advertisements
Maryland, substance abuse agency,
    contact information 592
Massachusetts
    adolescent alcohol consumption
        prevention 42
    community intervention programs
        154–55
    substance abuse agency, contact
        information 592
MAST *see* Michigan Alcoholism
    Screening Test
mast cells, described 251
McAuslan, Pam 455n
meclizine *299*
Medicaid, resource information 577
Medicare, resource information 577
medications
    age factor 300–302
    alcohol dependence 535–44, *538–39*
    alcohol interactions 3, 23, 24, 45, 84,
        92, 296–99
    alcoholism 534
    alcoholism treatment 18–19
    blood alcohol concentration 133
    kidney disorders 261–62
    substance abuse treatment 511–12

"Medications for Treating Alcohol
    Dependence" (AAFP) 535n
medium-chain triglycerides, alcoholic
    liver disease 191
memory deficit, heavy alcohol
    consumption 83
memory lapses, described 228–29
men
    alcohol abuse 75–77
    pancreatic cancer 215
menopause, osteoporosis 83
menstrual cycle, alcohol
    consumption 81
mental illness
    alcohol consumption 364–69
    post-traumatic stress disorder
        389–92
    substance abuse treatment 510
Messingham, Kelly A. N. 254n
metastasis, described 214
metformin *298*
methanol, hangovers 169
metoclopramide *298*
metronidazole *299*
MHC *see* major histocompatibility
    complex
Michigan, substance abuse agency,
    contact information 593
Michigan Alcoholism Screening Test
    (MAST) 477, 483
Micronase (glyburide) *298*
Milgram, Gail Gleason 161
milk thistle 551–52
minimal legal drinking age (MLDA)
    adolescent alcohol consumption 40
    alcohol consumption statistics 16
    defined 572
    described 137–38
Minnesota
    adolescent alcohol consumption
        prevention 42–43
    community intervention
        programs 155
    substance abuse agency, contact
        information 593
Minnesota Department of Health,
    publications
    caregiving, fetal alcohol syndrome
        326n, 332n, 333n, 336n

minorities *see* ethnic factors; racial factor

Mississippi, substance abuse agency, contact information 593

Missouri, substance abuse agency, contact information 593

mitochondria, adenosine triphosphate 565

MLDA *see* minimal legal drinking age

moderate drinkers, defined 572

moderate drinking
  described 4, 22, 184
  heart health 77
  heredity 27
  men 77

Molina, Brooke 394–95

monocytes, described 250

Montana, substance abuse agency, contact information 593

Monteiro, M. G. 475n

morbidity, defined 572

mortality, defined 572

Mothers Against Drunk Driving (MADD), contact information 585

motor vehicle accidents
  adolescent alcohol consumption 34, 116
  alcohol consumption statistics 12–13
  college drinking 73
  statistics 44, 141–42

Motrin (ibuprofen) *299*

MRI *see* magnetic resonance imaging

mucosal lining
  alcohol consumption 221–22
  defined 572

N

NAADAC *see* National Association of Alcoholism and Drug Abuse Counselors

NAADD *see* National Association on Alcohol, Drugs and Disability, Inc.

NAATP *see* National Association of Addiction Treatment Providers

NACOA *see* National Association for Children of Alcoholics

NALGAP *see* National Association of Lesbian and Gay Addiction Professionals

nalmefene *539*, 542

naltrexone
  defined 572
  described 511–12, 534, 535
  FDA approval 535
  genetic research 31
  overview 536–37, *539*

Naprosyn (naproxen) 172, *299*

naproxen 172, *299*

NASADAD *see* National Association of State Alcohol and Drug Abuse Directors

NASH *see* nonalcoholic steatohepatitis

National Association for Children of Alcoholics (NACOA), contact information 586

National Association of Addiction Treatment Providers (NAATP), contact information 586

National Association of Alcoholism and Drug Abuse Counselors (NAADAC), contact information 586

National Association of Lesbian and Gay Addiction Professionals (NALGAP), contact information 586

National Association of State Alcohol and Drug Abuse Directors (NASADAD), contact information 586

National Association on Alcohol, Drugs and Disability, Inc. (NAADD), contact information 586

National Cancer Institute (NCI), contact information 578

National Center for Complementary and Alternative Medicine (NCCAM), contact information 578

National Center for Health Statistics, contact information 578

National Center on Addiction and Substance Abuse at Columbia University, contact information 586

National Commission Against Drunk
Driving, Web site address 586
National Council on Alcoholism and
Drug Dependence (NCADD),
contact information 587
National Highway Traffic Safety
Administration (NHTSA)
contact information 578
publications
blood alcohol concentration 132n,
140n
substance-free parties 123n
National Institute of Allergy and
Infectious Diseases (NIAID),
immune system publication 246n
National Institute of Arthritis and
Musculoskeletal and Skin Diseases
(NIAMS), osteoporosis publication
285n
National Institute of Child Health
and Human Development (NICHD),
contact information 579
National Institute of Diabetes and
Digestive and Kidney Diseases
(NIDDK)
contact information 579
publications
cirrhosis 197n
liver biopsy 203n
National Institute of Drug Abuse
(NIDA), contact information 579
National Institute of Neurological
Disorders and Stroke (NINDS),
contact information 579
National Institute on Aging (NIA)
alcohol use publication 91n
contact information 579
National Institute on Alcohol Abuse
and Alcoholism (NIAAA)
contact information 579
publications
alcohol, cancer 282n
alcohol consumption 105n
alcoholism 17n
alcohol use screening 475n
children, alcohol 109n
college drinking 66n, 127n
diet and nutrition 180n
disorders co-occurrences 370n

National Institute on Alcohol Abuse
and Alcoholism (NIAAA), continued
publications, continued
heredity 29n
heredity, substance abuse 400n
minority alcohol use 85n
transportation safety 135n
treatment access 555n
underage drinking 34n
underage drinking trends 47n
women's health 79n
National Institute on Drug Abuse
(NIDA), drugged driving
publication 463n
National Institutes of Health (NIH),
depression publication 374n
National Library of Medicine (NLM)
see US National Library of Medicine
National Organization on Fetal
Alcohol Syndrome, contact
information 587
"National Survey Sharpens Picture
of Major Depression Among U.S.
Adults" (NIH) 374n
National Woman's Health
Information Center (NWHIC)
contact information 579
male alcohol abuse publication 75n
natural killer cells (NK cells) 250
NCADD *see* National Council on
Alcoholism and Drug Dependence
NCCAM *see* National Center for
Complementary and Alternative
Medicine
NCI *see* National Cancer Institute
Nebraska, substance abuse agency,
contact information 593
nefazodone *298*
nerve damage
alcohol abuse 425
alcohol consumption 265–69
neuron, defined 572
Neurontin (gabapentin) 541
neurotransmitters
defined 572
dopamine 569
gamma-aminobutyric acid 570
genetic research 31
serotonin 574

neutrophils, described 251
Nevada, substance abuse agency, contact information 594
New Hampshire, substance abuse agency, contact information 594
New Jersey, substance abuse agency, contact information 594
New Mexico, substance abuse agency, contact information 594
New York state, substance abuse agency, contact information 594
NHTSA *see* National Highway Traffic Safety Administration
NIA *see* National Institute on Aging
NIAAA *see* National Institute on Alcohol Abuse and Alcoholism
NIAID *see* National Institute of Allergy and Infectious Diseases
NICHD *see* National Institute of Child Health and Human Development
NIDA *see* National Institute of Drug Abuse
NIDDK *see* National Institute of Diabetes and Digestive and Kidney Diseases
NIH *see* National Institutes of Health
NINDS *see* National Institute of Neurological Disorders and Stroke
nitrofurantoin *299*
nitroglycerine *298*
nizatidine *298*
NK cells *see* natural killer cells
NLM *see* US National Library of Medicine
nonalcoholic steatohepatitis (NASH)
cirrhosis 198
see also steatosis
Norpramin (desipramine) *298*
North Carolina, substance abuse agency, contact information 594
North Dakota, substance abuse agency, contact information 594
nutrition supplements *see* supplements
Nux vomica 553

NWHIC *see* National Woman's Health Information Center (NWHIC)
Nydrazid (isoniazid) *299*

O

octanol 233
Oenothera biennis 551
Office of Minority Health, contact information 578
Ohio
substance abuse agency, contact information 595
underage drinking legislation 62–63
Oklahoma, substance abuse agency, contact information 595
older individuals, alcohol consumption 23, 81–84, 91–94
oncologists, defined 572
ondansetron 535, *539*, 541, 542
"Online Facts: The Effects of Alcohol" (Rutgers University Center of Alcohol Studies) 161n
oral cancers, alcohol consumption 276
oral cavity, alcohol consumption 221–22
Oregon, substance abuse agency, contact information 595
Orinase (tolbutamide) *298*
osteoporosis
alcohol consumption 82–83, 285–88
defined 572
outpatient treatment, defined 572
see also inpatient treatment; residential treatment
"Overview: Access to Recovery from Alcohol and Drug Use Disorders" (SAMHSA) 487n
oxidation, described 162
oxidative stress, defined 572
oxycodone *299*

P

pain management, palliative care 573
palliative therapy, defined 573
Panax ginseng 551
Panax quinquefolium 551

PanCAN *see* Pancreatic Cancer Action Network
pancreas
defined 573
described 207, 213–14
pancreatectomy, described 217
pancreatic cancer
distal pancreatectomy 568–69
overview 213–18
total pancreatectomy 575
Whipple procedure 575
Pancreatic Cancer Action Network (PanCAN), contact information 587
pancreatic duct, described 573
pancreatitis
alcoholism 207–12
defined 573
Pandey, Subhash C. 382–83
parents
alcoholics 419–22
alcohol use discussions 109–22
college drinking 67–70, 72
family issues 410–11
underage drinking 49–51
parotid glands
alcohol consumption 221
defined 573
parties, adolescent alcohol consumption 117, 123–25
Partnership for a Drug-Free America
contact information 587
interventions publication 469n
peak bone mass, described 82
see also osteoporosis
peer pressure, adolescent alcohol consumption 110, 116–17
Pennsylvania, substance abuse agency, contact information 595
pentoxifylline (PTX) 192
Percocet (oxycodone) *299*
Perkins, Kenneth 100–101
personality characteristics, adolescent alcohol consumption 36
PET *see* positron emission tomography
phagocytes, described 250–51
pharynx, defined 573
Phenergan (promethazine) *299*
phenobarbital *299*

phenotypes, alcoholism 30
phenytoin *299*, 541, 542
Philadelphia, underage drinking legislation 62
Phoenix House, contact information 587
physical dependence
alcoholism 17, 25, 76
defined 573
described 567
substance abuse 503
"PLWC Feature: Alcohol and Cancer" (American Society of Clinical Oncology) 276n
portal hypertension, cirrhosis 198
positron emission tomography (PET), alcoholic brain damage 234–35
post-traumatic stress disorder (PTSD), alcohol consumption 389–92
pregnancy
alcohol consumption 3, 22, 179, 239, 305–10, 322–24, 327
alcohol consumption statistics 13–14
alcohol use screening 482–83
brief interventions 497–98
heart health 24
unsafe sexual activity 450
Prevention Alert (SAMHSA) 377n
primary biliary cirrhosis, liver transplantation 186
primary tumors, described 214
probiotics, hangovers 171
problem drinking *see* alcohol abuse; drinking problems
promethazine *299*
Promising Practices, Web site address 587
proof
defined 573
described 178
propoxyphene *299*
ProSom (estazolam) *299*
protoporphyria 199
Prozac (fluoxetine) *538*, 540
"PTSD and Problems with Alcohol Use" (US Department of Veterans Affairs) 389n

PTX *see* pentoxifylline
Pueraria lobata 554
pyridoxine 191

Q

quality of life, palliative care 573
"Questions and Answers on Alcohol
    Consumption" (CDC) 3n

R

racial factor
    alcohol advertisements 60–61
    pancreatic cancer 215
radiation therapy
    defined 573
    pancreatic cancer 217
radio advertisements *see*
    advertisements
radiotherapy *see* radiation therapy
Randall, Carrie L. 384
ranitidine *298*
receptors, defined 573
Reglan (metoclopramide) *298*
relapse
    alcoholism 18
    defined 574
    substance abuse treatment 515
relapse prevention, defined 573
reproductive years, alcohol
    consumption 80–81
residential treatment, defined 574
    see also inpatient treatment;
        outpatient treatment
Restoril (temazepam) *299*
Revex (nalmefene) *539, 542*
ReVia (naltrexone) 19, 511, 534
Rhode Island, substance abuse
    agency, contact information 595
riboflavin 191
RID (Remove Intoxicated Drivers)
    USA, Inc., contact information 587
risk factors
    alcoholic cardiomyopathy 241
    alcoholism 18
    pancreatic cancer 214–15

risk taking
    adolescent alcohol consumption
        35, 39
    unsafe sexual activity 449–50
risky sexual behavior *see* sexually
    transmitted diseases; unsafe
    sexual activity
Robitussin A-C (codeine) *298*
rofecoxib *299*
Rowland, Belinda 167n
Rutgers University Center of
    Alcohol Studies
    alcohol effects publication 161n
    contact information 583

S

SADD *see* Students Against
    Destructive Decisions
S-adenosylmethionine (SAMe) 191
St. John's wort
    alcoholism treatment 552
    side effects 541
salicylates *299*
SAMe *see* S-adenosylmethionine
"Same Genes May Underlie Alcohol
    and Nicotine Co-Abuse" (NIAAA)
    400n
SAMHSA *see* Substance Abuse and
    Mental Health Services
    Administration
Saunders, J. B. 475n
Saving Lives Project (Massachusetts)
    154–55
school-based prevention programs
    adolescent alcohol consumption 41
    ethnic differences 88
screening *see* tests
"Screening for Alcohol Use and
    Alcohol-Related Problems"
    (NIAAA) 475n
"Screening for Alcohol Use
    Disorders with the AUDIT"
    (Babor, et al.) 475n
Scutellaria lateriflora 552
Secular Organization for Sobriety
    (SOS), contact information 587
selenium 550

self control, adolescent alcohol
consumption 44
self-help groups
defined 574
substance abuse treatment 509–10
self respect
adolescent alcohol
consumption 115
fetal alcohol spectrum disorders
316–17
fetal alcohol syndrome 341
senses, increased alcohol
consumption 100–101
Septra (sulfamethoxazole) *299*
Seromycin (cycloserine) *299*
serotonin
defined 574
genetic research 31
Serzone (nefazodone) *298*
"Severe Childhood ADHD May
Predict Alcohol, Substance Use in
Teen Years" (FDA) 393n
sexual assault
alcohol consumption 455–62
violence 450
sexually transmitted diseases (STD)
alcohol abuse 76
alcohol consumption statistics
14–15
substance abuse 448–49
see also unsafe sexual activity
SFP *see* Strengthening Families
Program
Silybum marianum 551
skullcap 552
sleep disorders, alcohol consumption
271–73
Smothers, Barbara A. 98
sober house, defined 570
Sober Truth on Preventing Underage
Drinking Act 62
social anxiety disorder, alcohol
consumption 384–88
social consequences
adolescent alcohol
consumption 112
minority groups 86
Soma (carisoprodol) *299*
Sominex (diphenhydramine) *299*

SOS *see* Secular Organization for
Sobriety
South Carolina, substance abuse
agency, contact information 595
South Dakota, substance abuse
agency, contact information 596
sphincters, defined 574
spirituality, twelve-step programs
545–48
spironolactone 243
spleen, described 248
Staphisagria 553
statistics
addiction 469
adolescent alcohol
consumption 112
alcohol abuse 19–20
alcohol consumption
adolescents 34–35, 47–49, 96–97
children 53, 96–97
overview 9–16
alcoholism 487–88
college drinking 66–67, 71, 72–73,
127–28
depression 375, 377
driving under influence 464–65
drug abuse 398–99
fetal alcohol syndrome 327
hepatitis C 193–94
pancreatic cancer 213
post-traumatic stress disorder 390
violent behavior 438
steatosis (fatty liver)
alcohol consumption 225
alcoholic liver disease 187–88
defined 569
described 184, 185
see also nonalcoholic steatohepatitis
stomach, alcohol consumption 222–24
stomatitis, defined 574
Strengthening Families Program
(SFP) 41, 88
stress
alcohol consumption 80
immune system 257
"Strict Graduated Driver Licensing
Laws Associated With Less Teen
Drinking and Driving" (SAMHSA)
147n

students
  alcohol consumption 34–35
  alcohol consumption statistics 11,
    14, 53
  alcohol use screening 484–85
  fetal alcohol syndrome 345–48
  see also college drinking; school-
    based prevention programs
Students Against Destructive
  Decisions (SADD), contact
  information 587
"Study Links Diet Quality with
  Alcohol Drinking Patterns"
  (NIAAA) 180n
substance abuse
  described 96, 501–3
  family issues 409–18
  treatment 503–17
  twelve-step programs 545–48
  unsafe sexual activity 445–54
  violent behavior 438–39
  workplace 423–35
Substance Abuse and Mental Health
  Services Administration (SAMHSA)
  contact information 580
  publications
    alcohol, age factor 300n
    alcoholism treatment 487n
    children, substance abuse
      treatment 519n
    driver licenses 147n
    families, substance abuse 409n
    fetal alcohol spectrum disorders
      311n
    substance abuse treatment 501n
"Substance Abuse Treatment and
  Family Therapy" (SAMHSA) 409n
"Substance Use and Risky Sexual
  Activity" (Kaiser Family
  Foundation) 445n
substance use disorders, defined 574
sudden cardiac death, alcohol
  consumption 237
suicides
  adolescent alcohol consumption 34
  alcohol consumption statistics 11
  college drinking 67
  depression 377–79
sulfamethoxazole *299*

supplements
  alcoholic liver disease 190–91,
    190–92
  alcoholism treatment 550–51
  hangovers 171
support groups
  defined 574
  interventions 21–22
"Supporting and Integrating Systems
  of Care" (NIAAA) 555n
supportive living, defined 574
surgical procedures
  distal pancreatectomy 568–69
  pancreatic cancer 217
  total pancreatectomy 575
synapse, defined 574

T

Tagamet (cimetidine) *298*
Taraxacum officinale 552
T cells, described 248–50
TEA-21 *see* Transportation Equity
  Act for the 21st Century
teenagers *see* adolescents
Tegretol (carbamazepine) 542
television advertisements *see*
  advertisements
temazepam *299*
Tennessee, substance abuse agency,
  contact information 596
teratogen, defined 574
tests
  alcoholic cardiomyopathy 242–43
  alcoholic hepatitis 184–85
  alcoholic liver disease 189–90
  alcohol-related problems 475–86
  alcohol withdrawal 525–26
  cirrhosis 199
  delirium tremens 530
  liver disorders 203–5
  nerve damage 266–67
  osteoporosis 287–88
  pancreatitis 208
Texas, substance abuse agency,
  contact information 596
therapeutic community, defined 574
"The secret of the 12 steps" (Clay) 545n

thiamine
  alcohol consumption 191, 230
  Wernicke-Korsakoff syndrome
    230–32, 550–51, 575
tobacco use
  alcohol abuse 400–401, 402–6
  osteoporosis 83
  pancreatic cancer 215
tolbutamide *298*
tolerance
  adolescent alcohol consumption 36
  alcoholism 17, 25, 76
  blood alcohol concentration 136
  defined 574
  described 567
  substance abuse 502
  tobacco abuse 403–4
Tonigan, J. Scott 547–48
Topamax (topiramate) *539*, 541–42
topiramate 535, *539*, 541–42
total pancreatectomy
  defined 575
  described 217
traditional Chinese medicine,
  alcoholism treatment 554
transitional apartments,
  described 574
Transportation Equity Act
  for the 21st Century (TEA-21;
  1998) 140–41
transportation safety, alcohol
  consumption 135–43
trazodone *298*
"Treatment for Alcoholism"
  (American Association for
  Clinical Chemistry) 534n
treatment plans
  access to care 555–62
  defined 575
  men 75
  older individuals 93–94
  substance abuse 503–17
  twelve-step programs 545–48
  see also comprehensive community
    programs; interventions
treatment teams
  defined 575
  described 503–5
Treno, Andrew J. 149n

Trexan (naltrexone) 536, *539*
triggers
  defined 575
  older individuals alcohol
    consumption 94
trimester, defined 575
twelve-step groups, defined 574
twelve-step programs 545–48
twins studies, alcoholism 26
Tylenol (acetaminophen) 205, *299*
Tylenol Cold and Flu
  (chlorpheniramine) *298*

U

ultrasound, pancreatitis 209, 210, 211
underage drinking
  heredity 26
  interventions 40–41
  prevention 39–43
  public health consequences 34–43
  statistics 11, 47–51, 53
"Underage Drinking: Why Do
  Adolescents Drink, What Are
  the Risks, and How Can
  Underage Drinking Be
  Prevented?" (NIAAA) 34n
unintentional injuries
  alcohol consumption statistics 13
  college drinking 72–73
  underage drinking 34–35, 44
University of Michigan Health System,
  sleep disorders publication 271n
unsafe sexual activity
  adolescent alcohol consumption 35,
    110, 116
  alcohol abuse 76
  alcohol consumption statistics 11, 12
  college drinking 66
  hepatitis C 193
  substance use 445–54
  see also sexually transmitted
    diseases
US Department of Education, contact
  information 580
US Department of Veterans Affairs,
  post-traumatic stress disorder
  publication 389n

US Food and Drug Administration (FDA)
    childhood attention deficit hyperactivity disorder publication 393n
    contact information 580
US National Library of Medicine (NLM), contact information 580
Utah, substance abuse agency, contact information 596

V

vaccines, hepatitis 201
valerian *299*
Valium (diazepam) 18, *298*
valproate 541
valproic acid 542
varices, cirrhosis 198
VCUG *see* voiding cystourethrogram
vehicle impoundments, alcohol abuse prevention 139
Vermont, substance abuse agency, contact information 596
Vicodin (hydrocodone) *299*
violence
    adolescent alcohol consumption 111
    alcohol consumption 438–41
    alcohol consumption statistics 13
    college drinking 66–67
    sexual assault 450, 455–62
Vioxx (rofecoxib) *299*
Virginia, substance abuse agency, contact information 596
vitamin B, alcoholism treatment 550
vitamin B1 *see* thiamine
vitamin E, fetal alcohol syndrome 233
voiding cystourethrogram (VCUG) 267

W

warfarin *298*, 541
Washington, DC *see* District of Columbia
Washington state, substance abuse agency, contact information 597

weight factor, blood alcohol concentration 133
Wernicke encephalopathy *see* Wernicke-Korsakoff syndrome
Wernicke-Korsakoff syndrome
    alcoholic liver disease 191
    defined 575
    overview 230–32
    thiamine 550
West Virginia, substance abuse agency, contact information 597
"What Are the Myths Vs. Facts About Alcohol and the Liver?" (American Liver Foundation) 183n
"What I Need to Know about Cirrhosis of the Liver" (NIDDK) 197n
"What Is Substance Abuse Treatment? A Booklet for Families" (SAMHSA) 501n
"What Parents Need to Know About College Drinking" (NIAAA) 66n
"What People Recovering from Alcoholism Need to Know About Osteoporosis" (NIAMS) 285n
"When Your Child Needs Substance Abuse Treatment" (SAMHSA) 519n
Whipple procedure
    defined 575
    described 217
WHO *see* World Health Organization
Williams, Steven H. 535, 542
Wills, Thomas Ashby 546–47
Wilson's disease, cirrhosis 199
wine
    adolescent alcohol consumption 46
    alcohol content 4, 178
    antioxidants 280
    described 161
    hangovers 169
    heart disease 238
Wisconsin
    community intervention programs 155
    substance abuse agency, contact information 597
withdrawal
    defined 575
    overview 524–27
    substance abuse 503

women
  alcohol consumption 79–84
  alcohol consumption effects
    229–30
  alcohol consumption statistics
    11–12
  alcohol effects 23
  alcoholic liver disease 189
  domestic violence 443
  drinking definitions 4
Women for Sobriety, Inc., contact
  information 588
workplace, alcohol abuse 423–35
World Health Organization
  (WHO), alcohol use screening
  publication 475n
Wyoming, substance abuse agency,
  contact information 597

X

Xanax (alprazolam) *298*

Y

YAAPST *see* Young Adult Alcohol
  Problems Screening Test
Young Adult Alcohol Problems
  Screening Test (YAAPST) 485
Youth Access to Alcohol Task Force 63
"Youth Violence and Alcohol/Drug
  Abuse" (Hazelden Foundation) 438n

Z

Zantac (ranitidine) *298*
Zawacki, Tina 455n
zero tolerance laws
  adolescent alcohol consumption
    40–41
  alcohol consumption statistics 11
  defined 575
  described 6, 138
zinc 550
Zofran (ondansetron) *539*, 541

Health Reference Series
COMPLETE CATALOG

List price $87 per volume. **School and library price $78 per volume.**

Adolescent Health Sourcebook, 2nd Edition

Basic Consumer Health Information about the Physical, Mental, and Emotional Growth and Development of Adolescents, Including Medical Care, Nutritional and Physical Activity Requirements, Puberty, Sexual Activity, Acne, Tanning, Body Piercing, Common Physical Illnesses and Disorders, Eating Disorders, Attention Deficit Hyperactivity Disorder, Depression, Bullying, Hazing, and Adolescent Injuries Related to Sports, Driving, and Work

Along with Substance Abuse Information about Nicotine, Alcohol, and Drug Use, a Glossary, and Directory of Additional Resources

Edited by Joyce Brennfleck Shannon. 650 pages. 2006. 0-7808-0943-2.

"It is written in clear, nontechnical language aimed at general readers. . . . Recommended for public libraries, community colleges, and other agencies serving health care consumers."
— *American Reference Books Annual, 2003*

"Recommended for school and public libraries. Parents and professionals dealing with teens will appreciate the easy-to-follow format and the clearly written text. This could become a 'must have' for every high school teacher." — *E-Streams, Jan '03*

"A good starting point for information related to common medical, mental, and emotional concerns of adolescents." — *School Library Journal, Nov '02*

"This book provides accurate information in an easy to access format. It addresses topics that parents and caregivers might not be aware of and provides practical, useable information."
— *Doody's Health Sciences Book Review Journal, Sep-Oct '02*

"Recommended reference source."
— *Booklist, American Library Association, Sep '02*

AIDS Sourcebook, 3rd Edition

Basic Consumer Health Information about Acquired Immune Deficiency Syndrome (AIDS) and Human Immunodeficiency Virus (HIV) Infection, Including Facts about Transmission, Prevention, Diagnosis, Treatment, Opportunistic Infections, and Other Complications, with a Section for Women and Children, Including Details about Associated Gynecological Concerns, Pregnancy, and Pediatric Care

Along with Updated Statistical Information, Reports on Current Research Initiatives, a Glossary, and Directories of Internet, Hotline, and Other Resources

Edited by Dawn D. Matthews. 664 pages. 2003. 0-7808-0631-X.

"The 3rd edition of the *AIDS Sourcebook*, part of Omnigraphics' *Health Reference Series*, is a welcome update. . . . This resource is highly recommended for academic and public libraries."
— *American Reference Books Annual, 2004*

"Excellent sourcebook. This continues to be a highly recommended book. There is no other book that provides as much information as this book provides."
— *AIDS Book Review Journal, Dec-Jan '00*

"Recommended reference source."
— *Booklist, American Library Association, Dec '99*

Alcoholism Sourcebook, 2nd Edition

Basic Consumer Health Information about Alcohol Use, Abuse, and Dependence, Featuring Facts about the Physical, Mental, and Social Health Effects of Alcohol Addiction, Including Alcoholic Liver Disease, Pancreatic Disease, Cardiovascular Disease, Neurological Disorders, and the Effects of Drinking during Pregnancy

Along with Information about Alcohol Treatment, Medications, and Recovery Programs, in Addition to Tips for Reducing the Prevalence of Underage Drinking, Statistics about Alcohol Use, a Glossary of Related Terms, and Directories of Resources for More Help and Information

Edited by Amy L. Sutton. 653 pages. 2006. 0-7808-0942-4.

"This title is one of the few reference works on alcoholism for general readers. For some readers this will be a welcome complement to the many self-help books on the market. Recommended for collections serving general readers and consumer health collections."
— *E-Streams, Mar '01*

"This book is an excellent choice for public and academic libraries."
— *American Reference Books Annual, 2001*

"Recommended reference source."
— *Booklist, American Library Association, Dec '00*

"Presents a wealth of information on alcohol use and abuse and its effects on the body and mind, treatment, and prevention." — *SciTech Book News, Dec '00*

"Important new health guide which packs in the latest consumer information about the problems of alcoholism." — *Reviewer's Bookwatch, Nov '00*

SEE ALSO *Drug Abuse Sourcebook, Substance Abuse Sourcebook*

627

Allergies Sourcebook, 2nd Edition

Basic Consumer Health Information about Allergic Disorders, Triggers, Reactions, and Related Symptoms, Including Anaphylaxis, Rhinitis, Sinusitis, Asthma, Dermatitis, Conjunctivitis, and Multiple Chemical Sensitivity

Along with Tips on Diagnosis, Prevention, and Treatment, Statistical Data, a Glossary, and a Directory of Sources for Further Help and Information

Edited by Annemarie S. Muth. 598 pages. 2002. 0-7808-0376-0.

"This book brings a great deal of useful material together. . . . This is an excellent addition to public and consumer health library collections."
— *American Reference Books Annual, 2003*

"This second edition would be useful to laypersons with little or advanced knowledge of the subject matter. This book would also serve as a resource for nursing and other health care professions students. It would be useful in public, academic, and hospital libraries with consumer health collections." — *E-Streams, Jul '02*

■

Alternative Medicine Sourcebook

SEE Complementary & Alternative Medicine Sourcebook, 3rd Edition

■

Alzheimer's Disease Sourcebook, 3rd Edition

Basic Consumer Health Information about Alzheimer's Disease, Other Dementias, and Related Disorders, Including Multi-Infarct Dementia, AIDS Dementia Complex, Dementia with Lewy Bodies, Huntington's Disease, Wernicke-Korsakoff Syndrome (Alcohol-Reated Dementia), Delirium, and Confusional States

Along with Information for People Newly Diagnosed with Alzheimer's Disease and Caregivers, Reports Detailing Current Research Efforts in Prevention, Diagnosis, and Treatment, Facts about Long-Term Care Issues, and Listings of Sources for Additional Information

Edited by Karen Bellenir. 645 pages. 2003. 0-7808-0666-2.

"This very informative and valuable tool will be a great addition to any library serving consumers, students and health care workers."
— *American Reference Books Annual, 2004*

"This is a valuable resource for people affected by dementias such as Alzheimer's. It is easy to navigate and includes important information and resources."
— *Doody's Review Service, Feb '04*

"Recommended reference source."
— *Booklist, American Library Association, Oct '99*

SEE ALSO Brain Disorders Sourcebook

Arthritis Sourcebook, 2nd Edition

Basic Consumer Health Information about Osteoarthritis, Rheumatoid Arthritis, Other Rheumatic Disorders, Infectious Forms of Arthritis, and Diseases with Symptoms Linked to Arthritis, Featuring Facts about Diagnosis, Pain Management, and Surgical Therapies

Along with Coping Strategies, Research Updates, a Glossary, and Resources for Additional Help and Information

Edited by Amy L. Sutton. 593 pages. 2004. 0-7808-0667-0.

"This easy-to-read volume is recommended for consumer health collections within public or academic libraries." — *E-Streams, May '05*

"As expected, this updated edition continues the excellent reputation of this series in providing sound, usable health information. . . . Highly recommended."
— *American Reference Books Annual, 2005*

"Excellent reference." — *The Bookwatch, Jan '05*

■

Asthma Sourcebook, 2nd Edition

Basic Consumer Health Information about the Causes, Symptoms, Diagnosis, and Treatment of Asthma in Infants, Children, Teenagers, and Adults, Including Facts about Different Types of Asthma, Common Co-Occurring Conditions, Asthma Management Plans, Triggers, Medications, and Medication Delivery Devices

Along with Asthma Statistics, Research Updates, a Glossary, a Directory of Asthma-Related Resources, and More

Edited by Karen Bellenir. 609 pages. 2006. 0-7808-0866-5.

"A worthwhile reference acquisition for public libraries and academic medical libraries whose readers desire a quick introduction to the wide range of asthma information." — *Choice, Association of College & Research Libraries, Jun '01*

"Recommended reference source."
— *Booklist, American Library Association, Feb '01*

"Highly recommended." — *The Bookwatch, Jan '01*

"There is much good information for patients and their families who deal with asthma daily."
— *American Medical Writers Association Journal, Winter '01*

"This informative text is recommended for consumer health collections in public, secondary school, and community college libraries and the libraries of universities with a large undergraduate population."
— *American Reference Books Annual, 2001*

■

Attention Deficit Disorder Sourcebook

Basic Consumer Health Information about Attention Deficit/Hyperactivity Disorder in Children and Adults, Including Facts about Causes, Symptoms, Diagnostic Criteria, and Treatment Options Such as Medications, Behavior Therapy, Coaching, and Homeopathy

Along with Reports on Current Research Initiatives, Legal Issues, and Government Regulations, and Featuring a Glossary of Related Terms, Internet Resources, and a List of Additional Reading Material

Edited by Dawn D. Matthews. 470 pages. 2002. 0-7808-0624-7.

"Recommended reference source."
— Booklist, American Library Association, Jan '03

"This book is recommended for all school libraries and the reference or consumer health sections of public libraries." — American Reference Books Annual, 2003

∎

Back & Neck Sourcebook, 2nd Edition

Basic Consumer Health Information about Spinal Pain, Spinal Cord Injuries, and Related Disorders, Such as Degenerative Disk Disease, Osteoarthritis, Scoliosis, Sciatica, Spina Bifida, and Spinal Stenosis, and Featuring Facts about Maintaining Spinal Health, Self-Care, Pain Management, Rehabilitative Care, Chiropractic Care, Spinal Surgeries, and Complementary Therapies

Along with Suggestions for Preventing Back and Neck Pain, a Glossary of Related Terms, and a Directory of Resources

Edited by Amy L. Sutton. 633 pages. 2004. 0-7808-0738-3.

"Recommended . . . an easy to use, comprehensive medical reference book." — E-Streams, Sep '05

"The strength of this work is its basic, easy-to-read format. Recommended." — Reference and User Services Quarterly, American Library Association, Winter '97

∎

Blood & Circulatory Disorders Sourcebook, 2nd Edition

Basic Consumer Health Information about the Blood and Circulatory System and Related Disorders, Such as Anemia and Other Hemoglobin Diseases, Cancer of the Blood and Associated Bone Marrow Disorders, Clotting and Bleeding Problems, and Conditions That Affect the Veins, Blood Vessels, and Arteries, Including Facts about the Donation and Transplantation of Bone Marrow, Stem Cells, and Blood and Tips for Keeping the Blood and Circulatory System Healthy

Along with a Glossary of Related Terms and Resources for Additional Help and Information

Edited by Amy L. Sutton. 659 pages. 2005. 0-7808-0746-4.

"Highly recommended pick for basic consumer health reference holdings at all levels."
— The Bookwatch, Aug '05

"Recommended reference source."
—Booklist, American Library Association, Feb '99

"An important reference sourcebook written in simple language for everyday, non-technical users. "
— Reviewer's Bookwatch, Jan '99

Brain Disorders Sourcebook, 2nd Edition

Basic Consumer Health Information about Acquired and Traumatic Brain Injuries, Infections of the Brain, Epilepsy and Seizure Disorders, Cerebral Palsy, and Degenerative Neurological Disorders, Including Amyotrophic Lateral Sclerosis (ALS), Dementias, Multiple Sclerosis, and More

Along with Information on the Brain's Structure and Function, Treatment and Rehabilitation Options, Reports on Current Research Initiatives, a Glossary of Terms Related to Brain Disorders and Injuries, and a Directory of Sources for Further Help and Information

Edited by Sandra J. Judd. 625 pages. 2005. 0-7808-0744-8.

"Highly recommended pick for basic consumer health reference holdings at all levels."
—The Bookwatch, Aug '05

"Belongs on the shelves of any library with a consumer health collection." — E-Streams, Mar '00

"Recommended reference source."
— Booklist, American Library Association, Oct '99

SEE ALSO Alzheimer's Disease Sourcebook

∎

Breast Cancer Sourcebook, 2nd Edition

Basic Consumer Health Information about Breast Cancer, Including Facts about Risk Factors, Prevention, Screening and Diagnostic Methods, Treatment Options, Complementary and Alternative Therapies, Post-Treatment Concerns, Clinical Trials, Special Risk Populations, and New Developments in Breast Cancer Research

Along with Breast Cancer Statistics, a Glossary of Related Terms, and a Directory of Resources for Additional Help and Information

Edited by Sandra J. Judd. 595 pages. 2004. 0-7808-0668-9.

"This book will be an excellent addition to public, community college, medical, and academic libraries."
— American Reference Books Annual, 2006

"It would be a useful reference book in a library or on loan to women in a support group."
— Cancer Forum, Mar '03

"Recommended reference source."
— Booklist, American Library Association, Jan '02

"This reference source is highly recommended. It is quite informative, comprehensive and detailed in nature, and yet it offers practical advice in easy-to-read language. It could be thought of as the 'bible' of breast cancer for the consumer." — E-Streams, Jan '02

"From the pros and cons of different screening methods and results to treatment options, Breast Cancer Sourcebook provides the latest information on the subject."
— Library Bookwatch, Dec '01

"This thoroughgoing, very readable reference covers all aspects of breast health and cancer. . . . Readers will find much to consider here. Recommended for all public and patient health collections."

—*Library Journal, Sep '01*

SEE ALSO *Cancer Sourcebook for Women, Women's Health Concerns Sourcebook*

■

Breastfeeding Sourcebook

Basic Consumer Health Information about the Benefits of Breastmilk, Preparing to Breastfeed, Breastfeeding as a Baby Grows, Nutrition, and More, Including Information on Special Situations and Concerns Such as Mastitis, Illness, Medications, Allergies, Multiple Births, Prematurity, Special Needs, and Adoption

Along with a Glossary and Resources for Additional Help and Information

Edited by Jenni Lynn Colson. 388 pages. 2002. 0-7808-0332-9.

"Particularly useful is the information about professional lactation services and chapters on breastfeeding when returning to work.... *Breastfeeding Sourcebook* will be useful for public libraries, consumer health libraries, and technical schools offering nurse assistant training, especially in areas where Internet access is problematic."

—*American Reference Books Annual, 2003*

SEE ALSO *Pregnancy & Birth Sourcebook*

■

Burns Sourcebook

Basic Consumer Health Information about Various Types of Burns and Scalds, Including Flame, Heat, Cold, Electrical, Chemical, and Sun Burns

Along with Information on Short-Term and Long-Term Treatments, Tissue Reconstruction, Plastic Surgery, Prevention Suggestions, and First Aid

Edited by Allan R. Cook. 604 pages. 1999. 0-7808-0204-7.

"This is an exceptional addition to the series and is highly recommended for all consumer health collections, hospital libraries, and academic medical centers."

—*E-Streams, Mar '00*

"This key reference guide is an invaluable addition to all health care and public libraries in confronting this ongoing health issue."

—*American Reference Books Annual, 2000*

"Recommended reference source."

—*Booklist, American Library Association, Dec '99*

SEE ALSO *Dermatological Disorders Sourcebook*

■

Cancer Sourcebook, 4th Edition

Basic Consumer Health Information about Major Forms and Stages of Cancer, Featuring Facts about Head and Neck Cancers, Lung Cancers, Gastrointestinal Cancers, Genitourinary Cancers, Lymphomas, Blood Cell Cancers, Endocrine Cancers, Skin Cancers, Bone Cancers, Sarcomas, and Others, and Including Information about Cancer Treatments and Therapies,

Identifying and Reducing Cancer Risks, and Strategies for Coping with Cancer and the Side Effects of Treatment

Along with a Cancer Glossary, Statistical and Demographic Data, and a Directory of Sources for Additional Help and Information

Edited by Karen Bellenir. 1,119 pages. 2003. 0-7808-0633-6.

"With cancer being the second leading cause of death for Americans, a prodigious work such as this one, which locates centrally so much cancer-related information, is clearly an asset to this nation's citizens and others."

—*Journal of the National Medical Association, 2004*

"This title is recommended for health sciences and public libraries with consumer health collections."

—*E-Streams, Feb '01*

"... can be effectively used by cancer patients and their families who are looking for answers in a language they can understand. Public and hospital libraries should have it on their shelves."

—*American Reference Books Annual, 2001*

"Recommended reference source."

—*Booklist, American Library Association, Dec '00*

SEE ALSO *Breast Cancer Sourcebook, Cancer Sourcebook for Women, Pediatric Cancer Sourcebook, Prostate Cancer Sourcebook*

■

Cancer Sourcebook for Women, 3rd Edition

Basic Consumer Health Information about Leading Causes of Cancer in Women, Featuring Facts about Gynecologic Cancers and Related Concerns, Such as Breast Cancer, Cervical Cancer, Endometrial Cancer, Uterine Sarcoma, Vaginal Cancer, Vulvar Cancer, and Common Non-Cancerous Gynecologic Conditions, in Addition to Facts about Lung Cancer, Colorectal Cancer, and Thyroid Cancer in Women

Along with Information about Cancer Risk Factors, Screening and Prevention, Treatment Options, and Tips on Coping with Life after Cancer Treatment, a Glossary of Cancer Terms, and a Directory of Resources for Additional Help and Information

Edited by Amy L. Sutton. 715 pages. 2006. 0-7808-0867-3.

"An excellent addition to collections in public, consumer health, and women's health libraries."

—*American Reference Books Annual, 2003*

"Overall, the information is excellent, and complex topics are clearly explained. As a reference book for the consumer it is a valuable resource to assist them to make informed decisions about cancer and its treatments."

—*Cancer Forum, Nov '02*

"Highly recommended for academic and medical reference collections."

—*Library Bookwatch, Sep '02*

"This is a highly recommended book for any public or consumer library, being reader friendly and containing accurate and helpful information."

—*E-Streams, Aug '02*

■

Cardiovascular Diseases & Disorders Sourcebook, 3rd Edition

Basic Consumer Health Information about Heart and Vascular Diseases and Disorders, Such as Angina, Heart Attacks, Arrhythmias, Cardiomyopathy, Valve Disease, Atherosclerosis, and Aneurysms, with Information about Managing Cardiovascular Risk Factors and Maintaining Heart Health, Medications and Procedures Used to Treat Cardiovascular Disorders, and Concerns of Special Significance to Women

Along with Reports on Current Research Initiatives, a Glossary of Related Medical Terms, and a Directory of Sources for Further Help and Information

Edited by Sandra J. Judd. 713 pages. 2005. 0-7808-0739-1.

■

Caregiving Sourcebook

Basic Consumer Health Information for Caregivers, Including a Profile of Caregivers, Caregiving Responsibilities and Concerns, Tips for Specific Conditions, Care Environments, and the Effects of Caregiving

Along with Facts about Legal Issues, Financial Information, and Future Planning, a Glossary, and a Listing of Additional Resources

Edited by Joyce Brennfleck Shannon. 600 pages. 2001. 0-7808-0331-0.

Child Abuse Sourcebook

Basic Consumer Health Information about the Physical, Sexual, and Emotional Abuse of Children, with Additional Facts about Neglect, Munchausen Syndrome by Proxy (MSBP), Shaken Baby Syndrome, and Controversial Issues Related to Child Abuse, Such as Withholding Medical Care, Corporal Punishment, and Child Maltreatment in Youth Sports, and Featuring Facts about Child Protective Services, Foster Care, Adoption, Parenting Challenges, and Other Abuse Prevention Efforts

Along with a Glossary of Related Terms and Resources for Additional Help and Information

Edited by Dawn D. Matthews. 620 pages. 2004. 0-7808-0705-7.

■

Childhood Diseases & Disorders Sourcebook

Basic Consumer Health Information about Medical Problems Often Encountered in Pre-Adolescent Children, Including Respiratory Tract Ailments, Ear Infections, Sore Throats, Disorders of the Skin and Scalp, Digestive and Genitourinary Diseases, Infectious Diseases, Inflammatory Disorders, Chronic Physical and Developmental Disorders, Allergies, and More

Along with Information about Diagnostic Tests, Common Childhood Surgeries, and Frequently Used Medications, with a Glossary of Important Terms and Resource Directory

Edited by Chad T. Kimball. 662 pages. 2003. 0-7808-0458-9.

■

Colds, Flu & Other Common Ailments Sourcebook

Basic Consumer Health Information about Common Ailments and Injuries, Including Colds, Coughs, the Flu, Sinus Problems, Headaches, Fever, Nausea and

Vomiting, Menstrual Cramps, Diarrhea, Constipation, Hemorrhoids, Back Pain, Dandruff, Dry and Itchy Skin, Cuts, Scrapes, Sprains, Bruises, and More

Along with Information about Prevention, Self-Care, Choosing a Doctor, Over-the-Counter Medications, Folk Remedies, and Alternative Therapies, and Including a Glossary of Important Terms and a Directory of Resources for Further Help and Information

Edited by Chad T. Kimball. 638 pages. 2001. 0-7808-0435-X.

"A good starting point for research on common illnesses. It will be a useful addition to public and consumer health library collections."
— American Reference Books Annual, 2002

"Will prove valuable to any library seeking to maintain a current, comprehensive reference collection of health resources. . . . Excellent reference."
— The Bookwatch, Aug '01

"Recommended reference source."
— Booklist, American Library Association, Jul '01

■

Communication Disorders Sourcebook

Basic Information about Deafness and Hearing Loss, Speech and Language Disorders, Voice Disorders, Balance and Vestibular Disorders, and Disorders of Smell, Taste, and Touch

Edited by Linda M. Ross. 533 pages. 1996. 0-7808-0077-X.

"This is skillfully edited and is a welcome resource for the layperson. It should be found in every public and medical library."   — Booklist Health Sciences Supplement, American Library Association, Oct '97

■

Complementary & Alternative Medicine Sourcebook, 3rd Edition

Basic Consumer Health Information about Complementary and Alternative Medical Therapies, Including Acupuncture, Ayurveda, Traditional Chinese Medicine, Herbal Medicine, Homeopathy, Naturopathy, Biofeedback, Hypnotherapy, Yoga, Art Therapy, Aromatherapy, Clinical Nutrition, Vitamin and Mineral Supplements, Chiropractic, Massage, Reflexology, Crystal Therapy, Therapeutic Touch, and More

Along with Facts about Alternative and Complementary Treatments for Specific Conditions Such as Cancer, Diabetes, Osteoarthritis, Chronic Pain, Menopause, Gastrointestinal Disorders, Headaches, and Mental Illness, a Glossary, and a Resource List for Additional Help and Information

Edited by Sandra J. Judd. 657 pages. 2006. 0-7808-0864-9.

"Recommended for public, high school, and academic libraries that have consumer health collections. Hospital libraries that also serve the public will find this to be a useful resource."   — E-Streams, Feb '03

"Recommended reference source."
—Booklist, American Library Association, Jan '03

"An important alternate health reference."
— MBR Bookwatch, Oct '02

"A great addition to the reference collection of every type of library." — American Reference Books Annual, 2000

■

Congenital Disorders Sourcebook

Basic Information about Disorders Acquired during Gestation, Including Spina Bifida, Hydrocephalus, Cerebral Palsy, Heart Defects, Craniofacial Abnormalities, Fetal Alcohol Syndrome, and More

Along with Current Treatment Options and Statistical Data

Edited by Karen Bellenir. 607 pages. 1997. 0-7808-0205-5.

"Recommended reference source."
— Booklist, American Library Association, Oct '97

SEE ALSO Pregnancy & Birth Sourcebook

■

Consumer Issues in Health Care Sourcebook

Basic Information about Health Care Fundamentals and Related Consumer Issues, Including Exams and Screening Tests, Physician Specialties, Choosing a Doctor, Using Prescription and Over-the-Counter Medications Safely, Avoiding Health Scams, Managing Common Health Risks in the Home, Care Options for Chronically or Terminally Ill Patients, and a List of Resources for Obtaining Help and Further Information

Edited by Karen Bellenir. 618 pages. 1998. 0-7808-0221-7.

"Both public and academic libraries will want to have a copy in their collection for readers who are interested in self-education on health issues."
—American Reference Books Annual, 2000

"The editor has researched the literature from government agencies and others, saving readers the time and effort of having to do the research themselves. Recommended for public libraries."
— Reference and User Services Quarterly, American Library Association, Spring '99

"Recommended reference source."
— Booklist, American Library Association, Dec '98

■

Contagious Diseases Sourcebook

Basic Consumer Health Information about Infectious Diseases Spread by Person-to-Person Contact through Direct Touch, Airborne Transmission, Sexual Contact, or Contact with Blood or Other Body Fluids, Including Hepatitis, Herpes, Influenza, Lice, Measles, Mumps, Pinworm, Ringworm, Severe Acute Respiratory Syndrome (SARS), Streptococcal Infections, Tuberculosis, and Others

Along with Facts about Disease Transmission, Antimicrobial Resistance, and Vaccines, with a Glossary and Directories of Resources for More Information

Edited by Karen Bellenir. 643 pages. 2004. 0-7808-0736-7.

■

Contagious & Non-Contagious Infectious Diseases Sourcebook

Basic Information about Contagious Diseases like Measles, Polio, Hepatitis B, and Infectious Mononucleosis, and Non-Contagious Infectious Diseases like Tetanus and Toxic Shock Syndrome, and Diseases Occurring as Secondary Infections Such as Shingles and Reye Syndrome

Along with Vaccination, Prevention, and Treatment Information, and a Section Describing Emerging Infectious Disease Threats

Edited by Karen Bellenir and Peter D. Dresser. 566 pages. 1996. 0-7808-0075-3.

SEE ALSO *Infectious Diseases Sourcebook*

■

Death & Dying Sourcebook, 2nd Edition

Basic Consumer Health Information about End-of-Life Care and Related Perspectives and Ethical Issues, Including End-of-Life Symptoms and Treatments, Pain Management, Quality-of-Life Concerns, the Use of Life Support, Patients' Rights and Privacy Issues, Advance Directives, Physician-Assisted Suicide, Caregiving, Organ and Tissue Donation, Autopsies, Funeral Arrangements, and Grief

Along with Statistical Data, Information about the Leading Causes of Death, a Glossary, and Directories of Support Groups and Other Resources

Edited by Joyce Brennfleck Shannon. 653 pages. 2006. 0-7808-0871-1.

Dental Care & Oral Health Sourcebook, 2nd Edition

Basic Consumer Health Information about Dental Care, Including Oral Hygiene, Dental Visits, Pain Management, Cavities, Crowns, Bridges, Dental Implants, and Fillings, and Other Oral Health Concerns, Such as Gum Disease, Bad Breath, Dry Mouth, Genetic and Developmental Abnormalities, Oral Cancers, Orthodontics, and Temporomandibular Disorders

Along with Updates on Current Research in Oral Health, a Glossary, a Directory of Dental and Oral Health Organizations, and Resources for People with Dental and Oral Health Disorders

Edited by Amy L. Sutton. 609 pages. 2003. 0-7808-0634-4.

■

Depression Sourcebook

Basic Consumer Health Information about Unipolar Depression, Bipolar Disorder, Postpartum Depression, Seasonal Affective Disorder, and Other Types of Depression in Children, Adolescents, Women, Men, the Elderly, and Other Selected Populations

Along with Facts about Causes, Risk Factors, Diagnostic Criteria, Treatment Options, Coping Strategies, Suicide Prevention, a Glossary, and a Directory of Sources for Additional Help and Information

Edited by Karen Belleni. 602 pages. 2002. 0-7808-0611-5.

■

Dermatological Disorders Sourcebook, 2nd Edition

Basic Consumer Health Information about Conditions and Disorders Affecting the Skin, Hair, and Nails, Such as Acne, Rosacea, Rashes, Dermatitis, Pigmentation Disorders, Birthmarks, Skin Cancer, Skin Injuries, Psoriasis, Scleroderma, and Hair Loss, Including Facts about Medications and Treatments for Dermatological

Disorders and Tips for Maintaining Healthy Skin, Hair, and Nails

Along with Information about How Aging Affects the Skin, a Glossary of Related Terms, and a Directory of Resources for Additional Help and Information

Edited by Amy L. Sutton. 645 pages. 2005. 0-7808-0795-2.

"... comprehensive, easily read reference book."
—*Doody's Health Sciences Book Reviews, Oct '97*

SEE ALSO *Burns Sourcebook*

Diabetes Sourcebook, 3rd Edition

Basic Consumer Health Information about Type 1 Diabetes (Insulin-Dependent or Juvenile-Onset Diabetes), Type 2 Diabetes (Noninsulin-Dependent or Adult-Onset Diabetes), Gestational Diabetes, Impaired Glucose Tolerance (IGT), and Related Complications, Such as Amputation, Eye Disease, Gum Disease, Nerve Damage, and End-Stage Renal Disease, Including Facts about Insulin, Oral Diabetes Medications, Blood Sugar Testing, and the Role of Exercise and Nutrition in the Control of Diabetes

Along with a Glossary and Resources for Further Help and Information

Edited by Dawn D. Matthews. 622 pages. 2003. 0-7808-0629-8.

"This edition is even more helpful than earlier versions.... It is a truly valuable tool for anyone seeking readable and authoritative information on diabetes."
—*American Reference Books Annual, 2004*

"An invaluable reference." —*Library Journal, May '00*

Selected as one of the 250 "Best Health Sciences Books of 1999." —*Doody's Rating Service, Mar-Apr '00*

"Provides useful information for the general public."
—*Healthlines, University of Michigan Health Management Research Center, Sep/Oct '99*

"... provides reliable mainstream medical information ... belongs on the shelves of any library with a consumer health collection." —*E-Streams, Sep '99*

"Recommended reference source."
—*Booklist, American Library Association, Feb '99*

Diet & Nutrition Sourcebook, 3rd Edition

Basic Consumer Health Information about Dietary Guidelines and the Food Guidance System, Recommended Daily Nutrient Intakes, Serving Proportions, Weight Control, Vitamins and Supplements, Nutrition Issues for Different Life Stages and Lifestyles, and the Needs of People with Specific Medical Concerns, Including Cancer, Celiac Disease, Diabetes, Eating Disorders, Food Allergies, and Cardiovascular Disease

Along with Facts about Federal Nutrition Support Programs, a Glossary of Nutrition and Dietary Terms, and Directories of Additional Resources for More Information about Nutrition

Edited by Joyce Brennfleck Shannon. 633 pages. 2006. 0-7808-0800-2.

"This book is an excellent source of basic diet and nutrition information." —*Booklist Health Sciences Supplement, American Library Association, Dec '00*

"This reference document should be in any public library, but it would be a very good guide for beginning students in the health sciences. If the other books in this publisher's series are as good as this, they should all be in the health sciences collections."
—*American Reference Books Annual, 2000*

"This book is an excellent general nutrition reference for consumers who desire to take an active role in their health care for prevention. Consumers of all ages who select this book can feel confident they are receiving current and accurate information." —*Journal of Nutrition for the Elderly, Vol. 19, No. 4, 2000*

SEE ALSO *Digestive Diseases & Disorders Sourcebook, Eating Disorders Sourcebook, Gastrointestinal Diseases & Disorders Sourcebook, Vegetarian Sourcebook*

Digestive Diseases & Disorders Sourcebook

Basic Consumer Health Information about Diseases and Disorders that Impact the Upper and Lower Digestive System, Including Celiac Disease, Constipation, Crohn's Disease, Cyclic Vomiting Syndrome, Diarrhea, Diverticulosis and Diverticulitis, Gallstones, Heartburn, Hemorrhoids, Hernias, Indigestion (Dyspepsia), Irritable Bowel Syndrome, Lactose Intolerance, Ulcers, and More

Along with Information about Medications and Other Treatments, Tips for Maintaining a Healthy Digestive Tract, a Glossary, and Directory of Digestive Diseases Organizations

Edited by Karen Bellenir. 335 pages. 2000. 0-7808-0327-2.

"This title would be an excellent addition to all public or patient-research libraries."
—*American Reference Books Annual, 2001*

"This title is recommended for public, hospital, and health sciences libraries with consumer health collections." —*E-Streams, Jul-Aug '00*

"Recommended reference source."
—*Booklist, American Library Association, May '00*

SEE ALSO *Eating Disorders Sourcebook, Gastrointestinal Diseases & Disorders Sourcebook*

Disabilities Sourcebook

Basic Consumer Health Information about Physical and Psychiatric Disabilities, Including Descriptions of Major Causes of Disability, Assistive and Adaptive Aids, Workplace Issues, and Accessibility Concerns

Along with Information about the Americans with Disabilities Act, a Glossary, and Resources for Additional Help and Information

Edited by Dawn D. Matthews. 616 pages. 2000. 0-7808-0389-2.

"It is a must for libraries with a consumer health section." —*American Reference Books Annual, 2002*

"A much needed addition to the Omnigraphics Health Reference Series. A current reference work to provide people with disabilities, their families, caregivers or those who work with them, a broad range of information in one volume, has not been available until now. . . . It is recommended for all public and academic library reference collections." —*E-Streams, May '01*

"An excellent source book in easy-to-read format covering many current topics; highly recommended for all libraries." —*Choice, Association of College & Research Libraries, Jan '01*

"Recommended reference source." —*Booklist, American Library Association, Jul '00*

■

Domestic Violence Sourcebook, 2nd Edition

Basic Consumer Health Information about the Causes and Consequences of Abusive Relationships, Including Physical Violence, Sexual Assault, Battery, Stalking, and Emotional Abuse, and Facts about the Effects of Violence on Women, Men, Young Adults, and the Elderly, with Reports about Domestic Violence in Selected Populations, and Featuring Facts about Medical Care, Victim Assistance and Protection, Prevention Strategies, Mental Health Services, and Legal Issues

Along with a Glossary of Related Terms and Resources for Additional Help and Information

Edited by Dawn D. Matthews. 628 pages. 2004. 0-7808-0669-7.

"Educators, clergy, medical professionals, police, and victims and their families will benefit from this realistic and easy-to-understand resource." —*American Reference Books Annual, 2005*

"Recommended for all collections supporting consumer health information. It should also be considered for any collection needing general, readable information on domestic violence." —*E-Streams, Jan '05*

"This sourcebook complements other books in its field, providing a one-stop resource . . . Recommended." —*Choice, Association of College & Research Libraries, Jan '05*

"Interested lay persons should find the book extremely beneficial. . . . A copy of *Domestic Violence and Child Abuse Sourcebook* should be in every public library in the United States." —*Social Science & Medicine, No. 56, 2003*

"This is important information. The Web has many resources but this sourcebook fills an important societal need. I am not aware of any other resources of this type." —*Doody's Review Service, Sep '01*

"Recommended reference source." —*Booklist, American Library Association, Apr '01*

"Important pick for college-level health reference libraries." —*The Bookwatch, Mar '01*

"Because this problem is so widespread and because this book includes a lot of issues within one volume, this work is recommended for all public libraries." —*American Reference Books Annual, 2001*

SEE ALSO Child Abuse Sourcebook

■

Drug Abuse Sourcebook, 2nd Edition

Basic Consumer Health Information about Illicit Substances of Abuse and the Misuse of Prescription and Over-the-Counter Medications, Including Depressants, Hallucinogens, Inhalants, Marijuana, Stimulants, and Anabolic Steroids

Along with Facts about Related Health Risks, Treatment Programs, Prevention Programs, a Glossary of Abuse and Addiction Terms, a Glossary of Drug-Related Street Terms, and a Directory of Resources for More Information

Edited by Catherine Ginther. 607 pages. 2004. 0-7808-0740-5.

"Commendable for organizing useful, normally scattered government and association-produced data into a logical sequence." —*American Reference Books Annual, 2006*

"This easy-to-read volume is recommended for consumer health collections within public or academic libraries." —*E-Streams, Sep '05*

"An excellent library reference." —*The Bookwatch, May '05*

"Containing a wealth of information, this book will be useful to the college student just beginning to explore the topic of substance abuse. This resource belongs in libraries that serve a lower-division undergraduate or community college clientele as well as the general public." —*Choice, Association of College & Research Libraries, Jun '01*

"Recommended reference source." —*Booklist, American Library Association, Feb '01*

SEE ALSO Alcoholism Sourcebook, Substance Abuse Sourcebook

■

Ear, Nose & Throat Disorders Sourcebook, 2nd Edition

Basic Consumer Health Information about Disorders of the Ears, Hearing Loss, Vestibular Disorders, Nasal and Sinus Problems, Throat and Vocal Cord Disorders, and Otolaryngologic Cancers, Including Facts about Ear Infections and Injuries, Genetic and Congenital Deafness, Sensorineural Hearing Disorders, Tinnitus, Vertigo, Ménière Disease, Rhinitis, Sinusitis, Snoring, Sore Throats, Hoarseness, and More

Along with Reports on Current Research Initiatives, a Glossary of Related Medical Terms, and a Directory of Sources for Further Help and Information

Edited by Sandra J. Judd. 659 pages. 2006. 0-7808-0872-X.

"Overall, this sourcebook is helpful for the consumer seeking information on ENT issues. It is recommended for public libraries."
—American Reference Books Annual, 1999

"Recommended reference source."
—Booklist, American Library Association, Dec '98

■

Eating Disorders Sourcebook

Basic Consumer Health Information about Eating Disorders, Including Information about Anorexia Nervosa, Bulimia Nervosa, Binge Eating, Body Dysmorphic Disorder, Pica, Laxative Abuse, and Night Eating Syndrome

Along with Information about Causes, Adverse Effects, and Treatment and Prevention Issues, and Featuring a Section on Concerns Specific to Children and Adolescents, a Glossary, and Resources for Further Help and Information

Edited by Dawn D. Matthews. 322 pages. 2001. 0-7808-0335-3.

"Recommended for health science libraries that are open to the public, as well as hospital libraries. This book is a good resource for the consumer who is concerned about eating disorders." —E-Streams, Mar '02

"This volume is another convenient collection of excerpted articles. Recommended for school and public library patrons; lower-division undergraduates; and two-year technical program students."
—Choice, Association of College & Research Libraries, Jan '02

"Recommended reference source."
—Booklist, American Library Association, Oct '01

SEE ALSO Diet & Nutrition Sourcebook, Digestive Diseases & Disorders Sourcebook, Gastrointestinal Diseases & Disorders Sourcebook

■

Emergency Medical Services Sourcebook

Basic Consumer Health Information about Preventing, Preparing for, and Managing Emergency Situations, When and Who to Call for Help, What to Expect in the Emergency Room, the Emergency Medical Team, Patient Issues, and Current Topics in Emergency Medicine

Along with Statistical Data, a Glossary, and Sources of Additional Help and Information

Edited by Jenni Lynn Colson. 494 pages. 2002. 0-7808-0420-1.

"Handy and convenient for home, public, school, and college libraries. Recommended."
—Choice, Association of College & Research Libraries, Apr '03

"This reference can provide the consumer with answers to most questions about emergency care in the United States, or it will direct them to a resource where the answer can be found."
—American Reference Books Annual, 2003

"Recommended reference source."
—Booklist, American Library Association, Feb '03

■

Endocrine & Metabolic Disorders Sourcebook

Basic Information for the Layperson about Pancreatic and Insulin-Related Disorders Such as Pancreatitis, Diabetes, and Hypoglycemia; Adrenal Gland Disorders Such as Cushing's Syndrome, Addison's Disease, and Congenital Adrenal Hyperplasia; Pituitary Gland Disorders Such as Growth Hormone Deficiency, Acromegaly, and Pituitary Tumors; Thyroid Disorders Such as Hypothyroidism, Graves' Disease, Hashimoto's Disease, and Goiter; Hyperparathyroidism; and Other Diseases and Syndromes of Hormone Imbalance or Metabolic Dysfunction

Along with Reports on Current Research Initiatives

Edited by Linda M. Shin. 574 pages. 1998. 0-7808-0207-1.

"Omnigraphics has produced another needed resource for health information consumers."
—American Reference Books Annual, 2000

"Recommended reference source."
—Booklist, American Library Association, Dec '98

■

Environmental Health Sourcebook, 2nd Edition

Basic Consumer Health Information about the Environment and Its Effect on Human Health, Including the Effects of Air Pollution, Water Pollution, Hazardous Chemicals, Food Hazards, Radiation Hazards, Biological Agents, Household Hazards, Such as Radon, Asbestos, Carbon Monoxide, and Mold, and Information about Associated Diseases and Disorders, Including Cancer, Allergies, Respiratory Problems, and Skin Disorders

Along with Information about Environmental Concerns for Specific Populations, a Glossary of Related Terms, and Resources for Further Help and Information

Edited by Dawn D. Matthews. 673 pages. 2003. 0-7808-0632-8.

"This recently updated edition continues the level of quality and the reputation of the numerous other volumes in Omnigraphics' Health Reference Series."
—American Reference Books Annual, 2004

"An excellent updated edition."
—The Bookwatch, Oct '03

"Recommended reference source."
—Booklist, American Library Association, Sep '98

"This book will be a useful addition to anyone's library." —Choice Health Sciences Supplement, Association of College & Research Libraries, May '98

". . . a good survey of numerous environmentally induced physical disorders . . . a useful addition to anyone's library."
— *Doody's Health Sciences Book Reviews, Jan '98*

Environmentally Induced Disorders Sourcebook

SEE *Environmental Health Sourcebook, 2nd Edition*

Ethnic Diseases Sourcebook

Basic Consumer Health Information for Ethnic and Racial Minority Groups in the United States, Including General Health Indicators and Behaviors, Ethnic Diseases, Genetic Testing, the Impact of Chronic Diseases, Women's Health, Mental Health Issues, and Preventive Health Care Services

Along with a Glossary and a Listing of Additional Resources

Edited by Joyce Brennfleck Shannon. 664 pages. 2001. 0-7808-0336-1.

"Recommended for health sciences libraries where public health programs are a priority."
— *E-Streams, Jan '02*

"Not many books have been written on this topic to date, and the *Ethnic Diseases Sourcebook* is a strong addition to the list. It will be an important introductory resource for health consumers, students, health care personnel, and social scientists. It is recommended for public, academic, and large hospital libraries."
— *American Reference Books Annual, 2002*

"Recommended reference source."
— *Booklist, American Library Association, Oct '01*

"Will prove valuable to any library seeking to maintain a current, comprehensive reference collection of health resources. . . . An excellent source of health information about genetic disorders which affect particular ethnic and racial minorities in the U.S."
— *The Bookwatch, Aug '01*

Eye Care Sourcebook, 2nd Edition

Basic Consumer Health Information about Eye Care and Eye Disorders, Including Facts about the Diagnosis, Prevention, and Treatment of Common Refractive Problems Such as Myopia, Hyperopia, Astigmatism, and Presbyopia, and Eye Diseases, Including Glaucoma, Cataract, Age-Related Macular Degeneration, and Diabetic Retinopathy

Along with a Section on Vision Correction and Refractive Surgeries, Including LASIK and LASEK, a Glossary, and Directories of Resources for Additional Help and Information

Edited by Amy L. Sutton. 543 pages. 2003. 0-7808-0635-2.

"... a solid reference tool for eye care and a valuable addition to a collection."
— *American Reference Books Annual, 2004*

Family Planning Sourcebook

Basic Consumer Health Information about Planning for Pregnancy and Contraception, Including Traditional Methods, Barrier Methods, Hormonal Methods, Permanent Methods, Future Methods, Emergency Contraception, and Birth Control Choices for Women at Each Stage of Life

Along with Statistics, a Glossary, and Sources of Additional Information

Edited by Amy Marcaccio Keyzer. 520 pages. 2001. 0-7808-0379-5.

"Recommended for public, health, and undergraduate libraries as part of the circulating collection."
— *E-Streams, Mar '02*

"Information is presented in an unbiased, readable manner, and the sourcebook will certainly be a necessary addition to those public and high school libraries where Internet access is restricted or otherwise problematic." — *American Reference Books Annual, 2002*

"Recommended reference source."
— *Booklist, American Library Association, Oct '01*

"Will prove valuable to any library seeking to maintain a current, comprehensive reference collection of health resources. . . . Excellent reference."
— *The Bookwatch, Aug '01*

SEE ALSO *Pregnancy & Birth Sourcebook*

Fitness & Exercise Sourcebook, 2nd Edition

Basic Consumer Health Information about the Fundamentals of Fitness and Exercise, Including How to Begin and Maintain a Fitness Program, Fitness as a Lifestyle, the Link between Fitness and Diet, Advice for Specific Groups of People, Exercise as It Relates to Specific Medical Conditions, and Recent Research in Fitness and Exercise

Along with a Glossary of Important Terms and Resources for Additional Help and Information

Edited by Kristen M. Gledhill. 646 pages. 2001. 0-7808-0334-5.

"This work is recommended for all general reference collections."
— *American Reference Books Annual, 2002*

"Highly recommended for public, consumer, and school grades fourth through college." — *E-Streams, Nov '01*

"Recommended reference source."
— *Booklist, American Library Association, Oct '01*

"The information appears quite comprehensive and is considered reliable. . . . This second edition is a welcomed addition to the series."
— *Doody's Review Service, Sep '01*

Food & Animal Borne Diseases Sourcebook

Basic Information about Diseases That Can Be Spread to Humans through the Ingestion of Contaminated Food or Water or by Contact with Infected Animals and Insects, Such as Botulism, E. Coli, Hepatitis A, Trichinosis, Lyme Disease, and Rabies

Along with Information Regarding Prevention and Treatment Methods, and Including a Special Section for International Travelers Describing Diseases Such as Cholera, Malaria, Travelers' Diarrhea, and Yellow Fever, and Offering Recommendations for Avoiding Illness

Edited by Karen Bellenir and Peter D. Dresser. 535 pages. 1995. 0-7808-0033-8.

"Targeting general readers and providing them with a single, comprehensive source of information on selected topics, this book continues, with the excellent caliber of its predecessors, to catalog topical information on health matters of general interest. Readable and thorough, this valuable resource is highly recommended for all libraries."
— *Academic Library Book Review, Summer '96*

"A comprehensive collection of authoritative information." — *Emergency Medical Services, Oct '95*

■

Food Safety Sourcebook

Basic Consumer Health Information about the Safe Handling of Meat, Poultry, Seafood, Eggs, Fruit Juices, and Other Food Items, and Facts about Pesticides, Drinking Water, Food Safety Overseas, and the Onset, Duration, and Symptoms of Foodborne Illnesses, Including Types of Pathogenic Bacteria, Parasitic Protozoa, Worms, Viruses, and Natural Toxins

Along with the Role of the Consumer, the Food Handler, and the Government in Food Safety; a Glossary, and Resources for Additional Help and Information

Edited by Dawn D. Matthews. 339 pages. 1999. 0-7808-0326-4.

"This book is recommended for public libraries and universities with home economic and food science programs." — *E-Streams, Nov '00*

"Recommended reference source."
— *Booklist, American Library Association, May '00*

"This book takes the complex issues of food safety and foodborne pathogens and presents them in an easily understood manner. [It does] an excellent job of covering a large and often confusing topic."
— *American Reference Books Annual, 2000*

■

Forensic Medicine Sourcebook

Basic Consumer Information for the Layperson about Forensic Medicine, Including Crime Scene Investigation, Evidence Collection and Analysis, Expert Testimony, Computer-Aided Criminal Identification, Digital Imaging in the Courtroom, DNA Profiling, Accident Reconstruction, Autopsies, Ballistics, Drugs and

Explosives Detection, Latent Fingerprints, Product Tampering, and Questioned Document Examination

Along with Statistical Data, a Glossary of Forensics Terminology, and Listings of Sources for Further Help and Information

Edited by Annemarie S. Muth. 574 pages. 1999. 0-7808-0232-2.

"Given the expected widespread interest in its content and its easy to read style, this book is recommended for most public and all college and university libraries."
— *E-Streams, Feb '01*

"Recommended for public libraries."
— *Reference & User Services Quarterly, American Library Association, Spring 2000*

"Recommended reference source."
— *Booklist, American Library Association, Feb '00*

"A wealth of information, useful statistics, references are up-to-date and extremely complete. This wonderful collection of data will help students who are interested in a career in any type of forensic field. It is a great resource for attorneys who need information about types of expert witnesses needed in a particular case. It also offers useful information for fiction and nonfiction writers whose work involves a crime. A fascinating compilation. All levels."
— *Choice, Association of College & Research Libraries, Jan '00*

"There are several items that make this book attractive to consumers who are seeking certain forensic data.... This is a useful current source for those seeking general forensic medical answers."
— *American Reference Books Annual, 2000*

■

Gastrointestinal Diseases & Disorders Sourcebook, 2nd Edition

Basic Consumer Health Information about the Upper and Lower Gastrointestinal (GI) Tract, Including the Esophagus, Stomach, Intestines, Rectum, Liver, and Pancreas, with Facts about Gastroesophageal Reflux Disease, Gastritis, Hernias, Ulcers, Celiac Disease, Diverticulitis, Irritable Bowel Syndrome, Hemorrhoids, Gastrointestinal Cancers, and Other Diseases and Disorders Related to the Digestive Process

Along with Information about Commonly Used Diagnostic and Surgical Procedures, Statistics, Reports on Current Research Initiatives and Clinical Trials, a Glossary, and Resources for Additional Help and Information

Edited by Sandra J. Judd. 681 pages. 2006. 0-7808-0798-7.

". . . very readable form. The successful editorial work that brought this material together into a useful and understandable reference makes accessible to all readers information that can help them more effectively understand and obtain help for digestive tract problems."
— *Choice, Association of College & Research Libraries, Feb '97*

Genetic Disorders Sourcebook, 3rd Edition

Basic Consumer Health Information about Hereditary Diseases and Disorders, Including Facts about the Human Genome, Genetic Inheritance Patterns, Disorders Associated with Specific Genes, Such as Sickle Cell Disease, Hemophilia, and Cystic Fibrosis, Chromosome Disorders, Such as Down Syndrome, Fragile X Syndrome, and Turner Syndrome, and Complex Diseases and Disorders Resulting from the Interaction of Environmental and Genetic Factors, Such as Allergies, Cancer, and Obesity

Along with Facts about Genetic Testing, Suggestions for Parents of Children with Special Needs, Reports on Current Research Initiatives, a Glossary of Genetic Terminology, and Resources for Additional Help and Information

Edited by Karen Bellenir. 777 pages. 2004. 0-7808-0742-1.

"This text is recommended for any library with an interest in providing consumer health resources."
— *E-Streams, Aug '05*

"This is a valuable resource for anyone wishing to have an understandable description of any of the topics or disorders included. The editor succeeds in making complex genetic issues understandable."
— *Doody's Book Review Service, May '05*

"A good acquisition for public libraries."
— *American Reference Books Annual, 2005*

"Excellent reference." — *The Bookwatch, Jan '05*

"Recommended reference source."
— *Booklist, American Library Association, Apr '01*

"Important pick for college-level health reference libraries." — *The Bookwatch, Mar '01*

Head Trauma Sourcebook

Basic Information for the Layperson about Open-Head and Closed-Head Injuries, Treatment Advances, Recovery, and Rehabilitation
Along with Reports on Current Research Initiatives

Edited by Karen Bellenir. 414 pages. 1997. 0-7808-0208-X.

Headache Sourcebook

Basic Consumer Health Information about Migraine, Tension, Cluster, Rebound and Other Types of Headaches, with Facts about the Cause and Prevention of Headaches, the Effects of Stress and the Environment, Headaches during Pregnancy and Menopause, and Childhood Headaches

Along with a Glossary and Other Resources for Additional Help and Information

Edited by Dawn D. Matthews. 362 pages. 2002. 0-7808-0337-X.

"Highly recommended for academic and medical reference collections." — *Library Bookwatch, Sep '02*

Health Insurance Sourcebook

Basic Information about Managed Care Organizations, Traditional Fee-for-Service Insurance, Insurance Portability and Pre-Existing Conditions Clauses, Medicare, Medicaid, Social Security, and Military Health Care
Along with Information about Insurance Fraud

Edited by Wendy Wilcox. 530 pages. 1997. 0-7808-0222-5.

"Particularly useful because it brings much of this information together in one volume. This book will be a handy reference source in the health sciences library, hospital library, college and university library, and medium to large public library."
— *Medical Reference Services Quarterly, Fall '98*

Awarded "Books of the Year Award"
— *American Journal of Nursing, 1997*

"The layout of the book is particularly helpful as it provides easy access to reference material. A most useful addition to the vast amount of information about health insurance. The use of data from U.S. government agencies is most commendable. Useful in a library or learning center for healthcare professional students."
— *Doody's Health Sciences Book Reviews, Nov '97*

Healthy Aging Sourcebook

Basic Consumer Health Information about Maintaining Health through the Aging Process, Including Advice on Nutrition, Exercise, and Sleep, Help in Making Decisions about Midlife Issues and Retirement, and Guidance Concerning Practical and Informed Choices in Health Consumerism

Along with Data Concerning the Theories of Aging, Different Experiences in Aging by Minority Groups, and Facts about Aging Now and Aging in the Future; and Featuring a Glossary, a Guide to Consumer Help, Additional Suggested Reading, and Practical Resource Directory

Edited by Jenifer Swanson. 536 pages. 1999. 0-7808-0390-6.

"Recommended reference source."
— *Booklist, American Library Association, Feb '00*

Healthy Children Sourcebook

Basic Consumer Health Information about the Physical and Mental Development of Children between the Ages of 3 and 12, Including Routine Health Care, Preventative Health Services, Safety and First Aid, Healthy Sleep, Dental Care, Nutrition, and Fitness, and Featuring Parenting Tips on Such Topics as Bed-

wetting, Choosing Day Care, Monitoring TV and Other Media, and Establishing a Foundation for Substance Abuse Prevention

Along with a Glossary of Commonly Used Pediatric Terms and Resources for Additional Help and Information.

Edited by Chad T. Kimball. 647 pages. 2003. 0-7808-0247-0.

"It is hard to imagine that any other single resource exists that would provide such a comprehensive guide of timely information on health promotion and disease prevention for children aged 3 to 12."
— *American Reference Books Annual, 2004*

"The strengths of this book are many. It is clearly written, presented and structured."
— *Journal of the National Medical Association, 2004*

SEE ALSO Childhood Diseases & Disorders Sourcebook

Healthy Heart Sourcebook for Women

Basic Consumer Health Information about Cardiac Issues Specific to Women, Including Facts about Major Risk Factors and Prevention, Treatment and Control Strategies, and Important Dietary Issues

Along with a Special Section Regarding the Pros and Cons of Hormone Replacement Therapy and Its Impact on Heart Health, and Additional Help, Including Recipes, a Glossary, and a Directory of Resources

Edited by Dawn D. Matthews. 336 pages. 2000. 0-7808-0329-9.

"A good reference source and recommended for all public, academic, medical, and hospital libraries."
— *Medical Reference Services Quarterly, Summer '01*

"Because of the lack of information specific to women on this topic, this book is recommended for public libraries and consumer libraries."
— *American Reference Books Annual, 2001*

"Contains very important information about coronary artery disease that all women should know. The information is current and presented in an easy-to-read format. The book will make a good addition to any library."
— *American Medical Writers Association Journal, Summer '00*

"Important, basic reference."
— *Reviewer's Bookwatch, Jul '00*

SEE ALSO Cardiovascular Diseases & Disorders Sourcebook, Women's Health Concerns Sourcebook

Heart Diseases & Disorders Sourcebook

SEE Cardiovascular Diseases & Disorders Sourcebook, 3rd Edition

Hepatitis Sourcebook

Basic Consumer Health Information about Hepatitis A, Hepatitis B, Hepatitis C, and Other Forms of Hepatitis, Including Autoimmune Hepatitis, Alcoholic Hepatitis, Nonalcoholic Steatohepatitis, and Toxic Hepatitis, with Facts about Risk Factors, Screening Methods, Diagnostic Tests, and Treatment Options

Along with Information on Liver Health, Tips for People Living with Chronic Hepatitis, Reports on Current Research Initiatives, a Glossary of Terms Related to Hepatitis, and a Directory of Sources for Further Help and Information

Edited by Sandra J. Judd. 597 pages. 2005. 0-7808-0749-9.

"Highly recommended."
— *American Reference Books Annual, 2006*

Household Safety Sourcebook

Basic Consumer Health Information about Household Safety, Including Information about Poisons, Chemicals, Fire, and Water Hazards in the Home

Along with Advice about the Safe Use of Home Maintenance Equipment, Choosing Toys and Nursery Furniture, Holiday and Recreation Safety, a Glossary, and Resources for Further Help and Information

Edited by Dawn D. Matthews. 606 pages. 2002. 0-7808-0338-8.

"This work will be useful in public libraries with large consumer health and wellness departments."
— *American Reference Books Annual, 2003*

"As a sourcebook on household safety this book meets its mark. It is encyclopedic in scope and covers a wide range of safety issues that are commonly seen in the home."
— *E-Streams, Jul '02*

Hypertension Sourcebook

Basic Consumer Health Information about the Causes, Diagnosis, and Treatment of High Blood Pressure, with Facts about Consequences, Complications, and Co-Occurring Disorders, Such as Coronary Heart Disease, Diabetes, Stroke, Kidney Disease, and Hypertensive Retinopathy, and Issues in Blood Pressure Control, Including Dietary Choices, Stress Management, and Medications

Along with Reports on Current Research Initiatives and Clinical Trials, a Glossary, and Resources for Additional Help and Information

Edited by Dawn D. Matthews and Karen Bellenir. 613 pages. 2004. 0-7808-0674-3.

"Academic, public, and medical libraries will want to add the *Hypertension Sourcebook* to their collections."
— *E-Streams, Aug '05*

"The strength of this source is the wide range of information given about hypertension."
— *American Reference Books Annual, 2005*

Immune System Disorders Sourcebook, 2nd Edition

Basic Consumer Health Information about Disorders of the Immune System, Including Immune System Function and Response, Diagnosis of Immune Disorders, Information about Inherited Immune Disease, Acquired Immune Disease, and Autoimmune Diseases, Including Primary Immune Deficiency, Acquired Immunodeficiency Syndrome (AIDS), Lupus, Multiple Sclerosis, Type 1 Diabetes, Rheumatoid Arthritis, and Graves' Disease

Along with Treatments, Tips for Coping with Immune Disorders, a Glossary, and a Directory of Additional Resources.

Edited by Joyce Brennfleck Shannon. 671 pages. 2005. 0-7808-0748-0

"Highly recommended for academic and public libraries." —*American Reference Books Annual, 2006*

"The updated second edition is a 'must' for any consumer health library seeking a solid resource covering the treatments, symptoms, and options for immune disorder sufferers. . . . An excellent guide."
—*MBR Bookwatch, Jan '06*

Infant & Toddler Health Sourcebook

Basic Consumer Health Information about the Physical and Mental Development of Newborns, Infants, and Toddlers, Including Neonatal Concerns, Nutrition Recommendations, Immunization Schedules, Common Pediatric Disorders, Assessments and Milestones, Safety Tips, and Advice for Parents and Other Caregivers

Along with a Glossary of Terms and Resource Listings for Additional Help

Edited by Jenifer Swanson. 585 pages. 2000. 0-7808-0246-2.

"As a reference for the general public, this would be useful in any library." —*E-Streams, May '01*

"Recommended reference source."
—*Booklist, American Library Association, Feb '01*

"This is a good source for general use."
—*American Reference Books Annual, 2001*

Infectious Diseases Sourcebook

Basic Consumer Health Information about Non-Contagious Bacterial, Viral, Prion, and Fungal, and Parasitic Diseases Spread by Food and Water, Insects and Animals, or Environmental Contact, Including Botulism, E. Coli, Encephalitis, Legionnaires' Disease, Lyme Disease, Malaria, Plague, Rabies, Salmonella, Tetanus, and Others, and Facts about Newly Emerging Diseases, Such as Hantavirus, Mad Cow Disease, Monkeypox, and West Nile Virus

Along with Information about Preventing Disease Transmission, the Threat of Bioterrorism, and Current

Research Initiatives, with a Glossary and Directory of Resources for More Information

Edited by Karen Bellenir. 634 pages. 2004. 0-7808-0675-1.

"This reference continues the excellent tradition of the *Health Reference Series* in consolidating a wealth of information on a selected topic into a format that is easy to use and accessible to the general public."
—*American Reference Books Annual, 2005*

"Recommended for public and academic libraries."
—*E-Streams, Jan '05*

Injury & Trauma Sourcebook

Basic Consumer Health Information about the Impact of Injury, the Diagnosis and Treatment of Common and Traumatic Injuries, Emergency Care, and Specific Injuries Related to Home, Community, Workplace, Transportation, and Recreation

Along with Guidelines for Injury Prevention, a Glossary, and a Directory of Additional Resources

Edited by Joyce Brennfleck Shannon. 696 pages. 2002. 0-7808-0421-X.

"This publication is the most comprehensive work of its kind about injury and trauma."
—*American Reference Books Annual, 2003*

"This sourcebook provides concise, easily readable, basic health information about injuries. . . . This book is well organized and an easy to use reference resource suitable for hospital, health sciences and public libraries with consumer health collections."
—*E-Streams, Nov '02*

"Practitioners should be aware of guides such as this in order to facilitate their use by patients and their families."
—*Doody's Health Sciences Book Review Journal, Sep-Oct '02*

"Recommended reference source."
—*Booklist, American Library Association, Sep '02*

"Highly recommended for academic and medical reference collections." —*Library Bookwatch, Sep '02*

Kidney & Urinary Tract Diseases & Disorders Sourcebook

SEE Urinary Tract & Kidney Diseases & Disorders Sourcebook, 2nd Edition

Learning Disabilities Sourcebook, 2nd Edition

Basic Consumer Health Information about Learning Disabilities, Including Dyslexia, Developmental Speech and Language Disabilities, Non-Verbal Learning Disorders, Developmental Arithmetic Disorder, Developmental Writing Disorder, and Other Conditions That Impede Learning Such as Attention Deficit/ Hyperac-

tivity Disorder, Brain Injury, Hearing Impairment, Kline-felter Syndrome, Dyspraxia, and Tourette's Syndrome

Along with Facts about Educational Issues and Assistive Technology, Coping Strategies, a Glossary of Related Terms, and Resources for Further Help and Information

Edited by Dawn D. Matthews. 621 pages. 2003. 0-7808-0626-3.

"The second edition of Learning Disabilities Sourcebook far surpasses the earlier edition in that it is more focused on information that will be useful as a consumer health resource."
— American Reference Books Annual, 2004

"Teachers as well as consumers will find this an essential guide to understanding various syndromes and their latest treatments. [An] invaluable reference for public and school library collections alike."
— Library Bookwatch, Apr '03

Named "Outstanding Reference Book of 1999."
— New York Public Library, Feb 2000

"An excellent candidate for inclusion in a public library reference section. It's a great source of information. Teachers will also find the book useful. Definitely worth reading."
— Journal of Adolescent & Adult Literacy, Feb 2000

"Readable . . . provides a solid base of information regarding successful techniques used with individuals who have learning disabilities, as well as practical suggestions for educators and family members. Clear language, concise descriptions, and pertinent information for contacting multiple resources add to the strength of this book as a useful tool." — Choice, Association of College & Research Libraries, Feb '99

"Recommended reference source."
— Booklist, American Library Association, Sep '98

"A useful resource for libraries and for those who don't have the time to identify and locate the individual publications." — Disability Resources Monthly, Sep '98

Leukemia Sourcebook

Basic Consumer Health Information about Adult and Childhood Leukemias, Including Acute Lymphocytic Leukemia (ALL), Chronic Lymphocytic Leukemia (CLL), Acute Myelogenous Leukemia (AML), Chronic Myelogenous Leukemia (CML), and Hairy Cell Leukemia, and Treatments Such as Chemotherapy, Radiation Therapy, Peripheral Blood Stem Cell and Marrow Transplantation, and Immunotherapy

Along with Tips for Life During and After Treatment, a Glossary, and Directories of Additional Resources

Edited by Joyce Brennfleck Shannon. 587 pages. 2003. 0-7808-0627-1.

"Unlike other medical books for the layperson, . . . the language does not talk down to the reader. . . . This volume is highly recommended for all libraries."
— American Reference Books Annual, 2004

"... a fine title which ranges from diagnosis to alternative treatments, staging, and tips for life during and after diagnosis." — The Bookwatch, Dec '03

Liver Disorders Sourcebook

Basic Consumer Health Information about the Liver and How It Works; Liver Diseases, Including Cancer, Cirrhosis, Hepatitis, and Toxic and Drug Related Diseases; Tips for Maintaining a Healthy Liver; Laboratory Tests, Radiology Tests, and Facts about Liver Transplantation

Along with a Section on Support Groups, a Glossary, and Resource Listings

Edited by Joyce Brennfleck Shannon. 591 pages. 2000. 0-7808-0383-3.

"A valuable resource."
— American Reference Books Annual, 2001

"This title is recommended for health sciences and public libraries with consumer health collections."
— E-Streams, Oct '00

"Recommended reference source."
— Booklist, American Library Association, Jun '00

Lung Disorders Sourcebook

Basic Consumer Health Information about Emphysema, Pneumonia, Tuberculosis, Asthma, Cystic Fibrosis, and Other Lung Disorders, Including Facts about Diagnostic Procedures, Treatment Strategies, Disease Prevention Efforts, and Such Risk Factors as Smoking, Air Pollution, and Exposure to Asbestos, Radon, and Other Agents

Along with a Glossary and Resources for Additional Help and Information

Edited by Dawn D. Matthews. 678 pages. 2002. 0-7808-0339-6.

"This title is a great addition for public and school libraries because it provides concise health information on the lungs."
— American Reference Books Annual, 2003

"Highly recommended for academic and medical reference collections." — Library Bookwatch, Sep '02

SEE ALSO Respiratory Diseases & Disorders Sourcebook

Medical Tests Sourcebook, 2nd Edition

Basic Consumer Health Information about Medical Tests, Including Age-Specific Health Tests, Important Health Screenings and Exams, Home-Use Tests, Blood and Specimen Tests, Electrical Tests, Scope Tests, Genetic Testing, and Imaging Tests, Such as X-Rays, Ultrasound, Computed Tomography, Magnetic Resonance Imaging, Angiography, and Nuclear Medicine

Along with a Glossary and Directory of Additional Resources

Edited by Joyce Brennfleck Shannon. 654 pages. 2004. 0-7808-0670-0.

"Recommended for hospital and health sciences libraries with consumer health collections."
— E-Streams, Mar '00

"This is an overall excellent reference with a wealth of general knowledge that may aid those who are reluctant to get vital tests performed."
— Today's Librarian, Jan '00

"A valuable reference guide."
— American Reference Books Annual, 2000

■

Men's Health Concerns Sourcebook, 2nd Edition

Basic Consumer Health Information about the Medical and Mental Concerns of Men, Including Theories about the Shorter Male Lifespan, the Leading Causes of Death and Disability, Physical Concerns of Special Significance to Men, Reproductive and Sexual Concerns, Sexually Transmitted Diseases, Men's Mental and Emotional Health, and Lifestyle Choices That Affect Wellness, Such as Nutrition, Fitness, and Substance Use

Along with a Glossary of Related Terms and a Directory of Organizational Resources in Men's Health

Edited by Robert Aquinas McNally. 644 pages. 2004. 0-7808-0671-9.

"A very accessible reference for non-specialist general readers and consumers." — The Bookwatch, Jun '04

"This comprehensive resource and the series are highly recommended."
— American Reference Books Annual, 2000

"Recommended reference source."
— Booklist, American Library Association, Dec '98

■

Mental Health Disorders Sourcebook, 3rd Edition

Basic Consumer Health Information about Mental and Emotional Health and Mental Illness, Including Facts about Depression, Bipolar Disorder, and Other Mood Disorders, Phobias, Post-Traumatic Stress Disorder (PTSD), Obsessive-Compulsive Disorder, and Other Anxiety Disorders, Impulse Control Disorders, Eating Disorders, Personality Disorders, and Psychotic Disorders, Including Schizophrenia and Dissociative Disorders

Along with Statistical Information, a Special Section Concerning Mental Health Issues in Children and Adolescents, a Glossary, and Directories of Resources for Additional Help and Information

Edited by Karen Bellenir. 661 pages. 2005. 0-7808-0747-2.

"Recommended for public libraries and academic libraries with an undergraduate program in psychology."
— American Reference Books Annual, 2006

"Recommended reference source."
— Booklist, American Library Association, Jun '00

■

Mental Retardation Sourcebook

Basic Consumer Health Information about Mental Retardation and Its Causes, Including Down Syndrome, Fetal Alcohol Syndrome, Fragile X Syndrome, Genetic Conditions, Injury, and Environmental Sources

Along with Preventive Strategies, Parenting Issues, Educational Implications, Health Care Needs, Employment and Economic Matters, Legal Issues, a Glossary, and a Resource Listing for Additional Help and Information

Edited by Joyce Brennfleck Shannon. 642 pages. 2000. 0-7808-0377-9.

"Public libraries will find the book useful for reference and as a beginning research point for students, parents, and caregivers."
— American Reference Books Annual, 2001

"The strength of this work is that it compiles many basic fact sheets and addresses for further information in one volume. It is intended and suitable for the general public. This sourcebook is relevant to any collection providing health information to the general public."
— E-Streams, Nov '00

"From preventing retardation to parenting and family challenges, this covers health, social and legal issues and will prove an invaluable overview."
— Reviewer's Bookwatch, Jul '00

■

Movement Disorders Sourcebook

Basic Consumer Health Information about Neurological Movement Disorders, Including Essential Tremor, Parkinson's Disease, Dystonia, Cerebral Palsy, Huntington's Disease, Myasthenia Gravis, Multiple Sclerosis, and Other Early-Onset and Adult-Onset Movement Disorders, Their Symptoms and Causes, Diagnostic Tests, and Treatments

Along with Mobility and Assistive Technology Information, a Glossary, and a Directory of Additional Resources

Edited by Joyce Brennfleck Shannon. 655 pages. 2003. 0-7808-0628-X.

". . . a good resource for consumers and recommended for public, community college and undergraduate libraries." — American Reference Books Annual, 2004

■

Muscular Dystrophy Sourcebook

Basic Consumer Health Information about Congenital, Childhood-Onset, and Adult-Onset Forms of Muscular Dystrophy, Such as Duchenne, Becker, Emery-Dreifuss, Distal, Limb-Girdle, Facioscapulohumeral (FSHD), Myotonic, and Ophthalmoplegic Muscular Dystrophies, Including Facts about Diagnostic Tests, Medical and Physical Therapies, Management of Co-Occurring Conditions, and Parenting Guidelines

Along with Practical Tips for Home Care, a Glossary, and Directories of Additional Resources

Edited by Joyce Brennfleck Shannon. 577 pages. 2004. 0-7808-0676-X.

"This book is highly recommended for public and academic libraries as well as health care offices that support the information needs of patients and their families."
— E-Streams, Apr '05

"Excellent reference." — The Bookwatch, Jan '05

■

Obesity Sourcebook

Basic Consumer Health Information about Diseases and Other Problems Associated with Obesity, and Including Facts about Risk Factors, Prevention Issues, and Management Approaches

Along with Statistical and Demographic Data, Information about Special Populations, Research Updates, a Glossary, and Source Listings for Further Help and Information

Edited by Wilma Caldwell and Chad T. Kimball. 376 pages. 2001. 0-7808-0333-7.

"The book synthesizes the reliable medical literature on obesity into one easy-to-read and useful resource for the general public."
— American Reference Books Annual, 2002

"This is a very useful resource book for the lay public."
— Doody's Review Service, Nov '01

"Well suited for the health reference collection of a public library or an academic health science library that serves the general population." — E-Streams, Sep '01

"Recommended reference source."
— Booklist, American Library Association, Apr '01

"Recommended pick both for specialty health library collections and any general consumer health reference collection." — The Bookwatch, Apr '01

■

Ophthalmic Disorders Sourcebook

SEE Eye Care Sourcebook, 2nd Edition

■

Oral Health Sourcebook

SEE Dental Care & Oral Health Sourcebook, 2nd Edition

■

Osteoporosis Sourcebook

Basic Consumer Health Information about Primary and Secondary Osteoporosis and Juvenile Osteoporosis and Related Conditions, Including Fibrous Dysplasia,

Gaucher Disease, Hyperthyroidism, Hypophosphatasia, Myeloma, Osteopetrosis, Osteogenesis Imperfecta, and Paget's Disease

Along with Information about Risk Factors, Treatments, Traditional and Non-Traditional Pain Management, a Glossary of Related Terms, and a Directory of Resources

Edited by Allan R. Cook. 584 pages. 2001. 0-7808-0239-X.

"This would be a book to be kept in a staff or patient library. The targeted audience is the layperson, but the therapist who needs a quick bit of information on a particular topic will also find the book useful."
— Physical Therapy, Jan '02

"This resource is recommended as a great reference source for public, health, and academic libraries, and is another triumph for the editors of Omnigraphics."
— American Reference Books Annual, 2002

"Recommended for all public libraries and general health collections, especially those supporting patient education or consumer health programs."
— E-Streams, Nov '01

"Will prove valuable to any library seeking to maintain a current, comprehensive reference collection of health resources. . . . From prevention to treatment and associated conditions, this provides an excellent survey."
— The Bookwatch, Aug '01

"Recommended reference source."
— Booklist, American Library Association, Jul '01

SEE ALSO Healthy Aging Sourcebook, Physical & Mental Issues in Aging Sourcebook, Women's Health Concerns Sourcebook

■

Pain Sourcebook, 2nd Edition

Basic Consumer Health Information about Specific Forms of Acute and Chronic Pain, Including Muscle and Skeletal Pain, Nerve Pain, Cancer Pain, and Disorders Characterized by Pain, Such as Fibromyalgia, Shingles, Angina, Arthritis, and Headaches

Along with Information about Pain Medications and Management Techniques, Complementary and Alternative Pain Relief Options, Tips for People Living with Chronic Pain, a Glossary, and a Directory of Sources for Further Information

Edited by Karen Bellenir. 670 pages. 2002. 0-7808-0612-3.

"A source of valuable information. . . . This book offers help to nonmedical people who need information about pain and pain management. It is also an excellent reference for those who participate in patient education."
— Doody's Review Service, Sep '02

"Highly recommended for academic and medical reference collections." — Library Bookwatch, Sep '02

"The text is readable, easily understood, and well indexed. This excellent volume belongs in all patient education libraries, consumer health sections of public libraries, and many personal collections."
— American Reference Books Annual, 1999

"The information is basic in terms of scholarship and is appropriate for general readers. Written in journalistic style ... intended for non-professionals. Quite thorough in its coverage of different pain conditions and summarizes the latest clinical information regarding pain treatment." — *Choice, Association of College and Research Libraries, Jun '98*

"Recommended reference source."
— *Booklist, American Library Association, Mar '98*

■

Pediatric Cancer Sourcebook

Basic Consumer Health Information about Leukemias, Brain Tumors, Sarcomas, Lymphomas, and Other Cancers in Infants, Children, and Adolescents, Including Descriptions of Cancers, Treatments, and Coping Strategies

Along with Suggestions for Parents, Caregivers, and Concerned Relatives, a Glossary of Cancer Terms, and Resource Listings

Edited by Edward J. Prucha. 587 pages. 1999. 0-7808-0245-4.

"An excellent source of information. Recommended for public, hospital, and health science libraries with consumer health collections." — *E-Streams, Jun '00*

"Recommended reference source."
— *Booklist, American Library Association, Feb '00*

"A valuable addition to all libraries specializing in health services and many public libraries."
— *American Reference Books Annual, 2000*

SEE ALSO *Childhood Diseases & Disorders Sourcebook, Healthy Children Sourcebook*

■

Physical & Mental Issues in Aging Sourcebook

Basic Consumer Health Information on Physical and Mental Disorders Associated with the Aging Process, Including Concerns about Cardiovascular Disease, Pulmonary Disease, Oral Health, Digestive Disorders, Musculoskeletal and Skin Disorders, Metabolic Changes, Sexual and Reproductive Issues, and Changes in Vision, Hearing, and Other Senses

Along with Data about Longevity and Causes of Death, Information on Acute and Chronic Pain, Descriptions of Mental Concerns, a Glossary of Terms, and Resource Listings for Additional Help

Edited by Jenifer Swanson. 660 pages. 1999. 0-7808-0233-0.

"This is a treasure of health information for the layperson." — *Choice Health Sciences Supplement, Association of College & Research Libraries, May '00*

"Recommended for public libraries."
— *American Reference Books Annual, 2000*

"Recommended reference source."
— *Booklist, American Library Association, Oct '99*

SEE ALSO *Healthy Aging Sourcebook*

Podiatry Sourcebook

Basic Consumer Health Information about Foot Conditions, Diseases, and Injuries, Including Bunions, Corns, Calluses, Athlete's Foot, Plantar Warts, Hammertoes and Clawtoes, Clubfoot, Heel Pain, Gout, and More

Along with Facts about Foot Care, Disease Prevention, Foot Safety, Choosing a Foot Care Specialist, a Glossary of Terms, and Resource Listings for Additional Information

Edited by M. Lisa Weatherford. 380 pages. 2001. 0-7808-0215-2.

"Recommended reference source."
— *Booklist, American Library Association, Feb '02*

"There is a lot of information presented here on a topic that is usually only covered sparingly in most larger comprehensive medical encyclopedias."
— *American Reference Books Annual, 2002*

■

Pregnancy & Birth Sourcebook, 2nd Edition

Basic Consumer Health Information about Conception and Pregnancy, Including Facts about Fertility, Infertility, Pregnancy Symptoms and Complications, Fetal Growth and Development, Labor, Delivery, and the Postpartum Period, as Well as Information about Maintaining Health and Wellness during Pregnancy and Caring for a Newborn

Along with Information about Public Health Assistance for Low-Income Pregnant Women, a Glossary, and Directories of Agencies and Organizations Providing Help and Support

Edited by Amy L. Sutton. 626 pages. 2004. 0-7808-0672-7.

"Will appeal to public and school reference collections strong in medicine and women's health. . . . Deserves a spot on any medical reference shelf."
— *The Bookwatch, Jul '04*

"A well-organized handbook. Recommended."
— *Choice, Association of College & Research Libraries, Apr '98*

"Recommended reference source."
— *Booklist, American Library Association, Mar '98*

"Recommended for public libraries."
— *American Reference Books Annual, 1998*

SEE ALSO *Breastfeeding Sourcebook, Congenital Disorders Sourcebook, Family Planning Sourcebook*

■

Prostate Cancer Sourcebook

Basic Consumer Health Information about Prostate Cancer, Including Information about the Associated Risk Factors, Detection, Diagnosis, and Treatment of Prostate Cancer

Along with Information on Non-Malignant Prostate Conditions, and Featuring a Section Listing Support and Treatment Centers and a Glossary of Related Terms

Edited by Dawn D. Matthews. 358 pages. 2001. 0-7808-0324-8.

"Recommended reference source."
—Booklist, American Library Association, Jan '02

"A valuable resource for health care consumers seeking information on the subject. . . . All text is written in a clear, easy-to-understand language that avoids technical jargon. Any library that collects consumer health resources would strengthen their collection with the addition of the Prostate Cancer Sourcebook."
—American Reference Books Annual, 2002

SEE ALSO *Men's Health Concerns Sourcebook*

Prostate & Urological Disorders Sourcebook

Basic Consumer Health Information about Urogenital and Sexual Disorders in Men, Including Prostate and Other Andrological Cancers, Prostatitis, Benign Prostatic Hyperplasia, Testicular and Penile Trauma, Cryptorchidism, Peyronie Disease, Erectile Dysfunction, and Male Factor Infertility, and Facts about Commonly Used Tests and Procedures, Such as Prostatectomy, Vasectomy, Vasectomy Reversal, Penile Implants, and Semen Analysis

Along with a Glossary of Andrological Terms and a Directory of Resources for Additional Information

Edited by Karen Bellenir. 631 pages. 2005. 0-7808-0797-9.

Public Health Sourcebook

Basic Information about Government Health Agencies, Including National Health Statistics and Trends, Healthy People 2000 Program Goals and Objectives, the Centers for Disease Control and Prevention, the Food and Drug Administration, and the National Institutes of Health

Along with Full Contact Information for Each Agency

Edited by Wendy Wilcox. 698 pages. 1998. 0-7808-0220-9.

"Recommended reference source."
—Booklist, American Library Association, Sep '98

"This consumer guide provides welcome assistance in navigating the maze of federal health agencies and their data on public health concerns."
—SciTech Book News, Sep '98

Reconstructive & Cosmetic Surgery Sourcebook

Basic Consumer Health Information on Cosmetic and Reconstructive Plastic Surgery, Including Statistical Information about Different Surgical Procedures, Things to Consider Prior to Surgery, Plastic Surgery Techniques and Tools, Emotional and Psychological Considerations, and Procedure-Specific Information

Along with a Glossary of Terms and a Listing of Resources for Additional Help and Information

Edited by M. Lisa Weatherford. 374 pages. 2001. 0-7808-0214-4.

"An excellent reference that addresses cosmetic and medically necessary reconstructive surgeries. . . . The style of the prose is calm and reassuring, discussing the many positive outcomes now available due to advances in surgical techniques."
—American Reference Books Annual, 2002

"Recommended for health science libraries that are open to the public, as well as hospital libraries that are open to the patients. This book is a good resource for the consumer interested in plastic surgery."
—E-Streams, Dec '01

"Recommended reference source."
—Booklist, American Library Association, Jul '01

Rehabilitation Sourcebook

Basic Consumer Health Information about Rehabilitation for People Recovering from Heart Surgery, Spinal Cord Injury, Stroke, Orthopedic Impairments, Amputation, Pulmonary Impairments, Traumatic Injury, and More, Including Physical Therapy, Occupational Therapy, Speech/Language Therapy, Massage Therapy, Dance Therapy, Art Therapy, and Recreational Therapy

Along with Information on Assistive and Adaptive Devices, a Glossary, and Resources for Additional Help and Information

Edited by Dawn D. Matthews. 531 pages. 1999. 0-7808-0236-5.

"This is an excellent resource for public library reference and health collections."
—American Reference Books Annual, 2001

"Recommended reference source."
—Booklist, American Library Association, May '00

Respiratory Diseases & Disorders Sourcebook

Basic Information about Respiratory Diseases and Disorders, Including Asthma, Cystic Fibrosis, Pneumonia, the Common Cold, Influenza, and Others, Featuring Facts about the Respiratory System, Statistical and Demographic Data, Treatments, Self-Help Management Suggestions, and Current Research Initiatives

Edited by Allan R. Cook and Peter D. Dresser. 771 pages. 1995. 0-7808-0037-0.

"Designed for the layperson and for patients and their families coping with respiratory illness. . . . an extensive array of information on diagnosis, treatment, management, and prevention of respiratory illnesses for the general reader."
—Choice, Association of College & Research Libraries, Jun '96

"A highly recommended text for all collections. It is a comforting reminder of the power of knowledge that good books carry between their covers."
—Academic Library Book Review, Spring '96

646

■

Sexually Transmitted Diseases Sourcebook, 3rd Edition

Basic Consumer Health Information about Chlamydial Infections, Gonorrhea, Hepatitis, Herpes, HIV/AIDS, Human Papillomavirus, Pubic Lice, Scabies, Syphilis, Trichomoniasis, Vaginal Infections, and Other Sexually Transmitted Diseases, Including Facts about Risk Factors, Symptoms, Diagnosis, Treatment, and the Prevention of Sexually Transmitted Infections

Along with Updates on Current Research Initiatives, a Glossary of Related Terms, and Resources for Additional Help and Information

Edited by Amy L. Sutton. 629 pages. 2006. 0-7808-0824-X.

■

Skin Disorders Sourcebook

SEE *Dermatological Disorders Sourcebook, 2nd Edition*

■

Sleep Disorders Sourcebook, 2nd Edition

Basic Consumer Health Information about Sleep and Sleep Disorders, Including Insomnia, Sleep Apnea, Restless Legs Syndrome, Narcolepsy, Parasomnias, and Other Health Problems That Affect Sleep, Plus Facts about Diagnostic Procedures, Treatment Strategies, Sleep Medications, and Tips for Improving Sleep Quality

Along with a Glossary of Related Terms and Resources for Additional Help and Information

Edited by Amy L. Sutton. 567 pages. 2005. 0-7808-0743-X.

■

Smoking Concerns Sourcebook

Basic Consumer Health Information about Nicotine Addiction and Smoking Cessation, Featuring Facts about the Health Effects of Tobacco Use, Including Lung and Other Cancers, Heart Disease, Stroke, and Respiratory Disorders, Such as Emphysema and Chronic Bronchitis

Along with Information about Smoking Prevention Programs, Suggestions for Achieving and Maintaining a Smoke-Free Lifestyle, Statistics about Tobacco Use, Reports on Current Research Initiatives, a Glossary of Related Terms, and Directories of Resources for Additional Help and Information

Edited by Karen Bellenir. 621 pages. 2004. 0-7808-0323-X.

■

Sports Injuries Sourcebook, 2nd Edition

Basic Consumer Health Information about the Diagnosis, Treatment, and Rehabilitation of Common Sports-Related Injuries in Children and Adults

Along with Suggestions for Conditioning and Training, Information and Prevention Tips for Injuries Frequently Associated with Specific Sports and Special Populations, a Glossary, and a Directory of Additional Resources

Edited by Joyce Brennfleck Shannon. 614 pages. 2002. 0-7808-0604-2.

■

Stress-Related Disorders Sourcebook

Basic Consumer Health Information about Stress and Stress-Related Disorders, Including Stress Origins and Signals, Environmental Stress at Work and Home, Mental and Emotional Stress Associated with Depression, Post-Traumatic Stress Disorder, Panic Disorder, Suicide, and the Physical Effects of Stress on the Cardiovascular, Immune, and Nervous Systems

Along with Stress Management Techniques, a Glossary, and a Listing of Additional Resources

Edited by Joyce Brennfleck Shannon. 610 pages. 2002. 0-7808-0560-7.

"Well written for a general readership, the *Stress-Related Disorders Sourcebook* is a useful addition to the health reference literature."
— *American Reference Books Annual, 2003*

"I am impressed by the amount of information. It offers a thorough overview of the causes and consequences of stress for the layperson. . . . A well-done and thorough reference guide for professionals and nonprofessionals alike." — *Doody's Review Service, Dec '02*

Stroke Sourcebook

Basic Consumer Health Information about Stroke, Including Ischemic, Hemorrhagic, Transient Ischemic Attack (TIA), and Pediatric Stroke, Stroke Triggers and Risks, Diagnostic Tests, Treatments, and Rehabilitation Information

Along with Stroke Prevention Guidelines, Legal and Financial Information, a Glossary, and a Directory of Additional Resources

Edited by Joyce Brennfleck Shannon. 606 pages. 2003. 0-7808-0630-1.

"This volume is highly recommended and should be in every medical, hospital, and public library."
— *American Reference Books Annual, 2004*

"Highly recommended for the amount and variety of topics and information covered." — *Choice, Nov '03*

Substance Abuse Sourcebook

Basic Health-Related Information about the Abuse of Legal and Illegal Substances Such as Alcohol, Tobacco, Prescription Drugs, Marijuana, Cocaine, and Heroin; and Including Facts about Substance Abuse Prevention Strategies, Intervention Methods, Treatment and Recovery Programs, and a Section Addressing the Special Problems Related to Substance Abuse during Pregnancy

Edited by Karen Bellenir. 573 pages. 1996. 0-7808-0038-9.

"A valuable addition to any health reference section. Highly recommended."
— *The Book Report, Mar/Apr '97*

". . . a comprehensive collection of substance abuse information that's both highly readable and compact. Families and caregivers of substance abusers will find the information enlightening and helpful, while teachers, social workers and journalists should benefit from the concise format. Recommended."
— *Drug Abuse Update, Winter '96/'97*

SEE ALSO *Alcoholism Sourcebook, Drug Abuse Sourcebook*

Surgery Sourcebook

Basic Consumer Health Information about Inpatient and Outpatient Surgeries, Including Cardiac, Vascular, Orthopedic, Ocular, Reconstructive, Cosmetic, Gynecologic, and Ear, Nose, and Throat Procedures and More

Along with Information about Operating Room Policies and Instruments, Laser Surgery Techniques, Hospital Errors, Statistical Data, a Glossary, and Listings of Sources for Further Help and Information

Edited by Annemarie S. Muth and Karen Bellenir. 596 pages. 2002. 0-7808-0380-9.

"Large public libraries and medical libraries would benefit from this material in their reference collections."
— *American Reference Books Annual, 2004*

"Invaluable reference for public and school library collections alike." — *Library Bookwatch, Apr '03*

Thyroid Disorders Sourcebook

Basic Consumer Health Information about Disorders of the Thyroid and Parathyroid Glands, Including Hypothyroidism, Hyperthyroidism, Graves Disease, Hashimoto Thyroiditis, Thyroid Cancer, and Parathyroid Disorders, Featuring Facts about Symptoms, Risk Factors, Tests, and Treatments

Along with Information about the Effects of Thyroid Imbalance on Other Body Systems, Environmental Factors That Affect the Thyroid Gland, a Glossary, and a Directory of Additional Resources

Edited by Joyce Brennfleck Shannon. 599 pages. 2005. 0-7808-0745-6.

"Recommended for consumer health collections."
— *American Reference Books Annual, 2006*

"Highly recommended pick for basic consumer health reference holdings at all levels."
— *The Bookwatch, Aug '05*

Transplantation Sourcebook

Basic Consumer Health Information about Organ and Tissue Transplantation, Including Physical and Financial Preparations, Procedures and Issues Relating to Specific Solid Organ and Tissue Transplants, Rehabilitation, Pediatric Transplant Information, the Future of Transplantation, and Organ and Tissue Donation

Along with a Glossary and Listings of Additional Resources

Edited by Joyce Brennfleck Shannon. 628 pages. 2002. 0-7808-0322-1.

"Along with these advances [in transplantation technology] have come a number of daunting questions for potential transplant patients, their families, and their health care providers. This reference text is the best single tool to address many of these questions. . . . It will be a much-needed addition to the reference collections in health care, academic, and large public libraries."
— *American Reference Books Annual, 2003*

"Recommended for libraries with an interest in offering consumer health information." — *E-Streams, Jul '02*

"This is a unique and valuable resource for patients facing transplantation and their families."
— *Doody's Review Service, Jun '02*

■

Traveler's Health Sourcebook

Basic Consumer Health Information for Travelers, Including Physical and Medical Preparations, Transportation Health and Safety, Essential Information about Food and Water, Sun Exposure, Insect and Snake Bites, Camping and Wilderness Medicine, and Travel with Physical or Medical Disabilities

Along with International Travel Tips, Vaccination Recommendations, Geographical Health Issues, Disease Risks, a Glossary, and a Listing of Additional Resources

Edited by Joyce Brennfleck Shannon. 613 pages. 2000. 0-7808-0384-1.

"Recommended reference source."
— *Booklist, American Library Association, Feb '01*

"This book is recommended for any public library, any travel collection, and especially any collection for the physically disabled."
— *American Reference Books Annual, 2001*

SEE ALSO *Worldwide Health Sourcebook*

■

Urinary Tract & Kidney Diseases & Disorders Sourcebook, 2nd Edition

Basic Consumer Health Information about the Urinary System, Including the Bladder, Urethra, Ureters, and Kidneys, with Facts about Urinary Tract Infections, Incontinence, Congenital Disorders, Kidney Stones, Cancers of the Urinary Tract and Kidneys, Kidney Failure, Dialysis, and Kidney Transplantation

Along with Statistical and Demographic Information, Reports on Current Research in Kidney and Urologic Health, a Summary of Commonly Used Diagnostic Tests, a Glossary of Related Terms, and a Directory of Resources for Additional Help and Information

Edited by Ivy L. Alexander. 649 pages. 2005. 0-7808-0750-2.

"A good choice for a consumer health information library or for a medical library needing information to refer to their patients."
— *American Reference Books Annual, 2006*

■

Vegetarian Sourcebook

Basic Consumer Health Information about Vegetarian Diets, Lifestyle, and Philosophy, Including Definitions of Vegetarianism and Veganism, Tips about Adopting Vegetarianism, Creating a Vegetarian Pantry, and Meeting Nutritional Needs of Vegetarians, with Facts Re-

garding Vegetarianism's Effect on Pregnant and Lactating Women, Children, Athletes, and Senior Citizens

Along with a Glossary of Commonly Used Vegetarian Terms and Resources for Additional Help and Information

Edited by Chad T. Kimball. 360 pages. 2002. 0-7808-0439-2.

"Organizes into one concise volume the answers to the most common questions concerning vegetarian diets and lifestyles. This title is recommended for public and secondary school libraries." — *E-Streams, Apr '03*

"Invaluable reference for public and school library collections alike." — *Library Bookwatch, Apr '03*

"The articles in this volume are easy to read and come from authoritative sources. The book does not necessarily support the vegetarian diet but instead provides the pros and cons of this important decision. The Vegetarian Sourcebook is recommended for public libraries and consumer health libraries."
— *American Reference Books Annual, 2003*

SEE ALSO *Diet & Nutrition Sourcebook*

■

Women's Health Concerns Sourcebook, 2nd Edition

Basic Consumer Health Information about the Medical and Mental Concerns of Women, Including Maintaining Health and Wellness, Gynecological Concerns, Breast Health, Sexuality and Reproductive Issues, Menopause, Cancer in Women, Leading Causes of Death and Disability among Women, Physical Concerns of Special Significance to Women, and Women's Mental and Emotional Health

Along with a Glossary of Related Terms and Directories of Resources for Additional Help and Information

Edited by Amy L. Sutton. 746 pages. 2004. 0-7808-0673-5.

"This is a useful reference book, which makes the reader knowledgeable about several issues that concern women's health. It is recommended for public libraries and home library collections." — *E-Streams, May '05*

"A useful addition to public and consumer health library collections."
— *American Reference Books Annual, 2005*

"A highly recommended title."
— *The Bookwatch, May '04*

"Handy compilation. There is an impressive range of diseases, devices, disorders, procedures, and other physical and emotional issues covered . . . well organized, illustrated, and indexed." — *Choice, Association of College & Research Libraries, Jan '98*

SEE ALSO *Breast Cancer Sourcebook, Cancer Sourcebook for Women, Healthy Heart Sourcebook for Women, Osteoporosis Sourcebook*

Workplace Health & Safety Sourcebook

Basic Consumer Health Information about Workplace Health and Safety, Including the Effect of Workplace Hazards on the Lungs, Skin, Heart, Ears, Eyes, Brain, Reproductive Organs, Musculoskeletal System, and Other Organs and Body Parts

Along with Information about Occupational Cancer, Personal Protective Equipment, Toxic and Hazardous Chemicals, Child Labor, Stress, and Workplace Violence

Edited by Chad T. Kimball. 626 pages. 2000. 0-7808-0231-4.

"As a reference for the general public, this would be useful in any library." — *E-Streams, Jun '01*

"Provides helpful information for primary care physicians and other caregivers interested in occupational medicine. . . . General readers; professionals."
— *Choice, Association of College & Research Libraries, May '01*

"Recommended reference source."
— *Booklist, American Library Association, Feb '01*

"Highly recommended." — *The Bookwatch, Jan '01*

■

Worldwide Health Sourcebook

Basic Information about Global Health Issues, Including Malnutrition, Reproductive Health, Disease Dispersion and Prevention, Emerging Diseases, Risky Health Behaviors, and the Leading Causes of Death

Along with Global Health Concerns for Children, Women, and the Elderly, Mental Health Issues, Research and Technology Advancements, and Economic, Environmental, and Political Health Implications, a Glossary, and a Resource Listing for Additional Help and Information

Edited by Joyce Brennfleck Shannon. 614 pages. 2001. 0-7808-0330-2.

"Named an Outstanding Academic Title."
— *Choice, Association of College & Research Libraries, Jan '02*

"Yet another handy but also unique compilation in the extensive Health Reference Series, this is a useful work because many of the international publications reprinted or excerpted are not readily available. Highly recommended." — *Choice, Association of College & Research Libraries, Nov '01*

"Recommended reference source."
— *Booklist, American Library Association, Oct '01*

SEE ALSO Traveler's Health Sourcebook

650

Teen Health Series
Helping Young Adults Understand, Manage, and Avoid Serious Illness

List price $65 per volume. **School and library price $58 per volume.**

Alcohol Information for Teens
Health Tips about Alcohol and Alcoholism

Including Facts about Underage Drinking, Preventing Teen Alcohol Use, Alcohol's Effects on the Brain and the Body, Alcohol Abuse Treatment, Help for Children of Alcoholics, and More

Edited by Joyce Brennfleck Shannon. 370 pages. 2005. 0-7808-0741-3.

"Boxed facts and tips add visual interest to the well-researched and clearly written text."
— *Curriculum Connection, Apr '06*

Allergy Information for Teens
Health Tips about Allergic Reactions Such as Anaphylaxis, Respiratory Problems, and Rashes

Including Facts about Identifying and Managing Allergies to Food, Pollen, Mold, Animals, Chemicals, Drugs, and Other Substances

Edited by Karen Bellenir. 410 pages. 2006. 0-7808-0799-5.

Asthma Information for Teens
Health Tips about Managing Asthma and Related Concerns

Including Facts about Asthma Causes, Triggers, Symptoms, Diagnosis, and Treatment

Edited by Karen Bellenir. 386 pages. 2005. 0-7808-0770-7.

"Highly recommended for medical libraries, public school libraries, and public libraries."
— *American Reference Books Annual, 2006*

"It is so clearly written and well organized that even hesitant readers will be able to find the facts they need, whether for reports or personal information. . . . A succinct but complete resource."
— *School Library Journal, Sep '05*

Cancer Information for Teens
Health Tips about Cancer Awareness, Prevention, Diagnosis, and Treatment

Including Facts about Frequently Occurring Cancers, Cancer Risk Factors, and Coping Strategies for Teens Fighting Cancer or Dealing with Cancer in Friends or Family Members

Edited by Wilma R. Caldwell. 428 pages. 2004. 0-7808-0678-6.

"Recommended for school libraries, or consumer libraries that see a lot of use by teens."
— *E-Streams, May 2005*

"A valuable educational tool."
— *American Reference Books Annual, 2005*

"Young adults and their parents alike will find this new addition to the *Teen Health Series* an important reference to cancer in teens."
— *Children's Bookwatch, Feb '05*

Diabetes Information for Teens
Health Tips about Managing Diabetes and Preventing Related Complications

Including Information about Insulin, Glucose Control, Healthy Eating, Physical Activity, and Learning to Live with Diabetes

Edited by Sandra Augustyn Lawton. 410 pages. 2006. 0-7808-0811-8.

Diet Information for Teens, 2nd Edition
Health Tips about Diet and Nutrition

Including Facts about Dietary Guidelines, Food Groups, Nutrients, Healthy Meals, Snacks, Weight Control, Medical Concerns Related to Diet, and More

Edited by Karen Bellenir. 432 pages. 2006. 0-7808-0820-7.

"Full of helpful insights and facts throughout the book. . . . An excellent resource to be placed in public libraries or even in personal collections."
— *American Reference Books Annual, 2002*

"Recommended for middle and high school libraries and media centers as well as academic libraries that educate future teachers of teenagers. It is also a suitable addition to health science libraries that serve patrons who are interested in teen health promotion and education."
— *E-Streams, Oct '01*

"This comprehensive book would be beneficial to collections that need information about nutrition, dietary guidelines, meal planning, and weight control. . . . This reference is so easy to use that its purchase is recommended."
— *The Book Report, Sep-Oct '01*

"This book is written in an easy to understand format describing issues that many teens face every day, and then provides thoughtful explanations so that teens can make informed decisions. This is an interesting book that provides important facts and information for today's teens." — *Doody's Health Sciences Book Review Journal, Jul-Aug '01*

"A comprehensive compendium of diet and nutrition. The information is presented in a straightforward, plain-spoken manner. This title will be useful to those working on reports on a variety of topics, as well as to general readers concerned about their dietary health." — *School Library Journal, Jun '01*

Drug Information for Teens, 2nd Edition

Health Tips about the Physical and Mental Effects of Substance Abuse

Including Information about Marijuana, Inhalants, Club Drugs, Stimulants, Hallucinogens, Opiates, Prescription and Over-the-Counter Drugs, Herbal Products, Tobacco, Alcohol, and More

Edited by Sandra Augustyn Lawton. 468 pages. 2006. 0-7808-0862-2.

"A clearly written resource for general readers and researchers alike." — *School Library Journal*

"This book is well-balanced. . . . a must for public and school libraries." — *VOYA: Voice of Youth Advocates, Dec '03*

"The chapters are quick to make a connection to their teenage reading audience. The prose is straightforward and the book lends itself to spot reading. It should be useful both for practical information and for research, and it is suitable for public and school libraries." — *American Reference Books Annual, 2003*

"Recommended reference source." — *Booklist, American Library Association, Feb '03*

"This is an excellent resource for teens and their parents. Education about drugs and substances is key to discouraging teen drug abuse and this book provides this much needed information in a way that is interesting and factual." — *Doody's Review Service, Dec '02*

Eating Disorders Information for Teens

Health Tips about Anorexia, Bulimia, Binge Eating, and Other Eating Disorders

Including Information on the Causes, Prevention, and Treatment of Eating Disorders, and Such Other Issues as Maintaining Healthy Eating and Exercise Habits

Edited by Sandra Augustyn Lawton. 337 pages. 2005. 0-7808-0783-9.

"An excellent resource for teens and those who work with them." — *VOYA: Voice of Youth Advocates, Apr '06*

"A welcome addition to high school and undergraduate libraries." — *American Reference Books Annual, 2006*

"This book covers the topic in a lucid manner but delves deeper into every aspect of an eating disorder. A solid addition for any nonfiction or reference collection." — *School Library Journal, Dec '05*

Fitness Information for Teens

Health Tips about Exercise, Physical Well-Being, and Health Maintenance

Including Facts about Aerobic and Anaerobic Conditioning, Stretching, Body Shape and Body Image, Sports Training, Nutrition, and Activities for Non-Athletes

Edited by Karen Bellenir. 425 pages. 2004. 0-7808-0679-4.

"Another excellent offering from Omnigraphics in their *Teen Health Series*. . . . This book will be a great addition to any public, junior high, senior high, or secondary school library." — *American Reference Books Annual, 2005*

Learning Disabilities Information for Teens

Health Tips about Academic Skills Disorders and Other Disabilities That Affect Learning

Including Information about Common Signs of Learning Disabilities, School Issues, Learning to Live with a Learning Disability, and Other Related Issues

Edited by Sandra Augustyn Lawton. 337 pages. 2005. 0-7808-0796-0.

"This book provides a wealth of information for any reader interested in the signs, causes, and consequences of learning disabilities, as well as related legal rights and educational interventions. . . . Public and academic libraries should want this title for both students and general readers." — *American Reference Books Annual, 2006*

Mental Health Information for Teens, 2nd Edition

Health Tips about Mental Wellness and Mental Illness

Including Facts about Mental and Emotional Health, Depression and Other Mood Disorders, Anxiety Disorders, Behavior Disorders, Self-Injury, Psychosis, Schizophrenia, and More

Edited by Karen Bellenir. 400 pages. 2006. 0-7808-0863-0.

"In both language and approach, this user-friendly entry in the *Teen Health Series* is on target for teens needing information on mental health concerns." — *Booklist, American Library Association, Jan '02*

"Readers will find the material accessible and informative, with the shaded notes, facts, and embedded glos-

sary insets adding appropriately to the already interesting and succinct presentation."
— *School Library Journal, Jan '02*

"This title is highly recommended for any library that serves adolescents and parents/caregivers of adolescents." — *E-Streams, Jan '02*

"Recommended for high school libraries and young adult collections in public libraries. Both health professionals and teenagers will find this book useful."
— *American Reference Books Annual, 2002*

"This is a nice book written to enlighten the society, primarily teenagers, about common teen mental health issues. It is highly recommended to teachers and parents as well as adolescents."
— *Doody's Review Service, Dec '01*

Sexual Health Information for Teens

Health Tips about Sexual Development, Human Reproduction, and Sexually Transmitted Diseases

Including Facts about Puberty, Reproductive Health, Chlamydia, Human Papillomavirus, Pelvic Inflammatory Disease, Herpes, AIDS, Contraception, Pregnancy, and More

Edited by Deborah A. Stanley. 391 pages. 2003. 0-7808-0445-7.

"This work should be included in all high school libraries and many larger public libraries. . . . highly recommended."
— *American Reference Books Annual, 2004*

"Sexual Health approaches its subject with appropriate seriousness and offers easily accessible advice and information." — *School Library Journal, Feb '04*

Skin Health Information for Teens

Health Tips about Dermatological Concerns and Skin Cancer Risks

Including Facts about Acne, Warts, Hives, and Other Conditions and Lifestyle Choices, Such as Tanning, Tattooing, and Piercing, That Affect the Skin, Nails, Scalp, and Hair

Edited by Robert Aquinas McNally. 429 pages. 2003. 0-7808-0446-5.

"This volume, as with others in the series, will be a useful addition to school and public library collections." — *American Reference Books Annual, 2004*

"There is no doubt that this reference tool is valuable."
— *VOYA: Voice of Youth Advocates, Feb '04*

"This volume serves as a one-stop source and should be a necessity for any health collection."
— *Library Media Connection*

Sports Injuries Information for Teens

Health Tips about Sports Injuries and Injury Protection

Including Facts about Specific Injuries, Emergency Treatment, Rehabilitation, Sports Safety, Competition Stress, Fitness, Sports Nutrition, Steroid Risks, and More

Edited by Joyce Brennfleck Shannon. 405 pages. 2003. 0-7808-0447-3.

"This work will be useful in the young adult collections of public libraries as well as high school libraries."
— *American Reference Books Annual, 2004*

Suicide Information for Teens

Health Tips about Suicide Causes and Prevention

Including Facts about Depression, Risk Factors, Getting Help, Survivor Support, and More

Edited by Joyce Brennfleck Shannon. 368 pages. 2005. 0-7808-0737-5.

Health Reference Series

Adolescent Health Sourcebook,
2nd Edition

AIDS Sourcebook, 3rd Edition

Alcoholism Sourcebook, 2nd Edition

Allergies Sourcebook, 2nd Edition

Alzheimer's Disease Sourcebook,
3rd Edition

Arthritis Sourcebook, 2nd Edition

Asthma Sourcebook, 2nd Edition

Attention Deficit Disorder Sourcebook

Back & Neck Sourcebook, 2nd Edition

Blood & Circulatory Disorders
Sourcebook, 2nd Edition

Brain Disorders Sourcebook, 2nd Edition

Breast Cancer Sourcebook, 2nd Edition

Breastfeeding Sourcebook

Burns Sourcebook

Cancer Sourcebook, 4th Edition

Cancer Sourcebook for Women,
3rd Edition

Cardiovascular Diseases & Disorders
Sourcebook, 3rd Edition

Caregiving Sourcebook

Child Abuse Sourcebook

Childhood Diseases & Disorders
Sourcebook

Colds, Flu & Other Common Ailments
Sourcebook

Communication Disorders Sourcebook

Complementary & Alternative Medicine
Sourcebook, 3rd Edition

Congenital Disorders Sourcebook,
2nd Edition

Consumer Issues in Health Care
Sourcebook

Contagious Diseases Sourcebook

Contagious & Non-Contagious Infectious
Diseases Sourcebook

Death & Dying Sourcebook, 2nd Edition

Dental Care & Oral Health Sourcebook,
2nd Edition

Depression Sourcebook

Dermatological Disorders Sourcebook,
2nd Edition

Diabetes Sourcebook, 3rd Edition

Diet & Nutrition Sourcebook,
3rd Edition

Digestive Diseases & Disorder
Sourcebook

Disabilities Sourcebook

Domestic Violence Sourcebook,
2nd Edition

Drug Abuse Sourcebook, 2nd Edition

Ear, Nose & Throat Disorders
Sourcebook, 2nd Edition

Eating Disorders Sourcebook

Emergency Medical Services Sourcebook

Endocrine & Metabolic Disorders
Sourcebook

Environmentally Health Sourcebook,
2nd Edition

Ethnic Diseases Sourcebook

Eye Care Sourcebook, 2nd Edition

Family Planning Sourcebook

Fitness & Exercise Sourcebook,
3rd Edition

Food & Animal Borne Diseases
Sourcebook

Food Safety Sourcebook

Forensic Medicine Sourcebook

Gastrointestinal Diseases & Disorders
Sourcebook, 2nd Edition

Genetic Disorders Sourcebook,
3rd Edition

Head Trauma Sourcebook

Headache Sourcebook

Health Insurance Sourcebook

Healthy Aging Sourcebook

Healthy Children Sourcebook

Healthy Heart Sourcebook for Women

Hepatitis Sourcebook

Household Safety Sourcebook

Hypertension Sourcebook

Immune System Disorders Sourcebook,
2nd Edition